The Mutual Fund Business

The
Mutual Fund
Business

2nd Edition

ROBERT C. POZEN

editorial assistance by
Sandra D. Crane, CFA

Houghton Mifflin Company

Boston   New York

To my loving and supportive wife Liz.

Executive Editor: George T. Hoffman
Senior Development Editor: Susan M. Kahn
Editorial Assistant: Julia Perez
Senior Project Editor: Rachel D'Angelo Wimberly
Editorial Assistant: May Jawdat
Production/Design Coordinator: Jodi O'Rourke
Manufacturing Manager: Florence Cadran
Marketing Manager: Steven W. Mikels
Marketing Associate: Lisa E. Boden

Cover image: Tony Stone Images/Lois & Bob Schlowsky

Printed in the U.S.A.

Library of Congress Control Number: 2001097978

ISBN: 0-618-16610-6

1 2 3 4 5 6 7 8 9 — DOW — 05 04 03 02 01

Contents

PART III   Marketing and Servicing of Mutual Fund Shareholders   287

Chapter 7   *Marketing of Mutual Funds*   288

Chapter 8   *Retirement Plans and the Fund Business*   345

Preface

While I was pleased with the popularity of the first edition of *The Mutual Fund Business,* I've sought to produce a second edition that is more than an updated version of the original. All information in the second edition is through the end of 2000 unless otherwise indicated. In specific, I've made several changes in response to the constructive comments I've received from users of the first edition.

Most importantly, I've tried to write a true textbook supplemented by a few excerpts from the literature, in contrast to the original format of a short introduction to each Chapter followed by an extensive group of outside readings. Since this textbook style results in a more integrated overview of each subject, it should appeal to readers looking for a primer on the mutual fund industry, including students in broader undergraduate courses on financial institutions or capital markets as well as new employees of fund complexes or service providers.

To better serve these readers, I've also expanded the initial three chapters of the book into a concise introduction to mutual funds. Chapter One now contains a brief history of the industry, as well as a discussion of mutual funds in their role as financial intermediaries. Chapter Two is substantially revised to explain in detail the various types of mutual funds and the main measures (peer groups and indexes) to gauge fund performance. Chapter Three is an enlarged summary of the regulatory framework for mutual funds — not only the SEC's disclosure requirements, but also recent developments on fund taxes, independent directors and electronic commerce.

At the same time, I've retained the detailed case studies and class exercises that accompany each Chapter. These cases and exercises are designed for more advanced analysis of each subject, especially courses at graduate schools of business. Chapter Five contains a new case study on stock picking for a small cap stock mutual fund. This new case study replaces the previous one on the Code of Ethics; this topic is now incorporated into the textbook portion of Chapter Three on fund regulation.

To better serve more advanced students of mutual funds, I've also expanded significantly the text in the three chapters on portfolio management. While Chapters Four and Five begin with a basic description of bonds and stocks respectively, they proceed to a higher level of discussion on techniques employed by research analysts and strategies pursued by portfolio managers. Similarly, while Chapter Six begins with a basic description of the U.S. stock markets, it proceeds to an in-depth look at the role of the fund trading desk and the complexities of best execution.

Chapters Seven, Eight and Nine continue to focus on marketing and servicing of mutual funds with a few additions. After reviewing the retail and intermediary channels of fund distribution, Chapter Seven discusses a few of the current trends cutting across all distribution channels like open architecture and advice products. After reviewing the 401(k) and IRA markets for mutual funds, Chapter Eight outlines a few retirement issues for the future, such as the distribution phase and Social Security reform. Chapter Nine on fund servicing includes new material on pricing practices of fund transfer agents and the fund industry's evolving use of technology. A discussion of technological influences, where relevant, on any specific subject in any part of the book replaces the separate and general Chapter on technology in the first edition.

Chapter Ten on the financial dynamics of mutual funds is enlarged to cover the spate of recent studies on mutual fund fees and the increasing number of acquisitions involving fund sponsors. Chapter Eleven on the role of mutual funds in corporate governance is expanded to review the empirical literature on institutional activism and the rights of mutual funds as shareholders in foreign companies. Chapter Twelve (formerly Chapter Thirteen) on internationalization of mutual funds reviews other issues for mutual funds investing in foreign companies and broadens the discussion of asset gathering outside of the U.S. to include foreign pension schemes.

Throughout the book, I've inserted "callouts" to provide a concrete illustration of a particular point. For example, there are callouts describing a fund complex's marketing approach, a significant takeover battle and a relevant piece of legislation. I've also divided the questions at the end of each Chapter into two groups — review questions aimed at understanding the specific concepts explained in the Chapter, and discussion questions designed to provoke debate on broader issues raised by the Chapter.

Acknowledgements

In the process of publishing this second edition, I was helped by many people at Fidelity Investments. My greatest thanks and appreciation go to Sandra Crane for her tremendous efforts in editing and producing the book, as well as creating the case studies for Chapters Five and Nine. Without Sandra, there simply would be no second edition.

Kathleen Miskiewicz was a major contributor to the book by developing the new Chapter Two as well as helping to integrate the initial three Chapters; moreover, Kathleen took the lead in completing the huge tasks of reviewing the edits to the manuscript and correcting the galleys. Judy Hogan also provided good editorial comments on Chapter Three.

Bill Eigen, as well as the Fidelity fixed income group, did an excellent job of expanding Chapter Four on managing bond funds, as did Mike Jenkins for Chapter Five on managing stock funds. Peter Lert, together with Eric Roiter, took the lead on enlarging Chapter Six on the fund trading desk.

Alice Lowenstein deserves special thanks for weaving together the disparate marketing issues into a coherent Chapter Seven, after initial research by Jennifer Brown. John Kimpel displayed his mastery of retirement issues in drafting Chapter Eight and Peter DeSilva drew on his extensive experience in fund servicing to put together Chapter Nine.

Karleton Fyfe assisted with research for Chapter Ten while he worked at Fidelity; subsequently, he died in the tragic events of September 11, 2001. I extend my deepest sympathies to Karleton's family.

The outstanding analysis of data on acquisitions in the fund industry was prepared by Greg Fleming and Jeff Laborsky of Merrill Lynch for Chapter Ten. David Jones then did a masterful job of drafting a textual explanation of this data analysis. Bill Wall and Don Cassidy worked well together in developing Chapter Eleven on mutual funds and corporate governance. Greg Merz displayed his elegant writing style in explaining the internationalization of mutual funds for Chapter Twelve.

Along the way, many other people lent their expertise to develop particular examples or sections in the book or spent time on reviewing the material. Specific thanks go to Dwight Churchill, Bob Dwight, Bob Gervis, Jenny McAuliffe, David Pearlman, David Potel and Anne Punzak. I'd like to thank Sara Leventhal and Rob Gowen for their help with research throughout the book; Debbie Casey, Kasia Kiladis and Leia Mezes for help with proofing; as well as Melinda Costanzo and Betty Donahue for typing and revising the manuscript.

I also want to express my strong appreciation for the editorial and production work done by Houghton Mifflin staff — Susan Kahn, Rachel D'Angelo Wimberly, Jodi O'Rourke and Florence Cadran.

Last, but not least, I am deeply grateful to my wife who gracefully put up with my late night and weekend work on this second edition.

The Mutual Fund Business

Structure, Measurement and Regulation of Mutual Funds

I

Part I provides a basic overview of mutual funds through three Chapters on the functions and main types of mutual funds as well as their regulatory framework.

Chapter One focuses on mutual funds as financial intermediaries between savers and a diversified pool of securities. It begins by looking at why savers might choose to invest in mutual funds, as opposed to individual securities. Next, it reviews the history of mutual funds, with an emphasis on current trends. Then it compares the structural characteristics of mutual funds to those of commercial banks. This comparison is explored in greater depth through a case study examining the characteristics of both shares in a money market fund and deposit accounts in a commercial bank.

Chapter Two reviews the main types of mutual funds, which are based on the assets in which they invest: money market, bond and stock funds as well as hybrid funds. For each type of mutual fund, the Chapter describes the two principal methods of measuring their performance: relative to peer groups of similar funds and relative to indexes of representative securities. For stock funds, it focuses on the debate between active and passive management. The Chapter also considers a few pooled alternatives to actively and passively managed mutual funds. It ends with an exercise involving asset allocation among various types of mutual funds.

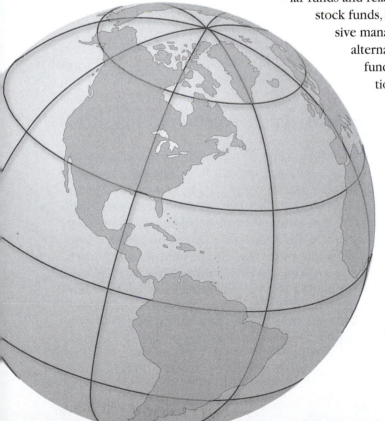

Chapter Three lays out the regulatory framework for mutual funds, with a focus on the applicable disclosure and advertising requirements. It also summarizes the recent regulations governing the electronic transmission of fund and customer information. Next, it discusses the substantive requirements imposed on mutual funds, with particular emphasis on the role of independent directors. Then it addresses the enforcement of both disclosure and substantive requirements for mutual funds, including the Code of Ethics. The Chapter ends with an exercise involving the design of a short-form prospectus for a mutual fund.

1

1

Indirect Investing Through Mutual Funds

Investors have a basic choice: they can invest directly in individual securities, or they can invest indirectly through a financial intermediary. A financial intermediary gathers savings from consumers and invests these monies in a portfolio of financial assets. A mutual fund is a type of financial intermediary—a corporation or trust—through which savers pool their monies for collective investment, primarily in publicly traded securities. Other types of financial intermediaries are commercial banks, insurance companies and pension plans.

A fund is "mutual" in the sense that all of its returns, minus its expenses, are shared by the fund's shareholders. A fund's returns consist of interest and dividends received from the fund's investments, as well as its realized and unrealized capital gains or losses. The fund's shared expenses consist primarily of an advisory fee for managing the fund's investments and a transfer agency fee for servicing the fund's shareholders, as well as sometimes an annual fee for distributing the fund's shares, called a 12b-1 fee after a Securities and Exchange Commission (SEC) rule.

This Chapter focuses on mutual funds as financial intermediaries. First, it discusses why investors might choose mutual funds as opposed to individual securities or managed accounts; second, it reviews the history of mutual funds with an emphasis on current trends; and third, it compares the structural characteristics of mutual funds to those of commercial banks. The case study expands on the final topic by looking at one type of mutual fund called a money market fund in contrast to a deposit account at a commercial bank.

I. Mutual Funds versus Individual Securities

In choosing investments, most people are seeking to maximize their returns and minimize their risks, but this combination is not easy to achieve because of the strong, positive relationship between return and risk. The return on an investment includes interest, dividends and capital gain or loss. Although there are many definitions of risk, it may be thought of generally as the potential range of returns from an investment. For example, a Treasury bill is a very low-risk investment because it is virtually certain to pay its specified interest rate if held to maturity. By contrast, the stock of a new biotech company is a very high-risk investment because its price could zoom up or fall to near zero. As these examples illustrate, investors seeking higher returns usually must take higher risks, while investors satisfied with lower returns need not take much risk.

Since most investors are risk averse—uncomfortable with risk—they typically seek higher returns with equivalent risks by trying to find "undervalued" securities—

2

securities whose prices do not yet reflect their actual value. However, securities markets generally are considered to be quite efficient in that any public information about any widely traded security is assimilated promptly in its price. This is often called the efficient market hypothesis (EMH). Because most securities markets tend to be governed by the EMH to a significant extent, it is very difficult to find "undervalued" securities on a regular basis.

This conclusion was reinforced during the 1960s and 1970s by a series of empirical studies, often referred to as the "random walk," showing that future changes in stock prices are randomly related to current stock prices. For example, if McDonald's is trading today at 50, it is as likely tomorrow to trade at 49 as 51. This is because today's price of 50 already incorporates all public information about McDonald's as a company and the trading market for its stock. As a result, any change in McDonald's stock price will be based on new information, and investors cannot tell in advance whether this new information will be positive or negative.

Both the random walk and the EMH are discussed in Reading 1.1. By contrast, Reading 1.2 discusses a different approach to the securities markets—sometimes called behavioral finance. This approach is based on the premise that most investors do not behave perfectly rationally. Rather, they are heavily influenced by psychological factors in making investment decisions. For example, it is well known that investors are more reluctant sellers of losing investments than winning investments, even if selling losing investments would make a lot of sense from a tax perspective. In addition, unsophisticated investors often use simple rules of thumb in choosing investments. For instance, if a pension plan offers five mutual funds, many participants will simply allocate their contributions evenly among the five choices.

As Reading 1.2 points out, the behavioral approach better explains certain investing phenomena than the EMH or random walk. One vivid illustration is the huge rise and sharp fall of Internet stocks. If the prices of Internet stocks efficiently reflected all public information about these companies, how could they zoom up so high until mid-March 2000 and then fall so quickly after that date? Did investors realize only after mid-March that most Internet companies were losing money with little chance of earning profits in the future? Or did many investors play follow the leader, investing in Internet stocks because they were popular among online traders regardless of the actual prospects of these companies?

More systematically, there is considerable evidence of reversion to the mean in the equity markets. For instance, if a company's stock rises a great deal over five years, it tends to go down over the next five years. Conversely, if a company's stock declines a great deal over five years, it tends to go up over the next five years.[1]

While the debate continues about the efficiency and psychology of the securities markets, there is a fairly strong consensus that investors can reduce their aggregate risk exposure by holding a diversified portfolio of securities. As elaborated in Reading 1.1, it is useful to think of securities as having two main types of risk, generally referred to as alpha and beta. Beta risk is based on the volatility of the market in general, while alpha risk is based on the fortunes of a specific company in that market. Company-specific risk (alpha) usually accounts for 50% to 70% of a security's price movement and market risk (beta) for 30% to 50%. In other words, all stocks will tend to rise in a bull market and fall in a bear market, although the fortunes of a particular company are generally more important to that company's stock price than the general bent of the stock market.

Diversification reduces the aggregate risk of a portfolio through investments in a variety of securities—thus, lowering the company-specific risk (alpha) of a securities portfolio. In other words, the losses from one particular security can be offset by the gains from another security. But a well-diversified portfolio of U.S. stocks still retains the risk of declines in the overall U.S. stock market (beta). To protect against such declines, an investor may hold several portfolios of securities, each from a different asset class—for example, a portfolio of U.S. stocks, a portfolio of Japanese stocks and a portfolio of U.S. bonds. This broader type of diversification lowers the market risk of holding U.S. stocks since the price movements of U.S. stocks, Japanese stocks and U.S. bonds do not generally coincide.

A mutual fund provides investors with the benefits of diversification by participating in a large pool of securities and thereby obtaining exposure to different industries and/or asset classes. Moreover, the mutual fund industry allows investors to choose among a wide range of diversified pools. Today, there are more than 8,000 mutual funds with many different types of investment objectives designed to meet different consumer needs—from bond funds with lower risk and lower returns to technology funds that are more volatile and have higher expected returns.

Investors have gravitated toward mutual funds not only because they provide diversification, but also because they offer other advantages such as securities expertise, administrative cost and convenience. Although some individual investors may have some investment knowledge, the securities expertise of most mutual fund managers is higher. Moreover, fund managers have more access to company management, an in-house team of research analysts and Wall Street research. In addition, fund managers have access to technology that makes these resources available at the touch of a button. Administrative costs generally are lower for mutual funds than individual investments. These include savings on record keeping and better executions of securities trades (which usually cost less on a per share basis for the amount a fund might trade versus what an individual might trade). Moreover, fund complexes offer their shareholders a way to invest conveniently through phones or the Internet 24 hours a day. Fund complexes also provide fund shareholders with a broad array of related services such as tax reporting, retirement planning and educational materials.

On the other hand, investing through mutual funds has some inherent disadvantages versus investing in individual securities. These include the need to pay advisory fees, the possibility of poor performance and the potential conflicts of interest involved in any fiduciary relationship. The increased diversification of a mutual fund decreases the chance of hitting the jackpot from betting everything on one security that soars. Moreover, the relative advantages of mutual funds with regard to reduced brokerage costs and better research access have declined as individual investors have gained access to online trading and securities research on the Internet.

A mutual fund also leaves investors with less control of their securities portfolio, especially on the timing of realized gains for tax purposes. A mutual fund is required to distribute to its shareholders almost all capital gains realized during that year. Thus, an investor may have to pay tax on capital gains even if he or she does not sell fund shares. (See Chapter Three for more on mutual fund taxation.) On the other hand, a mutual fund is allowed to deduct all its management and operating expenses before making any distributions to its shareholders. By contrast, an investor who pays a fee to a financial adviser for managing individual securities may not deduct that fee unless that fee (together with other nonfund advisory expenses) exceeds 2% of his or her adjusted gross income. This 2% floor effectively precludes most investors from deducting the advisory fees they pay to managers of accounts for individual securities.

Investors choosing between individual stocks and a stock mutual fund should consider the rising volatility of the U.S. equity market. A recent study concludes that over the 35-year period from mid-1962 to 1997, the volatility, or dispersion of returns, among individual stocks more than doubled, therefore increasing the need for diversification. The study suggests that investors must hold 50 stocks in their portfolios in order to achieve the same level of diversification of risk provided by a 20-stock portfolio years ago when individual securities were less volatile.[2] Another study concluded that a portfolio of more than 100 large-cap or small-cap stocks is necessary to remain within 5% of average risk (defined in the study as the average volatility of 40,000 simulated portfolios created for the study).[3] On the other hand, some professional money managers believe that a portfolio of 20 to 30 stocks provides investors with adequate diversification.

There are additional considerations for investors who are trying to decide between individual bonds or a bond mutual fund. Such investors frequently are focused on income: they want the yield on their bond investments to provide a steady income stream. To obtain this income stream, investors can buy individual bonds—for example, Treasury bonds, U.S. government agency bonds, corporate bonds or municipal bonds— and hold these bonds to their maturity date. Alternatively, investors can obtain an income stream by buying a diversified mutual fund that invests in bonds. There are pros and cons to each alternative. Investors who purchase most types of individual bonds receive an income stream fixed at the time of purchase and usually have a right to get back their principal at the bond's maturity date. These two features are important especially to an investor who buys a bond to hold until maturity. By contrast, bond mutual funds have neither fixed income streams nor an obligation to give investors back their principal at maturity.

On the other hand, there are higher minimums required to purchase most individual bonds (usually a $25,000 minimum, except Treasury bonds, which have a $1,000 minimum) than for mutual funds, whose minimums may be as low as $1,000. An investor who buys or sells an individual bond will always pay trading costs. These may be as much as 2% to 4% of the value of bonds that are not widely traded or for odd lots below $100,000 in most bonds. By contrast, an investor can buy or redeem mutual fund shares on any business day without paying any trading fees, although the fund itself may incur transaction costs if its total sales do not match its total redemptions. Most important, owning one $25,000 individual bond lacks the diversification that comes from investing in a bond mutual fund. Such diversification is especially significant for corporate and municipal bonds because a few default from time to time. In addition, bond mutual funds offer convenient services, such as monthly income payments, compared to individual bonds that generally have quarterly, semiannual or annual income payments.

As the bull market in U.S. stocks continued, individual investors put more and more of their assets into equities, including equity mutual funds rather than bank deposits, bonds or real estate. From 1989 to 1999, the ratio of discretionary equity holdings to total discretionary financial assets for households rose from 34% to 61%, and the share of households owning equities rose from 32% to 48%. Similarly, the portion of new mutual fund accounts invested in equity funds was 36% between 1989 and 1995 and 48% between 1995 and 1999.[4]

There is much anecdotal evidence to suggest that individual investors are shifting toward equity in the form of individual securities rather than mutual funds. For example, the Nasdaq stock market reported swelling trading volume in technology stocks in 1999 and attributed much of the growth to individual investors trading on the Internet. Many press articles at that time highlighted investors who sought higher returns from hot stocks and more control of their tax situation by directly buying stocks rather than purchasing equity mutual funds. On the other hand, since the spring of 2000 when the Internet stock bubble burst, the volume of online stock trading by individuals has dropped sharply, as many have returned to more conservative mutual funds. More broadly, statistics from the Federal Reserve Board and the Investment Company Institute (ICI) show that U.S. households overall have been net buyers of equity mutual funds and net sellers of individual stocks during the 1990s (see Figure 1.1). In 1998 and 1999, the gap between household purchases of equities through mutual funds versus

FIGURE 1.1

Purchases of equities by households ($ billions)

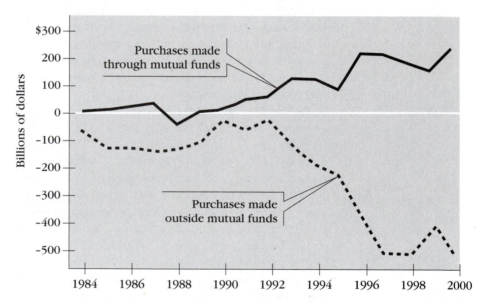

Note: Equities held directly or through mutual funds, bank personal trusts and estates, closed-end funds and defined contribution plans. Equity purchases made through mutual funds include purchases of equities made by mutual funds held in bank personal trusts and estates and mutual funds that are investment options in defined contribution plans. Equity purchases made outside mutual funds include purchases of equities made directly by bank personal trusts and estates, closed-end funds, and through direct purchase investment options in defined contribution plans.
Source: Federal Reserve Board; Investment Company Institute. Reprinted by permission of the Investment Company Institute.

other methods started to narrow, although the gap widened in 2000 as there was a relative increase in such equity purchases through mutual funds.

Besides online trading, another method for buying individual securities is the separate account—a portfolio of individual securities that is managed separately for a customer by a bank, broker or financial adviser. Historically, separate accounts were made available, usually by a trust bank or trust department of a commercial bank, to wealthy customers with account minimums of $1 million or higher. More recently, account minimums for certain types of separate accounts have dropped sharply to the range of $100,000 to $250,000, and in a few cases to $50,000. These newer types of separate accounts include consultant wraps and rep wraps, depending on whether the account is managed by a third-party adviser chosen by a consultant or a brokerage representative. The consultant or rep wrap for individual securities should be distinguished from a mutual fund wrap where a portfolio of mutual funds is managed for a customer. (See the exercise in Chapter Two for more on mutual fund wraps.)

In a consultant or rep wrap, the customer actually owns the specific securities in the account, rather than a share of a mutual fund that represents an undivided interest in a securities portfolio. As a result, the adviser can choose individual securities appropriate for the customer's particular objectives and can control the purchases and sales of securities in the account to reduce the tax impact on that customer. On the other hand, the advisory fee paid to the manager of a consultant or rep wrap is not deductible unless that fee (together with other advisory expenses) exceeds 2% of the customer's adjusted gross income. The advisory fee for a consultant or rep wrap generally ranges from 1.5% to 3% of assets under management per year, with no extra charge for brokerage commissions.

As the minimums have been lowered for consultant or rep wraps, the degree to which the selection of individual securities is customized for each investor has been reduced significantly. In many wrap programs, every investor is placed in one of several model portfolios, which buy and sell substantially the same securities for all accounts in that model through the use of a "cloning" technology. This trend toward "cloned" portfolios has spawned a spate of Internet-based wrap programs, such as RunMoney.com, with relatively low minimums and fees. In addition, several Internet companies, like Folio *fn,* have launched low-cost programs to construct and trade portfolios of stocks (sometimes called baskets). The investor can choose from prepackaged model portfolios constructed by the program sponsor, such as a growth portfolio of 50 stocks; or the investor can pick stocks for his or her own basket on the basis of criteria such as industry sector, market capitalization, price/earnings ratio or inclusion on an analyst's recommended list.

The two types of portfolios cater to different investors. The prepackaged model portfolio is similar to a mutual fund; it provides passive investors with little choice or customization. By contrast, baskets of stocks are a portfolio tool designed to appeal to active traders willing to delineate specific investment requirements for a basket. Prepackaged model portfolios and baskets of stocks also can be distinguished based on whether the portfolios are updated and rebalanced on a periodic basis through a service provided by the program sponsor. Most prepackaged models offer regular updates and rebalancing of their portfolios, while baskets of stocks generally do not. The active trader using baskets may change the criteria for the stocks in his or her basket or may request that some of the stocks in the basket be sold in favor of other asset classes.

Fidelity Investments and Charles Schwab both announced in early 2001 their intention to offer baskets of stocks. The SEC said that folios are not mutual funds so long as individual investors make their own investment decisions on their securities portfolio in light of their own particular needs and the investor maintains the rights of ownership with respect to each of the securities in the folio.

The expansion of separate accounts, through consultant and rep wraps as well as Internet-based programs, has attracted significant assets. Cerulli Associates estimates that, from 1998 through the end of 2000, assets in consultant wrap accounts grew by approximately 25% per year and rep accounts by 43% per year. At the end of 2000, assets in consultant wrap accounts were approximately $290 billion, and assets in rep wrap accounts were approximately $69 billion. In response, some traditional managers of mutual funds have created wrap programs involving securities for their high-net-worth customers in order to compete with those offered by banks, brokers and financial advisers. Other traditional managers of mutual funds have developed Internet-based tools to help their customers construct portfolios of individual securities and mutual funds. (See Chapter Seven for more on investment advice.)

II. *Mutual Funds: History and Current Trends*

Although historians have found pooled trusts in other places, the origins of the modern U.S. mutual fund industry can be traced to Boston. At the beginning of the twentieth century, Boston law firms formed trust divisions to manage the assets of wealthy Boston families. As these families grew and the wealth was dispersed, the mutual fund came into existence as a way to provide commingled management of multiple family accounts. During 1924 in Boston, there was the first public offering of a mutual fund—an "open-end" fund that stands ready to issue and redeem shares to investors on a daily basis. But the growth of the mutual fund industry was soon stymied by the stock crash of 1929 and the Depression of the 1930s. Determined to protect investors better, Congress passed legislation regulating investments and securities markets, including the Securities Act of 1933, which requires full disclosure in all public securities offerings.

In 1935, the SEC undertook a special study that led to the passage of the Investment Company Act of 1940 (1940 Act). The 1940 Act established the standards by which mutual funds and other types of investment companies must operate, including requirements (detailed in Chapter Three) for fund promotion, reporting, pricing and portfolio investing. Although the 1940 Act offered better protection to investors, the mutual fund industry grew very slowly during the 1940s and early 1950s.

The industry experienced a small growth spurt during the late 1950s and 1960s, when the economy was strong and the stock market was rising. At that time, most mutual funds invested in stocks and were sold by broker-dealers with front-end sales charges, or "loads," of 8½% of an investor's initial investment in a fund. But this growth spurt gave way to doldrums during the early 1970s; as the stock market declined steadily, it became very difficult to sell stock mutual funds. Instead, investors were interested mainly in short-term or income-oriented investments.

During the 1970s, the industry created money market funds, many of which were sold through direct advertising without the traditional sales load. Money market funds became the savior of the industry during the late 1970s and early 1980s as interest rates, and therefore returns to shareholders of these funds, climbed to double digits, while banks were legally prevented from paying more than a specified rate (e.g., 4% or 5%) on most small deposits. By the early 1980s, money market funds accounted for a larger percentage of industry assets than either stock or bond funds. Money market funds allowed fund companies to gather assets from individual investors, who could then exchange easily from money market funds into stock funds as the stock market took off during the 1980s. At the same time, money market funds became an attractive cash management vehicle for corporations, trust departments and other institutional investors.

In the late 1970s, the mutual fund industry also introduced tax-exempt funds based on legislation allowing them to pass through to their shareholders tax-exempt interest from municipal debt. These tax-exempt bond and money market funds became increasingly popular after 1986 when Congress eliminated or restricted many other tax-advantaged investment opportunities. Such tax-exempt funds remain one of the core vehicles to attract high-net-worth investors.

Over the past 15 years, mutual funds have grown at a fantastic pace. The total assets of mutual funds were less than $500 billion in 1985 and climbed to almost $7 trillion at the end of 2000—a compound annual growth rate of 19.3%. A number of factors were behind the rapid growth rate of mutual funds assets and accounts during the late 1980s and 1990s. These factors, which will be discussed in later Chapters, include a bull market in U.S. stocks, the expansion of tax-advantaged retirement vehicles, the creation of attractive new fund products and the introduction of enhanced services to shareholders. Another factor driving the rapid growth of fund assets and accounts has been the broad variety of distribution channels and pricing structures developed by the mutual fund industry. While later Chapters explore these developments in detail, it is useful to summarize the key distribution channels and pricing structures here.

Traditionally, mutual funds were distributed through intermediaries—mainly broker-dealers—who sold mutual funds for a front-end sales load charged to the investor at the time of purchase. These sales loads have gradually declined from 8½% in the 1960s to an average of 4% to 5% currently. In addition to (or in lieu of) loads, brokers now typically receive annual distribution and service fees called 12b-1 fees. These 12b-1 fees typically range from 0.25% to 1.00% per year of assets under management; they are paid by the fund, rather than the individual investor, to the distributor.

The advent of money market funds during the 1970s spurred the spread of direct-marketed funds. In the direct distribution channel, mutual fund distributors use print ads and mailers to solicit sales from investors who are comfortable making their own investment decisions. These investors respond by mail, by calling a toll-free number at the fund complex or by accessing the Internet. Most of these direct-marketed funds charge no sales loads and no 12b-1 fees (or 0.25% or less per year); they are called no-load funds.

Retirement plans represent a third distribution channel, partly institutional and partly retail. Mutual fund managers are attractive service providers to plan sponsors of

401(k) and other defined contribution plans because they offer a broad array of investment alternatives, quality record keeping and servicing features. After a mutual fund manager is chosen by the plan sponsor, the manager usually provides disclosure documents and educational materials to plan participants so they may individually choose to have their plan contributions invested in specific funds. Record keeping and other service fees (in addition to standard fund expenses) may be negotiated between the mutual fund manager and the employer or plan sponsor.

Over the past decade, intermediaries other than broker-dealers have begun to play a significant role in fund distribution and management. Banks began to offer money market and bond funds and, to a lesser degree, equity funds. Most bank-sponsored funds are sold with loads or 12b-1 fees, although some are sold no-load or with loads waived for fiduciary accounts. At the same time, insurance companies have joint-ventured with fund managers to sell variable annuities—annuity contracts wrapped around a set of mutual funds. These are contracts issued by insurance companies that allow investors to accumulate assets on a tax-deferred basis for retirement or other long-term goals.

More broadly, financial planners have become major sources of investment advice to mutual fund customers faced with an overwhelming array of choices. Financial planners help fund customers sort out their financial goals, design a general strategy and select specific funds to implement that strategy. In selecting mutual funds from several fund families, financial planners have been an important user of the mutual fund marketplaces. These marketplaces, created in the early 1990s, allow investors to purchase over 1,000 mutual funds offered by over 100 fund sponsors, typically through a single brokerage account.

Table 1.1 shows the asset growth between 1985 and 2000 of the three main types of mutual funds, which are based on the asset class of fund investments: stock funds, bond funds and money market funds. A fourth category of mutual fund is a hybrid fund, which invests in a combination of stocks, bonds and other securities. The Table indicates a marked shift in the relative importance of fund asset classes between 1985 and 2000—toward equity funds and away from money market funds. Figure 1.2 shows the number of households owning mutual funds, which went from 10.2 million in 1984 to 50.6 million in June 2000, the latter figure representing 49% of all U.S. households. Most mutual fund shareholders are in the middle class: according to the ICI, 58% have household incomes in the range of $25,000 to $74,999. Nine percent have household incomes below that range, and 33% have household incomes above that range.

Given the large percentage of U.S. households that own mutual funds, it should not be surprising that the mutual fund industry is an important source of capital for the U.S. economy.[5] Mutual funds help finance job creation and corporate growth by buying the stock of U.S. publicly traded companies. As of December 31, 1999, mutual funds owned almost 20% of the $17.5 trillion of publicly held U.S. equity outstanding. At the same time, mutual funds have provided companies with an alternative source (in addition to banks) of borrowed money, especially short-term borrowings (less than nine months) called commercial paper. As of December 31, 1999, mutual funds owned over 11% of the $4.6 trillion in total corporate and foreign bonds outstanding and almost 45% of the $1.4 trillion in total commercial paper outstanding. Moreover, mutual funds are big suppliers of capital to governmental entities. As of De-

TABLE 1.1

Mutual fund industry assets ($ billions)

			Fund Categories			
Years	Equity	Hybrid	Bond	Taxable Money Market	Tax-Exempt Money Market	Total
1985	116.9	12.0	122.6	207.5	36.3	495.4
1986	161.4	18.8	243.3	228.3	63.8	715.7
1987	180.5	24.2	248.4	254.7	61.4	769.2
1988	194.7	21.1	255.7	272.3	65.7	809.4
1989	248.8	31.8	271.9	358.7	69.4	980.7
1990	239.5	36.1	291.3	414.7	83.6	1,065.2
1991	404.7	52.2	393.8	452.6	89.9	1,393.2
1992	514.1	78.0	504.2	451.4	94.8	1,642.5
1993	740.7	144.5	619.5	461.9	103.4	2,070.0
1994	852.8	164.5	527.1	500.6	110.4	2,155.4
1995	1,249.1	210.5	598.9	630.0	123.0	2,811.5
1996	1,726.1	252.9	645.4	762.0	139.8	3,526.3
1997	2,368.0	317.1	724.2	898.1	160.8	4,468.2
1998	2,978.2	364.7	830.6	1,163.2	188.5	5,525.2
1999	4,041.9	383.2	808.1	1,408.7	204.4	6,846.3
2000	3,961.4	350.8	809.1	1,607.3	238.1	6,966.8

Note: The data contain a series break beginning in 1990. All funds were reclassified in 1990, and a separate category was created for hybrid funds. At the same time, data for funds that invest in other mutual funds were excluded from the series. Data prior to 1990 have been restated to create a consistent series back to 1984.
Source: Investment Company Institute. Reprinted by permission of the Investment Company Institute.

cember 31, 1999, mutual funds owned almost 8% of the $7.6 trillion of U.S. Treasury and agency securities outstanding—thus helping to finance the national debt and lower the cost of home mortgages through agencies like Fannie Mae. As of December 31, 1999, mutual funds owned 31% of the $1.53 trillion in total municipal securities outstanding—thus helping to fund public projects like bridges and schools for local governments.

A 1999 study by the ICI indicates that the mutual fund industry also has a significant role in the economy as an employer. According to the study, mutual fund complexes themselves provide approximately 166,000 jobs nationwide, and the mutual fund industry creates an additional 290,000 jobs in other areas of the economy—for example, organizations like banks, accounting firms and law firms that provide services to mutual funds, as well as brokers and other entities that sell a range of investment products including mutual funds.

As the mutual fund industry grew during the 1990s, there were many acquisitions of investment advisers to fund complexes. For example, Invesco acquired AIM, and Zurich Financial acquired Kemper and Scudder. In 2000 alone, there was a wave of

FIGURE 1.2

Number and percentage of U.S. households owning mutual funds, 1980–2000

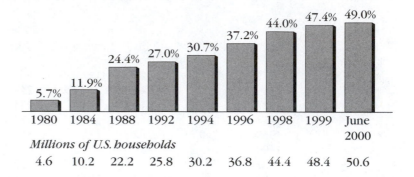

Note: U.S. households owning mutual funds in 1980 and 1984 were estimated from data on the number of accounts held by individual shareholders and the number of funds owned by fund-owning households. Data for 1980 through 1992 exclude households owning mutual funds only through employer-sponsored retirement plans. Data for 1994 through 2000 include households owning mutual funds only through employer-sponsored retirement plans. The data for 1998, 1999 and 2000 include fund ownership through variable annuities.
Source: Fundamentals: Investment Company Institute Research in Brief, Vol. 9, No. 4 (August 2000), Fig. 1. Reprinted by permission of the Investment Company Institute.

consolidations, including several acquisitions of U.S. fund complexes by international companies: UniCredito Italiano acquired Pioneer, CDC Asset Management acquired Nvest (adviser to the Oakmark funds) and Old Mutual acquired United Asset Management (parent of the adviser to the PBHG funds and other fund families). These consolidations have occurred mainly because of the increasing need to make large expenditures on technology, offer a broad array of products and achieve a global presence in order to stay competitive. (See Chapter Ten on mergers and acquisitions.) Yet the assets controlled by the largest 10 fund complexes have remained relatively stable, between 45% and 55% during the past decade, according to the ICI. This stability is the result of several factors—most important, the ease of entry of new managers into the fund industry and the very small number of acquisitions involving the managers of the industry's largest 25 fund complexes.

The ownership of U.S. mutual fund managers as of late 2000 reflects both the traditional and modern elements of the industry. The industry was historically dominated by narrowly focused fund management companies owned by their employees and/or founding families. Thus, 59% of mutual fund assets are managed by companies that are publicly held, and 41% of assets are managed by privately held companies. At the same time, half of the assets in the industry's largest 50 fund complexes were managed by subsidiaries of financial services conglomerates whose primary line of business is not mutual fund management. These conglomerates tend to be dominated by commercial banks, insurance companies and securities dealers seeking the relatively stable fee income derived from managing mutual funds.

III. The Structural Characteristics of Mutual Funds and Commercial Banks

A. Structure of Mutual Funds

Looking at mutual funds as financial intermediaries, what exactly is the relationship among their investors, the fund, the management company and other service providers? To answer this question, it is helpful to consider Figure 1.3.

Many people do not realize that a mutual fund is a separate entity—a trust or corporation—with its own board of directors, usually consisting of a majority of independent directors. On the basis of disclosure documents, shareholders (savers) provide their money to the fund, and they elect the independent directors of the fund. Each year, the independent directors approve an advisory contract with a management company, which invests fund assets in stocks and/or bonds according to the objectives specified in the fund's disclosure documents (e.g., a prospectus). (See Chapter Three for discussion of regulation and disclosure of mutual funds.)

Service providers to a mutual fund may be categorized by their relationship to shareholders, the mutual fund itself or the securities portfolio held by the fund. First, it is the management company (sometimes called the investment adviser or investment manager) that contracts with the mutual fund to invest its assets in a portfolio of securities. On the basis of research and analysis, the management company selects the securities in the fund's portfolio consistent with the investment objectives stated in the fund's prospectus. The management company is also usually the sponsor or creator of the fund.

A second category of service providers acts as links between the shareholders and the mutual fund; these include the underwriter (or distributor), which sells fund shares to investors, and the transfer agent, which services existing fund shareholders. These

FIGURE 1.3

Structure of a mutual fund

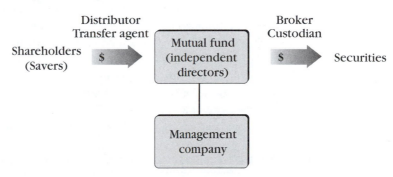

services include a variety of record-keeping tasks such as mailing shareholder account information, calculating and disbursing dividends and preparing tax information. Another key service is daily pricing of mutual fund shares so that investors can purchase or redeem these shares each day. While the transfer agent may be an affiliate of the management company or an unaffiliated firm, the underwriter is usually an affiliate of the management company.

Still other service providers act as links between the mutual fund and its portfolio of securities. This third category includes the custodians that hold the assets of the fund in a segregated account and the brokers that effect securities trades on behalf of the fund. Fund custodians are usually banks, which are required to hold mutual fund assets in segregated accounts. Fund brokers may be independent firms or a combination of independent and affiliates of the fund management company.

Most management companies advise an array of mutual funds including all three of the main categories: stock, bond and money market funds. Such an array of mutual funds, all advised by the same management company, is called a fund complex. Exhibit 4 of the case study for this Chapter lists the array of mutual funds in the T. Rowe Price fund complex. Shareholders usually are allowed to exchange freely among funds in the same complex. In addition, the funds in a complex typically have the same principal underwriter and transfer agent. Shareholders periodically receive a consolidated statement containing information on all their fund holdings within the complex. Shareholders can also make one phone call or visit one website to purchase or sell several funds in the same complex.

Similarly, newspapers report the daily prices of mutual funds organized by complex and then by alphabetical order. Newspapers show a bid (or buy price) and ask (or sell price) for each fund. The buy and sell prices will be different if the fund has a front-end sales load. If a fund does not have a front-end sales load, the newspaper indicates "N.L." for no-load. As explained in Figure 1.4, the newspapers add the letter "p" after the name of a fund that has a 12b-1 fee and the letter "r" after the name of a fund that has a back-end load or redemption fee. A back-end load is paid by a shareholder to the fund distributor when leaving a fund within a specified number of years. A redemption fee is paid by a shareholder to the fund itself if he or she leaves the fund within a short period such as 90 days or six months.

The price, or net asset value (NAV), of a fund is the market value of all the fund's securities and other holdings (if any), minus expenses, divided by the total number of shares outstanding. Mutual funds must calculate the NAV of their shares every business day (usually at 4:00 P.M. EST). Investors can place orders to buy or sell (redeem) some or all of their fund shares at any time and will receive the NAV next calculated for the fund. Thus, an investor who places an order to buy fund shares at 11:00 A.M. will buy those shares at the NAV of that fund calculated at 4:00 P.M. the same day. An investor who places an order to buy fund shares at 11:00 P.M. will buy those shares at the NAV of that fund calculated at 4:00 P.M. the next business day.

B. *Mutual Funds versus Commercial Banks*

As shown by Table 1.2, assets of major institutions and financial intermediaries have increased greatly in the past decade. However, mutual funds have gained assets at a more rapid pace than banks, insurance companies and other financial intermediaries. By

FIGURE 1.4

Mutual fund quotes in the newspaper

Apzbc:			
Axyte	9.95	10.73	...
Bxy Xer	10.37	11.33	-.01
Dar Rppe	7.38	8.07	+.09
Income	3.16	3.45	+.01
Tbq Ratl	9.97	10.47	+.01
Tbqr Dt	10.19	10.70	-.02
Xypr Ap r	10.05	10.98	-.01
Brlkd:			
Blgr Dfr	15.64	16.46	-.03
Bmo Pnc	8.54	N.L.	-.06
Bto Bmd	7.27	7.65	...
Cmyog:			
MIA p	11.86	12.79	+.01
MIX	11.44	12.33	+.03
MIY p	9.70	10.46	-.01
MBF	11.58	12.49	+.04
MBI	14.18	15.92	+.20
MBR	11.99	12.93	+.03
MRI	10.01	10.79	-.02
MII	7.66	8.26	+.02
MDX	10.00	10.50	...
DMX r	9.74	10.23	...
GYI	6.93	7.47	-.03
JAM	13.47	14.18	-.04
JEL	10.09	10.59	-.06
MTNC	10.25	10.76	-.02
MPRS r	10.12	10.62	+.02
Jellies	20.33	N.L.	+.01
Sulter	23.81	N.L.	+.13
Drxpg:			
Bakc Jau	8.19	8.53	-.01
Cryl Ba	20.68	22.12	+.05
Gryd 3	12.10	12.60	-.04
Frp Dur p	9.80	10.45	-.11
Fye Pm p	12.61	N.L.	...
Hy Finc	15.45	16.52	+.06
Hx Papie	10.96	11.42	-.06
Lerl Eiy t	10.02	10.95	+.02
Jxt RP	10.90	11.12	-.04
Lante	12.01	13.14	-.02
Mina Si	7.36	7.67	-.01
MsalT p	9.56	9.96	+.01
Nuz Bai	9.85	9.95	...
Oceana	16.49	17.64	+.12
Grxya	15.30	N.L.	+.04
Gsrxab r	12.96	N.L.	-.04
Hilt ltd	10.54	N.L.	-.02
Holpre r	8.40	N.L.	-.02
Hprl Rd	13.58	N.L.	+.07
Nev Sra	16.65	N.L.	-.01
Ow Nort r	13.53	N.L.	+.17
Sys Run	5.08	N.L.	+.01
Tqr Hyd	8.73	N.L.	+.02
Tuir IS	10.26	N.L.	-.03
Tvsa Ei	5.11	N.L.	+.01
Veersl Yr	9.49	9.87	+.07
Fdrlk:			
Uhd Eec	10.18	N.L.	+.03
Rho Qnd p	10.77	N.L.	+.02
Iro Nico t	8.54	N.L.	-.06
Gpprl:			
Allist B	24.00	N.L.	+.01
Cuy Nini t	10.76	N.L.	-.03
Eqryti	15.87	16.71	+.02
Ginta Ir	12.00	N.L.	+.01
Gvrt Lis	10.18	N.L.	+.03
Heai lec f	10.40	10.51	-.02
Jbd Hld	10.23	10.77	-.04

How to Read Newspaper Fund Quotes

The following is an example of how mutual fund tables appear in many newspapers.

The first column is the abbreviated fund's name. Several funds listed under a single heading indicate a family of funds.

The second column is the Net Asset Value (NAV) per share as of the close of the preceding business day. In some newspapers, the NAV is identified as the sell or the bid price—the amount per share you would receive if you sold your shares (less the deferred sales charge, if any). Each mutual fund determines its net asset value every business day by dividing the market value of its total net assets, less liabilities, by the number of shares outstanding. On any given day, you can determine the value of your holdings by multiplying the NAV by the number of shares you own.

The third column is the offering price or, in some papers, the buy price or the asked price—the price you would pay if you purchased shares. The buy price is the NAV plus any sales charges. If there are no initial sales charges, an "NL" for no-load appears in this column, and the buy price is the same as the NAV. To figure the sales charge percentage, divide the difference between the NAV and the offering price by the offering price. Here, for instance, the sales charge is 5 percent ($14.18 - $13.47 = $0.71; $0.71 ÷ $14.18 = 0.050).

The fourth column shows the change, if any, in net asset value from the preceding day's quotation—in other words, the change over the most recent one-day trading period. This fund, for example, gained six cents per share.

A "p" following the abbreviated name of the fund denotes a fund that charges an annual fee from assets for marketing and distribution costs, also known as a 12b-1 plan (named after the 1980 Securities and Exchange Commission rule that permits them).

If the fund name is followed by an "r," the fund has either a contingent deferred sales charge (CDSC) or a redemption fee. A CDSC is a charge if shares are sold within a certain period; a redemption charge is a fee applied whenever shares are sold.

A "t" designates a fund that has both a CDSC or a redemption fee and a 12b-1 fee.

An "f" indicates a fund that habitually enters the previous day's prices, instead of the current day's.

Other footnotes may also apply to a fund listing. Please see the explanatory notes that accompany mutual fund tables in your newspaper.

Source: Investment Company Institute, *Mutual Fund Fact Book* (2000). Reprinted by permission of the Investment Company Institute.

TABLE 1.2

Assets of major institutions and financial intermediaries ($ millions)

	1990R	1992R	1994	1996	1998	1999
Depository institutions	*$4,912,370*	*$4,998,460*	*$5,461,960*	*$6,072,190*	*$7,122,040*	*$7,560,620*
Commercial banks[a]	3,337,480	3,654,930	4,159,710	4,710,400	5,642,130	5,994,080
Credit unions[b]	217,240	264,700	293,600	330,110	391,480	415,130
Savings institutions[c]	1,357,650	1,078,830	1,008,650	1,031,680	1,088,430	1,151,410
Life insurance	*$1,367,370*	*$1,614,340*	*$1,862,890*	*$2,246,290*	*$2,769,520*	*$3,104,510*
Investment institutions	*$2,488,112*	*$3,531,252*	*$4,311,878*	*$6,353,023*	*$9,676,185*	*$7,004,779*
Bank-administered trusts[d]	1,368,666	1,791,526	2,043,197	2,684,453	3,999,321	N/A
Closed-end investment companies	52,554	93,467	113,285	142,300	151,655	158,225
Mutual funds[e]	1,066,892	1,646,259	2,155,396	3,526,270	5,525,209	6,846,339

a. Includes U.S.-chartered commercial banks, foreign banking offices in the United States, bank holding companies and banks in affiliated areas.
b. Includes only federal or federally insured state credit unions serving natural persons.
c. Includes mutual savings banks, federal savings banks and savings and loan associations.
d. Reflects only discretionary trusts and agencies.
e. Includes short-term funds; excludes funds of funds.
N/A = not available.
R = revised.
Source: Federal Reserve Board; Federal Financial Institutions Examination Council; Investment Company Institute. Reprinted by permission of the Investment Company Institute.

2000, the assets of the mutual fund industry were nearly $7 trillion, almost 6.5 times the size at the end of 1990. By contrast, depository institutions have grown only 53% over the same time period, to $7.5 trillion in assets, while life insurance assets have more than doubled to $3.1 trillion.

Let's consider the structure of a mutual fund as compared to the structure of another key financial intermediary—a commercial bank. A mutual fund is a relatively pure form of financial intermediary because there is an almost perfect pass through of money from the accounts of fund shareholders (savers) to the securities in which the fund invests. Shareholders are told in which types of securities their funds will be invested, and changes in the value of the securities held in the fund portfolio are translated on a daily basis directly to the value of the fund shares held by the fund shareholders. The management company receives a management fee based on the size of the fund (e.g., 0.6% of fund assets or 60 basis points, abbreviated 60 bp) for investing fund assets on behalf of fund shareholders. The management company does not participate in either the profits or losses of fund investments (except to the extent that an increase or decrease in the fund's assets affects the amount of the management fee).

By contrast, a commercial bank is not a pure pass-through type of financial intermediary. Through branches and other marketing efforts, the bank gathers deposits from savers, although they have no specific knowledge of how their deposits will be used. Bank officers invest the monies of savers in loans or securities the bank deems appropriate at the time. In return for use of their monies, bank depositors usually receive a specified rate of interest—for example, 5% per year—that does not change on a daily basis because of fluctuations in the financial markets. Nor do bank depositors share in the gains or losses of the bank's investments in loans or securities. Consequently, the management of a bank is not paid a management fee based on the current value of the bank's investments. Instead, bank management earns profits by generating a positive spread between the return on bank investments in loans or securities and the interest paid on bank deposits.

Thus, the shareholders of a mutual fund are its equity owners. They elect the directors of the fund and fully participate in the positive or negative returns of fund investments. By contrast, the depositors in a bank are its creditors. As creditors, they do not elect the bank's directors, who are chosen by the bank's shareholders. Nor do bank depositors participate in the positive or negative returns of a bank's loans or investments.

Because the changes in the value of a mutual fund's portfolio are translated daily into changes in the value of fund shares, it is very difficult for a mutual fund to mismatch its assets and liabilities. For this reason, the risk of bankruptcy for a mutual fund is extremely low, and a mutual fund share is not insured by any federal agency. By contrast, since bank depositors are entitled to receive a prescribed rate of interest regardless of the results of the bank's loans or investments, a bank may face a mismatch between its assets and liabilities. However, this risk of bankruptcy is effectively mitigated for bank depositors because their deposits are insured up to $100,000 per separate account by the Federal Deposit Insurance Corporation (FDIC). Reading 1.3 outlines the basic organization of a commercial bank.

In addition, many banks have trust departments that manage investments for trust, agency, pension and/or other fiduciary accounts. These trust accounts are managed in a similar fashion to separate accounts for individual securities, described above. To facilitate investments by these fiduciary accounts, some banks have established common or collective trust funds that operate to some degree like private mutual funds, though they are subject to different regulatory and tax regimes. Bank common and collective trust funds are discussed in Chapter Two.

Compare the diagram in Figure 1.5 of a commercial bank (without a trust department) to the diagram of a mutual fund in Figure 1.3. Note that the shareholders of the bank are different from its depositors (savers), while the savers and shareholders of a mutual fund are the same. Also note that the bank's managers are officers of the bank itself, as opposed to the fund managers, who are in a separate entity that has a contract with the fund.

In short, to use Robert Merton's terms, mutual funds are "translucent" financial intermediaries, and commercial banks are "opaque" financial intermediaries.[6] As Merton points out, customers of a financial intermediary have a very strong need to have their promised payoffs from the intermediary as insensitive as possible to the fortunes of the intermediary itself. In theory, these customers could seek to eliminate the risk of default by the intermediary through hedging or diversification; in practice, however, the crucial role of a financial intermediary is to provide services to many customers who themselves are not efficient hedgers or diversifiers. Thus, "opaque" commercial banks present their customers with a significant and difficult-to-understand risk of default, which is mitigated substantially by government insurance of deposits up to $100,000 per account. As "translucent" intermediaries, mutual funds present their cus-

FIGURE 1.5

Structure of a commercial bank

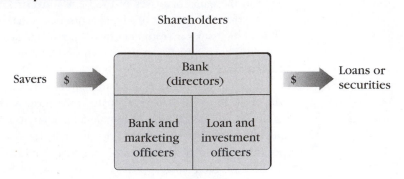

tomers with a less significant and easier-to-understand risk of default; as a result, fund customers have been willing to do business with mutual funds despite their lack of governmental insurance.

REVIEW QUESTIONS

1. What are the pros and cons of investing directly in individual stocks or bonds versus investing indirectly through a mutual fund?

2. What is the difference between alpha and beta risk? Which one can be reduced through diversification?

3. What is the difference between a sales load and a 12b-1 fee? Why did the advent of money market funds lead to no-load funds directly marketed to investors?

4. How does the money flow from shareholders to securities through a mutual fund? What roles do the service providers play for mutual funds?

5. If the interest from a money market fund's investments increases from 5% to 6% per year, what will happen to the return on the fund's shares and to the management fee of the fund's managers? If the interest from a bank's investments increases from 5% to 6% per year, what will happen to the return on the bank's deposits and to the profits of the bank?

6. What is the difference between a shareholder of a fund and a shareholder of a bank? Who is an "investor" in the bank? Who do the directors of a fund represent, as opposed to the directors of a bank?

DISCUSSION QUESTIONS

1. From 1982 through 1999, the U.S. stock market rose at a historically high rate, which obviously helped to attract assets to equity mutual funds. If the returns in the U.S. stock market revert to historical norms of 11% to 13% annual returns, what might that imply for the size and composition of the mutual fund industry?

2. The mutual fund industry is beginning to use the Internet to disseminate fund information and effect fund transactions. The Internet also makes it much easier for savers to obtain information about individual securities and much cheaper to trade these securities. As the Internet develops, will savers make their investment directly in individual securities rather through financial intermediaries such as mutual funds?

3. As the baby boomers have matured, they have become more oriented toward savings and more disposed toward mutual funds. The first wave of the baby boomers, born between 1946 and 1950, reaches normal retirement age between 2010 and 2015. What does the retirement of the baby boomers imply for mutual funds, directly in terms of savings patterns and indirectly in terms of the stock market?

4. Why do you think the mutual fund industry has experienced a decline in front-end sales loads and the introduction of 12b-1 fees? Do you believe that most sales of equity and bond funds will be in the direct marketing channel without loads or 12b-1 fees, or in the intermediary channel with loads and/or 12b-1 fees?

5. How do you think the roles of commercial banks and mutual funds as financial intermediaries will change in the future? Will their roles tend to converge or diverge?

6. Should the mutual fund industry push for government insurance of money market funds? Should federal insurance of bank deposits be reduced or eliminated?

NOTES

1. De Bondt and Thaler, "Does the Stock Market Overreact?" *Journal of Finance* 40(3), 793–805 (1985). See also Poterba and Summers, "Mean Reversion in Stock Prices: Evidence and Implications," *Journal of Financial Economics* 22, 26–59 (1988).
2. Campbell, Lettau, Malkiel and Xu, "Have Individual Stocks Become More Volatile? An Empirical Exploration of Idiosyncratic Risk," *Journal of Finance* 56(1), 1–43 (February 2001).
3. Newould and Poon, "Portfolio Risk, Portfolio Performance, and the Individual Investor," *Journal of Investing* 5, 72–78 (Summer 1996).
4. Bernstein Research, *The Future of Money Management in America*, 72–73, 76 (2000).
5. ICI, Mutual Fund Fact Book, 2000.
6. Merton, "A Functional Perspective of Financial Intermediation," *Financial Management* 24, 23–41 (Summer 1995).

READING 1.1

*Money Managers and Securities Research**

Robert C. Pozen

I. The Basic Framework of Portfolio Theory

Economists have developed an extensive body of portfolio theory[1] and empirical evidence on the stock markets. According to portfolio theory, it is a reasonable approximation to characterize every investment by two measures—expected return and risk.[2] Expected return is usually defined as the weighted average of all possible returns[3] from an investment.[4] Risk is usually defined as the average amount of variation among all the possible returns from an investment.[5] As a general rule, risk and return are positively correlated.[6] An investment with a low risk, like a U.S. savings bond, usually has a low return. An investment with a high risk, like a speculative stock, usually has a potential for a high return.

Portfolio theory generally assumes that investors are "risk averse": they will avoid investments with increased risks unless compensated by appropriate increases in expected returns.[7] This assumption of risk aversion is probably realistic for most investors, especially for the clients of institutional investors.[8] Although a few gamblers might prefer risky investments solely because of their riskiness, they can better express this preference for risks by trading directly in stock options than by depositing their savings in a financial intermediary with a relatively stable portfolio.[9]

Given the dual characteristics of investment opportunities and the normal preferences of their clients, money managers should try to construct portfolios with the highest return for any given risk level or, in other words, the lowest risk for any given return.[10] In theory, money managers might achieve this objective by either of two approaches—by finding "undervalued" stocks with higher returns than stocks of the same risk category, or by decreasing the aggregate risks of their portfolios without lowering the average returns. . . .

II. The Search for Higher Returns

Most of the securities research purchased by money managers is aimed at discovering undervalued stocks with higher returns than stocks in the same risk category.[11] From a group of 50 very stable stocks, for example, a money manager might try to select the 10 stocks that will show the largest gains during the next year. Researchers (often called analysts) try to discover such undervalued stocks by technical or fundamental analysis. In technical analysis, the researcher examines historical data on prices and volume of stock trading in an attempt to find recurring patterns for individual securities or for the stock market as a whole.[12] For instance, a technical analyst might attempt to predict stock prices on the basis of the volume of short-selling[13] in a particular stock. In fundamental analysis, the researcher examines historical data on corporate earnings and management in an attempt to predict future flows of corporate income for particular companies, industries or corporations generally. For example, a fundamental analyst might try to predict stock prices in airline companies by projecting the supply and demand for airline services.[14]

A. Technical Analysis. In an extensive set of empirical studies, economists have demonstrated that future changes in stock prices are randomly related to current stock prices.[15] These studies have failed to find any predictable connection of significant magnitude between future changes in stock prices and past data on stock prices, trading volume and the main chart patterns used by technical analysts.[16] Although these studies have found some statistical dependencies for stock prices within very short and very long time periods, the extra returns from trading strategies based on these dependencies are often offset by the transaction costs of such strategies.[17]

Moreover, technical analysis offers no economic theory of causation between past and future movements of stock prices.[18] It is based on the notion that "largely because of investor psychology, buying and selling patterns recur."[19] Technical analysis focuses exclusively on the internal dynamics of the stock markets; it ignores entirely the earnings of the corporations, which are the ultimate sources of value for the shares traded on the stock markets. . . .

* Robert C. Pozen, *Money Managers and Securities Research*, 51 *New York University Law Review.* Rev. 923 (1976), pp. 923–943. Reprinted with permission.

B. Fundamental Analysis. As technical analysts focus on the trading patterns of stocks, so fundamental analysts focus on the earnings of corporations. Since future changes in stock prices are significantly correlated with future changes in corporate earnings,[20] any fundamental analyst who could predict future changes in corporate earnings could thereby predict future changes in stock prices to a substantial degree. The main problem is that future changes in corporate earnings are themselves randomly related to past records of corporate earnings.[21] In other words, a corporation with earnings of $1 million in 1976 is as likely to have earnings of $0.8 million, as it is to have earnings of $1.2 million in 1977. For this reason, fundamental analysis will be of economic value only if the analyst uncovers new information about a company's earning potential[22] or makes a new interpretation of existing data about that company. . . .

C. The Social Benefits of Securities Research. [Adherents to the Efficient Market Hypothesis (EMH) do not claim that security analysis is a worthless pursuit. On the contrary, they hold that the workings of efficient markets are vitally dependent on the labors of thousands of analysts and investors; it is just that these poor fellows do not realize, or refuse to believe, that their efforts will not be rewarded. Moreover, we are also told that all those astute financial institutions are paying millions of dollars for research that will not benefit them but will rather fulfill the broader social purpose of keeping our security markets efficient. Adherents to EMH want us to believe this and more. Thus we are to believe that investors and analysts are only selectively rational, that is, they are rational in making the investment decisions which are necessary to keep our securities markets efficient but they are irrational in disbelieving the EMH, which disbelief is essential to the continued efficiency of our security markets. Why, we must ask, should we believe that such an inconsistency in rational behavior on the part of investors and security analysts actually exists? What would happen to the markets' efficiency if the investors and analysts refused to expend any longer efforts, which cannot benefit them personally? Can true believers in EMH continue to reap the benefits that the work of the disbelievers bestows on them? Can they buy and sell securities with the same degree of confidence as is possessed by those who expend efforts at research?][23]

III. Lower Risks Through Diversification

While money managers cannot easily find stocks with the same risk category, through diversification they can generally decrease the aggregate risk of their investments without decreasing aggregate returns. The basic principle of diversification is that the overall construction of the portfolio, rather than the selection of individual securities, should be the focus of investment decisions.[24] To the extent that the individual securities in the portfolio react differently to the same future events, the aggregate risks of a portfolio of securities are lower than the average of the risks of the individual securities.[25] To take a simplified example, suppose a portfolio consists of two shares of stock—one from Company A that manufactures oil heaters, the other from Company B that manufactures gas heaters. If only oil prices increase, the stock of Company A will decline but the stock of Company B will rise. Conversely, if only gas prices increase, the stock of Company A will rise but the stock of Company B will decline. Since the price movement of each share of stock is offset by the price movement of the other share of stock, the aggregate risk of this portfolio will be lower than the average of the risks of both shares. To decrease the aggregate risk of a portfolio, economists have suggested several types of diversification strategies. . . .

Building on Markowitz's work, William Sharpe proposed a simplified model for ascertaining the efficient frontier of portfolios.[26] Sharpe divided all the risks of a security into two components—alpha and beta coefficients. *Alpha* risk refers to that portion of the price variation of a security attributable to the unique characteristics of the issuer. Since alpha risk by definition is not correlated to the price movements of other securities, it can be eliminated through perfect diversification of a securities portfolio without reducing returns.[27] *Beta* risk refers to that portion of the price variation of a security attributable to the price movements of the stock market as a whole.[28] For example, a stock with a beta of 1.0 will tend to rise and fall with the stock market averages. A stock with a beta of 1.5 will tend to rise 50% more than the stock market when it is rising and to decline 50% less than the stock market when it is declining. Since beta risk by definition represents the degree to which each security reacts in the same way as all other securities, it is impossible to reduce beta risk through diversification without reducing the returns of the portfolio.[29] Thus, given the difficulty of finding undervalued stocks with higher returns than other stocks in the same risk category, Sharpe's efficient frontier is theoretically defined as the securities portfolio at each level of beta risk that has eliminated all alpha risk though perfect diversification. . . .

Notes

1. For a general introduction to the economic literature, see R. Brealey, *An Introduction to Risk and Return from Common Stocks* (1969). To be precise, the term "portfolio theory" refers to the abstract model on risk and return developed by Professor Harry Markowitz; the term "capital asset pricing theory" refers to the workable model for evaluation of portfolios developed by Professor William Sharpe. But this article uses portfolio theory to include the contributions of both Professors Markowitz and Sharpe.

2. For a discussion of reasonableness of this approximation, see Cohen, "The Suitability Rule and Economic Theory," 80 *Yale L.J.* 1604, 1618-19 (1971).

3. Returns include both price increases or decreases, and dividends (if any).

4. For example, suppose stock X had a .35 probability of a 9% return, a .40 probability of an 8% return, a .15 probability of a 7% return and a .10 probability of a 6% return. The expected return of stock X is the weighted average of all these possible returns according to their probability of occurrence, which in this example would be 8%, calculated as follows: $(.35)(9\%) + (.40)(8\%) + (.15)(7\%) + (.10)(6\%) = 8\%$. This example is adapted from Bines, "Modern Portfolio Theory and Investment Management Law: Refinement of Legal Doctrine," 76 *Colum. L. Rev.* 721, 738 (1976).

5. Using the same figures for stock X provided in note 4 supra, the variance of the returns of stock X can be calculated by (1) squaring the difference between each possible return and the expected return; (2) weighting the squares from step (1) according to their probability of occurrence; and (3) adding together all the weighted squares from step (2).
   In case of stock X, for example, the first step is to calculate the difference between each possible return and the expected return, and then to square the difference. The results are:
   $9\% - 8\% = 1\% \times 1 = 1\%$
   $8\% - 8\% = 0\% \times 0 = 0\%$
   $8\% - 7\% = 1\% \times 1 = 1\%$
   $8\% - 6\% = 2\% \times 2 = 4\%$
   The second step is to weight the squares from step (1) according to their relative probability of occurrence. The results are:
   $1\% \times .35 = .35\%$
   $0\% \times .40 = 0\%$
   $1\% \times .15 = .15\%$
   $4\% \times .10 = .40\%$
   The third step is to add together the weighted squares from the second step, which yields a variance of .9% for stock X.

6. J. Lorie & M. Hamilton, *The Stock Market: Theories and Evidence* 211-27 (1973). But see Modigliani & Pogue, "An Introduction to Risk and Return," *Financial Anaysts J.,* May-June 1974, at 69, 77-82, 84-85.

7. J. Cohen, E. Zinbarg & A. Zeikel, *Investment Analysis and Portfolio Management* 739 (1973).

8. Langbein & Posner, "Market Funds and Trust-Investment Law," 1976 *Am. B. Foundation Research J.* 7-8; cf. Friedman & Savage, "The Utility Analysts of Choices Involving Risk," 56 *J. Pol. Econ.* 279, 284, 300-01 (1948).

9. As Bines states: "Plainly, if pure chance is to be an element of a person's investment policy, he requires no professional help to roll the dice." Bines, *supra* note 4, at 759.

10. Money managers cannot simply choose stocks with higher returns at the same risk level because higher returns are generally associated with higher risk stocks. Nor can money managers simply increase returns by choosing high-risk stocks, because investors are generally risk averse. Thus, money managers should invest for the highest returns at the particular level of risk selected. Cohn, Zinbarg & Zeikel, *supra* note 7, at 742.

11. See R. Hagin & C. Mader, *The New Science of Investing* 97-106 (1973).

12. Cohen, Zinbarg & Zeidel, *supra* note 7, at 514.

13. A short sale is the sale of a security at time 1 by a seller who does not own the security at time 1, but who effectively promises to deliver by buying the security at time 2. Short sellers hope that the stock price will decline so that the price received for the sale at time 1 will be higher than the price required to buy the stock at time 2.

14. Fundamental and technical analysis can, of course, be used together; they are not mutually exclusive.

15. For a general review of these economic studies, see Fama, "Efficient Capital Markets: A Review of Theory and Empirical Work," 25 *J. Finance* 383 (1970). The randomness is between past data and the *direction* as well as the *amount* of future changes in stock prices. These are, of course, the two critical variables in making investment choices. A money manager who buys a stock at 200, for instance, wants to know whether it will go up to 220 or down to 180.

16. Hagin & Mader, *supra* note 11, at 61-83.

17. *Id.* At 68-69. *See also* Fama & Blume, "Filter Rules and Stock Trading," 39 *J. Bus* 226-41 (1966).

18. McQuown, "Technical and Fundamental Analysis and Capital Market Theory," *J. Bank Research,* Spring 1973, at 10-11.

19. Bines, *supra* note 4, at 789-90 (footnote omitted).

20. Brealey, *supra* note 1 at 77-81.

21. *Id.* At 88-103; Lorie & Hamilton, *supra* note 6, at 158-63.

22. Cohen, Zinbarg & Zekel, *supra* note 7, at 753.

23. Bernstein, "In Defense of Fundamental Analysis," *Financial Analysts J.,* Jan.-Feb. 1975, at 4-5.

24. Note, "Fiduciary Standards and the Prudent Man Rule Under the Employment Retirement Income Security Act of 1974," 88 *Harv L. Rev.* 960, 970-71 (1975).

25. Cohen, *supra* note 2, at 1611-12 & n.39.

26. Sharpe, "A Simplified Model for Portfolio Analysis," 9 *Management Sci.* 277 (1963). The simplified model is often referred to as the Sharpe-Lintner-Mossin model since Lintner and Mossin arrived at models similar to Sharpe's through different methodologies. See Lintner, "Valuation of Risk Assets and the Selection of Risky Investments in Stock Portfolios and Capital Budgets," 47 *Rev. Econ. & Statistics* 13 (1965); Mossin, "Equilibrium in a Capital Asset Market," 34 *Econometria* 768 (1966).

27. Bines, *supra* note 4, at 752-53; see Langbein & Posner, *supra* note 8, at 9-10

28. Studies indicate that beta accounts for 30-50% of the price movements of listed stocks; the remainder is accounted for by alpha. Cohen, Zinbarg & Zeikel, *supra* note 7, at 769-70 & n.41.

29. See Bines, *supra* note 4, at 753; Langbein & Posner, *supra* note 8, at 9-10. The beta of a portfolio as a whole is defined as the weighted average of the beta of each security in the portfolio. Cohen, Zinbarg & Zeikel, *supra* note 7, at 771.

READING 1.2
The End of Behavioral Finance*

Richard Thaler

. . . Why Behavioral Finance Cannot Be Dismissed

Modern financial economic theory is based on the assumption that the "representative agent" in the economy is rational in two ways: The representative agent (1) makes decisions according to the axioms of expected utility theory and (2) makes unbiased forecasts about the future. An extreme version of this theory assumes that every agent behaves in accordance with these assumptions. Most economists recognize this extreme version as unrealistic; they concede that many of their relatives and acquaintances—spouses, students, deans, government leaders, and so on—are hopeless decision-makers. Still, defenders of the traditional model argue that it is not a problem for some agents in the economy to make suboptimal decisions as long as the "marginal investor," that is, the investor who is making the specific investment decision at hand, is rational.

The argument that asset prices are set by rational investors is part of the grand oral tradition in economics and is often attributed to Milton Friedman, one of the greatest economists of the century and one of the greatest debaters of all time. But the argument has two fundamental problems. First, even if asset prices were set only by rational investors in the aggregate, knowing what individual investors are doing might still be of interest. Second, although the argument is intuitively appealing and reassuring, its adherents have rarely spelled it out carefully.

Suppose a market has two kinds of investors: rational investors (rationals), who behave like agents in economics textbooks, and quasi-rational investors (quasis), people who are trying as hard as they can to make good investment decisions but make predictable mistakes. Suppose also that two assets in this market, X and Y, are objectively worth the same amount but cannot be transformed from one into the other. Finally, assume that the quasis think X is worth more than Y, an opinion that could change (quasis often change their minds) while the rationals know that X and Y are worth the same. What conditions are necessary

to assure that the prices of X and Y will be the same, as they would be in a world with only rational investors?

The question is complex, but some of the essential conditions are the following. First, in dollar-weighted terms, such a market cannot have too many quasis (in order for the rational investors to be marginal). Second, the market must allow costless short selling (so that if prices get too high, the rationals can drive them down). Third, only rational investors can sell short; otherwise, the quasis will short Y when the two prices are the same because they believe X is worth more than Y. The result would be no equilibrium. Fourth, at some date T, the true relationship between X and Y must become clear to all investors. Fifth, the rationals must have long horizons, long enough to include date T. These conditions are tough to meet.

Consider the example of the Royal Dutch/Shell Group, as documented in Rosenthal and Young (1990) and Froot and Dabora (1999). Royal Dutch Petroleum and Shell Transport are independently incorporated in, respectively, the Netherlands and England. The current company emerged from a 1907 alliance between Royal Dutch and Shell Transport in which the two companies agreed to merge their interests on a 60/40 basis. Royal Dutch trades primarily in the United States and the Netherlands and is part of the S&P 500 Index; Shell trades primarily in London and is part of the Financial Times Stock Exchange Index. According to any rational model, the shares of these two components (after adjusting for foreign exchange) should trade in a 60-40 ratio. They do not: the actual price ratio has deviated from the expected one by more than 35 percent. Simple explanations, such as taxes and transaction costs, cannot explain the disparity.[1]

Why don't rational investors intervene to force the shares of Royal Dutch/Shell back to their rational 60-40 ratio? The answer is that hedge funds do make investments based on this disparity: They buy the cheaper stock and short the more expensive one. Indeed, Royal Dutch/Shell is one of many such investments Long-Term Capital Management [LTCM] had in place in the summer of 1998. In August 1998, when things started to unravel for LTCM, the Royal Dutch/Shell disparity was relatively large, so at a time when LTCM might have chosen to increase the money it was willing to bet on this anomaly, it had to cut back instead. Shleifer and Vishny (1997) envisioned this scenario in their article explaining the "Limits of Arbitrage."

The lesson from this example is that even when the relationship between two prices is easy to calculate and fixed by charter, prices can diverge and arbitrageurs are limited in their ability to restore the prices to parity. What, then, are the prospects for prices to be rational in more-complex settings?

Take the case of Internet stocks. Many, if not most, professional analysts believe that the valuations of Internet stocks are too high. In surveys of professional investors that I conducted in the spring of 1999, the median respondent thought that the intrinsic value of a portfolio of five Internet stocks (America Online, Amazon.com, eBay, Priceline.com and Yahoo!) was 50 percent of the market price. Suppose the "professionals" are right and these multibillion-dollar companies are worth only half of their current prices. Suppose further that this valuation is the consensus of Wall Street experts. How can such a situation exist? The answer is that it may be an equilibrium (although not a "rational equilibrium") as long as the Wall Street pessimism will not drive the price down because the supply of short sellers will then be too limited. Although some hedge funds are willing to bet on convergence for the Royal Dutch/ Shell disparity, few are willing to bet on the demise of the Internet frenzy, or at least too few to cause it to happen.

The analysis of Internet stocks applies with even greater force to the current level of the U.S. stock market. The consensus on Wall Street (and on similar streets around the world) is that the U.S. stock market is 20–30 percent overvalued; yet, prices can continue to increase because the investors who are willing to bet on a decline have too few dollars to prevail. First, in the U.S. market, the largest investors—pension funds, endowments and wealthy individuals—typically use some rule of thumb for asset allocation, such as 60 percent in equities, and are thus relatively insensitive to the level of asset prices. Second, such insensitivity is even more characteristic of individual investors in 401(k) plans, who rarely rebalance their portfolios.

Evidence That Should Worry Efficient Market Advocates

The previous section showed that the premise of behavioral finance—that cognitive biases may influence asset prices—is at least theoretically possible. But is it worth the trouble? What is the evidence that existing models cannot

do the job? Surely the Royal Dutch/Shell example, although striking, is not by itself enough to undermine the rational efficient market paradigm that has served the field well for so long. I will briefly discuss five areas in which behavior in the real world seems most at odds with the theories in textbooks.

Volume. Standard models of asset markets predict that participants will trade very little. The reason is that in a world where everyone knows that traders are rational (I know that you are rational, you know that I am rational, and I know that you know that I am rational), if I am offering to buy some shares of IBM Corporation and you are offering to sell them, I have to wonder what information you have that I do not. Of course, pinning down exactly how little volume should be expected in this world is difficult, because in the real world people have liquidity and rebalancing needs, but it seems safe to say that 700 million shares a day on the NYSE is much more trading than standard market models would expect. Similarly, the standard approach would not expect mutual fund managers to turn over their portfolios once a year.

Volatility. In a rational world, prices change only when news arrives. Since Robert Shiller's early work was published in 1981, economists have realized that aggregate stock prices appear to move much more than can be justified by changes in intrinsic value (as measured by, say, the present value of future dividends). Although Shiller's work generated long and complex controversy, his conclusion is generally thought to be correct: stock and bond prices are more volatile than advocates of rational efficient market theory would predict.

Dividends. Modigliani and Miller (1958) showed that in an efficient market with no taxes, dividend policy is irrelevant. Under the U.S. tax system, however, dividends are taxed at a higher rate than capital gains and companies can make their taxpaying shareholders better off by repurchasing shares rather than paying dividends.[2] This logic leaves us with two major puzzles, one about company behavior and the other about asset prices. Why do most large companies pay cash dividends? And why do stock prices rise when dividends are initiated or increased? Neither question has any satisfactory rational answer.[3]

The Equity Premium Puzzle. Historically, the equity premium in the United States and elsewhere has been huge. For example, a dollar invested in U.S. T-bills on January 1, 1926, would now be worth about $14; a dollar invested in large-cap U.S. stocks on the same date would now be worth more than $2,000. Although one would expect returns on equities to be higher, because they are riskier than T-bills, the return differential of seven percent a year is much too great to be explained by risk alone (Mehra and Prescott 1985).

Predictability. In an efficient market, future returns cannot be predicted on the basis of existing information. Thirty years ago, financial economists thought the most basic assumption of the efficient market hypotheses was true (Fama 1970). Now, everyone agrees that stock prices are at least partly predictable (see, for example, Fama 1991) on the basis of past returns, such measures of value as price-to-earnings or price-to-book ratios, company announcements of earnings, dividend changes, and share repurchases and seasoned equity offerings.[4] Although considerable controversy remains about whether the observed predictability is best explained by mispricing or risk, no one has been able to specify an observable, as opposed to theoretical or metaphysical, risk measure that can explain the existing data pattern (see, for example, Lakonishok, Shleifer, and Vishny 1994). Furthermore, the charge that these studies are the inevitable result of data mining is belied by the fact that the authors have covered every important corporate announcement that a company can make. Academics have not selectively studied a few obscure situations and published only those results. Rather, it seems closer to the truth to say that virtually every possible trigger produces apparent excess returns. . . .

Notes

1. See Froot and Dabora, who also studied the similar cases of Unilever N.V./PLC and SmithKline Beecham.
2. See Miller (1986) for a convincing summary of this argument.
3. The argument is sometimes made that prices increase when dividends increase because companies are using a change in dividend to signal something. Benartzi, Michaely, and Thaler (1997) found no evidence, however, that increases in dividends provide any information about future changes in earnings.
4. For a sampling of the empirical literature, see DeBondt and Thaler (1987), Lakonishok, Shleifer, and Vishny (1994), Bernard (1992), Michaely, Thaler, and Womack (1995), and Ikenberry, Lakonishok, and Vermaelen (1995). For an alternative interpretation of this literature, see Fama (1998).

READING 1.3

Industry Profile: How the Commercial Banking Industry Operates[*]

Commercial banks serve as intermediaries between customers who save money and customers who borrow it. Their principal activities are collecting deposits and disbursing loans.

Individual commercial banks may diverge widely in terms of markets served and earnings sources. . . . Other industry concerns that we consider are: costs related to obtaining and maintaining adequate funding sources; the inherent risks in financing at a given interest rate; Federal Reserve policies and their effect on interest rates; and competitive influences on the retail (consumer) and commercial strategies of regional and money center banks.

Business Types

There are two main categories of banks: money centers and regionals. Money center banks tend to be located in major U.S. financial centers and are typically involved in international lending and foreign currency operations. Regional banks tend to be focused in one or a few geographic areas or states, where their lending and deposit activities are generally focused.

The merger of several large regional banks in the late 1980s spurred the creation of a new type of regional bank, the so-called super-regional, which operates across many states or geographic areas and can be national in scope.

---

[*] "Commercial Banking" Industry Survey, Standard & Poor's, (November 2000). Reprinted by permission of Standard & Poor's, a division of the McGraw-Hill Companies, Copyright © 2001.

Bank Assets

A commercial bank's earnings are derived from a variety of sources. These sources, or "earning assets," include loans (commercial, consumer, and real estate) and securities (investment and trading account). . . .

Loans. Commercial and residential real estate loans, secured by customers' property, are generally long-term installment mortgages. Residential mortgages generate a predictable cash flow and are usually the least risky type of loan. Commercial real estate and interim construction loans are medium-term loans that generate high yields but also carry high risks.

Commercial and industrial (C&I) loans can be made on a short-term, medium-term, or long-term basis, and may be either secured or unsecured. Often the lowest yielding of a bank's loans, C&I loans usually include compensating balance requirements, commitment fees, or both, although these requirements are becoming less common in today's intensely competitive environment. Processing costs are relatively low for C&I loans, and pricing (i.e., interest rates and fees) is flexible.

Consumer loans, comprising installment and credit card lending, are usually medium-term in maturity, with predictable principal and interest payments that reliably generate cash flow. Credit risk and processing costs are generally higher than for business loans, and yields are subject to usury ceilings in some states.

Securities. Individuals and institutions such as banks purchase securities as investments. A security's value is typically based on the interest rate it receives, and will fluctuate with the market level of interest rates. Securities may be taxable (such as U.S. government bonds and other securities) or tax-exempt (such as state and local government securities). The maturities of these financial instruments vary widely.

Banks purchase securities as a means of earning interest on assets while maintaining the liquidity they need to meet deposit withdrawals or to satisfy sudden increases in loan demand. In addition, securities diversify a bank's risk, improve the overall quality of its earning asset portfolio, and help manage interest rate risk.

Investment securities are also an important source of a bank's earnings, particularly when lending is weak but funds for investing are plentiful. U.S. banks are major participants in the bond market. Municipal bonds generally have longer terms and less liquidity then U.S. government and Treasury bonds, but their tax-exempt feature is attractive in that it reduces taxable income.

Trading account securities are interest-bearing securities held primarily for realizing capital gains. Because their trading performance is strongly affected by interest rate trends, they carry a high risk. For that reason, banks have historically held them in small allotments. . . .

Bank Liabilities

A bank's principal liabilities include the following: consumer demand and time deposits, corporate demand and time deposits, foreign deposits and borrowings, negotiable certificates of deposit (jumbo CDs, usually sold in denominations of $100,000 or more), federal funds, other short-term borrowings (such as commercial paper), long-term debt, and shareholders' equity.

Deposits. Consumer savings plans with commercial banks consist of demand deposits (such as checking accounts) and time deposits (regular savings, money market, and negotiable order of withdrawal accounts, and six-month money market certificates). These sources of funds have historically proven to be stable and important for banks. The interest rates that they command vary with overall money market interest rates or the duration of the time deposit, and they must be competitive in order to attract and keep depositors.

With deposit interest in the range of 2% to 4% over the past few years, deposit growth has been sluggish as consumers have sought out investments with higher rates of return, such as mutual funds.

Interest Rate Risks

Assets and liabilities can mature or be repriced in periods ranging from overnight to 30 years. Most, however, mature in less than one year, and few extend beyond five years. Interest rate risk occurs when a liability matures or is repriced at a time that's not synchronized with the asset that it's funding.

As a rule, banks don't match assets and liabilities on a one-to-one basis. Instead, assets and liabilities are grouped together into specific time frames, such as overnight, 30 days, 90 days, one year, and the like. Thus, within a given period, banks can determine their interest rate sensitivity.

If more of a bank's liabilities mature or are repriced before assets, the bank is said to be "liability-sensitive," or to have a negative gap. If more assets mature than liabilities, the bank is said to be "asset-sensitive," or to have a positive gap. If a bank's assets and liabilities are evenly matched, it's said to be balanced. In a period of falling interest rates, a bank with a negative gap will see net interest margins widen. Conversely, a bank with a positive gap will benefit during a period of rising rates. . . .

Most bank loans now come with variable rates. On the funding side, much of the debt, deposits, and preferred stock dividends also carry variable rates. As a result, much of the interest rate risk has been shifted from the lender to the borrower. . . .

Interest Rates: The Key to Profits

The outlook for interest rates has important implications for bank profits. Because most profits are derived from net interest income (the interest income received on loans minus the interest expense for borrowed funds), interest rates determine to a large extent how much money a bank can make.

Net interest margin (a bank's net interest income divided by its average earning assets) is a common measure of a bank's ability to squeeze profits from its loans. Net interest margins widen or narrow depending on the direction of interest rates, the mix of funding sources underlying loans, and the duration (or time period until expiration) of the investment portfolio.

Falling interest rates have a positive effect on banks for several reasons. One is that they can make net interest margins expand, at least in the short term, because while banks are still earning a higher-than-market yield on loans to customers, the cost of funds goes down more quickly in response to the new, lower rates. Second, declining rates

enhance the value of a bank's fixed-rate investment portfolio, since a bond with a higher stated interest rate becomes more valuable as prevailing rates drop. Furthermore, falling rates lower the cost of credit, which often stimulates loan demand and reduces delinquency rates.

Of course not all banks are affected equally by rate decreases. Liability-sensitive banks—which rely more heavily on borrowed funds than on customer deposits to fund loan growth—typically reap greater benefits.

In the broadest sense, banks are inherently asset-sensitive because they derive a significant portion of their funding from essentially free sources, such as equity issues or demand deposits. This is especially true of the smaller regional banks that focus on garnering retail (consumer) deposits, and that have limited access to the purchased money markets. Unless they work to reduce their asset sensitivity, they tend to do better in periods of high or rising interest rates.

Money center banks, however, rely heavily on borrowed funds, and have a small retail deposit base relative to their asset size. Thus, they tend to be liability-sensitive and to benefit most during periods of falling rates.

Fluctuations in interest rates, while important, don't have an absolute influence over the net interest margins of commercial banks, primarily because of banks' ability to adjust to such fluctuations. In theory, banks can match the maturities of their assets (loans and investments) and liabilities (deposits and borrowings) so that rates earned and rates paid move more or less in tandem, while net interest margins remain relatively stable. In practice, however, banks can—and do—deviate from a perfectly balanced position. . . .

▪▪▪▪▪ CASE STUDY
Analyzing Credit Issues in a Money Market Fund

Money market funds (MM Funds) are the type of mutual fund that is most similar to bank deposits. Both pay income, both do not fluctuate in value and both are relatively safe. But there are crucial differences between an MM Fund and a bank deposit. The most important difference is that a bank deposit is insured by the Federal Deposit Insurance Corporation (FDIC)—a federally chartered corporation that insures deposits held by commercial banks and thrift institutions—up to $100,000, while MM Funds are not insured by any government agency.

Instead of being insured by the FDIC, MM Funds are subject to strict regulation by the Securities and Exchange Commission (SEC). With regard to taxable money market funds, the type involved in this Case Study, the SEC imposes three key regulatory restrictions. First, at least 95% of the MM Fund's assets must be invested in the highest-quality money market instruments (rated A-1, P-1 or equivalent), and the other 5% or less must be invested in issuers with the second highest rating (A-2, P-2 or equivalent). Second, the MM Fund may not invest more than 5% of its assets in any single top-rated issuer (other than the federal government) and no more than 1% of its assets in any second-rated issuer. Third, the average maturity of the MM Fund's assets may not exceed 90 days.

MM Funds must determine on a daily basis their net asset value or "NAV" (the current value of the fund's portfolio divided by the number of shares of the fund outstanding). MM Funds generally distribute all net income of the fund as it is earned and use an accounting technique to maintain a constant dollar value for each share, rather than a fluctuating value, as do the shares of stock and bond funds. By using amortized cost accounting, distributing all income as received and rounding NAV to the nearest penny, a MM Fund will usually be able to maintain a NAV of $1 per share. If a MM Fund were to incur losses of ½ of 1% or more on its portfolio, however, its NAV would drop below $1—called "breaking the buck." Such losses would occur mainly in the event of a credit default on a substantial position in one issuer held by a MM Fund, but could also occur in the event of a very severe movement in interest rates for a MM Fund with a relatively long maturity.

Despite these regulatory restrictions, one MM Fund has actually "broken the buck," and several have come close. In these situations, the investment manager of a MM Fund faces an unattractive set of alternatives, including letting the MM Fund "break the buck," or buying the defaulted paper at its face value from the MM Fund and absorbing the loss itself. This is precisely the situation faced by T. Rowe Price in the case study for this Chapter. These situations are not merely theoretical. For example, in January 2001, five investment managers revealed that they bought defaulted paper of California utilities to prevent their funds from breaking a buck. In 1994, investment managers for 39 funds bought distressed, unrated interest rate derivative securities for the same reason.

Discussion Questions

1. How and why do banks and mutual funds differ from the viewpoint of the sponsoring financial services company?
2. What are the major differences between a bank account and a money market fund from a customer's viewpoint?
3. From the consumer viewpoint, why would you choose a bank account over a money market fund, or vice versa?
4. Why would T. Rowe Price be so concerned about recognizing a loss in Prime Reserve? Please quantify the accounting issue. What would be the impact of a loss in Prime Reserve on money market funds of other fund sponsors?
5. What alternative courses of action were open to T. Rowe Price in relation to Prime Reserve's holding of MRT paper? What was the best alternative, and why? What was your evaluation of other alternatives?
6. Would T. Rowe Price's stock and bond mutual funds face the same challenge confronting the manager of the Prime Reserve Fund?
7. Would bank management ever face the situation confronting the manager of the Prime Reserve Fund?
8. What does it mean when a bank becomes insolvent? In that event, what happens to the bank depositor?
9. Can a money market fund become insolvent in the same sense as a bank? Can there be a run on a money market fund?

*Threatening to Break a Buck**

On March 12, 1990, Standard & Poor's downgraded the commercial paper of Mortgage & Realty Trust Co. (MRT) from A-2 to A-3. MRT's access to the commercial paper market was shut off overnight, and previously committed bank credit lines were withdrawn. On March 13, MRT missed a $13 million payment due on maturing medium term notes. A further $97 million of the trust's commercial paper and other indebtedness would be maturing by month's end, as would an additional $200 million within the year. MRT began negotiations with banks and other lenders to try to secure a line of credit sufficient to cover its near-term cash needs.

T. Rowe Price Associates, Inc. (TRPA) was the single largest holder of MRT paper: $65 million face value of which $42 million was in its Prime Reserve money market fund, and $23 million in various investment advisory accounts. TRPA had to decide whether to intervene and preserve Prime Reserve's unblemished record. Among various alternatives, TRPA could participate in the financing MRT was seeking, and/or it could purchase the MRT paper from the fund and other affected accounts.

Background on T. Rowe Price Associates, Inc.

T. Rowe Price was one of the largest money management organizations in the U.S. At the end of 1989, the firm had $28 billion in assets, of which $17 billion was in mutual funds and $11 billion in separate accounts (mostly pension funds and endowments). TRPA was one of the few publicly traded independent money management firms. It went public in 1986 at $12 per share, and in March 1990, was trading at around $30. Company insiders owned 23% of the 14.4 million shares outstanding. Exhibits 1–3 contain summary financials; Exhibit 4 gives a breakdown of the firm's mutual fund products. The following is an excerpt from the February 1990 Prime Reserve annual report:

> The 1980s were … kind to T. Rowe Price, and we begin the new decade as one of the largest independent investment management firms in the country. During the '80s, our staff tripled in size to over 1,000, the mutual fund assets we manage grew from about $5 billion to $17 billion, and the total number of shareholder accounts expanded from 350,000 to over 1.5 million.
>
> Nonetheless, these years of rapid growth have not changed our dedication to serving individual and institutional investors. We have had no other business since our founding in 1937.
>
> Our strategy, which we believe has served you and us well in good and bad times, rests on several long-held principles:
>
> - Integrity must prevail in every aspect of our business.
> - Our time and energy must be devoted to the investment management business, which we know well, and not to unrelated activities which could detract from our primary focus.
> - Our shareholders' and other clients' interests come first; if your interests are served, ours will be also over time.
> - The money you entrust to us is treated with the same respect and attention we accord our own.

EXHIBIT 1

T. Rowe Price income statement, December 31, 1989 (dollars in millions)

Management fees:	
Mutual funds	$80.9
Private accounts and other	38.0
Administrative fees	32.2
Investment income	5.6
Other revenues	2.8
Total revenues	$159.5
Advertising and promotion expense	11.8
Compensation, administrative, & general	98.7
Total expenses	$110.5
Income before taxes & minority interests	49.0
Income taxes	17.6
Minority interests in consolidates subsidiaries	1.6
Net income	$29.7
Earnings per share	$2.00

EXHIBIT 2

T. Rowe Price balance sheet, December 31, 1989 (dollars in millions)

Assets

Cash and cash equivalents	$40.0
Accounts receivable	24.4
Investments in mutual funds	16.4
Marketable debt securities	19.7
Limited partnership interests	10.5
Property and equipment	10.7
Other assets	5.9
	$127.6

Liabilities and stockholders' equity

Liabilities:	
Accounts payable and accrued expenses	$11.0
Accrued compensation and related costs	5.6
Income taxes payable	2.0
Dividends payable	2.2
Deferred revenues	1.1
Long-term debt	2.6
Minority interests in consolidated subs	1.7
Total liabilities	$26.2
Stockholders' equity	101.4
	$127.6

- We strive at all times to deliver the highest quality investment products and services at the lowest reasonable costs.
- We try to talk frankly and openly with you about all aspects of your investments with T. Rowe Price.

Recognizing there is no single or correct way to make money in the financial markets, we have responded to our shareholders' diverse needs by providing a wide range of investments, services, and timely information. In choosing what to offer, however, we try always to make sure we are adding real value and not latching onto short-term trends or fads.

The Prime Reserve Fund

The Prime Reserve Fund dated back to 1976. With assets of $4.8 billion in February 1990, it was by far T. Rowe Price's largest mutual fund. The fund's prospectus described the primary investment objective as:

> Preservation of capital, liquidity, and, consistent with these objectives, the highest possible current income by investing in a diversified portfolio of prime domestic and foreign U.S. dollar–denominated money market securities.

The fund's investment restrictions required it to hold at least 65% of total assets in prime money market instruments, i.e., instruments in the highest rating category of a major rating agency: A-1 (Standard & Poor's Corp.), or P-1

EXHIBIT 3

Composition of T. Rowe Price management fee revenues, December 31, 1989 (dollars in millions)

	Assets Managed	Management Fee Rate	Revenue Running Rate
Money market and short-term bond funds	$6,200	0.44%	$27.3
Equity funds	6,300	0.57	35.9
Fixed-income funds	2,800	0.57	16.0
Municipal bond funds	2,000	0.57	11.4
Total mutual funds	$17,300	0.52%	$90.6
Private accounts:			
Equity	$5,500	0.42%	$23.1
Fixed income	5,400	0.20	10.8
Total private accounts	$10,900	0.30%	$33.9
Total	$28,200	0.44%	$124.5

Source: Sandford C. Bernstein & Co., Inc., January 1990.

EXHIBIT 4

T. Rowe Price mutual funds

Fund (Year Commenced)	Primary Investment Objective
Money market	
Prime Reserve (1976)	Preservation of capital, liquidity and, consistent with these objectives, the highest possible current income by investing in a diversified portfolio of prime domestic and foreign US dollar–denominated money market securities.
Tax-Exempt Money (1981)	Preservation of capital, liquidity, and consistent with these objectives, the highest possible current income exempt from federal income tax by investing in high quality municipal securities which mature in one year or less.
US Treasury Money (1982)	Maximum safety of capital, liquidity, and consistent with these objectives, the highest available current income by investing primarily in short-term US Treasury securities and repurchase agreements on such securities.
California Tax-Free Money (1986)	Highest possible current income exempt from federal and California state income taxes consistent with preservation of principal and liquidity by investing in high quality municipal securities which mature in one year or less.
New York Tax-Free (1986)	Highest possible current income exempt from federal, New York State and New York City Money income taxes consistent with preservation of principal and liquidity by investing in high quality municipal securities which mature in one year or less.
Stock	
Growth Stock (1958)	Long-term growth of capital and increasing dividend income through investment primarily in common stocks of well-established growth companies
New Horizons (1960)	Long-term growth of capital through investment primarily in common stocks of small, rapidly growing companies.
New Era (1969)	Long-term growth of capital through investment primarily in common stocks of companies which own or develop natural resources and other basic commodities, and other selected, non–resource growth companies.
Internal Stock (1980)	Total return from long-term growth of capital and income principally through investments in marketable securities of established, non–United States issuers.
Growth & Income (1980)	Long-term growth of capital, a reasonable level of current income and an increase in future income through investment primarily in income-producing equity securities which have the prospects for growth of capital and increasing dividends.
New American Growth (1985)	Long-term growth of capital through investment primarily in the common stocks of U.S. companies which operate in the service sector of the economy.
Equity Income (1985)	High current income by investing primarily in dividend-paying common stocks of established companies with favorable prospects for increasing dividend income and, secondarily, capital appreciation.
Capital Appreciation (1986)	Maximum capital appreciation through investment primarily in common stocks.
Science & Technology (1987)	Long-term growth of capital through investment primarily in the common stocks of companies which are expected to benefit from the development, advancement and use of science and technology.
Small-Cap Value (1988)	Long-term capital growth through investment primarily in the common stocks of companies with relatively small market capitalizations which are believed to be undervalued and have good prospects for capital appreciation.

EXHIBIT 4 (CONTINUED)

International Discovery (1988)	Long-term growth of capital through investment primarily in the common stocks of rapidly growing, small and medium sized companies based outside the United States
European Stock (1990)	Long-term capital appreciation by investment primarily in a diversified portfolio of equity securities issued by companies domiciled in Europe.

Taxable bond

New Income (1973)	Highest level of income over time consistent with the preservation of capital through investment primarily in marketable debt securities.
High Yield (1984)	High level of income and, secondarily, capital appreciation through investment primarily in high-yielding, lower-medium and low quality, income-producing debt securities and preferred stocks (including convertible securities).
Short-Term Bond (1984)	Highest level of income consistent with minimum fluctuation in principal value and liquidity through investment primarily in short- and intermediate-form debt securities.
GNMA (1985)	Highest level of current income, consistent with preservation of principal and maximum credit protection by investment exclusively in securities backed by the full faith and credit of the U.S. government, primarily Government National Mortgage Association (GNMA) mortgage-backed securities, and other instruments involving these securities.
International Bond (1986)	High level of current income by investing in an international portfolio of high-quality, nondollar-denominated fixed income securities.
U.S. Treasury Intermediate (1989)	High level of current income consistent with maximum credit protection and an average portfolio maturity of three to seven years by investing primarily in U.S. Treasury securities and repurchase agreements involving such securities.
U.S. Treasury Long-Term (1989)	High level of current income consistent with maximum credit protection and an average portfolio maturity of fifteen to twenty years by investing primarily in U.S. Treasury securities and repurchase agreements involving such securities.

Tax-free bond

Tax-Free Income (1976)	High level of income exempt from federal income tax by investing primarily in longer-term investment-grade municipal securities
Tax-Free Short-Intermediate (1983)	Higher than money market yields by investing primarily in short- and intermediate-term, high and upper-medium quality municipal securities which make interest payments exempt from federal income tax.
Tax-Free High Yield (1985)	High level of income exempt from federal income tax by investing primarily in longer-term investment-grade municipal securities.
New York Tax-Free Bond (1986)	Highest level of income exempt from federal, New York State and New York City income taxes by investing primarily in long-term investment-grade municipal securities.
California Tax-Free Bond (1986)	Highest level of income exempt from federal and California state income taxes by investing primarily in long term, investment-grade municipal securities.
Maryland Tax-Free Bond (1987)	Highest level of income exempt from federal and Maryland state and local income taxes by investing primarily in long-term, investment-grade municipal securities.

Sources: Form 10K for year ended December 31, 1989 and *Barron's.*

(Moody's Investors Service), or F-1 (Fitch Investors Service), or equivalent. Securities could not be purchased if rated less than A-2 or P-2 or F-2 or the equivalent as judged by the fund's board of directors.

Investments could be made in certificates of deposit, bankers' acceptances, and other obligations of banks and savings and loan associations only if they had assets of at least $1 billion. In the case of smaller institutions, investments were limited to the federally insured $100,000 maximum.

Consistent with SEC restrictions, the fund could not purchase an instrument with a maturity greater than one year, and had to maintain an average portfolio maturity of 90 days or less. In addition, at most 5% of the portfolio could be invested (at the time of purchase) in the securities of any one issuer, and at most 25% in any one industry. The SEC restrictions did not apply to securities issued by the U.S. Government and its agencies, or certificates of deposit and bankers' acceptances, although Prime Reserves did limit investments in any one bank or Savings and Loan (S&L) to 5%.

As shown in Exhibit 5, the fund's twenty largest holdings accounted for 51.6% of the portfolio and were primarily Euro commercial paper of CDs. The issuers were all financial institutions and nearly all foreign. Exhibit 6 gives the largest holdings of other selected large money market funds including Merrill Lynch's CMA fund, which, at $30 billion, was more than twice the size of the next largest fund. Like some of the funds in Exhibit 6, Prime Reserve held no U.S. Treasury securities, even though Treasuries made up 26% of total money market fund assets (Exhibit 7).

As part of its investment strategy, TRPA tended to position the Prime Reserve portfolio at the most attractive part of the yield curve, viewed in terms of the firm's assessment of the interest rate environment. In March of 1990, the portfolio had an average maturity of 38 days. During the prior twelve months, the average maturity had varied between 22 and 53 days, at times deviating from the industry average by as many as 18 days.

Prime Reserve paid T. Rowe Price an annual management fee of 0.44% of assets (Exhibit 3). With other costs of 0.31%, its recent twelve-month expense ratio was 0.75%, in line with the current industry average, estimated at 0.73%.

Mortgage & Realty Trust Co.

Mortgage & Realty Trust Co. was a 20-year-old, publicly traded real estate investment trust. It invested primarily in loans secured by commercial real estate, including one- to two-year construction loans, intermediate-term loans used to acquire existing property for physical or economic rehabilitation, and participating loans which provided for sharing in revenues and capital appreciation, with terms of up to 15 years. The Trust also made direct purchases of real estate.

Exhibit 8 contains the Trust's unaudited March 1990 balance sheet. It had $594 million of assets, $405 million of liabilities, and $189 million of net worth. MRT's management argued the Trust was far from insolvent, and that it was merely experiencing a temporary liquidity crisis which asset sales soon would alleviate.

Other Mutual Fund Holders of MRT Paper

Reportedly, there were altogether 10 money market fund holders of MRT paper. Other than the Prime Reserve Fund, only two funds were publicly identified. Alliance Capital's Money Reserves fund held $8.7 million of the paper, and Raymond James Financial's Heritage Cash Trust fund held $12 million. Alliance Capital had $45 billion of assets under management, of which $1 billion was in Money Reserves. Raymond James, whose primary business was brokerage and underwriting, managed some $17 billion through various asset management subsidiaries. Its Heritage Cash Trust fund had $660 million in assets in March 1990.

Previous Cases of Investment Losses in Money Market Funds

The Mortgage & Realty situation was not without precedent. In June 1989, Integrated Resources, a real estate, insurance, and financial services concern, defaulted on some $1 billion of short-term debt. Most of this was in the form of commercial paper issued to fund front-end sales commissions.

The Value Line Cash Fund held $22.6 million (3.2% of its portfolio) of Integrated's paper; Unified Management Corp.'s Liquid Green money market fund held $9 million. Both Value Line and Unified Management chose to "bail out" their fund shareholders by buying the paper for their own accounts at full value. In 1989, Value Line took a $7.5 million after-tax charge to earnings on its holding of Integrated paper.

The Integrated Resources situation represented the first reported instance of default of an instrument purchased by a money market fund. However, it was not the first time money market funds had experienced investment losses. In 1980, anticipating a decline in interest rates, the

EXHIBIT 5

Largest holdings of the T. Rowe Price prime reserve fund (2/28/90) (dollars in millions)

Issuer	Value	% Total	Moody's	S&P
Mitsubishi Bank, Ltd. (London)	$231	4.8%	P-1	A-1+
Sanwa Bank, Ltd. (London)	230	4.8	P-1	*A-1+
Tokai Bank, Ltd. (London)	168	3.5	P-1	*A-1+
Sumitomo Bank, Limited (London)	150	3.1	P-1	*A-1+
Bank of New York (London)	150	3.1	P-1	A-1
Long Term Credit Bank of Japan (London)	136	2.8	P-1	A-1+
Dai-Ichi Kangyo Bank, Ltd. (London)	133	2.7	P-1	*A-1+
Sumitomo Trust & Banking Co. (London)	130	2.7	P-1	*A-1+
Dresdner Bank AG (London)	130	2.7	P-1	A-1+
Fuji Bank, Ltd. (London)	115	2.4	P-1	*A-1+
Svenska Handelsbanken (London)	113	2.3	P-1	A-1+
Chrysler Financial Corporation[1]	109	2.2	P-2	A-2
Société Générale (London)	100	2.1	P-1	NR
First Bank System, Inc.	99	2.0	P-2	A-2
Den Danske Bank A/S (London)	98	2.0	P-1	A-1
Citizen Fidelity Bank & Trust Company	95	2.0	P-1	A-1+
Royal Bank of Canada	81	1.7	P-1	A-1+
NCNB National Bank of North Carolina	78	1.6	P-1	A-1
Pugent Sound Bancorp	77	1.6	NR	A-2
National City Bank	75	1.5	P-1	A-1
Subtotal	$2,497	51.6%		
U.S. Government & Federal Agencies	0	0		
Total fund value	$4,842	100.0%		

Note: Ratings are as of March 1990.
1. Chrysler Financial Corporation downgraded to "A-3" on 6/14/90 and "P-3" on 6/29/90.
* Rating of the parent company.

Institutional Liquid Assets fund lengthened the maturity of its $1.4 billion portfolio of government securities to over 70 days.[1] Instead of falling, rates rose, hurting the fund's performance, and triggering more than $400 million in redemptions in just three days. $2 million of portfolio losses were incurred in selling securities to meet redemptions, an amount for which the fund was reimbursed by Salomon Brothers, the fund's distributor, and the First National Bank of Chicago, the fund's adviser. First National subsequently lost the advisory contract, which was awarded to Goldman Sachs & Co.

The Money Market Fund Industry

Money market mutual funds first appeared in 1974. Like other mutual funds, they were designed to offer small investors the benefit of economies of scale, including particularly diversification, professional management and investments in odd amounts. In addition, investors usually could receive free check writing and wire-transfer privileges (for amounts over some minimum), avoid the early withdrawal penalties of fixed maturity CDs, and receive automatic redemption and next day settlement. Many of the above benefits also were attractive to corporations and other institutions running small short-term portfolios.

EXHIBIT 6

Largest holdings of selected money market funds (dollars in millions)

Fidelity: Spartan (4/30/90)	Value	% Total	Moody's	S&P
Philip Morris Companies, Inc.	$300	4.0%	P-2	A-1
General Motors Acceptance Corp.	317	3.8	P-1	A-1+
General Electric Capital Corp.	298	3.6	P-1	A-1+
Citicorp[1]	285	3.4	P-1	A-1+
Sears Roebuck Acceptance Corp.	249	3	P-1	A-1
Svenska Handelsbanken, Inc.	234	2.8	P-1	A-1+
Goldman, Sachs & Co.	222	2.7	P-1	A-1+
Barclays Bank PLC	219	2.6	P-1	A-1+
Preferred Receivables Funding Corp.	206	2.5	P-1	A-1
Kansallis North America, Inc.	184	2.2	P-1	A-1+
Bayerische Landesbank GZ	179	2.2	P-1	A-1+
Ford Motor Credit Company	149	1.8	P-1	A-1+
Subtotal	$2,873	34.6%		
U.S. Government & Federal Agencies	1,490	17.9		
Total fund value	$8,311	100.0%		

Fidelity: Cash Reserves (11/30/89)	Value	% Total	Moody's	S&P
Sanwa Bank, Ltd.	$550	5.10%	P-1	A-1+
Saloman, Inc.	492	4.5	P-1	A-1
Chrysler Financial Corporation[2]	456	4.2	P-2	A-2
Eastman Kodak	359	3.3	P-1	A-2
Tokai Bank, Ltd.	356	3.3	P-1	*A-1+
Fuji Bank, Ltd. (Grand Cayman)	350	3.2	P-1	*A-1+
Philip Morris Companies, Inc.	295	2.7	P-2	A-1
Mitsubishi Bank, Ltd. (Grand Cayman)	285	2.6	P-1	A-1+
Grand Metropolitan PLC	281	2.6	P-2	A-1
Sumitomo Bank, Ltd.	260	2.4	P-1	A-1+
General Electric Capital Corp.	248	2.3	P-1	A-1+
Shearson Lehman Hutton Holdings, Inc.	203	1.9	P-1	A-1
Merrill Lynch & Co., Inc.	198	1.8	P-1	A-1
Subtotal	$4,334	39.9%		
U.S. Government & Federal Agencies	175	1.6		
Total fund value	$10,860	100.0%		

Dreyfus: Worldwide Dollar (4/30/90)	Value	% Total	Moody's	S&P
Chrysler Financial Corp.	$636	8.9%	P-2	A-2
Mitsubishi Bank, Ltd. (Grand Cayman)	509	7.1	P-1	A-1+
Fuji Bank, Ltd. (Grand Cayman)	426	6.0	*P-1	*A-1+
Chemical Bank (London)	376	5.3	*P-2	*A-2
Goldman, Sachs & Co.	340	4.8	P-1	A-1+
Commercial Credit Co.	288	4.0	P-2	A-2
Oryx Energy Co.	264	3.7	P-2	A-2
Sears Savings Bank	210	2.9	NR	A-2
Colombia Savings–Denver[4]	194	2.7	NR	WR
Philip Morris Companies, Inc.	183	2.6	P-2	A-1
Saitama Bank, Ltd. (London)	171	2.4	P-1	NR

EXHIBIT 6 (CONTINUED)

	Value	% Total	Moody's	S&P
Sumitomo Bank, Ltd. (London)	150	2.1	P-1	*A-1+
Yasuda Trust & Banking Co., Ltd.	135	1.9	P-1	A-1+
Chase Manhattan Corp.	130	1.8	P-2	A-2
Amerco	125	1.8	NR	A-2
Subtotal	$4,137	58.1%		
U.S. Government & Federal Agencies	0	0.0		
Total fund value	$7,127	100.0%		

Dreyfus: Liquid Assets (12/31/89)	Value	% Total	Moody's	S&P
First National Bank of Chicago	$655	8.4%	P-1	A-1
Greenwood Trust Co.	585	7.5	NR	NR
Goldman, Sachs & Co.	394	5.0	P-1	A-1+
Shearson Lehman Hutton Holdings, Inc.	379	4.8	P-1	A-1+
PKBanken North America, Inc.	325	4.1	P-1	A-1+
Morgan Stanley Group, Inc.	309	3.9	P-1	A-1+
Salomon, Inc.	300	3.8	P-1	A-1
Chase Manhattan Corp.	294	3.8	P-2	A-2
Continental Illinois National Bank	290	3.7	P-2	A-2
Chase Manhattan Bank, N.A.[3]	280	3.6	P-1	A-1
Tokai Credit Corp.	275	3.5	P-1	A-1+
State Bank of India Finance Inc.	209	2.7	P-1	A-2
Security Pacific Corp.	209	2.7	P-1	A-1+
Philip Morris Companies, Inc.	199	2.5	P-2	A-1
Citicorp[1]	155	2.0	P-1	A-1+
Subtotal	$4,856	62.0%		
U.S. Government & Federal Agencies	0	0.0		
Total fund value	$7,836	100.0%		

Merrill Lynch: CMA (3/31/90)	Value	% Total	Moody's	S&P
General Motors Acceptance Corp.	$1,091	3.7%	P-1	A-1+
General Electric Capital Corp.	891	3.0	P-1	A-1+
Ford Motor Credit Company	826	2.8	P-1	A-1+
Citibank, N.A.	805	2.7	P-1	A-1+
Sears Roebuck Acceptance Corp.	796	2.7	P-1	A-1
Dai-Ichi Kangyo Bank, Ltd. (New York)	750	2.5	P-1	A-1+
Fuji Bank, Ltd. (New York)	590	2.0	P-1	*A-1+
American Express Credit Corp.	521	1.8	P-1	A-1+
Associates Corp. of North America	448	1.5	P-1	A-1+
Mitsubishi Bank, Ltd. (New York)	443	1.5	P-1	A-1+
PepsiCo, Inc.	383	1.3	P-1	A-1
ITT Financial Corp.	348	1.2	P-1	A-1
E.I. duPont de Nemours & Co.	348	1.2	P-1	A-1+
Security Pacific National Bank	347	1.2	P-1	A-1+
Mitsui Bank, Ltd. (New York)	330	1.1	P-1	A-1+
Morgan Guaranty Trust Company (London)	313	1.1	P-1	A-1+
Shell Oil Co.	298	1.0	P-1	A-1
CIT Group Holdings, Inc.	298	1.0	P-1	
Subtotal	$9,828	33.0%		
U.S. Government & Federal Agencies	6,463	21.7		
Total fund value	$29,768	100.0%		

EXHIBIT 6 (CONTINUED)

Merrill Lynch: Ready Assets (12/31/89)	Value	% Total	Moody's	S&P
Dai-Ichi Kangyo Bank, Ltd.	$617	5.8%	P-1	A-1+
General Electric Capital Corp.	487	4.6	P-1	A-1+
General Motors Acceptance Corp.	440	4.1	P-1	A-1+
Citibank, N. A.	435	4.1	P-1	A-1+
Fuji Bank, Ltd. (New York)	340	3.2	P-1	A-1+
Goldman, Sachs & Co.	308	2.9	P-1	A-1+
Security Pacific National Bank	283	2.7	P-1	A-1+
Ford Motor Credit Co.	269	2.5	P-1	A-1+
Sony Capital Corp.	257	2.4	P-1	A-1+
Bankers Trust Company (London)	245	2.3	P-1	*A-1+
Chrysler Financial Corp.[2]	224	2.1	P-2	A-2
Sears Roebuck Acceptance Corp.	211	2.0	P-1	A-1+
Long-Term Credit Bank, Japan (New York)	205	1.9	P-1	A-1+
J.P. Morgan & Co., Inc.	200	1.9	P-1	A-1+
Subtotal	$4,521	42.5%		
U.S. Government & Federal Agencies	573	5.4		
Total fund value	$10,650	100.0%		

Note: Ratings are as of March 1990.
1. Citicorp downgraded to "P-2" on 5/22/90.
2. Chrysler Financial Corp. downgraded to "A-3" on 6/14/90 and "P-3" on 6/29/90.
3. Chase Manhattan Bank, N.A. downgraded to "P-2" on 6/11/90.
4. Columbia Savings' short-term debt rating of "A-1" withdrawn on 2/15/89; company subordinated debt downgraded to "D" on 1/6/89.
*Rating of the parent company.

EXHIBIT 7

Mix of industry money market fund assets (dollars in billions)

	1983	1984	1985	1986	1987	1988	Oct.1989
Assets	$162	$210	$208	$228	$255	$272	$357
U.S. Treasuries	30%	31%	33%	33%	32%	26%	26%
Certificates of deposit	28	21	17	18	22	23	20
Bankers' acceptances	12	9	6	5	4	4	2
Commercial paper	29	37	42	42	39	43	47
All other	1	1	2	3	3	3	4
Total	100%	100%	100%	100%	100%	100%	100%
Average maturity (days)	37	43	37	40	31	28	33
Number of funds	307	329	348	360	389	432	454

Money market funds grew phenomenally between 1978 and 1982 when interest rates surged and Regulation Q limited the rates banks and S&Ls could pay on savings and time deposits. By 1989, there were over 450 money market funds with assets exceeding $350 billion (Exhibit 7) and an estimated 20 million accounts. Investment advisory fees on these funds totaled $1.5 billion.

The commercial paper market burgeoned in parallel with money market funds. Corporations increasingly bypassed banks, raising short-term funds directly in the public markets. By the late 1980s, commercial paper issuance exceeded all bank commercial and industrial loans. Money market funds were large buyers, owning about 30% of the $653 billion of commercial paper outstanding in June 1990. In terms of Moody's credit ratings, this total was broken down as follows:

P-1	$462 billion
P-2	79
P-3	9
Non-Prime	6
Not rated	97
Total	$653

Foreign issuers accounted for an increasingly large share of top-rated commercial paper and CDs as the credit quality of U.S. financial institutions and corporations deteriorated.

Calculation of Net Asset Value

Most money market funds, including Prime Reserve Fund, priced their portfolios daily or even more frequently. Securities with maturities longer than 60 days were valued at market. Securities with maturities shorter than 60 days were valued at amortized cost unless this was deemed not to reflect fair value, in which case an alternative "good faith" determination of fair value had to be made.

It was also standard practice for money market funds to maintain a net asset value (NAV) of $1.00 per share. This was accomplished by distributing the net income of the fund as it was earned, and by rounding the NAV to the nearest penny. In addition, money market funds would keep to relatively short maturities, and try to "minimize" credit risk and other exposures. However, as Prime Reserve Fund's prospectus cautioned:

> Although [the] Fund believes that it will be able to maintain its net asset value at $1.00 per share under most conditions, there can be no absolute assurance that it will be able to do so on a continuous basis. If

the Fund's net asset value per share declined, or was expected to decline, below $1.00 (rounded to the nearest one cent), the Board of Directors of the Fund might temporarily reduce or suspend dividend payments in an effort to maintain the net asset value at $1.00 per share. As a result of such reduction or suspension of dividends, the investor would receive less income during a given period than if such a reduction or suspension had not taken place. Such action could result in an investor receiving no dividend for the period during which he holds his shares and in his receiving, upon redemption, a price per share lower than that which he paid.

Recent Price Competition in Money Market Fund Industry

Historically, yield was an important determinant of the flow of assets between money market funds and alternative savings vehicles like certificates of deposit. Yield was also an important dimension of competition within the mutual fund industry. With the industry expense ratio at 0.73%, low-cost producers like Vanguard—whose money market fund expense ratio was only 0.30%—had an enormous advantage.

In early 1989, in perhaps the most aggressive campaigns in industry history, Fidelity and Dreyfus began marketing their Spartan and Worldwide Dollar funds respectively. The expense ratios of these funds were completely absorbed by the sponsoring companies, giving considerable boost to their yields. When short-term rates were hovering at about 10%, Spartan and Worldwide Dollar were among the few funds able to advertise eye-catching double-digit yields (Exhibit 13). Both funds attracted billions of dollars in very short order. On April 30, 1990, Spartan had $8.3 billion in assets, while Worldwide Dollar had $7.1 billion (Exhibit 6).

Fidelity guaranteed to keep Spartan's expense ratio beneath 0.45% until 1992. In late 1989, the firm increased the fund's expense ratio to 0.10% (from zero). Dreyfus was less specific about its commitment to maintain a low expense ratio. As of July 1990, Worldwide Dollar's expense ratio was still at zero.

In addition to subsidizing Worldwide Dollar's expense ratio, Dreyfus invested the fund more aggressively than most in higher-yielding Eurodollar securities. Worldwide Dollar also operated under more liberal investment restrictions. For example, the fund could invest up to 15% of

EXHIBIT 8

Balance sheet of mortgage & realty trust, March 1990, unaudited (dollars in millions)

Assets		
Mortgage loans and investments:		
Construction loans	$91	
Standing loans	316	
Long-term amortizing loans	13	
Participating loans and investments	68	
Non-earning mortgage loans	14	
Total mortgage		$502
Real estate:		
Investments in real estate equities	51	
Properties acquired through foreclosure and held for sale:		
Earning	7	
Non-earning	20	
Less allowance for losses	(3)	
Total real estate		75
Cash		1
Short-term investments		2
Interest receivable and other assets		14
		$594

Liabilities and stockholders' equity		
Liabilities:		
Notes payable:		
Commercial paper	$167	
Medium-term notes	35	
Bank bid facility	50	
Total public debt	252	
Senior notes	123	
Revolving credit	20	
Total senior debt	395	
Convertible subordinated debentures	1	
Total debt		$396
Accounts payable and accrued expenses		9
Total liabilities		$405
Shareholders' equity		189
		$594

EXHIBIT 9

The U.S. household balance sheet, December 31, 1979 and 1989 (dollars in billions)

	1979	1989
Financial intermediaries:		
Checkable deposits and currency	$256	$490
Savings deposits	425	590
MMDAs	0	490
Small CDs	633	1,200
Large CDs	73	45
Total financial intermediaries	$1,387	$2,915
Open-market securities:		
Savings bonds	$80	$120
Treasury and agency debt	154	865
Municipal debt	77	295
Corporate and foreign debt	72	160
Open-market paper	38	140
Subtotal: debt securities	$420	$1,580
Equities	812	2,100
Total open-market securities	$1,232	$3,680
Packaged products:		
Money market & short-term bond funds	$40	$375
Long-term fixed-income funds	14	295
Equity mutual funds	30	200
Subtotal: mutual funds	$84	$870
Other packaged products	24	140
Credit balances at brokers	10	45
Total packaged products	$118	$1,055
Discretionary financial assets	$2,737	$7,650
Owner-financed mortgage	89	130
Life insurance reserves	207	325
Pension fund assets	767	2,900
Equity in non-corporate business	1,179	2,430
Total financial assets	$5,580	$13,435
Owner-occupied real estate and land	2,324	4,650
Consumer durables (autos, appliances)	925	1,910
Total assets	$8,829	$19,995

EXHIBIT 10

Relationship of fixed-income mutual fund inflows to S&L consumer deposit flows

	Money Market & Short-Term Bonds	Long-Term Bonds	Total	S&L Consumer Deposits
	New Inflows			
1982	$30.4	$4.7	$35.1	$(14.7)
1983	(43.7)	10.4	(33.3)	41.8
1984	48.8	15.3	64.1	22.5
1985	(5.4)	63.8	58.4	5.4
1986	34.0	99.3	133.3	(11.5)
1987	10.2	6.8	17.0	(9.9)
1988	0.1	(4.5)	(4.4)	(14.0)
1989	81.0	1.0	82.0	(70.0)

Source: Sanford C. Bernstein & Co., Inc., January 1990.

EXHIBIT 11

Comparison of short-term consumer interest rates

		Money Market Funds	Money Market Deposit Accounts	Thrift 6-Month CD's	6-Month Treasury Bills	A-1/P-1 CP
1984		9.90%	9.19%	10.35%	9.77%	10.12%
1985		7.70	7.51	7.97	7.65	7.95
1986	Q1	7.34%	6.88%	7.74%	6.96%	6.93%
	Q2	6.57	6.48	7.19	6.18	6.45
	Q3	5.88	6.00	6.60	5.60	5.73
	Q4	5.41	5.68	6.17	5.40	6.01
1987	Q1	5.56%	5.62%	6.16%	5.14%	6.23%
	Q2	5.90	5.72	6.59	5.98	6.94
	Q3	6.25	5.85	7.01	6.14	7.90
	Q4	6.73	6.05	7.43	6.46	7.01
1988	Q1	6.48%	6.00%	7.33%	6.04%	6.71%
	Q2	6.46	5.90	7.16	6.46	7.11
	Q3	7.34	6.04	7.60	7.25	8.02
	Q4	8.00	6.22	8.11	7.86	8.65
1989	Q1	8.91%	6.46%	8.72%	8.59%	9.53%
	Q2	9.50	6.61	9.50	8.33	9.70
	Q3	8.68	6.46	8.64	8.00	8.97
	Q4	8.44	6.40	8.34	7.91	8.62

EXHIBIT 12

The Dreyfus Corporation income statement, 1989, and summary balance sheet, year-end 1989 (dollars in millions)

Income statement:

Management fees	$186.5
Dreyfus Consumer Bank	10.2
Other revenues	6.2
Investment income	73.3
Total revenues	$276.2
Advertising & other selling expenses	40.0
Sales, general & administrative	107.4
Interest expense	8.2
Total expenses	$155.6
Income before taxes	120.6
Taxes	35.0
Ordinary income	$85.6
Gain on sale of credit card business	43.2
Net income	$128.8
Earnings per share	$3.16
Shares outstanding (millions)	41
Stock price per share (March 1990)	$36

Summary balance sheet:

Assets

Cash assets	$146
Receivables	59
Investments	677
Fixed and other assets	44
	$926

Liabilities and stockholders' equity

Accounts payable	$34
Other liabilities	175
Stockholders' equity	717
	$926

its assets in the securities of any one bank, a limitation that moreover applied to only 75% of fund assets. In the fund's prospectus, Dreyfus notes that SEC staff had expressed concern as to whether certain bank obligations should be subject to the statutory 5% limitation governing most mutual fund investments. As shown in Exhibit 6, Worldwide Dollar's largest holding on April 30 was 9% investment in Chrysler Financial. This paper was then rated A-2/P-2 but downgraded to A-3/P-3 in June 1990.

Note

1. *Barrons,* March 26, 1990.

EXHIBIT 13

Source: Wall Street Journal, 6/21/89.

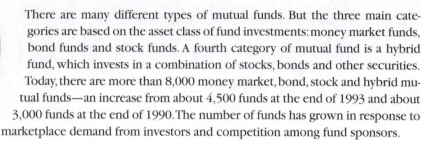

Choosing Among Mutual Funds

There are many different types of mutual funds. But the three main categories are based on the asset class of fund investments: money market funds, bond funds and stock funds. A fourth category of mutual fund is a hybrid fund, which invests in a combination of stocks, bonds and other securities. Today, there are more than 8,000 money market, bond, stock and hybrid mutual funds—an increase from about 4,500 funds at the end of 1993 and about 3,000 funds at the end of 1990. The number of funds has grown in response to marketplace demand from investors and competition among fund sponsors.

This Chapter focuses on understanding the main types of mutual funds from the viewpoint of investors—understanding the various ways in which funds are categorized and the various methods by which their performance is measured. It first discusses peer groups and key indexes for money market funds, bond funds and hybrid funds. Then it covers the more complicated peer groups and key indexes for equity funds, as well as the debate on active and passive management through index funds. Finally, it outlines a few pooled alternatives to mutual funds and presents an exercise on asset allocation among mutual funds.

Before we turn to the main types of funds, let us briefly introduce some concepts that will recur throughout the Chapter. There are three key ways to measure the performance of money market, bond, stock and hybrid mutual funds. All of these funds may be measured by total return, compared to peer groups of similarly situated funds or compared to indexes of securities.

The basic measurement of mutual fund performance is total return. According to the standard definition, the total return of a mutual fund is calculated by adding any distributions of income or capital gains made by a fund to its shareholders, together with any change in its net asset value (which can be positive or negative), and dividing the sum by the cost of the initial investment. For the purpose of calculating total return, all fund distributions are normally assumed to be reinvested in additional shares of the same fund. An example of a total return calculation follows.

Initial investment (per share)		$100
Income distribution		$4
Capital gains distribution		$2
Investment appreciation (shares now worth $104)		$4
Total return	=	$\dfrac{\text{Income} + \text{capital gain} + \text{appreciation}}{\text{Initial investment}}$
	=	$\dfrac{\$4 + \$2 + \$4}{\$100}$
	=	$\dfrac{\$10}{\$100}$
	=	10%

Net asset value changes used in computing total return take into account the annual operating expenses (total expenses) of a fund, such as the management fee, fees to service providers (e.g., transfer agency and custody fees) and 12b-1 fees used to pay for distribution expenses. Total return may or may not include sales loads paid by investors when shares are bought (front-end loads) or sold (back-end loads). Obviously, if a fund's total return does not include the sales load, the total return will be higher; if the total return reflects the sales load, the total return will be lower. A fund's total expenses and sales loads, if any, are found in the fee table near the front of the fund's prospectus. Although this standard definition of total return applies to all mutual funds, investors tend to focus on different components of total return for each fund type—for example, dividend yield for money market funds and capital appreciation for equity funds. As we discuss each type of fund below, we will describe its primary components of total return.

In choosing among funds, some investors are sensitive to total expenses and sales loads as separate items, while others focus on the more comprehensive concept of total return. Investors can review rankings of funds according to their total expenses within each fund type; such rankings are available in the media and over the Internet. Investors are especially sensitive to total expenses in money market and bond funds because expenses generally have a larger impact on their total return than the total return of equity funds or hybrid funds (which historically have higher returns). Investors can also divide mutual funds between load funds that impose a sales charge on investors and no-load funds that are sold without a sales charge. Mutual funds sold through an intermediary, such as a broker or bank, often involve a sales load—either a front-end load charged to the investor at the time of purchase or a back-end load charged to the investor at the time of redemption. As mentioned above, 12b-1 fees are included in total expenses of a fund, although they are effectively a sales charge paid in annual installments.

The second main way to measure mutual funds is to compare the total return of a fund to the total return of peer groups of similarly situated funds. Peer groups can be based on many different criteria, such as broad fund categories, investment objectives or fund holdings. Funds within each peer group are compared to other funds in the group. When used to measure or rank funds, the peer groups are referred to as a competitive universe. The funds in a competitive universe are ranked by total return and are often divided into four quartiles. The better performers (top 25%) compose the first quartile, while the poorer relative performers (bottom 25%) are in the fourth quartile. Independent measurement firms, such as Lipper Analytical Services and Morningstar, generate monthly, quarterly and annual rankings of mutual funds by their total returns relative to their competitive universes.

The definition of peer groups and measurements based on the peer groups are subject to debate for all fund types, especially for U.S. general equity funds because they are the most complicated to group and measure. For that reason, we cover U.S. general equity funds separately from other equity funds in our discussion of competitive universes. The intent of peer group comparisons is laudable: to measure the skill of the manager in selecting securities and constructing a fund portfolio, instead of whether a manager did well because his or her fund happened to be invested in a favored portion of the securities market (e.g., large-growth stocks in 1999). However, it is notoriously difficult to construct an appropriate set of peer groups. As we will see, peer groups can be broadly or narrowly defined. Broad peer groups are often criticized as including funds that are not similarly situated; thus, factors other than the skill of the manager may heavily influence rankings in broad peer groups. On the other hand, narrow peer groups are often criticized as too small for statistical validity; they also may present moving targets since funds can quickly slip in or out of narrowly defined groups.

One of the simplest and most popular forms of peer groups is based on broad categories of fund investments. Morningstar assigns star ratings within four broad categories: domestic stock funds, international stock funds, taxable bond funds and non-taxable bond funds. Morningstar assigns overall star ratings to funds based on a fund's historical risk-adjusted performance as of the most recent month end. Morningstar calculates its star ratings based on a fund's 3-, 5- and 10-year average annual total return in excess of the 90-day Treasury bill (including the sales load, if applicable) and a risk factor that reflects a fund's performance below the 90-day Treasury bill. The top 10% of funds in a category receive five stars, the next 22.5% receive four stars, the middle 35% receive three stars, the next 22.5% receive two stars and the bottom 10% receive one star. The 3-, 5- and 10-year ratings are weighted to arrive at the overall Morningstar star ratings, which are published every month. Morningstar does not rate funds that are less than three years old, so a new "hot" fund must build a record before obtaining a coveted four- or five-star rating.

Morningstar also groups and rates mutual funds within 48 narrower categories based on fund holdings over the past three years. The 48 categories are subsets of Morningstar's four main groupings. Funds within these narrower categories are rated using the same basic methodology as the star system, but category ratings do not include loads and cover only the most recent three-year period. The Morningstar categories are listed in Table 2.1. Instead of being assigned stars, funds in the Morningstar category-rating scheme are assigned a number from 1 to 5, with 5 being the highest rating.

Another way to group funds by peers is by investment objective—the primary investment focus of the fund. The Securities and Exchange Commission (SEC) requires a fund's investment objective to be included in its prospectus, and the investment objective usually may be changed only by a vote of the shareholders of the fund. In addition to requiring a stated investment objective, the SEC imposes a "name test" requirement on funds that have names implying a certain investment focus, such as Japanese funds or health care funds. The SEC recently announced that by July 31, 2002, such funds must invest at least 80% of their assets in the securities of companies that meet the name test, measured at the time of purchase of the securities (up from at least 65%). There are many ways to group funds by investment objective. Lipper categorizes funds according to 91 investment objectives based on prospectus policies and its review of the fund's investment characteristics. The Lipper objective-based categories are listed in Table 2.2. Many of Lipper's investment objective categories currently require that the fund invest at least 65% of its assets in a particular type of investment. For example, to be classified as a telecommunications fund by Lipper, a fund must invest at least 65% of its assets in the securities of companies in the telecommunications business. (In light of the recent change in the SEC's name test rule, Lipper will have to decide if it is going to change the criteria used to define its investment objective categories.)

TABLE 2.1

Morningstar "star rating" categories

Domestic Stock	*International Stock*
Large-Cap Value	Europe
Large-Cap Blend	Latin America
Large-Cap Growth	Diversified Emerging Markets
Mid-Cap Value	Pacific/Asia
Mid-Cap Blend	Pacific/Asia (no Japan)
Mid-Cap Growth	Japan
Small-Cap Value	Diversified Foreign
Small-Cap Blend	Diversified World
Small-Cap Growth	International Hybrid
Specialty Communications	
Specialty Financial	
Specialty Health	
Specialty Natural Resources	
Specialty Precious Metals	
Specialty Real Estate	
Specialty Technology	
Specialty Utilities	
Domestic Hybrid	
Convertible Bond Hybrid	

Non-Taxable Bond	*Taxable Bond*
Muni National Long	Government Long-Term
Muni National Intermediate	Government Intermediate Term
Muni Single State Long	Government Short-Term
Muni Single State Intermediate	General Long-Term
Muni Short-Term	General Intermediate-Term
Muni California Long	General Short-Term
Muni California Intermediate	General Ultrashort-Term
Muni New York Long	Specialty Emerging Markets Bond
Muni New York Intermediate	Specialty International
	Specialty High-Yield
	Specialty Multisector

In order to rank funds, Lipper considers each of the 91 investment objective categories separately. Lipper ranks funds within each investment objective competitive universe by total return (without sales load) and divides the funds into four quartiles. A fund's ranking can change over different time periods. For example, a fund may be in the first quartile of its competitive universe (i.e., ranked 18 out of 100 funds) based on one-year return, but in the third quartile (i.e., ranked 58 out of 80 funds) based on five-year return.

In addition to the peer groups already mentioned, Lipper and Morningstar group U.S. general equity funds by investment style into competitive universes based on historical fund holdings. Such groupings for U.S. general equity funds are complicated and will be detailed later. In short, both classify U.S. general equity funds by market capitalization—large, mid or small cap—based on an asset-weighted market capitalization of

TABLE 2.2

Lipper investment objective categories

General Equity Funds
1. Capital Appreciation
2. Growth
3. Growth & Income
4. Equity Income
5. Mid-Cap
6. Small-Cap
7. Micro-Cap
8. S&P 500 Index Objective

Sector and Specialty Equity Funds
9. Financial Services
10. Health/Biotechnology
11. Natural Resources
12. Real Estate
13. Science & Technology
14. Specialty & Miscellaneous
15. Telecommunications
16. Utility

World Equity Funds
17. Gold-Oriented
18. Global
19. Global Small-Cap
20. International
21. International Small-Cap
22. European Region
23. Pacific Region
24. Japanese
25. Pacific ex. Japan
26. China Region
27. Emerging Markets
28. Latin American
29. Canadian

Mixed Equity Funds
30. Flexible Portfolio
31. Global Flexible Portfolio
32. Balanced
33. Balanced Target Maturity
34. Convertible Securities
35. Income

Fixed Income Funds
36. Ultra Short Obligation Fund

Short/Intermediate-Term U.S. Treasury and Government Funds
37. Short U.S. Treasury
38. Short U.S. Government
39. Short-Intermediate U.S. Government
40. Intermediate U.S. Treasury
41. Intermediate U.S. Government

Short/Intermediate-Term Corporate Fixed-Income Funds
42. Short Investment Grade Debt
43. Short-Intermediate Investment Grade Debt
44. Intermediate-Investment Grade Debt

General Domestic Taxable Fixed-Income Funds
45. General U.S. Treasury
46. General U.S. Government
47. Adjustable Rate Mortgage
48. GNMA
49. U.S. Mortgage
50. Corporate Debt Funds A Rated
51. Corporate Debt Funds BBB Rated
52. General Bond
53. Multi-Sector Income
54. High Current Yield
55. Convertible Securities
56. Flexible Income
57. Target Maturity

World Taxable Fixed Income Funds
58. Short World Multi-Market Income
59. Short World Single-Market Income
60. Global Income
61. International Income
62. Emerging Markets Debt

Short/Intermediate Municipal Debt Funds
63. Short Municipal Debt
64. Short/Intermediate Municipal Debt
65. Intermediate Municipal Debt

General Municipal Debt Funds
66. General Municipal Debt
67. Insured Municipal Debt
68. High Yield Municipal Debt
69. Single-State Municipal Debt
70. Other States Short/Intermediate Municipal Debt
71. Other States Intermediate Municipal Debt
72. California Intermediate Municipal Debt
73. California Insured Municipal Debt
74. California Short/Intermediate Municipal Debt
75. Florida Intermediate Municipal Debt
76. Florida Insured Municipal Debt
77. Massachusetts Intermediate Municipal Debt
78. New York Intermediate Municipal Debt
79. New York Insured Municipal Debt
80. Ohio Intermediate Municipal Debt
81. Pennsylvania Intermediate Municipal Debt
82. Virginia Intermediate Municipal Debt

Money Market Funds (Taxable)
83. Institutional Money Market
84. Institutional U.S. Treasury Money Market
85. Institutional U.S. Government Money Market
86. Money Market Instrument
87. U.S. Government Money Market
88. U.S. Treasury Money Market

Money Market Funds (Tax Exempt)
89. Tax Exempt Money Market
90. Institutional Tax-Exempt Money Market
91. Single-State Tax-Exempt Money Market

the fund's holdings. (Lipper also has a multi-cap market capitalization classification for funds that do not fall clearly into either the large or mid-cap classifications.) Both also classify U.S. general equity funds by investment style within each market capitalization classification—growth, value or blend (blend is sometimes called core)—based on financial characteristics of the fund's holdings.

The third main way to measure mutual funds is to compare a fund's total return to the return of an index (sometimes called a benchmark). An index is a hypothetical portfolio of securities, representing a securities market or portion thereof, which is maintained by an independent provider. Some indexes provide a gauge of the activity of the general market (e.g., Standard & Poor's 500 index for the U.S. equity market), while others may focus on a particular country or region or market sector (e.g., Morgan Stanley Capital International Latin American index and Goldman Sachs Technology index). Index providers price each security in the market index periodically and calculate many statistics for the index, such as the price change and total return for stock indexes, and the average duration, yield and total return for bond indexes. Investors may choose among funds by comparing a fund's total return to the return of the index. However, the return of an index is a somewhat theoretical concept because it does not include the expenses that actually would be involved in establishing and maintaining a portfolio of securities for any group of investors. Even the return of an index fund reflects the operating expenses for running the portfolio and servicing fund shareholders as well as transaction costs such as brokerage commissions associated with buying and selling securities. Therefore, the comparison of a fund's total return to the return of an index is not an "apples to apples" comparison.

I. *Types of Non-stock Funds*

A. *Money Market Funds*

Money market funds invest in debt securities that mature in 13 months or less, and the average maturity of all their holdings may not exceed 90 days. Money market funds are either taxable or tax exempt. Taxable funds invest in debt securities, such as corporate or U.S. government debt, that are subject to federal income tax. Tax-exempt funds invest in debt securities that are exempt from federal income tax, although the securities may be subject to state or local tax. The income from tax-exempt funds may also be subject to the federal alternative minimum tax (AMT). Generally, tax-exempt funds may invest up to 20% of their assets in securities that are subject to the AMT (although many tax-exempt funds choose not to invest in any securities that are subject to the AMT); municipal money market funds are a subset of tax-exempt money market funds that may invest up to 100% of their assets in securities that are subject to the AMT.

As you saw in Chapter One, money market funds attempt to keep a $1.00 net asset value (NAV). Because money market funds aim to keep a $1.00 NAV, they distribute all net income to shareholders as dividends daily, although the daily dividends often accrue and typically are paid to shareholders monthly. Therefore, when comparing the total return of money market funds, investors focus primarily on a fund's dividend yield (computed after expenses are subtracted). Investors also are interested in the expense level of a money market fund; the median total expense for money market funds is approximately 59 basis points (bp).[1]

While all money market funds invest in high-quality, short-term securities with generally lower risk than other mutual funds, investors should recognize the differences among money market funds. The funds differ in quality and credit risk due to the securities in which they invest. On the taxable side, U.S. Treasury funds invest in Treasury securities that are backed by the full faith and credit of the U.S. Treasury and are generally considered to be of the highest quality and the lowest credit risk. U.S. government funds invest in U.S. government agency securities that are also of high quality and relatively low credit risk, although generally slightly lower quality and slightly higher credit risk than Treasury securities. Most agency securities are backed by the moral obligation of the U.S. government. Agency securities are issued by agencies such as Fannie Mae (FNMA) and Freddie Mac (FHLMC). General-purpose taxable money market funds (the case study in Chapter One focused on a general-purpose fund) primarily invest in commercial paper and certificates of deposit issued by corporations and banks with slightly lower quality and higher credit risk than U.S. government securities.

Some taxable money market funds may call themselves "rated" funds if the fund (as opposed to the securities in which the fund invests) meets criteria established by independent firms, such as Standard & Poor's (S&P) and Moody's. In order to meet the criteria necessary to call itself rated, a fund must meet requirements that are stricter than those required by the SEC for taxable money market funds. As discussed in the case study in Chapter One, there are three key SEC requirements for taxable money market funds: (1) at least 95% of the fund's assets must be invested in the highest-quality money market securities (rated A-1 or P-1 or equivalent), and the other 5% or less must be invested in money market securities with the second-highest rating (A-2, P-2 or equivalent); (2) the fund may not invest more than 5% of its assets in any single top-rated issuer (other than the federal government) and no more than 1% of its assets in any second-rated issuer; and (3) the average maturity of the fund's assets may not exceed 90 days. Generally, to receive the highest rating from S&P and Moody's, a money market fund must invest 100% of its assets in the highest-quality money market securities, and the average maturity of the fund's assets may not exceed 60 days.

There are fewer types of tax-exempt money market funds. The primary distinction in the funds is between national tax-exempt funds and single state tax-exempt funds. As the names indicate, national tax-exempt funds invest in high-quality, short-term securities that are exempt from federal income tax. Single state tax-exempt funds invest in high-quality, short-term securities that are exempt from state or local tax as well as federal income tax. Tax-exempt money market funds invest in securities, such as general obligation bonds issued by municipalities, backed by the credit and taxing power of the issuer; revenue bonds backed only by the revenues of the facilities being financed, or by a special tax on the facilities or users of the facility; and tax-exempt commercial paper, issued by nonprofits and state and local governments. General obligation bonds are usually considered stronger credits than revenue bonds or tax-exempt commercial paper issued by nonprofits, although any of these credits may be strengthened by insurance or standby letters of credit provided by third parties.

There are two competitive universe peer groupings commonly used to measure money market funds: Lipper and iMoneyNet (formerly IBC Financial Data, Inc.). Lipper categorizes money market mutual funds around nine standard investment objective peer groups for taxable and tax-exempt money market funds (see Table 2.2). Lipper has three main taxable fund objectives: U.S. Treasury, U.S. government and money market. Lipper also has corresponding objectives for institutional money market funds (funds with a very high investment minimum and lower relative expense ratio). Lipper's three objectives for tax-exempt money market funds are tax exempt, institutional tax exempt and single state tax exempt.

iMoneyNet, an independent measurement firm that covers money market funds, groups money market funds into four broad categories: taxable retail, tax-free retail, taxable institutional and tax-free institutional. The retail categories contain funds geared toward the individual investor, while, similar to Lipper, the institutional categories contain funds geared toward the institutional investor. iMoneyNet also has 14 narrower categories of money market funds. Key benchmarks for money market funds are the iMoneyNet peer averages, since there are no widely used indexes for money market funds.

B. *Bond Funds*

Bond funds also invest in debt securities, although the securities held by bond funds have longer maturities than securities held by money market funds. Bonds are issued by a much broader range of entities than money market securities, and the bonds held by bond funds do not have to meet the strict quality standards required for the securities held by money market funds. Like money market funds, bond funds are either taxable or tax exempt, depending on the securities in which the fund invests.

Taxable bond funds invest in debt securities that are subject to federal income tax, such as U.S. Treasury and U.S. government agency securities, asset-backed bonds like mortgage-backed securities, corporate bonds (either high-grade or below-investment-grade "junk" bonds) or foreign government bonds. U.S. Treasury securities are backed by the full faith and credit of the U.S. Treasury; most U.S. government agency securities are backed by the moral obligation of the U.S. government. Income from federal government bonds is generally subject to federal, but not state, income tax. Asset-backed securities such as Government National Mortgage Association (GNMA) securities are interests in pools of underlying securities, such as mortgage loans; the GNMA securities are backed by the full faith and credit of the U.S. Treasury. Most corporate bonds held by mutual funds are issued by publicly traded corporations. If the corporation has good credit, the bonds issued are considered high or investment grade. If the corporation has poorer credit, the bonds issued are generally considered below-investment grade or junk bonds (rated BB or lower by a credit rating agency such as Moody's or S&P). Junk bonds pay a higher yield to compensate for greater risk. Foreign government bonds are issued by non-U.S. governments of developed or emerging markets countries.

Tax-exempt bond funds invest in debt securities that are issued by jurisdictions across the nation or within a specific state. The income derived from national tax-exempt bond funds is not subject to federal income tax, but most of the income is likely to be subject to the income tax of some state. The income derived from state tax-exempt bond funds is "double-tax free"—subject to neither federal nor state income tax for residents of that state. Often the income derived from state tax-exempt bond funds is also free from local income tax as well as federal and state income tax—"triple-tax free"—for example, New York City bonds. As with money market funds, the income from tax-exempt funds may be subject to the AMT. Generally, tax-exempt funds may invest up to 20% of their assets in securities that are subject to the AMT (although many tax-exempt funds choose not to invest in any securities that are subject to the AMT); municipal bond funds are a subset of tax-exempt bond funds that may invest up to 100% of their assets in securities that are subject to the AMT.

Both taxable and tax-exempt bond funds may be distinguished by term (e.g., short term, intermediate term or long term). Term is based on the dollar-weighted average maturity of the funds' investments. (Dollar-weighted average maturity is the value of each investment multiplied by the time remaining until its maturity, added together and divided by the value of the fund's portfolio.) Normally, long-term bond funds pay higher yields than intermediate-term bond funds, which in turn pay higher yields than short-term bond funds. However, in general, the longer the dollar-weighted average maturity, the more a fund's NAV will fluctuate in response to changes in market interest rates.

S&P and Moody's rate the securities in which bond funds invest by credit quality, although they do not rate the funds themselves. Bonds issued by the federal government have the highest rating of AAA, and junk bonds have ratings of BB or lower. Some tax-exempt bond funds call themselves insured funds because they invest at least 80% (up recently from 65%; funds have until July 31, 2002, to comply with the new rule) of the fund's assets in securities insured by a firm, such as Municipal Bond Investors Assurance Corp. (MBIA), that backs the payment obligation of the security. The credit quality of bonds and bond ratings will be explored in greater detail in Chapter Four when we cover portfolio management of bonds.

Bond funds distribute net income to shareholders as dividends, but unlike money market funds, they do not maintain a $1.00 NAV; the NAV of bond funds changes daily. The income dividends of bond funds generally accrue daily and are distributed to shareholders monthly. Total return for a bond fund is based on the fund's dividend yield and capital gains. In addition to total return, bond funds also may quote the actual dividends paid by the fund, known as the distribution rate, and the daily rate of per share income, known as the mil rate. However, the total return of a bond fund is more important to investors than its distribution rate because a bond fund can report a high distribution rate while incurring significant capital losses. Investors are also interested in the expense level of a bond fund; the median total expense is approximately 99 bp for taxable bond funds and approximately 97 bp for municipal bond funds.

Bond funds may be grouped into competitive universes according to the three principal schemes discussed in the introduction to the Chapter. First, Morningstar groups bond funds into two broad categories—taxable bond and non-taxable bond— and assigns star ratings within each competitive universe. Second, Morningstar also groups bond funds into 20 narrower peer groups (11 taxable bond and 9 non-taxable bond) listed in Table 2.1 and assigns a category rating within the group, allowing investors to evaluate funds within a narrower competitive universe.[2]

Third, Lipper categorizes bond mutual funds around standard investment objectives for taxable and municipal bond funds listed in Table 2.2. Lipper has 27 taxable bond and 20 municipal bond investment objective categories. The taxable and municipal bond categories are primarily divided based on level of maturity and credit quality. In addition, there are five investment categories for world taxable fixed income funds including short world multi-market income, short world single-market income, global income (invests in debt securities of U.S. and non-U.S. issuers), international income (invests in debt securities of non-U.S. issuers) and emerging markets debt (invests in debt securities of emerging markets issuers). The more specific municipal bond fund categories include insured municipal debt funds, high-yield municipal debt funds and 14 investment objective categories covering single state municipal debt funds of different maturities.

Besides peer groups, the performance of actively managed bond funds is measured against the returns of bond indexes. (See Chapter Four for investment strategies used by bond fund managers in their efforts to beat the relevant bond index.) The key index for general-purpose taxable bond funds is the Lehman Brothers Aggregate Bond index—comprising investment-grade bonds, including Treasury, corporate and mortgage-backed securities, with maturities of one year or more. The key index for national tax-exempt bond funds is the Lehman Brothers Municipal Bond index—comprising a huge number of investment-grade municipal bonds with maturities of one year or more that were part of an offering of at least $50 million.

Other bond indexes focus on narrower parts of the taxable bond market: for example, the high-yield, below-investment-grade market (e.g., Merrill Lynch High Yield Master index), the intermediate-term investment grade and U.S. government markets (e.g., Lehman Brothers Intermediate Government/Credit Bond index and Lehman Brothers Intermediate Government Bond index), and the long-term U.S. government market (e.g., Salomon Smith Barney Treasury/Agency index). The Merrill Lynch High Yield Master index includes high-yield bonds with maturities of one year or more and a credit rating of lower than BBB-/Baa3. The Lehman Brothers Intermediate Government/Credit Bond index includes government and investment-grade corporate bonds with maturities of between one and 10 years. The Lehman Brothers Intermediate Government Bond index includes U.S. government bonds with maturities of between 1 and 10 years. The Salomon Smith Barney Treasury/Agency index includes U.S. government debt obligations with maturities of more than one year.

An example of a narrower index for the tax-exempt market is the Lehman Brothers 1–6-year Municipal Bond index in the short/intermediate-term municipal market. The Lehman Brothers 1–6-year Municipal Bond index includes municipal debt instruments with maturities of one to six years. There are many single state municipal indexes—for example, the Lehman Brothers Massachusetts Three Plus Year Enhanced Municipal Bond index that includes Massachusetts investment-grade municipal bonds with maturities of three years or more.

A key international bond index is the Salomon Brothers World Government Bond index that includes securities traded in 14 world bond markets. A key index in the emerging markets bond area is the J. P. Morgan Emerging Markets Bond Index Global, which includes debt instruments issued by entities in 27 emerging markets countries.

Some bond funds are passively managed index funds that attempt to track the return of an index. Bond index funds usually attempt to track the return of their index by purchasing a statistically representative sample of securities whose combined total return will approximate that of the index. Most bond index funds, such as the Merrill Lynch Aggregate Bond Index Fund, attempt to track the return of the Lehman Brothers Aggregate Bond index, which is considered to be representative of the taxable bond market, since an index often includes thousands of bonds. Other bond index funds have shorter terms, such as Vanguard's Intermediate-Term Bond Index Fund that attempts to track the return of the Lehman Brothers 5–10-year Government/Credit index.

C. Hybrid Funds

Hybrid funds—such as balanced or asset allocation funds—invest in a combination of equity, debt and other securities. Balanced funds generally invest about 60% of assets in equity securities and 40% of assets in debt securities, both short and long term. Other asset allocation funds invest in a mix of equity and debt securities, and may change that mix from time to time within stated parameters.

Total return for hybrid funds that invest in stock, bond and money market instruments has several components—capital appreciation, capital gains and dividends—just as hybrid funds have several asset classes of investments. The median total expense for hybrid funds is approximately 124 bp.

Hybrid funds may be grouped into competitive universes according to the three principal schemes discussed in the introduction to the Chapter. First, Morningstar includes hybrid funds in its international stock or domestic stock broad category and assigns star ratings to the funds within the broad competitive universe. Second, Morningstar groups hybrid funds into three narrower peer groups—domestic hybrid, convertible bond hybrid and international hybrid, listed in Table 2.1—and assigns a category rating within the group, allowing investors to evaluate funds in a narrower competitive universe.

Third, Lipper categorizes the funds around standard investment objectives listed in Table 2.2. Lipper includes hybrid funds as part of its equity fund investment objectives. There are six Lipper investment mixed equity fund objectives for hybrid funds: flexible portfolio, global flexible portfolio, balanced, balanced target maturity, convertible securities and income. Funds in Lipper's flexible portfolio objective allocate investments across various asset classes, including domestic common stocks, bonds and money market instruments with a focus on total return. Funds in Lipper's global flexible portfolio objective allocate investments across various asset classes, including domestic and foreign stocks, bonds and money market instruments with a focus on total return; generally, at least 25% of the funds' portfolios must be invested in securities traded outside the United States. Funds in Lipper's balanced objective seek to conserve principal by maintaining at all times a balanced portfolio of stocks and bonds, typically about 60% stocks and 40% bonds. Funds in the balanced target maturity objective invest to provide a guaranteed return of investment at maturity (targeted periods); a portion of the funds' assets are invested in zero coupon U.S. Treasury securities, and the rest is invested in equity securities for long-term growth of capital. Funds in the convertible securities objective invest primarily in convertible bonds and/or convertible preferred stock. Funds in the income objective normally seek a high level of current income through investing in income-producing stocks, bonds and money market instruments.

In contrast to this variety of peer groups, there are few indexes created by independent providers especially for hybrid funds, because the funds invest in several asset classes. Often benchmark indexes for hybrid funds are a composite of indexes representing the different asset classes, such as a composite of the S&P 500 for the equities and the Lehman Brothers Aggregate Bond index for the investment-grade bonds in a balanced fund.

II. Stock Funds

While all stock funds invest in equity securities, there are many different types of stock funds. Some broad categories are U.S. funds, international funds, global funds, regional funds and sector funds. U.S. funds generally invest in equity securities of U.S. companies. International funds generally invest in equity securities of companies outside the United States, while global funds invest in equity securities of U.S. companies and companies outside the United States. Regional funds invest in equity securities of companies in a specific region, like Latin America or Europe. Sector funds invest in the equity securities of U.S. companies and companies outside the United States in specific industries or fields, such as health care or technology. We will begin by covering competitive universe peer groups for equity funds other than U.S. general equity funds and then separately for U.S. general equity funds. Then we will cover indexes for equity funds, including the debate on active versus passive management through equity index funds.

Investors frequently focus on the total return for equity funds, which primarily consists of appreciation (or depreciation) of the fund securities and capital gains. Dividends are typically not a large component of total return for equity funds, with a few exceptions such as equity income funds, which generally seek to hold securities with higher dividends than the average company in the S&P 500. Investors are less interested in the expenses of an equity fund than a bond fund since such expenses typically make up a relatively small portion of an equity fund's total return. The median total expense is approximately 179 bp for international, global and regional equity funds, approximately 161 bp for sector equity funds and approximately 135 bp for U.S. general equity funds.

A. Competitive Universes

1. Equity funds (other than U.S. general equity funds)   Equity funds other than U.S. general equity funds may be grouped into competitive universes according to the three principal schemes discussed in the introduction to the Chapter. First, Morningstar groups the funds within two broad categories—international stock and domestic stock—and assigns star ratings within each competitive universe. Second, Morningstar groups international, global, regional and sector equity funds into 16 narrower peer groups (eight for international equity funds and eight for domestic equity funds), listed in Table 2.1, and assigns a category rating within each group, allowing investors to evaluate funds in a narrower competitive universe.[3]

Third, Lipper categorizes the funds around standard investment objectives listed in Table 2.2. There are 21 Lipper investment objectives for non-U.S. general equity funds, including 13 objectives covering international, regional and single country funds and eight objectives covering sector and specialty funds. The Lipper equity fund objectives are self-descriptive and generally require that the fund invest at least 65% of assets in equity securities of the particular region, country or sector, such as Latin America, Japan or financial services.

2. U.S. general equity funds   U.S. general equity funds may be grouped into competitive universes according to five principal schemes. Since we have already seen three of the schemes—Morningstar broad star groupings, Morningstar category peer groups and Lipper investment objective groups—we will briefly discuss these peer groups in this section as they apply to U.S. general equity funds. We have not yet reviewed two schemes for peer groups that are used primarily for U.S. general equity funds—Morningstar style boxes and Lipper style classifications—so we will discuss these two style peer groups in greater detail.

a. Standard peer groups   Morningstar includes U.S. general equity funds in its broad U.S. stock category and assigns star ratings within the competitive universe. Morningstar also groups U.S. general equity funds into nine narrower peer groups listed in Table 2.1 and assigns a category rating within the group, allowing investors to evaluate funds in a narrower competitive universe.

In addition, Lipper categorizes the U.S. general equity funds around standard investment objectives listed in Table 2.2. There are eight Lipper investment objectives for U.S. general equity funds: capital appreciation, growth, growth & income, equity income, mid-cap, small-cap, micro-cap and S&P 500 index. Funds in the Lipper capital appreciation objective aim at maximum capital appreciation; funds in the Lipper growth objective invest in companies with expectations of significant long-term earnings growth; funds in the growth & income Lipper objective combine an earnings growth orientation with a dividend requirement; and funds in the equity income Lipper objective seek high current income and growth of income by investing 65% or more of assets in dividend-paying equities, and the fund's gross (or net) yield must be at least 125% of that of the U.S. general equity funds universe. Within the peer groups oriented toward companies with lower market capitalizations, funds in the mid-cap Lipper objective invest primarily in companies with market capitalizations less than $5 billion at time of purchase; funds in the small-cap Lipper objective invest primarily in companies with market capitalization less than $1 billion at time of purchase; and funds in the Lipper micro-cap objective invest primarily in companies with market capitalizations less than $300 million at the time of purchase. Funds in Lipper's S&P 500 index objective are passively managed, with limited expenses, and are designed to replicate the performance of the S&P 500 index (index funds are discussed later in this Chapter).

Because some of the investment objective categories in Lipper's "old" system are not precisely defined, there can be considerable overlap between categories—particularly between the capital appreciation and growth investment objective categories. In addition, these two categories are quite diffuse: they include a large number of funds with a broad range of investment styles and median market capitalizations. Therefore, critics argue that peer groups based on investment objectives allow "style drift," so that investors cannot be sure what type of securities will be held by their funds. On the other hand, the Lipper investment objective categories allow equity funds to be compared with a large enough number of funds to constitute a representative sample of peers. These groups of funds are also very stable, since a shareholder vote is generally needed to change a fund's investment objective. Most important, supporters argue that investors want portfolio managers to have the flexibility to move their funds toward the market segment with the best performance instead of adhering to the abstract concept of style purity.

b. Style peer groups Both Morningstar and Lipper group U.S. general equity funds by investment style into competitive universes based on historical fund holdings. Morningstar and Lipper group funds by market capitalization and investment style into grids or style boxes and rank funds within each style group peer classification. Both of these style box systems have the advantage of comparing funds with a focused group of peers that are operating in the same segment of the stock market. Both have another advantage of being based on actual fund holdings rather than a fund's investment objective that can be circumvented in practice. On the other hand, the funds in any style box can change relatively quickly—for example, if a fund acquires new holdings or the price of its existing holdings rises sharply. In addition, these systems tend to pigeonhole a fund into one style box, although that style box may represent a weakly performing part of the stock market.

Morningstar classifies equity funds by small, medium or large market capitalization and within each capitalization classification by a value, growth or blend investment style. In classifying equity funds by market capitalization, Morningstar uses the weighted-median market capitalization of the fund's holdings. Within each capitalization classification, Morningstar groups equity funds by style using financial characteristics of the fund's holdings. While we will cover financial characteristics in more detail in Chapter Five, we will briefly review three terms here:

Price/earnings ratio—the price of a stock divided by its earnings per share
Price/book ratio—the price of a share of stock divided by its book value (the company's assets minus its liabilities) per share
Dividend yield—the annual dividend per share of a company divided by its current market price per share

Funds grouped as growth funds tend to invest in securities with relatively high price/earnings and price/book ratios, and have relatively low dividend yields. By contrast, funds grouped as value funds tend to invest in securities with relatively low price/earnings and price/book ratios, and have higher dividend yields. Funds grouped as blend funds invest in a mix of growth and value securities and fall in the middle of the growth/value scale.

Based on its analysis of the market capitalization and financial characteristics of the fund's holdings, Morningstar assigns each fund to one of the nine sectors of a style box on the Style*Map*ᴿᴹ illustrated in Figure 2.1.

The rows indicate a small, medium or large market capitalization, and the columns indicate a value, blend or growth investment style. A fund's current style box placement, symbolized by a circle, is based on its most recent holdings reported to Morningstar and gives a snapshot of the fund at one point in time. Style boxes are also useful for tracking the consistency of a fund's investment style over time. Historical characteristics are calculated at the end of each quarter for the past 12 quarters (or for the life of the fund for new funds), and a fund's historical style is indicated by the shaded area on the Style*Map*ᴿᴹ. For instance, the fund pictured on this Style*Map*ᴿᴹ is currently in the small-cap blend box but has also been in the small-cap growth box during the past three years.

Like Morningstar, Lipper has a "new" classification system of style boxes for U.S. general funds, divided into market capitalization (large cap, multi cap, mid cap or small

FIGURE 2.1

*Morningstar Style*Map[SM]

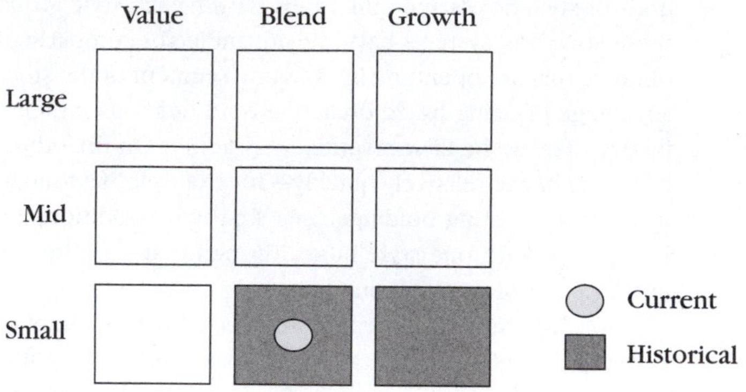

Reprinted with permission.

cap) and investment style (value, growth or core) on the basis of fund holdings. As explained previously, some of the investment objectives in Lipper's "old" system also have a capitalization focus (e.g., small cap). Mutual funds having an investment objective with a capitalization focus primarily hold securities of companies whose market capitalization is within a specified range, usually measured at the time that the fund purchases the security. Lipper's "new" system of style boxes, however, is based entirely on analysis of actual fund holdings, without regard to fund objectives. This analysis applies to all U.S. general equity funds, not just funds having an investment objective with a capitalization focus.

Lipper's style box system classifies funds by analyzing the financial characteristics of the fund's holdings at three different dates: the most recently available portfolio holdings, one-year-prior fiscal-year-end holdings and two-year-prior fiscal-year-end holdings. The most recent results are weighted 60%, the one-year-prior results are weighted 30% and the two-year-prior results are weighted 10%. The rows indicate market capitalization, and the columns indicate a growth or value investment style, or a mix of both (core).

Based on its analysis of the asset-weighted market capitalization of the fund's holdings at three different dates, Lipper classifies a fund as large cap, multi cap, mid cap or small cap. Lipper classifies funds that do not fall clearly into either large cap or mid cap as multi cap; a fund in the multi-cap sector has less than 75% of its assets in large-cap or mid-cap holdings. Lipper also classifies funds by value, growth or core investment style versus other funds within each capitalization classification based on analysis of financial characteristics, such as price/earnings ratio, price/book ratio and sales growth. As a result, the Lipper grid, illustrated in Figure 2.2, has 12 boxes (four capitalization categories and three style categories). In addition, Lipper ranks funds within four supergroups that include all styles for a particular capitalization level (i.e., across the

FIGURE 2.2

Lipper style box classifications

	Value	Core	Growth
Large cap			
Multi cap			
Mid cap			
Small cap			

row). For example, as illustrated by the shaded area in Figure 2.2, the large-cap super-group includes all value, growth and core funds that meet the large-cap criteria.

In short, although both Morningstar and Lipper classify funds by investment style based on historical fund holdings, there are differences in the two schemes. As noted previously, Lipper uses a multi-cap classification that includes funds whose asset-weighted market capitalization does not fall clearly into either the large-cap or mid-cap classifications. In addition, Lipper ranks funds two ways: within four "supergroup" market capitalization classifications and within 12 narrower market capitalization and style classifications. Moreover, Morningstar and Lipper use different measures for the market capitalization row determinations. Morningstar uses a tiered approach based on 5,000 stocks, while Lipper bases its market cap breaks on a sample of securities in the new S&P SuperComposite 1500 index. Both Morningstar and Lipper determine style columns within each market capitalization row based on financial characteristics of the fund's holdings against indexes.

B. Indexes, Active versus Passive Management and Index Funds

Here we will review the key indexes used to measure the performance of equity funds as well as the debate on active management of mutual funds versus passive management through index funds (funds with an investment objective to match the return of an index). Investment strategies employed by active and passive managers are covered in greater depth in Chapters Four and Five in the discussion of portfolio management of bond and equity mutual funds.

1. Indexes   The S&P 500 is the most popular and widely used index. It is designed to represent the overall market and is composed of stocks of 500 large companies that trade in the United States. Because the S&P 500 is market capitalization weighted, large-capitalization companies have a bigger influence on the index than smaller companies. For example, in 1998, 71% of the 28.6% return of the S&P 500 was from the performance of the largest 50 companies in the index. Another representation of the overall

U.S. stock market is the Wilshire 5000 Total Market Index, a market-capitalization-weighted index that includes all listed stocks of companies headquartered in the United States for which prices are readily available—about 7,000 stocks. At the end of 2000, the stocks in the S&P 500 represented approximately 78% of the market capitalization of the Wilshire 5000 Total Market Index.

Some indexes are well known but are narrowly focused and therefore are inappropriate comparative indexes for most funds. While the Dow Jones Industrial Average index is the oldest and most quoted U.S. stock indicator, it is composed of only the price-weighted average of 30 large stocks, without any capitalization weighting. It primarily represents only the largest industrial companies, though it has a few large technology companies. The Nasdaq Composite index is another popular index that represents only a part of the overall U.S. stock market. The Nasdaq Composite index is designed to represent the performance of the National Market System, which includes over 5,000 stocks traded only over-the-counter and not on an exchange. During 1999 and 2000, the Nasdaq was heavily concentrated in technology stocks, much more so than the U.S. stock market as a whole.

There are also narrower U.S. stock indexes that focus on stocks with particular financial characteristics. An illustration of the focus on specific financial characteristics is the division of the Russell 1000 index (largest 1,000 U.S. listed securities) into value and growth indexes. To create the style indexes, Russell ranks each stock in the Russell 1000 index by its price/book ratio and forecasted growth values. Russell creates a composite rating for each stock, ranks the stocks by composite rating and applies an algorithm to determine style membership weights. Russell classifies 70% of the stocks as all value or growth, and 30% are weighted proportionately to both value and growth. As a result, the Russell 1000 Value (R1V) includes the securities in the Russell 1000 that generally share certain characteristics, such as a relatively low price/earnings (P/E) ratio, a relatively low price/book ratio and a relatively high dividend yield. By contrast, the Russell 1000 Growth (R1G) includes the securities from the Russell 1000 that generally have a relatively high P/E ratio, a relatively high price/book ratio and a relatively low dividend yield. For small-capitalization stocks, a popular index is the Russell 2000, which comprises the next 2,000 largest U.S. stocks after the large-cap stocks in the Russell 1000 (i.e., the stocks ranked from 1,001 to 3,000 by market capitalization). There are also indexes focused on U.S. mid-cap stocks (e.g., S&P Mid-Cap 400) between the large- and small-capitalization companies and on specific market sectors (e.g., Goldman Sachs Health Care index and the Russell 3000 Utilities index).

Other stock indexes focus on international markets (e.g., MSCI EAFE index and MSCI All-Country World Free[4] index ex-U.S.), regions (e.g., MSCI Europe index and MSCI Latin America index) and countries (e.g., Toronto Stock Exchange 300 index for Canada and TOPIX for Japan). The MSCI EAFE index is designed to be representative of the developed markets other than the United States and Canada and includes approximately 1,000 securities of companies representing 21 countries. The MSCI All-Country World Free index ex-U.S. is designed to be representative of developed and emerging markets other than the United States. It includes approximately 1,725 securities of companies representing 48 countries (including Canada and 26 emerging markets). The MSCI Europe index is designed to represent the performance of developed markets in Europe and includes over 500 securities of companies representing 16 European countries. The MSCI Emerging Market Free–Latin America index is designed to represent the performance of markets in Latin America and includes approximately 150 securities of companies representing seven countries. The TSE 300 is designed to represent the performance of the Canadian market and includes 300 securities traded in Canada. The TOPIX is designed to represent the performance of the Japanese market and includes nearly 1,300 securities.

2. Active versus passive management   Most of our discussion in this Chapter has focused on actively managed mutual funds—funds where fundamental or technical analysis by employees of the management company is used to select individual securities in an effort to achieve high returns or outperform "the market" represented by a benchmark index. Actively managed mutual funds try to outperform the relevant benchmark index by various methods—for example, buying large positions in certain securities in the benchmark (security selection) or overweighting or underweighting sectors in the benchmark (sector weighting) (see Chapters Four and Five).

By contrast, index mutual funds are passively managed; their investment objective is to attempt to match the return of an index. This may be done by purchasing all of the component securities of the index in identical proportions to the index or purchasing a statistically representative sample of securities whose combined total return will approximate that of the index. Because index funds do not rely on fundamental or technical research, they usually have lower management fees and total expenses than actively managed funds. The median total expense is approximately 66 bp for U.S. equity index funds, approximately 94 bp for international equity index funds and approximately 40 bp for U.S. bond index funds, although the largest equity index funds have total expenses of less than 20 bp.

Passive investment management used by equity index funds is based on the efficient market hypothesis (EMH)—that stock prices already reflect all publicly available information and any new information is immediately absorbed in stock prices (see Reading 1.1 in Chapter One). It is difficult to obtain new information material to stock prices before anyone else (without engaging in illegal conduct). Therefore, according to EMH adherents, it is virtually impossible to outperform the market on a regular basis through active management and stock selection based on fundamental or technical research. Academic studies include data suggesting that over the long term, index funds are likely to outperform a majority of actively managed mutual funds of similar risk.[5] Along the same line, a recent study on performance and manager style found that neither the growth nor value investment styles outperformed indexes over the long term.[6] Expenses and transaction costs account for almost all of the difference in performance between the passive and active investing over the long term. However, most of these studies focus on highly liquid and closely followed portions of the U.S. stock markets. In other types of equity markets, indexes may be easier to beat. For example, active managers could beat the MSCI EAFE Index simply by overweighting Japan during the 1980s and underweighting Japan during the 1990s. Moreover, over shorter periods, skill by active managers in picking U.S. stocks has been shown to lead to outperformance by actively managed funds.[7] There is also some support for the conclusion that past fund performance is likely to be predictive of future performance over longer periods,[8] although this conclusion may be influenced by survivorship bias (i.e., weak-performing funds tend to be merged out of existence).[9]

Amid this academic debate, there is strong evidence showing that active managers tend to outperform passive managers when the performance of the U.S. equity market (represented by the S&P 500) is driven by a broad-based set of stocks of varying cap size, as opposed to a narrow band of the largest-cap stocks. In contrast, when the performance of the U.S. equity markets is led by the largest stocks in the S&P 500, which dominate that index by market capitalization, index funds based on the S&P 500 tend to do better than the average actively managed fund. This point is illustrated by Figure 2.3, based on data from December 1963 through December 2000.

In periods when passive investing outperforms active management, why do any investors buy actively managed funds? One reason is that many investors believe that they can select actively managed funds that are likely to beat the indexes. In every profession, the talented people will outperform the averages, while the mediocre people will not. This belief is bolstered by evidence that specific managers have beaten the indexes on a regular basis—for example, Peter Lynch of the Magellan Fund and William Miller of the Legg Mason Value Trust.

FIGURE 2.3

Active versus passive investing: Active management outperforms in broad markets 1963–2000

Note: The shaded areas represent broad markets (when the equal-weighted S&P 500 outperforms the cap-weighted S&P 500). Since 1963, 61.9% of yearly observations have shown active managers outperform when the market is broad.

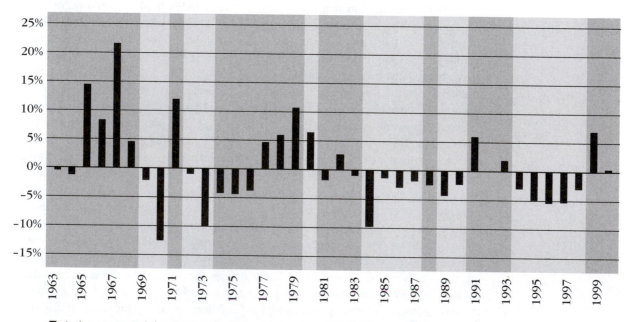

■ Active manager alpha (Lipper Growth universe minus S&P 500® cap-weighted)

Other investors may prefer to invest in mutual funds run by a well-known management company, regardless of the particular manager of the fund. These preferences are based on the premise that broad research coverage, a disciplined investment process and an experienced pool of managers are likely to produce above-average results. This premise is supported by a recent study by Morningstar, which examined mutual fund performance following a portfolio manager change. Funds that had performed well on a risk-adjusted basis relative to peers over a five-year period from 1990 to 1995 were divided into two groups: those that had a manager change during the five-year period and those that had not experienced a manager change. The study looked at fund performance for the next five-year period and found that funds that performed well continued to perform well, and funds that had not performed well continued to underperform, regardless of manager change.[10]

Academic authors have developed a more complex explanation of why there is persistency of good performance among certain mutual funds.[11] These authors begin by pointing out that contrary to most industries, the fees charged by good performing funds are not higher than those of poor performers. They then put forward the hypothesis: if there are funds with superior management whose fees do not reflect that superiority, then cash flows should go to those funds from investors who recognize this anomaly. To test this hypothesis, they look to see if the return for new cash flows into good performing funds is better than the average return for all investors in these funds. This appears to be at least partially true: cash flow of new money into and out of mutual funds follows predictions of future performance. In addition, the risk-adjusted returns earned on new cash flows over a 10-year study are positive and outperform the return of the average active and average passive funds over the same period.

Conversely, another academic study applies the psychological concept of cognitive dissonance to explain why investors hold on to persistently poorly performing funds. Cognitive dissonance is a process by which people tend to revise their beliefs to reduce apparent logical contradictions. The study shows that even well-informed investors tend to bias their perceptions positively about past performance of mutual funds that do not actually perform well. Because of this overly optimistic attitude, investors tend to be slow to sell poorly performing funds. Such investor inertia supports the study's finding that there is an unusually high frequency of poorly performing funds.[12]

3. Index funds   The performance of an index fund may differ from the performance of the index. As we have discussed, indexes do not have annual operating expenses, while index funds have expenses, such as management and custody fees, which limit the ability of the index fund to match the return of the index. In addition, index funds have transaction costs, such as brokerage commissions associated with buying and selling securities in response to changes in the composition of the index, as well as cash flows in and out of the index fund. Most important, index funds do not usually buy all the securities in the index, especially larger indexes, so the performance of a representative sample may deviate from the performance of the index. (See Chapter Three for a discussion of the tax efficiency of index funds.)

The most popular index funds are based on the S&P 500, such as Vanguard 500 Index Fund, which was at various times the first or second largest mutual fund in the United States during 2000. Other popular U.S. stock index funds are based on other indexes mentioned earlier, such as the Schwab Total Stock Market Index Fund or T. Rowe Price Total Equity Market Index Fund (based on the Wilshire 5000 Total Market index). Broad-based index funds such as the Total Market Index funds do not change their holdings frequently, as compared to index funds that track narrower indexes, which may be dramatically reconstituted as securities are added or subtracted. A good illustration of the narrower type is the Dreyfus Mid Cap Index Fund, which attempts to track the return of the S&P 400 MidCap index.

Most international equity index funds, such as AXP International Equity Index Fund, attempt to track the return of the MSCI EAFE index. The MSCI EAFE is a very well-known international index that is considered to be representative of developed markets outside the United States and Canada. Other international equity index funds attempt to track narrower international indexes, such as Vanguard European Stock Index Fund, which attempts to track the return of the MSCI Europe index (considered to be representative of developed markets in Europe). As explained in Chapter Twelve, the MSCI indexes are changing significantly as they move from the criterion of a company's market capitalization to the freely traded portion of its capitalization.

Some fund complexes offer enhanced index funds that combine passive and active management in an attempt to outperform the return of an index. The purest types of enhanced index funds are highly correlated to their index, have low tracking error and focus on picking top stocks. Some enhanced index funds invest a portion of assets passively by benchmarking to an index, and they invest other assets actively by selecting stocks or sectors that the fund manager believes will result in a higher return than the index. An example of this type of enhanced index fund is the TIAA-CREF Growth Equity Fund, based on the Russell 3000 Growth Index. Other enhanced index funds, such as ProFunds, use leverage in an attempt to outperform the benchmark index significantly. ProFunds' enhanced index funds leverage strategy is expected to result in a 15% increase in fund return if the index increases by 10%. A 10% decline in the index, however, is expected to result in a 15% decrease in fund return.

III. Alternatives to Mutual Funds (Other Pooled Investment Vehicles)

There are alternative investment pools that primarily compete with equity index funds, such as unit investment trusts (UITs) and exchange-traded funds (ETFs). There are also pooled investment vehicles such as hedge funds and common trust funds that are primarily offered to individuals with a high net worth and institutions. We will describe these other forms of pooled vehicles in the next sections. (For comments on managed accounts of individual securities, see Chapter One.)

A. Alternatives to Equity Index Funds

1. Unit investment trusts   UITs are passively managed pooled investment vehicles that offer interests in a fixed portfolio of securities; there is no significant change in the portfolio of securities held by a UIT after it is initially assembled. UITs are registered investment companies and have a specified termination date. The UIT investor purchases "units" of the UIT and receives a share of the principal and interest or dividends. When the UIT is terminated, the proceeds are paid to the unit holder. Because they are passively managed, UITs are often considered an alternative to index funds. However, unlike index funds—in which the holdings and proportion of assets invested in individual issuers change to reflect changes in the benchmark index—the holdings and weightings of UITs are fixed at their creation and do not change over the life of the UIT.

UITs are generally bought and sold through a brokerage firm. Some investors buy units of a UIT and hold them until the UIT terminates; other investors sell their UIT units on the secondary market, or redeem their UIT units through the UIT based on the net asset value of the UIT shares—the current market value of the securities held by the UIT. UITs generally have low annual expenses. Because there is no active management of the portfolio, the fund pays no management fee, and the fund incurs very few transaction fees because the UIT does not buy and sell securities. However, when investors initially buy a UIT, they must pay a sales charge, often 4% to 5% of the total purchase amount for long-term UITs. If investors exchange from one UIT to another, they must pay an additional sales charge on their purchase of the units of the new UIT, although sometimes a reduced sales charge is available for exchanges.

At the end of 2000, assets invested in traditional UITs totaled approximately $88.8 billion. There are different types of UITs—both traditional and newer products. "Dogs of the Dow" UITs are examples of a short-term equity UIT. Dogs of the Dow is an investment strategy whereby an investor buys the stocks in the Dow Jones Industrial Average index (30 large, primarily industrial stocks) with the highest dividend yields and lowest P/E ratios. Many brokerage firms like Merrill Lynch, Prudential and Salomon Smith Barney offer a Dogs of the Dow UIT that invest in the 10 highest-yielding Dow stocks from the previous year. The UITs generally begin on January 1 of each year and terminate on December 31. Investors purchase units in the UIT at the beginning of each year and hold their units until the year-end liquidation of the UIT. The investor must realize any capital gains when the UIT is liquidated at year-end. Expenses for Dogs of the Dow UITs include an approximately 175 bp annual fee and a 1.00% sales charge (payable on each purchase).

An example of newer equity UITs are HOLDRS [SM], fixed portfolios of securities (usually 20) generally created based on industry sectors. There are many sector HOLDRS, several focused on Internet subsectors, and others focused on the biotech, broadband, pharmaceutical, regional bank, semiconductor, telecom and utilities sectors. Together, all these types of HOLDRS represented approximately $5.3 billion in assets at the end of 2000.[13]

2. Exchange-traded funds   ETFs today are passively managed pooled investment vehicles that attempt to track an index, often an index based on a foreign country or an industry sector. Unlike UITs, ETFs buy and sell securities as the securities in the corresponding index change. At the end of 2000, there were over 80 ETFs with combined total assets of over $65 billion.[14] SPDRs, which track the S&P 500 index, are the oldest and largest ETF. They were launched in 1993 and have assets of over $25 billion. Nasdaq 100s, or QQQs, which track the Nasdaq 100 index, are the fastest-growing ETF. They were launched in 1999 and have assets of over $23 billion. iShares S&P 500 were launched in 2000 and already have assets of over $2.3 billion. There are also ETFs based on specific market sectors such as the Select Sector SPDRs launched in 1998 and the iShares Dow Jones Series launched in 2000. Other ETFs track indexes in foreign countries, such as the iShares MSCI Series, covering over 21 foreign countries, from Australia to the United Kingdom. Many of the iShares MSCI ETFs, such as iShares MSCI Belgium, were known formerly as WEBS and launched in 1996; other iShares MSCI, such as iShares MSCI South Korea, launched in 2000.

Technically, ETFs may be structured as open-end mutual funds or UITs, but they differ from traditional index mutual funds in several areas. Unlike traditional index mutual funds, ETF shares are bought and sold in two different ways. Institutions and large investors purchase and redeem ETF shares directly from the ETF in large creation units, generally of amounts above $1 million. Individual investors buy and sell ETF shares that are listed and traded on the stock exchange through a broker in much smaller amounts. Unlike traditional index mutual funds, ETFs may be traded on a stock exchange throughout the day. By trading throughout the day, ETFs appeal to short-term traders because they provide more flexibility than traditional mutual funds, which usually are priced once at the end of the day. ETFs are sometimes marketed as tax efficient because, like index funds, they have made relatively modest distributions of capital gains over the past few years, but intraday trading of EFTs tends to undermine their tax efficiency. (See Chapter Three on tax issues.)

Many ETFs based on traditional indexes have low expense ratios, often lower than traditional mutual funds or even index funds. However, the brokerage commissions payable by investors when they trade ETFs can be costly, especially if they trade frequently. Moreover, most trades of ETFs implicitly involve the payment of a spread (the difference between the bid and ask quotations) to the exchange specialist making a market in the ETF. (See Chapter Six on equity trading.) Total expenses for the SPDR and the Nasdaq 100 are 18 bp, for iShares S&P 500 are 9 bp and for the iShares Dow Jones Sector ETFs are 60 bp. Some ETFs, like the iShares MSCI and the Select Sector SPDRs, pay a trail commission in the form of a Rule 12b-1 fee to the broker (in addition to investor paid brokerage commissions). The trail commission is included in the expense ratio of these ETFs; the expense ratio of the iShares MSCI ranges from 84 bp to 153 bp and of the Select Sector SPDRs is approximately 57 bp.

Some see ETFs as a threat to the mutual fund industry, particularly to mutual funds focused on narrower sectors like technology. Others view ETFs as a niche product for day traders of equity indexes, although a few ETF sponsors are trying to find a way to create actively managed ETFs, which would have to surmount substantial practical and regulatory hurdles. In 2000, Vanguard announced that it would begin offering ETFs tracking the S&P 500 and several other indexes as lower-cost classes of its existing index funds. The firm cited ETFs' natural fit with Vanguard's emphasis on indexing as a reason for its decision. With some ETFs (such as iShares S&P 500) beginning to undercut Vanguard's positioning as offering very low expense index funds, competitive pressures may also have played a role in Vanguard's decision. The launch of some of Vanguard's ETF classes has been delayed due to a lawsuit over licensing rights to S&P indexes.

B. Pooled Vehicles Primarily for High-Net-Worth Investors

1. Hedge funds   Hedge funds are actively managed pooled investment vehicles that meet requirements for exemption from registration under the securities laws. The funds are generally organized as limited partnerships and are not publicly offered; the offering

is limited to fewer than 500 wealthy individuals and institutions in order to avoid SEC reporting and registration. Hedge funds are known for using aggressive investing techniques such as leverage—often investing borrowed money substantially in excess of shareholder contributions. In addition, hedge funds may bet that prices of individual stocks will fall by short selling. By contrast, the ability of mutual funds to invest borrowed monies or engage in short selling is severely restricted by SEC regulations. As a result, only a few mutual funds use leverage or short selling as a principal investment strategy.

As discussed in Chapter Three, mutual funds are subject to an extensive regulatory regime in many other areas—for example, disclosure of investment policies, conflicts of interest and daily pricing of shares. Hedge funds are not subject to any of these regulatory requirements, except the general anti-fraud provisions of the federal securities laws. Two areas of difference are of particular note. Shareholders of hedge funds may redeem infrequently, often only twice per year after a blackout period of one or two years from the initial offering. Shareholders of every mutual fund have the right to redeem every business day. Hedge funds charge high and asymmetrical management fees—typically 1% per year plus 20% of positive performance above a threshold (without a similar penalty for negative performance). The SEC prohibits such asymmetrical performance fees for managers of mutual funds.

As of the end of 2000, there were approximately 5,000 hedge funds with approximately $350 billion in assets under management. This represents a substantial increase from as recently as 1997, when there were approximately 2,800 hedge funds and approximately $210 billion in assets under management.[15] This increase was driven by a broadening of the regulatory exemptions for hedge funds and, more important, a perception that they were likely to deliver extraordinary returns even in down markets.

While certain hedge funds have done well, over the five years ending January 31, 2001, hedge funds on average returned 14.65% annually—underperforming the 18.36% annual return of the S&P 500 over the same period.[16] Similarly, a study based on data from 1990 through mid-1999 showed that hedge funds on average had a 14.2% annual return, as compared to an 18.8% annual return for the S&P 500 over the same period.[17] Yet this study concluded that hedge funds offered a better risk-return trade-off than the S&P 500, because the volatility of hedge fund returns was lower than the volatility of the S&P 500 during this period. By contrast, another study, based on six years of data, reportedly found that inaccurate pricing of holdings by some hedge funds understated the volatility of the returns from hedge funds.[18]

Some investment managers have asked for regulatory parity on performance fees between mutual funds and hedge funds in order to level the paying field to attract and retain portfolio management talent. Other mutual fund complexes offer hedge funds, although there is great variation as to whether the same individuals manage both mutual funds and hedge funds. The SEC staff has expressed concerns about potential conflicts of interest, based in part on the higher fees collected from hedge funds, when the same investment adviser manages both a mutual fund and a hedge fund. Others believe that an investment adviser should be able to manage both types of funds simultaneously, provided there are appropriate safeguards to prevent conflicts such as trade allocation policies.

2. Common trust funds   Common trust funds are pooled investment vehicles generally established by commercial banks and trust companies as one of their fiduciary services. Common trust funds are typically set up as two-tier structures. A bank establishes a trust with individual investors; then the assets of the individual trusts are commingled in a common trust fund, the pooled investment vehicle.

Common trust funds are subject to regulation by the Office of the Comptroller of the Currency but exempt from registration under securities laws. Therefore, common trust funds are not subject to the extensive regulatory restrictions of the Investment Company Act. (See Chapter Three.) Instead, they are subject to less onerous requirements imposed by the Comptroller of the Currency. For example, common trust funds must value their assets at least quarterly, while mutual funds must value their assets daily. Common trust funds are required to disclose their complete holdings annually, as opposed to semiannually for mutual funds.

However, common trust funds have several disadvantages relative to mutual funds. Most important, the Comptroller of the Currency substantially limits their marketing and advertising to investors. A bank may provide limited information about the performance of the common trust fund to customers in connection with their establishing a trust relationship with the bank. Moreover, a common trust fund may be used only to invest the assets of a bona-fide trust for which the bank serves as the trustee; a bank may not set up revocable trusts feeding into a common trust fund merely to avoid its registration as a mutual fund. These limitations on the use of common trust funds were further tightened by the Gramm-Leach-Bliley Act of 1999.

Because of these limitations, common trust funds have grown at a much slower pace than mutual funds. Indeed, in order to avoid these limitations, several banks have recently converted their common trust funds into mutual funds. For example, in 1999, First Union converted common trust funds it acquired from Core States and Signet Bank into eight Evergreen mutual funds. As of the end of 1999, there were just under $200 billion in assets under management in common trust funds up from just under $160 billion in assets under management in 1998.[19]

REVIEW QUESTIONS

1. Name the four main types of mutual funds. Describe each type.

2. What is the difference between measuring a mutual fund's performance relative to a peer group versus an index?

3. What is a mutual fund investment objective? Name several peer groups based on investment objectives.

4. Compare the boxes of a Morningstar style grid to the boxes of a Lipper style grid.

5. What is an index fund? What is the index that best reflects the whole U.S. stock market?

6. Explain the differences between active management and passive management.

7. How are exchange-traded funds (ETFs) and unit investment trusts (UITs) different from index mutual funds, and from each other?

8. What are the similarities and differences between a mutual fund and a common trust fund?

DISCUSSION QUESTIONS

1. Do you think fund expenses should be more important to investors in money market, bond or equity funds?

2. Which do you think is better: using peer groups based on investment objectives or peer groups based on fund holdings? Why? Does your answer depend on the type of fund?

3. What are the arguments for and against an index fund? Are these arguments stronger or weaker for funds investing in large-cap U.S. stocks, small-cap U.S. stocks and foreign stocks?

4. Do you think the rise of ETFs will hurt the mutual fund industry? Are there any advantages to the mutual fund industry from the proliferation of ETFs?

5. Should hedge funds be subject to many of the same regulations as mutual funds? Or should mutual funds have the flexibility of hedge funds with regard to leveraged investments and performance fees?

NOTES

1. Median total expenses for all fund types are based on data provided by Lipper for funds with fiscal years ending in 2000.

2. Morningstar also classifies bond funds using style boxes by quality (Treasury and agency, investment-grade corporate, or below-investment grade) and average maturity (short, medium or long). The Morningstar bond fund style boxes are not as widely used as the equity style boxes.

3. Morningstar also classifies international funds using style boxes. The Morningstar international equity fund style boxes are not as widely used as the U.S. equity fund style boxes.

4. MSCI Free indexes measure the investment opportunities generally available to the nondomestic institutional investor and exclude companies and share classes not available for purchase by foreigners. As explained in Chapter Twelve, the MSCI Indexes are changing significantly as they move from the criterion of a company's market capitalization to the freely traded portion of its capitalization.

5. See Elton, Gruber and Blake, "The Persistence of Risk-Adjusted Mutual Fund Performance," *Journal of Business* 69, 133-157 (April 1996); Gruber, "Another Puzzle: The Growth in Actively Managed Mutual Funds," *Journal of Finance* 51, 783-810 (July 1996); Carhart, "On Persistence in Mutual Fund Performance," *Journal of Finance* 52, 57-82 (March 1997).

6. See Davis, "Mutual Fund Performance and Manager Style," *Financial Analysts Journal*, 19-27 (January-February 2001).

7. See Hendricks, Patel and Zeckhauser, "Hot Hands in Mutual Funds: Short-Run Persistence of Performance, 1974-88," *Journal of Finance* 48, 93-130 (March 1993).

8. See Goetzmann and Ibbotson, "Do Winners Repeat?" *Journal of Portfolio Management* 20, 9-17 (Winter 1994); Elton, Gruber and Blake, pp. 134, 156; contra Carhart, p. 74.

9. See Brown, Goetzmann, Ibbotson and Ross, "Survivorship Bias in Performance Studies," *Review of Financial Studies* 5, 553-580 (1992).

10. Morningstar, "Manager Changes: Should You Stay or Should You Go?" *Cooley,* September 21, 2000.

11. See Gruber, 783-84, 807.

12. See Goetzmann and Peles, "Cognitive Dissonance and Mutual Fund Investors," *Journal of Financial Research* 20, 145-158 (Summer 1997).

13. HOLDRS assets of $5.3 billion are based on Strategic Insight year-end 2000 reported assets in ETFs and HOLDRS of $70.8 billion (excluding Telebras HOLDRS) less ICI year-end 2000 reported assets in ETFs of $65.5 billion.

14. Source: ICI

15. Source: Hedgeworld USA Inc.

16. "New Study Snips Away at Hedge Funds," *Wall Street Journal,* February 22, 2001, p. C1, citing Asness, Krail and Liew, "Do Hedge Funds Hedge?" AQR Capital Management, LLC, Preliminary Study (Dec. 2000).

17. Liang, "Hedge Fund Performance: 1990-1999," *Financial Analysts Journal* 11-18 (Jan.-Feb. 2001).

18. Asness, Krail and Liew, "Do Hedge Funds Hedge?" AQR Capital Management, LLC, Preliminary Study, December 2000.

19. Source: FDIC

EXERCISE 2.1

Allocating Assets Among Mutual Funds

What should an investor do once he or she has decided to invest his or her assets in a portfolio of mutual funds? How should an investor choose among over 8,000 mutual funds?

An important consideration when allocating assets among mutual funds is diversification. Diversification is a strategy whereby an investor attempts to reduce risk by spreading assets among different industries, market capitalizations, investment styles, countries and/or asset classes. A diversified portfolio makes it more likely that investors will be exposed to different industries, market capitalizations, investment styles and asset classes as they move in and out of favor with the market, reducing the overall risk of investors' portfolios. The top-performing investment style and asset class change over time. In some periods, large-cap growth stocks are best; in other periods, small-cap value stocks are best. Similarly, in some periods, bonds are the top performers, in other periods U.S. stocks are the top performers, while in other periods foreign stocks are best. Figures 2.4 and 2.5 illustrate how the top-performing investment style and asset class changed between 1985 or 1981 and 2000.

Of course, a mutual fund itself provides investors with a significant degree of diversification by participating in a large pool of securities. In addition, certain types of mutual funds are designed as asset allocation funds in order to provide more complete diversification in one fund. Some of these asset allocation funds invest directly in underlying securities, such as hybrid funds holding stocks and bonds; others are fund of funds, such as "life strategy" funds described below, which invest in other mutual funds. Another way to provide diversification and asset allocation is to pay a broker, financial adviser or other intermediary for advice in choosing mutual funds. Some investors pay an intermediary directly for advice; others invest in asset allocation programs involving mutual funds, sometimes called mutual fund wraps.

Asset Allocation Mutual Funds

An example of a hybrid asset allocation fund is a balanced fund that invests approximately 60% of its assets in stocks and 40% of its assets in bonds. There are also related sets of hybrid funds such as American Century's three Strategic Allocation funds, each with a different neutral asset mix and corresponding level of risk and return. The asset mix of the Strategic Allocation funds can vary from the neutral mix within prescribed ranges. Strategic Allocation: Aggressive has the highest risk and highest potential return, with a neutral mix of 78% of assets invested in stocks, 20% of assets in bonds and 2% of assets in short-term and money market instruments. Strategic Allocation: Moderate has a medium level of risk and potential return, with a neutral mix of 63% of assets invested in stocks, 31% of assets invested in bonds and 6% of assets invested in short-term and money market instruments. Strategic Allocation: Conservative has the lowest risk and lowest potential return, with a neutral mix of 45% of assets in stocks, 45% of assets in bonds and 10% of assets in short-term and money market instruments. Investors select the Strategic Allocation fund that corresponds most closely with their risk appetites and return objectives.

Life strategy funds are asset allocation mutual funds designed to assist with retirement planning by changing the neutral mix over time. A life strategy fund begins with a heavy weighting in stock funds and a light weighting in bond and money market funds—for example, 70% in stock funds and 15% in each of the other two fund types. As the target retirement date approaches, a life strategy fund reduces its weighting in stock funds and increases its weighting in bond and money market funds—for example, 20% in stock funds and 40% in each of the other two fund types. In a life strategy fund, the investor initially picks a fund based on his or her anticipated retirement date, and the asset allocation decisions are left to the fund manager.

Other fund of funds provide diversification and asset allocation. For example, Fidelity Four-in-One Index Fund invests a fairly fixed percentage of assets in four underlying Fidelity index funds—50% of assets in Spartan 500 Index Fund and 15% of assets in each of Spartan Extended Market Index Fund, Spartan International Index Fund and Fidelity U.S. Bond Index Fund. The investor gains exposure to the U.S. stock and bond markets and the international stock market through an investment in one mutual fund.

FIGURE 2.4

Sector rotations, 1985–2000

	Basic materials	Capital goods	Communication services	Consumer cyclicals	Consumer staples	Energy	Financials	Health care	Technology	Transportation	Utilities
1985	22.5%	23.4%	28.5%	25.1%	39.9%	13.4%	37.0%	38.1%	18.7%	28.2%	15.7%
1986	23.2	9.5	17.6	18.3	25.6	14.4	6.9	30.2	−5.2	9.2	13.9
1987	21.6	3.4	−1.9	−3.4	7.7	4.6	−19.4	5.1	12.7	−12.2	−13.6
1988	4.0	8.2	17.6	19.1	12.9	13.7	17.2	8.8	−4.4	14.4	8.2
1989	22.5	23.8	53.4	13.2	43.8	32.6	28.0	35.6	−5.8	15.3	25.0
1990	−13.4	−10.3	−19.0	−12.2	5.6	−1.2	−24.1	14.0	−1.0	−15.5	−7.3
1991	24.1	24.2	9.6	44.5	32.9	2.9	49.1	55.2	16.9	45.7	16.6
1992	5.9	6.8	10.2	18.3	6.9	−1.9	21.0	−17.8	2.3	7.3	0.8
1993	12.1	14.1	11.5	7.0	−1.6	11.0	7.8	−10.9	19.7	16.3	7.8
1994	5.1	−1.6	−9.9	−11.9	3.0	−0.1	−5.1	8.7	16.3	−15.8	−16.8
1995	16.6	33.3	37.7	14.4	34.4	25.9	49.3	53.5	39.2	34.8	25.6
1996	13.8	28.2	−2.0	15.0	18.5	21.6	32.2	18.4	40.9	14.2	0.8
1997	7.0	25.5	37.4	34.4	32.3	21.9	45.3	40.7	26.0	26.5	18.5
1998	−8.0	12.5	46.8	35.2	20.2	−1.1	12.6	42.4	74.9	−4.5	10.0
1999	26.0	29.1	19.2	22.5	−6.3	18.8	3.8	−8.1	74.2	−10.9	−9.0
2000	−14.5	2.8	−38.0	−20.5	4.7	14.0	26.2	37.3	−39.3	15.8	59.5

Notes: Shaded area represents top annual performer among S&P 500 sectors. All figures represent total annual returns.
Past performance is no guarantee of future results. An investor cannot invest directly in the index.

Source: Ibbotson.

But investors may want to invest in more than one fund or target their allocation differently than provided by the one-stop asset allocation funds. It is important to keep in mind that diversification is not achieved by investing in a certain number of funds; investing in three large-cap U.S. stock funds, all with high-technology weightings, does not provide diversification. But adding small-cap, international, industry sector and bond funds increases diversification. By selecting a portfolio of mutual funds that ranges across market capitalizations, countries, industry sectors, investment styles and asset classes, the investor is more diversified and is subject to less risk than investing in three large-cap U.S. stock funds.

Advice Programs and Tools

Some investors pay a broker, financial planner or other intermediary for advice in choosing mutual funds. Others want guidance on how to structure a mutual fund portfolio or information about mutual funds in order to buy them

FIGURE 2.5

Asset classes go in and out of favor

	Large-cap stocks	Foreign stocks	Small-cap stocks	Bonds	High yield bonds	Money markets
1981	−4.9%	−1.0%	2.0%	6.2%	10.4%	15.1%
1982	21.4	−0.9	25.0	32.6	36.3	11.3
1983	22.5	24.6	29.1	8.4	20.3	8.9
1984	6.3	7.9	−7.3	15.1	9.4	10.0
1985	32.2	56.7	31.1	22.1	28.7	7.8
1986	18.5	69.9	5.7	15.3	15.6	6.2
1987	5.2	24.9	−8.8	2.8	6.5	5.9
1988	16.8	28.6	24.9	7.9	11.4	6.8
1989	31.5	10.8	16.2	14.5	0.4	8.6
1990	−3.2	−23.2	−19.5	9.0	−6.4	7.9
1991	30.6	12.5	46.1	16.0	43.8	5.8
1992	7.7	−11.9	18.4	7.4	16.7	3.6
1993	10.0	32.9	18.9	9.8	18.9	3.1
1994	1.3	8.1	−1.8	−2.9	−1.0	4.2
1995	37.4	11.6	28.4	18.5	17.4	5.8
1996	23.1	6.4	16.5	3.6	12.4	5.3
1997	33.4	2.1	22.4	9.7	12.6	5.3
1998	28.6	20.3	−2.6	8.7	0.6	5.1
1999	21.0	27.3	21.3	−0.8	3.3	4.7
2000	−9.1	−14.0	−3.0	11.6	−5.7	5.9

Note: Shaded area represents top annual performer among S&P 500 sectors. All figures represent total annual returns.

Data: Large Stocks as measured by S&P 500; Foreign Stocks as measured by MSCI EAFE, Small Stocks as measured by Russell 2000® , Bonds as measured by Lehman Brothers Aggregate, Hi-Yield Bonds as measured by Credit Suisse First Boston High Yield, Money Markets as measured by T-Bill.

directly themselves. While advice can take many forms, it generally is a personalized investment recommendation by a financial intermediary such as a broker or investment adviser, usually for a fee. Guidance is hard to define. It is less than advice provided by a paid financial intermediary, but more than information about mutual funds found in disclosure documents or press articles or on the Internet. More and more fund sponsors are providing advice and guidance to investors on choosing among mutual funds, with or without an explicit fee.

One option available to investors is asset allocation programs involving mutual funds, called mutual fund wraps. In a mutual fund wrap, a broker, financial adviser or other intermediary manages a portfolio of mutual funds for a customer. The adviser provides advice to the customer and chooses the mutual fund mix that best meets the customer's objectives. The adviser is able to control the purchases and sales of mutual funds in the wrap account to reduce the tax impact on that customer. As was mentioned in Chapter One, the advisory fee paid to the manager of the mutual fund wrap is not deductible unless that fee (together with other advisory expenses) exceeds 2% of the customer's adjusted gross income. Cerulli Associates estimates that as of the end of 2000, wrap mutual fund accounts held $126 billion in assets, up from $104 billion at the end of 1999, $77 billion at the end of 1998 and $53 billion at the end of 1997. More than 60% of the mutual fund wraps are packaged with a preselected list of mutual funds. The other programs have broader fund options. Some mutual fund wraps also allow the investor to hold individual securities. (See Chapter One on separate accounts of individual securities.) The average wrap fee on mutual fund accounts at the end of 2000 was 1.25%, with typical account minimums in the range of $10,000 to $50,000.

Many tools are available to assist an investor with asset allocation decisions. The Internet sites of many mutual fund complexes, such as T. Rowe Price and INVESCO, include asset allocation tools. Many investment-oriented websites or online brokerages, like Quicken.com and Charles Schwab & Co., include asset allocation tools. Often the tools are designed to assist with planning for a specific goal, such as children's college education, a new home purchase or retirement. The tools generally ask questions about an investor's investment horizon, risk tolerance, assets and financial situation and then suggest a target asset allocation mix—for example, 55% large-cap U.S. funds, 15% small-cap U.S. funds, 15% international funds and 15% bond funds.

Whether based on advice obtained through a paid financial intermediary, guidance offered by a fund sponsor or information from a website, asset allocation and diversification are important considerations in choosing a mutual fund portfolio. This Exercise takes you through an asset allocation worksheet and helps you construct a diversified mutual fund portfolio. The worksheet is a self-assessment tool that requires potential investors to answer questions about their investment objectives and constraints, and then through self-scoring focuses on an appropriate target asset mix.

Discussion Questions

First, complete the Asset Allocation Planner worksheet that follows, using your personal experience and financial data or creating a fictitious investor. Then answer the following questions.

1. What is the objective of diversifying your portfolio? What are the benefits, if any? What are the drawbacks, if any?

2. If an investor's portfolio consisted of only an S&P 500 index fund, would the investor be adequately diversified? Would such a portfolio be inconsistent with other legitimate investor objectives?

3. What is the function of each of the three asset categories mentioned in the Asset Allocation Planner? What other categories, if any, would you add?

4. What are the relative merits of a portfolio of mutual funds versus a portfolio of individual securities?

5. What are the major nontax factors an investor should consider when building a suitable portfolio? What happens to the relative importance of these factors over time?

6. What consideration should be given to taxes in constructing a portfolio? What happens if one asset does much better than all other assets over time?

7. Does this worksheet provide sufficient guidance to investors seeking to build a suitable portfolio?

8. What are the advantages and disadvantages of using a worksheet versus receiving investment advice from a broker or financial adviser?

BUILDING AN INVESTMENT
STRATEGY WITH
ASSET ALLOCATION PLANNER

Fidelity Investments®

MANAGE YOUR INVESTMENT PORTFOLIO RESPONSIBLY

At Fidelity, we believe it's important for every individual to take control of his or her investment portfolio. After all, only you know the financial needs you have today—and the goals you've set for the future. To help you make responsible decisions about investing, look to Fidelity to help you develop long-term investment strategies and for information and tools to help you manage your money.

By adhering to an investment approach that combines the unique strength of our people, research process, investment philosophy, and long-range performance perspective, Fidelity has become the market leader* in mutual funds, managing more assets than any other mutual fund company nationwide.

Fidelity's powerful approach to money management.

Hire some of the best investment talent. Creating opportunity for shareholders begins with hiring talented people, and then training them within our investment management organization. Fidelity analysts rotate through different industries, sectors, and investment disciplines. An analyst who compiles a track record of excellence is rewarded with wider responsibilities.

> **Fidelity has some of the industry's most experienced managers.**
>
> - 79% of the stock fund assets at Fidelity are managed by professionals with at least 10 years' tenure at Fidelity.
>
> - The average experience of a manager who runs one of Fidelity's largest stock funds is 15 years.

Conduct exhaustive research. Fidelity's investment decisions are based on information. We believe that better information can lead to more informed investment decisions. We have hundreds of investment professionals researching opportunities worldwide. The most important component of our research comes from meeting directly with companies and their senior management—"kicking the tires" to see if an investment may be worthwhile.

Teamwork. At Fidelity we don't manage funds by committee. Each individual is ultimately responsible for his or her own results; however, analysts and fund managers have the support, guidance, and knowledge of the entire Fidelity team worldwide.

*With $950 billion total assets under management as of 9/30/00.

1

THE ASSET ALLOCATION PLANNER: HELPING
YOU BUILD A DIVERSIFIED INVESTMENT PORTFOLIO

Your money is too important to invest without a plan. That's why it's crucial to assess your current situation and analyze your goals—to better help you make responsible investment decisions when building or modifying your portfolio.

Using a thoughtful, step-by-step process, the Asset Allocation Planner Worksheet in this brochure helps you examine your needs and determine the mix of investments that may be right for you. It also introduces you to asset allocation strategies that can help you to diversify your investments across asset classes to balance maximizing return with minimizing risk. To make it easier for you to use the Asset Allocation Planner, we've organized this guide into three sections.

1. Laying the groundwork

This section reviews the factors that influence your investing strategy and explores and defines the principles of:

- diversification
- risk and return
- asset allocation

2. The Asset Allocation Planner Worksheet

Based on your own situation and how you answer the questions, the Asset Allocation Planner Worksheet can help you determine the mix of investments that might be right for you. Thirteen multiple-choice questions focus on the key factors that can influence your investment decisions, including:

- your time horizon
- your risk tolerance
- the role of an individual investment in your overall portfolio

3. Your next steps

Here's where you can put the Asset Allocation Planner method into action. With the Investment Check-Up chart, you can compare your current investments to the target asset mix provided by the Asset Allocation Planner Worksheet—and then decide on your next steps. Asset Allocation Planner presents an array of Fidelity mutual funds to consider as you implement (or modify) your investment plan, plus helpful information on other products and services available from Fidelity.

Reviewing your plan periodically

It's important that you review your investment plan at least once a year to determine whether it still meets your goals. As your financial objectives or needs change, as well as market conditions, you should review your investment strategy to be sure you're comfortable with your investments and that they still fit your goals.

THE IMPORTANCE OF **DIVERSIFICATION**

Diversification is a time-tested strategy that can help you reduce risk by spreading your money among many different kinds of investments, such as stocks, bonds, and short-term investments. It works typically because no two investments perform exactly the same way at the same time. Having a diversified portfolio can let you focus on building for the long term instead of trying to time the market.

Diversified portfolios also tend to provide less volatile returns over the long term and can help minimize downside risk. The chart at right compares the performance of a diversified portfolio — 60% common stocks (as measured by the S&P 500®), 30% long-term government bonds (as measured by 20-year U.S. Government bonds), and 10% cash equivalents (30-day U.S. Treasury bill) — with a non-diversified portfolio composed entirely of common stocks (as measured by the S&P 500®) during two major market declines.

During both the October 1987 and the August 1998 market declines, the diversi-fied portfolios did not fall as far as the all-stock portfolios during these market declines, and bounced back faster. Of course, past performance is no guarantee of future results.

Investing over time is a simple strategy that works.

At Fidelity, we believe that a regular investment plan over time is one of the most effective ways to help build a portfolio. Investing over time is important because the value of any investment will fluctuate. When you invest regularly at consistent intervals, also known as dollar cost averaging,[1] you buy at many different prices instead of trying to time the market. Even Wall Street experts can't always buy at the lowest price and sell at the highest.

Investing regularly over time is an effective way to help meet your investment goals. Although this strategy does not protect you from a loss in a declining market or assure you a profit, it may help lower the average cost of your purchase over the long term.

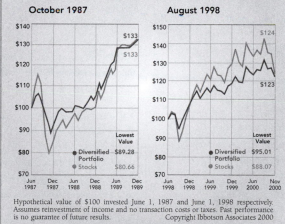

Diversified Portfolios and Market Declines

Historically, during market declines, diversified portfolios have not fallen as far as all-stock portfolios, and bounced back faster.

Hypothetical value of $100 invested June 1, 1987 and June 1, 1998 respectively. Assumes reinvestment of income and no transaction costs or taxes. Past performance is no guarantee of future results.   Copyright Ibbotson Associates 2000

[1]Dollar cost averaging does not assure a profit or protect against loss in declining markets. For the strategy to be effective, you must continue to purchase shares both in market ups and downs.

BALANCING RISK AND RETURN

Before you determine what investment mix (stocks, bonds, short-term instruments) may be best for you, it's important to take a closer look at risk and understand how selecting different types of investments can help you manage it. Each of the three types of investments, or "asset classes," has its own associated risks. And with investments, greater potential return usually indicates more risk.

Stock market investing

While the stock market as a whole has historically provided superior returns over the long term compared to bonds and short-term instruments,* it's important to consider market risk when investing in stocks. Market risk is the risk that your investment will fluctuate in value along with other securities in the market, and your shares may be worth less when you sell them.

Because the share price of a stock can fall as dramatically as it can rise, stock market investing may be more appropriate if you're investing for longer-term goals and have the time to wait out any short-term fluctuations in the market.

Investing in bonds

Bonds historically have been less volatile than stocks. Most pay interest and may be appropriate for investors who want regular income from their investments. Bonds are subject to credit risk, which is the risk of the issuer's defaulting on payment as well as the risk of a decline in the bonds' value when their credit standing deteriorates. Also, bonds do not provide the same opportunity for growth that stocks do.

Bond investors also need to understand interest-rate risk. That's the risk that interest rates will change and therefore affect the price of the bond investment you may be holding. For example, if you hold a bond paying 6% and interest rates rise to 10%, the market value of your bond will decline because current bonds are paying the higher interest rate. This can also work in reverse to produce a gain in your bond price if interest rates were to drop.

Short-term instruments

Short-term instruments—securities with maturities of one year or less—are the least volatile of the three asset classes. Short-term instruments can help you meet short-term investment goals. They also can add some liquidity or stability to a portfolio. Short-term instruments tend to pay lower rates than longer-term bonds, and you should keep in mind that not all short-term instruments are backed by government guarantees or insurance.

Investing in short-term instruments exposes you to the risk that you may lose ground to inflation. This inflation risk is the risk that the returns on your investment may not keep up with inflation. Inflation can eat away at your return, sometimes eroding it entirely. For example, during 1996, Treasury bills returned 5.30 percent on average. The same year, the Consumer Price Index, a measure of inflation, rose 3.30 percent. That means that the real return from Treasury bills was just 2.00 percent.

Setting up your plan

The Asset Allocation Planner Worksheet that begins on page 6 can help you develop an asset allocation strategy for a specific investment goal. If you have more than one goal—saving for a down payment and a college education, for instance—you should consider creating a separate plan for each.

*Past performance is no guarantee of future results.

MARKET CAPITALIZATION AND **INVESTMENT STYLE**

Other important ways to diversify within the stock asset class are by investment style: value vs. growth, and by size, the market capitalization of the companies, large vs. small cap stocks. Growth and value stocks tend to have differing risk and return characteristics and may behave differently during the various market cycles.

For example, research from the Frank Russell Company has shown that there has been significant variation in value and growth returns over time. Understanding the style of an investment fund can be a helpful tool when you analyze how an investment has performed. A brief explanation of investment style follows:

Growth

Growth stocks have higher Price/Earnings ratios than the market average, based on the market's belief that the companies have superior prospects for earnings growth. The Price/Earnings ratio is the market price of the stock divided by annual earnings per share.

Value

Value stocks have lower Price/Earnings ratios than the market average, based on concerns about the companies' prospects for earnings growth. Value companies might have hidden or undervalued assets, ranging from real estate holdings, to a great brand name, to a misunderstood industry, to underrated products or underperforming assets.

Blend

Blend is a combination of value and growth stock investment styles.

MARKET CAPITALIZATION

Stocks with different market capitalizations also have different levels of volatility and returns over time. Including stocks and stock funds with different market capitalizations in your portfolio can help to diversify your portfolio over the long term. Small

cap stocks may offer greater potential returns, but also greater potential risk, as the earnings of small caps can be more sensitive to the state of the economy.

Small Cap

- Under $1 billion in market capitalization
- Typically newer companies
- Usually does not pay dividends

Mid-Cap

- Between $1 billion and $5 billion in market capitalization
- Growing companies
- Usually does not pay dividends

Large Cap

- Over $5 billion in market capitalization
- Established companies
- Usually pays dividends

An easy way to visualize the investment styles of stocks is to review the investment style map below.

Valuation		
Value	Blend	Growth
Large Cap Value	Large Cap Blend	Large Cap Growth
Mid-Cap Value	Mid-Cap Blend	Mid-Cap Growth
Small Cap Value	Small Cap Blend	Small Cap Growth

(Capitalization: Large / Medium / Small)

5

ASSET ALLOCATION PLANNER WORKSHEET

Based on common investment principles, the Asset Allocation Planner Worksheet uses a point system to help you find an asset allocation strategy that can match your investment goals.

To complete the Worksheet, select your best answer for each question and enter the corresponding point value in the space to the right. The point values will vary by question, according to how each factor may influence an investment decision.

Once you've finished, add up the points from questions 2 and 3, then add up the points on questions 4–13. Subtract the sum of 4–13 from the sum of 2 and 3. Compare your total score to the target asset mixes you'll find on page 10 to find which one may be most appropriate for your current needs.

Naturally, the asset allocation that's indicated by your score is just a guide. The decision to invest more conservatively or aggressively than your target asset mix suggests is always yours to make. To help you with that decision, the following questionnaire takes into consideration your time horizon, current financial situation, and risk tolerance. While this tool can help identify an investment strategy, for many investors there are some circumstances where it may not be appropriate.

Regardless of your point score, if you're investing for fewer than two years, you may want to consider the Short-Term Portfolio, shown on page 10.

Please keep in mind that the Asset Allocation Planner is designed to help you plan for a specific investment goal. Should you have multiple investment goals—for short-term and long-term savings, for instance—consider completing a Worksheet for each one.

> Don't forget, too, that your score is based on your current assessment of a number of factors. If your personal situation—or market conditions—change, it makes sense to review your investment strategy. At a minimum, you should review your investment strategy on an annual basis.

Your Investment Goal

1. Is saving for retirement your current investment goal?*

❏ Yes
❏ No

*If you plan to invest for less than two years, you may want to skip the questionnaire and consider the Short-Term Target Asset Mix on page 10. Determining the time frame for your investment is critical to making an investment decision: the longer your investment horizon, the more aggressive you may want to be.

2. In how many years do you plan to retire?	Points	
a. Retired or plan to retire in less than 4 years	❏ 0	
b. 4 to 6 years	❏ 52	
c. 7 to 10 years	❏ 69	Points
d. 11 to 16 years	❏ 70	
e. 16+ years	❏ 71	

ASSET ALLOCATION PLANNER Worksheet

Your Investment Time Frame

3. Do you expect to withdraw more than one-third of the money in this account within seven years (for a home purchase, college tuition, or other major need)? If yes, when do you expect to withdraw from the account?

a. No ☐ 20

b. Within 3 years ☐ 0

c. Within 4 to 7 years ☐ 12

Points

A: 2 + 3

Total

How Does This Investment Fit into Your Total Financial Picture?

It is important to consider this investment in relationship to your total portfolio. The percentage of your portfolio that this investment represents will influence how conservative or aggressive you may want to be.

4. Approximately what portion of your total investable assets—the dollar amount of the investments you currently have—will this investment represent? (Do not include your principal residence or vacation home when figuring this total.)

a. Less than 25% ☐ 0

b. Between 25% and 50% ☐ 1

c. Between 51% and 75% ☐ 2

d. More than 75% ☐ 4

Points

Your expectation for future earnings will help determine how your assets should be allocated. If you're expecting significant earnings increases, it may be appropriate to be somewhat more aggressive.

5. Which ONE of the following describes your expected future earnings over the next five years? (Assume inflation will average 4%.)

a. I expect my earnings increases will far outpace inflation (due to promotions, new job, etc.). ☐ 0

b. I expect my earnings increases to stay somewhat ahead of inflation. ☐ 1

c. I expect my earnings to keep pace with inflation. ☐ 2

d. I expect my earnings to decrease (retirement, part-time work, economically depressed industry, etc.). ☐ 4

Points

If a large portion of your income goes toward paying debt, you may need to have cash available for unforeseen circumstances. Or, you may have responsibility for ongoing family obligations. Either can dictate a more conservative approach.

6. Approximately what portion of your monthly net income goes toward paying off installment debt (auto loans, credit cards, etc.) other than a home mortgage?

a. Less than 10% ☐ 0

b. Between 10% and 25% ☐ 1

c. Between 26% and 50% ☐ 2

d. More than 50% ☐ 6

Points

7

ASSET ALLOCATION PLANNER Worksheet

7. How many dependents do you support? (Include children you support, spouse, elderly parents, etc.)

		Points
a. None	❏ 0	
b. 1	❏ 1	
c. 2 to 3	❏ 2	
d. More than 3	❏ 4	

An emergency fund can provide a cushion against unexpected expenses, so you avoid having to draw on long-term investments to meet immediate needs.

8. Do you have an emergency fund (savings of three to six months' after-tax income)?

		Points
a. No	❏ 8	
b. Yes, but less than six months of after-tax income.	❏ 3	
c. Yes, I have an adequate emergency fund.	❏ 0	

9. What portion of your retirement income do you expect to come from this retirement investment?

		Points
a. Less than 20%	❏ 0	
b. 20% to 35%	❏ 1	
c. 36% to 50%	❏ 2	
d. More than 50%	❏ 4	

Your Personal Risk Tolerance

Your prior investment experience can help determine your attitude toward investment risk.

10. Have you ever invested in individual bonds or bond mutual funds (aside from U.S. savings bonds)?

		Points
a. No, and I would be uncomfortable with the risk if I did.	❏ 10	
b. No, but I would be comfortable with the risk if I did.	❏ 4	
c. Yes, but I was uncomfortable with the risk.	❏ 6	
d. Yes, and I felt comfortable with the risk.	❏ 0	

11. Have you ever invested in individual stocks or stock mutual funds?

		Points
a. No, and I would be uncomfortable with the risk if I did.	❏ 8	
b. No, but I would be comfortable with the risk if I did.	❏ 3	
c. Yes, but I was uncomfortable with the risk.	❏ 5	
d. Yes, and I felt comfortable with the risk.	❏ 0	

ASSET ALLOCATION PLANNER Worksheet

Your comfort level with investment risk influences how aggressively or conservatively you choose to invest. It should be balanced with the potential of achieving your investment goals.

12. Which ONE of the following statements best describes your feelings about investment risk?

    a. I would only select investments that have a low degree of risk   ❏ 12
       associated with them (i.e., it is unlikely I will lose my original investment).

    b. I prefer to select a mix of investments with emphasis on those with   ❏ 9
       a low degree of risk and a small portion in others that have a higher
       degree of risk that may yield greater returns.

    c. I prefer to select a balanced mix of investments—some that have   ❏ 5
       a low degree of risk, others that have a higher degree of risk that may
       yield greater returns.

    d. I prefer to select an aggressive mix of investments—some that have   ❏ 1
       a low degree of risk, but with emphasis on others that have a higher
       degree of risk that may yield greater returns.

    e. I would select an investment that has only a higher degree of risk   ❏ 0
       and a greater potential for higher returns.

Points ▢

13. If you could increase your chances of improving your returns by taking more risk, would you:

    a. Be willing to take a *lot* more risk with *all* your money.   ❏ 0
    b. Be willing to take a *lot* more risk with *some* of your money.   ❏ 2
    c. Be willing to take a *little* more risk with *all* your money.   ❏ 6
    d. Be willing to take a *little* more risk with *some* of your money.   ❏ 9
    e. Be unlikely to take much more risk.   ❏ 12

Points ▢

Scoring Directions:

A. Write your point score for Questions 2 and 3   ▢

B. Add your points from Questions 4 through 13   − ▢

C. Subtract "B" from "A"   ▢ Total Points

See next page for suggested portfolios.

Formula for your Asset Allocation Planner score:

<20 points = Conservative   **50 – 69 points = Growth**
(Please note, your score may be less than or equal to zero.)

20 – 49 points = Balanced   **70 + points = Aggressive Growth**

9

WHAT DOES YOUR SCORE MEAN?

Your Asset Allocation Planner score provides an indication of an asset allocation strategy that may be right for you. Each of the five target asset mixes below has a different mix of investments, so each one will strike a different balance between risk and return. If you need your money in two years or less, a portfolio made up of short-term/money market instruments can provide you with current income, liquidity, and an element of stability.

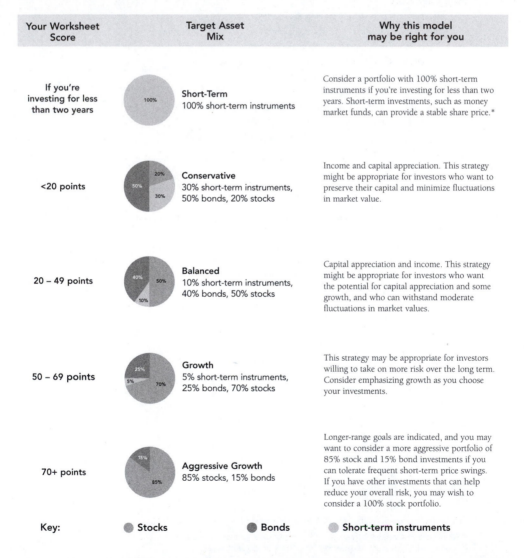

Your Worksheet Score	Target Asset Mix	Why this model may be right for you
If you're investing for less than two years	**Short-Term** 100% short-term instruments	Consider a portfolio with 100% short-term instruments if you're investing for less than two years. Short-term investments, such as money market funds, can provide a stable share price.*
<20 points	**Conservative** 30% short-term instruments, 50% bonds, 20% stocks	Income and capital appreciation. This strategy might be appropriate for investors who want to preserve their capital and minimize fluctuations in market value.
20 – 49 points	**Balanced** 10% short-term instruments, 40% bonds, 50% stocks	Capital appreciation and income. This strategy might be appropriate for investors who want the potential for capital appreciation and some growth, and who can withstand moderate fluctuations in market values.
50 – 69 points	**Growth** 5% short-term instruments, 25% bonds, 70% stocks	This strategy may be appropriate for investors willing to take on more risk over the long term. Consider emphasizing growth as you choose your investments.
70+ points	**Aggressive Growth** 85% stocks, 15% bonds	Longer-range goals are indicated, and you may want to consider a more aggressive portfolio of 85% stock and 15% bond investments if you can tolerate frequent short-term price swings. If you have other investments that can help reduce your overall risk, you may wish to consider a 100% stock portfolio.

Key: ● Stocks   ● Bonds   ● Short-term instruments

*An investment in a money market fund is not insured or guaranteed by the Federal Deposit Insurance Corporation (FDIC) or any other government agency. Although a money market fund seeks to preserve the value of your investment at $1.00 per share, it is possible to lose money by investing in the fund.

YOUR NEXT STEPS

Now that you've reviewed basic asset allocation concepts and have determined a target asset mix that may be right for you, consider these next steps to develop a plan to help you pursue your investment strategy.

Step 1: Developing Your Plan

Compare the target asset mix provided by the Worksheet score to your current portfolio mix. This chart can help you to determine adjustments you may want to consider for your investment strategy as you pursue your goals.

Investment Checkup*

	Current Investments Market Value	% of Total	Target Asset Mix % of Total	Change Suggested (+) or (–)[1]
Short-Term Investments				
CDs and other bank deposits	_____			
Money market funds[2]	_____			
Other	_____			
Total Short-Term Investments	$_____	_____%	_____%	_____%
Bonds[3]				
Individual bonds	_____			
Bond mutual funds	_____			
Other	_____			
Total Bonds	$_____	_____%	_____%	_____%
Stocks				
Individual stocks	_____			
Stock mutual funds	_____			
Other	_____			
Total Stocks	$_____	_____%	_____%	_____%
Total for Three Asset Classes	$_____	_____	_____	_____%

If your current holdings are within 5% of your target asset mix for all asset classes, you might want to remain within your current strategy.

* Include bank accounts and CDs, investments at other firms, and, if you're saving for retirement, assets you have in IRAs, 401(k)s, or other employer-sponsored retirement plans. Do not include investments such as real estate, precious metals, and limited partnerships.

[1] In order to move closer to your target asset mix, you may need to reallocate assets within your current portfolio or contribute additional money. Some approaches you may want to consider could include: investment of anticipated cash (e.g., bonus); sale of currently held short-term assets; systematic investment over time; or sale of currently held stock/bond assets.

Note: The sale of any asset may have tax consequences unless maintained in a tax-deferred or tax-free account. In addition, when considering a sale of individual securities or mutual funds, you may want to consider some or all of the same factors you consider in making a new investment. Consult your tax or financial adviser on your specific situation.

[2] An investment in a money market fund is not insured or guaranteed by the Federal Deposit Insurance Corporation or any other government agency. Although the fund seeks to preserve the value of your investment at $1.00 per share, it is possible to lose money by investing in the fund.

[3] Any fixed-income security sold prior to maturity may be subject to substantial gain or loss.

11

Fidelity makes it easy to **DIVERSIFY YOUR INVESTMENTS**

Whether you plan to invest in mutual funds, individual securities, or both to create a more diversified portfolio, Fidelity makes it easy to get started.

Step 2: Building Your Portfolio

After you determine the changes you may need to make to your investment mix to more closely match your target asset mix, your next step is to identify the most appropriate investments to fulfill your asset allocation plan. Fidelity offers a number of mutual fund options that you may want to consider.

One option is a one-step approach to diversification with Fidelity Asset Manager® funds. Or you can evaluate Fidelity and non-Fidelity fund options on **Fidelity.com** with our proactive online tools and information:

- Fund Evaluator℠ – Interactive research tool that helps self-directed investors evaluate investment options. Use Morningstar® data to compare and research our mutual funds.
- FundScreens™ – Narrow your search with this quarterly report of selected top-performing stock and bond funds.
- Growth Calculator – See how the growth of your investments can be affected by different factors.

Step 3: Start to Benefit from Your Strategy

When you open a Fidelity Account,℠ you can begin benefiting from the convenience and control the account has to offer.

To open your account, simply log on to **Fidelity.com** and go to "open an account" and complete the application online.

Step 4: Monitoring Your Investments with Your Fidelity Statement

Fidelity's easy-to-read statement, available online or by mail, provides you with comprehensive information on all your Fidelity non-retirement accounts. You can take a closer look at your total portfolio to help determine if your investment strategy is on track with your goals.

Fidelity Asset Manager® Funds – a one-step approach to diversification

Fidelity offers a convenient way to put the Asset Allocation Planner ideas to work with the Fidelity Asset Manager funds. With a single investment, these funds let you diversify your investment across a carefully allocated mix of domestic and foreign short-term and money market instruments, bonds, and stocks of all types.

Fidelity Asset Manager: Income®
Investors scoring up to 20 points on the Worksheet may wish to consider Fidelity *Asset Manager: Income.®* Its goal is a high level of income, and capital appreciation where appropriate. The fund's investments fluctuate around a neutral mix of 20% stocks, 50% bonds, and 30% short-term/money market instruments.

Fidelity Asset Manager: Growth®
Investors scoring between 50 and 69 on the Worksheet may wish to consider Fidelity *Asset Manager: Growth.®* Its goal is to maximize total return over the long term. The fund's investments fluctuate around a neutral mix of 70% stocks, 25% bonds, and 5% short-term/money market instruments.

Fidelity Asset Manager℠
Investors scoring between 20 and 49 points on the Worksheet may wish to consider Fidelity *Asset Manager.℠* Its goal is high total return with reduced risk over the long term. The fund's investments fluctuate around a neutral mix of 50% stocks, 40% bonds, and 10% short-term/money market instruments.

Fidelity Asset Manager: Aggressive℠
Investors scoring above 70 on the Worksheet may wish to consider Fidelity *Asset Manager: Aggressive.℠* Its goal is to maximize total return over the long term. The fund's investments fluctuate around a neutral mix of 85% stocks, 15% bonds and 0% short-term/money market instruments.

 Stocks   Bonds 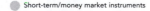 Short-term/money market instruments

CHOOSE FROM A WIDE ARRAY OF FIDELITY FUNDS

Another option is to create your own portfolio. As you consider investments for your goal, you may want to consider the following mutual funds from Fidelity. To help you select investments for your target asset mix, a select list of Fidelity funds are arranged by category. In addition to the Fidelity Asset Manager funds described on the previous page, we've included a further selection of Fidelity funds you may wish to consider as you make your investment decisions.

MONEY MARKET FUNDS*

Money market funds offer a place where your short-term investments can seek high current yields while remaining more stable and accessible than longer-term investments. They can also provide an interim investment while you are searching for a growth or income opportunity. All Fidelity money market funds offer checkwriting, so they are among the most liquid investments available. In addition, all of Fidelity's money market funds are offered without a sales charge. All money market funds seek to maintain a $1 share price.

Cash Reserves
Fidelity State Municipal Money Market Funds
(CA, CT, MA, MI, NJ, NY, OH)
Municipal Money Market Fund

BOND FUNDS

Bond funds can play an important role in your portfolio by adding balance and growth potential. They also may help you achieve a variety of investment objectives, including portfolio diversification, current income, protection of principal, and tax reduction. The chart below highlights just a few of Fidelity's bond funds. All are available without a sales charge.

Investment Grade
Fidelity Government Income Fund
Fidelity Intermediate Bond Fund
Fidelity Investment Grade Bond Fund
Fidelity Ginnie Mae Fund
Fidelity Short-Term Bond Fund

High-Yield[1]
Fidelity Capital & Income Fund
Fidelity High Income Fund

Municipal
Spartan® Short-Intermediate Municipal Income Fund
Spartan® Municipal Income Fund
Spartan® Intermediate Municipal Income Fund
Spartan® State Municipal Income Funds (AZ, CA, CT, FL, MA, MD, MI, MN, NJ, NY, OH, PA)

STOCK FUNDS

Stock funds can play an important role in your portfolio, particularly if your goal is long-term growth, because over time stocks historically have outperformed other types of investments. Of course, past performance is no guarantee of future results. Their potential for growth means stock funds can also serve as a hedge against inflation, helping to prevent erosion of an investment's value.

Some stock funds also pursue current income in combination with growth. The dividends that may be offered in growth and income stock funds may help to cushion your portfolio against the volatility typical of more aggressive stock funds that focus primarily on capital appreciation and growth.

Large Cap
Fidelity Aggressive Growth Fund
Fidelity Blue Chip Growth Fund
Fidelity Dividend Growth Fund
Fidelity Equity-Income Fund
Fidelity Export and Multinational Fund
Fidelity Fund
Fidelity Retirement Growth Fund
Fidelity Equity-Income II Fund
Fidelity Large Cap Stock Fund
Fidelity Disciplined Equity Fund

Mid/Small Cap[2]
Fidelity Capital Appreciation Fund
Fidelity Mid-Cap Stock Fund
Fidelity OTC Portfolio
Fidelity Small Cap Stock Fund
Fidelity Value Fund

International[3]
Fidelity Aggressive International Fund
Fidelity Diversified International Fund
Fidelity International Growth & Income Fund
Fidelity Overseas Fund

Index
Spartan® 500 Index Fund
Spartan® Extended Market Index Fund
Spartan® International Index Fund[3]

Fidelity also offers over 4,100 non-Fidelity mutual funds available through FundsNetwork® that you may want to consider.

Note: The mutual funds identified in these materials are examples of Fidelity funds investors may wish to consider. Nothing contained herein is a recommendation to buy or sell the mutual funds or any single fund listed, and there may be other investments that investors may consider more appropriate to satisfy their needs and goals.
*An investment in a money market fund is not insured or guaranteed by the Federal Deposit Insurance Corporation (FDIC) or any other government agency. Although a money market fund seeks to preserve the value of your investment at $1.00 per share, it is possible to lose money by investing in the fund.
[1]The funds invest in lower-quality debt securities, which generally offer higher yields, but also carry more risk.
[2]The securities of smaller, less-known companies may be more volatile than those of larger companies.
[3]Foreign international investments involve greater risk and may offer greater potential returns than U.S. investments. These risks include political and economic risks, as well as the risk of currency fluctuations.

13

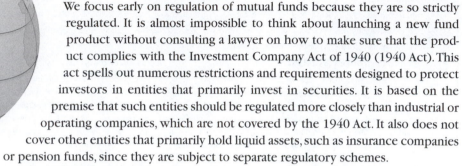

3 | Regulation and Disclosure for Mutual Funds

We focus early on regulation of mutual funds because they are so strictly regulated. It is almost impossible to think about launching a new fund product without consulting a lawyer on how to make sure that the product complies with the Investment Company Act of 1940 (1940 Act). This act spells out numerous restrictions and requirements designed to protect investors in entities that primarily invest in securities. It is based on the premise that such entities should be regulated more closely than industrial or operating companies, which are not covered by the 1940 Act. It also does not cover other entities that primarily hold liquid assets, such as insurance companies or pension funds, since they are subject to separate regulatory schemes.

Most of the laws covered in this Chapter are administered by the Securities and Exchange Commission (SEC), which was created by Congress in the early 1930s as part of the New Deal. The SEC is an independent regulatory agency aimed at providing protection to investors by enforcing the federal securities laws and issuing rules. The SEC focuses much of its efforts on promoting full disclosure of information to the investing public, though it also is involved in substantive regulation of the stock markets and investment companies.

This Chapter begins by describing the different types of investment companies and their tax treatment. It next outlines the disclosure and advertising rules applicable to mutual funds. Then it summarizes the issues involved in the electronic transmission of fund and customer information. It proceeds to a discussion of substantive requirements imposed on mutual funds, followed by a review of the role of their independent directors. The textbook portion of the Chapter closes by addressing the enforcement of all these rules, including the Code of Ethics for mutual fund complexes. At the end of the Chapter is an exercise involving the design of a short-form prospectus on the key points about a mutual fund.

I. Classification and Taxation

To begin, it is useful to understand generally the legal structure of a mutual fund and specifically to dispel the myth that a mutual fund is a mere product. A mutual fund is a legal entity, a trust or corporation organized under the laws of a state, distinct from the fund's investment manager. For this reason, fund trustees or directors are subject to fiduciary duties under state law. In addition, all mutual funds are subject to an elaborate layer of federal regulations. Broadly, the 1940 Act provides for three classes of investment companies: face amount certificate companies, unit investment trusts (UITs) and management companies. Mutual funds are classified as "open-end, management invest-

ment companies" under the 1940 Act and must meet certain diversification requirements as well as certain income distribution requirements of the Internal Revenue
Code (the Code).

As discussed in Chapter One, mutual funds have a dynamic portfolio of securities,
which may vary in composition as the portfolio manager buys and sells securities
based on the fund's investment objectives. In contrast, as discussed in Chapter Two,
passive investment companies like UITs offer interests in a fixed portfolio of securities;
there is no significant change in the portfolio of securities held by the unit investment
trust after it is initially assembled.[1]

Within the class of management companies, there are open-end and closed-end
funds. An open-end management company, also called a mutual fund, is the type of fund
that an average investor encounters most often. A mutual fund continuously sells
shares to the public and stands ready to redeem shares every day at its net asset value
(NAV), the value of a single share, computed by adding up the fund's assets, subtracting
its liabilities, and dividing the results by the number of shares outstanding. By contrast,
a closed-end fund generally offers new shares episodically (if at all) and does not provide a redemption privilege. Once issued, shares of a closed-end fund generally are
traded on an exchange similar to shares of industrial companies, and they may trade at,
above or below NAV. In most cases, closed-end funds trade at a price below their NAV
(i.e., at a discount).

Management companies are broken down further into diversified and nondiversified funds. Most mutual funds meet the 1940 Act's definition of diversification: as to
75% of the assets of the fund, the fund may not acquire more than 10% of the voting securities of any one issuer *and* it may not invest more than 5% of total fund assets in any
one issuer. Thus, in theory, a diversified mutual fund could invest 25% of its assets in 1
issuer and 75% of its assets in 15 issuers (i.e., 5% in each issuer), for a total of 16 positions in the fund. In practice, most diversified mutual funds hold more than 50 positions and rarely invest more than 10% of their assets in any one issuer. By contrast,
nondiversified mutual funds often concentrate their investments in a smaller number
of issuers.

Whether or not they meet the 1940 Act's tests for diversification, all mutual funds
must meet the diversification and income distribution requirements of the Code in order to qualify for tax pass-through treatment. A tax pass-through means that the mutual
fund (which is a corporation or trust) pays no corporate tax; instead, the dividends, interest and capital gains on its investments are distributed to fund shareholders, according to their proportionate ownership of the fund, who are then taxed on the
distributions on their individual federal and state income tax returns. In practice, most
fund shareholders choose to have their fund distributions automatically reinvested in
additional fund shares, so they do not receive cash for the distributions on which they
are required to pay income taxes.

Under the Code's diversification requirements, as to 50% of the assets of a fund, the
fund may not acquire more than 10% of the voting securities of any one issuer and may
not invest more than 5% of the total fund assets in any one issuer. With respect to the
remaining 50% of its assets, the fund may not invest more than 25% in any one issuer.
Thus, in theory, a fund meeting only the Internal Revenue Service (IRS) diversification

tests could hold only 12 positions (ten 5% positions and two 25% positions), although this almost never happens.

While the Code's diversification requirements are less stringent than those in the 1940 Act, its income distribution requirements force every mutual fund to pay out to its shareholders each year almost all dividends and interest payments received, as well as the net capital gains realized by the fund through its buying and selling of portfolio securities. Realized capital losses of a fund may be used to offset realized capital gains of the same fund before fund distributions, but realized capital losses in excess of realized capital gains are not distributed and instead are carried forward to the next tax year. While the tax pass-through is a big advantage for mutual funds, the annual distribution of all realized gains needed to qualify for pass-through reinforces a significant disadvantage to holders of mutual fund shares as compared to holders of individual securities: holders of mutual fund shares have no control over the timing of realized gains. For example, a fund shareholder cannot choose to delay the realization of a capital gain in appreciated shares sold by the fund, even if he or she would have preferred to wait until the next tax year. Thus, investors who buy and hold shares of a mutual fund face an annual income tax liability for any capital gains realized by that fund, even though they themselves have not sold any shares of that fund.

Because of these required fund distributions of realized capital gains (as well as interest and dividends), Congress has put pressure on the SEC to mandate disclosure of after-tax fund returns in addition to other fund performance measures. In response, the SEC has adopted rules requiring all mutual funds (except money market funds) to disclose their after-tax returns in fund prospectuses. Specifically, a fund prospectus must disclose not only its before-tax average annual return for 1-, 5- and 10-year periods (or the life of the fund, if shorter), but also its average annual return after taxes on fund distributions under both of two assumptions—assuming no redemption of fund shares by the fund shareholders during the relevant periods and redemption of all fund shares at the end of the relevant periods. The SEC requires such after-tax disclosures to be based on the highest marginal tax rate possibly applicable to a shareholder of the fund, even though most fund shareholders do not actually pay the top marginal tax rate. While the SEC did not require such after-tax disclosures to be included in any fund advertisement, these disclosures must be included in any advertisement by a fund representing that it is managed to limit the effect of taxes on its returns. Table 3.1 provides an example of the presentation of before-tax and after-tax average annual return.

Despite the SEC's new disclosure requirements, it is still unclear how important after-tax returns are to mutual fund investors. During 2000, there were only 50 funds with less than $40 billion in assets included in Morningstar's category of tax-managed equity and fixed income funds. Perhaps this relative lack of attention is because fund assets increasingly are held by retirement accounts that do not pay annual income taxes. Some high-net-worth investors who are very tax sensitive have migrated from mutual funds to separate accounts (as discussed in Chapter One). Other tax-sensitive investors have chosen index mutual funds because they have distributed very small amounts of capital gain over the past decade. Index funds have made minimal capital gain distributions because they generally have been experiencing net sales and therefore usually have not needed to sell a significant amount of portfolio securities. However, if index funds experience substantial redemptions, they will be forced to sell

TABLE 3.1

Average annual returns

For the Periods Ended December 31, 2000	Past 1 Year	Past 5 Years	Life of Fund[a]
Fidelity Dividend Growth—Return before taxes	12.25%	22.53%	22.71%
Fidelity Dividend Growth—Return after taxes on distributions	10.25	19.71	20.29
Fidelity Dividend Growth—Return after taxes on distributions and sale of fund shares	8.98	17.78	18.53
S&P 500 (reflects no deduction for fees, expenses or taxes)	−9.10	18.33	17.76

Note: After-tax returns are calculated using the historical highest individual federal marginal income tax rates, but do not reflect the impact of state or local taxes. Actual after-tax returns will differ depending on your individual circumstances. The after-tax returns shown are not relevant if you hold your shares in a retirement account or through another tax deferred arrangement. Returns are based on past results and are not an indication of future performance.
[a]From April 27, 1993.

securities in their portfolios and to realize capital gains. The potential capital gains held by many index funds are huge because of the bull market over the past decade, although the index funds may be able to sell relatively high-cost securities to meet an initial wave of redemptions. Moreover, index funds may distribute substantial capital gains as a result of changes in the constituent securities of the index. These changes occur if a security is moved from one index to another because of a large increase in its market capitalization. For example, in 1999 Standard & Poor's removed Qualcomm Inc. from its S&P MidCap 400 index because the market capitalization of Qualcomm had increased and the security was going to be added to the S&P 500 index. Index funds that attempted to match the return of the S&P MidCap 400 had to sell Qualcomm and realize significant capital gains because the security's price had risen sharply.

In June 2000, a Joint Economic Committee study for the U.S. Congress estimated that the current tax treatment of mutual funds causes fund investors to lose on average between 10% and 20% a year of the preliquidation rate of return (before selling fund shares). For example, given a $10,000 investment earning a 10% annual rate of return (before taxes), a 2.3% reduction in preliquidation rate of return because of income taxes would cost a mutual fund investor almost $82,000 over a 30-year period.[2] To eliminate this disadvantage, the Committee recommended moving the realization point that triggers a capital gains tax liability from the fund level—at the point where the mutual fund realizes a gain by selling shares of stocks or bonds in its portfolio—to the individual level—at the point where the shareholder sells (i.e., redeems) his or her own shares of the fund. Legislation along these lines has been introduced. If enacted, it would allow fund shareholders to defer recognition of all or some (e.g., up to $3,000 per person each year) of the capital gains realized by the fund until they decide to sell their fund shares.

II. *Disclosure and Advertising Rules*

The 1940 Act was passed a few years after Congress enacted the core disclosure statute for securities offerings: the Securities Act of 1933 (1933 Act), sometimes referred to as a "truth in securities" law. The 1933 Act requires registration with the SEC of most public offers and sales of securities. It also requires most public issuers of securities to disseminate a prospectus disclosing all material facts concerning such securities to potential investors. The prospectus requirements are aimed at providing accurate information regarding the material circumstances of the company and the securities it proposes to sell so that potential investors may make informed judgments in their purchases of such securities. The 1933 Act, together with other general antifraud provisions in the securities laws, also generally prohibits material misrepresentations and omissions in connection with the purchase or sale of securities. However, it does not prohibit or prescribe conduct by issuers, nor does it preclude securities offerings by risky, poorly managed or unprofitable companies. As long as these issuers are prepared to tell the world what they are doing, they have broad freedom to conduct their business as they please.

The Securities Exchange Act of 1934 (1934 Act) extended investor protections to securities traded on the national securities exchanges in the United States. Thirty years later, the Securities Exchange Act Amendments of 1964 expanded the 1934 Act to cover equity securities in the over-the-counter market if the issuer had assets over $1 million and more than 500 shareholders. The 1934 Act is designed to ensure fair and orderly securities markets by establishing annual and quarterly reporting requirements for publicly traded companies. It also authorizes the SEC to set the ground rules for the operation of the securities trading markets and the securities professionals (e.g., brokers and dealers) who operate in those markets.

In the disclosure area, mutual funds are subject to relatively strict rules because mutual funds are continuously offering their shares to investors. As a result, mutual funds are continuously subject to many of the same rules that apply to initial public offerings (IPOs) of industrial companies. Most important, a mutual fund must clear its prospectus through the SEC, which sets and interprets the rules for prospectus disclosure. Although the SEC never actually "approves" the issuance of any prospectus, it does have the right to stop a prospectus from being distributed. To avoid such a confrontation, mutual fund sponsors go through a lengthy comment and negotiation process with SEC staff about the contents and format of a fund's prospectus. In practice, a mutual fund must always have on hand a prospectus to send to new investors and also must send an updated prospectus approximately once a year to existing fund shareholders.

In addition to the disclosure requirements of the 1933 Act, the 1940 Act imposes special disclosure requirements on prospectuses of mutual funds. (See the prospectus at the end of this Chapter.) Most important, a mutual fund is required to disclose in its prospectus a description of its fundamental policies. These must include its status as a diversified or nondiversified fund and its policy with respect to borrowing money, underwriting securities, concentrating its investments in a particular industry, purchasing real estate, purchasing commodities and making loans. A fund must also disclose any other policy deemed fundamental and may not change any fundamental policy without the prior approval of shareholders. A fund subject to the SEC name test rule has a choice regarding policies associated with the fund's name (except for tax-exempt funds). Such a fund may adopt a fundamental policy to invest at least 80% of its assets in investments suggested by its name, which may not be changed without the prior approval of shareholders. Alternatively, a fund subject to the name test rule is allowed to adopt a policy that it will provide notice to shareholders at least 60 days prior to changing its name test policy.

In early 2001, the SEC adopted a rule, effective in mid-2002, that imposes an 80% name test on three main types of funds; this test is measured at the time a fund makes an investment under normal circumstances. First, the SEC requires any fund with a name suggesting that it focuses its investments in a particular type of security or a particular industry to invest at least 80% of its assets in that security or industry. For example, the Preferred Stock Fund and the Biotechnology Fund would both have to meet the 80% name test, but the Growth or Value Fund would not because the SEC considers these names to be investment strategies rather than security types. Second, the SEC requires funds with names suggesting that they focus on investments in a particular country (e.g., Mexico) or in a particular geographic region (e.g., Europe) to invest 80% of their assets in investments that are tied economically to that country or geographic region. The SEC requires funds with "foreign" in their names to meet the 80% test, although not funds with "international" and "global" in their name because the SEC believes these latter two names connote diversification among different countries. Third, the SEC requires funds with a name suggesting its distributions are exempt from federal or state income tax to meet the 80% test. For funds with "tax-exempt" in their names, with respect to 80% of their assets, the income from these investments must be exempt under alternative minimum tax rules as well as normal income tax rules; although for funds with "municipal" in their names, the income from investments may be subject to the alternative minimum tax.

Over the years, the SEC has developed a tiered approach to fund disclosure, with different levels of detail available to investors as they wish. For example, an investor can obtain on request a Statement of Additional Information (SAI) that provides more detail about a mutual fund's operations than its prospectus. On the other hand, since 1998, the SEC has permitted the use of a short-form prospectus (referred to as a Profile) by mutual funds. Investors may purchase shares of a fund based on a Profile provided that certain key information about the fund is disclosed in the Profile. This information in a Profile must be presented in a specified sequence so that funds can be compared easily. An investor who purchases fund shares based on a Profile must receive the full prospectus with the purchase confirmation. (The Exercise at the end of this Chapter involves the creation of a Profile, allowing you to choose the key information items about a mutual fund needed by prospective investors.)

In addition to sending out prospectuses, mutual funds are required by the SEC to send out reports twice a year to existing fund shareholders. These reports review the performance of the fund and include management's discussion of the fund's results during the reporting period. Currently, these reports must also list every security held at the end of the reporting period, along with the market value of each security as of that date. In 2000, the SEC's Division of Investment Management indicated it was considering whether shareholders really want or need the long listing of portfolio holdings in these semiannual fund reports or whether they would be more likely to read something shorter and less cumbersome. For instance, instead of listing all securities in its portfolio, a mutual fund could send a report that enumerates its top 50 holdings and summarizes, with graphs and charts, the overall investment characteristics of the fund. Fund sponsors would still be required to send a full list of fund holdings to any fund shareholder who requests such a list. On the other hand, a few critics are pressing the SEC to require mutual funds to publish their holdings on a more frequent basis—quarterly, monthly or even weekly. These critics maintain that fund shareholders have a right to know the holdings of their funds on a more frequent basis. In response, industry representatives point out that more frequent disclosure of fund holdings will hurt fund shareholders by enhancing the ability of hedge funds and other third parties to front-run (or trade the same stocks ahead of) the trading of mutual funds. Roughly 20% of all U.S. public equities are held by mutual funds, including large fund complexes that engage in extended buying and selling programs.

Because mutual funds are continuously offering their securities for sale to investors, these funds are particularly constrained by the SEC's restrictive rules for advertising during a public offering. To provide some flexibility on advertising, the SEC has adopted certain rules that allow for the use of fund advertisements. (See Reading 3.1 "Advertising the Fund" at the end of this Chapter.) "Generic" advertisements are used commonly to provide general explanatory or background information about mutual funds. These advertisements may contain information about categories of funds (e.g., money market funds) without mentioning any particular fund by name. The advertisements may invite inquiry for further information and prospectuses and must indicate the name of the dealer or fund sponsor. The SEC also allows mutual funds to publish more specific advertisements for their funds, historically called "tombstone ads." These advertisements may contain the name of specific mutual funds along with information on their investment objective, portfolio manager and other fund particular information. The information in these advertisements must be accompanied by special legends that specify how an investor may obtain further information about the fund.

Mutual funds that wish to publish performance information or even more detailed information about a fund may use an "omitting" prospectus, which may contain information the "substance of which" is found in a full fund prospectus. The performance information in these advertisements must adhere to detailed SEC guidelines (e.g., standardized average annual returns for 1-, 5- and 10-year or life-of-fund periods), which allow for comparison of returns across differing mutual fund advertisements. Other information included in these advertisements generally must be based on statements included in the fund's full prospectus. The SEC has been authorized by Congress to repeal the "substance of which" requirements, effectively eliminating any content restrictions on these advertisements, but it has not yet adopted rules implementing this authorization.

While the SEC sets the legal framework for fund advertising, this framework is interpreted and administered by the National Association of Securities Dealers, Inc. (NASD). The NASD is a self-regulatory organization for securities brokers and dealers, which has the power to discipline member firms for violating its rules. By contrast, see "Investment Company Institute." All sales and advertising material (other than prospectuses) that brokers or dealers use must be submitted for review to the NASD's independent subsidiary, NASD Regulation, Inc. In addition, mutual funds still must pay state registration fees for sales of fund shares to investors in that state, although states no longer review fund

CALLOUT

Investment Company Institute

The Investment Company Institute (ICI) is the organization that established the advisory groups on independent directors and personal trading discussed later in this Chapter. The best practices recommended by these groups have become industry standards and sometimes SEC requirements. However, the ICI is not a self-regulatory organization like the NASD; rather, it is a trade organization that represents the mutual fund industry on legislative and regulatory issues. The ICI also holds well-attended conferences for industry participants, generates useful materials for investor education and operates a mutual insurance company for the fund industry.

Founded in 1940, the ICI derives its strength from its excellent staff and broad membership. It effectively represents almost all of the significant fund complexes in the United States, with approximately 95% of the fund industry's assets held by more than 78 million individual shareholders. As of December 31, 2000, ICI membership included 8,444 mutual funds, 490 closed-end funds and 8 sponsors of UITs. This breadth generally has allowed the fund industry to speak with one voice before Congress, the SEC and the IRS; by contrast, there are several groups representing different segments of the banking and insurance industries. However, as more managers of fund complexes become part of larger financial conglomerates, it will be a challenge for the ICI to retain its historic role as an effective advocate for mutual funds.

prospectuses or advertising. Instead, the states focus on monitoring the activities of small investment advisers and policing the sales practices of local broker-dealers.

III. Internet and Privacy

With the rising popularity of the Internet, the mutual fund industry has tried to take advantage of electronic commerce to improve customer communications and reduce paperwork costs, while providing better disclosure to fund shareholders. However, the computerization of customer information has put new emphasis on their privacy concerns, especially in light of 1999 legislation that allowed banks to combine with other financial institutions more freely.

A. Electronic Disclosures

Since 1995, the SEC has permitted almost all disclosure documents of mutual funds to be delivered electronically to fund shareholders who consent to electronic delivery. In the past, the SEC has required that such consent by fund shareholders be in writing after receiving appropriate information. More recently, the SEC has allowed mutual funds and other financial intermediaries to obtain informed consent to electronic delivery by telephone in a manner that ensures the consent's authenticity. A record of the telephonic consent must be maintained with as much detail as any written consent, including whether the consent is global—that is, relating to all documents to be delivered. The SEC has made it clear that an investor with a brokerage account or an account at another type of intermediary may give a global consent to the electronic delivery of all documents of multiple issuers, including mutual funds from various fund complexes, as long as the consent is informed. Thus, most fund sponsors try to obtain one written or telephonic consent from every fund shareholder authorizing the electronic delivery of all fund documents. Furthermore, fund sponsors rely on intermediaries' distributing fund products and the operators of fund marketplaces to obtain global consents to electronic delivery of fund documents. (For electronic consents, see "Electronic Signatures.")

To service electronic customers, most fund complexes post on their websites all of the required disclosure documents for all the funds in the complex—current fund prospectuses, as well as annual and semiannual reports of the funds. In addition, the websites typically provide fund shareholders with their quarterly or monthly account statements, as well as confirmations of fund transactions (purchases, redemptions or exchanges). Such online disclosure and customer reporting results in substantial savings to funds in paperwork processing, while allowing fund shareholders to choose which documents they want to read electronically. In quarterly newsletters or account statements (or both), a fund sponsor usually provides a schedule of regular updates of its prospectuses, as well as the publication schedule of annual and semiannual fund reports. However, if a fund makes a significant unscheduled amendment to its prospectus (e.g., the imposition of a redemption fee), then the fund must mail or email notice of such amendment to all fund shareholders (including those who have consented to electronic delivery).

Besides legal disclosures and customer reports, these websites provide fund shareholders with a wealth of information about the fund complex. For example, websites typically include information on fund performance and the background of portfolio managers, a description of new fund products and an explanation of the various services offered by the complex, as well as an array of computerized tools for college or retirement planning. In addition, many websites of fund complexes offer hyperlinks whereby shareholders can access material from third parties that may be of interest to fund shareholders. These materials may include magazine articles on funds, commentary on pending legislation or advertisements for other financial products. The SEC has identified a list of relevant factors in determining whether the fund complex will be responsible legally for the accuracy of information on a third party's website hyperlinked to the complex's website. These factors include the context of the hyperlink on the complex's site, the layout of the hyperlinked information on the third party's site and the absence or presence of precautions against investor confusion about the source of the hyperlinked information.

The treatment of mutual fund advertising on the Internet raises special legal issues. As a general principle, the SEC has declared that when a securities issuer (including a mutual fund) embeds a hyperlink to a website within a document required to be filed or delivered under the federal securities laws, the issuer should always be deemed to have adopted the hyperlinked information for purposes of the antifraud provisions of those laws. Unlike other issuers of securities, however, mutual funds are required to file their advertisements with the NASD under the 1940 Act. Recognizing this unusual situation, the SEC has announced that mutual funds will not be automatically responsible for all hyperlinked information from fund advertisements; rather, responsibility will be determined under the facts and circumstances of each case according to factors such

CALLOUT
Electronic Signatures

In June 2000, Congress passed the Electronic Signatures in Global and National Commerce Act (E-Sign), which provides that signatures and contracts may not be denied legal validity or enforceability solely because they are in electronic form. By clarifying federal law and overriding state law (with limited exceptions), E-Sign generally facilitates the ability of fund complexes to establish and service customer accounts, conduct transactions and obtain or provide documentation on an electronic basis.

E-Sign sets forth detailed requirements for consumer consent to the use of electronic records or signatures, preceded by clear and conspicuous disclosures.

For any consent obtained prior to October 1, 2000, mutual funds may continue to rely on SEC rules. For consents obtained after that date, the SEC and other agencies are allowed to flesh out E-Sign's requirements in a manner consistent with their regulatory mandates.

E-Sign requires that when an electronic record is used to satisfy a legal requirement for a writing, the electronic record must be in a form that can be retained and accurately reproduced for later reference. Electronic records used for this purpose must accurately reflect the substantive information in the record that is required to be retained, as opposed to computer codes or other extraneous data. Thus, fund complexes should be able to use electronic records in connection with fund applications and transfers. Indeed, they should be able to convert into electronic form existing paper records, even those for which originals must be retained.

as the ones mentioned above for hyperlinks of fund websites. In the SEC's view, this approach will encourage fund sponsors to provide investors with third-party material that will assist them in making informed decisions, while discouraging funds from providing investors with inaccurate or misleading hyperlinks.

B. Customer Privacy

Although privacy has been a serious concern for investors over the years, this concern has been heightened recently by the confluence of two factors: the increasing collection of customer information on computer systems and the emergence of financial conglomerates combining a variety of financial services. When Congress broke down the remaining legal barriers among banks, insurance and securities firms in the Gramm-Leach-Bliley Act (GLB) of 1999, it adopted a federal set of privacy rules for individual customers of mutual funds and other financial institutions.

The scope of these privacy rules as applied to mutual funds is complicated. These privacy rules apply to any individual holder of mutual fund shares but not to corporations, trusts or partnerships. For instance, the privacy rules apply to individuals who establish an individual retirement account (IRA) with any financial institution, but not to a financial institution that serves as a trustee or fiduciary of a company's employee benefit plan. Nor do the federal privacy rules apply to an individual who makes anonymous use of online financial tools offered by a fund website or to an individual who merely requests a fund prospectus without submitting an application to purchase fund shares.[3] Moreover, an individual is not a customer of a mutual fund if he or she purchases fund shares through a broker-dealer that serves as record owner of the shares on the books of the fund. In that case, the individual would be a customer of the broker-dealer, which would be required to comply with the federal privacy rules. On the other hand, an individual is a customer of a mutual fund if he or she purchases fund shares through a broker-dealer and is the record owner of the shares on the books of the fund.

Under the GLB, every mutual fund and the mutual fund's distributor must send out a privacy notice explaining its privacy policies to fund customers and providing them with an opportunity to opt out of certain disclosures to certain persons. More specifically, the regulations permit a financial institution to disclose a customer's personal financial information to any affiliate, as long as that institution has sent that customer a privacy notice explaining its policies toward its affiliates. By contrast, disclosures of a customer's personal financial information to nonaffiliates generally are prohibited if the customer opts out after receiving a privacy notice. It bears emphasis that these federal privacy rules are subject to heated debate in Congress and that states retain the authority to impose stricter privacy rules than the GLB.

A fund as well as the fund's distributor must send to every customer an initial privacy notice on opening an account and subsequent notices on an annual basis. Many fund complexes send out joint privacy notices from the fund and the fund's distributor. If a fund complex's privacy policies change materially within the year, it must send an updated privacy notice to all its customers. The notice must explain clearly and accurately the categories of personal financial information that a fund complex collects from customers, the categories of personal financial information that a fund complex intends to disclose to its affiliates and the categories of affiliates (plus exceptions) to which such disclosures may be made. For this purpose, personal financial information potentially encompasses all information that a customer supplies to a financial institution or a financial institution otherwise obtains, in connection with providing a financial product or service to a customer. Such information also includes any nonpublic customer list (such as names, addresses or telephone numbers) that is derived from nonpublic personal financial information.

The affiliates of a mutual fund potentially cover the fund sponsor, its principal underwriter and the investment adviser, as well as those entities for other funds in the complex. The affiliates of a mutual fund may also cover banks, insurance companies and other financial institutions within the same financial conglomerate. Moreover, the GLB allows the sharing of a customer's personal financial information with certain entities that work together with the fund complex, although they technically might not qualify as affiliates under common control. One such entity would be an external transfer agent or operations center that is hired by the fund to process transactions or answer customer inquiries. Another such entity would be a firm that markets the financial institution's own financial products or services pursuant to a joint marketing agreement with that institution.

By contrast, a mutual fund or other financial institution may not provide a customer's personal financial information to any nonaffiliate (outside the exceptions mentioned above) unless the fund or financial institution provides the customer with an Opt-Out Notice. That notice must identify all categories of information that may be disclosed as well as all categories of nonaffiliates that may receive such information.

It also must provide a reasonable means by which the customer may exercise his or her right to opt out. It is not reasonable to require a customer to write a letter in order to opt out. Instead, a reasonable means to opt out includes a check-off box in a prominent position, a toll-free number to call, a printed reply form accompanying the notice or a form that can be sent back by email by fund customers who have already agreed to electronic delivery of fund documents.

IV. *Substantive Regulation*

In contrast to the prospectus requirements of the 1933 Act and the reporting requirements of the 1934 Act, which focus on the disclosure of information, the 1940 Act prohibits a broad range of conduct and mandates various types of behavior by the fund and its affiliates.

A. *Limits on Sales Charges*

First, the 1940 Act establishes limits on charges related to the sales of mutual fund shares. Front-end sales loads are commissions paid to a distributor by investors before they buy fund shares. Front-end sales loads may not exceed 8½%, although most front-end sales loads are in the 4% to 6% range. Back-end sales loads are paid by investors when they leave a fund; these often are called contingent deferred sales loads (CDSCs) because they decrease in amount as the holding period increases. For example, a CDSC might be 5% after the first year, 4% after the second year and so on. If an investor exchanges shares from one fund to another in the same complex, the investor is not allowed to be charged a CDSC; rather, the time spent in the initial fund is added to the time spent in the next fund for purposes of computing the holding period for the CDSC.

A 12b-1 fee is a fee paid annually by the fund to a distributor of its shares; it is effectively a sales charge paid on an installment plan instead of a lump sum. For example, a fund each year may pay 0.50%—50 basis points (bp)—of its assets to its distributor to compensate the distributor for its sales efforts. A fund may utilize a 12b-1 fee only or may combine a 12b-1 fee with some type of sales load. Under SEC rules, a fund must obtain shareholder approval before adopting a 12b-1 plan and director approval of such plan annually thereafter.

The NASD sets the detailed rules on sales loads and 12b-1 fees for mutual funds pursuant to the framework established by the 1940 Act and the SEC. NASD rules permit the waiver of sales loads for objectively defined classes, such as retirement plans, and allow reductions in sales loads for large purchases of fund shares. The NASD rules limit the amount of 12b-1 fees charged annually by a mutual fund, generally to 1% (100 bp) per year. The NASD also has an elaborate formula limiting the total amount of 12b-1 fees (plus sales loads) that a fund may charge over its lifetime. A fund with a Rule 12b-1 plan generally is limited to an aggregate sales charge of 7.25% or 6.25% (both with an annual interest rate adjustment), depending on whether the fund pays a service fee. The NASD allows a fund to be advertised as no load only if it charges no sales loads and has a 12b-1 fee no more than 0.25% (25 bp).

B. Limits on Portfolio Investments

Second, the 1940 Act establishes limits on the portfolio investments made by a mutual fund. A mutual fund must focus its investments on the investment objectives and strategies described in the fund's prospectus. In addition, the 1940 Act requires mutual funds to concentrate on relatively liquid securities that can be priced daily and can be converted quickly to meet redemption requests. Conversely, a mutual fund generally may not hold more than 15% of its assets in illiquid securities (10% for a money market fund). This liquidity requirement distinguishes mutual funds from other types of financial intermediaries; it forces mutual funds to buy mainly securities of public companies traded on established markets.

A mutual fund may choose to stop offering to sell its securities to all or some investors. For example, a fund may be closed to all new purchasers while continuing to sell shares to existing shareholders. However, a mutual fund must always stand ready to redeem its shares every day at their NAV next determined after the fund receives the redemption request. Accordingly, the 1940 Act requires mutual funds to determine a NAV once each business day (typically at 4:00 P.M., Eastern Time). This requirement imposes a more rigorous discipline on fund managers than financial institutions that mark to market their portfolios (place a current value on the securities in their portfolio) monthly or quarterly. Fund managers cannot delay addressing an issue materially affecting a security held by a fund, such as a bankruptcy threat or a tender offer; instead, they must value every portfolio security every day. Although a fund must price a redemption request at the next determined NAV, it normally makes payment to the redeeming shareholder (or another fund in the case of an exchange) on the next business day following the business day on which the redemption was received (but payment may be delayed up to seven days in exceptional circumstances). A fund may meet a redemption request from cash on hand or by selling securities in its portfolio (equity sales typically take three business days to settle).

The 1940 Act also establishes tight restrictions on the ability of mutual funds to issue debt securities or borrow money. These restrictions are designed to constrain mutual funds from becoming leveraged investment vehicles. For the same reason, a mutual fund is limited in effecting short sales, that is, selling a security one does not own in the hopes of buying it back later at a lower price. Accordingly, only a handful of mutual funds use leverage or short selling as a principal investment strategy.

C. Prohibitions on Transactions Between Mutual Funds and Affiliates

Third, Section 17 of the 1940 Act contains extensive prohibitions on transactions between mutual funds and their affiliates, broadly defined to include anyone holding more than 5% of the voting stock of a fund or its manager and any entity if more than 5% of its voting stock is held by the fund or its manager. As an illustration, if a company owns 6% of a fund's investment adviser, the company would be prohibited from buying portfolio securities from that fund. Similarly, if a bank owned 6% of a fund's shares, that fund generally would be prohibited from buying securities of that bank. This extensive range of prohibitions is designed to avoid situations raising possible conflicts of interests, even if they do not involve actual abuses. For this reason, the 1940 Act gives the SEC broad authority to grant exemptions to the Section 17 prohibitions on affiliated transactions—by order relating to a specific fund or by rule granting relief to all mutual funds. Since these prohibitions cover such an extensive range of situations, many of which do not involve actual abuse, the SEC has issued many exemptions under Section 17 with extensive conditions to protect the interests of fund shareholders.

More broadly, the 1940 Act provides the SEC with the authority to exempt any person, entity, security or transaction from any provision of the 1940 Act if the exemption meets certain general standards: the exemption must be necessary or appropriate in the public interest and consistent with the protection of investors. The SEC regularly uses this authority to issue rules that provide broad exemptions from specific provisions in the 1940 Act or to issue an exemption from a number of provisions in the 1940 Act for a specific transaction. For example, as a result of a rule, money market funds are permitted to value their assets using amortized cost rather than current market value as generally required under the 1940 Act. This flexibility to issue exemptions allows the SEC to adapt to market developments not foreseen when the 1940 Act was drafted without the delay and complexity involved with a legislative amendment.

V. *Independent Directors*

The 1940 Act gives special powers to "disinterested" directors or trustees of a mutual fund, often called the independent directors of a fund. Under the 1940 Act, an independent director may not be affiliated with the fund's investment adviser and must meet other tests of independence. Under the 1940 Act, independent directors must constitute at least 40% of all mutual fund boards and a majority of the board if the fund's principal underwriter is affiliated with the fund's adviser. In general, shareholders elect all directors, except that incumbent directors can appoint additional directors as long as at least two-thirds of the directors have been elected by the shareholders. In most funds, the independent directors act as a nominating committee for new directors; this procedure is required if a fund adopts a 12b-1 plan. Under the SEC's recently adopted rules, discussed below, independent directors will constitute a majority of almost all fund boards and will serve as the nominating committee for such boards.

Independent directors often serve on the boards of all funds in a complex, although some complexes have several sets of independent directors—for example, one set for money market funds and another set for equity funds. The total compensation of independent directors, which is disclosed in fund proxy statements, ranges from below $50,000 per year for smaller complexes to over $200,000 per year for the largest complexes. Critics have charged that independent directors cannot properly oversee all the funds in a large complex and that their interlocking directorships in a complex create an inherent conflict of interest. Defenders maintain that independent directors can split into several investment committees to review all funds in the complex on a regular basis. Defenders also explain that service on multiple boards in the same complex allows directors to make equitable allocations of expenses across all funds or groups of funds. For example, almost all complexes handle customer inquiries through a telephone system available to all funds, and many complexes organize equity research and trading to support all equity funds. After several rounds of litigation, the courts generally have concluded that service of directors on multiple boards in the same fund complex is permissible. Furthermore, director service on multiple boards in the same fund complex is considered "best practice" by the ICI Advisory Group on independent directors. (See "Advisory Group on Best Practices for Directors," recommendation 12.)

Independent directors generally are supposed to serve as watchdogs on behalf of fund shareholders—as their elected representatives, monitoring the activities of the fund adviser and other service providers. Under many SEC rules and exemptions, such as those under Section 17 discussed above, independent directors must approve in advance or review periodically specific actions by the fund's investment adviser. On an annual basis, the independent directors must negotiate and approve the contract between the fund and its transfer agent. (See Chapter Nine on transfer agency contracts.) Most important, the independent directors must annually approve the management contract between the fund and its investment adviser. Although independent directors rarely fire a fund's adviser, they do negotiate for lower fees and better services from the adviser.

As part of the annual review of the management contract, a fund's independent directors receive large volumes of materials from the investment adviser, as well as extensive data on fund performance and expenses prepared by third parties such as Lipper. These materials generally include statistics about the fund's performance relative to the market and its peers, the fund's level of sales and redemptions over various periods, the fund's fee structure and level compared to other funds and the fund's profitability to the investment adviser.

In addition, the investment adviser usually presents less statistical information on the nature and quality of the services it provides to the fund and fund shareholders. These services might include, for instance, voting of proxies for fund holdings, coordination with the fund's custodians and answering inquiries from fund shareholders. On the other hand, an adviser typically presents information on ancillary benefits that it or its affiliates may receive as a result of its relationship with the fund. These ancillary benefits might include, for instance, serving as trustee for pension accounts or brokerage commissions from fund trades.

With the significant growth and change in the mutual fund industry over the past decade, the role of independent directors has evolved. New types of funds, new distribution channels and complex relationships among funds, advisers, service providers, broker-dealers and others have made the role of independent directors more complicated and important. As a result, under the auspices of the ICI, an Advisory Group in 1999 identified "best practices" for independent directors to represent the interests of mutual fund shareholders effectively. (See "Advisory Group on Best Practices for Directors.")

In early 2001, the SEC adopted three sets of rules relating to the independence of directors. First, the SEC imposed several new preconditions for any fund seeking to take advantage of 10 commonly used SEC exemptive rules, such as the Section 17 rules exempting funds from the prohibitions on affiliated transactions (discussed previously):

1. Independent directors must constitute at least a majority of the fund's board of directors rather than the 1940 Act minimum of 40%.

2. Incumbent independent directors must select and nominate new independent directors, although the fund's adviser may be consulted during the process.

CALLOUT
Advisory Group on Best Practices for Directors

In summary, the Advisory Group recommended the following "best practices":

1. At least two-thirds of the directors of all investment companies be independent directors.
2. Former officers or directors of a fund's investment adviser, principal underwriter or certain of their affiliates not serve as independent directors of that fund.
3. Independent directors be selected and nominated by the incumbent independent directors.
4. Independent directors establish the appropriate compensation for serving on fund boards.
5. Fund directors invest in funds from the complex on whose boards they serve.
6. Independent directors have qualified investment company counsel who is independent from the investment adviser and the fund's other service providers, and have expressed authority to consult with the fund's independent auditors or other experts, as appropriate, when faced with issues that they believe require special expertise.
7. Independent directors complete on an annual basis a questionnaire on business, financial and family relationships with the adviser, principal underwriter, other service providers and their affiliates.
8. Fund boards establish Audit Committees, composed entirely of independent directors, pursuant to a written charter that spells out its duties and powers. The Audit Committee should meet with the fund's independent auditors at least once a year outside the presence of the investment adviser's representatives and secure from the auditor an annual representation of its independence from management.
9. Independent directors meet separately from the investment adviser in connection with their consideration of the fund's advisory and underwriting contracts and otherwise as they deem appropriate.
10. Independent directors designate one or more "lead" independent directors.
11. Fund boards obtain directors' and officers' errors and omissions, insurance coverage and/or indemnification from the fund that is adequate to ensure the independence and effectiveness of independent directors.
12. Fund boards of directors generally be organized either as a unitary board for all the funds in a complex or as cluster boards for groups of funds within a complex, rather than as separate boards for each individual fund.
13. Fund boards adopt policies on retirement of directors.
14. Fund directors evaluate periodically the board's effectiveness.
15. New fund directors receive appropriate orientation and all fund directors keep abreast of industry and regulatory developments.

3. If the independent directors choose to retain legal counsel, such counsel must be independent of the fund's investment adviser and principal underwriter.

Second, the SEC adopted rules incorporating certain best practices of independent fund directors:

1. Allow mutual funds and their affiliates to purchase joint insurance policies (e.g., errors and omissions insurance) only if they do not exclude coverage for litigation between the independent directors and the fund's advisers.
2. Encourage funds to maintain an independent audit committee by exempting any such fund from the obligation to have shareholders approve the fund's selection of an independent accountant.

3. Relax the definition of "disinterested" director to prevent the inappropriate disqualification of independent directors with tangential relations to a fund.

Third, the SEC required funds to disclose in their proxy statements and other documents additional information about fund directors, such as:

1. Background data about the identity, business experience of each director, number of funds overseen and other directorships outside the fund complex.

2. Dollar ranges of holdings in each fund as well as aggregate holdings in all funds within the fund complex that the director oversees.

3. Information about potential conflicts of interest as a result of relationships, interests and transactions involving at least $60,000 between the fund and the independent director (as well as his or her immediate family).

4. Description of the board's role in fund governance, including a description of each standing committee of the board and the board's basis for approving the current advisory contract.

VI. *Enforcement and Ethical Codes*

All the rules and regulations for mutual funds are enforced vigorously by public and private parties. The SEC may bring various types of enforcement actions against funds, their advisers and their directors for material violations of the federal securities laws. Similarly, the NASD may bring disciplinary proceedings against any member firm or employee thereof for material violations of fund advertising or sales rules. In addition, fund shareholders may bring individual or class actions under the 1933 Act or other federal antifraud provisions for material misrepresentations or omissions in their fund's prospectus. More broadly, shareholders of a fund or a publicly traded company may bring individual or class actions under Section 10(b) of the 1934 Act for fraud or manipulation in connection with the trading of securities by a fund, a fund management company or an affiliate thereof.

Furthermore, fund shareholders may bring suits under the 1940 Act as well as applicable state law for alleged breaches of fiduciary duty by the fund's adviser, its directors or certain affiliated persons. In most cases, these suits must be brought as derivative actions in the name of the fund—as opposed to individual or class actions. In most derivative actions, fund shareholders must make a demand on directors not involved in the litigation before a suit may commence. However, fund shareholders have an express direct right of action under Section 36(b) of the 1940 Act to bring lawsuits challenging a fund's advisory fee they believe is excessive. Courts have interpreted "excessive" to invalidate advisory fees if they are so large that they bear no reasonable relationship to the services provided and they could not have been the result of arm's-length bargaining. The following factors have been used by courts in determining whether a management fee is excessive:[4]

1. The nature and quality of the services provided to shareholders.

2. The profitability of the investment adviser with respect to the fund.

3. The economies of scale in operating a fund as it grows.

4. The fee structures of other funds.

5. The indirect profits to the investment adviser as a result of the relationship to the fund.

6. The independence and conscientiousness of the directors.

Subject to such a broad range of public and private lawsuits, most fund complexes have hired inside and outside counsel to help interpret the various disclosure and other requirements applicable to mutual funds and their advisers. The largest fund complexes typically have a legal department of significant size, as well as a compliance unit to monitor day-to-day adherence to the panoply of rules affecting mutual funds and their affiliates. In major cities, many law firms have large divisions specializing in mutual fund practice. The independent directors of most large fund complexes also retain legal counsel independent of the fund's adviser or principal underwriter. In litigation, judges have given considerable weight to the business judgment of the independent directors, especially if they were advised by independent counsel.

One unique aspect of mutual fund regulation involves the Code of Ethics (Code), which must be adopted and enforced by every mutual fund complex. The provisions of the Code often go beyond the restrictions in the federal securities laws by prohibiting practices that may be unethical though not necessarily illegal. For example, it is already illegal for a portfolio manager to front-run his or her fund by buying a stock for a personal account and then buying the same stock for a fund managed by him or her to boost the stock's price. The Code of Ethics prohibits a much broader range of personal trading by portfolio managers than front running. Moreover, each mutual fund complex is given considerable leeway in fashioning and implementing a Code that is appropriate for that complex. Thus, the Code represents a form of self-regulation.

Specifically, SEC Rule 17j-1 under the 1940 Act requires every mutual fund (except money market funds), its investment adviser and its principal underwriter to adopt a Code of Ethics meeting certain criteria. First, the Code must be designed reasonably to prevent fraudulent and manipulative practices. This has traditionally focused on personal trading of individual securities by portfolio managers, analysts and others involved in making investment decisions for the mutual funds. However, the Rule exempts trading in U.S. government securities, bank certificates of deposit and commercial paper as well as transactions in shares issued by mutual funds, because they do not present potential conflicts of interest between funds and fund employees. On the other hand, investments in public offerings and private placements by investment professionals must be preapproved specifically by the Code of Ethics officer.

Second, the Code must require "access persons" to file reports with the fund complex on their personal trading at least quarterly, as well as on their personal securities holdings initially upon becoming an access person and annually thereafter. The Rule broadly defines "access person" to include any employee of a fund or its investment adviser "who, in connection with his or her regular functions or duties, makes, participates in, or obtains information regarding the purchase or sale of a security by a registered investment company, on whose functions relate to the making of any recommendation with respect to the purchases or sales." This definition is so broad it may include fund accountants and lawyers, as well as portfolio managers and analysts.

Third, the Code must include reasonable procedures for a mutual fund complex to maintain records of personal trading and enforce the provisions of the Code. Through examination and inspections, the SEC reviews each complex's Code and its procedures for enforcing the Code's provisions. The SEC also has instituted enforcement actions in cases where it finds that fund personnel are violating the Code or provisions of the federal securities laws.

Fourth, the Code as well as any material changes to it must be approved by the directors, including a majority of the independent directors. In addition, the directors must receive annually a report that summarizes any material violations of the Code and certifies that the fund, investment adviser and principal underwriter each have adopted procedures reasonably designed to prevent access persons from violating their Code.

Fifth, the Statement of Additional Information for a fund is required to disclose that the fund and its investment adviser and principal underwriter have adopted a Code of Ethics and whether the Code permits access persons to engage in personal trading. In addition, the full text of a fund complex's Code of Ethics must be filed with the SEC as part of a fund's registration statement, which is accessible to the investing public through the SEC's electronic system for disclosure documents.

By contrast, neither federal nor state laws require Codes of Ethics for personal trading by employees of other financial institutions, such as commercial banks, insurance companies or pension funds. The employees of these financial institutions are subject mainly to general fiduciary restrictions against certain conflicts of interest. Indeed, the SEC does not impose the requirements of a Code of Ethics on investment advisers to entities other than mutual funds; for example, an investment adviser to a hedge fund has no SEC obligation to adopt a Code of Ethics.

Despite the stricter rules for personal trading by mutual fund employees as compared to employees of other financial institutions, the press ran many critical reports on personal trading by fund portfolio managers during the 1990s. These reports focused on allegations of personal trading at the expense of funds by a few well-known portfolio managers and generated concerns by mutual fund complexes about how they were being perceived by the investing public. As a result, the ICI appointed a Blue Ribbon Advisory Group in 1994 to make recommendations about bolstering the Code of Ethics. (See "Blue Ribbon Advisory Group on Personal Investing.") Although these recommendations did not have the force of law, they were adopted in substance by mutual fund complexes with over 95% of the industry's assets. Table 3.2 summarizes the key provisions of the Code of Ethics of the five largest mutual fund complexes in the mid-1990s. Some of these recommendations subsequently were incorporated into the SEC rules, discussed above; other recommendations became standard industry practice.

TABLE 3.2

Code of ethics: How investments are restricted . . . Here are the rules governing personal trading by fund managers and other employees with knowledge of fund trading that are in effect at the five largest mutual fund companies

	Fidelity Investments	Vanguard Group	Capital Research and Management	Merrill Lynch Asset Management	Franklin Templeton Group
Assets under management, [July 1996]	$391.9 billion	$208.5 billion	$155.1 billion	$147.0 billion	$106.8 billion
Participation in initial public offering	Prohibited	Prohibited	Prohibited	Prohibited	Prohibited
Private in placement investments	Restricted	Restricted	Restricted	Restricted	Restricted
Holding period (minimum time between purchase and sale of the same security)	60 calendar days	60 calendar days	60 calendar days	60 calendar days	60 calendar days
Blackout period (ban on trading in a security before and after the company's funds trade in it)	7 calendar days	7 calendar days If a Vanguard fund buys the same security within 7 days of an employee's purchase, the employee must hold the security for at least six months.	7 calendar days	After a Merrill Lynch fund buys a security, employees may not sell it for 30 days or buy it for 15 days. After a Merrill Lynch fund sells a security, employees may not sell it for 7 days or buy it for 30 days.	5 business days
Short selling	Employees may not sell short any securities in which Fidelity funds hold a long position, but short positions are allowed on securities Fidelity funds do not own, against the S&P100 and 500 indices, and "against the box."	Prohibited	Prohibited. Writing opinions is also prohibited.	Banned from selling a security short if the Merrill Lynch manager's fund or private account holds a long position in the same security.	No special restrictions

Source: Ann Wozencraft, "Managers' Personal Trades: What the SEC Wants You to Know," *New York Times*, July 21, 1996. Copyright © 1996 by the New York Times Co. Reprinted by permission.

CALLOUT
Blue Ribbon Advisory Group on Personal Investing

The recommendations of the Blue Ribbon Advisory Group fall into three main categories: substantive restrictions on personal investing, procedures for ensuring compliance with the Code and disclosure of the key provisions of the Code.

The substantive restrictions include a recommended prohibition against fund investment personnel acquiring securities in an IPO. This prohibition is designed to preclude the possibility of fund investment personnel obtaining an allocation in a sought-after IPO when that allocation could have gone to the fund. Another recommendation, subsequently adopted by the SEC, prohibits the purchase by fund investment personnel of securities in a private placement without express prior approval by the fund complex's Ethics officer. In most cases, mutual funds do not purchase securities in a private placement; such securities are not publicly tradable and therefore are illiquid. If the company subsequently goes public, the fund investment personnel should disclose his or her interest, and the fund's decision to participate in the IPO should be subject to an independent review.

More generally, the Advisory Group recommended that any access person be prohibited from executing a securities transaction on a day during which a mutual fund in his or her complex has a pending order in the same security, until that order is executed or withdrawn. Because this prohibition is designed to prevent personal trades from materially hampering the execution of fund trades, it permits exceptions for de minimis trades by fund personnel. A more stringent trading prohibition is recommended for trades by a portfolio manager in relation to trades by his or her own fund in order to prevent even the potential for a conflict of interest. No portfolio manager should buy or sell a security within seven calendar days before and after his or her fund trades in that security.

But what if a portfolio manager places a personal trade because he or she hears about the prospect of a transaction by another portfolio manager for another fund? The Advisory Group recommended that all investment personnel be required to disgorge any profits from the purchase and sale, or sale and purchase, of the same (or equivalent) security within 60 calendar days. This disgorgement rule is based on the premise that any impact of fund trading on the price of a security will be dissipated within 60 days given the volatility of securities markets.

In addition, the Advisory Group recommended a basic antibribery provision. The Code of Ethics should prohibit all investment personnel from receiving any gift or other thing of more than de minimis value from any person or entity that does business with the mutual fund complex. On the corporate governance front, the Advisory Group recommended that the Code of Ethics generally should prohibit investment personnel from serving on the board of directors of any publicly traded company. This prohibition is designed to constrain the flow of inside information from a public company to a mutual fund that might invest in the securities of such a company. However, exceptions may be granted if board service would further the interests of fund shareholders and a " Fire Wall" could be established to address insider-trading issues.

On procedures to ensure compliance with the Code, the Advisory Group made a broad array of recommendations, many of which were later integrated into SEC Rule 17j-1. The Code of Ethics should require all access persons to direct their brokers to supply the fund complex with duplicate copies of confirmations of all personal securities transactions, as well as copies of all periodic account statements. Some fund complexes require all access persons to execute all securities transactions through only one broker designated by the complex. Other fund complexes rely on the NASD rule requiring all broker-dealers to notify a registered investment adviser to a mutual fund complex if any of its employees opens a brokerage account.

The Code of Ethics should require all access persons to "preclear" all personal securities transactions with an official designated by the fund complex. Such preclearance procedures should be designed reasonably to identify any prohibition or limitation applicable to the proposed investment. The Code of Ethics should also establish procedures to monitor personal securities transactions after preclearance has been granted.

The Code of Ethics should require all investment personnel to report all personal securities holdings to the fund complex upon commencement of employment and thereafter on an annual basis. On an annual basis, all access persons should be required to certify that they have read and understand the Code of Ethics and that they have complied with all applicable Code requirements. Each year, the investment manager of a mutual fund complex should prepare a report concerning per-

sonal trading for review by the independent directors of the relevant funds. The report should identify Code violations requiring significant remedial actions during the past year and suggest changes, if needed, in the provisions of the Code.

Finally, the Advisory Group recommended that every mutual fund disclose in appropriate documents the restrictions and procedures on personal securities transactions. These disclosure requirements essentially were incorporated into SEC Rule 17j-1.

REVIEW QUESTIONS

1. What are the critical differences between mutual funds and closed-end funds? Why do you think closed-end funds have declined in popularity relative to mutual funds?

2. Why do sophisticated investors try not to buy shares of a mutual fund immediately before its annual distribution of realized capital gains? What happens to the unrealized capital gains of a mutual fund?

3. What is the focus of the 1933 Act versus the 1940 Act? What is the difference in regulatory approach between these two Acts?

4. What is the name test rule? Does the rule apply to any of the following funds: Small Cap Fund, Value Fund, Europe Fund or International Fund?

5. May a mutual fund complex share customer information with an external transfer agency retained to process fund transactions? May a mutual fund complex share customer information with a company marketing credit cards?

6. What is the NASD? How does the role of the NASD relate to the role of the SEC with regard to mutual funds?

7. What are the legal maximums for sales loads and 12b-1 fees? May a fund charge a 12b-1 fee and still be advertised as a no-load fund?

8. What is the unique procedure available to fund shareholders in challenging a fund adviser's management fees as excessive? What factors do courts use in determining excessive fees?

DISCUSSION QUESTIONS

1. Should mutual funds be subject to more extensive regulation than industrial companies under the federal securities laws? Does the 1940 Act regulate conflicts of interest too strictly or too leniently?

2. Should annual distributions by mutual funds be taxed if they are reinvested by fund shareholders? Does it matter whether these distributions are realized capital gains or other types of income?

3. What are some advantages that the Internet provides to mutual fund managers and fund shareholders? What concerns are raised by the extensive use of the Internet in the fund industry? Have these concerns been met by applicable legal rules?

4. Are independent directors of mutual funds more or less powerful than the independent directors of a publicly traded U.S. company? Do you believe that adoption of the proposals of the Advisory Group and the SEC would make independent directors of mutual funds effective watchdogs for fund shareholders?

5. Should Congress ban all personal trading by mutual fund employees? Is the Code of Ethics unnecessary since all mutual fund employees are already subject to the antifraud and anti-manipulation rules in the federal securities laws?

NOTES

1. Unit trusts in England and investment trusts in Japan can be actively managed.
2. U.S. Congress, Joint Economic Committee, *Encouraging Personal Savings and Investment: Changing the Tax Treatment of Unrealized Capital Gains* (June 2000).
3. The federal privacy rules apply to a more limited degree to individual consumers of mutual funds. Consumers are individuals who obtain a financial product or service for personal, family or household use (e.g., setting up a personalized page on a mutual fund website). Consumers have more limited interaction with the mutual fund than customers, who have a continuing relationship with the mutual fund and expect continuing service or communication.
4. *Gartenberg* v. *Merrill Lynch Asset Management, Inc.*, 694 F.2d 923 (2nd Cir. 1982).

READING 3.1

*Advertising the Fund**

Kirkpatrick & Lockhart LLP

Mutual Fund Advertisements

As the United States fund industry has become increasingly competitive and diverse, flexibility in advertising has become more important. Although the basic statutory premise, to treat a written offer of a security as a prospectus, has remained unchanged, a number of specially designed advertising rules permit mutual funds and their advisers and distributors to provide more information to potential investors than industrial companies would be permitted to provide in connection with an offer of their securities. This recognizes that securities are in reality the product that a mutual fund has to sell. Advertising and sales literature must, however, be distributed within the structure permitted by the Securities Act of 1933 (1933 Act).

A. Restrictions on Advertising—Section 5 of the 1933 Act
    When a new mutual fund is established and registered with the SEC, there are three distinct periods in the process, each governed by different advertising rules.
    1. Preregistration period
        No offers, sales, sales literature or promotional activities are permitted during the period immediately preceding the filing of a registration statement with the SEC.
    2. Registration period
        From the time a registration statement is filed with the SEC until it is declared effective, only the following promotional activities are permitted: (i) distribution of "red-herring" prospectuses, (ii) Rule 134 "Tombstone" advertisements, and (iii) Rule 482 "omitting prospectus" advertisements.
    3. Post-effective period
        After the registration statement is declared effective, the following rules apply:
        a) The full prospectus, often referred to as the statutory prospectus, may be distributed freely;
        b) Advertisements that comply with Rules 134 and 135a may be distributed without a prospectus;
        c) Fund profiles which comply with Rule 498 may be used in advertising and mailed to prospective investors (see fund profile discussion);
        d) An omitting prospectus which complies with Rule 482 may be used in newspaper, magazine, radio, and television advertising, or mailed to potential investors; and
        e) All other sales literature must be accompanied or preceded by the statutory prospectus. These materials are referred to as "supplemental sales literature."
        f) The foregoing controls are all designed to ensure the primacy of the statutory prospectus in the selling process.

B. SEC Advertising Rules
    Section 5 of the 1933 Act prohibits offers of securities unless offered by a Section 10 prospectus. The term "offer" is broadly defined under federal securities laws to include any written communications designed to engender investor interest in a security. Section 2(10) of the 1933 Act defines prospectus to include any "circular, advertisement, letter or communication . . . which offers any security for sale." Section 5 of the 1933 Act prohibits a person from distributing a prospectus for any security unless it complies with strict disclosure requirements imposed by Section 10 of the 1933 Act (the content of the statutory prospectus is dictated by Section 10(a); a "summary prospectus" is permitted under Section 10(b)). Investment company marketing materials generally fall within the definition of a prospectus and thereby are subject to these disclosure requirements. However, SEC regulations offer several means of creating marketing materials which can be used to solicit investors without containing the disclosures found in a statutory prospectus, as follows:
    1. Fund Profile—Rule 498:
        A profile is a summary prospectus under Section 10(b) of the 1933 Act. It provides investors with a summary of key information about a fund presented in a standardized sequence, thereby allowing easy comparison of funds.

a) A profile must include the following information:

  (1) Risk/Return Summary (substantially identical to that for a statutory prospectus under Form N-1A):

    (a) Fund's investment objectives/goals.

    (b) Fund's principal investment strategies.

    (c) Principal risks of investing in the fund, including a narrative discussion and the risk return bar chart and table—performance information in the table must be updated as of the end of each calendar quarter as soon as practicable after the completion of the quarter.

    (d) Fee table.

  (2) Identification of the investment adviser and subadviser(s), the name and length of time that the portfolio manager has managed the fund, and the portfolio manager's business experience for the last 5 years.

  (3) How to purchase fund shares, including the minimum initial or subsequent investment requirements, the initial sales load, and, if applicable, initial sales load breakpoints or waivers.

  (4) How to sell fund shares, including that shares are redeemable, the procedures for redeeming shares, and any charges or sales loads that may be assessed upon redemption (including the existence of any waivers).

  (5) The terms and conditions under which the fund makes distributions, the reinvestment options for those distributions, and the expected tax treatment of the distributions.

  (6) A brief summary of other services available to fund investors.

b) A profile may be distributed through any means, including direct mail, print media, broadcast and electronic media.

c) The profile may include an investment application. Investors who receive the fund profile have the option of purchasing fund shares directly from the profile or requesting and reviewing the fund's prospectus. Thus, the profile can be used as a direct sales document.

d) An investor who purchases fund shares based on the profile must receive the statutory prospectus with the purchase confirmation.

e) A profile may describe more than one fund and, therefore, could be a useful means of providing investors information about related investment alternatives offered by a single fund group.

f) Plain English disclosure requirements apply to profiles.

g) Rule 482 advertising materials (discussed below) may accompany profiles.

h) Legally, the profile is a summary prospectus under Section 10(b), and a misleading profile may result in liability under Section 12 of the 1933 Act. To avoid confusion with the statutory prospectus, however, the SEC does not permit profiles to be labeled "prospectuses."

2. Tombstone Advertisements—Rule 134

a) The Tombstone Rule exempts from the definition of the term "prospectus" a notice, circular, advertisement, letter, or other communication published or transmitted to any person after a registration statement has been filed if it includes only the information permitted or required by the Rule. The content of marketing materials prepared in accordance with the Rule is limited to the information specifically listed in the Rule. The types of permissible information are substantially broader for mutual funds than for other kinds of issuers.

b) The Rule permits an advertisement to contain some or all of the following information:

  (1) A fund's classification and its general attributes

  (2) A description of its investment objectives, policies, and methods of operation

  (3) Offers, descriptions, and explanations of a company's products and services that do not constitute securities, provided that such offers, descriptions, and explanations do not directly relate to the desirability of owning or purchasing a security issued by the company and that all references to the company's securities contain statements permitted by or required by the Rule

  (4) Any corporate symbol or trademark of the company or its investment adviser

(5) Identification of the fund's principal officers and its investment adviser

(6) A pictorial illustration which is appropriate for the fund's prospectus but which does not include performance figures

(7) The aggregate net asset value of the company or of all of the companies managed by the fund's investment adviser as of the most recent practicable date

(8) A description of general economic conditions, retirement plans, or other goals to which an investment in the company may be directed; provided that, such description does not directly or indirectly relate to past performance or suggest achievement of investment objectives

(9) Any graphic design or attention-getting headline that does not involve performance figures

(10) A description of an offer to shareholders of shares at a reduced price or without the regular sales load charged

c) The tombstone advertisement must contain the following:

   (1) A statement as to whether the security is being offered in connection with a distribution by the issuer or by a security holder, or both, and whether the issue represents new financing or refunding or both

   (2) A legend which provides the name and address of a person or persons from whom a written prospectus may be obtained and states that an investor should read the prospectus carefully before investing or sending money

   (3) In the case of a money market fund, the legend required by Rule 482(a)(7), stating that an investment in the fund is neither insured nor guaranteed by the U.S. government and there can be no assurance that the fund will maintain a stable $1.00 share price

d) Under Rule 134(a)(13), a mutual fund advertisement that complies with Rule 134 may be combined with an advertisement for other services if the following conditions are met:

   (1) The other offers, descriptions, and explanations may not relate directly to the desirability of owning or purchasing securities issued by any fund;

   (2) All direct references in such communications to a mutual fund's securities may contain only the statements required or permitted by the other provisions of the Rule; and

   (3) All references to any fund must be placed in a separate and enclosed area in the communication.

3. Generic Advertising—Rule 135a

A notice, circular, advertisement, letter, sign or other communication, published or transmitted to any person, which does not specifically refer by name to the securities of a particular fund, to the fund itself, or to any other securities not exempt under Section 3(a) of the 1933 Act, is not an offer of any security if the following conditions are fulfilled:

a) The communication may contain only:

   (1) Explanatory information relating to securities of funds generally, or to the nature of funds, or to services offered to shareholders of funds

   (2) The mention or explanation of funds of different generic types or having various investment objectives, such as "balanced funds," "growth funds," "income funds," "leveraged funds," "specialty funds," "variable annuities," "bond funds," and "no-load funds"

   (3) Offers, descriptions and explanations of various products and services which are not securities, if the offers, descriptions and explanations do not relate directly to the desirability of owning or purchasing a security issued by a fund

   (4) An invitation to inquire for further information

b) The communication must contain the name and address of the registered broker or dealer or other person sponsoring the communication. If the communication contains a solicitation of inquiries, and if prospectuses for fund securities are to be sent or delivered in response to such inquiries, the communication must state the number of funds involved, and the fact that the sponsor of the communication is the principal underwriter or investment adviser of the funds.

c) If the communication describes any type of security, service or product, the person sponsoring the communication must offer for sale the security, service or product described in the communication.

4. "Omitting Prospectus"—Rule 482

a) This rule under the 1933 Act permits mutual fund advertisements containing more information than can appear in a Tombstone Ad (under Rule 134); in particular, data regarding fund performance may be included. However, the content of Rule 482 ads is limited to information "the substance of which" is contained in the fund's prospectus or Statement of Additional Information. Because Rule 482 material need not contain all of the information in a Section 10(a) prospectus, it is commonly known as an "omitting prospectus." These ads are the primary vehicle for communicating performance data to prospective investors and are subject to the following conditions:

   (1) The advertisement concerns a fund which is selling or proposing to sell its securities pursuant to a registration statement which has been filed;

   (2) It appears in a newspaper or magazine or is used on radio or television, or is mailed to prospective investors;

   (3) It contains only information the substance of which is included in the prospectus (or SAI);

   (4) It states, conspicuously, from whom a prospectus may be obtained and that an investor should read that prospectus carefully before investing;

   (5) It contains the boilerplate disclosure that the advertisement is not a prospectus; and

   (6) It may not contain or be accompanied by an application to purchase shares.

b) These advertisements are treated as prospectuses by the SEC (hence, the name "omitting prospectus").

c) A Rule 482 omitting prospectus for a money market fund must include a legend that any investment in the fund is neither federally insured nor guaranteed. If the fund holds itself out as maintaining a stable net asset value, it must state that there can be no assurance that the fund will be able to maintain a stable net asset value.

d) As noted, unlike advertisements and sales material relying on Rule 134 or 135a, Rule 482 material may contain performance data, provided that the substance of this information is found in the fund's prospectus. This data must be calculated in accordance with the specific computation methods prescribed by the SEC. Rule 482 also regulates the manner in which performance data are presented. Performance data must be computed based on methods specified in Form N-1A. The following is a summary of the requirements for Rule 482 materials that contain performance information:

   (1) Total Return: If total returns are advertised, the piece must include the 1-, 5-, and 10-year average annual returns (or life of fund, if shorter) as of the most recently completed calendar quarter.

   (2) Yield for non–money market funds: Non–money market funds may quote a yield calculated using a specific formula for the most recent 30-day period practicable. All non–money market fund yield quotations must be accompanied by 1-, 5-, and 10-year average annual returns.

   (3) Yield for money market funds: Money market funds may quote a current yield or a current yield accompanied by an effective yield, calculated by a specific formula for the most recent 7-day period practicable. Money market fund yields need not be accompanied by average annual total returns.

   (4) Taxable-equivalent yields: Funds with significant tax-exempt income may quote current yield and taxable-equivalent yield calculated using a specific formula.

   (5) Sales load and other fees: If a sales load or any other nonrecurring fee is charged, the ad must disclose the maximum amount of the load or fee. Total returns, both average annual and cumulative, must include the effect of the load or fee.

(6) Load waivers: When a fund has its load waived for a specific time period, or for a specific group of investors, the load must still be included in the average annual total return calculation.

(7) Reimbursement: If a fund is in any level of reimbursement, this fact must be disclosed, and yields calculated without the effects of reimbursement must also be stated.

(8) Nonstandardized performance data is permitted, but it must include all elements of return, and be accompanied by standardized total return data, which is equally prominent.

e) Performance data must be as of the most recent practicable date. For Rule 482 ads, this requirement is met if the total return information is as of the most recent calendar quarter-end prior to submission of the ad for publication. However, the SEC staff has recently emphasized that a performance advertisement in technical compliance with Rule 482 may nevertheless violate the anti-fraud rules if it does not show a material decline in performance that occurred subsequent to the quarter end.

f) The requirements with respect to presentation of fund performance data apply to Rule 482 advertisements, regardless of medium. For example, telephone systems that provide investors with performance information must also comply with Rule 482.

g) Beginning October 1, 2001*, certain fund advertisements must also show after-tax performance for a recent 1-, 5-, and 10-year period (or life of fund, if shorter), based on the highest federal income tax rate. This standardized after-tax information must be included (1) if the fund includes any after-tax returns in its advertisement or (2) if the fund includes other performance information together with representations that the fund is managed to limit taxes.

5. Sales Literature—Rule 156

Sales literature is advertising material that is preceded or accompanied by a statutory prospectus. It is defined to include "any communication (whether in writing, by radio, or by television) used by any other person to offer to sell or induce the sale of securities of any investment company." Sales literature is subject to fewer rules than tombstone, performance, or generic advertising.

Rule 156 under the 1933 Act reiterates general anti-fraud standards found elsewhere in the securities laws that relate to advertisements. The emphasis of the Rule is on the need for a balanced, truthful discussion of risks and benefits. Moreover, the Rule identifies areas which, in the SEC's experience, have provided the greatest opportunity for misleading statements. Rule 156 applies to all types of mutual fund sales material and advertising, not only to sales literature.

a) The main principle of Rule 156 is that in connection with the offer or sale of securities, investment companies may not use any form of sales literature that is materially misleading. Sales literature is considered misleading if it:

(1) contains an untrue statement of a material fact;

(2) omits to state a material fact necessary in order to make a statement made, in light of the circumstances of its use, not misleading; or

(3) contains statements about possible benefits connected with services to be provided without giving equal prominence to any associated limitations or risks.

b) Legends

(1) In a Rule 156 piece (supplemental sales literature), unless the text of the piece makes it clear that a prospectus was sent previously or that a prospectus is enclosed, the following disclaimer should appear in the piece:

"Not authorized for distribution unless preceded or accompanied by a current fund prospectus."

6. Rule 34b-1: This Rule requires sales literature to contain certain legends. It also requires any performance information presented in sales literature to meet the requirements of Rule 482 under the 1933 Act, including those governing the manner of calculation. The Rule provides that any mutual fund sales literature will be considered materially misleading if it fails to contain the information specified by the Rule.

---

* The SEC recently delayed the date for compliance with the rule covering after-tax performance in certain fund advertisements until December 1, 2001.

7. Newsletters: Some investment company complexes use newsletters to communicate with current shareholders or prospective investors. Newsletters contain a variety of articles, including those that describe new products or services offered by the investment company, or general articles intended to educate or inform readers on broad topics, such as retirement investing. Because most newsletters contain offering material, they must be filed with the NASD or the SEC, as applicable.

a) Rule 134 Material in Newsletters

   (1) A newsletter may contain Rule 134 material.

   (2) Rule 134 material may appear in the same newsletter as Rule 482 material.

   (3) Rule 134 material for more than one fund may be included in a single article if it is segregated so as to compose a single unit (Rule 134 unit).

   (4) More than one Rule 134 unit may appear in the same newsletter provided that each unit can be identified and tested to determine its compliance with Rule 134.

   (5) Each Rule 134 unit requires a legend, unless more than one Rule 134 unit appears on a page. In this case, a single legend satisfies the rule, provided that it is placed in such a way that it clearly applies to each unit on the page.

b) Rule 482 Material in Newsletters

   (1) Rule 482 material (each, a "482 unit") appearing in a newsletter must be segregated and presented as a separate unit. This requirement applies to a 482 unit that is part of a larger article.

   (2) If a Rule 482 unit relates to more than one fund, the information relating to each fund must be separate so that it can be identified and tested to determine its compliance with Rule 482.

   (3) If 482 material is included in a textual article, the following content and format requirements must be met:

   (4) The 482 material must appear as a distinct unit, separate from the rest of the article;

   (5) The content of the article must comply with Rule 482; and

   (6) Fund-specific material must be able to be identified as relating only to that fund.

c) Rule 482 Legends

   (1) Each 482 unit requires a legend, unless more than one Rule 482 unit appears on a page. In this case, a single legend satisfies the rule, provided that it is placed in such a way that it clearly applies to each unit on the page.

   (2) In a brochure or similar document that contains only Rule 482 material relating to a single fund, a legend may appear only once.

   (3) If 482 material is set forth in a table, legend(s) may be included only once at the end of the table, provided that they clearly relate to all of the funds in the table.

d) Rule 135a Material in Newsletters

   (1) Rule 135(a) material (generic advertising) may not appear in a newsletter that includes Rule 134 and Rule 482 material.

   (2) Rule 135(a) material may be included in newsletters that include only 135(a) material and non-offering material.

e) Free Writing (Non-Rule) Material in Newsletters

   (1) Free writing, while it may not be an offer when considered separately from the rest of a newsletter, may be an offer in the context of the newsletter. It must be tested with respect to:

     (a) the securities of each fund being offered or about to be offered by the investment company distributing the newsletter; and

     (c) the context of the newsletter and any accompanying materials.

f) Free writing that encourages investors to invest in a specific fund or funds offered by the investment company would likely be deemed an offer.

g) Free writing that is nonoffer material may be included in a newsletter, provided that it is segregated from Rule 134 and Rule 482 material.

h) Free writing that is an offer may be included in a newsletter only if it meets certain other requirements. . . .

:::::
:::::   **EXERCISE 3.1**

Designing a Short-Form Prospectus

Almost everyone agrees that the full prospectus for a mutual fund is too long, too complex and simply too boring for most investors. As a result, most investors do not read the entire full prospectus; instead, at most they read a few pages of the full prospectus and usually rely on other sources of information such as press articles, rating services and friends' suggestions.

To make fund disclosure documents simpler and more readable, the SEC and the fund industry have developed a short-form prospectus called the Profile. The Profile is designed to provide investors with the key items of information about a fund in an easy-to-read format such as questions and answers. The SEC requires all funds to address the same subjects in the same sequence in order to facilitate comparisons. According to the SEC, the profile should address nine subjects:

1. The fund's goals or objectives
2. The fund's main investment strategies
3. The main risks of investing in the fund
4. The fund's fees and expenses
5. The fund's investment adviser and portfolio manager
6. How investors may buy fund shares
7. How investors may sell fund shares
8. The fund's distributions and tax information
9. A summary of services available to typical investors

However, the Profile does not do away with the full prospectus. The cover or the beginning of the Profile must offer an 800 number for investors to call if they want to be sent the full prospectus before purchasing a fund. In addition, the Profile must offer to send investors a copy of other information about the fund (such as the fund's latest annual or semiannual report) if they wish to learn more about it. After an investor chooses to purchase a fund on the basis of the Profile, the investor must receive the full prospectus along with the confirmation of the purchase.

Thus, the Profile is part of a multi-tier system of disclosure. An investor may obtain more or less information from fund disclosure documents depending on the investor's needs or desires. The Profile is designed to provide the key information necessary for a purchase; an existing shareholder may use a full prospectus to find out more detailed information about taxes or fund wires. But some investors may want the full prospectus and the fund's annual report before purchasing; these documents can be obtained easily for free by making a call to an 800 number.

In the light of this background information, the Exercise asks you to draft your own Profile based on the full prospectus, which follows, for the Fidelity Dividend Growth Fund.

Discussion Questions

After considering the information an investor needs to make a decision about a fund, draft the contents of a readable short-form prospectus as a Profile for the Fidelity Dividend Growth Fund. In drafting the Profile, keep in mind the following questions:

1. What are the key pieces of information an investor needs to decide whether to invest in a fund?
2. How would you report fund performance? Which time periods would you choose, and why? Do you think funds should be required to compare past performance with a benchmark? How do you recommend that performance numbers be updated?
3. How do you recommend that the Profile disclose the risks associated with investing in the fund, so that prospective investors could compare the relative risks of different funds?
4. What fees should the fund company be required to disclose? Would you require that all fees that appear in the full prospectus also appear in the Profile?
5. What information does the investor need to know about the process of purchasing or selling shares of the fund? And what other information does the investor need regarding the logistics of doing business with the fund company?
6. In your opinion, should the Profile be distributed to prospective investors in lieu of the Section 10(a) prospectus? Or should the Profile always be accompanied by the more detailed prospectus?
7. Do you think all fund companies should be required to distribute Profiles in the same format (with the same questions)? Or should there be different rules for different types of funds, such as money market versus bond versus stock funds?
8. Should there be special types of Profiles for investors in mutual funds used in 401(k) plans, as compared to retail investors? Should fund Profiles be allowed to be displayed on the Internet?

Fidelity®

Dividend Growth
Fund

(fund number 330, trading symbol FDGFX)

Prospectus
September 28, 2000

82 Devonshire Street, Boston, MA 02109

Contents

Fund Summary

Investment Summary

Investment Objective

Dividend Growth Fund seeks capital appreciation.

Principal Investment Strategies

Fidelity Management & Research Company (FMR)'s principal investment strategies include:

• Normally investing primarily in common stocks.

• Normally investing at least 65% of total assets in companies that it believes have the potential for dividend growth by either increasing their dividends or commencing dividends, if none are currently paid.

• Investing in domestic and foreign issuers.

• Investing in either "growth" stocks or "value" stocks or both.

• Using fundamental analysis of each issuer's financial condition and industry position and market and economic conditions to select investments.

Principal Investment Risks

The fund is subject to the following principal investment risks:

• *Stock Market Volatility.* Stock markets are volatile and can decline significantly in response to adverse issuer, political, regulatory, market, or economic developments. Different parts of the market can react differently to these developments.

• *Foreign Exposure.* Foreign markets can be more volatile than the U.S. market due to increased risks of adverse issuer, political, regulatory, market, or economic developments and can perform differently from the U.S. market.

• *Issuer-Specific Changes.* The value of an individual security or particular type of security can be more volatile than the market as a whole and can perform differently from the value of the market as a whole.

An investment in the fund is not a deposit of a bank and is not insured or guaranteed by the Federal Deposit Insurance Corporation or any other government agency.

When you sell your shares of the fund, they could be worth more or less than what you paid for them.

Performance

The following information illustrates the changes in the fund's performance from year to year and compares the fund's performance to the performance of a market index and an average of the performance of similar funds over various periods of time. Returns are based on past results and are not an indication of future performance.

Fund Summary - continued

Year-by-Year Returns

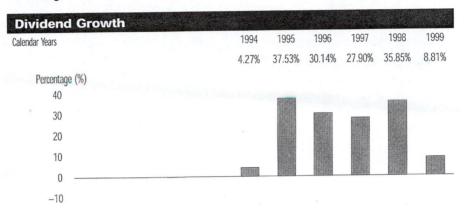

Dividend Growth						
Calendar Years	1994	1995	1996	1997	1998	1999
	4.27%	37.53%	30.14%	27.90%	35.85%	8.81%

During the periods shown in the chart for Dividend Growth, the highest return for a quarter was 19.53% (quarter ended December 31, 1998) and the lowest return for a quarter was –9.56% (quarter ended September 30, 1999).

The year-to-date return as of June 30, 2000 for Dividend Growth was 7.86%.

Average Annual Returns

For the periods ended December 31, 1999	Past 1 year	Past 5 years	Life of fund[A]
Dividend Growth	8.81%	27.61%	24.37%
S&P 500®	21.04%	28.56%	22.42%
Lipper Growth Funds Average	29.27%	25.04%	X

[A] *From April 27, 1993*

[X] *Not available*

Standard & Poor's 500[SM] Index (S&P 500®) is a market capitalization-weighted index of common stocks.

The Lipper Funds Average reflects the performance (excluding sales charges) of mutual funds with similar objectives.

Fee Table

The following table describes the fees and expenses that are incurred when you buy, hold, or sell shares of the fund. The annual fund operating expenses provided below for the fund do not reflect the effect of any reduction of certain expenses during the period.

Shareholder fees (paid by the investor directly)

Sales charge (load) on purchases and reinvested distributions	None
Deferred sales charge (load) on redemptions	None
Annual account maintenance fee (for accounts under $2,500)	$12.00

Annual fund operating expenses (paid from fund assets)

Management fee	0.54%
Distribution and Service (12b-1) fee	None
Other expenses	0.23%
Total annual fund operating expenses	0.77%

A portion of the brokerage commissions that the fund pays is used to reduce the fund's expenses. In addition, through arrangements with the fund's custodian and transfer agent, credits realized as a result of uninvested cash balances are used to reduce custodian and transfer agent expenses. Including these reductions, the total fund operating expenses would have been 0.74%.

This **example** helps you compare the cost of investing in the fund with the cost of investing in other mutual funds.

Let's say, hypothetically, that the fund's annual return is 5% and that your shareholder fees and the fund's annual operating expenses are exactly as described in the fee table. This example illustrates the effect of fees and expenses, but is not meant to suggest actual or expected fees and expenses or returns, all of which may vary. For every $10,000 you invested, here's how much you would pay in total expenses if you close your account at the end of each time period indicated:

1 year	$ 79
3 years	$ 246
5 years	$ 428
10 years	$ 954

Fund Basics

Investment Details

Investment Objective

Dividend Growth Fund seeks capital appreciation.

Principal Investment Strategies

FMR normally invests the fund's assets primarily in common stocks.

FMR normally invests at least 65% of the fund's total assets in companies that FMR believes have the potential for dividend growth by either increasing their dividends or commencing dividends, if none are currently paid.

The fund's strategy is based on the premise that dividends are an indication of a company's financial health and companies that are commencing or increasing their dividends have an enhanced potential for capital growth. Although FMR uses income to evaluate the fund's investments, the fund does not invest for income.

FMR may invest the fund's assets in securities of foreign issuers in addition to securities of domestic issuers.

FMR is not constrained by any particular investment style. At any given time, FMR may tend to buy "growth" stocks or "value" stocks, or a combination of both types. In buying and selling securities for the fund, FMR relies on fundamental analysis of each issuer and its potential for success in light of its current financial condition, its industry position, and economic and market conditions. Factors considered include growth potential, earnings estimates, and management.

FMR may lend the fund's securities to broker-dealers or other institutions to earn income for the fund.

FMR may use various techniques, such as buying and selling futures contracts, to increase or decrease the fund's exposure to changing security prices or other factors that affect security values. If FMR's strategies do not work as intended, the fund may not achieve its objective.

Description of Principal Security Types

Equity securities represent an ownership interest, or the right to acquire an ownership interest, in an issuer. Different types of equity securities provide different voting and dividend rights and priority in the event of the bankruptcy of the issuer. Equity securities include common stocks, preferred stocks, convertible securities, and warrants.

Principal Investment Risks

Many factors affect the fund's performance. The fund's share price changes daily based on changes in market conditions and interest rates and in response to other economic, political, or financial developments. The fund's reaction to these developments will be affected by the types of securities in which the fund invests, the financial condition, industry and economic sector, and geographic location of an issuer, and the fund's level of investment in the securities of that issuer. When you sell your shares of the fund, they could be worth more or less than what you paid for them.

The following factors can significantly affect the fund's performance:

Stock Market Volatility. The value of equity securities fluctuates in response to issuer, political, market, and economic developments. In the short term, equity prices can fluctuate dramatically in response to these developments. Different parts of the market and different types of equity securities can react differently to these developments. For example, large cap stocks can react differently from small cap stocks, and "growth" stocks can react differently from "value" stocks. Issuer, political, or economic developments can affect a single issuer, issuers within an industry or economic sector or geographic region, or the market as a whole.

Foreign Exposure. Foreign securities, foreign currencies, and securities issued by U.S. entities with substantial foreign operations can involve additional risks relating to political, economic, or regulatory conditions in foreign countries. These risks include fluctuations in foreign currencies; withholding or other taxes; trading, settlement, custodial, and other operational risks; and the less stringent investor protection and disclosure standards of some foreign markets. All of these factors can make foreign investments, especially those in emerging markets, more volatile and potentially less liquid than U.S. investments. In addition, foreign markets can perform differently from the U.S. market.

Issuer-Specific Changes. Changes in the financial condition of an issuer, changes in specific economic or political conditions that affect a particular type of security or issuer, and changes in general economic or political conditions can affect the value of an issuer's securities. The value of securities of smaller, less well-known issuers can be more volatile than that of larger issuers.

In response to market, economic, political, or other conditions, FMR may temporarily use a different investment strategy for defensive purposes. If FMR does so, different factors could affect the fund's performance and the fund may not achieve its investment objective.

Fundamental Investment Policies

The policy discussed below is fundamental, that is, subject to change only by shareholder approval.

Dividend Growth Fund seeks capital appreciation.

Valuing Shares

The fund is open for business each day the New York Stock Exchange (NYSE) is open.

The fund's net asset value per share (NAV) is the value of a single share. Fidelity normally calculates the fund's NAV as of the close of business of the NYSE, normally 4:00 p.m. Eastern time. However, NAV may be calculated earlier if trading on the NYSE is restricted or as permitted by the Securities and Exchange Commission (SEC). The fund's assets are valued as of this time for the purpose of computing the fund's NAV.

Fund Basics - continued

To the extent that the fund's assets are traded in other markets on days when the NYSE is closed, the value of the fund's assets may be affected on days when the fund is not open for business. In addition, trading in some of the fund's assets may not occur on days when the fund is open for business.

The fund's assets are valued primarily on the basis of market quotations. Certain short-term securities are valued on the basis of amortized cost. If market quotations are not readily available or do not accurately reflect fair value for a security or if a security's value has been materially affected by events occurring after the close of the exchange or market on which the security is principally traded (for example, a foreign exchange or market), that security may be valued by another method that the Board of Trustees believes accurately reflects fair value. A security's valuation may differ depending on the method used for determining value.

Shareholder Information

Buying and Selling Shares

General Information

Fidelity Investments was established in 1946 to manage one of America's first mutual funds. Today, Fidelity is the largest mutual fund company in the country, and is known as an innovative provider of high-quality financial services to individuals and institutions.

In addition to its mutual fund business, the company operates one of America's leading discount brokerage firms, Fidelity Brokerage Services LLC (FBS LLC). Fidelity is also a leader in providing tax-advantaged retirement plans for individuals investing on their own or through their employer.

For account, product, and service information, please use the following web site and phone numbers:

• For information over the Internet, visit Fidelity's web site at www.fidelity.com.

• For accessing account information automatically by phone, use Fidelity Automated Service Telephone (FAST®), 1-800-544-5555.

• For exchanges, redemptions, and account assistance, 1-800-544-6666.

• For mutual fund and brokerage information, 1-800-544-6666.

• For retirement information, 1-800-544-4774.

• TDD – Service for the Deaf and Hearing-Impaired, 1-800-544-0118 (9:00 a.m. – 9:00 p.m. Eastern time).

Please use the following addresses:

Buying Shares

Fidelity Investments
P.O. Box 770001
Cincinnati, OH 45277-0002

Overnight Express
Fidelity Investments
2300 Litton Lane – KH1A
Hebron, KY 41048

Selling Shares

Fidelity Investments
P.O. Box 660602
Dallas, TX 75266-0602

Overnight Express
Fidelity Investments
Attn: Redemptions – CP6I
400 East Las Colinas Blvd.
Irving, TX 75039-5587

You may buy or sell shares of the fund through a retirement account or an investment professional. If you invest through a retirement account or an investment professional, the procedures for buying, selling, and exchanging shares of the fund and the account features and policies may differ. Additional fees may also apply to your investment in the fund, including a transaction fee if you buy or sell shares of the fund through a broker or other investment professional.

Certain methods of contacting Fidelity, such as by telephone or electronically, may be unavailable or delayed (for example, during periods of unusual market activity). In addition, the level and type of service available may be restricted based on criteria established by Fidelity.

Shareholder Information - continued

The different ways to set up (register) your account with Fidelity are listed in the following table.

Ways to Set Up Your Account

Individual or Joint Tenant
For your general investment needs

Retirement
For tax-advantaged retirement savings

- **Traditional Individual Retirement Accounts (IRAs)**
- **Roth IRAs**
- **Rollover IRAs**
- **401(k) Plans and certain other 401(a)-qualified plans**
- **Keogh Plans**
- **SIMPLE IRAs**
- **Simplified Employee Pension Plans (SEP-IRAs)**
- **Salary Reduction SEP-IRAs (SARSEPs)**
- **403(b) Custodial Accounts**
- **Deferred Compensation Plans (457 Plans)**

Gifts or Transfers to a Minor (UGMA, UTMA)
To invest for a child's education or other future needs

Trust
For money being invested by a trust

Business or Organization
For investment needs of corporations, associations, partnerships, or other groups

Buying Shares

The price to buy one share of the fund is the fund's NAV. The fund's shares are sold without a sales charge.

Your shares will be bought at the next NAV calculated after your investment is received in proper form.

Short-term or excessive trading into and out of the fund may harm performance by disrupting portfolio management strategies and by increasing expenses. Accordingly, the fund may reject any purchase orders, including exchanges, particularly from market timers or investors who, in FMR's opinion, have a pattern of short-term or excessive trading or whose trading has been or may be disruptive to the fund. For these purposes, FMR may consider an investor's trading history in the fund or other Fidelity funds, and accounts under common ownership or control.

The fund may stop offering shares completely or may offer shares only on a limited basis, for a period of time or permanently.

When you place an order to buy shares, note the following:

- All of your purchases must be made in U.S. dollars and checks must be drawn on U.S. banks.

- Fidelity does not accept cash.

- When making a purchase with more than one check, each check must have a value of at least $50.

- Fidelity reserves the right to limit the number of checks processed at one time.

- If your check does not clear, your purchase will be canceled and you could be liable for any losses or fees the fund or Fidelity has incurred.

Certain financial institutions that have entered into sales agreements with Fidelity Distributors Corporation (FDC) may enter confirmed purchase orders on behalf of customers by phone, with payment to follow no later than the time when the fund is priced on the following business day. If payment is not received by that time, the order will be canceled and the financial institution could be held liable for resulting fees or losses.

There is no minimum account balance or initial or subsequent purchase minimum for investments through Fidelity Portfolio Advisory Services[SM], a qualified state tuition program, certain Fidelity retirement accounts funded through salary deduction, or accounts opened with the proceeds of distributions from such retirement accounts. In addition, the fund may waive or lower purchase minimums in other circumstances.

Minimums

To Open an Account	**$2,500**
For certain Fidelity retirement accounts[A]	$500
To Add to an Account	**$250**
Through regular investment plans	$100
Minimum Balance	**$2,000**
For certain Fidelity retirement accounts[A]	$500

[A] *Fidelity Traditional IRA, Roth IRA, Rollover IRA, SEP-IRA, and Keogh accounts.*

Key Information

Phone 1-800-544-6666	**To Open an Account** • Exchange from another Fidelity fund. Call the phone number at left. **To Add to an Account** • Exchange from another Fidelity fund. Call the phone number at left. • Use Fidelity Money Line[®] to transfer from your bank account.
Internet www.fidelity.com	**To Open an Account** • Complete and sign the application. Make your check payable to the complete name of the fund. Mail to the address under "Mail" below. **To Add to an Account** • Exchange from another Fidelity fund. • Use Fidelity Money Line to transfer from your bank account.
Mail **Fidelity Investments** **P.O. Box 770001** **Cincinnati, OH** **45277-0002**	**To Open an Account** • Complete and sign the application. Make your check payable to the complete name of the fund. Mail to the address at left. **To Add to an Account** • Make your check payable to the complete name of the fund. Indicate your fund account number on your check and mail to the address at left. • Exchange from another Fidelity fund. Send a letter of instruction to the address at left, including your name, the funds' names, the fund account numbers, and the dollar amount or number of shares to be exchanged.
In Person	**To Open an Account** • Bring your application and check to a Fidelity Investor Center. Call 1-800-544-9797 for the center nearest you. **To Add to an Account** • Bring your check to a Fidelity Investor Center. Call 1-800-544-9797 for the center nearest you.

Prospectus

Shareholder Information - continued

Wire	**To Open an Account** • Call 1-800-544-6666 to set up your account and to arrange a wire transaction. • Wire within 24 hours to: Bankers Trust Company, Bank Routing # 021001033, Account # 00163053. • Specify the complete name of the fund and include your new fund account number and your name. **To Add to an Account** • Wire to: Bankers Trust Company, Bank Routing # 021001033, Account # 00163053. • Specify the complete name of the fund and include your fund account number and your name.
Automatically	**To Open an Account** • Not available. **To Add to an Account** • Use Fidelity Automatic Account Builder® or Direct Deposit. • Use Fidelity Automatic Exchange Service to exchange from a Fidelity money market fund.

Selling Shares

The price to sell one share of the fund is the fund's NAV.

Your shares will be sold at the next NAV calculated after your order is received in proper form.

Certain requests must include a signature guarantee. It is designed to protect you and Fidelity from fraud. Your request must be made in writing and include a signature guarantee if any of the following situations apply:

• You wish to sell more than $100,000 worth of shares;

• Your account registration has changed within the last 15 or 30 days, depending on your account;

• The check is being mailed to a different address than the one on your account (record address);

• The check is being made payable to someone other than the account owner; or

• The redemption proceeds are being transferred to a Fidelity account with a different registration.

You should be able to obtain a signature guarantee from a bank, broker (including Fidelity Investor Centers), dealer, credit union (if authorized under state law), securities exchange or association, clearing agency, or savings association. A notary public cannot provide a signature guarantee.

When you place an order to sell shares, note the following:

• If you are selling some but not all of your shares, leave at least $2,000 worth of shares in the account to keep it open ($500 for retirement accounts), except accounts not subject to account minimums.

• Normally, Fidelity will process redemptions by the next business day, but Fidelity may take up to seven days to process redemptions if making immediate payment would adversely affect the fund.

• Redemption proceeds (other than exchanges) may be delayed until money from prior purchases sufficient to cover your redemption has been received and collected. This can take up to seven business days after a purchase.

• Redemptions may be suspended or payment dates postponed when the NYSE is closed (other than weekends or holidays), when trading on the NYSE is restricted, or as permitted by the SEC.

• Redemption proceeds may be paid in securities or other property rather than in cash if FMR determines it is in the best interests of the fund.

• You will not receive interest on amounts represented by uncashed redemption checks.

• Unless otherwise instructed, Fidelity will send a check to the record address.

Key Information

Phone **1-800-544-6666**	• Call the phone number at left to initiate a wire transaction or to request a check for your redemption. • Use Fidelity Money Line to transfer to your bank account. • Exchange to another Fidelity fund. Call the phone number at left.
Internet **www.fidelity.com**	• Exchange to another Fidelity fund. • Use Fidelity Money Line to transfer to your bank account.
Mail **Fidelity Investments** **P.O. Box 660602** **Dallas, TX** **75266-0602**	**Individual, Joint Tenant, Sole Proprietorship, UGMA, UTMA** • Send a letter of instruction to the address at left, including your name, the fund's name, your fund account number, and the dollar amount or number of shares to be sold. The letter of instruction must be signed by all persons required to sign for transactions, exactly as their names appear on the account. **Retirement Account** • The account owner should complete a retirement distribution form. Call 1-800-544-6666 to request one. **Trust** • Send a letter of instruction to the address at left, including the trust's name, the fund's name, the trust's fund account number, and the dollar amount or number of shares to be sold. The trustee must sign the letter of instruction indicating capacity as trustee. If the trustee's name is not in the account registration, provide a copy of the trust document certified within the last 60 days. **Business or Organization** • Send a letter of instruction to the address at left, including the firm's name, the fund's name, the firm's fund account number, and the dollar amount or number of shares to be sold. At least one person authorized by corporate resolution to act on the account must sign the letter of instruction. • Include a corporate resolution with corporate seal or a signature guarantee. **Executor, Administrator, Conservator, Guardian** • Call 1-800-544-6666 for instructions.

Shareholder Information - continued

In Person	**Individual, Joint Tenant, Sole Proprietorship, UGMA, UTMA**

• Bring a letter of instruction to a Fidelity Investor Center. Call 1-800-544-9797 for the center nearest you. The letter of instruction must be signed by all persons required to sign for transactions, exactly as their names appear on the account.

Retirement Account
• The account owner should complete a retirement distribution form. Visit a Fidelity Investor Center to request one. Call 1-800-544-9797 for the center nearest you.

Trust
• Bring a letter of instruction to a Fidelity Investor Center. Call 1-800-544-9797 for the center nearest you. The trustee must sign the letter of instruction indicating capacity as trustee. If the trustee's name is not in the account registration, provide a copy of the trust document certified within the last 60 days.

Business or Organization
• Bring a letter of instruction to a Fidelity Investor Center. Call 1-800-544-9797 for the center nearest you. At least one person authorized by corporate resolution to act on the account must sign the letter of instruction.
• Include a corporate resolution with corporate seal or a signature guarantee.

Executor, Administrator, Conservator, Guardian
• Visit a Fidelity Investor Center for instructions. Call 1-800-544-9797 for the center nearest you.

Automatically • Use Personal Withdrawal Service to set up periodic redemptions from your account.

Exchanging Shares

An exchange involves the redemption of all or a portion of the shares of one fund and the purchase of shares of another fund.

As a shareholder, you have the privilege of exchanging shares of the fund for shares of other Fidelity funds.

However, you should note the following policies and restrictions governing exchanges:

• The fund you are exchanging into must be available for sale in your state.

• You may exchange only between accounts that are registered in the same name, address, and taxpayer identification number.

• Before exchanging into a fund, read its prospectus.

• Exchanges may have tax consequences for you.

• The fund may temporarily or permanently terminate the exchange privilege of any investor who makes more than four exchanges out of the fund per calendar year. Accounts under common ownership or control will be counted together for purposes of the four exchange limit.

• The exchange limit may be modified for accounts held by certain institutional retirement plans to conform to plan exchange limits and Department of Labor regulations. See your plan materials for further information.

• The fund may refuse exchange purchases by any person or group if, in FMR's judgment, the fund would be unable to invest the money effectively in accordance with its investment objective and policies, or would otherwise potentially be adversely affected.

The fund may terminate or modify the exchange privilege in the future.

Other funds may have different exchange restrictions, and may impose trading fees of up to 2.00% of the amount exchanged. Check each fund's prospectus for details.

Account Features and Policies

Features

The following features are available to buy and sell shares of the fund.

Automatic Investment and Withdrawal Programs. Fidelity offers convenient services that let you automatically transfer money into your account, between accounts, or out of your account. While automatic investment programs do not guarantee a profit and will not protect you against loss in a declining market, they can be an excellent way to invest for retirement, a home, educational expenses, and other long-term financial goals. Automatic withdrawal or exchange programs can be a convenient way to provide a consistent income flow or to move money between your investments.

Fidelity Automatic Account Builder
To move money from your bank account to a Fidelity fund.

Minimum	Frequency	Procedures
$100	Monthly or quarterly	• To set up for a new account, complete the appropriate section on the application.
		• To set up for existing accounts, call 1-800-544-6666 or visit Fidelity's web site for an application.
		• To make changes, call 1-800-544-6666 at least three business days prior to your next scheduled investment date.

Direct Deposit
To send all or a portion of your paycheck or government check to a Fidelity fund.[A]

Minimum	Frequency	Procedures
$100	Every pay period	• To set up for a new account, check the appropriate box on the application.
		• To set up for an existing account, call 1-800-544-6666 or visit Fidelity's web site for an authorization form.
		• To make changes you will need a new authorization form. Call 1-800-544-6666 or visit Fidelity's web site to obtain one.

[A] *Because its share price fluctuates, the fund may not be an appropriate choice for direct deposit of your entire check.*

Shareholder Information - continued

Fidelity Automatic Exchange Service
To move money from a Fidelity money market fund to another Fidelity fund.

Minimum	Frequency	Procedures
$100	Monthly, bimonthly, quarterly, or annually	• To set up, call 1-800-544-6666 after both accounts are opened. • To make changes, call 1-800-544-6666 at least three business days prior to your next scheduled exchange date.

Personal Withdrawal Service
To set up periodic redemptions from your account to you or to your bank account.

Frequency	Procedures
Monthly	• To set up, call 1-800-544-6666. • To make changes, call Fidelity at 1-800-544-6666 at least three business days prior to your next scheduled withdrawal date.

Other Features. The following other features are also available to buy and sell shares of the fund.

Wire
To purchase and sell shares via the Federal Reserve Wire System.

• You must sign up for the wire feature before using it. Complete the appropriate section on the application when opening your account, or call 1-800-544-6666 to add the feature after your account is opened. Call 1-800-544-6666 before your first use to verify that this feature is set up on your account.

• To sell shares by wire, you must designate the U.S. commercial bank account(s) into which you wish the redemption proceeds deposited.

Fidelity Money Line
To transfer money between your bank account and your fund account.

• You must sign up for the Money Line feature before using it. Complete the appropriate section on the application and then call 1-800-544-6666 or visit Fidelity's web site before your first use to verify that this feature is set up on your account.

• Most transfers are complete within three business days of your call.

• Minimum purchase: $100

• Maximum purchase: $100,000

Fidelity On-Line Xpress+®
To manage your investments through your PC.

Call 1-800-544-0240 or visit Fidelity's web site for more information.

• For account balances and holdings;

• To review recent account history;

• For mutual fund and brokerage trading; and

• For access to research and analysis tools.

Fidelity Online Trading
To access and manage your account over the Internet at Fidelity's web site.

• For account balances and holdings;

• To review recent account history;

• To obtain quotes;

• For mutual fund and brokerage trading; and

• To access third-party research on companies, stocks, mutual funds, and the market.

FAST
To access and manage your account automatically by phone using touch tone or speech recognition.

Call 1-800-544-5555.

• For account balances and holdings;

• For mutual fund and brokerage trading;

• To obtain quotes;

• To review orders and mutual fund activity; and

• To change your personal identification number (PIN).

Policies

The following policies apply to you as a shareholder.

Statements and reports that Fidelity sends to you include the following:

• Confirmation statements (after transactions affecting your account balance except reinvestment of distributions in the fund or another fund and certain transactions through automatic investment or withdrawal programs).

• Monthly or quarterly account statements (detailing account balances and all transactions completed during the prior month or quarter).

• Financial reports (every six months).

Shareholder Information - continued

To reduce expenses, only one copy of most financial reports and prospectuses may be mailed to households, even if more than one person in the household holds shares of the fund. Call Fidelity at 1-800-544-8544 if you need additional copies of financial reports or prospectuses. If you do not want the mailing of these documents to be combined with those for other members of your household, contact Fidelity in writing at P.O. Box 5000, Cincinnati, Ohio 45273-8692.

Electronic copies of most financial reports and prospectuses are available at Fidelity's web site. To participate in Fidelity's electronic delivery program, call Fidelity or visit Fidelity's web site for more information.

You may initiate many **transactions by telephone or electronically.** Fidelity will not be responsible for any losses resulting from unauthorized transactions if it follows reasonable security procedures designed to verify the identity of the investor. Fidelity will request personalized security codes or other information, and may also record calls. For transactions conducted through the Internet, Fidelity recommends the use of an Internet browser with 128-bit encryption. You should verify the accuracy of your confirmation statements immediately after you receive them. If you do not want the ability to sell and exchange by telephone, call Fidelity for instructions.

When you sign your **account application,** you will be asked to certify that your social security or taxpayer identification number is correct and that you are not subject to 31% backup withholding for failing to report income to the IRS. If you violate IRS regulations, the IRS can require the fund to withhold 31% of your taxable distributions and redemptions.

Fidelity may deduct an **annual maintenance fee** of $12.00 from accounts with a value of less than $2,500, subject to an annual maximum charge of $24.00 per shareholder. It is expected that accounts will be valued on the second Friday in November of each year. Accounts opened after September 30 will not be subject to the fee for that year. The fee, which is payable to Fidelity, is designed to offset in part the relatively higher costs of servicing smaller accounts. This fee will not be deducted from Fidelity brokerage accounts, retirement accounts (except nonprototype retirement accounts), accounts using regular investment plans, or if total assets with Fidelity exceed $30,000. Eligibility for the $30,000 waiver is determined by aggregating accounts with Fidelity maintained by FBS LLC or which are registered under the same social security number or which list the same social security number for the custodian of a Uniform Gifts/Transfers to Minors Act account.

If your **account balance** falls below $2,000 (except accounts not subject to account minimums), you will be given 30 days' notice to reestablish the minimum balance. If you do not increase your balance, Fidelity may close your account and send the proceeds to you. Your shares will be sold at the NAV on the day your account is closed.

Fidelity may charge a **fee for certain services,** such as providing historical account documents.

Dividends and Capital Gain Distributions

The fund earns dividends, interest, and other income from its investments, and distributes this income (less expenses) to shareholders as dividends. The fund also realizes capital gains from its investments, and distributes these gains (less any losses) to shareholders as capital gain distributions.

The fund normally pays dividends and capital gain distributions in September and December.

Distribution Options

When you open an account, specify on your application how you want to receive your distributions. The following options may be available for the fund's distributions:

1. Reinvestment Option. Your dividends and capital gain distributions will be automatically reinvested in additional shares of the fund. If you do not indicate a choice on your application, you will be assigned this option.

2. Income-Earned Option. Your capital gain distributions will be automatically reinvested in additional shares of the fund. Your dividends will be paid in cash.

3. Cash Option. Your dividends and capital gain distributions will be paid in cash.

4. Directed Dividends® Option. Your dividends will be automatically invested in shares of another identically registered Fidelity fund. Your capital gain distributions will be automatically invested in shares of another identically registered Fidelity fund, automatically reinvested in additional shares of the fund, or paid in cash.

Not all distribution options are available for every account. If the option you prefer is not listed on your account application, or if you want to change your current option, call Fidelity.

If you elect to receive distributions paid in cash by check and the U.S. Postal Service does not deliver your checks, your distribution option may be converted to the Reinvestment Option. You will not receive interest on amounts represented by uncashed distribution checks.

Tax Consequences

As with any investment, your investment in the fund could have tax consequences for you. If you are not investing through a tax-advantaged retirement account, you should consider these tax consequences.

Taxes on distributions. Distributions you receive from the fund are subject to federal income tax, and may also be subject to state or local taxes.

For federal tax purposes, the fund's dividends and distributions of short-term capital gains are taxable to you as ordinary income, while the fund's distributions of long-term capital gains are taxable to you generally as capital gains.

Shareholder Information - continued

If you buy shares when a fund has realized but not yet distributed income or capital gains, you will be "buying a dividend" by paying the full price for the shares and then receiving a portion of the price back in the form of a taxable distribution.

Any taxable distributions you receive from the fund will normally be taxable to you when you receive them, regardless of your distribution option.

Taxes on transactions. Your redemptions, including exchanges, may result in a capital gain or loss for federal tax purposes. A capital gain or loss on your investment in the fund generally is the difference between the cost of your shares and the price you receive when you sell them.

Fund Services

Fund Management

Dividend Growth is a mutual fund, an investment that pools shareholders' money and invests it toward a specified goal.

FMR is the fund's manager.

As of March 31, 2000, FMR had approximately $639.1 billion in discretionary assets under management.

As the manager, FMR is responsible for choosing the fund's investments and handling its business affairs.

Affiliates assist FMR with foreign investments:

• Fidelity Management & Research (U.K.) Inc. (FMR U.K.), in London, England, serves as a sub-adviser for the fund. FMR U.K. was organized in 1986 to provide investment research and advice to FMR. FMR U.K. may provide investment research and advice on issuers based outside the United States and may also provide investment advisory services for the fund.

• Fidelity Management & Research (Far East) Inc. (FMR Far East) serves as a sub-adviser for the fund. FMR Far East was organized in 1986 to provide investment research and advice to FMR. FMR Far East may provide investment research and advice on issuers based outside the United States and may also provide investment advisory services for the fund.

• Fidelity Investments Japan Limited (FIJ), in Tokyo, Japan, serves as a sub-adviser for the fund. As of September 28, 1999, FIJ had approximately $16.3 billion in discretionary assets under management. FIJ may provide investment research and advice on issuers based outside the United States.

Beginning January 1, 2001, FMR Co., Inc. (FMRC) will serve as a sub-adviser for the fund. FMRC will be primarily responsible for choosing investments for the fund. FMRC is a wholly-owned subsidiary of FMR.

Charles Mangum is vice president and manager of Fidelity® Dividend Growth Fund, which he has managed since January 1997. He also manages other Fidelity Funds. Since joining Fidelity in 1990, Mr. Mangum has worked as a research analyst and manager.

From time to time a manager, analyst, or other Fidelity employee may express views regarding a particular company, security, industry, or market sector. The views expressed by any such person are the views of only that individual as of the time expressed and do not necessarily represent the views of Fidelity or any other person in the Fidelity organization. Any such views are subject to change at any time based upon market or other conditions and Fidelity disclaims any responsibility to update such views. These views may not be relied on as investment advice and, because investment decisions for a Fidelity fund are based on numerous factors, may not be relied on as an indication of trading intent on behalf of any Fidelity fund.

The fund pays a management fee to FMR. The management fee is calculated and paid to FMR every month. The fee is determined by calculating a basic fee and then applying a performance

Prospectus

Fund Services - continued

adjustment. The performance adjustment either increases or decreases the management fee, depending on how well the fund has performed relative to the S&P 500.

$$\underset{\text{fee}}{\text{Management}} = \underset{\text{fee}}{\text{Basic}} +/- \underset{\text{adjustment}}{\text{Performance}}$$

The basic fee is calculated by adding a group fee rate to an individual fund fee rate, dividing by twelve, and multiplying the result by the fund's average net assets throughout the month.

The group fee rate is based on the average net assets of all the mutual funds advised by FMR. This rate cannot rise above 0.52%, and it drops as total assets under management increase.

For July 2000, the group fee rate was 0.2740%. The individual fund fee rate is 0.30%.

The basic fee for the fiscal year ended July 31, 2000 was 0.58% of the fund's average net assets.

The performance adjustment rate is calculated monthly by comparing over the performance period the fund's performance to that of the S&P 500.

The performance period is the most recent 36 month period.

The maximum annualized performance adjustment rate is ± 0.20% of the fund's average net assets over the performance period. The performance adjustment rate is divided by twelve and multiplied by the fund's average net assets over the performance period, and the resulting dollar amount is then added to or subtracted from the basic fee.

The total management fee for the fiscal year ended July 31, 2000, was 0.54% of the fund's average net assets.

FMR pays FMR U.K. and FMR Far East for providing sub-advisory services. FMR Far East in turn pays FIJ for providing sub-advisory services.

FMR will pay FMRC for providing sub-advisory services.

FMR may, from time to time, agree to reimburse the fund for management fees and other expenses above a specified limit. FMR retains the ability to be repaid by the fund if expenses fall below the specified limit prior to the end of the fiscal year. Reimbursement arrangements, which may be discontinued by FMR at any time, can decrease the fund's expenses and boost its performance.

Fund Distribution

FDC distributes the fund's shares.

The fund has adopted a Distribution and Service Plan pursuant to Rule 12b-1 under the Investment Company Act of 1940 that recognizes that FMR may use its management fee revenues, as well as its past profits or its resources from any other source, to pay FDC for expenses incurred in connection with providing services intended to result in the sale of fund shares and/or shareholder support services. FMR, directly or through FDC, may pay significant amounts to intermediaries, such as banks, broker-dealers, and other service-providers, that provide those services. Currently, the Board of Trustees of the fund has authorized such payments.

If payments made by FMR to FDC or to intermediaries under the Distribution and Service Plan were considered to be paid out of the fund's assets on an ongoing basis, they might increase the cost of your investment and might cost you more than paying other types of sales charges.

To receive payments made pursuant to a Distribution and Service Plan, intermediaries must sign the appropriate agreement with FDC in advance.

FMR may allocate brokerage transactions in a manner that takes into account the sale of shares of the fund, provided that the fund receives brokerage services and commission rates comparable to those of other broker-dealers.

No dealer, sales representative, or any other person has been authorized to give any information or to make any representations, other than those contained in this prospectus and in the related statement of additional information (SAI), in connection with the offer contained in this prospectus. If given or made, such other information or representations must not be relied upon as having been authorized by the fund or FDC. This prospectus and the related SAI do not constitute an offer by the fund or by FDC to sell shares of the fund to or to buy shares of the fund from any person to whom it is unlawful to make such offer.

Appendix

Financial Highlights

The financial highlights table is intended to help you understand the fund's financial history for the past 5 years. Certain information reflects financial results for a single fund share. The total returns in the table represent the rate that an investor would have earned (or lost) on an investment in the fund (assuming reinvestment of all dividends and distributions). This information has been audited by PricewaterhouseCoopers LLP, independent accountants, whose report, along with the fund's financial highlights and financial statements, are included in the fund's annual report. A free copy of the annual report is available upon request.

Selected Per-Share Data and Ratios

Years ended July 31,	2000	1999	1998	1997	1996
Selected Per-Share Data					
Net asset value, beginning of period	$ 31.14	$ 28.11	$ 25.07	$ 17.24	$ 16.04
Income from Investment Operations					
Net investment income	.15 [B]	.17 [B]	.17 [B]	.20 [B]	.11
Net realized and unrealized gain (loss)	1.89	5.18	5.21	8.09	2.25
Total from investment operations	2.04	5.35	5.38	8.29	2.36
Less Distributions					
From net investment income	(.14)	(.13)	(.15)	(.09)	(.09)
From net realized gain	(2.14)	(2.19)	(2.19)	(.37)	(1.07)
Total distributions	(2.28)	(2.32)	(2.34)	(.46)	(1.16)
Net asset value, end of period	$ 30.90	$ 31.14	$ 28.11	$ 25.07	$ 17.24
Total Return [A]	7.00%	21.90%	23.81%	49.21%	15.44%
Ratios and Supplemental Data					
Net assets, end of period (in millions)	$ 10,432	$ 14,283	$ 7,371	$ 4,368	$ 1,220
Ratio of expenses to average net assets	.77%	.87%	.89%	.95%	1.02%
Ratio of expenses to average net assets after expense reductions	.74% [C]	.84% [C]	.86% [C]	.92% [C]	.99% [C]
Ratio of net investment income to average net assets	.52%	.58%	.64%	.99%	.86%
Portfolio turnover rate	86%	104%	109%	141%	129%

[A] The total returns would have been lower had certain expenses not been reduced during the periods shown.
[B] Net investment income per share has been calculated based on average shares outstanding during the period.
[C] FMR or the fund has entered into varying arrangements with third parties who either paid or reduced a portion of the fund's expenses.

Additional Performance Information

Lipper has created new comparison categories that group funds according to portfolio characteristics and capitalization, as well as by capitalization only. The Lipper Large-Cap Value Funds Average reflects the performance (excluding sales charges) of mutual funds with similar portfolio characteristics and capitalization. The Lipper Large-Cap Supergroup Average reflects the performance (excluding sales charges) of mutual funds with similar capitalization. The following information compares the performance of the fund to two new Lipper comparison categories.

Average Annual Returns

For the periods ended December 31, 1999	Past 1 year	Past 5 years	Life of fund[A]
Dividend Growth	8.81%	27.61%	24.37%
Lipper Large-Cap Value Funds Average	11.23%	22.35%	X
Lipper Large-Cap Supergroup Average	24.93%	26.34%	X

[A] *From April 27, 1993*

[X] *Not Available*

You can obtain additional information about the fund. The fund's SAI includes more detailed information about the fund and its investments. The SAI is incorporated herein by reference (legally forms a part of the prospectus). The fund's annual and semi-annual reports include a discussion of the fund's holdings and recent market conditions and the fund's investment strategies that affected performance.

For a free copy of any of these documents or to request other information or ask questions about the fund, call Fidelity at 1-800-544-8544. In addition, you may visit Fidelity's web site at www.fidelity.com for a free copy of a prospectus or an annual or semi-annual report or to request other information.

The SAI, the fund's annual and semi-annual reports and other related materials are available from the Electronic Data Gathering, Analysis, and Retrieval (EDGAR) Database on the SEC's web site (http://www.sec.gov). You can obtain copies of this information, after paying a duplicating fee, by sending a request by e-mail to publicinfo@sec.gov or by writing the Public Reference Section of the SEC, Washington, D.C. 20549-0102. You can also review and copy information about the fund, including the fund's SAI, at the SEC's Public Reference Room in Washington, D.C. Call 1-202-942-8090 for information on the operation of the SEC's Public Reference Room.

Investment Company Act of 1940, File Number: 811-4118

Fidelity Investments &(Pyramid) Design, Fidelity, Fidelity Money Line, Fidelity Automatic Account Builder, Fidelity On-Line Xpress+, FAST, and Directed Dividends are registered trademarks of FMR Corp.

Portfolio Advisory Services is a service mark of FMR Corp.

1.700756.103   DGF-pro-0900

Portfolio Management and Equity Trading

II

Part II examines the investment process of mutual funds through three chapters on the securities professionals who manage stock portfolios and bond portfolios as well as those who effect trades for such portfolios.

Chapter Four addresses bond funds. It begins with a description of the main sectors of the bond market and the main characteristics of bonds. It proceeds to look at the investment goals of bond funds and the key strategies used to achieve those goals. It then examines the roles played by portfolio managers, analysts and traders in managing bond funds. The Chapter ends with a case study on a portfolio manager confronted with a set of difficult investment decisions for a municipal bond fund.

Chapter Five addresses securities research and portfolio management of stock funds. It begins with an outline of the main characteristics and measures of common stock. It next reviews the process of researching stocks, with an emphasis on fundamental analysis. It then discusses the strategies employed by portfolio managers of stock funds, with an emphasis on active management. The Chapter ends with a case study of an analyst asked to recommend stocks for the launch of a small-cap stock fund.

Chapter Six addresses the trading process for stock mutual funds. It begins with a description of the main types of markets for the trading of U.S. stocks. It proceeds to a discussion of the role of fund trading desks, with emphasis on the strategies employed in placing fund orders. It then examines the fiduciary obligations of fund traders, including review by independent fund directors. The Chapter ends with a case study on fund traders who are attempting to execute very large orders for several mutual funds.

145

4

Portfolio Management of Bonds

In contrast to equities, bonds are unique in that investors who buy and hold bonds receive a return that is contractual in nature and known in advance. However, this "contractual" return can be affected by several micro- and macroeconomic forces, including changes in the credit quality of the issuer, the liquidity of the bond market and the fluctuation in interest rates. The impact of these forces on bonds, as we'll learn, lend themselves well to both quantitative and fundamental analysis.

This Chapter focuses on three primary areas related to bonds (often referred to as "fixed income securities"). First, it outlines bond mechanics, with an emphasis on types, characteristics and normal return patterns. Next, it discusses bond funds, including a review of their investment goals and the key strategies employed to attain those objectives. Then it looks at each of the players involved in fixed income fund management: portfolio managers, analysts and traders. The Chapter ends with a case study of a portfolio manager of a bond fund who is confronting a difficult set of investment decisions.

I. Bonds: Tradable IOUs

Bonds represent borrowings by companies or governmental institutions needing capital. These monies can be supplied by banks through loans or by securities underwriters through the issuance of bonds. A borrower will consider the relative costs, repayment dates and other factors in deciding whether to take out a loan or issue a bond. In both cases, the monies being provided to the borrower are directly or indirectly being supplied by savers. If a borrower issues bonds, they will be bought by individuals or by financial intermediaries like mutual funds, which have gathered monies from savers. If a borrower takes out a bank loan, the loan will be funded by bank deposits, which have been gathered from savers. Savers will consider the relative risks and returns of buying bonds directly, purchasing shares in a bond fund or making deposits in a bank.

A bond represents a contractual obligation by the issuing company or governmental entity, as opposed to equities (stocks), which represent equity ownership in the company. In essence, a bond certificate is a formal IOU written by a borrower (e.g., corporation, government agency or municipality) to an investor or group of investors (e.g., individual, mutual fund or pension fund). Interest and principal repayments are specified for each bond at issuance, thus making the future cash flows relatively certain (unless the issuer declares bankruptcy). In contrast, the periodic cash flow from equities—dividends, if any—is subject to a discretionary vote of the company's directors.

Further, the company's obligations to pay its bonds are senior to any claims of its stockholders. This gives bondholders a distinct advantage relative to common shareholders in the event of an adverse development affecting the issuer. Most important, in the event of bankruptcy, bondholders are likely to receive partial returns on their bonds, while common shareholders are likely to receive nothing. For these reasons, bonds generally are considered less risky than stocks. In contrast to bondholders, however, equity holders stand to benefit from positive company developments through higher stock prices and possibly higher dividends. In most cases, bondholders are entitled only to periodic interest payments (at the bond coupon rate) and receipt of principal (par value) at maturity.

Some investors simply want to buy and hold a few specific bonds to maturity. But many other investors buy bonds and sell them before maturity in an effort to obtain an attractive "total return" at a reasonable level of risk. The total return from a bond is its periodic interest payments plus its appreciation (or depreciation) during the period between the purchase and sale of the bond, divided by the bondholder's initial investment. Bonds generally appreciate in price when interest rates go down and generally depreciate in price when interest rates go up. In addition, the price of bonds issued by a specific company or governmental entity may rise or fall as the financial condition of the issuer improves or deteriorates.

Bond funds provide investors seeking total return with an easy way to buy and sell a diversified pool of bonds managed by professionals for a modest fee. Bond funds also provide several convenient features, including monthly distribution for investors who need a regular income flow. Most bond funds concentrate on a particular segment of the bond market (e.g., U.S. government, corporate or municipal) and a specified average maturity (e.g., short term or long term). (For the various categories of bond funds, see Chapter Two.) The diversified nature of bond funds is attractive particularly to investors interested in corporate or municipal bonds because they involve credit risk.

There are two principal strategies for managing bond funds. One category of investment strategies involves "passive" management of a bond fund. The simplest form of passive management is buy and hold. Here the bonds are simply bought and held to maturity. Another type of passive management is known as indexing. Indexing is a strategy that attempts to replicate the bond market or a sector of the bond market by using an index as a proxy for the market or a specific sector.

The second category of investment strategies is "active" management of bond funds. Most bond funds are actively managed; that is, the portfolio manager (PM) attempts to outperform the return of a relevant index or a peer group of bond funds with similar objectives. As explained later in this Chapter, active PMs try to outperform by employing strategies such as duration management, yield curve positioning and sector selection.

In managing a bond fund, a PM must understand the many different sectors and security types comprising the bond market, each possessing different risk/return characteristics. As we'll learn, bond prices do not react in a uniform fashion across different sectors. Although bonds are most influenced by changes in interest rates, bonds of similar maturity and structure issued by different companies will trade at different yields due to issuer-specific credit factors, such as leverage, working capital liquidity and funds available for debt service.

A. Major Sectors of the Bond Market

The total size of the U.S. dollar bond market is very large—approximately $16.2 trillion as of year-end 2000. By comparison, the U.S. equity market was valued at $14.4 trillion (based on the Wilshire 5000 total market index). Although the dollar value of the two markets is not vastly different, this is not true for the number of issues that comprise each market. While the U.S. equity market comprises several thousand issues, the U.S. bond market is made up of 2 to 3 million different issues.

There are five major sectors of the bond market: governments, mortgage-backed securities, corporates, municipals and foreign government bonds. In addition, derivatives, which are "synthetic" securities, make up a sixth category. Since U.S. mutual fund managers focus primarily on dollar-denominated bonds, we will concentrate here on the size and composition of the U.S. bond market (see Table 4.1).

1. U.S. government   The U. S. government borrows to finance its ongoing operations. Over the past few decades, large budget deficits have resulted in Treasury issuance of up to $300 billion per year. Because of a recent budget surplus, however, the U.S. Treasury has allowed debt to mature and initiated a buyback of existing debt obligations, with a particular emphasis on longer-maturity (30-year) securities. Regardless of the day-to-day condition of the national budget, obligations of the U.S. Treasury are thought to be among the most secure investments in the world. This is because the United States is a large and wealthy country and U.S. dollars are widely accepted as a base currency around the world. The Treasury issues bonds on a monthly and quarterly basis and had approximately $3.4 trillion in outstanding debt as of the end of 2000.

TABLE 4.1

Major sectors of the U.S. dollar bond market at year-end 2000

Sector	Nominal Value Outstanding (billions)	Percentage of Total
U.S. government	$3,357	21%
Mortgage-backed securities	2,492	15
Corporate	4,523	28
Municipal	1,568	10
Foreign[a]	1,685	10
Asset-backed securities	742	5
Other government agencies[b]	1,825	11
Total	$16,192	100%

[a]Yankee and Eurodollar bonds, as of December 31, 1998.
[b]Includes bonds of other federal agencies not included in mortgage-backed securities total.
Source: Federal Reserve Flow of Funds; Salomon Smith Barney, "How Big Is the World Bond Market?" April 7, 2000, for foreign bond levels.

2. Mortgage-backed securities   Mortgage-backed securities (MBS) are packages of home mortgage loans that are combined and structured to suit the needs and preferences of investors. The most common type of MBS is known as a "pass-through" security, because all principal and interest payments from the mortgages of which they are composed pass through from the homeowners to bondholders in a prespecified manner. The largest issuers of MBS are Fannie Mae (FNMA) and Freddie Mac (FHLMC), shareholder-owned corporations with a special relationship to the U.S. government; the third member of the trio is Ginnie Mae (GNMA), a government-owned entity within the Department of Housing and Urban Development. Because homeowners may prepay home mortgage loans at any time, MBS are highly susceptible to early prepayment (e.g., the risk of receiving principal payments earlier than expected), thus making it difficult to project exact maturity dates. The size of the MBS market was approximately $2.5 trillion as of year-end 2000.

3. Corporate bonds   Corporate bonds are issued mainly by large corporations to finance their operations or acquisitions. Smaller corporations generally finance their operations with bank loans. As of year-end 2000, the size of the corporate bond market was roughly $4.5 trillion; of that amount, approximately $258.9 billion, or 5.8%, represented the market value of debt of high yield issuers.[1] "Junk bonds" are the high yielding subset of the corporate bond market for corporations with poorer credit. (See "Information on High Yield Bonds.") Those corporate sectors that are the principal issuers of corporate bonds are public utilities, transportation companies, industrials, telecommunication companies and banks and finance companies.

4. Municipal bonds   Municipal bonds are issued by states and local municipalities in the United States. The proceeds of these bonds are used generally to finance the construction of capital projects, such as hospitals, highways and schools. Periodic interest payments or coupon income from municipal bonds typically are exempt from federal income taxes as well as state and local income taxes of the jurisdiction issuing the bonds. Although there is a chance of default for these bonds, about half of all municipal bonds issued are insured by bond insurers, such as MBIA, Inc. or Ambac Insurance Corporation, which guarantee the repayment of principal due when the insured bond matures. Although the insurers usually do not cover contractual obligations of municipal bond issuers to make periodic interest payments, they remove much of the downside risk for investors by guaranteeing the payment of principal on many municipal bonds. As a result of such insurance, municipal bonds are attractive to high-net-worth individuals who want the tax exemption but are unwilling or unable to follow the changing credit profile of a particular municipal issuer. Thus, the bond insurers are important players in the municipal market. The size of the municipal market was roughly $1.6 trillion as of year-end 2000.

5. Foreign government bonds   Foreign government bonds include those issued by large industrialized nations, such as Germany and Japan, and smaller "emerging markets," such as Argentina and Thailand. Portfolio managers in the United States most commonly hold two types of foreign bond issues: Eurodollar bonds and Yankee bonds.

Eurodollar bonds are denominated in U.S. currency, issued and traded outside the jurisdiction of any single country and are underwritten by an international syndicate. Although Yankee bonds also are denominated in U.S. dollars, they are issued in the United States by foreign domiciled issuers that register with the Securities and Exchange Commission (SEC). As such, Yankee bonds are often viewed in the same light as U.S. corporate bonds, while Eurodollar bonds are viewed as "foreign bonds." Eurodollar and Yankee bonds represent a relatively small portion of total outstanding debt of corporate and governmental foreign issuers. As of December 31, 1998, the market for Eurodollar and Yankee bonds was roughly $1.7 trillion, while foreign governments had about $9.2 trillion in outstanding bonds, and foreign companies had about $4.1 trillion in outstanding bonds.[2]

6. Derivatives   Derivatives are not actual fixed income securities; rather, they are contracts, which derive their value from an underlying instrument. Fixed income portfolio managers use derivatives to increase or decrease a portfolio's exposure to a particular interest rate, index, credit or group of credits in a manner not available in the cash (or regular bond) markets. The most widely used derivative product in the fixed income market is the bond futures contract, which is traded on the Chicago Board of Trade. This contract is a proxy for the long end of the Treasury market—that is, for long Treasury bonds with maturities of 20 years and greater. As the amount of long Treasury bonds in the market has declined due to the government buyback program, the Treasury futures contract has provided liquidity to the Treasury market. Futures also exist for Treasury debt with shorter maturities as well as for municipal bonds. The futures contracts for municipal bonds trade on the basis of the value of 40 municipals bonds included in an index called the Bond Buyer Index.

B. Basic Characteristics of Bonds

Bonds have four key characteristics set at the time of issuance, which can be ascertained from the bond certificate (if applicable) and supporting documentation (the indenture or prospectus): par value, coupon rate, maturity and optional features.

1. Par value   Par value (or face value) is the principal amount that investors will be repaid when the bond reaches its maturity date. It also serves as the basis for which periodic interest payments will be made. For instance, if an investor owned $10,000 par value of an 8%, five-year maturity annual pay bond, that investor would be entitled to receive $800 per year in interest payments and $10,800 ($10,000 par value plus $800 final interest payment) when the bond matured.

2. Coupon or nominal rate   Coupon or nominal rate is the rate of interest the bond will pay, expressed as an annual percentage of the par value. The term "coupon" is derived from the traditional practice of bondholders' "clipping coupons" from bond certificates and exchanging them for cash at a financial institution. For instance, an investor who held $10,000 par value of a bond with a 6% coupon would receive $600 per year in coupon payments. Some bonds have coupon rates that are reset periodically according to a prespecified benchmark, for example, 200 basis points (bp) over

CALLOUT

Information on High Yield Bonds

A high yield bond (sometimes referred to as a "junk" bond) is a bond issued by a company that is considered to be a relatively high credit risk. This means that the chance of default with high yield bonds is significantly greater than the chance for higher-quality bonds. To compensate for their higher credit risk, high yield bonds pay higher yields than bonds of better credit quality. Studies have demonstrated that diversified portfolios of high yield bonds have higher aggregate returns than other bond portfolios; these studies suggest that the higher yields of junk bonds more than compensate for their higher default risk over time.

High yield bonds derive their name from their issuer and income characteristics. Bonds considered to have an acceptable risk of default are "investment grade," which encompass BBB- rated bonds and higher. Bonds rated below BBB (e.g., BB or B) are called "speculative grade," "high yield" or "junk" bonds and have a higher risk of default. High yield bonds normally have interest rates 4% to 7% above Treasury bonds of comparable maturities. In addition, a minority of high yield bonds pay interest in kind—additional high yield bonds—instead of in cash.

Before the 1980s, most junk bonds were created by a decline in credit quality of formerly investment-grade issuers (known as "fallen angels"). This was a result of a major change in business conditions or the assumption of too much financial risk by the issuer. Investors and researchers soon began to observe that the "risk-adjusted" returns for diversified portfolios of junk bonds were quite attractive. In many cases, the higher yield of these bonds was found to more than compensate the investor for the actual credit losses incurred on such bonds. In response, underwriters in the 1980s began to issue new bonds for issuers that were less than investment grade. This trend was led by Drexel-Burnham, where Michael Millken headed a major charge into junk bonds. This era ended with government lawsuits against Millken, the bankruptcy of Drexel-Burnham and the collapse of many lower-rated issuers of junk bonds. In the 1990s, however, the junk bond market recovered and is currently vibrant.

Many mutual funds have been established that invest in high yield bonds exclusively. Most individual investors have chosen to invest through a diversified mutual fund in high yield bonds because of their large minimum size of trades, the need for specialized credit knowledge and the high default risk for any one issue. Most of these high yield funds have provided investors with competitive returns over time, particularly when viewed relative to investment-grade bond funds (see the table). But the returns of high yield bonds tend to be more volatile than the returns of most investment-grade alternatives. In addition, the risk of loss, particularly over short time periods, can be much higher. An extreme example, calendar year 2000, illustrates well the potential risks of high yield bond investing. While the 10-year Treasury note finished the year up 8% and investment-grade bonds up almost 12%, high yield bonds were down 5%.

1990–2000 Returns of investment grade bonds versus high yield bonds

Year	Merrill Lynch Domestic Master	Merrill Lynch High Yield Master II
1990	9.1	−4.36
1991	15.85	39.17
1992	7.58	17.44
1993	10.02	16.69
1994	−2.82	−1.03
1995	18.52	20.46
1996	3.58	11.27
1997	9.65	13.27
1998	8.87	2.95
1999	−0.96	2.51
2000	11.73	−5.12

Source: Bloomberg/Merrill Lynch Index system.

Because of their significant risk of default and volatility of returns, high yield bonds usually are considered by investment professionals as "hybrid" securities—possessing risk/return characteristics of both stocks and bonds. The return on high yield bonds is less related to overall changes in interest rates and more related to the continued financial health of the issuer. Accordingly, credit analysis for high yield bonds is similar to equity analysis in that it focuses more on issuer fundamentals, in a bottom-up process, than on macroeconomic factors like interest rates. Specifically, credit analysis of high yield bonds concentrates on the downside risk of default and the individual characteristics of issuers. To lower the aggregate credit risk of their funds, portfolio managers often diversify their high yield bonds by industry group and issue type.

the 10-year Treasury rate. These are known as floating-rate securities. In contrast to fixed-rate securities, the periodic interest payments on floating-rate bonds rise or fall according to movements in a prespecified benchmark interest rate.

Not all bonds make periodic coupon payments. Most important, zero coupon bonds have no periodic coupon payments. Rather, they are issued to investors at prices significantly below their stated maturity (par) value and accrue value over time according to a prescribed schedule. For instance, an investor may buy a 10-year zero coupon bond with a par value of $1,000 at a price of $800. While not providing any periodic interest payments, the zero coupon bond will accrue $20 in value each year and pay its par value of $1,000 at maturity, thus compensating the investor for the capital commitment. In addition, the amount of the annual accrual on a zero coupon bond usually is taxed as ordinary income, even though the holder receives no annual cash payment on such a bond. For this reason, zero coupon bonds are often most appropriate for tax-sheltered vehicles such as individual retirement accounts (IRAs).

A bond's coupon payments are an important element of its total return profile. Coupon size is a primary determinant of price volatility for bonds. Given their larger periodic cash flows, higher coupon bonds are usually less reactive to interest rate changes than lower coupon bonds. Accordingly, zero coupon bonds are among the most volatile securities available.

3. Maturity   Maturity is the date on which the bond comes due; the issuer is required to pay investors their principal on the maturity date. For instance, a bond with 10 years to maturity from 1/1/98 would mature on 1/1/2008. Most bonds mature within 30 years of their issuance date, although bonds have been issued with up to a 100-year maturity (a century bond). A bond with 1- to 5-year maturity generally is considered short term, intermediate-term bonds mature between 5 and 12 years and long-term bonds mature in more than 12 years. In the Treasury market, securities issued by the Treasury with a year or less to maturity at the time of issuance are referred to as "bills," securities with maturities of more than 1 but not less than 10 years are referred to as "notes" and securities that mature in more than 10 years are referred to as "bonds."

The time frame, or maturity, of a bond is important. It defines not only the time period in which the holder of the bond will receive coupon payments, but also the year the principal will be paid in full. Market interest rates fluctuate over the life of a bond, causing market prices of bonds to rise or fall according to the magnitude of the interest rate changes. As a bond approaches maturity, its market price will approach its par value (absent a significant risk of default). Given their longer term until receipt of principal, long-maturity bonds have higher risk profiles (and thus more volatile price patterns) than bonds with intermediate- or short-term maturities.

4. Option features embedded in bonds   Many bonds contain optional features that can change their risk/return patterns significantly. While several different features can be found in bonds of varying types, the most common are call provisions, put provisions and conversion features.

Call provisions written into the bond contract are stipulations that allow the issuer to redeem (or "call") the bond before the final maturity. Issuers often exercise call options in order to refinance their debt at lower interest rates. Treasury bonds typically are issued without call options; therefore, unless they are repurchased by the U.S. Treasury in the open market, they will remain outstanding until maturity. However, many corporate and municipal bonds, as well as all MBS, have the possibility of early retirement. Some callable bonds contain a "make-whole" provision that compensates investors in the event of a call because they must now reinvest their money at a lower rate.

Mortgage loans have a "built-in" call provision, as borrowers have the right to pay off mortgage loans (which serve as the building blocks—or collateral—for mortgage-backed securities) at any time, in whole or part, before the maturity date of the loan. In some but not all cases, borrowers will be required to pay a prepayment fee. The prepayment experience of the underlying mortgage pool is often "passed through" to all bondholders in an equal fashion, although some MBS are structured such that prepayments are spread unevenly among various tranches—different bond classes, which each have varying maturities—of the securities.

In contrast to a call provision, which gives rights to the bond issuer, a *put provision* gives a bondholder the right to sell a bond back to an issuer at par value (or another pre-specified price) on designated dates. This feature is advantageous to a bondholder, particularly if interest rates rise (and the bond's price falls below par value) after the issue date.

Bonds with a *conversion feature*—allowing conversion from a debt to an equity instrument—are known as convertible bonds and are considered "hybrid" securities, offering characteristics and risk/return profiles akin to debt and equity securities. Most convertible bonds offer investors the right to exchange their bonds for a specific number of shares of common stock when prescribed conditions are met. In light of the potential value of this conversion feature (particularly if the underlying stock price rises significantly), convertible bonds are sold with lower coupon rates than otherwise similar bonds without conversion features.

C. Elements of Bond Analysis

A coupon-bearing bond can be thought of as a contractual set of cash flows, consisting of periodic coupon payments (interest) plus a final principal payment at maturity. A bond's price will be a function of several factors, including present value of the promised cash flows, likelihood of default (i.e., nonpayment of coupon or principal, or both) and features specific to the issue being analyzed. Thus, by their very nature, bonds lend themselves well to quantitative analysis pursuant to several measures that are helpful in making decisions on relative value. The following six measures are among the more popular used by analysts and investors when comparing the return and/or risk characteristics of different bonds.

1. Current yield   Current yield is found by dividing the annual coupon interest of a bond by its current market price. This is in contrast to *coupon or nominal* yield, which simply divides the annual coupon interest by par value (usually 1,000). Although current yield is a measure of return, it ignores other sources of return that will affect the total yield of a bond, such as interest earned on interim coupon payments and the gain or loss experienced over the purchase price of the bond at maturity.

2. Yield to maturity (YTM)   YTM is the annual rate of return an investor would realize if he or she bought a bond at a particular price, received all the coupon payments, reinvested the coupons at this same YTM rate and received the principal at maturity. In contrast to current yield, yield to maturity takes into account the *horizon return* impact of the difference between the actual price paid for a bond and its "terminal value" (usually par). For instance, an investor purchasing a five-year 8% coupon bond at a price of $900 (and maturing at par value, or $1,000) will reap a higher return over the life of the bond than an investor purchasing a similar bond at par value. YTM recognizes these differences by quantifying the annual effective return an investor is likely to receive if the bond is held to maturity and all interim cash flows (i.e., coupon or interest payments) are reinvested at the calculated YTM. Yield to maturity is also known as the bond's internal rate of return (IRR). The YTM calculation allows investors to compare bonds with different coupons, maturities and prices. Bonds typically are quoted for trading purposes using YTM.

3. Price   Price is the amount that an investor pays for a bond, expressed as a percentage of par value. Thus, a price of 97.5 for a $10,000 par value bond means that the investor pays $9,750 (97.5% of $10,000) for the bond. The YTM is a by-product of the firm's price. All else held equal, bonds with lower prices have higher YTMs (and vice versa). The formula equating price and yield for a bond paying annual coupons for *n* years is:

$$\text{Price} = \frac{\text{Coupon}_1}{(1+\text{YTM})^1} + \frac{\text{Coupon}_2}{(1+\text{YTM})^2} + ... + \frac{\text{Coupon}_n + \text{Principal}}{(1+\text{YTM})^n}$$

Since YTM is in the denominator of the fraction, the price and yield of a bond will move in opposite directions: if the yield rises, the price will fall; if the price rises, the yield will fall. This inverse relationship is the most basic principle of bond price behavior and is very important when evaluating portfolio management–related decisions. For example, no one will pay full price for a bond with a 5% coupon rate when other similar bonds pay 8%; the 5% bond will sell at a discount from par, or less than 100 cents on the dollar. The exact price would be worked out from the formula above; the bond in the example would sell for a price that produces a YTM of 8%.

4. Yield curve   The yield curve is a graph showing yields for bonds of various maturities, typically using a benchmark group of bonds such as U.S. Treasuries. An example of a yield curve is shown in Figure 4.1, with YTM on the *y*-axis and years to maturity on the *x*-axis. In general, longer maturities offer higher yields, so the yield curve is upward sloping. It is upward sloping because investors generally require more compensation in return for lending capital for longer periods of time. For example, all else being equal, an investor requires more enticement (usually in the form of a higher coupon rate) to buy a 10-year bond (in which the principal repayment will be made at the end of 10 years) than a 5-year bond. In addition, longer maturities typically carry more risk of inflation or other adverse developments. In Figure 4.1, 90-day Treasuries are priced to yield around 5.2%. The yield of each successive maturity is higher than the yield of the previous maturity, with 30-year Treasuries priced to yield almost 6.7%.

5. Yield spread   A yield spread is the yield of a particular bond minus the yield of a benchmark yield curve at the bond's maturity. For example, in Figure 4.1, a 10-year corporate bond that has a yield of 7.25% (shown as Bond C) corresponds to the 10-year

FIGURE 4.1

Sample U.S. treasury yield curve

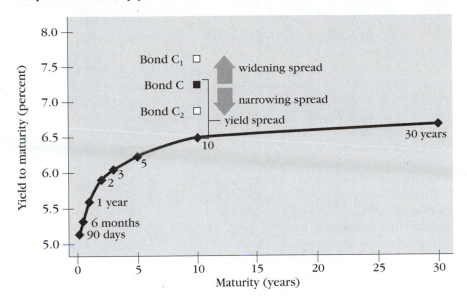

U.S. Treasury yielding 6.51% and would have a yield spread of 0.74% (the 7.25% corporate yield minus the corresponding 6.51% Treasury yield, represented by a thin vertical line). In general, a yield spread represents compensation for risk; it is a premium the bond pays to induce investors to take risk above a benchmark security. (See "Evolution of an Alternative Benchmark.") In the example described above, the yield spread of 74 bp is most likely compensation for risk of default (otherwise known as credit risk) on the corporate bond versus the U.S. Treasury. However, a portion of the spread could also be due to risk of early repayment (call) or other features attached to the corporate issue in question.

Note that if the yield of Bond C in Figure 4.1 increases (shown by Bond C_1) while the corresponding Treasury yield remains the same, the yield spread is said to "widen." Conversely, if the yield of Bond C begins to decrease (shown by Bond C_2) relative to the corresponding Treasury yield, the yield spread is said to "narrow" or "tighten." A widening yield spread for Bond C may indicate an increase in the credit risk for that specific issuer. Widening of yield spreads in general may indicate more risk in the market overall—possibly at a time when there is concern about the economy's experiencing deceleration of growth or even moving into a recession. Conversely, a narrowing of yield spreads may indicate lower credit risk for that specific issuer or a more favorable view of the economy generally.

6. Duration Duration is the percentage a bond's price will change if its yield is changed by 1% (100 bp). For instance, if a bond has a duration of seven and its yield rises from 5% to 6%, we would expect the price to drop (remember that price and yield

CALLOUT
Evolution of an Alternative Benchmark

U.S. Treasury securities are often viewed as the "risk-free" security when determining yield spreads; as such, they most often serve as the benchmark in determining spread levels for other sectors of the U.S. bond market. Recent developments in the U.S. debt market, including an "inversion" of the yield curve (whereby long-maturity securities actually yield less than some of their shorter-maturity counterparts) and stepped-up debt buybacks by the U.S. Treasury (and therefore less outstanding Treasuries to measure), have resulted in the utilization of some alternative benchmarks for determining spread levels.

The most significant alternative benchmark is the *swap curve*, a benchmark used extensively in global bond markets and increasingly in the U.S. market. In very basic terms, a swap curve represents the relationship of the cash flows exchanged by parties involved in a fixed-to-floating interest rate swap and quantifies that fixed-to-floating swap rate as a function of maturity. In other words, the swap curve is the series of fixed rates for different maturities at which a large AA-rated international bank can borrow and then enter into an interest rate swap agreement to repay the borrowed money at a floating rate (i.e., the London Interbank Offered Rate, or LIBOR). Although the swap rate is not entirely risk free (there is always a chance—albeit small—that an AA bank borrower could default on its obligation), it is the closest approximation to a risk-free rate in the corporate markets and therefore is gaining gradual acceptance. Corporate, mortgage-backed and asset-backed bonds are quoted increasingly by U.S. trading desks in terms of a spread to swaps as well as to Treasuries, although the Treasury curve is still the preferred benchmark for participants in the U.S. bond market.

The figure shows a swap curve relative to a Treasury curve. Note that both curves have a similar shape but that the swap curve—because it does have some default risk—is above that of the Treasury curve.

U.S. treasury yield curve versus a swap yield curve

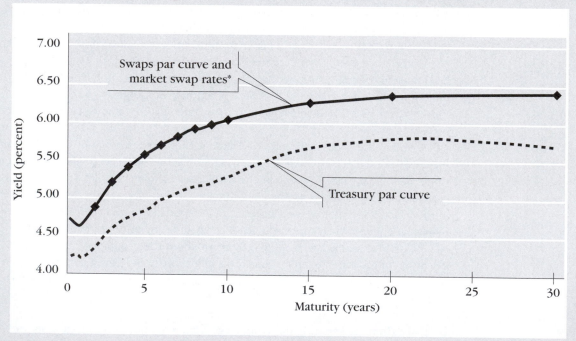

*Swap rates, specified by diamonds, denote actual or observed rates; the line between such rates has been interpolated.

move in opposite directions) by 7% (duration of seven multiplied by 1% change in yield). Duration can be thought of as the average time it takes for investors to recoup their initial investment from the bond's principal and interest payments, weighted by the present value of these payments. The most important factor in determining a bond's duration is its maturity; longer maturities result in longer durations. A bond's duration will be shorter than its maturity if the investor receives interest payments before the bond matures. Conversely, a zero coupon security will have a duration equal to its maturity, a result stemming from its lack of interim cash flows (coupon payments) prior to maturity. As shown by Table 4.2, in the U.S. Treasury market on March 28, 2001, 5-year maturities had durations of approximately 4.0, 10-year maturities had durations of approximately 7.7 and 30-year maturities had durations of 14.6.

D. Risks of Bond Investment

Like all other capital market investments, bonds carry their own special set of risks. For the buy-and-hold investor, the main risk is the disruption of periodic interest and principal payments. Investors who plan on trading fixed income securities (selling prior to stated maturity dates) subject themselves to additional risks relative to the buy-and-hold investor. Although there are several different ways to classify these risks, they can be divided into five main types: market (interest rate) risk, reinvestment risk, credit risk, call risk and event risk.

1. Market risk   Market risk addresses the inverse relationship between market interest rates and bond prices (see Figure 4.2). It is by far the largest single risk universally faced by bond investors. In the simplest sense, market risk is the risk of bond price erosion due to upward movements in interest rates. For example, assume you purchase a 6% five-year Treasury security today at par value. Tomorrow, five-year market interest rates move up to 7%. The only way to sell your 6% security in this new 7% interest rate environment would be to lower the price to compensate the buyer for the yield difference—the fact that your five-year bond pays a rate below the current market rate.

TABLE 4.2

Comparison of duration, coupon rate and yield to maturity for various bond categories

	Duration	Coupon Rate	Yield to Maturity
2-year Treasury	1.893	4.25%	4.24%
5-year Treasury	3.96	5.75	4.62
10-year Treasury	7.682	5.0	4.97
30-year Treasury	14.60	5.375	5.48
Merrill Lynch Domestic Master Index	5.00	6.90	5.97
Merrill Lynch Treasury/ Agency Master Index	5.52	6.72	5.15

Note: Data as of March 28, 2001.

FIGURE 4.2

Inverse relationship between interest rates and bond prices

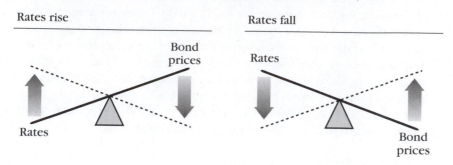

Accordingly, you will face a capital loss if you choose to sell your bond at this time, a prime example of market risk. It is important to note that the exact degree of movement in the bond's price from changes in interest rates depends on the multiple characteristics of a bond, including coupon rate, maturity and any options attached to the issue.

2. Reinvestment risk   Reinvestment risk relates to the variability in bond returns that result from fluctuations in the interest rate at which interim cash flows (coupon payments) are reinvested. The cash flows received from a bond usually are assumed to be reinvested. The amount of additional income from reinvestment (sometimes referred to as "interest on interest") will depend on interest rate levels available at the time of reinvestment. If interest rates fall and interim cash flows are reinvested at successively lower rates, then the investor will realize a return that is less than indicated by the original YTM calculation, which assumes reinvestment of coupons at the same YTM rate. It bears emphasis that reinvestment risk and interest rate risk work in opposite directions—while falling interest rates boost bond prices, they reduce the return from reinvestment of cash flows. Accordingly, a bond with a long maturity and a high coupon is most sensitive to reinvestment risk.

3. Credit risk   Credit risk is the threat that the issuer of a bond may default (i.e., become unable to make interest or principal payments as scheduled). This type of risk is gauged by a quality rating from independent commercial rating companies such as Moody's Investors Service, Standard & Poor's Corporation (S&P) and Fitch. (See Table 4.3 for a detailed description of ratings by the major agencies.) All of the major rating agencies designate debt quality by assigning a letter rating to an issue. Moody's further qualifies some ratings by adding a numeral, whereas S&P and Fitch add a plus or minus. In general, Triple A is the strongest rating given to an issuer—for example, the U.S. government has a credit rating of Triple A. Bonds with Triple A ratings to Triple B ratings are considered investment grade. Bonds rated below Triple B are not considered investment grade—for example, high yield or "junk" bonds are those with Double B ratings or lower. Bonds in the C or D categories are considered predominantly speculative and may already be in default.

TABLE 4.3

Bond rating symbols by major rating agencies

Moody's	S&P	Fitch	Summary Description
Investment grade: High creditworthiness			
Aaa	AAA	AAA	Gilt edge, prime, maximum safety
Aa1	AA+	AA+	
Aa2	AA	AA	High-grade, high credit quality
Aa3	AA–	AA–	
A1	A+	A+	
A2	A	A	Upper-medium grade
A3	A–	A–	
Baa1	BBB+	BBB+	
Baa2	BBB	BBB	Lower-medium grade
Baa3	BBB–	BBB–	
Speculative: Lower creditworthiness			
Ba1	BB+	BB+	
Ba2	BB	BB	Low grade, speculative
Ba3	BB–	BB–	
B1		B+	
B2	B	B	Highly speculative
B3		B–	
Predominantly speculative, substantial risk or in default			
	CCC+	CCC+	In poor standing, substantial risk
Caa	CCC	CCC	
Ca	CC	CC	May be in default, very speculative
C	C	C	Extremely speculative
	CI		Income bonds—no interest being paid
		DDD	
		DD	Default
	D	D	

Source: Frank J. Fabozzi and T. Dessa Fabozzi, *The Handbook of Fixed Income Securities,* Fourth Edition. Copyright © 1995 by The McGraw-Hill Companies. Reprinted by permission of the McGraw-Hill Companies.

Bonds with higher default risk will trade at successively lower prices than otherwise similar Treasury securities because the market will demand higher yields to compensate for the increased risk of default. As default risk continues to increase, the market will demand a successively higher yield and thus push the price of the bonds lower. For example, an investor may purchase a high-quality bond priced to yield 7%, only to see the issuer's credit deteriorate to an upper medium grade. The market would likely demand a yield above 7% to compensate for the increase in credit risk, which would cause the price of the bond to drop. Regardless of the likelihood of default, perceptions of credit risk also can have an immediate and significant impact on bond price, a particularly worrisome characteristic for an investor who plans on selling a bond prior to maturity.

4. Call risk   Call risk relates to the risk an investor faces when buying a bond with an embedded call option attached: that the bond will be "called," or retired, prior to the stated maturity date. In other words, call risk is the risk that an investor's bond gets "called away" at an inopportune time, such as when interest rates are falling. The call provision limits potential price appreciation, makes future cash flows uncertain and can force an investor to reinvest proceeds in a lower interest rate environment than when the bond was originally purchased. Picture an investor who recently purchased a 10-year, 11% callable bond at par value. Assume interest rates fall over the next year, and the issuer decides to exercise the call option. The bond gets called, the high coupon payments stop and the investor is now forced to reinvest the proceeds at a lower interest rate level—an undesirable situation for the investor but a clear benefit for the issuer. Call provisions always have a potential benefit to bond issuers, since they offer the ability to call in higher interest debt when interest rates fall. Accordingly, callable bonds are sold with higher yields than comparable noncallable bonds unless the bonds have a make-whole feature, as mentioned previously.

5. Event risk   Event risk involves circumstances unforeseen at the time of purchase that can have a large adverse effect on bond prices. Examples include buyouts, management restructuring, natural disasters and acts of war. By its nature, event risk relates to events that can rarely be foreseen or predicted with any accuracy but nonetheless must be recognized as having a potential impact on bond prices.

II. Managing a Bond Mutual Fund

While some investors purchase individual bonds, others invest in bonds through mutual funds. Mutual funds offer investors professional management of a diversified pool of bonds with many convenient features at a modest cost. In choosing a particular bond fund, investors expect the PM to concentrate investments in the sector of the bond market and the maturity range described in the fund's prospectus and advertising materials; for example, a long-term, investment-grade bond fund is not expected to own many (if any) short-term, high-yield securities. Within these parameters, investors expect the PM to draw on his or her expertise, backed by research on bonds, to pursue strategies designed to outperform the applicable index or peer group.

A. Investment Objectives and Benchmarks

In selecting bonds for any bond fund, the PM must follow the fund's investment objective as stated in its prospectus. The SEC currently requires a fund to invest at least 80% (up from 65% as of mid-2002) of its assets according to the security type or geographic area suggested by its name (for further details, see Chapter Three). For example, generally at least 80% of the assets of a U.S. Treasury bond fund must be invested in bonds issued by the U.S. Treasury. Another key constraint on the PM is the stated maturity of the bond fund. Short-term bonds have maturities in the range of 1 to 5 years, intermediate-term bonds in the range of 5 to 12 years and long-term bonds more than 12 years. The weighted average maturity of the bond fund, although not necessarily every bond held by the fund, should be in the stated range.

There is also a key distinction between taxable and tax-exempt bond funds. In the taxable area, bond funds may invest primarily in high-grade corporate bonds, high yield bonds (below investment grade), asset-backed bonds (e.g., MBS), foreign bonds or U.S. government bonds. Interest derived from U.S. government bonds is generally subject to federal, but not state, income tax. In the tax-exempt area, bond funds can be invested in municipal bonds from jurisdictions across the nation or within a specific state. The income derived from national tax-exempt bond funds is not subject to federal income tax, but most of the income is likely to be subject to state income tax. The income derived from state tax–exempt bond funds is "double-tax free"—subject to neither federal nor state income taxes in the state issuing the bonds.

Consistent with the bond fund's investment objective, the active PM selects bonds in an effort to beat the return of the market, defined in terms of a market index and/or a competitive universe (for more detail, see Chapter Two). A market index is a hypothetical portfolio of bonds designed to represent a segment of the bond market. The index is created and maintained by an independent provider (two of the largest providers of bond indexes are Lehman Brothers and Salomon Smith Barney). The providers price each bond in the market index periodically and calculate many statistics for the index, including its average duration, yield and total return. A PM can use these indexes to understand what constitutes a neutral position in line with the relevant segment of the bond market. The PM can then choose to buy more or less of a particular bond or market sector than it makes up proportionately of the index. For example, one of the most widely used indexes for general-purpose taxable bond funds is the Lehman Aggregate Bond Index. As of April 2001, this index was composed of 5,341 bonds, representing three main segments: 20.7% were investment-grade corporate bonds, 41.0% were mortgage-backed bonds, and 36.8% were U.S. Treasury bonds (including Treasuries and government agencies excluding MBS). The remaining 1.5% were bonds of other kinds of asset-backed securities.

A competitive universe (or peer group) is a set of bond funds with similar investment objectives. For example, all of the short-term U.S. government bond funds would constitute a competitive universe. The competitive universe is created and maintained by an independent measuring firm such as Lipper. On a monthly, quarterly and yearly basis, these firms rank all funds in the competitive universe according to their total returns. The first quartile represents the best-performing funds of the competitive universe, while the fourth quartile represents the worst-performing funds.

Instead of trying to outperform an index or competitive universe, a relatively small number of bond funds simply aim to equal the return of a particular market segment. To achieve that objective, the PM would buy bonds (or a representative sample of such bonds) in the same proportion as that of the relevant index. These bond funds are known as "index funds," and their management is called "passive." Bond fund index management represents challenges in that many widely followed indexes contain an extremely high number of securities (in some cases, over 5,000) and certain bonds that are illiquid or not available for purchase. Accordingly, passive managers use one of several replication techniques in order to mimic the behavior of an index. A popular method is known as stratified sampling, whereby the index is broken up into components (or cells), and selected securities from each cell are chosen for representation.

This Chapter concentrates on investment strategies for actively managed bond funds. The PMs for such funds are compensated by a relatively modest base salary plus a significant bonus opportunity based on performance relative to the appropriate index or peer group. In most fund complexes, performance for bonus purposes is measured over several time periods—for instance, 1, 3 and 5 years—though the weightings may be different for each time period. In most fund complexes, the majority of a PM's bonus depends on quantitative measures of the PM's own performance. However, a smaller portion of bonus payouts typically depends on the quantitative performance of a broader group (e.g., all bond funds or all municipal bond funds) and qualitative measures of other contributors to the investment management function (e.g., analyst mentoring, recruitment efforts and marketing presentations). In addition, fund sponsors usually offer PMs some form of equity participation, through shares or stock options, in the fortunes of the whole mutual fund enterprise including distribution and servicing as well as investment management.

Table 4.4 sets forth the results of a 2001 survey on compensation of fixed income PMs and analysts. But it should be recognized that the compensation of top PMs managing large bond funds in well-known fund complexes often runs in multiples of the medians reported in this survey.

B. Investment Strategies for Active Management

A PM of an actively managed bond fund usually employs one or more strategies in an attempt to "beat the market"—to add value relative to an appropriate benchmark or index. Some managers may focus on big-picture strategies, such as duration management, yield curve positioning or sector selection strategies, while others may focus on methods of selecting specific bonds or credits (referred to as "bottom-up" strategies). Still

TABLE 4.4

*Summary of results of AIMR/Russell Reynolds compensation survey
for mutual fund company respondents*

| Position | 2001 Median Compensation | | | | 90th Percentile |
	Salary	Bonus	Noncash	Total	
Head of fixed income	$180,000	$185,000	$120,000	$388,000	$3,035,000
Portfolio manager, domestic fixed income	140,000	100,000	35,000	317,500	987,000
Portfolio manager, global fixed income	125,000	150,000	10,000	315,000	854,000
Securities analyst, domestic fixed income	98,000	62,500	9,000	166,250	375,000
Securities analyst, global fixed income	110,000	53,000	1,000	197,500	330,000

Source: Association for Investment Management and Research, *2001 Investment Management Compensation Survey.*

others may choose to apply more quantitative methods, such as employing credit derivatives, predicting calls or prepayments and calculating "option adjusted spreads" (OAS).

1. Duration management   Interest rate movements have a powerful impact on bond prices. Accordingly, a PM can dramatically influence the return of a portfolio of bonds by adjusting the portfolio's sensitivity to anticipated interest rate movements, a practice commonly referred to as *duration management*. This strategy involves altering the average duration of the bonds in a fund depending on the PM's outlook for interest rates. The general level of interest rates fluctuates over time, depending on such macroeconomic factors as inflation, economic growth and the Federal Reserve's monetary policy. A PM who expects yields to fall would buy bonds with longer durations and sell bonds with shorter durations. The PM would need to do this until the average duration in the fund was longer than the market's average duration. Then, if yields fell as expected, the portfolio would rise in price more than average. In other words, it would beat the market. Conversely, a PM who expected yields to rise would shorten up the fund's average duration.

Duration management is a powerful performance tool. If a PM can predict accurately the course of interest rates, the fund will surely beat the market. Unfortunately, predicting the direction of interest rates is very difficult to do in practice. Making calls on macroeconomic variables amounts to predicting what vast numbers of people, companies and governments will do—which is never easy. In addition, the market quickly incorporates into bond yields any new information that will affect interest rates. This market efficiency makes it hard for any fund manager consistently to predict interest rates correctly.

2. Yield curve positioning   The yield curve for U.S. Treasury securities shows the relationship between their yields and maturities. The shape of the yield curve changes over time. A yield curve strategy seeks to capitalize on expected changes in this shape.

The yield curve can shift in a variety of ways. In some cases, it will shift in a parallel fashion—that is, all yields across the maturity spectrum will shift up or down by the same amount. It can also shift in a nonparallel fashion, whereby the yields for different maturities change by different amounts. A PM with an outlook for a particular yield curve shape can try to capitalize on that future shape by implementing a yield curve strategy. Among the strategies available for implementation, two of the more common ones are *bullet* and *barbell* maturity strategies.

With a *bullet* strategy, a portfolio manager concentrates the maturities of the bond holdings at a particular point on the yield curve. With a *barbell* strategy, a portfolio manager concentrates the maturities of the bond holdings at two extreme maturities. For example, a bullet strategy might be to create a portfolio with maturities concentrated around 10 years, while a corresponding barbell strategy might be to create a portfolio with 5-year and 20-year maturities (see Figure 4.3). In both cases, the portfolios have a similar "average" maturity—with similar sensitivity to general interest rate changes—although each has a different maturity structure.

Each of these strategies will result in different performance when the yield curve shifts in a nonparallel fashion. In the example in Figure 4.3, suppose the yield curve undergoes a "steepening shift" from 5- to 30-year maturities, whereby 5-year yields fall 20

FIGURE 4.3

Illustrations of two common yield curve strategies

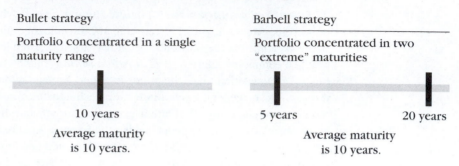

bp while yields of longer maturities (10- and 20-year bonds) remain unchanged. In this scenario, the barbell portfolio would likely outperform the bullet portfolio. Why? Remember that as interest rates fall, bond prices rise. It is likely that the price increase resulting from the drop in 5-year yields would cause the combined performance of the barbell strategy (with half of the portfolio's assets invested in 5-year maturities) to outpace the bullet portfolio (with the entire portfolio in 10-year maturities), which would not realize any price appreciation from a drop in 5-year yields.

Although yield curve strategies are not as powerful as active duration management, they have a meaningful impact on portfolio performance. PMs pay particular attention to yield curve positioning and often utilize the services of quantitative analysts to identify potential yield curve trading and portfolio positioning strategies.

3. Sector selection   As discussed earlier in the Chapter, different sectors of the bond market can vary widely in terms of risk/return characteristics. A PM wishing to exploit this variance may engage in active sector selection, a strategy whereby different sectors of the bond market are over- or underweighted relative to a prespecified benchmark allocation. For example, suppose a PM is managing a taxable bond fund against the Lehman Aggregate Bond index, which has three main components: U.S. Treasuries, investment-grade corporates and mortgage-backed securities. A PM expecting a firming economy and improving company fundamentals may wish to overweight corporate bonds relative to U.S. Treasuries in the index. In this case, the PM's view is that corporate bonds will outperform other sectors represented within the index because the better financial health of companies generally will be reflected in reduced credit risk and therefore an increase in prices. Conversely, a manager believing the economy is on the verge of a recession may wish to overweight U.S. Treasuries relative to all other bond sectors. In this case, the PM believes that a difficult economic environment may lead to favorable relative performance for U.S. Treasuries since they are not subject to the credit risk that is inherent in corporate bonds.

As illustrated in Table 4.5, Portfolio A is overweighted in all non-Treasury sectors of the market (sometimes referred to as "spread" sectors) relative to the benchmark. In this case, the PM believes he or she can generate excess return by maintaining a higher allocation in corporate bonds and mortgage-backed securities relative to the bench-

TABLE 4.5

Active portfolio allocation versus benchmark

Sector	Portfolio A Weight	Benchmark Weight	Relative Weight
Treasuries	29%	47%	−18%
Agencies	5	4	1
Corporates	30	24	6
Mortgage-backed securities	27	22	5
Asset-backed securities	4	3	1
Cash	5	0	5

mark—a view that is probably predicated on a positive economic outlook as well as other factors, such as appealing fundamentals of particular bonds within the spread sectors and the relative attractiveness of these sectors according to a quantitative model. In any event, the PM will benefit if corporate bonds and mortgages outperform Treasuries over future periods. On the other hand, the PM is taking the risk of underperforming the index should Treasuries outperform the spread sectors.

A consistently successful sector allocation can have a significant impact on relative performance for a bond fund. However, such success depends heavily on a correct assessment of macroeconomic factors and their differential effects on key sectors of the bond market. Although not quite as challenging as predicting interest rates, correctly assessing the macroeconomic implications for bond sectors is very difficult.

4. Credit selection   Another important strategy is known as credit selection: overweighting the bonds of certain issuers and underweighting the bonds of others in anticipation of a ratings change. A rating issued by a credit agency tells investors about an issuer's ability to pay interest and principal—in other words, the risk of default. A bond's credit rating is an important factor in determining its yield spread, since the rating constitutes an evaluation—based on extensive analysis by the rating agencies—of a significant risk associated with holding such a bond. Because of the reputation of the agencies, the breadth of companies followed and the ease of access to such ratings, the market normally factors in the agency rating when pricing a bond.

However, there are a tremendous number of issues in the bond market compared to the number of analysts at credit agencies. In particular, the credit agencies have been criticized for being slow to change their ratings in the face of changing credit conditions. Agency officials feel an obligation to focus their ratings on long-term (versus short-term) prospects of a company and also tend to move bond ratings based on actual or highly probable events versus rumors. These timing differences provide an opportunity for credit analysts at fund management companies (and elsewhere) to identify bonds that appear poised for a rating change ahead of when the agencies and the overall market signify such a change. (See "FINOVA: A Divergence Between Rating Agencies and the Market.") As a result of such credit analysis, for example, a PM might choose a bond in anticipation of an upgrade in the bond's credit rating. If the PM is right and the credit rating of the bond is subsequently upgraded, the yield spread of the bond is likely to tighten. A tightening spread causes a bond's price to rise relative to the market, thus providing the bond with a superior return.

Although credit selection is an important performance tool, it is not as powerful as duration management. A fund may own many bonds poised for upgrade, but it would take quite a few to equal the impact of one correct interest rate forecast. On the other hand, a change in credit quality is more amenable to analysis than the course of interest rates, since credit judgments require understanding of only one company at a time.

5. Credit derivatives   In periods of economic downturn or significant market volatility, PMs increasingly look to manage the credit risk in their portfolios through the use of credit derivatives; that is, they may look to either increase or decrease their portfolio's exposure to a particular credit, group of credits or an index in a manner not available in the cash markets. The most common vehicle for managing credit risk—and the mainstay of the current credit derivative market—is the credit default swap. In its simplest form, a credit default swap is a bilateral agreement that enables an investor to buy protection against the risk of default by, or deterioration in the credit quality of, a particular issuer. Typically, if such an event occurs, the investor receives an agreed-on payment, which compensates him or her for the loss incurred. The buyer of protection pays a fee to the protection seller, usually in the form of a cash payment over the life of the transaction. The transaction thus has created a synthetic short position in a credit, insulating the portfolio from the impact of a payment default or other impairment of the market value of a given security or securities. Conversely, an investor may want exposure to a particular credit but may be unable to purchase that issuer's debt in the cash market. By entering into a default swap as a seller of protection, the investor is able to gain exposure to that credit without actually buying the debt in the cash market.

Mutual funds today remain a relatively small player in the derivatives market due to restrictions on the ability of some funds to enter into swap agreements. Banks, securities firms and insurance companies are the dominant players in the market. However, as the credit derivative market becomes more liquid and the documentation of these transactions becomes more standardized, these restrictions are likely to be lifted so as to allow more widespread use of credit derivatives by mutual funds.

6. Predicting calls or prepayments   A sixth strategy is prepayment prediction. As noted previously, call provisions in many bonds allow the issuer to repay them before maturity. This is a serious potential problem for holders of bonds, who are likely to have high yielding bonds bought back from them if interest rates drop (thus forcing reinvestment of the proceeds in a lower interest rate environment). Accordingly, one of the PM's strategies may be to hold callable bonds with low prepayment risk relative to their yield spread. The most important application of this strategy involves MBS.

MBS are highly vulnerable to early retirement through calls because the home mortgages underlying them usually are refinanced when interest rates fall. Bond analysts study the patterns of these prepayments and create models that predict how quickly MBS with different coupons will be retired. By comparing the output of such models with the yield spreads available in the market, the PM tries to forecast which MBS will do well and which will do poorly, and will adjust the fund's holdings accordingly. Although forecasting the speed of prepayments for MBS is a less powerful per-

CALLOUT

FINOVA: A Divergence Between Rating Agencies and the Market

Often the market anticipates rating changes, moving the price of an issuer's bonds before any action by the credit rating agencies. In the following example, the bonds began to trade at noninvestment grade levels prior to the company's ratings being reduced to noninvestment grade (see the accompanying figure). The example also shows that divergences between the market and the rating agencies can occur when rumors begin to affect a company's bonds. Unlike the market, where rumors often affect the price of a company's stocks or bonds, rating agency ratings reflect only actual or highly probable events.

The FINOVA Group offers commercial financing to small and midsize businesses. In January 2000, the company's bonds were rated Baa1 by Moody's and A− by S&P.

The market began to drive down the price of FINOVA's bonds in March 2000 as concerns developed about the quality of the company's loan portfolio following its write-off of a $70 million loan. These concerns were exacerbated by the departure of the company's CEO.

In response to these events, S&P downgraded FINOVA's bonds to BBB+ on March 31, 2000. On May 8, 2000, after the company was forced to draw down on the lines of credit supporting its commercial paper program, Moody's downgraded its rating one notch to Baa2. The next day, May 9, S&P put its rating on "watch developing," based on FINOVA's management announcement that the company was exploring its strategic options, including a sale of the company.

Although these downgrades by the rating agencies still left the FINOVA bonds with an investment-grade rating, market concerns about the company's liquidity position had already pushed down the price of FINOVA's bonds to noninvestment-grade or junk bond levels. More negative news about the company's loan portfolio hit the market in the summer, and the price of FINOVA

FINOVA group bonds with a 7.25% coupon rate and maturity date of 7/12/2006 versus credit ratings

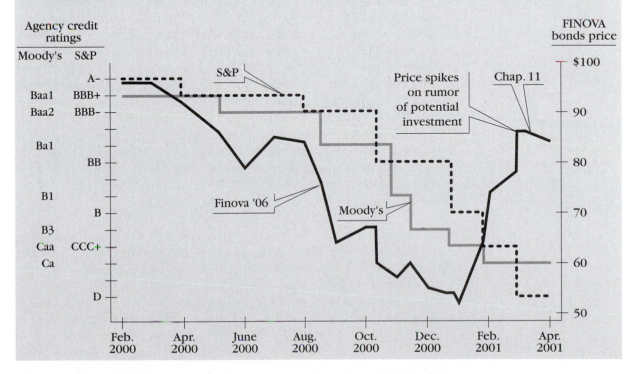

bonds dropped further. S&P downgraded the company once again to BBB− when a buyer had not materialized by late July. Moody's followed suit in mid-August, dropping its rating to Ba1, the first noninvestment-grade rating for the company.

By then, FINOVA's bonds were trading at a level substantially below their rating level. As FINOVA announced more negative news, both rating agencies continued to downgrade their ratings. Although these downgrades further reduced the price of the bonds, most of the price decline had already occurred because the market had already anticipated these downgrades.

In December 2000, as the rating agencies continued to reduce FINOVA's rating due to a high probability that the company was going to file for bankruptcy, the price of

FINOVA's bonds reversed dramatically as rumors of a potential investment in the company, to be undertaken in conjunction with bankruptcy proceedings, circulated among bondholders. Bond prices recovered almost half of their previous value by the end of February 2001. But the rating agencies did not change FINOVA's ratings at this time because there was no indication from management that an investment was imminent. On March 7, 2001, FINOVA filed for bankruptcy. As of July 2001, the company is still in bankruptcy and is rated Caa2 by Moody's and D by S&P. Although FINOVA has received a commitment for a loan from the outside investor, its ratings are expected to remain at current levels until the company's debt is restructured and it removes itself from bankruptcy.

formance tool than duration management, it is more achievable. Prepayment prediction involves analyzing fewer aspects of the behavior of fewer people than does predicting interest rates.

7. Option adjusted spread strategies   A PM interested in exploiting perceived pricing inefficiencies between bonds with embedded options (e.g., callable bonds) and "conventional" bonds may utilize a process known as option adjusted spread (OAS) analysis. OAS is a measure of yield spread that takes into account the fact that bonds with embedded options (such as call options and prepayments) are inherently riskier than "straight" bonds. The spread is "option adjusted" in the sense that the positive or negative effects of the option are taken into account when valuing the cash flows of the security. While involving a complex calculation, OAS results can supply useful insights to a PM. For instance, a PM may choose to overweight bonds with high OAS scores. More broadly, OAS provides the PM with an additional tool in evaluating bonds for a fund portfolio. An OAS-based strategy is obviously most useful for PMs who use securities with embedded options (such as callable bonds and MBS) as part of their approach to portfolio diversification. Working closely with a quantitative analyst, a PM can determine an optimal mix of bonds based on OAS analysis.

All of these seven strategies can be used separately to beat the benchmark, or they can be used in combination by a bond fund manager. In implementing each strategy, the PM must choose not only which bonds to acquire but also how much risk to take. PMs want to ensure that the market is providing adequate compensation for the risk taken. In the case of duration management, this means deciding how much of a difference in duration the portfolio should have relative to the overall market and evaluating the sufficiency of the additional yield provided for any increase in duration. In the case of credit selection, this means deciding how large a percentage of the portfolio a particular company or municipality should represent and analyzing the additional yield provided for accepting higher credit risk. In short, the PM of a bond fund tries to obtain higher returns than its benchmark while balancing the market's risk/return relationships.

III. *Roles of Investment Professionals*

There are four main categories of bond fund professionals: portfolio managers, credit analysts (and municipal analysts), quantitative analysts and traders. Successful bond fund management is usually the result of a team approach—with the PM, analysts and traders working and communicating together to make better-informed investment decisions than they would make individually. Although operating in their own areas, bond analysts and traders are expected to communicate effectively with the PM to help in making decisions about the choice of particular bonds and the structure of the overall portfolio. For instance, effective bond traders do not just execute buy and sell orders. Rather, they provide regular communication on market tone, trading ideas and issue-specific items to the PM. As we'll discuss, the role of an effective bond fund investment professional is quite challenging, requiring independent thought and team play.

A. *The Portfolio Manager: Putting It All Together*

1. General functions of PMs   The PM makes buy and sell decisions for one fund or a group of similar funds. As discussed, the PM must keep the fund invested within its written guidelines. In looking for bonds that will outperform the market, an effective PM needs to keep current on events and developments affecting the bond market generally and key issuers specifically. For this reason, a PM will review reports, meet with companies and attend industry conferences. Moreover, in selecting an array of bonds for the fund, the PM must manage its aggregate risk exposure, including the construction of an adequately diversified portfolio. The PM must also regularly monitor the liquidity of the fund's holdings and its cash position. This also involves investing new cash in times of shareholder purchases and selling bonds to raise cash to meet shareholder redemptions.

An effective bond PM usually has close ties to the firm's traders and analysts. While the PM makes ultimate buy or sell decisions and acts as a fiduciary with respect to fund shareholders, traders and analysts usually offer much input in the day-to-day decision-making process. For instance, by maintaining close communications with bond issuers, an analyst can offer in-depth perspective on existing and emerging bond opportunities. Once the decision to buy or sell is made, the trader can offer input about issue liquidity, trading size and market tone. In addition, traders can offer information about securities that are trading in an abnormal fashion that might create buying or selling opportunities. The PM's job is to synthesize information from all sources when making decisions about security selection and portfolio construction.

A PM's job goes beyond picking bonds for inclusion in the portfolio. This manager is ultimately responsible for the bond fund's performance and must be able to justify all holdings. These responsibilities involve the following activities:

- *Monitoring portfolio risk exposures.* A PM must be aware of all risk exposures within his or her funds, including exposures from security and sector allocations, as well as the risk impact of proposed trades.

- *Monitoring internal compliance limits.* A PM must keep the fund within its compliance limits—for instance, maximums on its total allocation to cash and its percentage ownership of single bond issues.

- *Reviewing performance for external audiences.* A PM usually must explain the performance of the fund regularly to its independent directors at board meetings and its shareholders through semiannual reports, as well as occasionally to representatives of the media and the measurement firms (e.g., Morningstar and Lipper).

2. Special considerations for municipal bond fund managers   Like their counterparts on the taxable bond side, municipal bond fund PMs handle all day-to-day decisions on security selection and portfolio construction. However, as the name implies, a municipal bond fund manager is focused on a relatively small segment of the bond market: municipal (tax-free) securities.

The municipal bond market is often said to trade based on "technicals." This refers to the fact that the market is very supply and demand driven. Although all markets are affected by supply and demand considerations, influences such as tax law, which governs the supply of municipal bonds, and state tax rates, which affect the demand for municipal bonds, can exacerbate the supply and demand imbalances. Understanding the supply and demand factors that influence different parts of the municipal market can help a municipal PM identify undervalued municipal bonds.

Supply and demand imbalances for bonds issued by a single state can lead to trading opportunities. Demand for bonds of a particular state is largely determined by the state tax rates that are levied on income or investment income. The supply of a particular state's bonds is a function of the amount of bonds issued by the state and municipal entities within the state. For example, Maryland bonds often trade at a high premium relative to other municipal bonds because the state has a high state tax rate and there is a limited supply of Maryland bonds. Periodically, events might lead to an increase in issuance of Maryland bonds; a knowledgeable municipal portfolio manager would use this opportunity to increase the fund's exposure to Maryland bonds, expecting their yield spread to tighten when available supply subsequently dissipates.

A drop in interest rates can lead to a sharp increase in the available supply of municipals due to a phenomenon called *advance refunding.* Advance refunding is the procedure by which a municipal issuer refinances its outstanding debt. Tax law limits the number of advance refundings a municipal issuer can undertake and imposes certain profitability restrictions. Thus, a substantial drop in interest rates is typically necessary in order for a refunding to be economically feasible to an issuer. After interest rates have fallen, however, the overhang of potential supply due to anticipated refunding deals coming to market often limits the upside price performance of municipals.

Cyclical participants in the municipal market also affect the demand for municipals. Insurance companies invest in municipal bonds during periods of profitability but become sellers during periods of losses. Additionally, crossover buyers—institutional investors that trade municipal bonds based on historical relationships to other sectors—can affect the municipal market. Crossover buyers enter the market when municipals have underperformed relative to taxable bonds. As this relationship changes and municipals begin to outperform, the crossover buyers sell the municipals and invest back into taxables. Watching closely the relative value of municipals to taxables enables the municipal PM to predict when crossover buyers will enter the market.

Because of these technical constraints, PMs of municipal bond funds may find it difficult at times to implement a particular portfolio strategy. Thus, a municipal bond fund manager must pay special attention to the related issues of liquidity and pricing. The liquidity of municipal bonds varies widely among issuers. (See "Liquidity Risk of High Yield Municipal Bonds.") While the yield on a given issue might be tempting, a PM should check the liquidity status of the issue to ensure compatibility with the fund's trading needs. Similarly, pricing varies widely among municipal dealers, as well as between municipal bonds that are bought "new" in the primary market and similar bonds that are traded in the secondary market. Accordingly, a portfolio manager must make particular efforts to ensure that the bonds in his or her portfolio are priced accurately on a daily basis.

In addition, a PM of a municipal bond fund must cope with the special legal issues that impact municipal bonds. These include:

- *Tax issues.* Managers of municipal funds must be keenly aware of tax code developments, since even a general tax change could have a profound impact on supply or demand conditions within the municipal market. For instance, if the top federal income tax rate on ordinary income is lowered, this change would reduce the value of tax-exempt interest to high-income investors and therefore decrease the demand for municipal bonds.

- *Legal opinion.* Legal opinions are important in choosing a municipal bond since they support the qualifications for tax exemption. A bond manager must have a member of his or her team review and understand the legal opinion prior to a municipal bond transaction.

- *Default issues.* Government issuers are often subject to different rules on bankruptcy and reorganizations than are shareholder-owned companies. Therefore, PMs must consider the relative safety of the bond being considered, including remedies available in the event of financial difficulties for the issuers.

3. Performance attribution   Measuring the success or failure of active investment strategies is a final important step in the bond management process. A bond fund's total return is available to the public every day. On a monthly, quarterly and annual basis, the total return of every bond fund is compared to that of its index and ranked relative to its peer group by outside measuring firms. While these performance comparisons and ratings are important to PMs as well as to fund shareholders, PMs and their investment supervisors try to understand the drivers of such performance. In particular, portfolio managers of bond funds take a keen interest in quantifying the impact of various investment strategies on fund returns and the risk taken to generate such performance. The performance attribution process attempts to break down a fund's returns relative to the returns of a prespecified benchmark and explain why the returns are different by attributing the returns to changes in underlying bond valuation factors. These factors encompass both market-wide parameters and security-specific events. For example, the market-wide parameters include changes in the shape of the yield

CALLOUT
Liquidity Risk of High Yield Municipal Bonds

Municipal bond investors don't expect to see the value of their fund plummet nearly 70% in a single day, but that's exactly what happened to the shareholders of Heartland's High Yield Municipal Bond Fund on October 16, 2000. The reason for the dramatic drop was a reevaluation of the outdated pricing on the fund's holdings of municipal high yield bonds—many of which were infrequently traded—to reflect current market conditions. As

a result of this reevaluation, shareholders of the Heartland Municipal Bond Fund saw its net asset value per share (NAV) drop to $2.45 from $8.01 the day before.

While quite dramatic in magnitude, Heartland's "mark-down" illustrates well one of the primary risks of investing in below-investment-grade securities issued by municipalities: liquidity risk. During market downturns, a combination of cautious bond dealers and lack of buyers can result in dramatic price movements for thinly traded bonds such as high yield municipal bonds. Despite their above-market yields, these bonds are among the first to become illiquid when the market environment turns sour.

curve, changes in sector or quality spreads or changes in market volatility; security-specific events include changes in credit quality, special paydowns or refundings. Performance attribution plays a critical role in the overall bond fund investment process as it enables a PM to understand why his or her fund performed the way it did during the relevant period.

For instance, a PM may wish to know the impact of an active overweight in corporate bonds relative to a diversified benchmark (i.e., one that includes Treasuries, corporates and mortgages). In the simplest sense, the manager could look at the fund's average weighting in corporate bonds relative to their weighting in the benchmark and compare the returns of the corporate bond index allocation to the overall index. However, such an approach is one-dimensional; it doesn't take into account several factors that could have a substantial impact on the bond fund's performance.

Table 4.6 shows a performance attribution report for Diversified Portfolio A, a taxable bond fund investing in multiple sectors of the bond market. For the prior six-month period, the 3.2% total return of Portfolio A exceeded the 2.5% index return by 0.7. How was this excess return generated? This particular report breaks performance into four main factors (plus a residual not shown here for simplicity's sake). The table lists the contribution of each factor to the total return of Diversified Portfolio A as well as to its benchmark index. It also lists the difference in contribution for each component by absolute numbers as well as by percentage of total difference.

The *static return* measures the contribution to return of the fund's holdings as they move toward maturity or "roll down the yield curve." For example, bonds bought at a discount will exhibit "automatic" price appreciation as they get closer to maturity. Holding these bonds "static" in the portfolio during the measurement period will provide a positive contribution to return. In the example in Table 4.6, the bonds held by Portfolio A produced a static return of 0.89%, which exceeded the return of the index by 19 basis points (19 bp or 0.19).

TABLE 4.6

Portfolio A: Performance attribution report for past six-month returns

Risk Factor	Diversified Portfolio A Returns (%)	Index Return (%)	Difference	Percentage of Total Return Difference
Static return	0.89	0.70	0.19	27
Interest-sensitive return	2.56	1.90	0.66	94
Spread change return	−0.23	−0.10	−0.13	−19
Trading return	−0.02	0.00	−0.02	−2
Total	**3.2**	**2.5**	**0.7**	**100%**

The *interest-sensitive return* data help to identify the impact of duration on performance. The contributions to return from this factor come mostly from the strategies of duration management or yield curve positioning and are attributable to changes in the level, slope and shape of the yield curve. In the case of Portfolio A, much of the manager's absolute and excess return relative to the benchmark (66 bp or 0.66) was derived from this source. While further documentation might be necessary, it seems probable that the portfolio benefited from having a longer duration (and higher degree of interest sensitivity) than the index as interest rates fell (which is likely since both the return for the portfolio and the index are positive over the time period).

The *spread change return* measures sector and security selection decisions on overall performance. This factor is the portion of a portfolio's return attributable to changes in yield spreads for the bond sectors and individual securities selected by the PM; returns from such changes in yield spreads are probably the result of the sector selection and credit selection strategies discussed previously. In the case of Portfolio A, returns from such spread changes appear to have produced a negative impact of 13 bp (−0.13) on the fund's return relative to its index.

The *trading return* measures the return component attributable to changes in portfolio composition relative to a simple buy-and-hold strategy. Since an index is primarily a buy-and-hold portfolio of bonds, the contribution to its return for this component is expected to be zero. An active portfolio manager, however, is charged with buying and selling bonds as appropriate to outperform the index as well as a peer group. In this case, Portfolio A experienced a negative return of two bp (−0.02) that is attributable to trading.

The attribution report shown in Table 4.6 is a very basic report. There are numerous, and more complex, reports that give much greater detail on the performance drivers of a fund, such as detailed sector and security-level reports. By understanding each factor that is contributing to a fund's performance as well as the interaction among factors, a PM can learn from the past. He or she can try to avoid repeating the same type of mistake and continue to take advantage of similar successful strategies.

B.   The Credit Analyst: Evaluating Company-Specific Opportunities

1. General company and industry considerations   Much like an equity analyst, a credit analyst is concerned with company prospects, fundamentals and financial position. Both corporate and municipal bond analysts follow systematic approaches when evaluating bonds. Most often, they begin the analytic process by examining an issuer's preliminary offering statement (P.O.S). This document offers a host of information, including a description of the corporation or municipality, its business risks, competitive environment, income statement and balance sheet, as well as the details about this particular bond offering. Armed with this information and the evaluation of the rating agencies, the analyst obtains a better sense of the attributes of the issuer and the particular bond.

There are many general questions that a credit analyst seeks to answer when analyzing a bond issuer. These questions explore the issuer's historic and projected financial performance, the current status of its balance sheet, the competitive and regulatory environment, the potential for event risk and the quality of management. A credit analyst attempts to answer these questions by studying financial statements, reading trade journals, attending conferences and reviewing Wall Street research. A credit analyst also tries to talk with the bond issuer's management as well as its customers, suppliers and competitors.

Credit analysts typically interview customers, suppliers and competitors (among others) to understand their perspective and potential impact on the company and bond issue in question. These interviews may be backed up with on-site visits to the company or facility, which may include detailed discussions with the chief financial officer and other senior executives. While many site visits have the atmosphere of a prepackaged tour, the analyst gains additional perspective by visiting the physical location of the issuer and examining differences between perception and reality. For instance, an analyst examining an outstanding bond issue for a hospital might have read in the original offering documents that the hospital runs at 96% capacity. In the analyst's site visit, however, the hospital appeared to be operating now at 80%. Moreover, an analysis of this hospital's main competitors reveals they are aggressively pursuing strategies to increase their market share and these strategies may be the cause of the hospital's lowered operating level. Such insights may lead to follow-up questions, which must be answered to the analyst's satisfaction prior to rendering an educated buy-or-sell decision.

Corporate and municipal analysts for fund management companies (called the "buy" side) also talk with "sell" side analysts—for example, analysts representing Goldman Sachs or Merrill Lynch. In many cases, information exchange of this type can enhance the quality of the buy-side analyst's evaluation of a bond issuer. For instance, an analyst from a mutual fund manager may gain additional insight into company management by speaking with a particular sell-side analyst who has a long-standing relationship with management. More generally, dialogue with the sell side may be particularly beneficial for a credit analyst who is relatively new to a particular industry;

the analyst can be brought up to speed on the history and characteristics of the industry by a seasoned veteran at a major Wall Street firm.

High yield and investment-grade analysts often differ in their utilization of outside research providers. High yield securities—given their hybrid characteristics and higher risk of default than investment-grade securities—lend themselves well to intense company-level analysis. As such, high yield analysts often work closely with outside research providers (including the sell side) to gain insights on issuer financials, company management and business prospects. By contrast, investment-grade analysts often emphasize rating changes as part of their overall process, since these changes can have a profound impact on corporate bond prices. An analyst of investment-grade bonds is often interested in gaining a deep understanding of the rating process, the inputs involved and key drivers that may lead to a rating change. Accordingly, such an analyst would spend time with representatives of the rating agencies.

Based on all these inputs, an analyst can then create projections for the company or municipal issuer. Then the credit analyst can develop his or her own proprietary credit rating, which can be compared with public credit ratings of this particular bond and ratings on similar bonds to help determine the relative value of the issuer. If the credit analyst is more positive on the bond issuer than the market or rating agencies are, he or she will recommend purchase of the bonds, hoping that the yield spread of the bonds will tighten. A successful credit analyst is one who can predict changes in credit ratings and yield spreads ahead of the rest of the market.

2. Ratio analysis   Ratio analysis is one of the cornerstones of careful credit analysis. The main objective of ratio analysis is to assess quantitatively an issuer's ability to repay its obligations. Equity and credit analysts tend to differ in terms of their areas of concentration when examining a company. An equity analyst takes a keen interest in elements of a company's income statement that can have a direct impact on share prices, including earnings power and revenue growth. In many cases, an equity analyst can become comfortable with a high debt load relative to the issuer's equity if this capital structure can contribute to higher profits in the future. By contrast, a credit analyst's primary concerns are tilted toward the balance sheet of the issuer—specifically, the liability side. A credit analyst must focus on an issuer's overall debt load and its degree of leverage—the ratio of its debt to its equity. The critical job of the analyst is to evaluate the security and growth of the cash flows that will support the payments of interest and principal of a given bond.

In analyzing the ability of a corporate issuer to service its debt, a credit analyst will apply various types of ratios: debt, interest coverage and profitability ratios (see Table 4.7).

Within the broad category of debt ratios, two subcategories typically are utilized: short-term solvency and capitalization ratios. Short-term solvency ratios are used to judge the adequacy of an issuer's liquid assets for meeting obligations as they come due. The most common measure of this subcategory is the current ratio. This ratio is derived by dividing current assets by current liabilities. A high current ratio is indicative of strong liquidity. Capitalization ratios are used to examine the degree of leverage employed by a bond issuer relative to its earnings and cash flow potential. The two most

TABLE 4.7

Common ratios used in credit analysis

Ratio	Calculation	What It Measures
Debt Ratios		
Current ratio	Current assets/current liabilities	Coverage ability of a firm's liquid assets to satisfy current liabilities
Long-term debt to capitalization	Long term debt/long-term debt + shareholders' equity	Financial leverage
Total debt to capitalization	Current liabilities plus long-term debt/long term debt + shareholders' equity	Financial leverage
Interest Coverage Ratios		
Earnings before interest and taxes (EBIT) coverage ratio	EBIT/annual interest expense	Funds available to cover obligations related to a firm's debt burden
Operating cash flow to total debt	Operating cash flow/total debt	Overall debt repayment potential
Profitability Ratios		
Return on equity	Net income/equity	Profitability growth
Return on assets	Net income/total assets	Profitability growth
Profit margin (net margin)	Net income/sales	Profitability growth
Asset turnover	Sales/total assets	Profitability growth

common ratios utilized for this purpose are long-term debt to capitalization and total debt to capitalization. In both cases, the higher the ratio, the higher the degree of financial leverage employed at the firm.

Coverage ratios are used to examine the degree to which cash flows generated through earnings are sufficient to cover current interest and lease obligations. While several ratios are often examined, two in particular tend to be utilized most often: the earnings before interest and taxes (EBIT) coverage ratio and operating cash flow to total debt ratio. The EBIT coverage ratio gives the analyst an idea about funds available to cover obligations related to a firm's debt burden; the higher the ratio, the safer the analyst may feel about the issuer's ability to satisfy interest payments on debt. An analyst may be interested in further examining a company's coverage capabilities by observing the actual cash-generating capabilities of a firm. For instance, a firm may currently have "adequate" liquidity ratios, but its operations may impose an increasing drain on cash. In such cases, the analyst may choose to examine operating cash flow (basic cash flow less increases in working capital) as a percentage of debt to provide more insight into an issuer's future potential to repay its debts.

Profitability ratios typically are used to assess the drivers of a company's earnings. They represent the combined effects of liquidity, asset and debt management on the net income of the company. While equity analysts pay close attention to these ratios in order to gauge potential earnings per share growth and the potential impact on share price, credit analysts are interested in these ratios since it is profitability that ultimately allows a company to meet its debt obligations. Key profitability ratios include return on equity, return on assets, profit margin and asset turnover.

A good credit analyst will observe both the levels and trends of the ratios being used over several time periods. A snapshot of an issuer at one point in time may be misleading. Similarly, a good credit analyst will not view any one ratio in isolation. For instance, an abnormally high ratio of total debt to capitalization may be reasonable in light of good interest coverage ratios and strong profitability ratios. A good credit analyst will also make adjustments for factors unique to the company and the industry being studied. For example, an analyst would not necessarily expect ratio levels to be similar for companies in different industries. A large, profitable corporation in the consumer industry would certainly look different from a ratio analysis perspective than would a young, currently unprofitable telecommunications company. Analysts recognize these differences and incorporate them into their analysis.

CALLOUT
A Successful Call by a Credit Analyst

Bob Brown is a telecom credit analyst examining RZN Communications, a relatively new telephone company that competes with local Bell companies on fixed wire lines. RZN's bonds currently are rated BBB by S&P. Brown begins his analysis by taking a close look at recent industry developments. He finds that margins for rural access lines (fixed wire lines in rural communities) seem to be expanding, fueled by enhanced technology that allows for the transmission of both voice and data over the installed network. The local Bell companies for the most part have dismissed rural access lines because the cost of maintaining quality service to customers in remote locations overshadows revenue and income growth opportunities. Instead, these local Bells have decided to spend time and money defending their major metropolitan areas that were being attacked by competitors. By contrast, RZN has been very acquisitive over the past several years, purchasing more than 2 million rural access lines at favorable prices. Through enhanced technology, these lines can now transmit traditional voice services as well as new data services at costs below those in previous years (and therefore enhancing revenue and income potential).

Working with historical financial spreadsheets (income statement, balance sheet and cash flow), Brown builds a model that analyzes recent trends in revenue, operating margins and income, as well as recent changes in working capital, leverage and cash flows. Besides historical numbers, he looks at projected numbers to establish whether the company's credit profile is improving or getting worse. His models show that RZN's operating margins are improving, reflecting the company's ability to offer new data services at lower costs in addition to being able to offer multiple products over the same access line. He estimates that RZN's enhanced profile will be reflected in stronger coverage ratios (i.e., earnings coverage for debt interest payments). Brown's discussions with company management also reveal positive information. RZN management wants to improve the company's balance sheet and is planning to reduce debt and slow its pace of acquisitions. Brown ups his personal credit rating to A—a one-notch boost—and recommends purchase of the security.

Brown's analysis is on target. Higher margins and operating income materialize during the next quarter, leading the commercial credit rating agencies (such as S&P) to raise the credit rating of RZN Communications to A. Brown's recommendation to purchase the bonds prior to the upgrade by the credit agencies pays off as enthusiastic market participants eagerly purchase the newly upgraded securities, thus narrowing their yield spread relative to otherwise equivalent Treasury securities by 25 bp and causing a price improvement of over 2.5%.

C. *Municipal Analysts*

Although the job of corporate and municipal analysts is similar, the actual analysis differs somewhat because of the difference in issuer types. A municipal analyst may evaluate the creditworthiness of a particular municipality (for example, the city of New York) or a particular project that will be financed with municipal bonds (for instance, a stadium) or a tax-exempt entity that issues in the municipal market (such as a hospital or a private college). While the basic approach to financial and ratio analysis is the same as in the corporate market (i.e., modeling short-term liquidity, cash flow generation and leverage to determine the likelihood an issuer will repay principal and interest on time), the financial statements and accounting conventions of tax-exempt entities differ markedly from those in the taxable market. Many smaller municipalities still do not publish audited financial statements. Similarly, because securities issued in the municipal market are exempt from the SEC registration and reporting requirements applicable to the corporate markets, information about the issuer (particularly smaller, infrequent issuers) can be more difficult to obtain after the bond is issued. This presents a particular challenge for the municipal analyst.

In addition, municipal analysts must recognize the differences between companies and municipalities with regard to their capital sources. A company's capital is supplied by its shareholders. Therefore, a corporate issuer of bonds must pay attention to the demands of its shareholders as well as its obligations to bondholders. For instance, shareholders may press a company to buy back its stock, while bondholders may want the company to conserve its capital. By contrast, a municipality derives its "capital" from tax payments by local citizens. Therefore, a municipal issuer must be sensitive to the needs of its voters, which may not be totally consistent with the desires of its bondholders. For instance, voters may press for higher expenditures on public projects and lower taxes, while bondholders may be concerned about municipal deficits.

There are two principal types of municipal bonds: general obligation bonds and revenue bonds.

1. *General obligation bonds*   These bonds are issued typically by states, counties, cities and other municipalities. They are secured by the issuer's unlimited taxing power on individuals and corporations. Credit analysis of general obligation bonds involves an examination of the municipality's ability and willingness to repay its obligations. To assess these attributes, a municipal credit analyst needs to consider economic, political and social factors, as well as the current financial condition of the issuer. Following are the principal areas of analysis for general obligation bonds:

a. The economy   The municipal analyst must take a keen look at the municipality's current economic situation and assess its outlook for the future. Even in the midst of a strong national economic expansion, there will be municipalities that are struggling. Factors such as population growth, average age of the population and the amount of new residential and commercial construction will give the analyst insight into the economic prospects for the municipality. Additionally, the municipal analyst will look at the growth of new businesses and the fundamental outlook for large employers.

b. Quality of tax revenues   Property taxes are usually the principal source of revenue for a municipality. To assess the quality of these revenues, the credit analyst needs to look at the largest taxpayers. If one company dominates tax revenues, the municipal analyst needs to understand the financial outlook for that particular company. States and larger municipalities also have tax revenue from sales taxes and income taxes. The analyst needs to assess the prospect for growth of all tax revenue. Although a municipality may have the political ability to increase tax rates, businesses will leave if tax rates become too burdensome, and their departure will reduce future flows of tax revenues.

c. Reliance on intergovernmental revenues   For some municipalities such as school districts, intergovernmental payments received from the state compose a large percentage of revenues. The analyst needs to examine the reliability of these payments by looking at the state's financial situation and budgetary process.

d. Budget process   A reliable and conservative budget process is essential. The analyst needs to look at past budgets to determine the ability of the issuer to maintain balanced budgets and fund reserves. Wage pressures from employee unions and demands for social services need to be examined closely. A growing municipality might be attracting new businesses and future tax revenues but have sharply rising expenditures due to rising infrastructure costs.

e. Debt burden   The analyst needs to understand how much debt the municipality has outstanding currently and how much it plans to issue in the future that will be supported by the general taxing powers of the issuer. In addition to the general obligation bonds outstanding, leases need to be determined.

f. Sample questions to ask   The following are examples of questions a credit analyst might ask an issuer of general obligation bonds:

- What are the major revenue sources (sales tax, income tax, property tax), and what are the major expenditures? Does the governmental entity maintain balanced financial operations?

- Who are the major employers and taxpayers? Is the local population wealthy or poor? Has there been growth in employment, population and full-value tax base?

- How much debt has the governmental entity issued in recent years? What are the plans for future borrowing? What percentage of total expenditures is allocated for debt service annually?

- Does the governmental entity maintain reserves to protect itself during slowdowns in the economy? Does the governmental entity have strict policies on required reserve levels or a fund balance target used for budget purposes?

- Are there any extraneous factors that could affect creditworthiness—for example, are there potentially adverse legal settlements, unfunded pension liabilities, contentious union contract negotiations or political conflict that might have a negative impact on the municipality's financial condition?

2. Revenue bonds   Revenue bonds are issued by municipal issuers to finance a specific project. Revenues generated by the project are pledged to bondholders to finance debt service. Examples of projects financed by revenue bonds include hospitals, colleges and universities, airports, public power plants and water and sewer systems. Although the nature of the project will direct much of the specific analysis, some of the common factors a municipal credit analyst considers when analyzing a revenue bond are the following.[3]

a. Essentiality of the project   How essential is the project to region? What is the outlook for utilization of the project? Is utilization expected to increase in the future? For example, a public utility issuer pledging revenues collected from providing essential services such as water and sewer is likely to be a fairly stable credit. By contrast, an issuer pledging revenues from a municipal parking garage that can be subject to discretionary spending and competition from the private sector may represent greater credit risk.

b. Debt service coverage   This is one of the most critical ratios for a municipal analyst when evaluating revenue bonds. The municipal analyst will examine the nature of revenues available for debt service and assess the reliability of this revenue stream. Furthermore, the municipal analyst needs to assess whether future debt issuance will be necessary and, if so, the impact this will have on debt service coverage.

c. Economic factors   Because revenue bond projects are dependent on the local economy for utilization, it is necessary to have an understanding of current and projected local economic fundamentals.

d. Management evaluation   Similar to the analysis of a company, the municipal analyst will evaluate the experience and capability of the managers for the project supporting the revenue bonds. Strong management and effective leadership are as important in a municipal entity as in a Fortune 500 company.

e. Legal provisions   The legal provisions contained in the bond indenture take on greater importance with revenue bonds because of the dependence on revenues generated by the project to pay debt service. It is necessary to understand whether any other claims can be made on this stream of revenues, the ability of the issuer to increase rates and under what conditions the issuer can issue additional debt that would share the same legal claim to the issuer's revenues.

f. Sample questions to ask   Following are examples of questions a credit analyst might ask an issuer of hospital revenue bonds:

- Have you experienced positive growth in admissions and outpatient visits? Are you gaining or losing market share on your various services compared to your competitors?

- What percentage of your revenues do Medicare, Medicaid, Blue Cross, managed care, commercial payers and self-pay customers represent, and how profitable are each of these payers for you?

- What are your revenues, operating surplus, net surplus and debt service coverage levels, and how do these compare to prior years?

- How strong is your balance sheet in terms of your available cash levels, total outstanding debt and net assets?

- What is the governance structure and informal communication process between the board of directors, hospital management and the physicians?

D. The Quantitative Analyst

The quantitative analyst provides security valuation and portfolio risk measures. For security valuation, he or she researches the structural aspects of bonds to compute yield spreads and price sensitivity measures (e.g., duration). He or she also quantifies the risks and rewards of portfolio strategies under different yield curve reshaping and spread movement scenarios. Quantitative analysts apply sophisticated mathematical modeling techniques to large sets of historical data. These data include market information (such as prices and yields), macroeconomics and demographic variables.

An effective quantitative analyst creates sophisticated, dynamic tools for relative value assessment to capture potential security and market-level opportunities. These tools, sometimes called models, generate meaningful results and recommendations from reams of numerical data. The models may be based on historical data relationships (e.g., correlations and volatilities) and assumptions about the future (e.g., interest rates, spreads or mortgage prepayments). The specific duties of the quantitative analyst (also referred to as the "quant") may include the following:

- *Examining the analytical building blocks of bonds.* This involves assessing common aspects of bond price behavior such as the price/yield relationship, the value of embedded options and the systematic component of mortgage prepayments.

- *Processing security and portfolio information to produce valuation and risk parameters.* A quantitative analyst will make valuation recommendations related to historical trading patterns, profitable trading strategies and optimal risk/return trade-offs at the security, sector or portfolio level. The quantitative analyst may also provide recommendations on yield curve positioning and sector allocation.

- *Examining and providing assessment of quantifiable risk characteristics among securities and sectors.* The quantitative analyst will try to quantify risk among current and potential fund holdings, including forecasted price behavior in alternative economic and market scenarios.

The quantitative analyst often works closely with the PMs, traders and credit analysts to identify mispriced securities and provide numerical perspective on existing and potential fund holdings. Armed with the knowledge of a PM's overall intentions, an effective quantitative analyst can help identify an array of appropriately priced securities across different risk exposures within the PM's fund. This array provides the portfolio manager with an optimal set of securities from which to add or reduce exposure across a variety of sectors.

To see a quantitative analyst's role in making trade recommendations, look at Figure 4.4. The figure illustrates the price difference between two classes of mortgage-backed securities issued by Fannie Mae: 30-year 7% bonds (FN 7s) versus 15-year 6.5% bonds,

FIGURE 4.4

Sample scatter plot showing pricing relationships between two securities (daily data, 6/1/93–4/20/01)

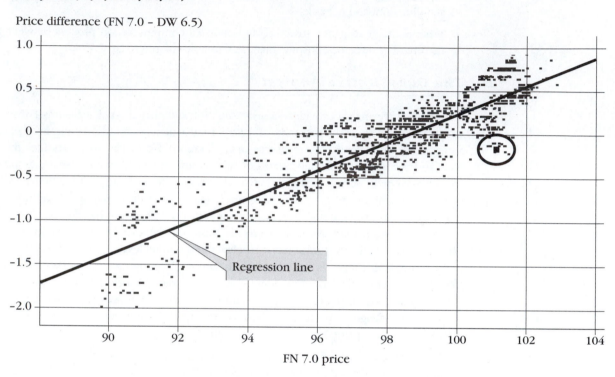

sometimes referred to as "dwarfs" (DW 6.5s). The quantitative analyst generated this graph by examining and plotting historical price data on the two securities to illustrate their pricing relationship over the past seven years. This relationship could signify a potential trading opportunity. Each dot represents the relationship on a given day; the *x*-axis gives the price of FN 7s, and the *y*-axis shows the price difference between the FN 7s and the DW 6.5s. The chart indicates a strong positive and linear relationship between the two securities. Specifically, as the price of FN 7s increases, the difference between the price of the FN 7s and the DW 6.5s grows at a relatively constant rate (measured by the slope of the regression line). However, the current pricing relationship between these two, highlighted in the graph with a black circle, is significantly below the normal range of this pricing relationship. In other words, the difference between the prices of the two securities is currently less than would be expected given their historical relationship and the current price of FN 7s. This observation suggests that the FN 7s are "cheap" relative to the DW 6.5s. Accordingly, the PM may want to consider a swap out of the 6.5s and into the 7s to exploit this potentially significant pricing abnormality.

E. The Trader

1. Current trading procedures

In order to carry out an active portfolio strategy, bonds have to be purchased and sold over time in order to keep the portfolio appropriately positioned relative to the market. Many large mutual fund complexes have made a transition to a centralized trading desk that comprises traders specializing in various market sectors (i.e., governments, corporates and municipals). If a trading desk has not been established, the trading function is generally left in the hands of the individual PM.

Virtually all bonds traded in the institutional market are traded over the counter, meaning that there is no centralized market or exchange. Bonds can trade anywhere and at any time during the day. Generally in the U.S. market, bond dealers and institutional investors begin trading through telephone conversations around 8:00 A.M. EST and end the trading day around 5:00 P.M.; however, trading can continue in the United States or offshore at all hours as long as two qualified parties are willing to transact.

The trader's primary job is to act as an intermediary in executing transactions on behalf of a portfolio with a Wall Street bond dealer who is willing to take the other side of a trade. In addition to specializing in trade execution, the trader is constantly surveying the market in order to understand supply and demand trends and other anomalies. As part of the investment process, the trader is considered the eyes and ears of the market. The trader closely coordinates his or her activities with those of the PMs and analysts to ensure that portfolio strategies are executed effectively.

By centralizing trading with specialist traders, larger mutual fund complexes can compete more effectively with Wall Street and therefore can reduce potential transaction costs. Controlling these transaction costs is a critical component of the execution process. Bond dealers are in the business of making money through maintaining a bid/offer spread when they "make a market" in various bond issues they are willing to trade. In attempting to negotiate a smaller-than-proposed bid/offer spread, such as buying a security more cheaply than it is offered, the trader can decrease transaction costs and increase value to the portfolio strategy. Furthermore, the specialization of traders enhances their ability to track the nuances of different market events and increases the ability of the PM to manage multiple portfolios. As new opportunities arise or market conditions change, the trader becomes aware of them and can communicate these developments quickly to the PMs and analysts.

2. Bond trading in the future

The process of trading bonds over the counter by iterative telephone conversations has been common practice for decades. The trader's responsibilities included calling multiple dealers, comparing prices, communicating with the PM and making the final trade decision. Given improvements in technology, the telephone conversation is now being augmented and eventually may be replaced entirely with more efficient electronic communications. These developments hold the promise of lowering costs for dealers and investors, providing more comprehensive market surveillance for smaller institutions and yielding more transparent pricing for everyone.

The initial steps in this direction are electronic replacements for phone calls in the negotiation and settlement phases of bond trades. After looking at the bonds quoted by named dealers on a screen, the trader submits a bid offer via the screen, and perhaps a series of counterproposals, before reaching an agreement on the transaction and submitting it via an electronic link to the settlement process. A good example of this limited form of electronic trading is TradeWeb, a consortium owned by several major dealers.

In terms of more significant changes, systems are being developed to allow direct negotiation and transaction similar to the platforms that have evolved in the over-the-counter equity markets. (See Chapter Six.) While substantive differences exist between the way that over-the-counter bonds and equities trade, technology should narrow the gap, allowing bonds to catch up with the real-time quotations systems available in equities. One of the most important differences between these markets is the number of and nature of the securities that have been created, producing a hurdle for developing trading systems. The U.S. bond market comprises 2 to 3 million different issues, compared to a relatively small U.S. equity market with several thousand issues. With so many securities in the bond market, trading activity for any given issue can range from very active to infrequent or almost nonexistent. Thus, the less liquid markets, such as high yield corporates and municipals, will take more time to develop effective electronic solutions to replace the phones.

But technology is well suited to provide an electronic execution facility for the most liquid, actively traded issues, such as U.S. Treasuries and high-grade corporate bonds; therefore, early systems have targeted these markets. This next generation is well illustrated by BondBook, another consortium owned by several major bond dealers. BondBook supplies a computer screen with anonymous live quotes from bond dealers and institutional investors in high-grade corporate bonds. Then, without any further negotiation, by computer or phone, an investor can execute the trade instantaneously by "hitting" the quote on the screen. The confirmation of the trade is then electronically transmitted to the settlement process.

In summary, the PM, credit analyst, quantitative analyst and trader work together as an investment team. Each has specialized skills and access to critical information in order to generate an optimal set of portfolio decisions. They share their perspectives and information in a collaborative approach to the management of bond funds. Their goal as a team is to deliver as high a return as practical while keeping the fund within its investment objectives and risk parameters. Each role is critical to the success of a team-oriented approach to portfolio management of bond funds.

REVIEW QUESTIONS

1. What advantages and disadvantages do bonds offer investors relative to stocks? What types of investors are likely to be interested in bond funds versus stock funds?

2. What are the advantages and disadvantages of owning a bond fund versus individual U.S. Treasury bonds? Is the answer different for individual municipal bonds or high yield bonds?

3. If a bond with a duration of 3.0 experienced a widening of its yield spread from 0.40% to 0.60%, by how much would its price change?

4. If a company's credit rating is upgraded, what will be the impact on the yield spread and price of the company's bonds? Why?

5. Does a bond with a higher coupon rate have higher risk than a comparable bond with a lower coupon rate? Does a bond with a higher yield to maturity (YTM) have higher risk than a comparable bond with a lower YTM?

6. Which bond fund has higher risk (all else being equal): a fund with an average maturity of 10 years or a fund with an average duration of 9 years?

7. What is the difference between passive management and active management of a bond fund?

8. What are the functions of the credit analyst, the quantitative analyst and the trader in the process of managing a bond fund?

DISCUSSION QUESTIONS

1. Why does the yield curve normally slope upward? In what circumstances would the yield curve slope downward?

2. Should investment managers of bond funds employ credit analysts when there are public ratings on so many bonds issued by the rating agencies? Does your answer depend on the type of bond fund?

3. If you were a manager of a taxable investment-grade bond fund, what are the pros and cons of using the following strategies: duration positioning, sector selection, and security selection?

4. What are the main differences and similarities between managing a municipal bond fund and managing a taxable corporate bond fund? Between the research performed by a municipal analyst and a taxable corporate analyst?

5. Why has the development of electronic trading been so much slower in the U.S. bond market than the U.S. equity market?

6. If you were a high yield bond analyst, would you spend a lot of time talking with any of the following: credit rating agencies, Wall Street analysts, fund equity analysts, company executives and government officials? Why?

NOTES

1. Using the Merrill Lynch High Yield Master II index as a proxy for the total high yield market size.
2. From Salomon Smith Barney, "How Big Is the World Bond Market," April 7, 2000.
3. The following paragraphs on analysis of revenue bonds draw to some degree on the excellent work of S. Feldstein, "Guidelines in the Credit Analysis of General Obligation and Revenue Municipal Bonds," in F. J. Fabozzi and T. D. Fabozzi (eds.), *The Handbook of Fixed Income Securities,* 4th ed. (New York: McGraw-Hill, 1995).

::::: CASE STUDY

Trustworthy Municipal Bond Fund

This case study puts you in the position of a bond fund portfolio manager who is confronted with a challenging set of decisions. Anne Preston previously had purchased some bonds issued by Hillsborough Water and Sewer System (HW&S), located in southern Florida, with the expectations that the yield on the bond would go down, the bonds would appreciate in value and the fund would sell them for a significant gain. The exact opposite has happened: the yield on the bond has gone up, the price of the bond has gone down and the fund is now facing a loss.

At the same time, Preston was being shown by an in-house analyst bonds issued by the state of Massachusetts. This was back in 1993, when Massachusetts was just finishing a very difficult economic time and was starting to show some credit improvement, which was starting to be recognized by the rating agencies. Moreover, the in-house analyst believed that these Massachusetts bonds might be upgraded again by the rating agencies.

As portfolio manager, Preston has several alternatives. First, she could simply admit that she had been wrong on HW&S, sell the bonds at a loss and put the money into cash. Second, she could add to her position in HW&S at the higher yield, assuming she had sufficient cash flow to support the purchase. Third, she could sell the Hillsborough bonds at a loss and reinvest the proceeds in these Massachusetts general obligation bonds (GOs).

The questions that follow are intended to take you through the same steps in the investment process as would the portfolio manager. These include consulting the credit analyst and the trader, evaluating the relative risks of the two bonds and assessing the implications for her whole portfolio. The final question focuses on the relationship between the case and the general points made in this Chapter about managing a bond portfolio.

Discussion Questions

1. What questions should Preston ask the credit analyst about Massachusetts GOs?
2. What questions should Preston ask the trader about Massachusetts GOs?
3. What questions should Preston ask the credit analyst about HW&S?
4. What questions should Preston ask the trader about HW&S?
5. What are the relative risks of these two bonds?
6. What questions should Preston ask herself about diversification and liquidity?
7. What bond portfolio management strategies are exemplified by these investment decisions?

EXHIBIT 1

Hillsborough W&S and Massachusetts GO: A comparison

Current Date	8/5/93			
Issuer	Hillsborough W&S		Massachusetts GO	
Coupon	5.25%		5.50%	
Maturity	8/1/2000		8/1/2007	
Rating	BBB+		A	
Modified duration	5.8		9.7	
	YTM	**Price**	**YTM**	**Price**
	4.75%	102.94	5.00%	104.99
	4.85	102.35	5.10	103.97
	4.95	101.75	5.20	102.96
	5.05	101.16	5.30	101.96
	5.15	100.58	5.40	100.97
	5.25	100.00	5.50	100.00 <= Current
Current =>	5.35	99.42	5.60	99.04
	5.45	98.85	5.70	98.09
	5.55	98.28	5.80	97.15
	5.65	97.72	5.90	96.23
	5.75	97.15	6.00	95.31

EXHIBIT 2

Treasury yield curve versus Hillsborough and Massachusetts bonds

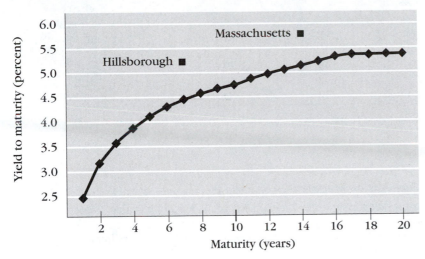

EXHIBIT 3

Municipal bond defaults

Year	Number of Issues	Volume (millions)
1983	25	$2,300
1984	47	498
1985	56	374
1986	150	1,287
1987	175	1,683
1988	139	899
1989	105	1,091
1990	162	1,964
1991	252	4,919
1992	174	2,081

Note: "Default" includes bond issues in which technical abrogations of covenants have occurred but principal and interest payments remain on schedule. Some of these defaults need not result in any losses to investors.
Source: Bond Investors Association and Fidelity Investments.

EXHIBIT 4

Number of municipal ratings changes by Standard & Poor's

	1990	1991	1992	1993 (through September 1993)
Upgrades	140	145	396	127
Downgrades	465	607	478	157
Upgrades/downgrades	30%	24%	83%	81%

Source: Bond Investors Association and Fidelity Investments.

EXHIBIT 5

Description of Standard & Poor's Corporation municipal bond ratings

AAA Debt rated AAA has the highest rating assigned by Standard & Poor's to a debt obligation. Capacity to pay interest and repay principal is extremely strong.

AA Debt rated AA has a very strong capacity to pay interest and repay principal and differs from the highest-rated debt and issues only in a small degree.

A Debt rated A has a strong capacity to pay interest and repay principal. Whereas it normally exhibits adequate protection parameters, adverse economic conditions or changing circumstances are more likely to lead to a weakened capacity to pay interest and repay principal for debt in this category than in higher-rated categories.

BBB Debt rated BBB is regarded as having an adequate capacity to pay interest and repay principal. Whereas it normally exhibits adequate protection parameters, adverse economic conditions or changing circumstances are more likely to lead to a weakened capacity to pay interest and repay principal for debt in this category than in higher-rated categories.

BB Debt rated BB has less near-term vulnerability to default than other speculative issues. However, it faces major ongoing uncertainties or exposure to adverse business, financial or economic conditions, which could lead to inadequate capacity to meet timely interest and principal payments.

B Debt rate B has greater vulnerability to default but currently has the capacity to meet interest payments and principal repayments. Adverse business, financial or economic conditions will likely impair the capacity or willingness to pay interest and repay principal. The B rating category is also used for debt subordinated to senior debt that is assigned an actual or implied BB or BB– rating.

CCC Debt rated CCC has a currently identifiable vulnerability to default and is dependent on favorable business, financial and economic conditions to meet timely payment of interest and repayment of principal. In the event of adverse business, financial or economic conditions, it is not likely to have the capacity to pay interest and repay principal.

CC Debt rated CC is typically applied to debt subordinated to senior debt, which is assigned an actual or implied CCC debt rating.

C The rating of C is typically applied to debt subordinated to senior debt, which is assigned an actual or implied CCC– debt rating. The C rating may be used to cover a situation where a bankruptcy petition has been filed but debt service payments are continued.

CI The rating CI is reserved for income bonds on which no interest is being paid.

D Debt rated D is in payment default. The D rating category is used when interest payments or principal payments are not made on the date due even if the applicable grace period has not expired, unless S&P believes that such payments will be made during such grace period. The D rating will also be used upon the filing of a bankruptcy petition if debt service payments are jeopardized.

Note: The ratings from AA to CCC may be modified by the addition of a plus or a minus sign to show relative standing within the major rating categories.
Source: Standard & Poor's Corp.

*Trustworthy Municipal Bond Fund**

The Situation

Trustworthy Investments was a large manager of mutual funds. At Trustworthy, tax-exempt funds were managed by a group consisting of 8 portfolio managers, 15 analysts and 3 traders (see Exhibit 6). Anne Preston, one of the portfolio managers, described the fund management process at Trustworthy as "a team effort with the portfolio managers working closely with the bond analysts and traders. I view the portfolio manager as a coordinator of resources, and the decisions he or she makes are based on market information provided by the traders and the credit information provided by analysts."

Since Trustworthy employed its own traders, the portfolio managers were freed from monitoring the execution of the trade and were able to manage more than one fund. Preston managed a number of tax-exempt bond funds, including the Trustworthy Municipal Bond Fund.

The Trustworthy Municipal Bond Fund was designed for investors seeking income exempt from federal income taxes (see Exhibit 8). Municipal Bond Fund investors tended to be extremely tax conscious, and many wanted to avoid as much federal taxation as possible. The fund's prospectus required it to be in bonds rated BBB. In addition, the fund was invested in bonds all along the yield curve, generally maintaining a dollar-weighted average duration of seven to eight years.

The portfolio managers gave close consideration to a number of factors when evaluating an investment opportunity. These included attempting to anticipate possible changes in interest rates and positioning the duration of the portfolio at a level consistent with this outlook but also in accordance with fund objectives. In addition, the portfolio managers would pay close attention to their in-house credit analysis rather than be dependent simply on credit ratings. Preston explained: "The credit agencies for the most part lag the market. The market may start to price a particular bond higher if it feels that there is a change in the underlying credit or a change in the environment, which will benefit the bond issuers. Rating agencies, however, are slow to revise their ratings due to the large number of issuers in the market and the difficulties associated with following all of them minutely. Our analysts try to stay ahead of the rating agencies and alert us to the possibility of any such changes so that we may benefit from them."

The portfolio managers also had to make trade-offs between choosing a bond for its high current income or

*This case is not a depiction of actual events. It was written for discussion purposes only.

buying a bond that was selling at a discount for its capital gain opportunity. Internally, Trustworthy evaluated the performance of its portfolio managers on the basis of total return, measured against other funds with similar objectives (total return is the sum of coupon income or dividends and any change in principal value).

Finally, the portfolio managers had to remain cognizant of the need to be diversified not only to control portfolio risk but also to preserve liquidity so that the fund could move out of its investments fairly quickly if necessary. Liquidity was needed especially in environments where portfolio managers feared large fund redemptions by investors, which in turn could force them to sell in a declining market. With higher-rated bonds generally being more liquid than lower-rated bonds, portfolio managers frequently yield against buying a stronger bond with a lower yield.

Hillsborough Florida Water and Sewer Bonds

Hillsborough Water and Sewer Utility (HW&S) was a municipality that supplied water and sewer facilities to residents in southern Florida. HW&S derived revenues from two sources: connection fees charged to new subscribers and usage fees charged to all subscribers depending on their monthly water usage.

In 1991, HW&S had proposed a debt offering consisting of a mixture of current income and zero coupon bonds.[1] In their proposed offering, HW&S had projected an optimistic revenue growth rate of 7% to 8% per annum, with about 40% of the debt repayment being dependent on connection fees to be collected from new customers. When S&P was approached to rate the new issue, it expressed concerns about the ability of the utility to meet the debt repayment schedule principally because it was so dependent on acquiring new customers. Furthermore, S&P pointed out that because the utility already had the highest water rates in the state—it recently had modernized its equipment—there was little possibility that it could increase its revenues from further rate increases. As a result, the new issue was only able to get a rating of BBB+ (see Exhibit 5). Prior to the offering, HW&S had been rated A− by S&P and Baa by Moody's. Moody's continued to rate HW&S as Baa.

The lower rating by S&P had a number of unfavorable consequences. Among these consequences was the fact that most retail investors (mostly older wealthy individuals) were reluctant to buy lower-rated bonds. Due to the subsequent lack in demand, the bonds sold at a substantial discount when issued in 1991.

Commonwealth of Massachusetts General Obligation Bonds

As with other general obligation bonds, the Commonwealth of Massachusetts GOs are secured by a pledge of the full faith and credit and taxing power of the state. In the late 1980s and the early 1990s, Massachusetts faced a difficult period both financially and economically. Indeed by 1991, the "Massachusetts miracle" touted by Governor Michael Dukakis during the 1988 presidential campaign had all but disappeared. From 1988 to 1991, the Commonwealth lost more than 10% of its employment base and saw its unemployment rate rise to 9.0% compared with 6.8% for the nation as a whole. The state, which historically had operated with modest surplus or balanced operations, faced the emergence of a structural imbalance where its revenues were not sufficient to pay its ongoing operating expenses. As a result, Massachusetts weighed in with poor financial performance punctuated by operating deficits that ballooned to more than $1.2 billion in 1990. The net effect of this trying financial period was the complete drawdown of the Commonwealth's existing budgetary reserves and significant increases in the overall debt burden of the State. In response, Moody's and S&P downgraded the credit ratings of Massachusetts from Aa and AA in 1988 to Baa and BBB.

In 1991, Dukakis was replaced as governor by the more fiscally conservative William Weld. Weld set about reducing the size of state government, effectuating tax cuts to stimulate the economy and undertaking deficit financings to resolve the accumulated deficit. Fortunately, from 1991 to 1993, Massachusetts saw its economy stabilize and, following from the imposition of fiscal discipline on state finances, a return to balanced operations. Moreover, the Commonwealth continuously added to its Stabilization Fund, with the fund balance growing to more than $309 million in 1993 from just $59 million in 1991. To recognize some of this improvement, Massachusetts GOs had been upgraded to A by Moody's Investor Service and A by Standard & Poor's in 1992.

What to Do About Hillsborough Water & Sewer

On July 7, 1993, the bonds of HW&S were brought to Anne Preston's attention by Bill Roche, a bond trader at Trustworthy. The bonds were now trading at a yield of 5.35%, 90 basis points higher than typical AAA rated bonds. Municipal bonds had lagged the tremendous run-up in the stock and taxable bond markets, mainly due to municipal issuers' taking advantage of low interest rates and refining

their debt and the uncertainty about President Clinton's plan to raise taxes. She was, however, willing to purchase the bonds for their short-term capital gain potential.

Before deciding, Preston had consulted Joe Brown, the Trustworthy credit analyst following HW&S. He described current market opinion as viewing HW&S as a BBB credit with little room for future improvement. However, he felt that the credit actually had improved in light of a number of changes. HW&S no longer had the highest water rates in Florida; a number of other water and sewer facilities had raised their rates after being forced to update their equipment to ensure compliance with safe drinking water legislation. In addition, HW&S now was able to meet 100% of its debt service requirements through usage fees due to an impressive growth in its customer base. Preston could hope that the credit improvement would be recognized by the rating agencies. She decided to invest $9.25 million in the HW&S bonds on July 7 for the account of the Trustworthy Municipal Bond Fund.

It was now August 5, and the bonds had declined in price to yield 5.35%. Preston tried to evaluate her options. She could sell the bonds now and cut her losses, or she could hold the bonds and wait for the market to recognize the credit improvement in HW&S. However, if the bill to raise taxes currently before Congress was defeated, municipal bonds could fall further.

A third alternative was to purchase Massachusetts GO bonds. Preston knew that Susan DiAngelo, the analyst following the Commonwealth of Massachusetts' credit for Trustworthy, felt that the ongoing improvement in the economic and financial conditions of the state warranted an internal rating of A+. DiAngelo saw additional upside in the bond over the longer term and anticipated upgrades from both Moody's and S&P over the next six months to A1 and A+, respectively. Because DiAngelo saw this potential upside for the bonds, there was a substantial possibility that yield spreads on these bonds relative to an AAA bond would decrease as a result. Preston knew that she could sell the Hillsboroughs and purchase these bonds. Trader Bill Roche remarked that he expected if the 5.50% Massachusetts GOs were upgraded to A+, the bonds would trade at a price to yield 5.30%.

Note

1. Zero coupon bonds were typically more expensive to issue in an environment in which the market desired current income. However, HW&S had insufficient revenues to pay interest on current income bonds. The issuer believed that with a rising customer base and rising water rates, it would have little difficulty redeeming the zero coupon bonds at maturity.

EXHIBIT 6

Trustworthy tax-exempt fixed income resources

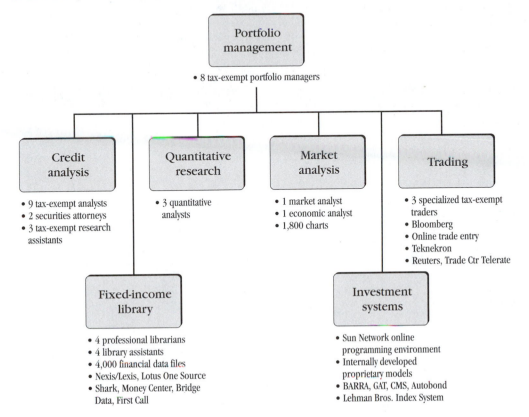

EXHIBIT 7

Relationship between duration, maturity, coupon and yield to maturity (calculated assuming semiannual coupon payments)

Yield to Maturity	5-Year Coupon	Duration (years)				
		10-Year Maturity	15-Year Maturity	20-Year Maturity	30-Year Maturity	Maturity
3%	0%	5.0	10.0	15.0	20.0	30.0
	3%	4.7	8.7	12.2	15.2	20.0
	5%	4.5	8.2	11.2	13.8	18.0
	7%	4.4	7.8	10.6	13.0	16.9
5%	3%	4.7	8.6	11.8	14.3	17.7
	5%	4.5	8.0	10.7	12.9	15.8
	7%	4.3	7.6	10.1	12.0	14.9
7%	3%	4.6	8.4	11.3	13.3	15.4
	5%	4.5	7.8	10.2	11.9	13.7
	7%	4.3	7.4	9.5	11.1	12.9

Note: The duration of a bond is the weighted-average time to receipt of its coupons and principal. The duration of fixed-rate debt is also an approximate measure of sensitivity of price to changes in yield to maturity. Specifically, the percentage change in price is approximately equal to the negative of the duration of the bond multiplied by the change in yield to maturity.

EXHIBIT 8

Trustworthy municipal bond fund

Fund Manager: Anne Preston Portfolio Breakdown—Net assets: $1,005,604,218

The Municipal Bond Fund's objective is to obtain a high level of current tax-exempt income consistent with preservation of capital. The Fund generally acquires longer-term (20–40 years) tax-exempt bonds that have credit characteristics consistent with rating agencies' definitions of A or better, although it may purchase bonds with BBB credit characteristics.

Categories		12/31/94		12/31/93
State general obligations		7.1		3.5
Local general obligations		6.1		4.7
Special tax		9.4		6.0
Lease rental		8.3		8.2
Water, sewer & gas utilities		7.2		10.3
Electric utilities		16.6		21.4
Ind. Revenue/pollution control		1.8		3.6
Transportation		10.2		6.0
Health care		14.8		20.5
Universities/student loans		4.1		6.9
Housing		3.2		3.5
Pooled loans/other		1.7		0.2
Escrowed/special obligation/pre-ref.		4.8		3.8
Total municipal bonds		95.3		98.6
Short-term obligations		6.9		2.1
Receivables less liabilities		2.1		−0.8
		100.0%		99.9%
Net assets ($000)		1,005,604		1,258,068
Net asset value ($)		7.36		8.69
Weighted average years to maturity		17.0		21.4
Duration		8.8		8.6
Ratings breakdown (as a % of total net assets)	AAA	40.3		36.7
	AA	23.9		25
	A	25.7		27.7
	BBB	12.2		11.4
		102.1%		100.8%
	Years			
Maturity distribution (as a % of total net assets)	0–1	6.9		2.1
	1–5	3.2		2.4
	5–10	6.7		3.1
	10–15	16.3		8.2
	15–20	32.2		22.0
	20+	36.8		63.0
		102.1%		100.8%
Top five states by % of net assets	CA	12.9	CA	14.1
	NY	11.6	PA	8.6
	MA	8.8	NY	8.5
	TX	8.6	MA	5.9
	IL	5.7	WA	5.6

* Hypothetical: For description purposes only.

Portfolio Management of Stocks

5

The capstone of the investment process is portfolio management: making the decisions about which securities to hold and in what proportions. The equity portfolio manager (PM) stands at the intersection of two major participants in the capital markets: companies that have issued equity securities and investors who have entrusted assets to the manager's fund. The PM's role is to select equity securities that are consistent with the fund's objectives and have good potential for high returns.

The Chapter begins with the basics of equity securities, including the main analytic measures used to describe common stocks. The next section describes different approaches to the equity research function, with emphasis on fundamental research. Then the Chapter turns to management of equity mutual funds, with a focus on active management. The Chapter ends with a case study on an analyst recommending stocks for the launch of a new mutual fund.

I. Overview of Equity Securities

A. Characteristics of Common Stock

Companies need money to maintain and grow their businesses. They often begin small, nurtured by investments from their founders. As they grow and require more capital to develop new products or build facilities, they turn to outside sources of funding. These sources may include bank borrowings or debt offerings (covered in Chapter Four), or they could involve *equity financing*. Selling equity in the firm means giving up some portion of the firm's ownership in exchange for additional funding. The ownership stake may be sold to private investors, such as venture capitalists, or to public investors. When a firm "goes public," it sells ownership to the general investor populace in the form of *stock* and receives the proceeds of the sale. This initial sale to the public constitutes the *primary market* for stocks, while subsequent stock transactions between investors constitute the *secondary market*. The company does not receive any capital from equity trading in the secondary market (described in Chapter Six). Most purchases and sales of stock take place in the secondary market, the primary focus of this Chapter.

A share of stock represents fractional ownership of a company and participation in the firm's profits or losses. Ownership of common stock also carries voting rights. Generally, shareholders do not vote on aspects of the firm's routine affairs, which are handled by the company's management (its officers). Rather, shareholders elect directors who are charged with representing their interests, together with hiring and overseeing the firm's management. Shareholders also vote on matters of corporate control, such as whether to accept a merger proposal from another firm. (Corporate governance is discussed in Chapter Eleven.) Most public companies issue common stock; some also issue another equity class known as *preferred stock*. Preferred stock typically has a higher dividend rate than does common stock, and it also has a relatively preferential claim on dividend payments. If a company encounters financial difficulty, it must pay interest on its bonds first, followed by dividends on its preferred stock. Only when these obligations are satisfied may dividends be paid to common stockholders. In exchange for this higher rank in the company's capital structure, preferred stock doesn't normally carry voting rights (with limited exceptions, such as when dividends are in arrears or when a proposal would materially alter the rights of preferred stockholders).

Stockholders of a company get "paid" in one of two ways: capital appreciation of their shares and dividend payments from the company. If a company is profitable, management may choose to reinvest profits in the business, creating retained earnings on the company's balance sheet. Companies with prospects for strong business growth typically reinvest higher percentages of their earnings than do companies in more mature industries. The objective of such reinvestment is to finance profitable products or ventures and keep the firm's overall growth rate steady or accelerating. The alternative is to pay out the earnings to stockholders in the form of dividends. Dividend payments are made at the discretion of the company's board of directors and may be eliminated if business conditions deteriorate. Though typically paid in cash, dividends are sometimes paid in the form of additional shares.

Most stockholders own shares for their capital appreciation potential. Equity ownership is generally riskier than holding debt, as profits and share price appreciation are less certain than interest payments. Investors weigh these risks alongside the potential for significant capital gains if companies succeed. Capital gains are simply increases in the price of a share of the company's common stock. Though macroeconomic trends and investor sentiment for the broad stock market affect the price of individual shares, the most influential factors are the firm's business fundamentals and investor expectations about the firm's prospects. Over time, stock price performance tends to reflect the company's underlying business performance. However, business fundamentals and stock price trends can diverge, sometimes for extended periods. Recognizing these disparities and capitalizing on them is the essence of securities research and active portfolio management.

Before turning to securities research and portfolio management, it will be helpful to understand the basic measures used to describe common stocks.

B. Measures of Stocks

The current value of a company—its *market capitalization* (or *market cap*)—is based on the total value of its outstanding stock. The market capitalization of a company is determined by multiplying the number of its outstanding shares of common stock by the current market price of each share. For example, a company with 10 million shares of common stock outstanding selling for $21 per share would have a market cap of $210 million. Portfolio managers may use market capitalization as a screen for investments (e.g., a mid-cap manager may concentrate on companies with market caps between $1 billion and $7 billion). Security analysts may compare the market cap to book value (the company's assets minus its liabilities) for an indication of how investors value a company's future prospects.

The market price of a share of common stock is typically analyzed in terms of various financial measures:

Price/earnings ratio (P/E), also known as the P/E multiple, is simply the price of a share of stock divided by its earnings per share (sometimes most recent reported, sometimes projected). This ratio gives an indication of how much investors are willing to pay for a company's potential earning power. The higher the multiple, the more that investors are willing to pay and the more "expensive" the stock is said to be. Stocks are often classified by their P/E ratio: those with a high P/E (e.g., 50 or 60) are typically young or fast-growing companies, while those with a low P/E (e.g., 8 or 10) are typically low-growth or mature industries. Low P/E stocks also may include companies that have underperformed recently or are in socially disfavored industries (e.g., tobacco).

Price/cash flow ratio (P/CF) is found by dividing the price of a share of stock by a measure of cash flow per share (often net income plus depreciation). P/CF is often used as a supplement to P/E, since cash flow is less subject to accounting distortions than are net earnings.

Price/book ratio (P/B) is computed by dividing the price of a share of stock by its book value (the company's assets minus its liabilities) per share and is often used as a measure of relative value for stocks. Analysts may compare the stock's P/B ratio to its historical range or to comparable industry ratios. The P/B ratio, like P/E, is often used in determining the attractiveness of a security. If a company has a relatively high P/B, investors are signaling that they see more profit potential than the hard assets on the company's books would suggest (e.g., an information technology company). Conversely, if a company has a relatively low P/B, its hard assets do not have good prospects of generating future earnings (e.g., a coal mining company).

Dividend yield is the rate of return paid on a stock, as measured by dividends. This measure is expressed as a percentage of the current market price of a share of stock. For example, a stock selling for $25 per share that pays an annual dividend of $1 has a dividend yield of 4% ($1/$25). As a general rule, low P/E stocks have higher dividend yields than high P/E stocks, which sometimes pay no dividends at all. However, this distinction has become less apparent as the dividend yield of the S&P 500 dropped from 3.7% in 1990 to 2.2% in 1995 to 1.2% in 2000. Also, many companies have bought back their own shares, instead of increasing dividends, because it was more tax efficient: investors receive capital gains when their shares are bought back by the company, and capital gains are taxed more favorably than dividends.

Stocks are also typically placed into one of several categories based on the anticipated movement of company earnings:

Cyclical stocks represent ownership interest in companies that tend to experience upward and downward changes in their net earnings that are correlated with the health of the economy in general. Earnings tend to rise quickly when the economy turns up and fall quickly when the economy turns down. Examples of cyclical industries are automobiles and housing.

Growth stocks represent ownership interests in companies with opportunities for above-normal increases in revenue or earnings. Because of their growth potential, these companies (e.g., Cisco) often sell at relatively high P/E ratios. Since these companies tend to reinvest earnings back into the business rather than pay dividends, growth stocks tend to have relatively low dividend yields.

Value stocks represent ownership interests in companies in mature industries with relatively low prospects for earnings and revenue growth, or companies with assets whose value has not yet been recognized by other investors. These stocks (e.g., electric utilities) often sell at low P/E ratios or tend to have relatively high dividend yields, or both.

II. Equity Research

A. Types of Research

Portfolio managers of most funds rely on research analysts to supply investment recommendations concerning which stocks to buy or sell. Most larger investment advisers have in-house analysts (commonly referred to as buy-side research) who produce proprietary research for their own PMs. In addition, most PMs obtain research from outside analysts at Wall Street firms (commonly referred to as Street research or sell-side research).

The career track for a security analyst varies depending on the structure of the investment adviser. In some firms, the research department is an entry point for talented young people to gain well-rounded experience in analyzing companies. In this model, successful analysts often go on to become PMs. An alternative approach is to have career analysts with a long-term commitment to a single industry. This approach is effective for Wall Street's sell-side analysts, as well as a few mutual fund managers. Although this approach provides continuity and expertise, it does not build the broad experience and market exposure required to manage a diversified mutual fund.

There are many different research methodologies used by mutual funds. The main types of research are fundamental, technical and quantitative (which can be either fundamental or technical).

Fundamental analysts rate stocks based on their research into the operations and finances of a company with a focus on estimating its future earnings. These analysts pore over the public disclosures of companies, interview company management and gather data from industry sources in order to make buy and sell recommendations.

Technical analysts look at data such as past price movements and trading volume to estimate future prices rather than looking at earnings of companies. Observations from the general stock market as well as trading patterns for individual securities can lead to the development of trading techniques and, ultimately, investment recommendations. See "The 'Head and Shoulders' Top in IBM: Technical Research in Action."

Quantitative analysts, who may use fundamental or technical data or a combination of both, develop mathematical models to assist in finding stocks that meet certain investment criteria. These analysts input vast amounts of data into a computerized model, which can then act as a screen for desirable stocks, categorized according to previously assigned criteria.

The next section concentrates on fundamental research, the most important type of securities analysis for the majority of mutual fund managers. But it is useful to un-

CALLOUT

The "Head and Shoulders" Top in IBM: Technical Research in Action

Sacred cows can be slaughtered. In late 1991, the stock of International Business Machines (IBM) completed a bearish technical formation and had a precipitous fall during a period of market strength and technology leadership. From its 1993 low, IBM rallied nearly 14-fold over the next six years. Were these moves forecastable? To a technical analyst, price patterns were a prelude.

In the late 1980s and early 1990s, IBM formed a bearish reversal pattern that technical analysts call a "head and shoulders" top (marked S-H-S in the figure shown here). The formation consists of an exhaustion rally (the "head") separated by two smaller rallies (the "shoulders"). The pattern is completed when the stock declines below the "neckline," or the lows of the entire formation. There are three attributes of the head and shoulders: (1) it is reliable, (2) the complexity of the pattern gives the analyst advance warning to anticipate the subsequent price decline, and (3) the depth of the formation yields a downside target. IBM had peaked relative to the market in 1970 and had considerably lagged the market in the post-1987 crash recovery as the stock

carved out its "right shoulder." The profile of the pattern was evident throughout the stock's 1988–1991 trading range and was completed by the break of the neckline at $25 (split adjusted) in November 1991. The $14 downside target was calculated by projecting the range from the neckline to the top of the head, downward from the neckline to the target ($25/$44 = 0.57, 0.57 × $25 = $14.25). This downside target was substantially exceeded as IBM bottomed at $10 in August 1993.

While the head-and-shoulders top preceded IBM's 1992 rout, the stock formed a bullish head and shoulders bottom in 1993–1994 (marked s-h-s in the figure). Note that in 1993–1994, the head was lower than the two shoulders. The upside target of this formation was a more modest $23, which was achieved in April 1995 as IBM played catch-up to the secular bull market in technology stocks.

Were these patterns obvious in advance to all Wall Street and buy-side technicians? No, because technical analysts use different tool kits and bring analytical biases to their work. For example, a short-term-oriented technician working at a hedge fund may have never seen the long-term pattern on his or her charts. A buy-side analyst may have feared the peer pressure of a negative rating on a large holding. Also, good analysis is a blend of quantitative skill and qualitative judgment, supplemented by experience.

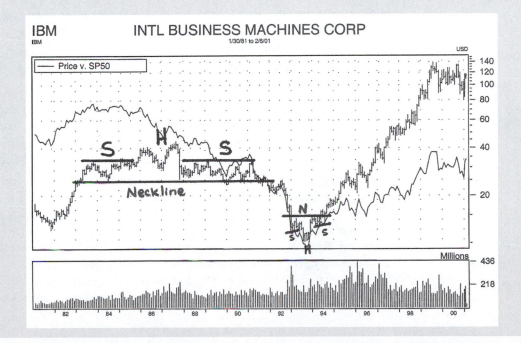

derstand a little more about the difference between quantitative and technical research. When asked to explain the difference, Richard Bernstein, chief quantitative strategist at Merrill Lynch & Company, said, "Market technicians believe you can extract all necessary information by simply looking at a stock price chart. Quantitative analysts are going to use a little more probability theory. It is more mathematical than visual."[1]

B. *Fundamental Research*

Fundamental equity research involves evaluating not only a specific company, but also its competitive position within its industry, as well as the industry's position in the market. The following are general questions that a fundamental equity analyst may ask:

- **Historical financial performance**: What has the trend been in revenues, costs and profit margins? Are the drivers of that performance still in place, or has the situation changed significantly?

- **Projected performance**: What is the projected trend in unit growth versus pricing? What is the breakdown of revenues by operating units? What areas will experience growth versus areas that might stagnate?

- **Breakdown of financial performance**: Is demand for the company's products strong? What is the supply relative to demand? Are prices for its raw materials stable or subject to increases? Does the company have excess cash flow from operations, and what is management's intended use for that cash flow?

- **Current financial position:** What is the current cash position? Are receivables going up or down? How are sales? What is the current inventory level? Any lost contracts?

- **Competitive environment**: Who are the important competitors the company faces? How large and strong are those competitors, and what are their announced plans? Is there pricing pressure?

- **Regulatory environment**: Do the existing regulations protect the company from competition? Are those regulations likely to change in an adverse way?

- **Event risk**: Are there impending regulatory or legislative changes? If the company has foreign operations, could currency fluctuations in a country affect the firm? Is there risk of adverse government actions, such as an oil embargo?

- **Quality of management**: Are the senior managers of the company experienced, with strong track records? As unanticipated problems occur, are they likely to make good decisions about how to respond?

The fundamental analyst typically approaches these questions by studying financial statements, touring facilities and talking with management, competitors and suppliers. The fundamental analyst also reads trade journals, attends conferences and reads Wall Street research. By assimilating information from a variety of sources, analysts develop an understanding of an industry and how an individual company stacks up against its competition. They also make contacts who can help them evaluate market rumors about a company. See "Trying to Differentiate Between Rumor and Fact."

Fundamental analysts used to rely heavily on management guidance about the likely future path of corporate revenues and earnings. However, management guidance

CALLOUT
Trying to Differentiate Between Rumor and Fact

The most carefully researched investment positions can come under sudden and unexpected challenges. In May 2000, the shares of EMC Corp. came under selling pressure as investors grew nervous about the company's ability to ship one of its newest products. EMC is one of the world's largest producers of computer storage systems. At the time, it was preparing to ship an eagerly anticipated new storage product that included multiple high-speed disk drives.

On May 26, a Wall Street analyst began cautioning investors that EMC's new product shipments would be delayed because of a shortage of the component disk drives. Although EMC had several sources for disk drives, the drives of its primary suppliers had failed to qualify under EMC's specifications for the new high-speed application. The Street analyst feared the remaining suppliers had insufficient capacity to fill the gap in time for EMC to

ship on schedule. If true, EMC would be in danger of missing projections for revenues and earnings, a fear that drove the stock 8% lower during the day.

Holding substantial positions in EMC stock, analysts and portfolio managers at Trustworthy Mutual Funds were concerned. Was the issue real or not, and if so, how would it affect EMC? Trustworthy's analysts worked overnight to contact different players in EMC's supply chain. They received assurances from the remaining disk drive manufacturers that EMC's needs could be filled. Pressing further, the analysts contacted Asian suppliers to the disk drive makers, including providers of the drives' semiconductors and high-speed spindle motors. None foresaw any problem in boosting production for EMC.

Trustworthy's analysts concluded the Street rumors were exaggerated and recommended holding the firm's positions. The call proved correct: EMC's shipments of new products came through as planned, and the stock recovered and moved sharply higher in the following months (see the figure).

EMC stock price performance

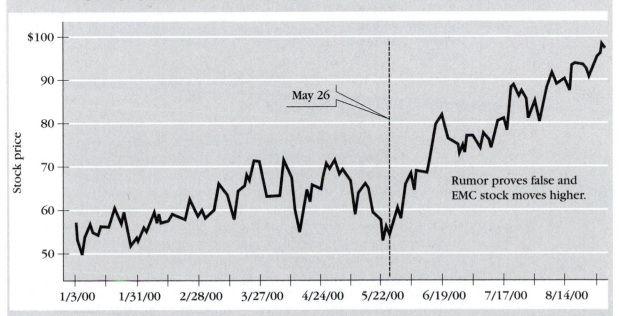

has become much less useful to fundamental analysts over the past few years. Quarterly earnings reports are now announced on conference calls, often involving several hundred listeners. Management presentations on these calls tend to be polished scripts written by lawyers and public relations staff; these calls are not a good vehicle for a candid exchange of ideas. In addition, Securities and Exchange Commission (SEC) Regulation FD ("Fair Disclosure") now prohibits top management from providing material items of information to analysts without promptly disseminating such items in a press release. Since the SEC has not precisely defined what is "material," executives of some companies have decided not to risk legal liability by meeting one-on-one with analysts. As a result of both these factors, fundamental analysts must rely less on management guidance and more on nonmanagement sources of information—for example, customers and suppliers. Moreover, fundamental analysts can still obtain from company management items of information that would not be significant to the average investor but are meaningful to the mosaic developed by an expert analyst.

Most fundamental analysts build models of the stocks they research. A model is a quantitative representation of a company's operations, typically created in a computer spreadsheet. The analyst populates the model with estimates of the company's revenue, expenses, margins, growth rates and other key variables. A model serves two important purposes: it allows an analyst to forecast a company's earnings, the primary driver of stock price performance, and it provides a framework to evaluate new information about the company.

Suppose, for example, that news stories begin hinting at a slowing of cellular phone handset sales in Europe. An analyst following a U.S. maker of semiconductors used in the phones could evaluate the impact on the company's stock by adjusting his model to see what would happen to the firm's operating results. The slowing demand will probably soften prices for chips, squeezing margins and profits if the company cannot trim operating costs quickly. If the slowdown is severe enough, it could even cause a collapse in semiconductor pricing and a serious earnings miss with a significant impact on the company's stock price. A well-constructed model allows the analyst to test a variety of assumptions and scenarios quickly.

C. Buy Side versus Sell Side

The research conducted by analysts at a fund adviser is proprietary, used for the benefit of the shareholders of the funds managed by that adviser. Shareholders of these funds have paid for the research—through the management fees charged to the fund—and reasonably expect that they should be its primary beneficiaries. Sharing the research publicly would undermine its value. Market prices quickly reflect new information about a company, giving an advantage to the analyst who uncovers it first. If an analyst finds an attractive investment opportunity, the goal is to establish positions in the stock before other investors recognize that opportunity.

In contrast to the proprietary nature of buy-side research conducted by fund advisers, the sell-side research generated by Wall Street firms is disseminated broadly. While this sell-side research is designed partly to help brokerage clients make good stock picks, it often has a different purpose. Most Wall Street firms derive the majority of their revenue and earnings from investment banking and securities underwriting services provided to corporations. In a speech to the Economic Club of New York on

October 18, 1999, SEC Chairman Arthur Levitt spoke bluntly about the closeness of these relationships between Street analysts and their firms' corporate clients: "If analysts continue to view the world through rose-colored lenses, they doom themselves to irrelevance. As more and more investors, even retail investors, recognize 'sell-side' analysis as a marketing tool, they will increasingly turn elsewhere for reliable research." Because of these underwriting relationships, Street analysts rarely assign sell recommendations to securities and instead use terms such as "neutral" or "hold" (which the knowledgeable investor may equate with "avoid"). (See "When a Buy Is Not a Buy.") In response to criticisms about potential conflicts of interest, the National Association of Securities Dealers, Inc. (NASD) has proposed rules requiring analysts to disclose personal ownership and investment banking relations with any company they cover, and several Wall Street firms have announced that their research analysts will be barred from buying stock in the companies they cover.

Nevertheless, Wall Street research does serve important functions to analysts at fund advisers. Since Street analysts often follow an industry for years, they can develop in-depth expertise on the companies within that industry. As a result, an individual Street analyst may be the private source of new stock ideas or cutting-edge analysis of existing positions, regardless of what is contained in the published reports of the Wall Street firm. More broadly, Wall Street estimates of company earnings help shape the consensus expectation of a company's future profits and growth rate, two factors that become embedded in its stock price. Any changes in those expectations are quickly reflected in the stock. Therefore, it is important for a mutual fund analyst to be aware if his or her own earnings estimate for a company is above or below the Street consensus. For example, suppose that an analyst at a fund adviser is forecasting an automaker's upcoming quarterly earnings report at $1.40 per share. She likes the company and is confident in her estimate, but knows that the consensus of sell-side analysts is $1.65

CALLOUT
When a Buy Is Not a Buy

When Jack Grubman upgraded AT&T stock to a buy in November [1999], the star Salomon Smith Barney analyst made big headlines. AT&T, long criticized by Mr. Grubman, was thrilled. And Salomon, a Citigroup unit, soon won a lucrative spot helping to manage the $10.6 billion initial public offering of AT&T Wireless Group.

Everyone seemed to win—everyone, that is, except investors who heeded his call and bought AT&T stock.

It turns out Mr. Grubman's high-profile call came just as AT&T's stock price was close to its high for the past year. The stock since has been halved as the entire telecom sector has plunged. So what has Mr. Grubman done about it? Well, nothing: He has kept his "buy" rating

on AT&T and most of the 34 other stocks he follows. . . . Still, Mr. Grubman contends that most sell-side analysts (those at Wall Street brokerage firms) don't post negative ratings, anyway. "Let's call a spade a spade," he says. "Nobody on the sell side puts negative ratings on stocks. Very few people have anything less than a positive rating."*

On October 6, 2000, "Mr. Grubman downgraded AT&T to an 'outperform' from a 'buy,' " and noted that "the reason the downgrade wasn't more drastic, to a lower 'neutral' rating, was that the stock had already declined 53% from its 52-week high."**

*Source: *Wall Street Journal,* October 4, 2000, **Wall Street Journal* October 9, 2000.

per share. If she is correct—and the company reports $1.40—the stock will fare badly, as most investors had been expecting better results. (See "The Cost of an Earnings Miss Can Be High.")

D. Valuation

1. Company valuation   Building an accurate picture of a company's operations and business prospects is important, but it is only part of the investment process. Research becomes investing when all the carefully accumulated information is used to form a buy or sell decision. Valuation is typically the determining factor, with the analyst and PM trying to assess whether a company's prospects are fully reflected in its stock price. (Reading 5.1 gives specific detail on two approaches to valuing common stock.)

An earlier portion of this Chapter introduced various quantitative measures of stocks. Two of the most widely used for valuation are the price-to-earnings (P/E) and price-to-cash flow (P/CF) ratios, although they do not dictate a buy or sell decision on their own. For example, is a networking equipment stock with a P/E ratio of 50 too expensive to buy? Not necessarily. The analyst must put the valuation statistics in context: How fast are the company's earnings growing? At what P/E ratios are its competitors trading? Is the analyst modeling bigger revenue increases than those expected by the Street? After weighing these variables, the analyst may assign a buy recommendation to the stock, calculating that it is undervalued even at 50 times earnings.

The shares of Cisco Systems provide an illustration of how a seemingly expensive stock can become more so. In late 1998, shares of Cisco were trading at a P/E of 71 times the consensus estimate for the company's July 1999 fiscal year. At a valuation level far above the market averages, it would have been logical for an analyst to shy away from the stock. Yet Cisco shares continued to dominate the U.S. equity market. In late 1999—after gaining 131%—the stock was trading at 96 times the earnings estimate for July 2000! Only in late 2000 did Cisco's P/E contract sharply, while remaining substantially above the average P/E of the S&P 500.

The drivers of Cisco's enormous market appreciation were twofold. To begin with, the fundamental outlook for the firm's earnings improved, and earnings estimates were rising. That alone would have helped the stock, other factors being equal. Even better for Cisco shareholders, investors were showing tremendous interest in anything Internet related. Cisco's products provided critical infrastructure for companies building Internet businesses, yet it was not dependent on the success on any single dot.com business model. Even at more than 70 times earnings, many investors viewed Cisco as a relatively safe way to invest in the Internet. That thesis led investors to pay more for each dollar of the company's earnings—to 96 times the forward earnings estimate. Such an increase in the P/E ratio of a stock is known as "multiple expansion."

This sort of positive sentiment about their prospects can bias valuations upward, leaving the stocks "priced to perfection." This means they are very vulnerable to any hint that the good news is tapering off. If the company warns of slowing business conditions, investors can drive down the price of the stock in a hurry.

2. Market valuation   Valuation of an individual stock or industry cannot be done in isolation. Considering value in the context of the overall market—or *relative valuation*—gives the analyst a yardstick by which to gauge individual companies. Unlike a fixed

CALLOUT
The Cost of an Earnings Miss Can Be High

In the second half of 1999, the share price of Procter & Gamble (P&G) had been a strong performer, advancing 37% from $86 on July 1, 1999, to a high of $117 on January 11, 2000. Despite an ongoing restructuring program, a sluggish business climate in Europe and a strong dollar versus the euro, P&G's overall business fundamentals still appeared solid to most investors. Even in the face of these challenges, the stock carried a rich valuation. Trading at nearly $100 per share in late January, P&G's shares carried a price/earnings ratio of approximately 30 times the $3.22 consensus estimate of P&G's earnings per share for their upcoming June 30, 2000, fiscal year end. It was particularly expensive for an "old economy" firm with an expected long-term growth rate of 12% to 13% per year, but P&G had demonstrated years of reliable earnings growth while delivering few negative surprises to investors.

Things changed quickly on the morning of March 7, 2000, with the bad news spelled out in a 7:00 A.M. press release from the company: "P&G said that it expects core third quarter earnings per share (EPS) on a diluted basis to be 10% to 11% *below* a year-ago, compared to its previous guidance of a 7–9 percent *increase*. . . . Resulting core net earnings per-share-growth for the fiscal year are expected to be about 7 percent, versus the 13 percent originally anticipated" (emphasis added). The company went on to detail several factors that had caused the shortfall, but there was no way to soften the message: investors' expectations for P&G's earnings were too high.

The reaction in the marketplace was swift and painful, with P&G shares opening sharply lower. From the previous day's close of $87 7/16, the stock fell 30% to finish the day at $61 on a volume of nearly 70 million shares, more than six times the stock's typical daily volume at the time. The sell-off pared nearly $38 billion from the company's market capitalization. As the figure shows, P&G shares remained below $70 until October 2000.

Procter & Gamble price history

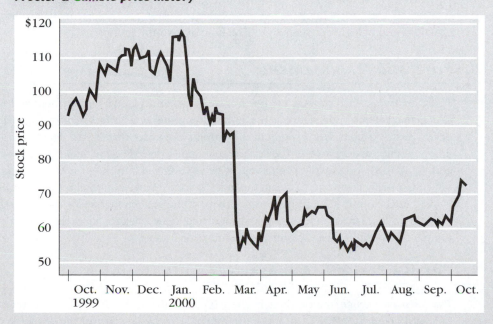

marker, however, valuation levels for the overall equity market have fluctuated significantly through time. Using the aggregate price/earnings ratio of the S&P 500 index, Figure 5.1 shows how widely the valuation level of the U.S. market has ranged since 1994. Three factors stand out as heavily influencing the overall level of equity market valuation:

Earnings growth.   A company's stock price represents the present value of the firm's future earnings, taking into account its balance sheet assets. If investors' expectations for earnings growth increase, so too will the value of the stock. In strong economic times, with estimates of growth rates rising for many companies, the P/E ratios for individual stocks and market indexes tend to increase.

Interest rates.   Rising interest rates tend to depress equity valuations. They make it more expensive for companies to access credit or service debt, and could slow the economy enough to put future earnings growth in doubt. Rising rates signal expectations of higher inflation, rendering a company's future earnings less valuable. Rising interest rates also mean higher yields on fixed income securities, making them more attractive as alternatives to equities. Conversely, declining interest rates tend to support higher equity valuations.

Investor sentiment.   Although difficult to observe directly, psychology plays a role in setting equity valuations. If the economy and the political scene are stable, investors may be willing to pay higher P/E multiples for equities. In such an environment, investors may believe there is a higher likelihood that companies will meet their expectations for earnings growth. Investors perceive the risk to be lower and are willing to pay more for the asset. The result is the type of P/E multiple expansion that occurred between 1995 and mid-1999, as shown in Figure 5.1. Conversely, if the economy is weakening and the political scene is unstable, investor psychology tends to bring down P/E multiples for equities. (See "The Role of Investor Sentiment.")

III. *Portfolio Management*

There are two main approaches to portfolio management: passive management and active management. Understanding the difference requires a little background on indexes. A stock index is a hypothetical portfolio of stocks that is maintained by an independent provider; two of the largest stock index providers are Standard & Poor's and Frank Russell Company. The providers price each stock in the market index periodically (usually daily) and calculate the index's price change and total return. Indexes were created to provide a gauge of the activity of the general market, or a certain size or type of company, by measuring and reporting value changes for a representative sample of securities. (See Chapter Two for more on indexes.)

A. *Passive Portfolio Management*

Passive management is an approach where the objective is simply to match the return of a market index. Passive managers try to minimize *tracking error,* or the deviation of the fund's return from the return of the index. This could be done by purchasing all of

FIGURE 5.1

P/E ratio of the S&P 500 index over time

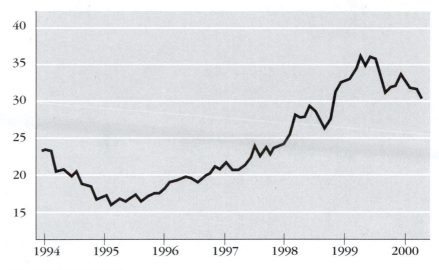

Source: The Conference Board.
Note: Actual P/E ratio for the S&P 500 is based on 12-month trailing earnings.

the component securities of the index in those same proportions in the fund, a practice known as *full replication.* Because some indexes contain a large number of stocks and trading many stocks can be costly, passive managers often purchase only a statistically representative subset of stocks in a practice known as *sampling.* Through quantitative modeling, they can assemble a basket of securities whose combined total return and volatility will closely approximate that of the index most of the time. However, significant differences can arise when securities markets or individual components of an index experience unusual volatility.

Because an index itself has no fees, an index fund must carefully control fees and other expenses to track the index closely. Most index funds charge very low management fees since they do not require securities analysts or securities research. In addition, portfolio managers of index funds generally receive lower compensation than successful active managers of mutual funds. However, shareholders of index funds typically expect the same high level of service afforded to shareholders of actively managed funds in the same complex. Index funds also incur custodial, audit and registration fees. Scale is an advantage, allowing the index fund's management fees and other expenses to be spread over a large asset base.

Although an index fund manager does not make active investment decisions, most index funds must still trade each day in response to shareholder activity. The manager must buy securities in the index as shareholders buy shares of the fund and must sell securities in the index as shareholders redeem shares of the fund—while keeping the fund closely aligned with its index. One key to minimizing the impact of shareholder

CALLOUT
The Role of Investor Sentiment

Investor sentiment can play a large role in securities valuation, especially in bull markets when a long-running stream of successes can prompt investors to pay ever-higher prices for stocks in favored categories. Initial public offerings (IPOs) of Internet retailing stocks in 1999 provided a graphic example. Following the well-documented surges in first-day trading of many dot.com IPOs, the phenomenon became self-fulfilling. Investors clamored for allocations of new offerings, even as the quality of the new firms' business plans deteriorated and earnings were nowhere on the horizon. On July 28, 1999, an Internet retailer named drugstore.com came public at an offering price of $18 per share. It soared more than 179% in secondary market trading, closing its first day at $50.25. Although it traded as high as $67½ in its first few weeks, business realities soon set in. The company found that acquiring new customers came at a high cost, including promotions, coupons and a $100 million licensing fee to place a tab on Amazon.com's website. It also found customers more prone to purchase low-margin pharmacy items than high-margin prescriptions, and order fulfillment costs were relatively high. As a result, estimates of when the company would turn profitable began to push further into the future. As the company's cash drew lower, it would need to return to an increasingly reluctant equity market for more financing. By October 2000, little more than a year after a stunning IPO, drugstore.com's stock traded below $3 per share.

drugstore.com price history

cash flows on tracking error is to have good advance information about the magnitude and direction of the transactions. Most fund complexes have sophisticated cash management systems that monitor pending shareholder activity during the trading day. These help the manager execute the net trade at the end of the day. Many index funds also carry positions in index futures, which track their underlying index very closely. Since most trading in index futures is low cost and very liquid, the futures can be bought or sold daily to absorb the fund's cash flows. Using index futures makes it unnecessary to disturb the individual securities positions that represent the bulk of the fund's assets.

Perhaps the biggest headache for an index fund manager is a change in the composition of the index itself. Whether due to a merger, bankruptcy or a desire by the index provider to include a more representative security, index changes are common. Russell indexes are rebalanced annually at the end of June, with hundreds of securities moving in and out of popular indexes such as the Russell 2000 index of small-capitalization stocks. Even the most widely used index, the Standard and Poor's 500 Index, has a surprising number of changes in a year (see Table 5.1).

There is considerable evidence showing that stocks that are to be included in the S&P 500 index tend to experience abnormally high relative returns in the period leading up to their inclusion in the index and then experience abnormally low relative returns in the period following their inclusion in the index. This insight has led some index managers to buy stocks as soon as it is announced that they will be added to the S&P 500 in order to achieve returns above that of the index and offset some of the index fund's operating expenses. However, this strategy can be dangerous in the event of adverse market movements for a manager trying to track an index closely. (Remember that passive managers attempt to replicate the exact return of a market index. Since their objective is to reduce tracking error, or the deviation of the fund's return from the return of the index, any strategy that might lead to such a deviation could undermine that objective.) For example, suppose today it is announced that XYZ stock will be added to the index a week from now. The manager of an index fund buys today at $42 per share all the shares of XYZ that the index fund will need a week from now. However, during this week before XYZ's inclusion in the index, XYZ announces a series of layoffs, causing its share price to tumble to $30 at the time it is included in the index.

TABLE 5.1

Constituent changes to the S&P 500 index

Year	S&P 500 Index Changes	Notable Additions
2000	57	Metlife, Palm, Harley-Davidson
1999	34	America Online, Yahoo!, Qualcomm
1998	46	Gateway, Nextel, FEDEX
1997	23	Omnicom, KLA-Tencor, Charles Schwab

The index fund manager is stuck with a $12 loss on its XYZ shares, which the fund could have avoided by waiting until the stock joined the index.

B. *Active Portfolio Management*

Active management is an approach where the manager's objective is to beat the return of an index. It is founded in the belief that diligent research can uncover opportunities where a security's price does not accurately reflect a company's true prospects. The active PM is responsible for the day-to-day buy and sell decisions in the fund. The manager selects securities from among the hundreds available in the relevant universe, allocates them in specific weights in a portfolio and produces a new asset (the mutual fund) that acts differently from any individual stock it holds.

Active management is framed by an overall process, which can vary from one fund complex to another. Within any given process, individual managers execute specific strategies and tactics in the daily challenge of portfolio management. The portfolio management process can take a number of forms, and many investment advisers employ elements of more than one. This is particularly true in larger fund complexes that can support broad product lines and multiple investment approaches.

Top-down managers form a macro view of the economy and capital markets and use that as a framework to identify attractive sectors, industries and securities. For example, an expectation that gross domestic product (GDP) growth is slowing may lead a top-down manager away from cyclically sensitive industries and toward steady unit growth companies in the consumer and health care sectors. Purchase decisions about individual stocks come at the end of this process.

In contrast, **bottom-up** managers begin with the selection of individual securities. They may narrow the choices with a variety of screening methods, such as minimum values for profitability or growth rate or a maximum level of P/E ratio. But they choose securities with the most attractive investment prospects, with little regard for macroeconomic forecasts. The fund's sector weightings are the by-products of individual stock selection decisions instead of an overall sector strategy.

Quantitative managers make extensive use of models and screening techniques, factoring dozens or even hundreds of variables into security selection and weighting decisions. Although subjective factors like the buy ratings on a stock may play a role in such models, quantitative managers tend to rely more on objective data about the financial trends for specific companies or the general economy.

Each of these investment approaches would come within the rubric of fundamental portfolio management, based on the measures of stocks and valuation statistics covered earlier in this Chapter. Individual PMs sometimes incorporate selected technical data, such as trading trends in price or volume, to guide the timing of buy and sell decisions. In addition, certain quantitative managers emphasize technical data in running their computer models. The models can be based on technical and/or fundamental approaches.

Most mutual funds are run by one individual, though some fund complexes employ alternative approaches to managing funds. One is the *team approach,* in which a number of investment professionals work together on one or more funds with similar objectives. Benefits of this structure include the sharing of ideas among investment professionals and good continuity of management if someone leaves the firm. The primary drawback is the potential diffusion of investment responsibility, with no one person fully accountable for fund results.

Another variant is the *composite approach,* which combines a team concept with individual accountability. In this approach, one manager is responsible for each component of a fund, with a different manager responsible for overall coordination and asset allocation. In a global fund, for instance, one manager could be responsible for U.S. equities, a second manager for European equities and a third manager for all other equities. In addition, a fourth manager could allocate assets among regions and coordinate industry weightings.

C. *Portfolio Construction and Strategy*

The day-to-day strategy employed by a PM is typically more flexible than the processes described above. While the overall process represents the PM's core philosophy, the PM's strategy must be consistent with the fund's objectives and constraints, while attempting to beat the relevant benchmarks for fund performance.

1. Investment objectives and constraints   The fund's investment objective sets the basic parameters for a fund's investment strategy. Featured prominently in a fund's prospectus, the investment objective is the manager's overriding goal; it represents the general expectation that shareholders have when buying shares in the fund. Investment objectives in many prospectuses tend to be worded broadly, such as "growth," "capital appreciation" or "income." Such broad objectives in effect define the outer limits of the fund's investment strategy; they leave the manager with considerable discretion in constructing a portfolio.

If the name of a fund has a specific meaning (e.g., the Energy Services Fund), then the PM is obliged to invest a certain percentage of the fund's assets in securities covered by the fund's name. Under the current rules of the SEC (effective in mid-2002), 80% of a fund's assets, measured at the time of security acquisition must meet a description of securities or companies implied by the fund's name—for example, the Mid-Cap Fund (see Chapter Three for more detail). However, the names of some funds are derived more with marketing in mind—for example, Putnam Voyager or American Century Ultra. These funds are not subject to the SEC's name test because their names do not imply a specific set of securities or companies. Moreover, the SEC has concluded that "growth" and "value" are not subject to the name test because these terms are insufficiently precise.

Most mutual funds must meet the diversification requirements in the Investment Company Act and Internal Revenue Code (see Chapter Three). However, these requirements are relatively loose. For example, a diversified fund could hold 20% of its assets in two 10% positions and 80% of its assets in twenty 4% positions. Therefore, a manager must decide as a matter of investment strategy the amount and nature of portfolio diversification.

As explained in Chapter One, the overall risk of a fund portfolio is determined by how its individual holdings move relative to one another. For example, a stock may be very volatile if held alone, but if paired with another that reacts in the opposite direction to market events, the combination could be relatively low risk. Although it is rare to find stocks that have perfectly negative correlation with one another, the real world does offer some good approximations. Consider the relationship between oil stocks and airline stocks. While falling oil prices have a negative impact on oil and energy service companies, they benefit airlines by lowering their fuel costs. Therefore, in constructing a portfolio, a manager must decide how much individual security risk to assume—which stocks to include in which proportions and whether to counterbalance the risk of some securities by selecting other securities that tend to move in the opposite direction.

While a diversified portfolio can reduce its individual security risk (or alpha risk), a diversified portfolio still is subject to the risk posed by the possible rise or fall of the overall equity market (or beta risk). As mentioned in Chapter One, market or beta risk determines on average between 30% and 50% of the price movement of a stock. Therefore, depending on his or her view of macroeconomic trends, a manager can change the fund's sensitivity to overall market risk (or beta risk). A manager who believes that conditions are favorable for a strong general advance in the equity market can increase the fund's beta by various techniques. For example, the manager could reduce cash to zero and concentrate the fund assets in mid-cap tech stocks, which tend to have high betas. Alternatively, if the manager expects equities to rise sharply out of a recessionary bear market, the manager may choose to concentrate the fund in cyclical stocks that often move first and fastest in such a situation. Conversely, if a manager expects the general equity market to correct downward, the manager could bring the fund's cash to a relatively high level and concentrate its assets in defensive stocks. For instance, stocks of drug manufacturers and electric utilities generally have low betas; they tend to outperform the general equity market when it is falling.

Closely related questions are: How many stocks should a fund hold, and how big should its largest positions be? The answer depends on several factors, including the fund's objective and the PM's investment strategy. A fund managed for aggressive capital appreciation may have fewer holdings, as well as larger individual positions, than a more conservative fund with a growth & income objective. The impact of a few stocks in the portfolio is much greater if they represent positions of 5% or 6% of a fund's assets rather than 1% or 2%. For this reason, the number and size of a fund's holdings should be influenced by the manager's degree of conviction that a particular stock will outperform, as well as his or her general skill in picking outperformers. A Morningstar study on concentrated funds reached the following conclusion:

> Remember, concentration produces extreme performance, but it isn't actually better on average. The portfolio manager makes the biggest difference in terms of whether or not the fund will succeed, because the effect of stock picking is magnified in a focused portfolio. Without the talent, the typical focused fund isn't likely to compensate investors for the additional individual stock risk they are taking on.[2]

The number and size of fund holdings also are affected by a range of practical factors. The PM of a highly concentrated fund with a few large positions may have difficulty selling fund holdings quickly if market conditions change or shareholder redemptions accelerate. These factors are particularly relevant to funds that hold relatively illiquid securities such as small company stocks or emerging market stocks. Furthermore, mutual funds with large assets tend to hold more names than funds with

FIGURE 5.2

Number of securities held in diversified U.S. equity mutual funds

Percent of all diversified U.S. equity funds

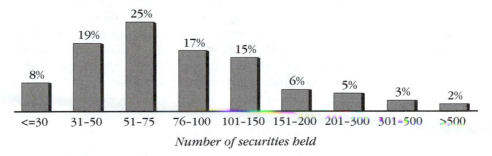

Number of securities held

Source: Morningstar Principia, July 2000.

smaller asset bases. On the other hand, there are diminishing benefits to diversification beyond a point. Position sizes become too small to affect the fund's results, regardless of how well the stock may perform. Also, keeping track of hundreds of stocks will tax even the most diligent portfolio manager. As shown by Figure 5.2, few funds hold fewer than 30 positions, with most diversified equity funds holding from 50 to 150 positions.

Cash flows and liquidity are other important constraints on PMs. Steady inflows of cash to a fund compel the manager to look for ways to put that cash to work quickly, by buying more of current security positions or seeking additional security names. Heavy redemptions may require the sale of some of the fund's holdings in order to handle the cash outflows, even if the timing is not optimal. Cash flow can be particularly high in sector funds or other funds that concentrate investments in a specific security type. Liquidity of securities (the ability to buy and sell quickly without unduly moving a stock's price) is especially important in thinly traded markets, such as certain foreign markets and the U.S. market for small-capitalization stocks.

2. Beating indexes and peers   While the investment objectives and constraints on a fund set its basic parameters, a manager's behavior is more specifically influenced by the criteria used in determining his or her compensation. In most complexes, PMs receive a relatively low base salary plus a potentially high bonus based primarily on the fund's performance relative to its benchmarks. In most complexes, bonus performance is measured over more than one time period—perhaps one year, three years or five years—although the weightings on each time period may be different. Most complexes have a qualitative or subjective component of a PM's bonus, in addition to this quantitative component based on fund performance. These qualitative or subject components may encompass the manager's efforts in recruiting at universities, mentoring analysts, presenting to client groups and supporting the overall investment process. Most complexes also have some form of compensation based on the performance of a group or entity larger than the manager's own fund in order to encourage idea sharing and build team spirit. These may include the quantitative performance of all funds in the complex or all funds in a particular category (e.g., all international funds), as well as the financial performance of the mutual fund complex as a whole (including distribution and servicing). This last category of compensation often takes the form of shares, stock options or other noncash vehicles.

As mentioned above, the largest portion of a PM's compensation generally depends on how well his or her fund did relative to designated performance criteria. Some complexes measure fund performance relative to a security index, others relative to a peer group and still others relative to a combination of index and peer group. The total compensation of portfolio managers and analysts for equity mutual funds is shown in Table 5.2, although the total compensation of a top-performing PM running a large mutual fund is likely to be a multiple of those medians.

a. Stock indexes   Indexes are groups of stocks that attempt to represent the performance of a whole stock market or market segment, such as technology stocks or small-cap stocks. Common stock indexes serve as benchmarks for portfolio managers—the baseline against which their performance is measured. Active portfolio managers try to beat their benchmarks by selecting what they believe are undervalued stocks or by overweighting industries they believe will be relative outperformers. Passive managers (index funds) try to track their indexes as closely as possible by selecting securities designed to be representative of all securities in the index.

Almost everyone has heard of the Dow Jones Industrial Average index (DJIA), but it is composed of only 30 large, primarily industrial stocks with a few large technology companies. Although it is the oldest and most quoted U.S. stock indicator, it represents only a narrow part of the performance of the overall U.S. stock market and therefore is rarely used by mutual funds. Another popular index is the Nasdaq composite. But this

TABLE 5.2

Summary of results of AIMR/Russell Reynolds compensation survey for mutual fund company respondents

Position	2001 Median Compensation				90th Percentile
	Salary	Bonus	Noncash	Total	
Chief investment officer	$310,000	$1,000,000	$200,000	$1,175,000	3,450,000
Head of equities	250,000	100,000	100,000	450,000	2,575,000
Portfolio manager, domestic equities	175,000	185,000	50,000	402,500	1,550,000
Portfolio manager, global and international equities	140,774	100,000	30,000	266,500	875,000
Securities analyst, domestic equities	110,000	70,000	12,657	217,000	570,000
Securities analyst, international equities	125,000	75,000	8,000	225,000	590,000

Source: Association for Investment Management and Research, *2001 Investment Management Compensation Survey.*

index is heavily laden with technology companies and does not reflect the composition of the U.S. stock market generally. Instead, many U.S. equity funds utilize the S&P 500 index, which is designed to represent the overall market and is composed of stocks of 500 large companies that trade in the United States. Even broader is the Wilshire 5000 index, which includes all listed stocks of companies headquartered in the United States for which prices are readily available. A small minority of U.S. equity funds use the Wilshire 5000 index.

There are literally hundreds of other indexes composed of U.S. or international stocks that are designed to represent entire markets, subsets defined by geographical regions or market capitalization ranges or styles of growth or value. (See the discussion of indexes in Chapter Two.) A good illustration of style indexes is provided by the Russell 1000 index (the largest 1,000 U.S. listed securities) divided into value and growth indexes. The Russell 1000 Value (R1V) includes the securities in the Russell 1000 that share certain characteristics, such as a relatively low P/E ratio, a relatively low P/B ratio and a relatively high dividend yield. By contrast, the Russell 1000 Growth (R1G) includes the securities from the Russell 1000 that share opposite characteristics, such as a relatively high P/E ratio, a relatively high P/B ratio and a relatively low dividend yield. For small-capitalization stocks, a popular index is the Russell 2000, which comprises the next 2,000 largest U.S. stocks after the large-cap stocks in the Russell 1000 (the stocks ranked from 1,001 to 3,000 by market capitalization). There are also indexes focused on mid-cap stocks (e.g., S&P Mid-Cap 400), between the large- and small-capitalization companies.

The fund's index is a major determinant of portfolio strategy. An index is used for performance evaluation and is identified in a fund's prospectus and marketing materials. It shapes investment strategy in two important ways. At a general level, it describes the type or style of securities that represent the investment objective and focus of a fund. For example, XYZ Large Cap Growth Fund may have the Russell 1000 Growth Index as its benchmark index. It includes those stocks with growth characteristics from among the 1,000 largest in the United States, making it a good proxy for the types of companies suggested by the fund's name.

More specifically, an index will bear on the weighting decisions for individual security positions in the fund. Stocks with the largest weighting in an index usually have the largest impact on its performance. Because active management is focused on outperforming an index, PMs carefully weigh decisions to "overweight" or "underweight" a security, and to what degree. An active weight, or "bet," is one where the fund's allocation to a stock differs from the stock's weight in the benchmark; the typical mutual fund has several hundred active weights. A positive active bet is holding a larger portion of a fund portfolio in a stock than it represents in the index. Avoiding a stock entirely or holding a relatively small position is a negative active bet and can be just as risky for the PM as holding a large overweight in another stock. If the absent stock turns out to be one of the stronger performers, it can cause the fund to lag the index. Yet another type of bet is to hold a security not included in the index. This is called an "out-of-benchmark bet."

Consider the following example of a positive bet. On the basis of the firm's research efforts, the manager may believe that a new drug being developed by Merck & Co. will receive approval by the Food and Drug Administration (FDA) sooner than generally expected. The effect would be to boost revenues and earnings for Merck faster than anticipated by Wall Street analysts. The PM would buy Merck shares in the fund and hold it at a weight greater than its weight in the index, creating an overweighted position. If the analysis is correct and Merck shares rally, the fund's larger position will allow it to gain ground on the index.

Negative bets are more easily misunderstood by investors. A stock may be in the top 10 holdings of a mutual fund yet still represent a negative bet by that fund's manager. Certain stocks like General Electric have been large components of the S&P 500, constituting as much as 4% of that index at one time. Therefore, even if a mutual fund holds 2% of its assets in General Electric, it would be making a large negative bet against the stock (i.e., it would be only half weighted in General Electric) (see Table 5.3).

Just as a fund manager can make a positive or negative bet on a stock within an index, so can the manager make a positive or negative bet on a sector in an index. Set forth in Table 5.4 are the neutral sector weights for the S&P 500 index as of December 31, 2000, as compared to the sector weights of the hypothetical Trustworthy U.S. Equity Fund. As you can see, this fund was significantly overweighted in Utilities and Health Care, while being significantly underweighted in Technology and Energy. The fund was close to market weighted in the other sectors.

b. Peer groups   Mutual fund managers are also judged by their performance relative to a competitive universe. A competitive universe is a group of competing mutual funds investing in a similar manner. The funds in a competitive universe are ranked by total return and are typically divided into four quartiles. The better performers (top 25%) compose the first quartile, and the poorer relative performers (bottom 25%) are in the fourth quartile. Independent measuring firms, such as Lipper and Morningstar, generate monthly, quarterly and annual rankings of mutual funds by their total returns relative to their competitive universes. (For a more detailed discussion of peer groups, see Chapter Two.)

The key question in these peer rankings is whether a fund is being considered in the appropriate competitive universe. Under Lipper's old system, the competitive uni-

TABLE 5.3

Security weights for Trustworthy U.S. Equity Fund versus S&P 500 index as of 12/31/00

Company Name	% in Fund	% in S&P	Variance
General Electric	2.0	4.0	−2.0
Exxon Mobil Corp	2.0	2.6	−0.6
Pfizer Inc	2.5	2.5	0.0
Cisco Systems Inc	2.0	2.4	−0.4
CitiGroup Inc	2.5	2.2	0.3
Wal-Mart Stores	2.1	2.0	0.1
Microsoft Corp	1.5	2.0	−0.5
American International Group	2.2	1.9	0.3
Merck & Co.	1.7	1.8	−0.1
Intel Corp	1.5	1.7	−0.2

TABLE 5.4

Sector weights for Trustworthy U.S. Equity Fund versus S&P 500 index as of 12/31/00

Sector	Mutual Fund Sector Weight	S&P 500 Sector Weight	Variance
Utilities	16.6	9.8	6.8
Health Care	17.5	13.3	4.2
Construction and Real Estate	1.2	0.3	0.9
Industrial Machinery	6.9	6.1	0.8
Transportation	1.5	0.7	0.8
Finance	18.1	17.5	0.6
Durables	2.1	1.8	0.3
Aerospace and Defense	2.0	1.7	0.3
Basic Industry	3.3	3.2	0.1
Retail and Wholesale	5.7	5.8	−0.1
Services	0.4	0.6	−0.2
Media and Leisure	3.5	3.9	−0.4
Nondurables	6.0	6.6	−0.6
Energy	3.1	6.6	−3.5
Technology	12.1	21.9	−9.8
	100.0	100.0	0.0

verses are grouped around several prospectus investment objectives—for example, capital appreciation, growth and equity income. These peer groups remain relatively stable over time. However, some of these old Lipper competitive universes are very large—for example, the growth universe contains over 1,700 peers. Moreover, other old Lipper competitive universes are quite diffuse—for example, capital appreciation is subject to a wide range of interpretation.

Therefore, while fund managers running against old Lipper peer groups know with certainty which funds are in their competitive universe, they often complain that they are losing out to funds that are "cheating"—that is, investing in a manner at odds with the average positioning of the peer group. For example, the Janus Balanced Fund was heavily loaded with technology stocks despite the generally conservative bent of that peer group. This heavy technology weighting helped that fund outperform its peers in 1999 but hurt its peer group performance in 2000.

In 1998, Lipper introduced a new peer group system based on a fund's actual holdings rather than its prospectus objective. The peer categories are organized in a grid according to market capitalization (large-cap, multi-cap, mid-cap and small-cap) and style (value, blend and growth). The new Lipper peer groups are similar to Morningstar's three-by-three box system, illustrated in Table 5.5, except that Morningstar has only three capitalization levels instead of the four levels used by "new" Lipper (Lipper adds a multi-cap row between large cap and mid cap).

Fund managers running against Lipper or Morningstar peer boxes have the advantage of competing with a group of funds focused on similar types of securities—for instance, large-cap value funds or small-cap growth. However, such fund managers can

TABLE 5.5

Morningstar Style Map℠

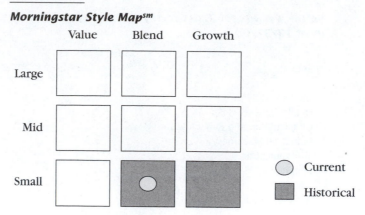

Reprinted with permission.

never be certain which funds will be in their peer box over typical periods for performance measurement (e.g., one, three and five years). Because the boxes are based on the holdings as of the last reporting date, there is a tendency for funds to shift boxes from time to time. This tendency is exacerbated because different fund complexes use different reporting dates, so that holdings from any one complex may be stable relative to other complexes. Moreover, the criteria for the boxes can inadvertently work against the best-performing funds. For instance, suppose the manager of a small-cap value fund picks such great stocks that they rise dramatically in price. Because of the higher P/E ratios and market capitalizations of such stocks, the fund could be pushed into small-cap blend, or even mid-cap blend, where the fund's peer ranking might be quite different.

Academics have examined how PMs react to their relative peer group position by applying a "tournament" theory to the fund industry. Since funds with the highest returns attract the most assets, the tournament theory suggests that rational managers will attempt to maximize their compensation by altering the composition of their portfolios based on their relative performance during the calendar year. One study found that funds losing in the growth peer group during the calendar year increase portfolio risk to a greater degree than funds winning in that peer group toward the latter half of the year.[3] Another study found that mutual funds experience unusual price rises on the last day of the calendar year and explains this finding as an effort by portfolio managers to increase their relative performance and thereby their annual compensation.[4] While these studies are provocative, it is unclear how much boosting performance on one day would affect the compensation of PMs since they are typically paid for performance over multiple time periods involving several years. Moreover, the tournament studies are somewhat undercut by the fact that some complexes use a calendar year, while others use a fiscal year for measuring fund performance (e.g., 12, 36 and 60 months ending September 30). On the other hand, toward the end of a quarter, certain managers have been known to buy stocks that have done very well during the quarter.

This type of window dressing allows these managers to appear to have selected the winning stocks for their funds, which often publish a list of top holdings as of quarter end.

D. *Performance Attribution*

Mutual fund managers live in glass houses, with their performance results published daily. Each night, fund complexes calculate the net asset value (NAV) for all funds and report them to the public. A fund's total return is calculated by summing any dividends received and any change in NAV during the period (which can be positive or negative), and dividing the sum by the cost of the initial investment at the start of the period. Total return calculations assume all fund distributions are reinvested in additional shares of the same fund.

On the basis of total return, the performance of every mutual fund is ranked relative to its index and its peer group. These relative performance numbers are then dissected by pundits in the media, measuring firms (e.g., Lipper and Morningstar) as well as fund shareholders. No other profession is subjected to this intense scrutiny based on such precise numbers. Suppose the performance of every dentist or lawyer were measured to the second decimal point, ranked quarterly against the performance of all other dentists or lawyers, and published widely in the media. Imagine the additional pressure on these professions!

Given these external pressures, the effort within a fund management company is to understand fund performance rather than criticize it. Even an outstanding fund manager will pick winners only two-thirds of the time and losers the rest of the time. The point is to understand performance so managers can repeat their successes and learn from their mistakes. Performance attribution is a process, based on extensive data analysis, by which a PM can understand why his or her fund performed the way it did during the relevant period.

Active managers make many different types of decisions in the attempt to outperform their fund's index and peer group. Performance attribution is the process of analyzing how effective those decisions were. Each decision can be measured and its positive or negative impact on the fund characterized in terms of *relative contribution*. For example, a PM may choose to overweight financial stocks in the fund compared to their weight in the fund's index. If financial stocks outperform the overall index during the subsequent period, the decision was a good one. Performance attribution captures that benefit, measuring both how big an overweight, or "active weight," the manager elected to carry and the degree to which the overweighted position beat the index. The combination of both factors is the decision's relative contribution to the fund's performance, expressed in basis points.

Performance attribution analysis is generated by sophisticated computer systems. Some mutual fund complexes develop and maintain their own proprietary systems, while others use commercially available products. The systems are loaded with weighting percentages and returns for individual securities positions in both funds and indexes and then calculate the performance impact of the manager's decisions. It is helpful to think of a fund's index as a neutral portfolio, providing the standard against which the system evaluates a PM's active decisions. Active equity managers typically make three main types of decisions: asset allocation decisions, sector or industry weighting decisions and individual security selection decisions.

1. Asset allocation decisions   An active asset allocation choice involves holding asset classes that are outside the fund's benchmark index. For the typical fund with an S&P 500 index, holding anything other than equities in that index constitutes an active asset allocation decision by the PM. Equity funds commonly have some allocation to other asset classes, although the portions are usually modest. Foreign stocks are often held in "domestic" equity funds, particularly shares of companies in global industries such as autos, oil or telecommunications. Equity income funds frequently hold debentures or convertible bonds to help meet their income objective.

The most common nonequity asset held by equity mutual funds is cash equivalents. All funds hold some allocation of cash to respond to shareholder redemptions, typically 3% to 7% of assets. Cash balances above 10% of assets often represent a strategic decision by the PM to reduce the fund's equity market exposure, a practice sometimes referred to as market timing. Attempting to predict short-term fluctuations in market direction is extraordinarily difficult, and few managers have successful track records at such predictions. Moreover, since the U.S. equity markets have returned between 11% and 13% on average over substantial historical periods, cash tends to be a drag on long-term fund performance. Therefore, most PMs try to limit cash holdings and minimize the impact of this asset class on fund performance.

2. Sector weighting decisions   As illustrated in the financial sector example above, most funds carry active sector weights. Some active sector weights are conscious, driven by top-down sector analysis. One PM may feel that a healthy economy and strong profit growth will favor technology stocks and accordingly build an over-weighted position in the sector. Another may be bearish on the prospects of the U.S. economy and accordingly choose to emphasize defensive stocks like consumer staples. Other active sector weights are the by-product of individual security selection by a bottom-up manager. As an illustration, a PM may like the relative earnings growth of several drug companies and thereby wind up with an overweighting in health care. Regardless of their methodology, all of these managers are making a sector bet and should understand whether it succeeded or failed.

Consider the sector bets and attribution analysis in the sample fund described in Table 5.6. (The sample attribution report is for one month, though many complexes view such reports on a quarterly basis.) The largest positive sector bets (in the relative weight column) were on energy, health and precious metals (in that order). But the overweighting of each of these three sectors resulted in modest negative contributions—see the sector selection column—as the performance of those three sectors lagged the performance of the S&P 500. The largest negative sector bets were on retail and nondurables (e.g., Coca-Cola). The negative bet on nondurables was the largest positive contributor in the sector selection column, as nondurables significantly underperformed the S&P 500. By contrast, the negative sector bet on retail was a negative contributor in the sector selection column, as retail outperformed the S&P 500.

3. Security selection decisions Decisions concerning which stocks to buy and sell are the ones most commonly thought of as "portfolio management." As with sector weighting decisions, holding an individual stock at a weight other than its benchmark percentage represents an active position in the fund. Attribution analysis measures the impact of each active bet in the fund—positive or negative. Most PMs carry several hundred active weights, even in funds with only 100 or 125 holdings; in such funds, managers are also making numerous negative bets. Consider a fund using the S&P 500 index as its benchmark and holding 125 stocks. The PM has made conscious decisions *not* to hold the other 375 stocks, so each one represents an active underweight. Performance attribution measures the impact of what is held in the fund, as well as the

TABLE 5.6

Sample performance attribution analysis
December 1, 1999–December 31, 1999
Benchmark: S&P 500
Relative Performance: +5.20%

Sector	Fund Weight	Bench-mark Weight	Relative Weight	Fund Return	Bench-mark Return	Relative Return	Stock Selection	Sector Selection	Total Relative Contrib.
Technology	26.46	25.67	0.79	29.14	17.94	11.20	2.96	0.10	3.06
Health	12.12	10.69	1.43	1.90	−8.98	10.89	1.32	−0.21	1.11
Basic Industrials	4.18	3.33	0.85	27.81	12.49	15.32	0.64	0.06	0.70
Retail	3.79	6.35	−2.55	23.23	11.15	12.08	0.46	−0.14	0.32
Nondurables	3.64	6.97	−3.33	−5.95	−3.68	−2.28	−0.08	0.32	0.23
Finance	12.69	14.46	−1.78	−1.29	−1.88	0.58	0.07	0.14	0.21
Media Leisure	4.65	4.49	0.16	10.43	8.08	2.35	0.11	0.00	0.11
Transportation	0.00	0.72	−0.72	NA	−4.51	NA	0.00	0.07	0.07
Durables	0.00	2.21	−2.21	NA	2.68	NA	0.00	0.07	0.07
Energy	8.73	5.87	2.87	2.09	−0.20	2.29	0.20	−0.17	0.03
Industrial Machinery	4.03	5.60	−1.57	16.96	13.38	3.58	0.14	−0.12	0.03
Construction	0.00	0.32	−0.32	NA	1.53	NA	0.00	0.01	0.01
Currency	0.00	0.00	0.00	NA	NA	NA	0.00	0.00	0.00
Aerospace Defense	0.92	1.34	−0.42	1.42	3.56	−2.14	-0.02	0.01	−0.01
Precious Metals	1.54	0.19	1.35	2.95	−2.22	5.17	0.08	−0.11	−.03
Expenses/other	0.00	0.00	0.00	NA	NA	NA	0.00	0.00	−0.06
Services	0.01	0.56	−0.55	NA	21.49	NA	0.00	−0.09	−0.08
Utilities	11.52	11.23	0.29	0.11	2.35	−2.25	−0.26	−0.01	−0.27
Cash	5.72	0.00	5.72	NA	NA	NA	0.00	0.00	−0.31
Totals	100.00	100.00	0.00	11.00	5.80	0.00	5.63	−0.07	5.20

impact of benchmark securities not held. A stock that goes up strongly but isn't held in the fund is just as painful as holding one that falls.

The example in Table 5.6 illustrates the significance of stock selection in determining fund performance. The largest total contribution to this fund came from technology (3.06). This contribution derived overwhelmingly from stock selection (2.96) and only minimally from sector selection (0.10). In other words, the PM was very skillful in picking the right technology stocks during the period, although the manager held only a modest overweight (0.79) in the technology sector. The table also illustrates the drag on performance resulting from holding cash (−0.31) in up markets, mentioned previously in this Chapter.

4. Interaction and process   While portfolio attribution tends to isolate each factor contributing to a fund's performance, in reality the interaction of these factors is more complex. As shown in Table 5.6, a PM can make an incorrect call on sector allocation but recover through good security selection decisions. This manager held a modestly overweighted position (1.43) in health care, the market's worst-performing sector during the period—producing a negative impact (−0.21) on fund performance. However, the specific health care stocks that the manager held far outperformed the health care sector of the S&P 500 (1.32). Those security selections more than compensated for the sector decision, resulting in a combined total relative contribution (1.11) from the fund's health care positions. In this case, the PM gets credit for finding good investments in a generally poor corner of the market.

By understanding each factor contributing to a fund's performance as well as the interaction among factors, a PM can learn from the past. He or she can try to avoid repeating the same types of mistakes and continue to take advantage of similar successful strategies. For example, some managers might learn that they are good at stock selection but not sector allocation; such managers might decide to stay relatively sector neutral and concentrate on picking individual stocks. Other managers might learn that they were hurt more by their negative bets than positive bets on individual stocks; such managers might decide to focus more heavily on what securities within the index they are not owning. Thus, portfolio management should be seen as an iterative process, in which past results are regularly analyzed and become inputs into future decisions.

REVIEW QUESTIONS

1. What is the difference between the book value and market capitalization of a company? What is the relationship of each of these financial measures to a company's earnings?

2. Can a domestic growth fund or international stock fund beat its index but fall within the third quartile of its competitive universe? Or can it lose to its index but be in the top quartile of its competitive universe?

3. Would the price movement of a stock relative to other stocks in the same industry over the past year be significant to a technical analyst, a fundamental analyst or a quantitative analyst? Why?

4. Suppose a PM who is managing against the Russell 1000 as a benchmark invests the fund so that the percentage of its assets invested in each sector matches each sector's percentage weight in the index. How does that PM expect to add value through active management of the fund?

5. Suppose a PM who manages against the S&P 500 as the fund's benchmark puts 1% of the fund's assets in the common stock of General Electric. Is the PM betting for or against General Electric and other stocks in the S&P 500?

6. Can fund holdings in a sector that underperforms the index during the relevant period make a positive total contribution to a fund's performance during that period? How?

DISCUSSION QUESTIONS

1. What generally is the effect of interest rate changes on stock prices? Can a country have low interest rates and low stock prices?

2. If you are worried about a sharp decline in the stock market, would you generally be better off holding a stock with a high P/E ratio or a stock with a high dividend yield? Is dividend yield still important? Why?

3. Which is a more powerful tool for security selection: fundamental or technical analysis? Are there any differences in time frames?

4. If you were managing an S&P 500 index fund, would you buy a security a week before it was included in that index? Why?

5. Should a manager of a U.S. stock fund be permitted to hold 5%, 10%, 20% or 30% of the fund's assets in cash? Any exceptions?

6. Should attribution analysis be done against peers as well as indexes? Where would the data come from?

NOTES

1. *New York Times,* Business Section at 8 (November 19, 2000).
2. Morningstar, "The Truth About Focused Funds," Summary, November 21, 2000.
3. Brown, Harlow, and Starks, "Of Tournaments and Temptations: An Analysis of Managerial Incentives in the Mutual Fund Industry," *Journal of Finance* at 85 (March 1, 1996).
4. Carhart, Kaniel, Musto, and Reed, "Mutual Fund Returns and Market Microstructure," The Rodney L. White Center for Financial Research, University of Pennsylvania (November 1999).

READING 5.1

Two Illustrative Approaches to Formula Valuations of Common Stocks*

Benjamin Graham

Of the various approaches to common stock valuation, the most widely accepted is that which estimates the average earnings and dividends for a period of years in the future and capitalizes these elements at an appropriate rate. This statement is reasonably definite in form, but its application permits the widest range of techniques and assumptions, including plain guesswork. The analyst has first a broad choice as to the future period he will consider; then the earnings and dividends for the period must be estimated, and finally a capitalization rate selected in accordance with his judgment or his prejudices. We may observe here that since there is no *a priori* rule governing the number of years to which the valuer should look forward in the future, it is almost inevitable that in bull markets investors and analysts will tend to see far and hopefully ahead, whereas at other times they will not be so disposed to "heed the rumble of a distant drum." Hence arises a high degree of built-in instability in the market valuation of growth stocks, so much so that one might assert with some justice that the more dynamic the company the more inherently speculative and fluctuating may be the market history of its shares.[1]

When it comes to estimating future earnings few analysts are willing to venture forth, Columbus-like, on completely uncharted seas. They prefer to start with known quantities—e.g., current or past earnings—and process these in some fashion to reach an estimate for the future. As a consequence, in security analysis the past is always being thrown out of the window of theory and coming in again through the back door of practice. It would be a sorry joke on our profession if all the elaborate data on past operations, so industriously collected and so minutely analyzed, should prove in the end to be quite unrelated to the real determinants of the value—the earnings and dividends of the future.

Undoubtedly there are situations, not few perhaps, where this proves to be the rueful fact. But in most cases the relationship between past and future proves significant enough to justify the analyst's preoccupation with the statistical record. In fact the daily work of our practitioner consists largely of an effort to construct a plausible picture of a company's future from his study of its past performance, the latter phrase inevitably suggesting similar intensive studies carried on by devotees of a very different discipline. The better the analyst he is, the less he confines himself to the published figures and the more he adds to these from his special study of the company's management, its policies, and its possibilities.

The student of security analysis, in the classroom or at home, tends to have a special preoccupation with the past record as distinct from an independent judgment of the company's future. He can be taught and can learn to analyze the former, but he lacks a suitable equipment to attempt the latter. What he seeks, typically, is some persuasive method by which a company's earnings record—including such aspects as the average, the trend or growth, stability, etc.—plus some examination of the current balance sheet, can be transmuted first into a projection of future earnings and dividends, and secondly into a valuation based on such projection.

A closer look at this desired process will reveal immediately that the future earnings and dividends need not be computed separately to produce the final value. Take the simplest presentation:

(1) Past earnings times X equal future earnings.
(2) Future earnings times Y equal present value.
This operation immediately foreshortens to:
(3) Past earnings times XY equal present value.

It is the XY factor, or multiplier of past earnings, that my students would dearly love to learn about and to calculate. When I tell them that there is no dependable method of finding this multiplier they tend to be incredulous or to ask, "What good is security analysis then?" They feel that if the right weight is given to all the relevant factors in the past record, at least a reasonably good present valuation of a common stock can be produced, one that will take probable future earnings into account and can be used as a guide to determine the attractiveness or the reverse of the issue at its current market price.

In this article I propose to explain two approaches of this kind, which have been developed in a seminar on common-stock valuation. I believe the first will illustrate reasonably well how formula operations of this kind may be worked out and applied. Ours is an endeavor to establish a comparative value in 1957 for each of the 30 stocks in the Dow Jones Industrial Average, related to a base valuation of 400 and 500, respectively, for the composite or group. (The 400 figure represented the approximate "Central Value" of the Dow Jones Average, as found separately by a whole series of formula methods derived from historical relationships. The 500 figure represented about the average market level for the preceding twelve months.)

As will be seen, the valuations of each component issue take into account the four "quality elements" of profitability, growth, stability, and dividend pay-out, applying them as multipliers to the average earnings for 1947–56. In addition, and entirely separately, a weight of 20% is given to the net asset value.

The second approach is essentially the reverse of that just described. Whereas the first method attempts to derive an independent value to be compared with the market price, the second starts with the market price and calculates therefrom the rate of future growth expected by the market. From that figure we readily derive the earnings expected for the future period, in our case 1957–66, and hence the multiplier for such future earnings implicit in the current market price.

The place for detailed comment on these calculations is after they have been developed and presented. But it may be well to express the gist of my conclusions at this point, viz.:

(1) Our own "formula valuations" for the individual stocks, and probably any others of the same general type, have little if any utility in themselves. It would be silly to assert that Stock A is "worth" only half its market price, or Stock B twice its market price, because these figures result from our valuation formula.

(2) On the other hand, they may be suggestive and useful as composite reflections of the past record, taken by itself. They may even be said to represent what the value would be, assuming that the future were merely a continuation of past performances.

(3) The analyst is thus presented with a "discrepancy" of definite magnitude, between formula "value" and the price, which it becomes his task to deal with in terms of his superior knowledge and judgment. The actual size of these discrepancies, and the attitude that may possibly be taken respecting them, are discussed below.

Similarly, the approach which starts from the market price, and derives an implied "growth factor" and an implied multiplier therefrom, may have utility in concentrating the analyst's attention on just what the market seems to be expecting from each stock in the future, in comparison or contrast with what it actually accomplished in the past. Here again his knowledge and judgment are called upon either to accept or reject the apparent assumptions of the marketplace.

Method I: A Formula Valuation Based Solely on Past Performance in Relation to the Dow Jones Industrial Average as a Group

The assumptions underlying this method are the following:

(1) Each component issue of the Dow Jones Industrial Average may be valued in relation to a base value of the average as a whole by a comparison of the statistical records.

(2) The data to be considered are the following:

(a) *Profitability*—as measured by the rate of return on invested capital. (For convenience this was computed only for the year 1956.)

(b) *Growth of per-share earnings*—as shown by two measurements: 1947–56 earnings vs. 1947 earnings, and 1956 earnings vs. 1947–56 earnings. (It would have been more logical to have used the 1954–56 average instead of the single year 1956, but the change would have little effect on the final valuations.)

(c) *Stability*—as measured by the greatest shrinkage of profits in the periods 1937–38 and 1947–56. (The calculation is based on the percentage of earnings retained in the period of maximum shrinkage.)

(d) *Payout*—as measured by the ratio of 1956 dividends to 1956 earnings. In the few cases where the 1956 earnings were below the 1947–56 average we substituted the latter for the former, to get a more realistic figure of current payout.

These criteria demonstrate the quality of the company's earnings (and dividend policy) and thus may control the multiplier to be applied to the earnings. The figure found under each heading is divided by the corresponding figure for the Dow Jones group as a whole, to give the company's relative performance. The four relatives were then combined on the basis of equal weights to give a final "quality index" of the company as against the overall quality of the group.

The rate of earnings on invested capital is perhaps the most logical measure of the success and quality of an enterprise. It tells how productive are the dollars invested in the business. In studies made in the relatively "normal" market of 1953 I found a surprisingly good correlation between the profitability rate and the price-earnings ratio, after introducing a major adjustment for the dividend payout and a minor (moderating) adjustment for net asset value.

It is not necessary to emphasize the importance of the growth factor to stock-market people. They are likely to ask rather why we have not taken it as the major determinant of quality and multipliers. There is little doubt that the expected future growth is in fact the major influence upon current price-earnings ratios, and this truth is fully recognized in our second approach, which deals with growth expectations as reflected in market prices. But the correlation between market multipliers and past growth is by no means close.

Some interesting figures worked out by Ralph A. Bing show this clearly.[2] Dow Chemical, with per-share earnings growth of 31% (1955 vs. 1948), had in August 1956 a price-earnings ratio of 47.3 times 1955 earnings. Bethlehem Steel, with corresponding growth of 93%, had a multiplier of only 9.1. The spread between the two relationships is thus as wide as fourteen to one. Other ratios in Mr. Bing's table show similar wide disparities between past growth and current multipliers.

It is here that the stability factor asserts its importance. The companies with high multipliers may not have had the best growth in 1948–55, but most of them had greater than average stability of earnings over the past two decades.

These considerations led us to adopt the simple arithmetical course of assigning equal weight to past growth, past stability, and current profitability in working out the quality coefficient for each company. The dividend payout is not strictly a measure of quality of earning power, though in the typical case investors probably regard it in some such fashion. Its importance in most instances is undeniable, and it is both convenient and plausible to give it equal weight and similar treatment with each of the other factors just discussed.

Finally, we depart from the usual Wall Street attitude and assign a weight of 20% in the final valuation to the net assets per share. It is true that in the typical case the asset value has no perceptible influence on current market price. But it may have some long-run effect on future market price, and thus it has a claim to be considered seriously in any independent valuation of a company. As is well known, asset values invariably play some part, sometimes a fairly important one, in the many varieties of legal valuations of common stocks, which grow out of tax cases, merger litigation, and the like. The basic justification for considering asset value in this process, even though it may be ignored in the current market price, lies in the possibility of its showing its weight later, through competitive developments, changes in management or its policies, merger or sale eventuality, etc.

The above discussion will explain, perhaps not very satisfactorily, why the four factors entering into the quality rating and the fifth factor of asset value were finally assigned equal weight of 20% each. The actual application of our illustrative method can now be explained by working through the figures for the first company in the group, Allied Chemical & Dye. Following are data used in computing the "value" of ACD relative to a 400 and a 500 valuation for the Dow Jones Industrial Average (see Table 1).

In Table 2 we supply the "valuation" reached by this method for each of the 30 stocks in the Dow Jones Industrial Average. Our table includes the various quality factors, the average earnings, and the asset values used to arrive at our final figures.

In about half the cases these "valuations" differ quite widely from the prices ruling on August 5 last, on which date the D. J. Average actually sold at 500. Seven issues were selling at 20% or more above their formula value, and an equal number at 20% or more below such value. At the extremes we find Westinghouse selling at a 100% "premium," and United Aircraft at about a 50% "discount." The extent of these disparities naturally suggests that our method is technically a poor one, and that more plausible valuations could be reached—i.e., ones more congruous with market prices—if a better choice were made of the factors and weights entering into the method.

A number of tests were applied to our results to see if they could be "improved" by some plausible changes in the technique. To give these in any detail would prolong this report unnecessarily. Suffice it to say that they were unproductive. If the asset-value factor had been excluded, a very slight change would have resulted in favor of the issues which were selling at the highest premium over their

TABLE 1

	D.J. Ind. Av.	Allied C&D	"Quality" factors: Ratio of ACD to D.J.
Earned per share			
1956	$36.00	$4.74	
1947–1956	27.00	4.50	
1947	21.80	3.73	
1938 (unadjusted)	6.01	5.92	
1937 (unadjusted)	11.49	11.19	
Dividends 1956	23.15	3.00	
Net asset value 1956	275.00	40.00	
Profitability:			
1956 earnings/1956 net assets	13.0%	11.85%	91%
Growth			
A: 1947–56 vs. 1957–59	26%	21%	
B: 1956 vs. 1947–56	30%	5%	
A plus B	56%	26%	46%
Stability:			
1938 earnings/1937 earnings	52.3%	53%	101%
Payout:			
1956 dividend/1956 earnings	64.3%	64%	100%
Average of four quality factors			84%

Formula to produce value of 400 for D.J. Ind. Av:
  "Value" equals 1/5 net assets plus 12.5 x 1947–56 earnings or 55 plus 12.5 x 27.50 or 400
Corresponding "valuation" of Allied Chem. & Dye, (including Quality Factor of 84%):
  Value equals 1/5 x 40 plus 0.84 x 12.5 x 4.50 or 55.
Formula to produce value of 500 for D.J. Ind. Av.:
  Value equals 1/5 net assets plus 16.2 x 1947–56 earnings or 500.
Corresponding "valuation" of Allied Chem. & Dye, (including Quality Factor of 84%):
  Value equals 1/5 x 40 plus 0.84 x 16.2 x 4.50 or 69.

formula value. On the other hand, if major emphasis had been placed on the factor of past growth, some of our apparently undervalued issues would have been given still larger formula values; for Table 2 shows that more of the spectacular growth percentages occur in this group than in the other—e.g., United Aircraft, International Nickel, and Goodyear.

It is quite evident from Table 2 that the stock market fixes its valuation of a given common stock on the basis not of its past statistical performance but rather of its expected future performance, which may differ significantly from its past behavior. The market is, of course, fully justified in seeking to make this independent appraisal of the future, and for that reason any automatic rejection of the market's verdict because it differs from a formula valuation would be the height of folly. We cannot avoid the observation, however, that the independent appraisals made in the stock market are themselves far from infallible, as is shown in part by the rapid changes to which they are subject. It is possible, in fact, that they may be on the whole a no more dependable guide to what the future will produce than the "values" reached by our mechanical processing of past data, with all the latter's obvious shortcomings.

Method 2

Let us turn now to our second mathematical approach, which concerns itself with future growth, or future earnings, as they appear to be predicted by the market price itself. We start with the theory that the market price of a representative stock, such as anyone in the Dow Jones

TABLE 2

Formula valuations of Dow Jones Industrial issues

Company	Quality factors				Avg. Factor	Earnings 1947–56	Book Value	Indicated value basis		Price 8/5/57
	Profit.	Growth	Stability	Payout				D.J. 400	D.J. 500	
Allied Ch.	91	46	94	100	84	4.50	40	55	69	89
Am. Can	81	70	137	107	99	2.61	28	39	48	44
Am. S. & Ref.	101	39	100	81	80	5.43	51	65	85	54
Am. T. & T.	54	40	163	130	97	9.90	150	151	185	173
Am. Tob.	98	27	111	104	85	6.58	59	82	102	72
Beth. St.	95	138	0	97	83	2.88	31	36	45	49
Chrysler	91*	0	38	51	45	8.15	74	66	80	77
Corn. Prod.	100	65	114	98	94	1.96	40	31	37	31
Du Pont	154	198	100	109	140	5.60	41	107	136	199
East. Kod.	136	100	148	85	117	3.49	28	57	63	104
Gen. Elec.	139	129	84	127	120	1.87	14	31	39	68
Gen. Foods	138	99	141	79	114	2.42	20	39	49	49
Gen. Motors	160	119	95	104	120	2.48	20	42	53	45
Goodyear T.	108	207	129	83	132	4.18	43	78	98	76
Int. Harv.	58*	0	91	98	62	3.70	49	39	47	35
Int. Nickel	164	263	119	90	159	3.86	31	83	105	92
Int. Paper	100	46	0	101	62	6.40	55	61	76	101
Johns Man.	93	96	44	100	83	3.07	29	38	47	45
Nat. Dist.	73*	0	62	118	63	2.47	26	25	31	26
Nat. Steel	95	96	101	88	95	5.71	68	79	99	75
Proc. & Gam.	110	46	105	103	91	2.61	21	34	42	49
Sears Roe.	112	56	144	84	99	1.82	15	26	32	28
S. O. Cal.	124	113	134	65	109	3.09	24	47	59	58
S.O.N.J.	130	166	97	80	118	2.85	24	47	59	67
Texas Corp.	126	171	81	66	11	3.48	34	56	70	74
Un. C. & C.	138	92	108	100	110	3.73	27	53	67	117
Un. Aircr.	158	361	181	66	192	3.65	35	96	121	62
U.S. Steel	99	239	0	67	101	3.51	47	54	67	69
Westinghouse	65*	0	0	83	37	3.79	43	27	32	64
Woolworth	69*	0	116	109	74	3.58	40	41	51	42
D.J. Ind. Av.	(13.0)	(56)	(52.3)	(64.3)	100	27.50	275	400	500	500

*Based on 1947–56 Average earnings vs. 1956 book value plus adj.

group, reflects the earnings to be expected in a future period, times a multiplier which is in turn based on the percentage of future growth. Thus an issue for which more than average growth is expected will have this fact shown to a double degree, or "squared," in its market price—first in the higher figure taken for future earnings, and second in the higher multiplier applied to those higher earnings.

We shall measure growth by comparing the expected 1957–66 earnings with the actual figures for 1947–56.

Our basic formula says, somewhat arbitrarily, that where no growth is expected the current price will be 8 times both 1947–56 earnings and the expected 1956–66 earnings. If growth G is expected, expressed as the ratio of 1957–66 to 1947–56 earnings, then the price reflects such next decade earnings multiplied by 8 times G.

From these assumptions we obtain the simple formula:

Price equals $(E \times G) \times (8 \times G)$, or $8G^2 \times E$, where E is the per-share earnings for 1947–56.

To find *G,* the expected rate of future growth, we have only to divide the current price by 8 times 1947–56 earnings, and take the square root.

When this is done for the Dow Jones Average as a whole, using its August 5, 1957, price of 500, we get a value of 1.5 for *G*—indicating an expected growth of 50% for 1957–66 earnings vs. the 1947–56 actuality. This anticipates an average of $41.00 in the next decade, as against $27.50 for the previous ten years and about $36.00 in 1956. This estimate appears reasonable to the writer in relation to the 500 level. (In fact he started with this estimate and worked back from it to get the basic multiplier of 8 to be applied to issues with no expected growth.) The price of 500 for the D. J. Average would represent in turn a multiplier of 8 × 1.5, or 12, to be applied to the expected future earnings of $41. (Incidentally, on these assumptions the average current formula value of about 400 for the Dow Jones Average would reflect expectations of a decade-to-decade growth of 35%, average earnings of $37.10 for 1957–66, and a current multiplier of 10.8 for such future earnings.)

In Table 3 we set forth the results of applying this second approach to the 30 Dow Jones issues. (The figures for Am. Tel. & Tel. might well be ignored, since utility issues should take a different basic formula.) The main interest in the table lies in the disparities it indicates between the expected future growth, implicit in the market prices, and the actual growth during the past decade. Ten of the companies (plus AT&T) sold at prices anticipating at least twice the Dow Jones Average rate of growth, comparing 1957–66 with 1956. Of these only two, Du Pont and General Electric, had actually shown distinctly better than average growth in the last ten years. Conversely, eight of the companies were indicating less than half the average expected rate of growth, including five for which actual declines from 1956 levels were apparently predicted. Yet of these eight companies, no less than five had actually shown far greater than average growth in the past decade.

This leads us to our final observations, which tie our two tables together. The ten companies previously mentioned, for which unusually rapid growth is anticipated, include seven of those shown in Table 2 as selling significantly above their formula valuation. Again, the eight for which subnormal or no growth is expected include six, which were selling substantially below their formula valuations.

We conclude that a large part of the discrepancies between carefully calculated formula values and the market prices can be traced to the growth factor, not because the formulas underplay its importance, but rather because the market often has concepts of future earnings changes which cannot be derived from the companies' past performance. The reasons for the market's breaking with the past are often abundantly clear. Investors do not believe, for example, that United Aircraft will duplicate its brilliant record of 1947–56, because they consider that a company with the United States Department of Defense as its chief customer is inherently vulnerable. They have the opposite view with regard to Westinghouse. They feel its relatively mediocre showing in recent years was the result of temporary factors, and that the electric manufacturing industry is inherently so growth-assured that a major supplier such as Westinghouse is bound to prosper in the future.

These cases are clear cut enough, but other divergencies shown in our table are not so easy to understand or to accept. There is a difference between these two verbs. The market may be right in its general feeling about a company's future, but the price tag it sets on the future may be quite unreasonable in either direction.

It is here that many analysts will find their challenge. They may not be satisfied merely to find out what the market is doing and thinking, and then to explain it to everyone's satisfaction. They may prefer to exercise an independent judgment—one not controlled by the daily verdict of the marketplace, but ready at times to take definite issue with it. For this kind of activity one or more valuation processes, of the general type we have been illustrating, may serve a useful purpose. They give a concrete and elaborated picture of the past record, which the analyst may use as a point of departure for his individual exploration and discoveries in the field of investment values.

Notes

1. On this point the philosophically inclined are referred to the recent article of D. Durand, "Growth Stocks and the Petersburg Paradox," *Journal of Finance* (September 1957): 348-363. His conclusion is that "the growth-stock problem offers no great hope of a satisfactory solution."
2. R. A. Bing, "Can We Improve Methods of Appraising Growth Stocks?" *Commercial and Financial Chronicle,* September 13, 1956.

TABLE 3

Formula calculations of expected growth of earnings of Dow Jones Industrial issues, as indicated by August 5, 1957, price

Company	Price 8/5/57	Average earnings 1947–56	Exp. Growth 1957–66 vs. 1947–56	Indicated earnings 1957–66	Indicated multiplier*	Earnings 1956	Exp. Incr. 1957–66 vs. 1956	Act. Incr. 1956 vs. 1947–56
Allied Ch.	89	$4.50	+58%	$7.22	12.6	$4.74	+52%	+6%
Am. Can.	44	2.61	46	3.83	11.6	2.92	33	12
Am. S. & R.	54	5.43	12	6.1	9	6.67	(−8)	23
Am. T. & T.**	173	9.9	47	14.7	11.8	10.74	36	14
Am. Tob.	72	6.58	18	7.8	9.4	7.51	4	14
Beth. St.	49	2.88	44	4.15	11.5	3.83	8	33
Chrysler	77	8.95	4	9.28	8.3	2.29	(large)	(−76)
Corn. Prod.	31	1.96	41	2.76	11.4	2.36	18	12
Du Pont	199	5.6	112	11.85	17	8.2	45	47
East. Kod.	104	3.49	93	6.62	15.4	4.89	36	37
Gen. Elec.	68	1.87	113	4	17	2.45	62	31
Gen. Foods	49	2.42	59	3.86	12.7	3.56	9	45
Gen. Motors	45	2.48	51	3.74	12.1	3.02	24	22
Goodyear T.	76	4.18	42	5.96	11.4	6.03	(−1)	47
Int. Harv.	35	3.7	8	4.02	8.6	3.14	29	(−15)
Int. Nickel	92	3.86	62	6.3	13	6.5	(−3)	68
Int. Paper	101	6.4	40	9.03	11.2	7.05	28	11
Johns Man.	45	3.07	36	4.21	10.9	3.5	20	14
Nat. Dist.	26	2.47	15	2.86	9.2	2.11	36	(−15)
Nat. Steel	75	5.71	28	7.32	10.2	7.09	3	25
Proc. & Gam.	49	2.61	53	3.99	12.2	3.05	30	20
Sears Roebuck	28	1.82	38	2.53	11	2.2	16	18
S. O. Cal.	58	3.09	55	4.78	12.4	4.24	12	39
S. O. N. J.	67	2.85	72	4.99	13.8	4.11	21	44
Texas Corp.	74	3.48	62	5.66	13	5.51	3	59
Un. C. & C.	117	3.73	99	7.43	15.9	4.86	53	32
Un. Air	62	3.65	45	5.31	11.6	7.66	(−32)	93
U.S. Steel	69	3.51	57	5.55	12.6	6.01	(-8)	73
Westinghouse	64	3.79	45	5.53	11.6	0.01	(large)	(−97)
Woolworth	42	3.58	22	4.39	9.8	3.57	23	0
D.J. Ind. Av.	500	$27.50	50	$41.25	12	$35.80	15	30

*Dec. 1956 Price ÷ —Indicated 1957–66 Earnings.
**The basic formula is less applicable to AT&T than to industrial issues.

::::: CASE STUDY

Managing a Stock Fund

Selecting an investment for a mutual fund involves more than analyzing an individual security. As you learned in this Chapter, active portfolio managers must select securities that fit within the overall investment objectives of the fund and within the many investment constraints on the fund in an effort to beat their benchmarks. These benchmarks usually are a stock index or a peer group (or both) made up of funds with similar investment objectives.

This case study is designed to put you in the position of a portfolio assistant for a stock fund who is confronted with a challenging set of decisions. She is assisting a portfolio manager who needs to complete the initial trades for the launch of a new fund. Currently, the manager has chosen enough stocks in weights to equal 70% of the fund's beginning assets. The portfolio assistant must try to recommend other names in weights equal to an additional 25% of assets (assuming the fund will start with 5% of its assets in cash).

The discussion questions set forth below are intended to make you go through some of the same steps in the investment process as would the portfolio assistant. These include assessing stocks on an individual basis as a fit for the portfolio; calculating valuation measures and conducting some relative valuation analysis; and offering stock selection and asset weighting recommendations.

Discussion Questions

1. Given the fund's prospectus and Trustworthy's internal policies, what are the specific categories of stocks that should be considered for the fund?
2. How would you describe to the consultants the investment strategy Paul Douglas is using to manage the Small Cap Stock Fund?
3. Of the stocks listed in Exhibit 4, which ones would you exclude based on fit for the fund, and why?
4. Looking further at Exhibit 4, which valuation measures do you think would be most helpful in conducting relative valuation comparisons for the securities not excluded in question 3?
5. Using your answers to questions 3 and 4 plus the information given at the industry level in Exhibit 5, which

stocks in Exhibit 4 would you recommend for the fund, and why?
6. Focusing only on the quantitative data provided on trucking companies in Exhibit 6, would you recommend investing in any of the trucking companies, and if so, which one(s) and in what weight?
7. Using the research notes in Exhibits 7 and 8 as well as the quantitative data in Exhibit 6, would your recommend either of the two trucking companies for the fund?
8. Using the recommendations given for questions 5, 6 and 7, what would be the new composition of the fund, and how would this new composition be consistent with the fund's objectives and constraints?

The Trustworthy Small Cap Stock Fund

Background on Trustworthy Investments

Trustworthy Investments started as a private pension fund management company in 1970. It expanded into the mutual fund business in the late 1970s when interest rates soared into double digits and money market funds became popular. Trustworthy began to offer stock mutual funds in the early 1980s and went public in 1986. It added bond funds in the late 1980s and international funds in the early 1990s.

By the year 2000, the Trustworthy complex offered 14 mutual funds, including 8 stock funds. Although Trustworthy primarily had distributed its funds through the retail channel for the past 20 years, the retirement market was representing a bigger and bigger percentage of new fund flows. As Trustworthy focused its sales efforts on this growing market segment, management spent a lot of time with fund consultants. The consultants had generally praised the complex's consistency of results and quality of shareholder service, but had also pointed out some holes in Trustworthy's product line that reduced the complex's attractiveness to retirement plans. Exhibit 1 shows an example of a popular categorization scheme used by many of the fund consultants who met with Trustworthy.

In response to the consultants' findings, the company reviewed its existing product offerings, market demand and availability of investment resources, and determined that the most viable new product to pursue would be a small-cap growth fund, benchmarked against the Russell 2000 and in a small-cap peer universe. They then quickly began the process of launching this new fund. Trustworthy's management company presented the idea to the board of trustees and obtained approval for the filing of the fund registration statement (including the fund's prospectus) with the SEC. During the 75-day SEC review period, the investment committee of the management company decided on a portfolio manager and obtained approval from the board of trustees for all of the contractual arrangements for the fund (e.g., the fees for the management company, as well as for all service providers to the fund). Once the contracts were approved and the 75-day review period passed without significant SEC comments, the fund was ready for launch. Marketing set a launch date of September 15; a few days ahead of this date, the management company set aside $1 million for the initial investments of the fund (which would be replaced later by investor money). Exhibit 2 outlines the fund's objective as well as principal investment strategies found in the fund's prospectus. It also lists other fund constraints imposed by the SEC or Trustworthy Investments.

Portfolio Management

On September 13, 2000, Paul Douglas sat on the train flipping through the research reports he'd received the night before. The Trustworthy Small Cap Stock Fund, the new small-cap equity mutual fund he had been chosen to manage for Trustworthy Investments, was set to launch in two days, and he wanted to finish putting together the initial portfolio trades as soon as possible.

Douglas was thrilled that he had been chosen as manager for the new fund. He had started work as an equity analyst for Trustworthy after finishing his M.B.A. in 1990. Over the next eight years, he covered several industries, including machinery, retailers and computer companies. As part of career development at Trustworthy, management often assigned analysts as portfolio assistants to existing fund managers. In 1998, Douglas had been given the additional responsibility of being portfolio assistant for the Capital Appreciation Fund and had done a superb job over the past two years. Managing the new Small Cap Stock Fund was his first opportunity to manage a fund himself, and he was very anxious about the fund's initial positions.

Douglas's approach for managing the portfolio would be based on his outlook for the economy and the resulting implications for industries and the companies within those industries. He has been keeping a keen eye on consumer demand and other macroeconomic factors and was concerned that the economy was showing strength such that

the Federal Reserve might be looking to increase interest rates. This could lead to a change in economic growth patterns and have a significant effect on any sector positioning he chose to implement.

Douglas glanced at a relative positioning report for his proposed fund, which showed the percentage of total assets invested in each major sector of the market versus the percentage weights held in the fund's benchmark index, the Russell 2000 (see Exhibit 3). Thus far, he had begun to position the fund as he thought appropriate for the current state of the economy and his future outlook on many of the economic sectors. At the launch of the fund (with 100% of fund assets invested), his targeted relative positioning would include overweights in the Technology and Health Care sectors and underweights in Finance, Utilities and Manufacturing. He planned to set all other sector weights close to the weights in the benchmark index for the fund. Finally, although he was open to buying value as well as growth stocks, he wanted to make sure the fund exhibited growth characteristics on average.

So far, Douglas had chosen 25 stocks in which to invest, equaling 70% of the fund's initial assets. The three biggest positions in the fund were each near a 7% weight and totaled 22% of the fund's assets. Paul wanted to find another 5 to 10 stocks to buy to diversify the portfolio further and bring the initial cash level down to 5%. (Although the targeted cash level for the fund would be around 3%, the Trustworthy trading desk asked Douglas to prepare his initial trade requests using a slightly higher cash level to allow for market volatility on the first day of trading for the fund.)

From the current pool of analysts, Trustworthy management had chosen Sara Powell to be Douglas's portfolio assistant for the new fund. She was currently covering the Transportation sector and was excited about the chance to work with Douglas on the construction of the new portfolio. She was combing through stock data to search for additional buy recommendations for the portfolio and was going to meet Douglas during the morning to go over several names that might be appropriate for the fund's objective. In preparation for her meeting, she had pulled data on some securities that had not been followed by Trustworthy's analysts very recently but might turn out to be good buying opportunities for the fund. Exhibit 4 shows the initial data she pulled for the securities, and Exhibit 5 sets forth some industry averages for securities in the Russell 2000.

Douglas had also asked her to specifically recommend the portfolio's positioning (if any) in the Transportation

Morningstar StyleMap℠

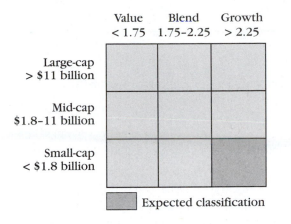

	Value < 1.75	Blend 1.75–2.25	Growth > 2.25
Large-cap > $11 billion			
Mid-cap $1.8–11 billion			
Small-cap < $1.8 billion			

☐ Expected classification

Reprinted with permission.

sector by looking at some trucking companies. Exhibit 6 contains some quantitative measures that Sara compiled for the Transportation industry and two trucking companies. Exhibits 7 and 8 are excerpts from research notes on the two trucking companies.

Amid the coughing and sniffling of his fellow commuters, Douglas settled into his seat and read the reports he had with him.

Explanatory Note on StyleMap℠

The style box (Exhibit 1) measures the typical size and valuation of companies in a fund. Market capitalization is shown from top to bottom, and valuation is shown from left to right. Morningstar ties market cap to the relative movements of the top 5,000 stocks in the domestic market. The top 5% of stocks are classified as large-cap, the next 15% are mid-cap, and the remaining 80% are small-cap. As of August 31, 2000, the boundary between large-cap and mid-cap was about $11 billion, and the cutoff between mid-cap and small-cap was about $1.8 billion. Morningstar determines a fund's market cap by ranking the stocks in its portfolio from the biggest to the smallest and then calculating the average weighted market capitalization of the stocks in the middle quintile (middle 40th percentile to 60th percentile) of the portfolio. After a fund's market cap has been determined, Morningstar places the fund in the large-cap, mid-cap or small-cap group according to where its market cap falls among the market's top 5,000 names. (For purposes of this case study, assume a fund would be considered small-cap if roughly 50% of its equity assets were invested in companies with market caps of less than $1.8 billion.)

To determine valuation, Morningstar categorizes a fund by comparing the P/E and P/B of the stocks in its portfolio with the most relevant of the three market cap groups. For example, for a fund completely made up of small-cap names, the P/E and P/B of each of its holdings are divided by the weighted median P/E and P/B (respectively) of the bottom 80% of companies. These ratios are called P/E and P/B scores. To determine a valuation classification, Morningstar looks at the average weighted P/E and P/B score of the middle quintile of the fund's portfolio. For each measure, a score of 1.00 represents an average valuation. If the sum of the fund's P/E and P/B scores is above 2.25, the fund is categorized as growth. If the sum of the two scores is below 1.75, the fund is categorized as value. Finally, if the sum is between 1.75 and 2.25, the fund is categorized as blend. (For purposes of this case study, assume that a fund would be considered growth—in the small-cap category—if its P/E were at least 17.85 and its P/B were at least 2.96.)

Current Data (8/31/00)	P/E	P/B	% Assets invested in companies with market caps above $1.8 billion
Russell 2000 index	27.4	4.9	NA
Trustworthy Small Cap Stock Fund (using initial trades equal to 70% of total assets)	29.2	5.5	50%

EXHIBIT 2

The Trustworthy Small Cap Stock Fund: Excerpts from the prospectus:

Investment Summary

Investment Objective

Trustworthy Small Cap Stock Fund seeks long-term growth of capital.

Principal Investment Strategies

Trustworthy Small Cap Stock's principal investment strategies include (for 80% of its assets):

- Normally investing the fund's assets in common stocks of companies with small market capitalizations. Small market capitalization companies are those whose market capitalization is similar to the market capitalization of companies in the Russell 2000 at the time of the fund's investment. Companies whose capitalization no longer meets this definition after purchase continue to be considered to have a small market capitalization for purposes of this policy. As of August 31, 2000, the Russell 2000 included companies with capitalizations between $22.7 million and $4.7 billion. The size of companies in the Russell 2000 changes with market conditions and the composition of the index.

- Investing in domestic issuers.

- Investing in companies it believes have above-average growth potential (stocks of those companies are often called "growth stocks"). In buying and selling securities for the fund, Trustworthy relies on fundamental analysis of each issuer and its potential for success in the light of its current financial condition, its industry position and economic and market conditions. Factors considered include growth potential, earnings estimates and management.

Other Fund Constraints:

Diversification

Trustworthy Small Cap Stock Fund is a diversified portfolio of securities. According to the Investment Company Act of 1940, this means that as to 75% of the assets of the fund, the fund may not acquire more than 10% of the voting securities of any one issuer and may not invest more than 5% of total fund assets in any one issuer. As an internal policy, Trustworthy prohibits owning more than 10% of any single security and investing more than 8% of total fund assets in any one issuer.

EXHIBIT 2 (CONTINUED)

Industry Diversification

Trustworthy Small Cap Stock Fund will invest to diversify across industries. The fund will not concentrate its holdings in any one industry in a weight greater than 25% of its assets at the time of purchase.

Liquidity

As an internal Trustworthy policy, managers are required to invest in fairly liquid securities. The management company has set a "liquidity" floor for each fund that relates to both the size of the trade and the daily volume of shares traded for a stock. Each fund may invest in stocks in an amount such that the trade is less than 25% of the average daily volume (usually calculated from trading information over the prior six months) at time of share purchase.

Types of Investments

Marketing has expressed a desire for the fund to remain in the small-cap growth category. The fund manager has explicitly expressed a desire to stay in the Morningstar small cap growth box.

EXHIBIT 3

Trustworthy Small Cap Stock Fund performance attribution: Industry positioning review (initial 70% of fund assets)

Major Industry	Trustworthy Small Cap Stock Fund Weight	Russell 2000 Index, 8/31/00 Weight	Fund Relative Weight
Commercial Services	4.00	4.12	−0.12
Communications	3.00	2.43	0.57
Consumer Durables	4.00	3.81	0.19
Consumer Nondurables	4.00	2.92	1.08
Consumer Services	4.00	4.64	−0.64
Distribution Services	2.00	1.67	0.33
Electronic Technology	5.50	15.04	−9.54
Energy Minerals	0.00	2.12	−2.12
Finance	5.50	18.39	−12.89
Health Services	2.00	3.38	−1.38
Health Technology	3.00	9.63	−6.63
Industrial Services	0.00	1.65	−1.65
Non-Energy Minerals	2.00	1.71	0.29
Process Industries	1.00	4.44	−3.44
Producer Manufacturing	0.00	6.03	−6.03
Retail Trade	9.00	4.07	4.93
Technology Services	21.00	8.21	12.79
Transportation	0.00	1.71	−1.71
Utilities	0.00	4.03	−4.03
Total	70.00	100.00	−30.00

EXHIBIT 4

Initial securities data

Ticker	Company Name	Major Industry	8/31/00 Price ($)	Market Cap ($M)	Daily Vol ($Mil)1	3 yr. Revenue growth	3 yr. EPS Growth	Trailing 1 yr. sales	Mean Sales est. FYI	Mean Sales est. FY2	Trailing 1 yr eps	Mean EPS est. FYI	Mean EPS est. FY2	Div. Yield	P/B	beta vs. S&P	ROE	Free cash flow per share
CTCO	COMMONWLTH TELE ENTE	Communications	38.63	870.4	2.00	-8.50	13.82	260.9	288.7	322.7	0.99	0.53	0.80	0.00	5.7	1.16	13.43	-2.14
WGO	WINNEBAGO INDUSTRIES	Consumer Durables	12.81	272.6	1.06	12.09	66.66	667.7	755.8	760.0	1.99	2.19	2.15	1.00	1.9	0.62	33.29	0.40
KCP	COLE KENNETH PROD IN	Consumer Non-Durables	44.06	900.0	4.55	26.12	27.82	310.3	354.5	465.0	1.24	1.66	2.06	0.00	7.4	0.99	25.05	1.58
HAIN	HAIN CELESTIAL GROUP	Consumer Non-Durables	31.25	572.2	10.31	45.72	64.39	206.0	328.5	476.1	0.81	0.84	1.38	0.00	4.0	0.97	13.51	0.61
APPB	APPLEBEES INTL INC	Consumer Services	22.69	607.1	10.08	18.25	16.10	669.6	693.4	761.3	1.91	2.36	2.69	0.34	2.4	0.62	19.71	1.55
EDMC	EDUCATION MANAGEMENT	Consumer Services	25.25	728.5	4.24	20.87	41.26	260.8	356.2	408.4	0.64	0.89	1.06	0.00	7.7	0.85	22.04	-0.48
AVCT	AVOCENT CORP	Electronic Technology	48.63	1,134.5	25.60	46.12	54.32	107.3	145.3	200.0	0.94	1.29	1.79	0.00	11.7	1.29	25.94	0.18
CCBL	C-COR.NET CORP	Electronic Technology	19.50	658.4	12.45	5.79	28.75	171.3	319.0	424.0	0.58	0.62	0.85	0.00	5.8	1.02	18.75	0.40
LLTC	LINEAR TECHNOLOGY CO	Electronic Technology	71.94	22,522.8	211.04	11.92	16.41	506.7	997.3	1,272.9	0.64	1.24	1.51	0.20	24.4	1.57	23.37	0.72
MRCY	MERCURY COMPUTER SYS	Electronic Technology	28.34	606.4	9.40	23.25	40.98	106.6	175.0	218.0	0.66	1.18	1.53	0.00	7.5	2.54	19.44	-0.51
RNBO	RAINBOW TECHNOLOGIES	Electronic Technology	39.63	497.4	7.12	14.14	40.98	121.1	172.6	212.3	0.71	1.15	1.59	0.00	4.7	0.77	8.56	0.54
CNT	CENTERPOINT PROPERTI	Finance	43.81	909.7	1.39	29.46	15.39	138.9	160.7	178.3	2.02	3.32	3.74	5.22	1.9	0.13	11.29	1.40
NDB	NATIONAL DISC BROKER	Finance	36.19	651.3	4.15	28.44	41.80	385.8	431.6	556.0	1.92	1.34	1.10	0.00	2.1	1.05	14.20	-0.77
RWY	RENT WAY INC	Finance	24.50	596.1	5.85	111.79	18.52	494.4	598.0	780.7	0.71	1.83	2.58	0.00	1.9	0.41	7.75	-0.52
ADVP	ADVANCE PARADIGM INC	Health Services	26.63	573.4	4.91	94.60	79.40	1968.4	2511.8	2,838.0	0.97	1.08	1.37	0.00	5.8	0.38	24.39	0.28
RHB	REHABCARE GROUP INC	Health Services	37.38	550.7	6.90	42.02	40.71	309.4	440.6	526.6	1.15	1.44	1.74	0.00	6.4	0.41	21.89	0.59
CRY	CRYOLIFE INC	Health Technology	26.88	331.7	1.06	21.44	-2.17	66.7	77.7	99.9	0.36	0.65	0.83	0.00	4.1	0.10	10.54	-0.23
CDIS	CAL DIVE INTERNATION	Industrial Services	57.50	904.4	5.14	29.36	17.62	161.0	172.3	245.6	1.13	1.25	1.98	0.00	5.9	2.05	12.78	-3.46
OII	OCEANEERING INTERNAT	Industrial Services	17.44	399.5	2.90	4.90	-0.97	416.8	448.6	540.4	0.74	0.61	1.20	0.00	2.0	0.90	8.95	-1.22
ROG	ROGERS CORP	Process Industries	34.88	520.3	0.31	19.90	7.38	247.8	245.2	283.8	1.24	1.57	1.88	0.00	4.4	0.19	16.44	1.25
LFUS	LITTLEFUSE INC	Producer Manufacturing	36.31	730.4	4.02	6.12	8.18	296.4	382.0	438.5	1.29	1.75	2.05	0.00	5.2	0.88	19.28	0.96
SGR	SHAW GROUP INC	Producer Manufacturing	55.69	397.2	10.21	32.22	16.25	494.0	777.8	1,606.2	1.52	1.84	2.54	0.00	3.8	1.30	10.51	0.75
CWTR	COLDWATER CREEK INC	Retail Trade	32.00	332.3	2.75	31.89	2.83	328.3	413.0	470.3	1.38	1.66	1.97	0.00	4.3	0.83	20.74	1.35
OMX	OFFICEMAX INC	Retail Trade	5.19	584.8	2.59	15.07	-45.29	4842.7	5075.0	5,556.2	0.09	0.17	0.37	0.00	0.5	1.07	0.89	1.33
CTSH	COGNIZANT TECH SOLUT	Technology Services	42.75	794.0	1.62	98.62	87.57	88.9	131.6	178.1	0.61	0.82	1.10	0.00	17.4	1.95	28.78	0.69
GPSI	GREAT PLAINS SOFTWAR	Technology Services	27.19	472.4	6.04	51.22	8.67	194.9	306.0	410.0	0.34	1.04	1.36	0.00	1.8	0.41	2.77	-0.74
IGTE	IGATE CAPITAL CORP	Technology Services	7.28	367.0	2.58	60.18	50.07	471.5	367.0	480.0	0.72	0.17	0.53	0.00	2.0	1.76	21.15	0.56
SPSS	SPSS INC	Technology Services	27.88	271.9	1.35	18.14	31.46	141.9	164.0	198.5	1.61	1.93	2.13	0.00	4.4	0.80	29.45	0.54
ATO	ATMOS ENERGY CORP	Utilities	20.75	658.7	0.15	10.51	-18.49	690.2	751.5	808.5	0.58	1.00	1.91	5.38	1.7	0.11	4.74	-1.95
SRP	SIERRA PACIFIC RESOU	Utilities	17.69	1,387.1	7.41	16.73	-17.30	1309.1	1794.0	3,376.0	0.83	1.12	1.83	5.76	0.9	0.23	4.52	-3.26

1. Daily Volume ($M) is calculated using the average share volume over the last 6 months multiplied by the current price

EXHIBIT 5

Industry averages for selected securities, Russell 2000

Major Industry	3 yr. Revenue growth	3 yr. EPS Growth	Trailing 1 yr sales	Mean Sales est. FY1	Mean Sales est. FY2	1-year Trailing P/E	Forward FY1 P/E	Forward FY2 P/E	P/B	beta vs. s&p	ROE	Free cash flow per share
Commercial Services	39.64	29.41	1,189.1	1,435.1	1,642.2	54.79	25.03	19.75	5.70	0.94	17.99	0.73
Communications	17.13	19.01	631.2	62,993.5	68,116.6	24.98	29.49	29.83	3.13	1.17	16.96	-0.27
Consumer Durables	24.49	29.02	2,063.5	2,238.6	2,434.9	18.35	19.05	5.13	2.50	0.92	21.80	1.49
Consumer Non-Durables	18.87	17.31	1,908.0	2,087.5	2,228.9	21.26	14.54	12.32	2.92	0.93	17.45	1.35
Consumer Services	24.39	22.97	1,024.8	1,274.5	1,396.0	30.09	23.84	20.86	3.88	0.86	15.72	0.52
Distribution Services	35.73	15.17	7,736.8	8,804.3	10,024.0	26.27	20.12	16.20	3.42	0.90	15.22	-0.41
Electronic Technology	25.64	23.67	553.0	628.3	740.8	97.68	59.32	34.59	8.57	1.23	17.00	0.92
Energy Minerals	3.59	-11.25	203.6	302.6	336.6	85.58	17.40	14.90	3.87	0.69	15.78	-0.63
Finance	33.07	18.88	837.5	1,207.8	1,452.4	16.62	14.79	10.41	2.12	0.63	14.59	1.59
Health Services	40.41	23.66	1,421.0	1,673.3	1,863.5	172.38	23.18	17.83	4.71	0.87	20.03	1.27
Health Technology	17.94	17.16	520.6	567.2	641.0	57.09	7.11	36.51	5.63	0.66	15.02	0.53
Industrial Services	31.56	23.09	843.4	970.1	1,158.9	135.35	36.01	21.60	3.85	1.15	10.63	0.12
Non-Energy Minerals	10.66	16.23	1,859.6	1,989.5	2,095.2	12.91	13.20	10.39	2.79	0.92	135.54	0.35
Process Industries	15.28	7.22	1,548.3	1,689.6	1,802.5	22.48	12.17	13.06	3.14	0.74	18.35	0.87
Producer Manufacturing	22.83	21.52	2,179.4	2,375.4	2,484.5	23.12	14.20	11.72	3.11	0.94	20.81	1.29
Retail Trade	23.17	29.29	3,231.0	3,549.4	3,886.8	21.79	17.16	13.67	3.36	1.14	18.59	0.63
Technology Services	40.09	26.24	495.9	569.1	674.3	83.26	46.24	26.66	5.91	1.18	17.91	0.74
Utilities	9.70	3.95	1,891.9	1,947.0	2,079.4	15.52	14.00	12.38	1.80	0.23	12.21	-0.72

EXHIBIT 6

Transportation industry data

	SWFT Swift Transport	CHRW C H Robinson	Industry Average
Valuation			
Current price ($)	14.00	49.50	
Latest twelve months P/E	14.0	33.2	15.4
Next twelve months P/E	12.7	29.5	13.5
Price/Book	2.2	7.7	3.0
Price/Cash Flow	5.8	47.3	14.4
Price/Sales	0.8	0.8	0.5
Sales Growth (%)			
Latest quarter	20.6	29.6	19.0
Latest twelve months	21.6	21.8	17.9
EPS Growth (%) Data from First Call			
Latest quarter	−3.7	29.4	33.1
Next quarter estimated	−11.6	21.2	8.3
Latest twelve months	5.3	28.4	35.1
Next twelve months estimated	10.1	12.6	18.0
Selected Financials (LTM)			
Sales ($ millions)	1,171.8	2,573.4	
Earnings before interest, taxes & depreciation	176.5	117.7	
Earnings before interest & taxes	115.7	103.9	
Net income	64.4	62.7	
EPS—diluted ($)	1.00	1.49	
Gross margin	9.8	13.9	
Free cash flow per share ($)	−2.03	0.35	
Market Value			
Market value	885.3	2,092.8	
+ Net short & long-term debt	225.0	−39.6	
= Enterprise value	1,110.3	2,053.2	
Profitability			
Net margin	5.5	2.4	3.3
Free cash flow margin	−10.9	0.6	−2.9
Net return on assets	8.1	11.6	7.2
Net return on equity	16.7	27.2	18.5

EXHIBIT 7

Excerpt from research note on SWFT

15 Aug 2000

Trucking/Leasing

Rating: Buy

Swift Transportation Company Inc (SWFT)

Market Cap: $1,042 M

Business Description

Swift Transportation is a regional truckload carrier operating throughout the U.S. The company avoids competition with long-haul carriers and railroads by focusing on short- to medium-haul services; average hauls are about 540 miles. Swift operates more than 23,600 trailers and vans and about 6,900 tractors from a network of 34 terminals. Goods carried include paper products, nonperishable foods, and retail and discount store merchandise. To provide real-time tracking, the firm has installed two-way satellite communications systems in most of its tractors.

News and Outlook

After speaking with the mgmt and reviewing valuations, I believe SWFT is a good stock to own here.

1) Fundamentals are not strong, but SWFT is gaining share at the expense of the smaller trucking companies. After more than 12 months of high fuel prices and recruiting expense, mid to small trucking companies are no longer able to break even on a cash flow basis. Their services to customers deteriorate increasingly as their driver turnover increases. SWFT, on the other hand, has strong financial conditions and continues to attract drivers due to its attractive equipment, facilities and compensation. In fact recruiting is getting easier. Thus SWFT is able to gain share by picking up new customers (such as COSTCO) and penetrating further existing customers' businesses.

2) SWFT will be able to make attractive acquisitions. Historically, SWFT has been a very successful acquirer. The CFO has repeatedly complained that trucking company executives are asking for unrealistic prices when looking to sell their business. He commented that recently the prices are getting very reasonable. SWFT, due to its relatively large scale and strong mgmt, has one of the highest operating margins in the industry. They excel in bringing down the cost structure after acquiring companies.

3) '01 comparison will be relatively easier as fuel cost has probably peaked. Industry bankruptcies and consolidation also help supply and demand, which will help rate increases.

4) On the negative side, the economy is weakening. Also, potential legislation allowing Mexican trucking companies to enter the U.S. will impact SWFT somewhere down the road by increasing competition.

EXHIBIT 8

Excerpt from research note on CHRW

8 Sep 2000

Trucking/Leasing

Rating: Buy   **CH Robinson Worldwide Inc (CHRW)**

Market Cap: $2,485 M

Business Description

One of the largest third-party logistics (3PL) providers in North America, CHRW provides international logistics and multimodal transportation services through the trucks belonging to other firms (as well as trains, boats and airplanes). It contracts with 20,000 motor carriers. With more than 130 offices in North and South America and Europe, CHRW handles more than 1.5 million shipments per year. It also buys, sells and transports fresh produce throughout the U.S. and provides the T-Chek "smart card" fueling service for motor carriers.

News and Outlook

After meeting with the mgmt, I believe that CHRW is a long-term winner, despite challenging short-term issues such as valuation and a tightening trucking capacity.

1) First, there is a secular trend for shippers to move towards a single source, which benefits larger, established companies such as CHRW. Second, the efficiency and productivity of a company's drivers are essential to returning an acceptable economic profit, and CHRW has by far the best incentive system to attract and retain top sales people and drive productivity. Third, it has the best IT system, which ensures high service and adds value to customers. Therefore, in the long run, CHRW will be able to gain share from traditional trucking companies. Note that CHRW's business model is very different from a typical trucker as it is not asset intensive. It utilizes mid- to small-size trucking companies for capacity. Thus, long-term share gains will drive CHRW's financial performance.

2) Potential legislation allowing Mexican trucking companies to enter the U.S. is beneficial as it will create another source of capacity for CHRW.

3) Due to its non–asset based model, CHRW has a different sensitivity to the trucking industry supply-demand cycle. It benefits less as supply-demand is tightening (since it has to pass thru rate increases to its capacity suppliers). But it also suffers less when the supply-demand cycle is not benign. In fact, CHRW's margins tend to increase during over-capacity as co. is able to get attractive rates from suppliers.

4) Weakening economy is also a concern since CHRW's topline growth is likely to slow down a touch. 4Q'00 comparison will be tough due to the year 2000 comparison in 4Q'99.

5) Finally, management has a good track record and is quite focused on objectives. I believe they will meet the goals and exceed expectations.

6

Brokerage Transactions for Mutual Funds

Nearly all investment decisions made by portfolio managers are implemented by trading: buying or selling securities. Since the prices obtained in such trades have an important effect on the performance of the fund, the trader is a partner to the portfolio manager in accomplishing the investment objectives of the fund. Most advisers to mutual fund complexes have a relatively small trading division, or "desk," that is separate from the corresponding portfolio management group for several reasons. First, this separation allows the portfolio managers to concentrate on their primary task of selecting stocks and structuring portfolios, normally with an investment horizon measured in months or years. Second, the separation allows the fund traders to develop specialized expertise in the dynamics of the market and to add value in implementing investment decisions within a time horizon of hours, days or even minutes. Third, the separation provides an independent check on the relations between portfolio managers and Wall Street firms (or the counterparties to fund transactions) in order to prevent inappropriate forms of collaboration.

The decisions by all the trading desks in the mutual fund industry have a significant impact on the market. Table 6.1 lists the market capitalization of each major U.S. stock market and the total amount across all three U.S. stock markets relative to the assets in U.S. domestic equity funds. This table shows that mutual funds as a whole have grown in their ownership of the U.S. market for publicly traded equities and held over 20% of that market at the end of 2000. Table 6.2 details the average daily trading volumes of the same three U.S. stock markets. Although precise data are not available, it can be estimated that the mutual fund industry's share of trading volume in these U.S. stock markets is even higher than its ownership share, perhaps reaching 30% of such trading volume.

TABLE 6.1

Size of major U.S. markets and mutual fund share

Date	Market Capitalization of Exchange ($M)				Domestic Equity Mutual Fund Assets ($M)	
	NYSE	Amex	Nasdaq	Total	Total	% of Market
1990	2,692,123	102,302	310,800	3,105,225	250,187	8.10%
1991	3,484,340	124,454	490,685	4,099,479	372,846	9.10
1992	3,798,238	88,797	618,774	4,505,809	494,701	11.00
1993	4,212,956	105,116	791,706	5,109,778	680,555	13.30
1994	4,147,937	86,036	793,669	5,027,642	748,526	14.90
1995	5,654,815	103,147	1,159,940	6,917,902	1,091,503	15.80
1996	6,841,988	97,911	1,511,824	8,451,723	1,445,017	17.10
1997	8,879,631	124,606	1,737,510	10,741,747	1,981,356	18.40
1998	10,271,900	126,307	2,524,360	12,922,567	2,481,684	19.20
1999	11,437,597	101,294	5,204,620	16,743,512	3,203,191	19.10
2000	11,442,383	82,828	3,578,592	15,103,804	3,145,725	20.80

Sources: Market capitalization of exchange: FIBV (International Federation of Stock Exchanges); includes domestic companies only (see http://www.fibv.com). Domestic equity mutual fund assets: Strategic Insight; includes assets of U.S.-focused mutual funds only.

TABLE 6.2

Trading volume of major U.S. markets

Date	Average Daily Trading Volume ($M)			
	NYSE	Amex	Nasdaq[a]	Total
1990	5,238	149	894	8,271
1991	6,009	162	1,371	9,533
1992	6,872	166	1,754	10,784
1993	9,025	167	2,668	13,853
1994	9,739	232	2,876	14,841
1995	12,234	289	4,758	19,276
1996	15,999	360	6,500	24,855
1997	22,836	566	8,857	34,256
1998	29,039	1,143	10,950	43,130
1999	35,497	NA	20,769	58,265
2000	43,889	3,752	39,283	88,924

[a]Includes correction for "double counting." See note 1 of text.
Source: FIBV; includes domestic and foreign stocks (see http://www.fibv.com)

This Chapter focuses on equity trading by mutual funds. It begins by outlining the operation of U.S. stock exchanges and over-the-counter equity markets, then focuses on the role of the fund trader in the equity investment process and moves to the fiduciary aspects of fund trading for equity mutual funds. The Chapter ends with a case study about a fund trader who is attempting to execute large orders for several equity funds in a mutual fund complex.

I. Overview of U.S. Equity Markets

Nearly all of the domestic stocks held in mutual funds trade on one of two major markets in the United States: the New York Stock Exchange (NYSE) or the National Association of Securities Dealers automated quotation system (Nasdaq). Most broker-dealer firms are members of both the NYSE and Nasdaq, which were both organized as cooperatives historically controlled by their members. The Nasdaq recently sold equity interests primarily to its large members and listed companies. Both markets recently have raised the possibility of public ownership.

The NYSE and Nasdaq remain different and competing marketplaces, although changes in technology and regulation are tending to lessen those differences. The NYSE is the largest stock exchange in the world, with average daily trading in 2000 of $44 billion and 1 billion shares. Located at 11 Wall Street in Lower Manhattan, the NYSE provides a single physical location for all the trading in each of the more than 3,000 stocks listed by public companies for trading on the exchange. By contrast, Nasdaq is a purely electronic market that uses telecommunications networks to bring stock quotations and other data for more than 5,000 stocks listed for trading to the computer screens of participating broker-dealers and other traders. Nasdaq now trades about the same amount of shares and dollars as the NYSE.[1]

Besides the NYSE and Nasdaq, there are a number of regional exchanges.[2] More important, as reviewed below, a number of new electronic trading systems have begun to present major challenges to the NYSE and Nasdaq. Whatever entities may emerge as the eventual winners and losers in the competition for trading activity within this rapidly changing landscape, the trading of U.S. equities is likely to continue at multiple marketplaces with increased choices on where and how to trade.

A. The New York Stock Exchange

Historically, the NYSE has operated its market as a continuous auction where participants compete on the basis of the prices they are willing to pay or receive in stock trades. The auction process serves to narrow the difference (called the *spread)* between the highest offer to purchase (called the *best bid*) and the lowest offer to sell (called the *best offer*) to attract the orders of current stockholders and other investors. Those willing to buy or sell a stock only at a specified price (or more favorable price) use "limit" orders, while those willing to accept the prevailing price use "market" orders.

When orders in an NYSE-listed stock are sent to the NYSE floor, they are brought to the post of the one and only "specialist" assigned to that stock by the NYSE, or held by a broker in the trading "crowd" congregating around such specialist's post. The specialist performs a unique role on the NYSE, acting at certain times as a neutral "auctioneer" and at other times as a trader—as either an agent for customers or as principal for its own account. As agent, the specialist maintains a "book" of limit orders at prices that are below (in the case of buy orders) or above (in the case of sell orders) the current price at which a given stock is trading. The specialist continually displays the highest price that a buyer (including the specialist) is willing to pay (the "best bid") and the lowest price that a seller (including the specialist) is willing to take (the "best offer"),[3] along with share quantities (size) that indicate how much stock is being bid for or offered. This Best Bid and Offer (BBO) is reported immediately by the NYSE and distributed by vendors to millions of market participants worldwide.[4]

Bids and offers come to the specialist's post both electronically (through an order routing system called SuperDOT), and through "floor brokers" in the trading "crowd" before the specialist's post (see Figure 6.1).[5] The specialist is responsible for conducting the continuous auction in a given stock among the trading crowd of floor brokers; in that auction, the specialist represents the limit orders on the book, as well as its own proprietary bid and offer. When a participant is willing to "hit a bid" (and sell) or "take

FIGURE 6.1

A *specialist's post* at the New York Stock Exchange

© New York Stock Exchange. Used with the permission of the New York Stock Exchange.

an offer" (and buy) quoted by the specialist, then a trade is effected. Such transactions may be executed by the specialist's matching limit orders on its book with market orders: a buy market order[6] will be executed at the current offer price, and a sell market order[7] will trade at the current bid price. Alternatively, the specialist can effect a transaction by itself, taking one side of a trade, thereby providing liquidity to the market. In doing so, the specialist hopes to complete another transaction quickly by taking the other side of a trade in the same stock (unwind the position) in order to generate income, as well as lower its risk and free up its capital. To lower its risk and free up its capital, the specialist also tries to reduce the size of its inventory in a given stock as much as possible at the end of the day. The NYSE has extensive rules concerning the actions of the specialist, who is required to maintain a liquid market by matching orders in accordance with price priority, to give priority to customer orders over its own proprietary trading and to maintain an "orderly market" in which price changes are not too large. In addition, two floor brokers in the crowd before the specialist post can agree on a price between the best bid and best offer quoted by the specialist. Such brokers generally are acting as agents for customers. Figure 6.2 depicts the chronological flow of an order to purchase and an order to sell on the NYSE, which are both executed at price Y.

After trades are effected on the NYSE floor, they are reported over the "consolidated tape," which is made widely available to market participants and investors by brokerage firms and vendors. The matching of buy and sell orders then leads to a process (currently completed within three days after the trade date)[8] in which the participating member firms exchange securities for cash in a centralized clearance and set-

FIGURE 6.2

Example of chronological flow of an order on the NYSE

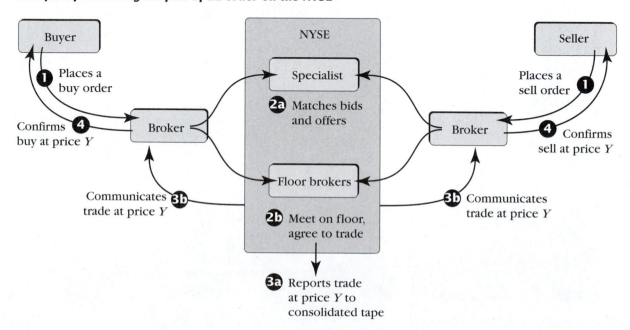

tlement system. The member firms charge commissions to their customers for acting as their agents in executing trades on the NYSE. Average commissions charged by NYSE member firms to mutual funds and other institutional investors are about 5 cents per share.[9] Such commissions represent charges for the services of the member firm in their brokerage functions, the use of the NYSE floor and trade clearance and settlement.

B. *Nasdaq*

In contrast to the NYSE where customer orders may be matched against each other, the over-the-counter (OTC) market operating through Nasdaq historically has been a market in which all trades occur through dealers who buy and sell for their own account. Although recent changes in Nasdaq have made it feasible for matches to occur directly between customer orders, trades on Nasdaq are still more likely to occur between a customer on one side and a dealer trading for its own account on the other side. However, in contrast to the NYSE, where one specialist is given a monopoly in trading each listed stock, Nasdaq allows for competition among multiple market makers in the same OTC stock. Subject to satisfying certain capital requirements, any NASD member firm can be designated as a market maker in any stock and compete with other market-making firms for order flow in that stock. In this competition, all market makers are required by Nasdaq to maintain both bids and offers (two-sided quotes) in any stock in which they participate, and trades are effected first by the dealer with the best bid or offer. Quotes indicate both the price level and size (amount of shares) for which the quote is applicable. The quoting dealer is required to "stand behind" his or her quote and execute up to that amount if any order is received. If news breaks or other orders arrive that move the market price, a slow dealer can get "picked off" by another participant if he or she does not move the quote quickly enough. Because of this exposure to getting picked off and the perception that showing larger size does not actually attract more orders, Nasdaq quotes generally show only a nominal amount (e.g., 1,000 shares). Figure 6.3 is a printout of a Nasdaq screen showing bid and offer quotes for Microsoft. Note that there are numerous dealers in this stock and that the spread between the bid and ask is quite narrow. These are both indications of a liquid stock.

If there are a public (i.e., nondealer) buyer and a public seller, then a dealer will try to buy from the seller at the bid price and sell to the buyer at the offer price, thus capturing the difference between the two prices (the "spread") as revenue. Both transactions are reported publicly.[10] Like the specialist on the NYSE, the Nasdaq dealer has an economic incentive to end the day by reducing its inventory of stock as much as possible. In this way, the dealer reduces its exposure to the risk that the value of the stock may drop by the opening of the market on the following day and maintains a high level of free capital that is necessary to support further trading activities.

The dealer generally cannot realize the entire spread as revenue. For example, the dealer runs the risk after buying stock from a seller that the buyer will change his mind or that the offer price will change through competition from other dealers and their order flow. Such a change of mind or price could reduce or eliminate the dealer's profit, or even turn it negative, before the dealer has an opportunity to enter into an offsetting sale. In many situations, one dealer has a buyer and another dealer has a seller, so the

FIGURE 6.3

Nasdaq screen (level ii) detailing quotes for Microsoft

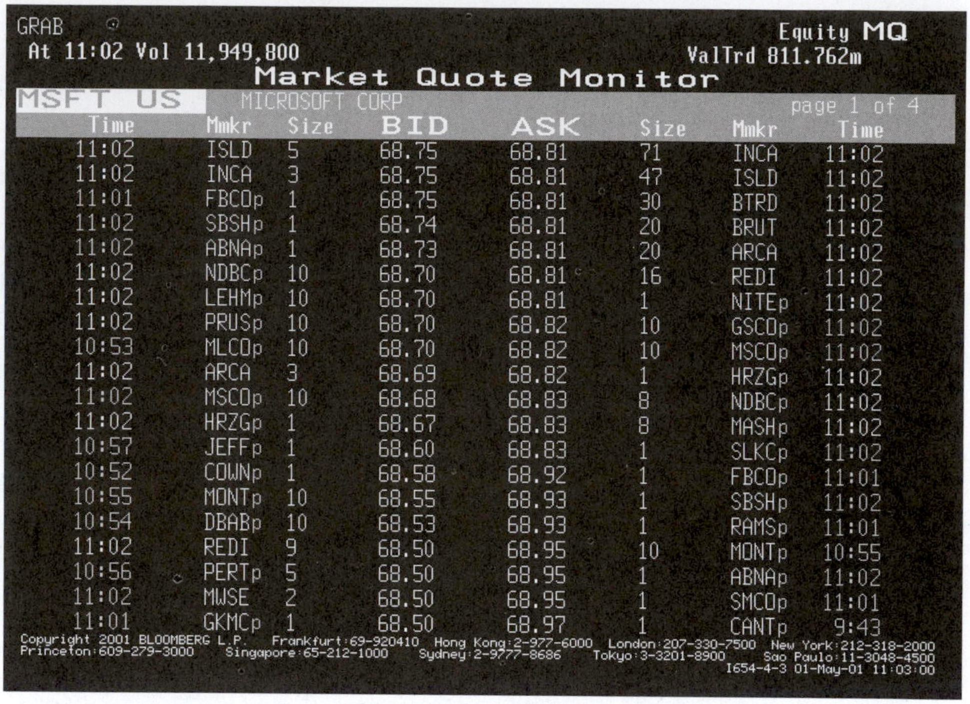
GRAB Equity MQ
At 11:02 Vol 11,949,800 ValTrd 811.762m
Market Quote Monitor
MSFT US MICROSOFT CORP page 1 of 4

Time	Mmkr	Size	BID	ASK	Size	Mmkr	Time
11:02	ISLD	5	68.75	68.81	71	INCA	11:02
11:02	INCA	3	68.75	68.81	47	ISLD	11:02
11:01	FBCOp	1	68.75	68.81	30	BTRD	11:02
11:02	SBSHp	1	68.74	68.81	20	BRUT	11:02
11:02	ABNAp	1	68.73	68.81	20	ARCA	11:02
11:02	NDBCp	10	68.70	68.81	16	REDI	11:02
11:02	LEHMp	10	68.70	68.81	1	NITEp	11:02
11:02	PRUSp	10	68.70	68.82	10	GSCOp	11:02
10:53	MLCOp	10	68.70	68.82	10	MSCOp	11:02
11:02	ARCA	3	68.69	68.82	1	HRZGp	11:02
11:02	MSCOp	10	68.68	68.83	8	NDBCp	11:02
11:02	HRZGp	1	68.67	68.83	8	MASHp	11:02
10:57	JEFFp	1	68.60	68.83	1	SLKCp	11:02
10:52	COWNp	1	68.58	68.92	1	FBCOp	11:01
10:55	MONTp	10	68.55	68.93	1	SBSHp	11:02
10:54	DBABp	10	68.53	68.93	1	RAMSp	11:01
11:02	REDI	9	68.50	68.95	10	MONTp	10:55
10:56	PERTp	5	68.50	68.95	1	ABNAp	11:02
11:02	MWSE	2	68.50	68.95	1	SMCOp	11:01
11:01	GKMCp	1	68.50	68.97	1	CANTp	9:43

Copyright 2001 BLOOMBERG L.P. Frankfurt:69-920410 Hong Kong:2-977-6000 London:207-330-7500 New York:212-318-2000
Princeton:609-279-3000 Singapore:65-212-1000 Sydney:2-9777-8686 Tokyo:3-3201-8900 Sao Paulo:11-3048-4500
I654-4-3 01-May-01 11:03:00

two dealers can effect a net transfer from buyer to seller by trading with each other. In such situations, the two dealers are likely to split the spread, though intervening market movements may cause one dealer to profit at the other's expense. In addition, most mutual funds and other large institutional investors will negotiate with a dealer to obtain a price "inside" the spread, in effect taking back from the dealer some of the spread profit.

While retail investors sometimes use a broker to reach a dealer in OTC trades, institutional investors like mutual funds do most of their OTC trades directly with a dealer, so they typically pay no commissions on such trades. Instead, the dealer makes profits from the spread, in exchange for taking the other side of the institution's trade and thereby providing liquidity. No dealer is required to make a market in any OTC stock. As a result, popular and heavily traded stocks attract many market makers, and their competition tends to reduce the average size of the spread. Thinly traded or obscure stocks may have no market maker, and if there is one, the spread may be unusually large. Figure 6.4 depicts the chronological flow of an order to purchase and an order to sell an OTC security traded through Nasdaq. The buyer is a retail investor us-

FIGURE 6.4

Example of chronological flow of an order on Nasdaq

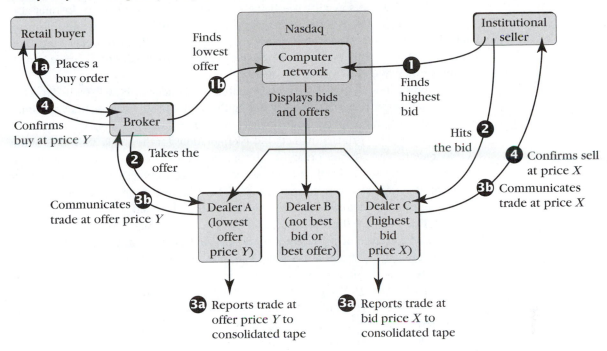

ing a broker; the seller is an institution going directly to one of the multiple dealers in the stock. After each of the orders is executed with a different Nasdaq dealer, the trades are reported on the consolidated tape and processed through a centralized clearance and settlement system.

C. Electronic Communication Networks and Other Trading Venues

In addition to the NYSE and Nasdaq, a number of other markets compete for order flow in the trading of stocks. The American Exchange (AMEX) in New York is a longstanding, although minor, rival to the NYSE. Regional exchanges are other traditional alternatives: Boston, Cincinnati, Philadelphia, Chicago and the Pacific Exchange. Trades and quotes at these exchanges are "consolidated" with those at the NYSE (plus those in any other U.S. market venue) to provide a single national view of the market in any listed stock. The AMEX and the regionals together account for only about 15% of the total consolidated trading in listed stocks.[11]

With advances in telecommunications and computer technology, a number of electronic networks have developed to allow trading directly between investors without the intermediation of traditional brokers or dealers. The oldest such trading system is Instinet (currently owned by Reuters), which came into wide use during the late

1980s. Instinet provides an electronic connection to trading desks of both institutions and broker-dealers, with software that displays Instinet quotes and messages along with Nasdaq quotes. It is used by institutional traders mainly for OTC stocks as a means of trading inside the spread that is being maintained by market makers. Instinet also provides a means for traders to negotiate privately for larger trades, while still maintaining anonymity. Its share volume has steadily increased to about 10% of Nasdaq's volume on average. Instinet generates revenue by charging both sides of the trade a small commission (about 2 to 3 cents per share).

Another trading system often used by mutual fund traders is POSIT (owned by ITG, Inc), which began being used widely during the 1990s. In this system, traders submit orders to a central computer that matches buys and sells, using as a price for the trade the midpoint of the primary market's bid-ask quotations for the stock. Both sides of the cross-trade receive a better price than the spread and pay only a small commission (2 to 3 cents per share) to POSIT for the execution service. Although POSIT prices are attractive, this system poses a disadvantage for the mutual fund trader because the matching process normally happens only at four prescheduled times during the trading day, and even then there is no guarantee of a match. As a result, the execution of an order may be delayed or perhaps not occur at all. In fact, most orders in the POSIT system do not match with a contrary order, and only a portion of a given trader's order is likely to be executed in a given matching round.

During the late 1990s, a number of other electronic trading systems were developed—so-called electronic communication networks (ECNs). This development was prompted by a new Securities and Exchange Commission (SEC) rule requiring any OTC dealer who accepts customer limit orders to display any such order if it is at a higher bid or lower offer than the dealer's own quoted bid or offer, so that other market participants can see and trade with the more favorably priced customer order. Instinet is actually an older version of an ECN mainly for institutional trades; newer versions include Island, Brut, Archipelago, Btrade and Redibook. Like Instinet, these ECNs have been used primarily (or exclusively) for the trading of OTC stocks, and together they have grown to comprise 30% or more of Nasdaq's volume as of 2000. The ECNs display the entire "book" of bids and offers available in their system, allowing participants to see greater depth of the market compared to the Nasdaq display of each dealer's BBO (the "top" of the book). Each ECN also provides a means for instantaneous execution against posted quotes—settling and guaranteeing the trade for both parties. The recently developed ECNs afford a mutual fund trader a new opportunity to work orders directly in the market and to interact directly with retail order flow (in addition to institutional order flow through Instinet or POSIT). At this early stage in their development, however, trading through ECNs often is very time intensive and can significantly increase the trader's work load because most ECN trades are small in size relative to the usual size of institutional orders. By affording an opportunity for investors' orders to interact through a computer network, ECNs represent an emerging hybrid market—bearing some of the characteristics of the OTC market (having neither a physical trading floor nor a specialist) and an exchange market (allowing direct interaction among investors' buy and sell orders and affording priority to orders based on price).

D.   *Current Developments Affecting Institutional Investors*

A major evolutionary step in the U.S. stock markets was the recent switch to decimalization. Traditionally, quotes have been displayed and trades have been executed at only a limited number of price points: typically at ⅛ or ¹⁄₁₆ of a dollar (e.g., 70.375 and 70.4375 cents); by contrast, the rest of the major industrialized markets quote prices in decimals with increments of one penny (e.g., 70.40 and 70.41 cents). Under the direction of the SEC, the NYSE and Nasdaq agreed to move to decimal prices for trades and quotes in 2001. From the institutional investor's perspective, the change to decimalization has both positive and negative implications. Many participants expect that decimal prices will lead to more efficient markets by reducing spreads between bid and ask prices of widely traded stocks. On the other hand, because orders will appear at 100 (rather than 8 or 16) price points per dollar, decimalization is likely to reduce the depth of orders at the best bid and ask price at any given price level. Early studies suggest that decimalization has led to lower prices paid for smaller orders typically placed by retail investors, while prices for larger orders of mutual funds and other institutional investors have not declined.[12] However, complaining that decimalization has sharply narrowed spreads, broker-dealers are asking institutional clients to consider paying commissions on OTC trades in addition to spreads.

Moreover, decimalization may give specialists and market makers an increased incentive to "step ahead" of large institutional orders through a practice called "pennying" or "penny jumping," thereby taking arguably unfair advantage of their access to market information. For example, if a specialist knows that a mutual fund is looking to buy 100,000 shares of Wal-Mart at $52.35, the specialist could buy Wal-Mart shares at $52.36 in anticipation that the stock price will rise as the fund raises its bid slightly—thus allowing the specialist to sell its shares at a profit. If the specialist is mistaken and the fund maintains (but does not increase) its bid, the specialist can nonetheless sell the shares at a loss of only one penny per share at $52.35. By contrast, under the earlier fractional pricing of stocks, a specialist stepping ahead of a large order risked a potential loss that was over six times greater even at ¹⁄₁₆ of a dollar (6.25 pennies versus 1 penny). Decimalization thus has the potential for significantly reducing the number and size of institutional limit orders because they can be easily bettered by orders of plus or minus one penny from market professionals.

Other significant developments point toward the gradual convergence of the different markets—ECNs, exchanges and Nasdaq—combining aspects of the traditional auction-based exchanges and the dealer-based OTC markets. Archipelago, one of the leading ECNs, has completed its purchase of the equity trading portion of the Pacific Stock Exchange (a regional) and plans to reconstitute it as a fully electronic exchange. Meanwhile, the NYSE has announced plans for an ECN-type facility for listed stocks and public display of the depth of limit orders on the specialist's book. Nasdaq has gained approval from the SEC to launch its "SuperMontage," which would include limit orders from ECNs as well as quotes from OTC market makers and their customers. SuperMontage represents a large step toward a consolidated limit order book for OTC stocks; it displays (at least partially) the depth of its "book" and provides rapid execution capabilities through the system. SuperMontage is a crucial move toward allowing an auction among customer orders in Nasdaq stocks, although it allows for certain exceptions from auction execution rules based strictly on price priority (highest bid and lowest offer). Finally, with the demise of Rule 390 of the NYSE, which prohibited NYSE member firms from making markets in NYSE-listed stocks off the floor of the NYSE, Nasdaq and the NYSE will compete directly for order flow by each providing facilities for trading stocks that are listed on the other marketplace. As a result of all these changes, mutual fund traders are likely to have an increasing number of choices as to where and how to trade stocks.

While the proliferation of alternative venues for executing trades in the same stock tends to benefit mutual funds, this proliferation has generated concerns about the adverse effects of market fragmentation. These concerns arise from a basic economic assumption that interaction of orders among all possible participants in a single trading venue (or interconnected trading venues) will inevitably lead to more efficient pricing of securities trades than would occur on multiple, separated markets. Advocates of a national market have pushed for the establishment of centralized facilities such as a central limit order book (CLOB) in which all limit orders from all markets in the United States would be stored and executed in accordance with strict time and price priority. However, critics contend that a CLOB, by channeling all orders into one computer system, would stifle innovation and necessitate public utility regulation. Critics also point out that large block trades from institutional investors like mutual funds would be very difficult to execute in a CLOB, which would hold many small orders with different time and price priorities.

II. *Roles and Responsibilities of Mutual Fund Traders*

In most mutual fund complexes, portfolio managers make investment decisions that are implemented by a separate group of investment professionals called fund traders. The trader seeks to accomplish the manager's goals, in accordance with any instructions received from the manager, in the most advantageous way for the fund shareholders—usually called seeking the "best execution." Seeking the best execution has become a more complex task because of the significant changes in the structure of the U.S. equity markets discussed above. In seeking to obtain the best execution for mutual fund orders, a trader may take into account not only the bid or offer price quoted in a particular market or by a particular market participant, but also the probability of trade completion, the depth and liquidity of a given market, the speed at which a trade can be carried out, as well as the commissions and other costs associated with executing a trade.

Mutual fund trading desks usually are organized around the portfolio managers that they serve; this organization allows for a trader to become familiar with a manager's portfolio, investment style and trading patterns. By contrast, a few large fund complexes have organized their trading desks more around the markets they trade in: domestic markets by sector or industry and international markets by country. Since the industry or sector organization of trading desks is similar to that of the trading desks of Wall Street firms, it allows traders to acquire experience in the individual stocks they trade consistently from day to day. But industry or sector organization requires fund traders to make special efforts to maintain close relationships with the fund managers.

Let's consider the chronology of a typical fund trade. The trade usually starts with an order to the fund trader from the portfolio manager (e.g., "buy 100,000 shares of Motorola") that includes some instructions, explicitly (e.g., "with a limit of 47") or implicitly ("if you can do that size without pushing the price too much"). The trader wants to get the trade done at the best possible price consistent with these instructions. The trader first must choose an approach to executing the order, which may be called *trading strategy* (discussed below). Having chosen the strategy, the trader must then choose the particular firm (e.g., broker, market maker or ECN) to carry out that strategy and transmit the order to that firm along with appropriate instructions. In making these decisions, the trader usually employs a number of mostly electronic information sources, including market information (last trades and current quotes), news feeds and perhaps vendor analytics, as well as internal research and analysis generated by the management company. The fund trader will then monitor the progress of the firm with the order, by telephone or electronic message, until the trade is complete (or another stopping point is reached). Next, the trader takes a report from the firm summarizing the trade (e.g., "you bought 100,000 shares of Motorola at an average price of 46.43"), which the trader then relays to the fund's back office so that the trade can be settled (by the exchange of cash and securities) and the results can be reflected in the fund's holdings.

The formal completion of the trade is accomplished by the fund's custodian, ordinarily a bank chosen by the fund to hold the stocks and cash (plus other assets) of the fund in a segregated account. (For a list of the largest custodians to mutual funds, see Table 6.3.) The custodian delivers cash (dollars or other relevant currency) to complete a purchase and delivers shares to complete a sale, typically to the Depository Trust Clearinghouse (DTC) or other securities depository to settle the trade. DTC nets all of the trades by institutions (and by brokers on behalf of individuals) and sees to the redistribution of cash or securities in accordance with that day's market transactions. DTC accomplishes this using "book-entry" settlement of the trades, without the physical transfer of stock certificates (see Figure 6.5).

TABLE 6.3

Top 10 mutual fund custodians by 1940 Act domestic fund assets

2000 Rank	Custodian	Assets ($M)
1	State Street Corp.	2,111,882
2	Bank of New York	928,458
3	Chase Manhattan Bank	900,376
4	Brown Brothers Harriman	410,444
5	PFPC Trust Company / PNC Bank	401,718
6	Deutsche Bank AG	345,100
7	First Union National Bank	251,635
8	Citibank N.A.	214,803
9	Mellon Trust	168,468
10	Investors Bank & Trust	125,041

Source: Thompson Financial, "The 2000 Custody Service Guide," September 2000.

FIGURE 6.5

Parties involved in execution and settlement of an order traded on an exchange

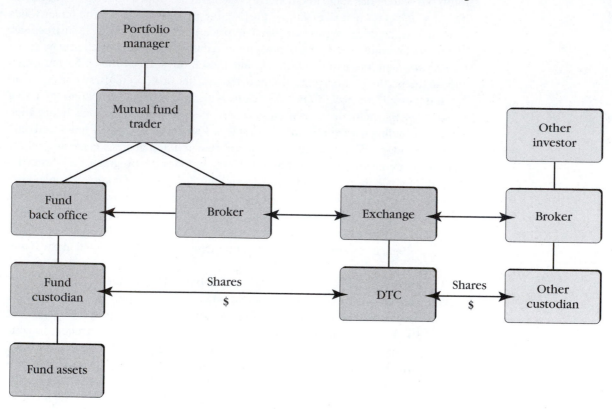

At the end of each day is an accounting cycle to reconcile a fund's accounts and portfolio holdings to reflect the fund's purchases and sales of securities during the day. An agent for the fund—typically the fund's administrator or pricing and bookkeeping agent—will price all of the fund's holdings and compute a total net asset value (NAV) for the fund. (See Chapter Nine for further discussion of fund pricing.)

A. Trading Strategies

Most trading orders from mutual funds are for trades much larger than the usual retail order from an individual investor. Individual fund orders are routinely for 10,000 to 50,000 shares, and it is not unusual for funds to trade 1 million shares or more. This size necessitates care, so that the fund will incur as little "market impact" as practical. Fund traders can pursue either of two main strategies: retain a broker as agent to work an order for the fund, or go directly to the market maker or electronic facility to execute the fund order. The former strategy generally is used for exchange trades, while the latter strategy generally is used for OTC trades, though these generalities have broken down in light of the dramatic changes in market structure discussed above. In addition, as discussed later in this Chapter, buy and sell orders in the same stock from two different funds within a complex can be crossed in an interfund trade.

The most common trading strategy for mutual fund traders with orders for exchange-listed stocks is to retain a broker, who will "work" the order as agent for the fund throughout the trade day.[13] The fund trader may not give the broker the entire order at once, but instead place part of the order, perhaps with a limit ("take 25,000 Motorola to buy with a 46.50 top"). As the trade progresses, the fund trader can increase the order with the broker until the entire amount is placed, as long as the broker's actions meet the expectations of the fund trader. If the broker does not produce the expected results, then the fund trader may terminate the order with the broker, cancel any remaining shares not yet executed and place the remainder of the order with another broker.

The most common strategy for mutual fund traders with orders in OTC stocks is to go directly to the market maker displaying the best quotes over Nasdaq. However, fund traders may choose to seek better executions for particularly large orders in OTC or exchange-listed stocks by using electronic facilities like Instinet or POSIT, described above, which specialize in institutional trading; or by hiring a Wall Street firm to put together a block trade, described later in this Chapter, where a Wall Street firm actively shops a large order in the "upstairs market" outside the NYSE or Nasdaq. In addition, the NYSE recently introduced Institutional Xpress, an electronic gateway for institutions to execute orders of at least 25,000 shares in an NYSE-listed stock directly against certain quotes displayed at the NYSE.

Another trading strategy used by mutual fund traders is the "basket trade" (also known as a program trade, portfolio trade or list trade). This strategy may be advantageous when a trader has a number of trades to accomplish, and the risk inherent in the group of orders is less than the total risk of the individual trades taken separately. In one version of a basket trade, the whole list of orders is executed with one dealer, with the dealer taking the opposite side of the trade directly. This is known as a "principal" basket trade, as opposed to an "agency" basket trade, where the broker agrees to trade the whole list but generally does not take part in any trades except as an agent. Often basket trades are constructed by the fund trader and offered to a limited number of brokers or dealers on a competitive basis, with a particular pricing scheme ("individual trades priced on the close"). In such situations, the competition between brokers is reflected in the commission rate at which they offer to do the trade.

For small orders, the fund trader may choose the strategy of executing the trade electronically. The NYSE's SuperDOT system allows orders to be electronically routed to the specialist's post, where they are executed when possible. Although SuperDOT will take orders up to 30,000 shares, most executions are for 3,000 shares or fewer, and the average trade size for many stocks is fewer than 1,000 shares. Thus, a trader can execute a small order directly through SuperDOT; a trader may also execute a larger order by dividing it into several smaller orders that are executed at various points throughout the day. In pursuing an electronic trading strategy, the trader must choose individual order sizes and times at which to send the orders.

In another type of electronic trading, a fund trader can work a relatively small order in a Nasdaq stock directly through an ECN, such as Archipelago, mentioned above. In this strategy, the fund trader takes an offer when buying, for example, if the offer appears to be a "good" price. Again, the trader's judgment goes into deciding when to trade and in what size. Usually Nasdaq quotes are for 1,000 shares or fewer on an ECN, so a fund order is ordinarily traded in several increments.

In implementing the trading strategies discussed above, the trader can specify several different types of instructions when placing an order. The most common types are market orders and limit orders (defined earlier in this Chapter). Traders use a limit order in an attempt to get a better price than the current market price. However, a limit order entails the risk that the market price will move against the order; then, in order to accomplish the trade, the order may have to be executed at a worse price than the original current market.

The trade-off between price and time is a basic element of trading and indicates the kind of risks that fund traders must address in accomplishing their trades. Reading 6.1 discusses the various strategies used by traders on the "buy side"—the side of institutional investors— as opposed to the "sell side" on Wall Street. By making trading decisions that are successful in terms of achieving good prices, a trader can make a substantial contribution to the performance of the fund. For this reason, traders usually are included in the category of investment professionals in the fund management firm. Traders typically are paid a salary plus a performance bonus, and compensation levels for traders at large fund complexes rose substantially during the 1990s. According to a survey by the Association for Investment Management and Research, the median annual compensation of a fund trader was $155,500 in 2001, with the top performers in large complexes at multiples of that median.

B. Broker-Dealer Selection and Services

As discussed above, fund traders typically use broker-dealers to access the market and accomplish the execution, although sometimes fund traders go directly to market makers and electronic networks. Broker-dealers provide two basic benefits to fund traders: search services ("finding the other side") and anonymity for large orders. In addition, some brokers supply research services to fund complexes.

Search services can include "shopping" the order in the upstairs market, as well as working the order on the exchange floor or in Nasdaq. In the upstairs market, a broker-dealer sends "indications of interest" (IOI) messages to client desks in order to find a "natural" counterparty to the trade—that is, to find a seller when the broker has a buy order (and vice versa). The broker-dealer itself may facilitate the order by selling out of its own inventory a portion of the stock being bought (or buying a portion being sold). In this case, the broker-dealer is using its own capital to facilitate the client's trade, hoping that it will be able to "unwind" (reverse) the position profitably. Alternatively, the broker-dealer may buy the block of stock from the mutual fund and then immediately sell most of the shares to institutions that have committed to different amounts of the block, perhaps retaining a small portion of the block for the firm's own account. Block trading, especially the decisions that must be made by a fund trader, is further illustrated by the case study at the end of this Chapter and in "Shopping a Block: Conversation at a Fund Trading Desk."

In shopping the block, the broker-dealer must be careful to avoid adverse market impact. For example, possible counterparties may see a large buy order coming to the market and choose to buy ahead of it in anticipation of a price rise that will be caused

CALLOUT
Shopping a Block: Conversation at a Fund Trading Desk

SCOTT [junior trader]: I'm really worried about selling this 300,000-share block of Softserve. The portfolio manager seems anxious to sell before the upcoming announcement of quarterly earnings, which he's obviously concerned about.

SANDRA [senior trader]: Yeah, but the recent trading volume in Softserve has been less than 100,000 shares a day. We're going to really push the price down selling 300,000 shares. We may do better by trading the shares at once as a block. What are the market makers showing on Nasdaq?

SCOTT: [looking at screen] UBS Paine Webber has the highest bid at 20.25, but it's showing only 5,000 shares bid at that price. There are only a few major market makers in this stock, and the bids fall pretty quickly down to 19.

SANDRA: That's a big drop in price. We might do better with a block trade. What about calling Goldman Sachs? They've indicated that they're accumulating some big positions in software stocks for a few foreign buyers.

SCOTT: Yeah, that's a good idea. With our levels of business, we should be able to get Goldman to take on the risk of buying some of the block themselves if they can't place the whole trade with clients.

SANDRA: Let's give Jennifer a call on the direct line; she's the senior block trader at Goldman, and she's already working some other positions with us. But let's see what she can offer before we tell her what

we're looking for. We don't want to give her a chance to drop the price right off the bat.

SCOTT: [Scott reaches Jennifer by phone.] Jennifer, how's it going? We're wondering if you could give us a picture of customer interest in Softserve.

JENNIFER: Hold on—let me check the screen and our data. . . . Looks like we can line up buyers for 100,000 shares. As for sellers, we have some stock to go ourselves and could sell up to 50,000 shares. What are you looking to do?

SCOTT: We're looking to *sell*, but only at reasonable levels. Can you give us a menu? At what prices are you willing to buy the stock?

JENNIFER: Let me check with our sales desk and risk manager.

SANDRA: We'll stay on hold. [A few minutes go by.]

JENNIFER: I'm back with some pretty good bids. At UBS Paine Webber's current quote of 20.25, we can buy up to 50,000 shares. The price will have to fall for trades any bigger than that. We can buy a 100,000 block at 20 and a 200,000 block at 19.55.

SANDRA: For customers or your own account?

JENNIFER: Mostly customers.

SCOTT: Well, 19.55 sounds pretty low for 200,000 shares. You're cutting price by 70 cents a share just for the block, which you can place.

JENNIFER: But this is a volatile stock, and that's a large block. We may have to buy some of this ourselves, so we need a margin for error.

SCOTT: How about we accept the 19.55 if you take on an additional 100,000 shares for your own account?

JENNIFER: A total of 300,000 shares at 19.55?

SCOTT: Right.

JENNIFER: Okay, we'll take it.

by the coming large order. If so, this "front-running" will itself raise the price that the fund will pay in executing a block trade. As we have seen, the change to decimal pricing increases the incentives (and decreases the risk) for those engaging in this practice. The worst outcome of such an effort would be for the price to rise so high in anticipation of a block trade that it becomes unattractive for the fund to execute that trade at all.

Anonymity is another key service provided by a broker-dealer. Because each mutual fund is required to report its complete holdings semiannually (plus quarterly filings for aggregate holdings by any manager of mutual funds with $100 million or more in assets under management), the secrecy concerning fund positions is short-lived. When a fund is known to have a large position in a stock and can be observed to be selling that stock, then a reasonable presumption would be made by the market participants that a large amount of the stock is going to be sold. A savvy floor trader, observing that the fund is selling, might try front-running the fund's order in hopes of profiting from the market impact of a large sell order bearing down on the market. In doing so, the floor trader would cause a price impact that the fund would subsequently pay. Since front-running is a serious concern for mutual fund traders, they are quite sensitive to the possibility of information leakage about their orders or their positions. However, if a large fund order is handled anonymously by a broker-dealer that is a regular player in U.S. equities, there is much less chance of adverse market impact from someone discovering the identity of the mutual fund placing the order.

In addition to search services and anonymity, some broker-dealers provide research services to support the portfolio manager's effort to make successful investment decisions. Trading commissions used to compensate the broker for these services are called "soft dollars"—"soft" because the research is paid for through higher commissions or through directing more business to the broker rather than by a separate "hard" cash remittance. (The SEC rules on soft dollars are discussed later in this Chapter.) In many fund complexes, the portfolio managers are given some input into commission flow to provide them with a means of rewarding broker-dealers for valuable research. To implement this approach, a fund complex may create a budget of "points," where each point corresponds to a given amount of commissions to be generated in the upcoming period. The portfolio managers can then "vote" the points to broker-dealers, who provide them with particularly valuable research. This voting system provides an incentive to broker-dealers to deliver good research services in order to maintain and expand the incremental commission income from the voted points, subject to their ability to deliver high-quality executions.

C. Other Functions of the Trading Desk

1. Market information   In many fund complexes, the traders serve as the portfolio managers' eyes and ears on the market. Because fund traders are continuously in touch with brokers, who have representatives on the NYSE floor and good connections to other trading venues, fund traders can keep a close watch on the market from moment to moment. Many traders consider it an important job of the broker to pass along whatever rumors may be flowing through the market, as well as warnings of impending corporate events and other news with financial implications. Such information is then communicated by the fund traders to the portfolio managers, who tend to spend their time analyzing data, going to industry conferences and meeting with companies. Portfolio managers often depend on their traders to keep them abreast of breaking news and intraday price movements. This division of functions allows portfolio managers to keep focused on a longer-term investment horizon, while not missing shorter-term opportunities to buy or sell securities.

2. Fund cloning   In many fund complexes, one manager may be in charge of multiple versions of the same portfolio. For example, a portfolio manager may manage one fund for the direct channel serving retail investors and similar funds serving pension plans or customers of broker-dealers. To serve these different marketing channels while retaining the efficiency of managing one pool, fund complexes typically ask the portfolio manager to select stocks for the primary fund and leave the replication, or "cloning," of similar funds to someone else. Such cloning is often a role played by the trading desk. Typically, the portfolio manager focuses on one large mutual fund, and the trading desk operates in such a way as to keep the holdings of clone funds as closely aligned as practical with the holdings of the mutual fund (the master). This involves the implementation of both trading and allocation rules to accommodate the vagaries of trading (such as round lot effects and compliance limits), as well as any special constraints that may be imposed by the cloned fund—for example, the exclusion of tobacco stocks from a pension fund.

3. Cash management   Another challenge for the mutual fund trader is to maintain an appropriate level of cash in a fund that is actively trading portfolio securities as the fund's own shareholders purchase and redeem its shares. As explained above, funds usually do not receive cash from stock sales until three business days after trade date. By contrast, redemptions by shareholders generally must be met on the next business day. Typically, the firm's trading system will not allow a trader to create an order to buy stock for which there is no available cash in the fund's account. In order to accomplish a purchase for a fund, it must have cash, or a sale of its portfolio securities must be in process. Often the safest procedure is to execute the sale orders first and then execute the purchase trades for the same fund. But this would be a counterproductive approach if the market were trending up. In other cases, buys and sells of the same fund can be paired, so that they are accomplished at the same time and net out the cash effects. To help maintain cash at appropriate levels, fund managers typically develop computerized monitoring systems. These systems provide portfolio managers and traders with real-time information on cash from fund shareholder activity as well as fund trading activity.

4. Compliance function   There are often restrictions on fund holdings imposed by statute, regulation or the policy of a fund or investment manager. For example, federal banking law prohibits any fund complex from holding more than 10% of any bank holding company, and most complexes will not own in aggregate more than 15% of the common stock of a publicly traded company in order to reduce liquidity problems and avoid triggering "poison pills" (which dilute outstanding shares through the issuance of additional shares at prices far below current market price). Therefore, fund traders must be careful to check whether each proposed trade violates any such restrictions. Most fund managers have built compliance limits into their computer systems that apply before securities purchases may be executed by any fund in the complex. These systems are designed to block the entry of trades that would breach a compliance limit or to alert the trader to the potential violation of such a limit. These limits usually are relevant mainly for securities purchases; securities sales often have no compliance implication unless a firm has a policy concerning selling behavior in particular circumstances. In addition, most fund managers have developed systems for monitoring compliance limits after trades are completed. These systems are designed typically to run a number of compliance checks at the end of each trading day. If a trader has made an error and purchases shares in violation of a compliance limit, the shares usually must be sold as soon as the error is detected. Moreover, if there is a material loss to the fund as a result of a negligent error by the fund manager it may be required to compensate the fund for the loss.

5. Interface with the back office   After the fund trader effects a trade, there is a substantial amount of processing and communication among the broker, the fund accounting facility and the fund's custodian bank to ensure that the trade is settled correctly and accurately reflected in the fund's subsequent holdings. This "back office" activity interacts with the trading desk mainly when there is some discrepancy concerning the trade. When the trader's data concerning the security, price, commission or number of shares in a fund transaction do not agree with those of the broker, the problem is referred to the trading desk for resolution before the trade can be settled. Usually the discrepancy is due to some error in the entry of data by either the fund trader or the broker, which can be readily resolved. Other back office issues for the trading desk include corporate actions such as a stock split, a name change or a merger. Occasionally, a trader will see that a corporate action is not being represented correctly in the fund's holdings, particularly when the error is interfering with trading the security. There also can be situations in which securities that are owned by the fund are held in escrow and cannot be traded, such as when they are out on loan or have been transferred formally to the fund but have not actually been received by the custodian. Particularly when these types of problems interfere with the trader's ability to trade the stock, the trading desk will work with back office personnel to understand the issue and resolve the problem to the extent practical.

III. *Fiduciary Responsibilities of a Mutual Fund Trader and Oversight by the Fund Board*

As an investment professional, the mutual fund trader has a fiduciary duty to try to trade securities in ways that advance the best interests of the fund and its shareholders. The core of this fiduciary duty is the general obligation to seek "best execution" of fund trades. As we will see, the definition and measurement of this general obligation are very complex. In addition, the fiduciary duty of fund traders encompasses four specific areas: (1) use of a broker affiliated with a fund, (2) use of "soft dollars" for research and other services, (3) allocation of trades among two or more sister funds, and (4) "interfund" trades within a fund complex. The federal regulatory scheme under the Investment Company Act of 1940 (1940 Act) places special responsibilities on a fund's board of directors to oversee how well mutual fund traders perform these general and specific duties. These oversight responsibilities may be carried out by the full board or a brokerage committee of the board.

A. Best Execution

The fund trader's primary responsibility is to seek to obtain "best execution" for fund trades. This is an obligation as well of the broker to whom a fund trader sends an order for execution. While neither the SEC nor the courts have ever precisely defined what constitutes best execution, the SEC has recognized that the duty to seek best execution does not require that trades be carried out at the lowest commission cost available from any broker. For example, if a broker sold shares at $30 instead of $29.90 per share, this difference in sale price would far exceed a difference of one or two cents in commission rate.

Rather, the duty to seek best execution entails the balancing of a number of factors to seek the most favorable overall terms reasonably available under the circumstances in choosing among competing brokers to whom orders are entrusted and among market centers to which orders are routed. Factors recognized as bearing on best execution include the price at which a trade can be effected, the level of commissions and other transaction costs, the operational and financial resources of a broker, the speed and likelihood of obtaining a trade execution, the liquidity and depth afforded by a market center, the reliability and technological resources of a market center and the degree of anonymity that a particular market center or broker can provide its customers (particularly institutional investors).

The SEC has also recognized that the duty to seek best execution should not be judged by focusing on individual trades, but rather should be assessed over a course of dealings with particular brokers and market centers. This is especially important for mutual fund complexes that are handling a large volume of trades on a daily basis. Under these circumstances, the duty of best execution contemplates that the fund's traders on a periodic basis review the quality of executions achieved through different brokers to whom orders are sent. The corresponding role of the fund's board of directors is to exercise oversight with regard to the periodic assessments of execution quality made by the fund's traders.

To assist both fund traders and fund directors in evaluating the execution quality achieved on behalf of mutual funds and other institutional investors, firms such as Abel/Noser and Plexus have developed sophisticated analytical models that use trading data from each of their clients. Figure 6.6 illustrates an evaluation of execution quality achieved by a hypothetical Fund A based on the analytic model developed by Abel/Noser.

The Abel/Noser model provides a measure of execution quality that defines the "cost" of trades for a fund on any given day by comparing the purchases or sales price with the volume-weighted average prices (VWAP) of all market trades in the given security for that day. Figure 6.6 provides a comparison of the cost of trades by Fund A against the cost experienced by the Abel/Noser universe of clients for the period beginning in the third quarter of 1997 through the second quarter of 2000. The graph

FIGURE 6.6

Compilation of trading costs reported by Abel/Noser for listed domestic equities

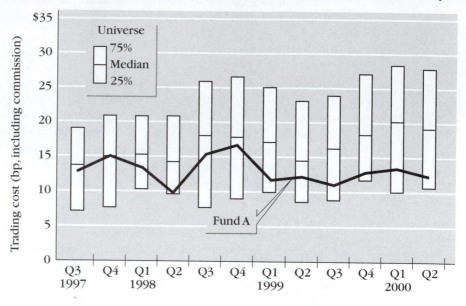

indicates that Fund A's trading costs were below the median of the Abel/Noser universe for all quarters, except for the fourth quarter of 1997 (97Q4), when those costs were at the median. This comparison provides considerable support for the traders and directors of Fund A in determining that on a relative basis, it received good execution quality for its trades during these periods. One limitation of the Abel/Noser approach, however, is that it does not account for the extent to which Fund A's trades impact the market price, since Fund A's trades are measured against an average price for the trading day that includes the effect of Fund A's trading activity.

An alternative model for execution quality is offered by Plexus. The Plexus approach attempts to take into account the impact that Fund A's own trades have on execution quality by comparing the prices of Fund A's trades against a "pretrade" market price. The pretrade price is the market price of a stock when the order is received, or the open price of the day for orders received before the market opens. To allow for comparisons across firms, Plexus provides a measure of "expected cost" for trades based on their clients' trade experience, using certain factors that take into account the size of trades, price volatility and market liquidity. Figure 6.7 illustrates that Fund A's actual trading cost ("experienced cost") was below expected cost for most of the period except for the third quarter of 1997. This relative comparison provides considerable support, within the framework applied by Plexus, to Fund A's traders and directors in concluding that Fund A received reasonably satisfactory execution quality during the periods examined.

FIGURE 6.7

Compilation of trading costs reported by Plexus for listed domestic equities

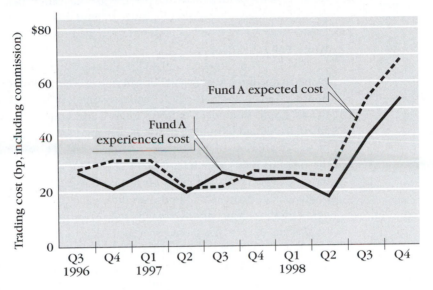

B. Specific Fiduciary Issues

1. Use of a broker affiliated with a fund   A fund management company may have an affiliated broker-dealer and may use that broker-dealer to trade under certain circumstances. For example, Merrill Lynch may act as a broker on behalf of a fund advised by Merrill Lynch Asset Management and in that capacity may bring an order for the fund to the NYSE for execution against an order held by another broker in the trading crowd or an order held by the NYSE specialist. Rules adopted by the SEC under the 1940 Act generally permit a broker who is affiliated with a fund's adviser to effect trades for the fund as an agent, so long as the commission charged is no more that the "usual and customary" commission prevailing in the market. The SEC's rules require a fund's board of directors to adopt procedures that are designed to monitor compliance in this regard and to make determinations on at least a quarterly basis that all trades carried out by a fund's affiliated broker meet the "usual and customary" commission standard.

Although an affiliated broker may act as *agent* for the fund (and receive a brokerage commission for executing the fund's trades), the 1940 Act broadly prohibits a fund's adviser and affiliates of an adviser from acting as a *dealer* in relation to the fund—that is, from selling any security or other property to (or purchasing any security or property from) the fund. This core provision of the regulatory scheme is intended to preclude conflicts of interest that could arise if a fund's affiliated broker "dumps" unwanted securities from its inventory into the portfolio of the fund.

However, in certain instances (often involving municipal securities), there may be a scarcity of supply in the market or a limited number of market makers, and a broker-dealer affiliated with a fund's adviser may be the leading market maker in the security. To allow for sales of securities in these circumstances, the SEC considers requests from broker-dealers for limited exemptions from the prohibition against trading as principal with an affiliated fund.

The 1940 Act contains a related prohibition that prevents a fund from purchasing shares being distributed in a public offering in which a broker-dealer affiliated with the fund's adviser participates in the underwriting syndicate. This prohibition is intended to address the potential conflict of interest that could lead the broker-dealer to cause an affiliated fund to purchase securities in an offering, although such securities might be unattractive or unfavorably priced. By rule, the SEC has allowed a limited exception that permits funds to purchase up to 25% of the securities distributed in such an offering, provided that the funds do not purchase directly from the adviser's affiliated broker-dealer participating in the syndicate and that the affiliated broker-dealer does not participate in any profits from the funds' purchases from other syndicate members. Here again, the SEC has placed special responsibility on the fund's board of directors to adopt procedures to monitor compliance with this limited exception and to make quarterly determinations that fund purchases in underwritings in which an affiliated broker participates comply with the rule's conditions.

2. Use of soft dollars   Historically, brokers have offered "bundled" rates for the execution of trades and the provision of research and related brokerage services. This practice arose during the era of fixed commission rates (which were finally abolished in 1975). By receiving research and other services from brokers in return for the payment of brokerage commissions, institutional investors could obtain indirectly what they could not obtain directly before 1975: discounts from fixed commission rates. Bundled rates have survived the deregulation of commission rates, as brokers (other than so-called discount brokers) have sought to avoid posting rates for trade execution-only services. The lack of transparency in the pricing of institutional brokerage services has enabled brokers to negotiate different arrangements among their institutional customers, including mutual funds, for the provision of research and other related services for so-called soft dollars—that is, the portion of a brokerage commission that exceeds the level that might otherwise be paid for "execution-only" services.

When Congress amended the securities laws in 1975 to eliminate fixed commission rates, it added a provision, Section 28(e) of the Securities Exchange Act of 1934, that permits a fund adviser or other investment manager to pay commissions to a broker that exceed the rates offered by other brokers if the adviser makes a good-faith determination that the commissions are reasonable in relation to the brokerage and research services provided by the broker. Under the statute, the research services obtained through the payment of soft dollars need not benefit the particular client whose commissions paid for the research but may instead benefit other clients (or all clients) of the adviser—for example, all funds in a complex. For these purposes, "research" services are construed broadly by the SEC to include the full range of services that assist a manager in carrying out its investment decision-making responsibilities. Research services encompass the generation of investment ideas; financial, economic, political or legal analyses bearing on prospects for a company or industry; the transmission of securities trade and quotation data as well as financial news; the measurement or analysis of fund trading and other aspects of fund performance; and computer hardware and software used to transmit or store research.

In reliance on this broad authorization, a fund's trader may decide not to send trades to a discount broker with low commissions for execution-only services and instead send those trades to a full-service broker that regularly provides useful securities research to the adviser or actively shops for matches on difficult fund trades. The research may be generated by the broker executing trades for the funds or may be obtained by that broker from another source (so-called third-party research). The research need not take the form of investment analysis, but may consist of electronic "feeds" of trade and quotation data from vendors such as Reuters or Bloomberg.

In managing the execution of fund orders, a fund's trader has other possible objectives in addition to trade execution and research. First, although some brokers may be unwilling to negotiate explicit discounts from their posted bundled rates, they may be willing to remit or rebate part of their commission to offset other expenses of their institutional customers. A mutual fund may thereby be able to reduce some of its custody expenses or transfer agent expenses—for example, when a broker agrees to direct some of the commissions it receives to the custodian or transfer agent of the fund. Such "recapture" of a portion of a brokerage commission directly benefits the fund generating the commission by reducing its operating expenses.

Second, a fund's trader may direct commissions to broker-dealers who also distribute the fund's shares. Under the rules of the NASD, such "directed brokerage" is permitted so long as the practice does not undermine the ability of the fund to seek the best execution of its trades and the fund discloses in its prospectus the policy of considering the sale of fund shares as a factor in the selection of broker-dealers to execute portfolio transactions. The NASD rules also prohibit binding contractual commitments or conditions for the award of brokerage commissions to a broker-dealer in exchange for its distribution of fund shares.

3. Allocation of trades among sister funds   When a single investment manager is responsible for a number of funds, the trading of such funds usually is consolidated in a single trading department or trading desk. Maintaining multiple trading desks for separate funds would be expensive and inefficient for the management firm, besides raising questions from a fiduciary perspective. If trading is not pooled, it might be difficult for the investment manager to avoid favoring one fund over another in trading a given stock. If trades for one fund were completed ahead of trades for another fund, the later trading fund would have to bear the market impact of the earlier-trading fund.

Because trades from multiple funds in the same complex are bunched together for execution, the complex must have a procedure for allocating the executed trades to the participating funds in a way that is fair. There are several different types of rules that usually are considered to produce fair allocations. One such rule allocates executed trades in proportion to order sizes. Another rule, often applicable to purchases, allocates trades in proportion to the asset size of the respective funds, subject perhaps to a de minimis exception to protect the smallest funds from being precluded from obtaining a meaningful share in a bunched trade. A third rule might take into account the timing of the orders, giving priority to the funds that provided the earliest orders to the fund trader in the course of a trading day.

While there is no universal rule specifying allocation procedures, it is the responsibility of the fund manager to establish a fair set of allocation rules. Otherwise, the possibility of favoring one fund over another may allow the adviser to place its own interests ahead of those of the shareholders—for example, by allocating "hot" initial public offering shares to the fund with the highest management fee. For this reason, the independent directors of sister funds, as part of their oversight of trading carried out for the funds, typically review the allocation policies followed by the funds' traders and approve any proposed changes to those policies.

4. Interfund trades   While sister funds may compete with one another in bunched trades in some cases, in other situations they may help reduce their costs and obtain better prices for their trades by entering into trades directly between or among themselves—without using any broker-dealer or going to any market center. Such trades are called *crosses* or *interfund* trades. Let's take a simple illustration from a fund complex that gives each portfolio manager full responsibility to select securities (i.e., the complex does not have an approved list of securities). If the portfolio manager of Fund A sends the trading desk an order to sell 40,000 common shares of General Electric at 90, and soon afterward a different portfolio manager for Fund B in the same complex sends the trading desk an order to buy 40,000 common shares of General Electric at 90.20, the trader may "cross" the two orders at the last reported price of an NYSE trade (e.g., at 90.10). In such a cross, neither fund pays any brokerage commissions, and both funds save 10 cents per share on the bid-ask spread.

Such interfund trades are permitted under SEC rules as long as no commission is paid to any broker and the price at which the trades are executed corresponds to the last independent price at which a trade in the relevant security has been carried out in the trading day; or, if no independent trades have occurred on that day, the price is midway between the highest independent bid and lowest independent offer. Consistent with the approach taken by the SEC to other potential conflict of interest situations, SEC rules governing interfund trading require a fund's board of directors to adopt procedures to govern such trading and to make quarterly determinations that such interfund trades meet the conditions in these rules.

REVIEW QUESTIONS

1. What is the difference between a primary offering and secondary market for stock? Why does the management of the issuer of stock—the company—care about the trading price of its stock?

2. What are the functions and limitations of an NYSE specialist in a listed stock? Compare and contrast the role of an NYSE specialist to the role of a Nasdaq market maker in a widely traded and sparsely traded stock?

3. What is the role of the fund custodian in the trading process? In what type of situations would fund traders become involved in discussing issues with a fund custodian?

4. Suppose a fund trader requests a broker affiliated with the fund's adviser to execute an OTC trade as agent for the fund. Does such an execution violate the affiliated-person rules of the 1940 Act or present any other conflict of interest?

5. Suppose a fund trader places an order to buy 5,000 shares of an exchange-listed stock with Broker F, which charges a commission of 5 cents per share, although Broker D would charge a commission of 4 cents per share for the same trade. Is such a placement permissible? If so, on what grounds?

6. Suppose a trader receives a market order to buy 20,000 shares of Ford from Fund B and a limit order to sell 20,000 shares of Ford at 80.25 from Fund S in the same complex. If the last reported trade for Ford on the consolidated tape was at 80.10, may the trader cross these two trades at 80.25 to save transaction costs for both Funds?

DISCUSSION QUESTIONS

1. What are the factors suggesting that decimalization will decrease the cost of trading? What are the factors suggesting that decimalization will increase the cost of trading? Which factors are likely to be most significant for which mutual funds?

2. Should the mutual fund industry support or oppose a proposal to centralize all trading in U.S. equities in one computer? What would be the arguments on either side?

3. Are there any economies of scale in a trader's bunching together orders from five funds in the complex, each to buy 2,000 shares of Intel? Would your answer be the same if each of the five funds wanted to buy 100,000 shares of Intel?

4. Suppose a complex has a $1 billion diversified growth fund and a $100 million financial services fund. Both place orders on the day to buy 100,000 shares of an initial public offering of an insurance company. If the trader received only 150,000 shares of the offering, how should they be allocated between the two funds?

5. Should managers of mutual funds (and other institutional investors) be prohibited from paying higher brokerage commissions in exchange for research and brokerage services? If Section 28(e) of the Securities Exchange Act of 1934 were repealed, what would be the likely effects on mutual funds and brokerage firms?

NOTES

1. The structure of the Nasdaq implies that these figures are normally "double-counted" relative to the way trading is reported on the NYSE, and so the size of the "actual" business is often viewed as half of the reported amount. The figures reported in Table 6.2 have been adjusted by this correction.
2. The American Exchange, now owned by Nasdaq, is best viewed as one of a group of regional exchanges.
3. If the difference (or "spread") between the highest bid and lowest offer widens too much, the specialist has a responsibility to step in as principal with its own bid or offer to limit the spread.
4. The BBO are sometimes called the "quotes."
5. For each "seat" purchased by a member firm, the firm is allowed to maintain one representative on the floor, called a floor broker. Floor brokers can represent client orders as well as orders for the firm's account. A few exchange members trade only for their own account.
6. A buy market order will be executed against the current best offer up to the size of that offer; a larger buy order would then be executed against the next best offer; and so forth.

7. A sell market order will be executed against the current best bid up to the size of that bid; a larger sell order would then be executed against the next best bid; and so forth.

8. There is discussion about moving to settlement one day after trade date for U.S. equities.

9. S. A. Berkowitz. and D. E. Logue, "Transaction Costs," *Journal of Portfolio Management* (Winter 2001): 65–74.

10. This typically results in a double counting of transactions relative to the NYSE, since the economic result of the two trades is equivalent to a single transaction between the buyer and seller, with the dealer receiving the spread in return for facilitating the trade. U.S. Securities and Exchange Commission, "Report on the Comparison of Order Executions Across Equity Market Structures," January 8, 2001.

11. According to data from the International Federation of Stock Exchanges, which uses the French abbreviation FIBV (see www.fibv.com).

12. G. Sofianos and J. Bacidore, "Decimalization and Trading Stocks in Pennies," Goldman Sachs Equity Derivatives Research, Feb. 9, 2001. See also C. Jones and M. Lipson, "Sixteenths: Direct Evidence on Institutional Execution Costs," *Journal of Financial Economics* 59, no. 2 (2001): 253–278, for a study of the effect of the reduction in minimum tick size on the NYSE from ⅛ to ⅟₁₆ that occurred in 1997.

13. Many fund firms prefer to trade a given stock through a single broker at a time. If multiple brokers were working portions of the same order simultaneously, they might compete among themselves for available liquidity, incurring a larger market impact than would be expected.

READING 6.1

*The Buy Side Trading Desk (excerpt)**

David Cushing

Introduction

Many years ago, investment management firms regarded trading as a clerical function, a necessary part of the "plumbing" of the equity portfolio management process. Virtually all of the emphasis was placed on stock selection and it was widely believed that paying up a few cents per share was a manageable cost of doing business, especially given that a stock pick was expected to appreciate many dollars per share. Since those days, nothing short of a revolution in attitudes and practices has taken place and a time traveler would hardly recognize the trading desk of today. As techniques were developed for measuring the total cost of trading and its impact on portfolio returns,[1] managers were horrified to learn that most of the value of their investment insights was leaking out through the plumbing.[2] This insight, coupled with the growing competitiveness of the industry, forced investors to radically rethink the role of implementation in their overall process and to innovate to stay alive.

Today, this revolution is nearly complete: trader and

*David Cushing, Inference Group LLC, March 31, 2001.

the portfolio manager are regarded as peers, trading desk IT budgets are among the largest in the investment firm, and the sophistication of the tools and techniques used by today's trader is truly impressive. What follows is a report on the state of the art in institutional equity trading.

The Effect of Investment Style on Trading

As anyone in the investment industry can tell you, there are a wide variety of investment styles in use today. At one end of the spectrum are the fundamental, buy-and-hold investors, who pore over financial statements, meet management face-to-face and pick stocks one at a time. At the other end of the spectrum are the highly technology–dependent investors, whose investment processes utilize electronic, parameterized inputs that are manipulated using sophisticated quantitative techniques. Often, the high-tech practitioner doesn't care about the particulars of a portfolio company, as long as its characteristics satisfy the investment model. Moreover, holding periods for these kinds of processes tend to be much shorter and turnover is correspondingly higher. In between these extremes lie a rich middle ground with a wide array of investment styles, each with its own unique characteristics. It should come as no surprise, then, that the trading requirements of professional investors are also highly varied. Over time, as portfolio management innovations have occurred, trading innovations have followed to better serve their emergent needs. As a result, today's trading toolkit is better-equipped than ever. We will first define and consider the core infrastructure elements, i.e., those tools that are common to most trading styles. Then we will describe how they are used in coordination with more specialized practices and technologies during "a day in the life" of two trading archetypes: the block trader and the portfolio trader. These terms are defined in detail in that section.

Core Trading Infrastructure

The technological foundation of the trading desk has been the most affected by change over past decade. Many of the elements that are considered essential on today's trading desk hadn't even been invented 10 years ago. They break down into three main categories: Trade Order Management & Routing, Trading Venues, and Trade Allocation, Reporting & Clearance.

Trade Order Management & Routing

The trade order management system, or TOM, is increasingly the nerve center of the buy-side trading desk. As the name implies, a TOM is a software application that receives, routes, tracks and otherwise processes the orders received by the desk. According to research by consultant TowerGroup, over 90% of large investment management firms (assets over $100 billion) have an order management system of some kind; however, that proportion decreases to about two-thirds for medium-sized firms ($10–$100 billion), and plummets to 20% or less for small firms ($1–$10 billion).

Most systems are either supplied by third-party vendors or custom-developed internally or by consultants. Vendor-supplied systems are increasingly the norm and many custom solutions have aged to the point of becoming "legacy" systems. Leading third-party vendors include Eze Castle Software, MacGregor Group (which also owns Merrin Financial), Advent Software, Charles River Development and LongView Group.

The trader's day is built around the TOM and for good reason. Among other things, it automates many functions that were previously manual, tedious and error-prone, such as taking reports from executing brokers, computing allocations and running restricted-list checks. Moreover, they are most responsible for the stunning productivity increase that most desks that adopt them have enjoyed. Far from leading to the layoffs predicted by some, the leverage

that TOMs provide have made each trader that much more valuable to his or her firm.

Most trade order management systems are integrated with the firm's portfolio management system, so that orders can be received and blocked efficiently. They are similarly linked to post trade settlement processes, such as custody reporting and electronic allocation systems like Thomson Financial's OASYS™ system. Finally, these systems are often tied to points of execution, such as exchange floors, Nasdaq and brokerage firms. The connectivity between TOMs and third parties usually occurs over one of a growing number of secure, high-speed private networks using an industry standard protocol known as FIX, which is an acronym for Financial Information Exchange. FIX was developed by an industry consortium starting in the early 1990s and has continued to evolve to meet a growing number of trading style requirements, such as portfolio trading. See Figure 1 for a schematic illustration of a typical institutional trading desk technology configuration.

While the benefits of TOMs are numerous, they do not come for free:

First, adopting such a system is inherently disruptive and expensive, especially for the initial round of integration and workflow changes, and will cause at least some pain in the short run.

Secondly, for a variety of reasons, TOM providers have been slow to add new functionality, especially the custom features that an organization requires. It is usually uneconomic for TOM vendors to develop features for a single user, and high switching costs make it difficult for users to walk away if they are unhappy.

Thirdly, TOM vendors historically have not been well capitalized, which in and of itself gives rise to business risk.

Lastly, since so much of the TOM's resources are consumed by the demanding requirements of processing and routing orders, little is left over to provide more than rudimentary analytics. As a result, analytics are most often provided by separate systems that offer varying degrees of integration.

Overall, however, a TOM's benefits typically substantially outweigh these costs, and a combination of consolidation among providers and the development of next-generation technology should eventually overcome many of these drawbacks . . .

Trade Allocation, Reporting & Clearance

As mentioned in the earlier section on trade order management, the TOM system generally handles both pre- and

A typical institutional trading desk technology configuration

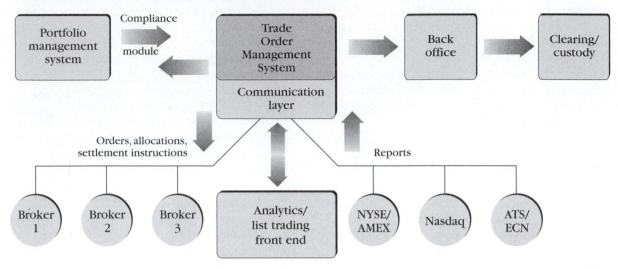

post-trade processing. In addition to running pre-trade compliance checks and blocking orders for execution, many TOMs compute post-trade allocations and transmit them to the executing broker or dealer, either directly or indirectly through a system like OASYS™. Most TOMs also report trade details to the firm's portfolio management system so that positions can be updated.

Electronic handling of post-trade processing confers numerous benefits. Error rates (and hence trading costs) are reduced, productivity and/or capacity is enhanced, a uniform standard for trade allocation is assured, and an audit trail is automatically generated for compliance and record-keeping purposes.

A Day in the Life

We have surveyed the primary tools and venues currently used by trading professionals and how they function in the wake of considerable regulatory change and technological evolution in recent years. Now our attention turns to a day in the life of the trader, who uses this core functionality in coordination with a variety of specialized techniques and technologies in order to carry out the job of achieving best, lowest-cost execution. For clarity's sake, we have divided trade execution into two idealized forms, block trading and portfolio trading. We define block trading to be the execution of single order that is typically large both in number of

shares and as a proportion of average daily volume. Such orders often take more than one day to execute and require a great deal of skill and patience. Portfolio trades usually involve the coordinated execution of a large number of orders, often under a variety of constraints such as maintaining dollar balance. Portfolio traders also require patience and a variety of technical skills, albeit somewhat different ones than their block trading counterparts.

The Block Trader

From the moment a block order hits the trade blotter, the name of the game is information. The trader's first objective is to quickly and efficiently gather as much information as possible about the stock being traded. The more important questions include:

- Who has been active in the name recently?
- What has the recent price action been?
- What is the motivation for the trade?
- When will earnings be released and what are expectations?
- Are there any rumors going around?
- Has an analyst recently issued a change of outlook?
- How actively does the stock trade and how volatile is it?
- Is there likely to be more stock to trade after this order is complete?

Once these inputs have been gathered, the trader can begin to formulate a strategy for execution and select an opening move. Generally speaking, she must decide between an approach that seeks immediacy and one that spreads the order out over time. The pretrade analysis will often indicate which approach is likely to achieve the better result. She must also decide which intermediary, if any, will be used to carry out the trade. If there is a clear "axe" in a given name—i.e., a dealer who has been actively trading the name, then the probability of finding liquidity at that dealer is higher and that dealer may well be selected to execute the order. However, if the trader has settled on using a broker in an agency capacity, she may well want to steer clear of the axe in order to preserve anonymity. The need to satisfy trading obligations for services such as research, access to new issues and capital commitment may also factor into broker selection, provided the choice is consistent with the principles of best-execution.

Regardless of which general approach is selected, an equally important decision must be made regarding how much information to share with the intermediary and how much discretion to give. Not surprisingly, the degree of sharing depends critically on the level of trust in and experience with a broker that the trader has. It also depends on what capacity the intermediary is acting in. For an OTC stock, there is a high probability that the trader will be interacting with a dealer that makes a market in the stock for its own account. For a listed stock, it is more common for the broker to act as agent; however, listed block positioners who act as principal are frequently employed. With respect to these decisions, there are no hard and fast rules and trader judgment is key. Some of the best executions are obtained in situations where the trader opened up to the broker and/or gave discretion in handling the order. Many would argue that this gives the broker a license to steal, while others would claim that it is in the broker's long-term interest to do a good job and not abuse the information.

Increasingly, traders are eliminating the order handling function of brokers and using direct electronic access to the exchange floors, Nasdaq and alternative trading vehicles such as crossing systems. For listed stocks, they are also increasing the use of so-called "direct access" brokers on the exchange floors, who are typically small, independent brokers who are not expected to shop orders to other institutions or to commit capital. Proponents of direct access like the increased level of control that they have over their orders and feel they can get better execution with less information leakage, even if it means chopping a large order into very small pieces and trading it patiently. . . . The ability to get one's bids and offers displayed directly in the National Best Bid Offer (NBBO) has increased the appeal of this approach.

Once the core approach has been chosen and the trade has been initiated, the trader continuously monitors market conditions and activity in the stock. She then adjusts the trading strategy accordingly and may even suspend trading if she feels the order is having a disproportionate impact on price. An almost countless number of scenarios can unfold, from news, to a competing order showing up, to surprise market events or volatility, and the trader must be prepared to respond in real time to anything that comes her way. It is important to note that, on a typical day, a trader may be handling a number of such orders, further increasing the demand and complexity of the trader's job. This process iterates until the trade is either completed or, as sometimes happens in the case of extreme adverse price movement or lack of liquidity, cancelled.

Once the order is executed, post-trade processing and analysis begins. The executed shares must be allocated and transmitted to the executing broker, as well as forwarded to the portfolio management system. Equally important is the measurement of execution quality. The average executed price on the trade is compared to a benchmark that is most suitable[3] for it and assessed. While it is difficult to draw conclusions from a single trade, the grouping and analysis of similar trades can lend significant insights into how well a particular technique or venue is performing.

The Portfolio Trader

While the block trader is busy moving a million shares of General Electric, her portfolio-trading counterpart is sitting further down the desk executing the two hundred or so orders that make up the weekly rebalance of a quantitatively driven fund. Where the TOM system, the telephone and a market data service are the key technologies for the block trader, the portfolio trader is most likely sitting in front of a special-purpose portfolio analysis and trading system. The orders he is trading may have started out the day in the TOM system for compliance checks, but they have been moved over to a system that is designed around the needs of trading portfolios and will help him execute his orders accurately and cost-effectively. Examples of such systems include ITG QuantEX® and FlexTrade Systems' FlexTrader™.

By definition of his task, the portfolio trader must orchestrate both the strategy and the tactics of execution, since his actions and the results they produce only have meaning in the context of the portfolio of orders. Although the techniques used are very different, the fundamental steps in the portfolio trade process are the same: pretrade analysis and trade strategy formulation, execution, and post-trade analysis.

Pretrade analysis for portfolio trading means understanding the liquidity and risk characteristics of the portfolio as a whole and also for the individual names in it. The aggregate characteristics are used to determine, for example, how many hours or days should be taken to trade the portfolio and whether there are significant risk exposures that need to be monitored and managed. They also are used to form an expectation about the cost of trading. Unlike single block trades, portfolio trades have a much narrower range of expected cost outcomes because of diversification, and cost estimates are therefore more reliable. Individual orders are analyzed to see if any of them should be handled separately on the basis of liquidity, volatility or both. This analysis requires some fairly sophisticated underlying models and databases, and may be carried out using systems that are internally developed or, as is more typical, are provided by third parties. These are often the same systems that are used to trade the portfolio through direct links to trading venues.

Once the trade list characteristics and constraints are understood, the portfolio trader has two high-level decisions to make. The first is whether to request a principal (guaranteed) bid for all or a part of the list from a dealer. The second is whether to allow a broker to execute the portfolio as agent on his behalf. The principal bid decision is driven by a number of factors, cost being chief among them. Typically, a portfolio trade is priced on a characteristics basis, meaning a summary of portfolio liquidity and risk is transmitted to one or more dealers, who are requested to provide a firm price (premium) at which they would be willing to execute the portfolio. There are numerous variations on this basic theme, such as requesting bids on a fully disclosed basis or carving out certain difficult names.

Derivatives-linked transactions are an important and often cost-effective subcategory of principal trades. If a portfolio trader is executing a swap from stock index futures to physical stock, he might be able to obtain a very aggressive bid for that swap because the market risk is relatively small. Similarly, he might be able to carve out an index-like basket from a larger portfolio trade and obtain swap-like benefits by requesting a bid on the "basis," or dif-

ference in price between the derivative and the cash portfolio. Some of the larger institutional desks employ derivative specialists to execute both outright and cash-linked trades.

If the best principal portfolio bid is deemed favorable, the portfolio trader can "hit the bid" and the deal will be consummated, typically after normal trading hours, using the 4:00 close as a reference price. The administrative convenience and reduced error potential of this method is one of its attractions.

However, if none of the bids is acceptable, the trader is now faced with the choice of handling the trade himself or forwarding it to a broker for execution as agent on a best-efforts basis. Assuming he chooses to execute it himself, the next step will be to finalize the choice of trading tactics and begin. Portfolio orders are usually submitted in "waves" representing a subset of the total order. Waves are selected in such a way as to balance the competing considerations of expected return, liquidity and risk. Managing waves is one of the key capabilities of the trader's portfolio trading system, and the better systems support customized, automated trading strategies that manage the many orders in a wave in response to changes in real-time market conditions. This capability frees the trader to deal with the more illiquid orders and "blow-ups" (large adverse price moves) that inevitably affect at least some of the stocks on the list, as well as to manage the aggregate characteristics of the list, such as dollar imbalance, risk exposure and completion rate. The better systems will also have connectivity to all the major execution venues, such as exchanges, ECNs and crossing systems, and also to the brokers of the trader's choice.

The more sophisticated trade execution systems will support custom automated trading strategies based on real-time data to handle the routine aspects of submitting, canceling and correcting orders.

Once the trade is complete, the same post-trade processing and analysis steps are performed, but on a portfolio basis. Again due to diversification, more insights can be gleaned from a single portfolio than can be from a single block trade, and pretrade cost estimates can and should be more closely compared to the realized cost of trading . . .

Notes

1. Cushing, David et al., "The Transaction Cost Challenge: A Comprehensive Guide for Institutional Equity Investors and Traders," New York: ITG Inc., 1999.
2. Edwards, Mark, and Wayne Wagner. "Capturing the Research Advantage," *Journal of Portfolio Management,* Volume 24, No. 3, pp. 16–24.
3. Benchmark suitability is determined by a number of factors, including the nature of the underlying investment strategy, the implementation strategy used and the trading horizon.

CASE STUDY

Executing a Block Trade

A fund trader has a fiduciary obligation to seek the best execution for fund orders. But best execution is a complex concept; it does not simply mean the lowest commission rate. A fund could pay a low commission while paying a higher purchase price for a stock and wind up worse off than an execution with a normal commission rate. Also, OTC trades are done "net," without any explicit commission.

Moreover, as mentioned in the Chapter text, in selecting a securities broker, a fund trader is legally permitted to take into account the quantity and quality of research provided by different brokers to portfolio managers in the fund complex. In this regard, many fund complexes maintain a point system that rates the research of various Wall Street houses. Subject to the duty to seek best execution, fund traders will try to allocate fund orders to brokers who have provided the most useful research to the fund complex.

In a fund complex that is regularly trading, other factors may influence a fund trader's decisions. For example, a fund trader may be given buy orders in the same stock by several portfolio managers on the same day. The fund trader must find a way to allocate the purchases of this stock in a fair manner among the relevant funds. Alternatively, a fund trader may be asked to execute many orders from many funds over a short period. In such a situation, a fund trader needs to consider the relative time sensitivity of various trades.

This case study focuses on a fund trader who is trying to execute a block trade for a fund: a very large trade relative to the normal daily volume for that stock.

Discussion Questions

1. Did Greg make a wise decision to go first to Kidder? Why? Were his reasons for going to Kidder short-term or long-term reasons?
2. In trying to sell Avantek alone, what were Greg's two main alternatives to the approach he took? What are the pros and cons of each alternative?
3. Why did Greg decide to include the Tandem buy in his proposal to Goldman Sachs? Was the Tandem buy more or less time sensitive than the Avantek sale?
4. Should Greg accept or reject Michael's offer? Should Greg make a counteroffer or go to a third dealer?

5. If Greg makes a counteroffer of selling Avantek at 24 ⅜ and buying Tandem at 15¼, should Michael accept? Why or why not?
6. If Greg makes a counteroffer of selling Avantek at 24 and buying Tandem at 15¼, should Michael accept? Why or why not?
7. Is it reasonable for a mutual fund to incur higher transaction costs for larger trades? Aren't there economies of scale involved in executing a 180,000-share trade in Avantek versus an 8,000- or 100-share trade in Avantek?
8. How would the sale of Avantek be different if it were traded only on the New York Stock Exchange? Is the exchange or OTC market superior for executing block trades? From whose viewpoint?

At the T. Rowe Price Trading Desk*

Tuesday, August 21, 1984

It was 9:58 A.M. and the markets were about to open. Greg Donovan, one of two traders for the T. Rowe Price New Horizons Fund (and accounts holding similar securities), was going over the list of buys and sells that he was hoping to execute during the day. Greg thought the market would be up that day, especially after speculation on the part of the traders he had dealt with the previous day that several large institutions were in the process of increasing their equity positions. Greg saw his most difficult task being the sale of a large block of Avantek stock. Avantek, traded on the OTC, had been fluctuating around $25/share during the previous few weeks, after being as low as $18 in May. (Exhibit 1A). The T. Rowe Price analyst covering the company thought that an earnings disappointment was imminent, and that news to that effect would cause the stock's price to plummet back into the teens. The analyst liked the stock on a long-term basis, however, and only wanted to trim down T. Rowe Price's current position of around 600,000 shares. Greg's instructions were to sell 183,000 shares at a price no lower than $23.

At 10:30 the Dow was up 7.50. Greg looked at the screen of his NASDAQ machine and saw that Kidder Peabody was the highest bidder for Avantek at $24⅜. Several brokers were at $24½ bid, with yet several others, including Goldman Sachs, at $24⅜. (These bids were all for

*Harvard Business School Case 9-285-041. This case was prepared by Andre F. Perold as the basis for class discussion rather than to illustrate either effective or ineffective handling of an administrative situation. Reprinted by permission of *Harvard Business Review*. From, "At the T. Rowe Price Trading Desk," by Andre Perold. Copyright © 1984 by the Harvard Business School Publishing Corporation; all rights reserved.

EXHIBIT 1A

Avantek price and volume charts, February–August 1984

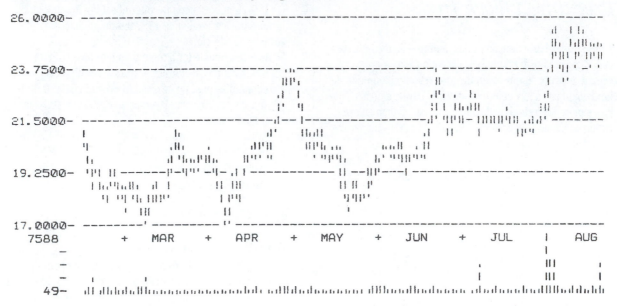

Note: Daily volume in hundreds of shares traded.

only 100 shares.) Goldman, knowing that T. Rowe Price had a large position in Avantek, had called earlier that morning to say that it was a buyer of the stock in sizeable quantities. Goldman was the largest and most preeminent OTC dealer, and would regularly offer to deal in large positions (50,000 shares or more) for its own account.

Greg decided to try Kidder first. Kidder, which had previously not committed much of its capital to the OTC market, had recently been moving towards becoming a more prominent player in this market. It had seemed to Greg that he might get a better execution from Kidder since a trade of this magnitude was the kind of trade on which they might even be willing to lose a little money in order to gain visibility. In addition, T. Rowe Price liked Kidder's research, and here was an opportunity to compensate them, in part, for that service.[1] Greg in any event often looked for opportunities to trade with brokers other than Goldman Sachs. This was because T. Rowe Price tended to get the best execution from Goldman, and so typically did a dis-

proportionately large share of its trading through that firm; that is, out of proportion to the degree to which it availed itself of Goldman's research.

At 10:40 he somewhat nervously picked up the phone.

GREG: (Talking to Steve, a Kidder trader): "Hi Steve, I see you're interested in some Avantek. How much do you want to buy?"

STEVE: "Let me see. I'll call you right back?"

Two minutes later.

STEVE: "I can do 12,000 shares at [24]⅝."

GREG: "I am interested in a more medium sized quantity. Can you do better?"

STEVE: "I don't really think so. But, let me look again. Don't do anything until I get back to you."

Ten minutes later.

STEVE: "Look, the best I can do is 20,000 shares."

EXHIBIT 1B

Daily price ranges and volume for Avantek, July 26, 1984–August 20, 1984

Date	High	Low	Volume (100's shares)
July 26	21⅝	21¼	125
27	21¾	21¼	439
30	21⅝	21½	668
31	22⅜	21⅜	1,053
Aug. 1	22½	21¾	7,588
2	23⅝	22⅛	4,550
3	25¼	23¾	4,576
6	25½	24½	1,159
7	24¾	23⅞	638
8	24½	23½	632
9	24⅝	23½	407
10	25½	24¾	1,522
13	24¾	24	555
14	25½	24½	1,003
15	25¼	24⅞	410
16	25⅛	24⅛	587
17	24¾	24	1,245
20	24¾	24½	116

GREG: "That's not enough. It seems as if I am going to have to go elsewhere. Is that OK?"

STEVE: (After a pause) "If I do more, say up to 35,000 shares, will you then deal?"

GREG: "No, that's still not enough. I'm just going to have to go elsewhere. OK?"

STEVE: "I suppose you'll have to."

Greg was upset with himself. He had hoped to be able to do a large trade with Kidder. However, all Steve had done was to try to get him on the "hook," and he was not going to bite. The "hook" was a term traders used to describe a situation where if you did one trade with a dealer and had more of the same stock to trade, then by the implicit rules of the game you would be obligated to give that dealer a first right of refusal on what remained. This was because the dealer would typically have taken part of the other side of the trade on his or her own account, a position that would be endangered if you then went and off loaded the rest of your position elsewhere. Greg was afraid that, if he did do an initial trade with Steve, the price of this

EXHIBIT 1C

Avantek trades on August 21, 1984, 10:00 A.M.–12:20 P.M.

Time	Price	Shares (100's)
10.17	24½	5
10.53	24½	4
10.53	24¾	10
11.03	24⅞	5
11.03	24⅞	45
11.33	24⅝	25
11.41	24⅞	1

lightly traded stock might fall by as much as one or even several dollars as Steve scurried around looking for more buyers knowing that he most likely had Greg on the hook for a lot more. Not all was lost at this point, however. By getting Steve to answer affirmatively when he had asked if he could go elsewhere, Greg had at least obtained an implicit commitment from Steve not to tell other traders of T. Rowe Price's intention to sell a large quantity of Avantek. At least, not immediately.

At this point Greg felt that his only option was to call Michael, a trader at Goldman Sachs. He wanted to move quickly and knew that Goldman would be willing to do the whole deal for its own account if necessary, as evidenced in particular by the early morning phone call. The trouble was that Greg now had to tell Michael that Steve already knew about the deal. Thus, since Goldman's position would now be riskier, Michael was unlikely to give them as good a price as he might have had Greg gone to him first.

Greg decided that perhaps the best way to approach Michael was to offer him a swap. For several weeks New Horizons had been adding to an already substantial long term position in Tandem (also traded OTC) and had done several of these trades through Michael. In fact, Goldman had mentioned that morning that they knew of a seller of Tandem. New Horizons and related accounts were interested in acquiring up to another 320,000 shares of this stock in the near term. It was up to Greg to choose how and when to acquire it. Greg's decision was to offer Michael both the Tandem purchase and the Avantek sale as a package deal.

At 11:25 he placed the call. At this point Kidder still showed up on the screen at $24⅝ bid on Avantek, with Goldman at $24⅜. During the course of the morning, small

EXHIBIT 1D

Institutional holdings in Avantek on 3/31/84** (Price = $19⅜, 18.7 million shares outstanding)

	3-Month Chg in Shares	Shares Held	Value 000$
Aetna Life & Casualty Co	−61,500	255,000	5,069
Allstate Insurance Co	313,100	622,700	12,379
American Natl B&T/Chicag	1,400	25,700	511
Ameritrust Company	−10,900	0	0
Associated Banc-Corp	600	14,300	284
Bank of Boston Corp	31,405	263,655	5,241
Bank of California N A		43,000	855
Bank One of Dayton N.A.	−21,500	0	0
Campbell Advisors Inc.	140,300	407,400	8,099
Campbell William G & Co.		43,400	863
Capital Research & Mgmt	233,000	233,000*	4,632
College Retire Equities	0	65,000	1,292
Comerica Inc		21,750	432
Dean Mitter Rey Intercap	35,600	125,600	2,497
Eaton & Howard Vance Snd	−2,184	26,033	518
Eberstadt Asset Mgmt Inc	121,800	371,500	7,385
Exxon Corporation	0	80,600	1,602
Fiduciary Tr Co/New York	−1,800	32,900	654
First Interstate Bancorp		20,420	406
First Manhattan Co	2,300	13,850	275
First Wisconsin Corp	0	26,500	527
Fleet National Bank	10,975	96,585	1,920
Franklin Resources Inc	0	12,000	239
G T Capital Management	11,200	117,000	2,326
Gardner & Preston Moss	−86,270	0	0
Hancock John Mutual Life	78,300	362,000	7,197
Harris Associates Inc	0	84,000	1,670
Harris Trust & Svgs Bank	−59,000	416,000	8,270
Hartford Stean Boiler	5,300	5,300*	105
Harvard College		4,000	80
Hongkong & Shanghai Bkg	−22,400	0	0
IDS Growth Fund Inc	0	500,000	9,940
IDS New Dimensions Fund	32,500	200,000	3,976
Investors Research Corp	175,000	175,000*	3,479
Jennison Assoc Capital	315,000	657,600	13,073
Kemper Finl Services	−181,900	94,300	1,875
Kidder Peabody & Co	3,700	27,700	551
Lincoln First Banks Inc		406,500	8,081
Merchants Natl Bk/Ced Rp	−900	25,000	497
Metropolitan Life Insur	0	9,500	189
Morgan Stanley Inc	124,344	460,844	9,162
National City Bk/Cleveld	0	11,000	219
Natl Westminster Bk Plc	0	31,000	616
Philadelphia Natl Bank		27,500	547
Price T Rowe Associate	38,735	871,410	17,324
Provident Life & Acc Ins	3,800	32,900	654
Reimer & Koger Assoc		51,900	1,032
Republicbank Corp	−96,100	15,785	314

EXHIBIT 1D (CONT.)

	3-Month Chg in Shares	Shares Held	Value 000$
Rice Hall James & Assoc	−15,500	0	0
Rothschild Asset Mgmt	−61,000	0	0
Russell Frank Co Inc	−31,300	0	0
Seligman JW & Company	−655,000	0	0
Shawmut Corporation		14,300	284
SIT Investment Assocs.		15,000	298
Smith Barney Inc		1,389	28
Sperry Capital Mgmt	10,000	110,000	2,187
State Street Resr & Mgmt	−89,100	204,900	4,073
Stein Roe & Farnham	−520	42,560	846
Torchmark Corporation	−60,000	0	0
Travelers Corp	0	55,000	1,093
USAA Investment Mgmt		25,000	497
United Missouri Bank/KC	0	56,000	1,113
United States Trust/NY	2,000	13,800	274
United Virginia Bkshares	−92,800	102,450	2,037
University of Rochester	0	404,000	8,032
Wech & Forbes Inc	790	51,830	1,030
Wells Fargo Bank N.A.	−3,150	43,900	873
Wisconsin Investmt Board	0	60,000	1,193
59 Mgrs 45.9% Shs Out	138,325	5,857,261	170,715

Source: "The Spectrum 3," Computer Directions Advisors, Silver Spring, MD.
*New position.
**This was the most recently available data on 8/21/84.

lots of Avantek stock had traded at levels as high as $24⅞ (Exhibit 1C.) Tandem, being much more active, had traded in small lots in the range of $15¼–$14⅞, with a 10,000 share block having just traded at $14⅞. (Exhibit 2C.) Currently, the lowest asking price for Tandem was $15⅛ (Kidder, Salomon, Merrill), with Goldman asking $15⅜. The Dow was up 11.81 for the day so far on volume of 40 million shares.

GREG: "I'd like to do a swap of 183,000 Avantek for 320,000 Tandem."

MICHAEL: "Now those are the kinds of deals I just love! Is it a package deal? A one shot deal? What? I like one shot deals."

GREG: "One shot." Then, apologetically, "Listen, I've already talked to Kidder but didn't give him any number. I did it because they're good on research. But, he only wanted to bid for medium size."

MICHAEL: "I'll get back to you."

15 minutes later, Michael called back to say that the Tandem side of the deal was easy to do, but that the Avantek part was harder; no prices as yet. He called back once again at 12:22.

MICHAEL: "I can do Avantek at $23½ and Tandem at $15¼."

Background

T. Rowe Price Associates, Inc. was an independent investment counseling firm, founded in 1937 and located in Baltimore, Maryland. In 1984 the firm had $15.5 billion under management. This was divided about equally amongst fixed-income and equities, and also about equally amongst 12 mutual funds on one hand and separately managed accounts on the other, the latter consisting mostly of large corporate pension plan accounts.

The New Horizons Fund was founded in 1960 and, in 1984, was the largest and oldest emerging growth mutual fund in the U.S. The Fund's objectives were to invest in companies in the early stages of their corporate life cycle,

EXHIBIT 2A

Tandem price and volume charts, February–August 1984. (Daily volume in hundreds of shares traded)

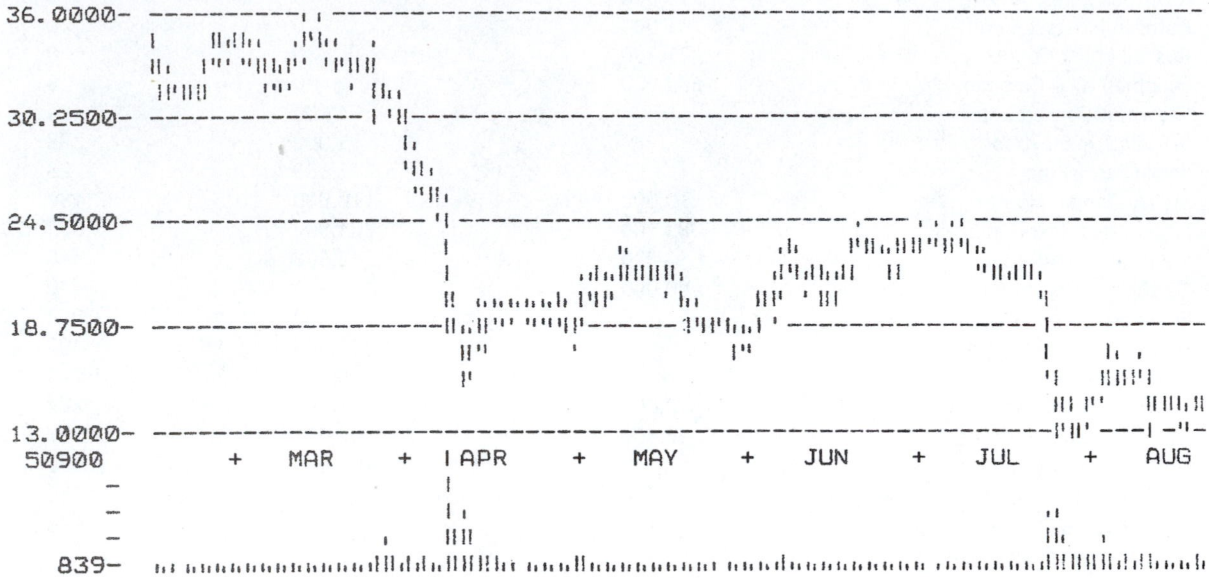

EXHIBIT 2B

Daily price and volume ranges for Tandem, July 26, 1984–August 20, 1984

Date	High	Low	Volume (100's shares)
July 26	16⅞	13⅜	26,807
27	15¾	14¼	14,909
30	15¾	13¼	7,759
31	14¼	13	11,108
Aug. 1	15⅜	14¼	11,240
2	15⅝	15⅛	9,057
3	16¾	15¼	134,43
6	18	16	7,646
7	17½	16⅛	4,615
8	16¾	16	6,506
9	16¾	16	4,849
10	17⅝	16⅝	10,791
13	17	13½	7,596
14	15⅜	14½	4,708
15	15⅝	14½	2,392
16	15½	15	5,806
17	15⅜	14⅜	4,084
20	14⅞	13¾	3,209

EXHIBIT 2C

Tandem trades on August 21, 1984, 10:00 A.M.–12:20 P.M

Time	Price	Shares (100's)	Time	Price	Shares (100's)
10.00	15	25	10.36	15	5
10.01	14⅞	10	10.37	15	1
10.01	14⅞	5	10.41	15	4
10.03	14⅞	3	10.43	15	1
10.03	14⅞	5	10.43	15	3
10.03	15⅛	50	10.43	15	5
10.05	15	3	10.44	15⅛	10
10.05	15⅛	10	10.44	15⅛	10
10.06	14¾	10	10.48	15	3
10.06	15⅛	5	10.49	15	25
10.06	15⅛	3	10.54	14⅞	1
10.06	15⅛	5	11.00	14⅞	32
10.07	15	1	11.01	15	2
10.07	15⅛	5	11.04	15	4
10.07	15	2	11.05	15	2
10.07	15⅛	13	11.09	15	1
10.07	15	10	11.09	15	3
10.08	15⅛	10	11.09	15	2
10.09	15⅛	10	11.18	15	5
10.11	15⅛	20	11.25	14⅞	100
10.11	15⅛	20	11.28	15	5
10.12	15⅛	9	11.30	15	5
10.14	15⅛	10	11.32	14⅞	270
10.20	15⅛	30	11.32	15	217
10.22	15⅛	100	11.32	15	5
10.22	15¼	49	11.33	15	10
10.23	15⅛	25	11.36	15	1
10.25	15⅛	5	11.37	15	10
10.26	15¼	3	11.42	15	10
10.26	15¼	3	11.44	15	10
10.26	15⅛	10	11.44	15⅛	2
10.27	15⅛	5	11.48	15	1
10.27	15¼	10	11.49	15⅛	10
10.31	15⅛	250	11.49	15⅛	20
10.32	15⅛	2	11.49	15	20
10.32	15⅛	18	11.49	15⅛	2
10.32	15	10	11.53	15⅛	2
10.21	15	10	11.54	15⅛	4
10.34	15⅛	3	12.15	15⅛	1
10.35	15	5			

EXHIBIT 2D

Institutional holdings in tandem on 3/31/84**

	3-Month Chg in Shares	Shares Held	Value 000$
Aetna Life & Casualty Co	67,200	178,700	5,429
American Natl B&T/Chicag	85,900	138,300	4,202
American Security Bank	151,700	411,700	12,507
American Tel & Tel Index	39,600	39,600*	1,203
Ameritrust Company	–12,600	18,000	547
BEA Associates Inc		15,000	456
Bankamerica Corp	11,350	11,350*	345
Bank of Boston Corp	–2,200	176,020	5,347
Bank of California N A		61,900	1,881
Bank of New England Corp	–3,000	11,256	342
Bank of New York	–22,550	28,035	852
Bankers Trust N Y Corp		401,350	12,193
Batterymarch Finl Mgmt	81,700	81,700*	2,482
Bernstein Sanford C & Co	1,587,815	1,587,815*	48,238
Boston Company Inc	0	10,810	328
Brokaw Capital Mgmt Co	–13,010	866,995	26,339
Capital Guardian Trust		75,100	2,282
Capital Holding Corp	–10,000	0	0
Capital Research & Mgmt	40,700	530,700	16,123
Centerre Bancorporation	100	78,000	2,370
Century Capital Assoc	–460,200	870,400	26,443
Chase Manhattan Corp	29,100	37,500	1,139
Cigna Corporation	–115,000	109,100	3,314
Citicorp	–60,572	571,070	17,349
College Retire Equities	60,000	170,000	5,165
Commerce Bankshares Inc	0	3,000	91
Criterion Group Inc	87,950	228,050	6,928
Crocker National Corp		170,400	5,177
Dauphin Deposit Bk & Tr	0	32,500	987
Dean Witter Rey Intercap	7,000	77,000	2,339
Donaldson Lufkin & Jen	–341,500	1,506,100	45,755
Duke Endowment	–9,900	17,100	519
Eaton & Howard Vance Snd	0	1,108	34
Eberstadt Asset Mgmt Inc	–100,000	425,000	12,911
Endowment Mgmt & Research	454,200	454,200*	13,799
Equitable Life Assur/Us	1,600	1,600*	49
Essex Investment Mgmt Co	–35,800	0	0
Exxon Corporation	22,100	22,100*	671
FMR Corp	–714,800	241,900	7,349
Fidelity Internatl Ltd	5,000	55,000	1,671
Financial Programs Inc		200,000	6,076
First Bank System Inc	–20,700	0	0
First City Bancorp/Texas	–12,200	0	0
First Interstate Bancorp		127,50	3,863
First Natl Bk/Palm Beach	–4,000	7,500	228
First Seneca Bank	–200	12,900	392
First Tennessee Natl Co	0	17,800	541

EXHIBIT 2D (CONT.)

First Trust Co/St Paul	4,500	12,664	385
Frontier Capital Mgmt Co	−55,000	418,200	12,705
G T Capital Management	−6,600	240,900	7,319
Gardner & Preston Moss	10,128	10,128*	308
General Elec Invt Corp	−30,000	0	0
Geocapital Corporation	67,100	190,200	5,778
Hancock John Mutual Life	−1,100	204,900	6,225
Harris Trust & Svgs Bank	6,000	106,000	3,220
Hongkong & Shanghai Bkg	−3,550	89,075	2,706
IBM Retirement Plan	33,700	33,700*	1,024
IDS/American Express Inc	11,050	69,150	2,101
IDS Growth Fund Inc	0	880,000	26,734
Investors Research Corp	278,400	965,300	29,326
Investors Vari Paymnt Fd	−200,000	200,000	6,076
Irving Trust Company	−2,300	0	0
Jennison Assoc Capital	−256,600	3,788,670	115,100
Jundt/Capen Associates	48,600	82,500	2,506
Kemper Finl Services	375,000	1,272,800	38,668
Lehman Brothrs Kuhn Loeb	−210,000	0	0
Liberty Natl B&T/Okla Ct	0	10,000	304
Lincoln First Banks Inc		18,000	547
Lincoln Natl Corp	−122,925	31,200	948
Manufacturers Hanover Co	13,270	354,200	10,761
Manufacturers Natl Corp	100	35,400	1,075
Markston International	0	19,000	577
McCohan Associates Inc		392,000	11,909
McRae Capital Mgmt	−17,100	0	0
Mellon National Corp		98,708	2,999
Merrill Lynch Asset Mgmt	66,300	134,300	4,080
Metropolitan Life Insur	1,500	1,500*	46
Morgan J P & Co Inc	26,000	127,000	3,858
Morgan Stanley Inc	−74,717	166,424	5,056
National City Bk/Cleveld	−6,000	52,000	1,580
National Life Insurance	−9,000	8,000	243
New York St Teachers Ret	0	118,000	3,585
Northern Trust Corp	4,800	29,250	889
Norwest Corporation	0	12,000	365
Oppenheimer Holdings Inc	−6,800	81,400	2,473
PNC Financial Corp	6,800	62,550	1,900
Pacific Mutual Life Ins	8,000	24,000	729
Potomac Asset Mgmt. Inc	35,000	35,000*	1,063
Price T Rowe Associate	−428,900	863,245	26,225
Prudential Ins Co/Amer	113,000	113,000*	3,433
Prudential-Bache Secs.	22,272	22,272*	677
Rice Hall James & Assoc	−825	7,965	242
Rockefeller & Company	0	9,687	294
Rosenberg Capital Mgmt	−51,300	662,300	20,121
Rothschild Asset Mgmt	−28,400	154,600	4,697
Russell Frank Co Inc	−5,300	156,700	4,761
Safeco Corporation	−39,000	0	0

EXHIBIT 2D (CONT.)

St Paul Companies Inc	−7,000	33,000	1,003
Scudder Stevens & Clark	−1,600	14,000	425
Sears Investment Mgmt	26,500	360,000	10,937
Seattle First Natl Bank	47,200	66,600	2,023
Shawmut Corporation		3,000	91
Siebel Capital Mgmt	140,000	176,300	5,356
Smith Barney Inc		95,755	2,909
Society Corporation	−150	8,450	257
Southtrust Bank/Alabama		35,000	1,063
State Street Boston Corp		42,500	1,291
State Univ Ret Sys/Ill		100,000	3,038
Stein Roe & Farnham	61,500	313,245	9,516
Toledo Trustcorp Inc		14,200	431
Trainer Wortham & Co	1,300	1,300*	39
Travelers Corp	35,000	93,400	2,837
United Missouri Bank/KC	0	678,000	20,598
United States Trust/NY	−5,650	109,863	3,338
University of Texas Sys	2,500	20,000	608
Value Line Inc.	9,300	9,300*	283
Wachovia Corporation	−7,756	0	0
Wall Patterson Mcgrew	−30,250	0	0
Warburg Pincus Counsellr	0	20,000	608
Weigarten Mgmt Corp	40,000	40,000*	1,215
Weiss Peck & Greer		714,175	21,697
Wells Fargo Bank N.A.	118,405	214,705	6,523
111 Mgrs 65.3% Shs Out	826,205	25,607,490	777,955

Source: "The Spectrum 3," Computer Directions Advisors, Silver Spring, MD.
*New position.
**This was the most recently available date on 8/21/84.

and before they became widely recognized. On June 30, 1984, the Fund had $1.2 billion in assets, of which 88% was invested in the common stocks of 161 companies with five-year EPS growth rates estimated to be at least 25% per year. The remaining 12% was in short-term fixed income securities.

The New Horizons Fund investment decisions were made by an investment advisory committee consisting of the president of the Fund, a trader (Greg), and five analysts who spent most of their time researching emerging growth companies. The analysts each managed a position of the Fund corresponding to their areas of expertise, and could make individual stock selection decisions without prior committee approval. They were also responsible for coordinating and overseeing the trading in their stocks. The committee actively allocated the Fund's assets across these analysts, and based its decisions on their and the president's collective judgments. Generally it favored those sec-

tors of the market with greater growth potential, better fundamentals and lower relative valuations.

T. Rowe Price employed six equity traders in all, including the head trader who had been with the firm for 25 years. Greg had the title of Vice President and had thus far spent six years at the firm, having previously had 10 years of trading experience elsewhere on the buy-side. In addition to serving on the investment advisory committee of the New Horizons Fund, he had some discretion to trade in stocks already owned by the Fund. For example, he could of his own accord increase an existing holding if there was a seller desperate enough to accept a very low price.

T. Rowe Price considered a college education to be a minimum qualification for a trading position, and would at times hire individuals with no previous trading experience. The salary and bonus levels for traders at T. Rowe Price were about in line with those of other large buy-side firms, where traders typically were paid somewhat less than their

EXHIBIT 3

Miscellaneous financial data on Avantek and Tandem (1983–84)

	Avantek	Tandem
P/E ratio	30	33
P/Book ratio	4.9	1.9
5-year EPS growth rate	27%	50%
Dividends	None	None
Revenues ($ mil)	119	464
L.T. debt/capitalization	2.3%	6.7%

portfolio manager and analyst counterparts. However, remuneration usually was widely distributed within any one of these groups. Traders and analysts on the sell-side earned more on average than their buy-side counterparts, with a few earning relatively very high sums of money.

In 1983 the equity trading desk did about 23,000 trades, averaging $36,000 per trade, and totaling $8.1 billion. These trades were split 50-50 between purchases and sales. The market capitalizations of the companies traded averaged $5.5 billion. The New Horizons Fund accounted for 18% of this trading in companies whose market capitalizations averaged $750 million. (See Exhibit 5.)

Recent Developments vis à vis Avantek and Tandem

T. Rowe Price's initial position in Avantek dated back to 1978 with the purchase of 320,000 shares at $1¾ (split adjusted) by the New Horizons Fund. The firm's position in this stock increased over the years, reaching 871,410 shares on March 31, 1984 (see Exhibit 1D). The bulk of this increase occurred in portfolios other than New Horizons. Some selling and repurchasing took place during these years based on occasional near term fundamental concerns on the part of the Aerospace/Defense analyst covering the company.

In June 1984, this analyst traveled to California to meet with the managements of several New Horizons Fund holdings. Upon his return, he issued the following update on Avantek with the stock then trading at $23⅛.

> Volume at AVAK continues to increase in both military and commercial lines. The production problems on the high frequency amplifier lines appear to be resolved. AVAK shipped $3.0 million within the most re-

cent month, up from recent periods under $2.0 million. A quarter-end push was clearly a factor, but I believe AVAK has made the strides it promised. Orders continue to flood in on the military side, although we should expect the rate to slow in coming quarters. On the commercial side, low noise amplifiers for the home satellite television (TVRO) market continue to sell in high volume. After holding up for a surprisingly long time, prices have finally collapsed, due in part to a flock of new entrants. AVAK is the low-cost producer and has steadily reduced costs on the TVRO line through engineering changes and limited automation. Operating margins, which exceeded 30% in 1983, should be no more than half that in 1984. TVRO should represent about 20% of sales this year. It is hard to tell where the TVRO market is going, but there is no reason to expect reduced pressure on prices. The potential for a serious problem exists with TVRO, and I will continue to monitor the situation closely.

> On balance, I was very satisfied by my visit to AVAK. My calendar 1984 estimate of $0.89 is probably too low by a few cents. Sell-side estimates have come down to the $0.90–$0.95 level. With rising margins on the military side, AVAK should be able to discover excellent earnings comparisons for the foreseeable future. I continue to be a buyer of AVAK below $18 and a seller at $24.

With the surge in the stock market in early August, Avantek rose above $24, and the New Horizons Fund and related accounts sold about 200,000 shares of Avantek between $24–$25 on August 2 and August 3.[2] No further selling took place prior to August 21, 1984, when, based on further research by the analyst, a sale recommendation was written with the stock at $24⅝. Excerpts are as follows:

> The pricing on low noise amplifiers (LNA) for the home satellite television (TVRO) market continues to collapse. While this business represents only 22% of AVAK's revenues, it has had considerably higher margins than the company's other lines; I expect that the margin squeeze will cause third quarter EPS to fall below the $0.21 reported in the June quarter, which would be a major disappointment. I have revised my third quarter estimate downward to $0.18 from $0.23 (versus $0.11 a year ago). Although the TVRO problem may be a reflection of the seasonal summer slowdown, I see no way the company can make up the

EXHIBIT 4

The Twenty-five largest holdings in the New Horizons Fund, June 30, 1984

Company	Initial Purchase	Market Value (000)	Percent of Fund
Molex	1973	$24,663	2.1%
Home Depot	1983	24,087	2.0
Service Corporation International	1982	21,743	1.9
Liz Claiborne	1982	20,193	1.7
Analog Devices	1980	19,340	1.6
Toys "R" Us	1979	16,840	1.4
LIN Broadcasting	1981	16,147	1.4
Manor Care	1981	15,528	1.3
United Stationers	1982	14,368	1.2
Granger Associates	1983	13,887	1.2
Network Systems	1980	13,483	1.1
Kelly Services	1978	13,471	1.1
Intergraph	1981	12,932	1.1
Micom	1981	12,749	1.1
ACCO World	1983	12,445	1.1
Anixter Bros.	1983	12,371	1.1
Safety-Kleen	1983	12,218	1.0
Unitrode	1982	11,981	1.0
Viacom International	1979	11,446	1.0
Circuit City Stores	1983	11,415	1.0
Barry Wright	1982	11,267	1.0
Nordstrom	1978	10,971	0.9
Payless Cashways	1975	10,961	0.9
Esterline	1983	10,298	0.9
National Education	1982	10,265	0.9
Total		$365,069	31.0%

earnings in the fourth quarter. With the drop in my estimate for the year, and the possibility of a protracted profit squeeze in TVRO, AVAK's valuation goes from rich to ridiculous. I recommend immediate sale.

AVAK is a leading producer of microwave amplifiers, components, and telecommunications equipment. By product line, sales break out as follows: defense components, 40%; telecommunications components and systems, 24%; TVRO components, 22%; and test equipment components, 14%. Over the past year, AVAK's growth has come from defense components and TVRO. On the defensive side, the company has been a major supplier of high frequency amplifiers to the electronic warfare systems contractors. The entire components industry was caught off guard by massive orders for high frequency amplifiers in 1982 and 1983. Everyone, AVAK included, had production problems, followed rapidly by earnings disappointments. AVAK bounced back most rapidly among all components suppliers. Part of this can be attributed to management, which turned around the high frequency product line. The second key factor, though, was a diversification. AVAK's business was not dependent exclusively on the high frequency product line, and when profits were hurt, other lines took up the slack. The biggest boost came from TVRO, which uses a high quality amplifier to boost the satellite TV signal received in the owner's backyard.

The TVRO business came out of nowhere in 1982, and AVAK was perfectly positioned to address it. As the

EXHIBIT 5

New Horizons Fund trading characteristics

	1983 First Half	1983 Second Half	1984 First Half
Dollars traded ($ million)	806	652	411
Percent purchases	40%	50%	44%
Percent net trades[1]	54%	63%	67%
Total trades (thousand)	4	3	2
Avg. trade size ($ thousand)[2]			
Purchases	178	202	136
Sales	208	237	260
Avg. price volatility (%)[3]	35	35	35
Avg. share price ($)	28	25	18
Avg. company capitalization ($ billion)	0.9	0.6	0.4
Avg. comm.[4] (¢/share)	8¢	9¢	7¢
Avg. comm.[4] (% principal)	0.29%	0.27%	0.35%
Avg. price impact of transactions[5] (% principal)			
Purchases: Commission trades	0.63%	−0.42%	−1.23%
net trades	−0.57%	0.28%	−0.30%
Sales: Commission trades	1.04%	−0.53%	0.24%
net trades	2.35%	1.38%	1.50%

[1]Trades done on a spread rather than commission basis.
[2]Average dollar value of a trade.
[3]Annualized standard deviation of daily returns.
[4]Commission purchase trades only.
[5]Price impact as estimated by SEI Funds Evaluation, Inc. This is, roughly, the price at which the trade took place less the subsequent day's industry-adjusted closing price. For both purchases and sales, a positive number is a cost, and a negative number is a benefit. For net trades, these numbers are SEI's estimates of total transaction costs. Total costs for commission trades = price impact + commissions.

market grew, AVAK worked to become the low-cost producer, and now has about a 30% share, principally at the high end of the quality spectrum. New entrants have caused prices to collapse, but until this quarter, TVRO remained AVAK's most profitable business. The Japanese have just entered the market, having diverted unused direct broadcast satellite (DBS) capacity to TVRO. AVAK has a big head start, but I doubt that the seasonal upswing in September can overcome the margin pressures at work in the marketplace.

The problem here is that Wall Street has very high expectations for AVAK. Everyone is looking for a 50% EPS gain this year, followed by 35% or more next year.

EXHIBIT 6

Performance record of the New Horizons Fund:

Annualized Compounded Returns for the Periods Ending 6/30/84	New Horizons	S&P 500
5 years	18.6%	14.0%
10	15.3	11.3
15	8.6	7.8
20	13.4	7.5
24	10.9	8.5

EXHIBIT 7

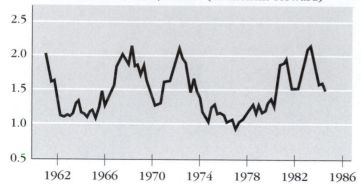

T. ROWE PRICE NEW HORIZONS FUND
P/E ratio of the fund's portfolio securities relative
to the S&P "500" P/E ratio (12 months forward)

This chart is intended to show the history of the average (unweighted) P/E ratio of the fund's portfolio companies compared with the P/E ratio of the S&P "500" index. Earnings per share are estimated by the fund's investment advisor from each quarter end.

It is too early to tell what will happen in 1985, since military components margins could rise dramatically, but 1984 will not meet the consensus estimate of $0.90 without a miracle in TVRO. In any case, the good news is in the stock. This is a well-managed company with good products in good markets. It is my judgment that the stock price today is out of line with AVAK's prospects. I recommend sale, with an eye to repurchasing in the $18–19 range.

Regarding Tandem, the New Horizons Fund and related accounts began accumulating a position in the stock in late 1981 and early 1982, and reached a position of over a million shares at an average cost of approximately $22 per share by the end of 1982. Based on some short-term fundamental concerns, this position was reduced in the first quarter of 1983 by about 200,000 shares at an average sale price of $28–$29 per share. The analyst however remained intrigued in the longer term with Tandem's niche market position in fault-tolerant computers and continued to like Tandem's long-term growth prospects.

The remaining position was held through the balance of 1983 and the stock performed quite well closing the year at $35⅛. The company, however, experienced fundamental problems in the first half of 1984 relating to revenue shortfalls and the stock plummeted from $35⅛ to a low of $13 in August 1984. On August 1 the analyst issued the following comments on Tandem, with the stock at $13⅞.

Tandem (TNDM) has once again disappointed with its latest quarterly EPS report and its stock has sharply retreated to mid-1980 price levels. I am concerned about TNDM's "anemic" revenue growth this year relative to my expectations of mid-1983 and now believe a 25% secular revenue growth forecast is much more reasonable than my prior 35% forecast. TNDM has been planning for 30%–35% revenue growth and operating profit margins have remained depressed as revenues have fallen short of budgeted amounts. I have reduced my FY1984 EPS estimate from $1.01 to $0.80 and my FY1985 estimate from $1.60 to $1.25. I have also reduced my secular growth rate assumption from 35% to 25%. In spite of the prevailing gloom about the company, I remain encouraged by TNDM's product capability, balance sheet strength, and much improved financial control. I believe TNDM will produce excellent investment returns from current levels over the next 12–24 months but would not expect TNDM to outperform other cyclically sensitive technology stocks near term. For those whose valuation instincts were better than mine over the past six months, my congratulations. At current price levels, however, I suggest another serious look, with the price being right but timing perhaps still premature.

New Horizons Fund and related accounts began adding to positions in Tandem in late July, accumulating another 600,000 shares prior to August 21, 1984.

Notes

1. Unlike trades on the NYSE and AMEX, which were on a commission basis (10¢/share was typical for a large institution), OTC trades were done purely on a spread basis, i.e., the dealer found a buyer willing to pay an asking price and a seller willing to receive a bid price (hopefully lower than the asking price), and pocketed the difference.
2. Related accounts had sold approximately 70,000 shares between March 31 and July 31 for reasons unrelated to any research recommendations.

Marketing and Servicing of Mutual Fund Shareholders

Part III discusses the relationships between mutual funds and their shareholders in two Chapters on marketing and servicing fund shareholders generally and one Chapter on these two subjects within the retirement context.

Chapter Seven addresses the marketing of mutual funds to nonretirement investors. It reviews the intermediary and direct channels for distributing mutual funds, including mutual fund supermarkets. It then elaborates on several themes that cross-cut all distribution channels: the move toward open architecture, the appetite for investment advice and needs-based marketing. The Chapter ends with a case study of a midsize bank's strategy for marketing mutual funds to its customers.

Chapter Eight explores the marketing and servicing of fund shareholders in the retirement channel. It analyzes the shift to defined contribution plans and the implications for mutual funds. Similarly, it analyzes the role of mutual funds in the market for individual retirement accounts. Then it touches on two future trends in retirement as they affect mutual funds and finishes with an exercise on designing 401(k) plans for different employee populations.

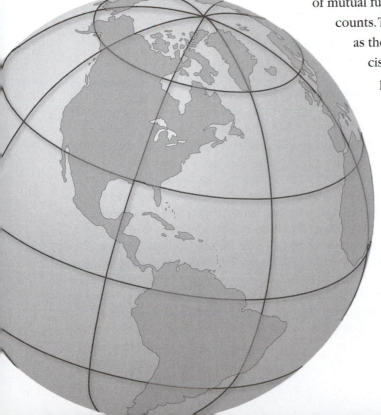

Chapter Nine deals with the servicing of mutual fund shareholders outside the retirement channel. It reviews the main functions of the transfer agent in servicing fund shareholders. It outlines the structure of the transfer agency industry and the technological changes driving that industry. It looks at the selection and pricing of transfer agency services by fund directors. The Chapter closes with a case study on a fund experiencing short-term trading by a small group of its shareholders.

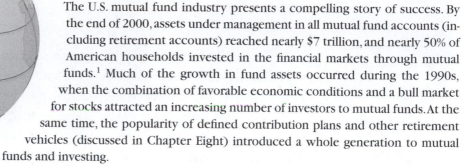

7

Marketing of Mutual Funds

The U.S. mutual fund industry presents a compelling story of success. By the end of 2000, assets under management in all mutual fund accounts (including retirement accounts) reached nearly $7 trillion, and nearly 50% of American households invested in the financial markets through mutual funds.[1] Much of the growth in fund assets occurred during the 1990s, when the combination of favorable economic conditions and a bull market for stocks attracted an increasing number of investors to mutual funds. At the same time, the popularity of defined contribution plans and other retirement vehicles (discussed in Chapter Eight) introduced a whole generation to mutual funds and investing.

The fund industry facilitated this growth by aggressively expanding its lineup of products as a means of encouraging and responding to consumer demand. In the early history of mutual funds, from their beginnings in the 1920s through their first growth spurt in the 1960s, investors were basically confined to stock funds. Money market and tax-free bond funds came into vogue during the 1970s and early 1980s; still, the product mix was limited. But by the end of the century, investors faced a dizzying selection, ranging from funds that encompass entire U.S. and foreign markets to those that invest in a single industry such as regional banks or the Internet. Indeed, by 2000, there were approximately 8,000 funds—two and a half times the number offered in 1989, according to the Investment Company Institute (ICI).

While this tremendous growth embodies the fund industry's success, it also presents the industry's greatest challenge. There are signs that the U.S. fund industry has begun to mature, as redemptions have increased and holding periods have decreased. For example, in 1999, a banner year for the stock market, long-term mutual funds (all mutual funds other than money market funds) had gross sales of $1.2 trillion. However, in the same year, more than $1 trillion flowed out in redemptions of long-term funds,[2] leaving net sales for long-term funds at less than $200 billion (see Table 7.1). Moreover, the average holding period for shareholders of long-term funds was 2.7 years in 1999, as compared to 9.2 years in 1975.[3]

Sweeping changes across the financial services sector, including many introduced by fund sponsors, drove this higher redemption rate and shorter holding period. Today, investment information abounds. Individual investors can turn to the popular and financial press, local and cable television as well as countless Internet sites for easy access to reams of data and analysis on securities markets and financial planning. The fund industry has facilitated comparison among funds by embracing open architecture, whereby fund sponsors allow their products to be distributed by their competitors. Individual investors can go to a single source for mutual funds from a wide variety of sponsors. At the same time, Internet-based trading platforms and robust telephone trading systems have made all types of securities transactions simple and convenient.

TABLE 7.1

Net new cash flow to mutual funds, 1999–2000 ($billions)

	Equity	Bond	Hybrid	Money Market	Total	Total Mutual Fund Assets
1990	13	6	2	23	44	1,065
1991	39	59	8	5	112	1,393
1992	79	71	22	−16	155	1,643
1993	129	73	39	−14	228	2,070
1994	119	−65	21	9	84	2,155
1995	128	−11	5	89	212	2,812
1996	217	3	12	89	321	3,526
1997	227	28	16	102	374	4,468
1998	157	75	10	235	477	5,525
1999	188	−5	-12	194	364	6,843
2000	309	−48	−32	160	389	6,967

Source: Investment Company Institute. Reprinted by permission of the Investment Company Institute.

Meanwhile, a host of new financial products, such as separate accounts involving discretionary management of individual securities, have gained recognition as potential investment alternatives to mutual funds. In this environment, competition for investor loyalty has been fierce, forcing fund sponsors to reinforce old strategies and create new strategies to retain market share.

One surefire route to growth of fund assets is outstanding performance. Investor decision making is influenced heavily by fund performance. Although the standard financial disclaimer, "Past performance is no guarantee of future results," has been proven true time and time again, investors increasingly chased funds with hot short-term performance. In the late 1990s, as technology stocks rallied, aggressive growth funds—and fund complexes that specialized in that style—posted dazzling returns. Investors responded by funneling assets to those areas almost exclusively. In 1999, for example, Sanford Bernstein reported that just 10 equity funds accounted for 44% of the industry's net inflow into equity funds, as the Nasdaq Composite Index had its best year ever, finishing up 85.6%. Performance-based success can be fleeting, however. In 2000, aggressive growth funds posted huge negative returns, and the Nasdaq Composite Index, a possible proxy for the aggressive growth segment of the market, had its worst year on record, finishing down 39.3%.

Beyond performance, distribution and service are widely cited as critical factors for increasing or retaining customers. This Chapter focuses on distribution. (Chapter Nine focuses on service.) Funds are sold through three main distribution channels:

1. The *intermediary* channel comprises brokerage firms of all stripes, banks and insurance companies, as well as financial planners and registered investment advisers.

2. The *direct* channel enables a consumer to purchase funds directly from the fund sponsor or through fund supermarkets (adjuncts to the direct channel that offer products from a variety of fund families).

3. The *retirement* channel encompasses 401(k) and other defined contribution plans plus individual retirement accounts. (Chapter Eight covers the retirement channel.)

This Chapter focuses on key practices and characteristics of the intermediary and direct channels. In doing so, it deliberately oversimplifies these subjects for learning purposes. Clear-cut distinctions between distribution channels are blurring as financial services companies compete to satisfy consumer demands for convenience, flexibility and product choice. Yet it is important to understand the history of each channel in order to grasp the significance of current trends and their potential for further change. Thus, this Chapter discusses fund distribution through the main types of intermediaries and then through direct marketers, including fund supermarkets. Next, it reviews important marketing trends that cut across both channels. This Chapter concludes with a case study about a medium-size bank's decisions on how to market mutual funds to its customers.

I. The Intermediary Channel

In discussing intermediaries, it is first necessary to define the types of financial firms within this channel. The Cerulli Intermediary Matrix (Table 7.2) provides a good starting point by highlighting key members of this channel. Historically, full-service securities firms dominate the intermediary group. This category includes wire houses, which offer a complete line of investment services through an integrated office network; and national brokerage firms, which are similar in geographic reach, but may offer more limited investment services in many cases. Other brokerage firms may be classified by their regional orientation, though this distinction is diminishing as many seek national scope. Another significant player in this channel is the independent brokers, which are typically small shops staffed by investment professionals, many of whom left larger firms in pursuit of different compensation structures and a wider variety of products. For purposes of this Chapter, we use the term "broker-dealer" to encompass all four types of firms: wire houses, national brokerages, regional and independent broker-dealers. Another member of the intermediary channel is banks, which can be further divided into broker-dealer functions of banks and their trust departments, with the latter typically concentrating on asset management services to high-net-worth individuals. Insurance companies are yet another member of the intermediary channel, typically operating through broker-dealer subsidiaries. Finally, registered investment advisers, a category that can also include financial planners, tend to exist as a network of small shops providing a range of financial services.

Certain recent trends have affected all members of the intermediary channel. Probably the most general trend is the ongoing shift from transaction-based services to advice-based services. The Internet has provided not only financial data and analysis, but also easy access to inexpensive trading and do-it-yourself investment solutions. As a result, financial intermediaries have been forced to expand their roles, moving from simply facilitating trades and providing information to managing portfolios and offering broad financial planning. This evolution from transaction-based to advice-based services has had an impact on pricing strategies for all members of the intermediary channel. Historically, financial professionals earned their primary compensation through

TABLE 7.2

Intermediary matrix

	Securities Firms	Regional Broker/Dealers	Independent Broker/Dealers	Banks	Insurance Agencies	Registered Investment Advisors
Statistics	Number of Representatives: 70,000+ 57,000 New York-based Wirehouse 13,000 National Full-Service	Number of Representatives: 17,000+	Number of Representatives:* 70,000+ *Includes part-time representatives.	Number of Representatives.* 30,000+ *Includes part-time representatives.	Number of Representatives.* 30,000+ *Represents agents primarily selling investment products.	Number of Representatives: 9,500 (firms), 30,000 (professionals) *Excludes high net worth money managers and IBD affiliates.
Definition	These firms provide all types of securities products and services to retail and institutional investors. Two Types of Firms • **Wire houses:** Full-service broker/dealer with an extensive and national and international branch network and proprietary products. • **National Full-Service:** Similar to wirehouses in distribution, offer full range banking capabilities. Limited high net worth and estate planning services.	Regionals provide all types of securities products and services to retail and institutional investors. Similar wirehouses, but in general regionals have fewer resources. Strong regional branch networks.	IBD reps function as independent contractors rather than employees. IBDs exert little control over which products and services reps offer individuals. Firms vary widely in size, training, and sophistication.	Bank brokerages are retail-oriented, branch-based operations that employ primarily salaried Series 7 dedicated reps or Series 6 part-time reps, or a mix of both.	Insurance agencies are subsidiaries of insurance companies comprised of a captive sales force. Commission-based reps were organized around selling traditional insurance products. Agencies are transforming themselves into financial planning firms, by emulating the independent broker/dealer model.	RIAs are single or small groups of advisors running their own shop independent of a larger firm affiliation. RIAs may hang their securities and insurance licenses with small brokerages or create an in-house b/d. Some fee-only RIAs are not NASD licensed. Other RIAs only create financial plans and do not manage assets.
Comments	**Wire house:** • Immense distribution. • Payout of commissions to reps at 35%–45%. • Shift toward financial planning and asset-based compensation. • Emphasis on proprietary products. • State of the art technology. • Complete range of investment services & resources. **National Full-Service:** • National presence • Wide-range of products and services • Personalized attention. • No proprietary products.	• Solidifying home markets and developing strong regional identities. • Most of the larger firms have been acquired by banks and insurance companies within the past five years. The few remaining independent regional firms are likely acquisition targets. • Vary in size.	• Heavy emphasis on packaged products such as mutual funds, variable annuities and wrap programs. • Payout of commissions to reps at 90% or more is significantly higher than securities firms. • Have embraced fee-based compensation (e.g., LPL's SAM wrap program). • Reps rely on their own reputation to prospect for clients. • Attract highly self-reliant, entrepreneurial brokers. • Extensive product and planning.	• Larger and mid-size banks brought brokerage activity in-house to establish their own full-service capabilities. • Smaller banks still rely on third-party marketers to deliver investment advice and products to bank customers. • Strong community ties. • Convenience for customers interested in one-stop shopping. • Limited proprietary products. • Heavy emphasis on packaged products such as mutual funds.	• Commission-dominant sales environment, but migrating to fee-based via mutual fund wrap programs. • Proprietary product oriented. • Heavy emphasis on insurance sales. • Slow growth in expanding product offering and non proprietary menu. • Sub-par technology capabilities. • Reps becoming more independent-oriented. • Moving toward independent B/D model. • Focusing on HNW market and specialized estate planning services.	• Highly independent and entrepreneurial environment. • Predominantly fee-based. • Strong community ties. • Prospecting is often referral based. • Highly personalized services. • Limited technology resources. • No brand recognition.

Sources: Securities Industry Association, *Financial Planning*; Cerulli Associates, *Cerulli Edge* (August 2000).

commissions on initial sales of mutual funds or individual securities. Recently, financial professionals have begun shifting toward a fee-based pricing model, charging clients a flat annual fee expressed as a percentage of assets managed by the professional. This Chapter examines this general trend in greater detail as it discusses each type of intermediary.

A. *Broker-Dealers*

Full-service broker-dealers were among the first purveyors of mutual funds. As the largest distributor of funds,[4] they remain a powerful force in the fund industry. Brokerage firms (including wire houses, national full-service firms, regionals and independents) employed nearly 160,000 representatives and made up approximately 65% of the intermediary market for mutual funds at the end of 2000.[5]

Originally focused on stocks, which they sold to clients for a commission, many broker-dealers were resistant when mutual funds had their initial growth spurt in the mid-1960s. Professional investment expertise is a key service provided by brokers (who may prefer to be called financial consultants), so their concern was that a professionally managed mutual fund would render their advice less valuable. However, while broker-dealers continue to work extensively with individual securities, they have come to consider mutual funds an important component of their product lineup—requiring advice on fund choice and creating lucrative potential for sale.

Broker-dealers typically sell mutual funds sponsored by two sources. On one hand are firms such as American Express, Morgan Stanley Dean Witter, Salomon Smith Barney and Merrill Lynch, which manage and market proprietary funds sponsored by investment advisers affiliated with the broker-dealer. On the other hand, many of these firms have made use of funds managed by independent fund sponsors (called "independent funds") that do not have captive sales forces. Among independent fund sponsors, American Funds, Putnam, Franklin and AIM have been important third-party providers of mutual funds to broker-dealers. As of early 2000, for example, these four firms made up more than half the assets in the independent fund segment.[6]

In earlier decades, a broker-dealer often had a big financial incentive to sell the firm's proprietary products. However, today's instant access to mutual fund information, especially regarding fund performance, has made it easier for clients to compare various offerings and has increased the pressure to sell the best-performing funds—proprietary or not. In general, compensation systems now give less preference to the selling of in-house fund brands. Moreover, the performance of proprietary funds run by certain investment advisers affiliated with broker-dealers has not kept up with the performance of funds advised by independent companies that focus exclusively on asset management. As a result, independent fund sales account for an increasing portion of broker-dealer fund sales.

As compensation for selling mutual funds, the broker-dealer used to look primarily to sales commissions, called loads. Originally, broker-dealers sold mutual funds with a front-end sales load that was charged to the investor at the time of purchase. During the 1960s, loads were as high as 8.5% of the amount invested in a mutual fund; they have since declined to an average of 4% to 5%. In 1980, the Securities and Exchange Commission (SEC) allowed mutual funds to add a distribution charge, called a 12b-1 fee, to the annual fees charged to fund assets. This fee provided fund sponsors with an annual stream of revenue (of up to 1% per year of fund assets under management) to cover the cost of advertising, promoting and servicing the fund. Loads and 12b-1 fees were combined in various ways to create funds with multiple share classes for the intermediary channel. For example, such funds typically offer a Class A with a high front-end load and a low 12b-1 fee, as well as a Class B with no front-end load and a high 12b-1 fee together with a declining back-end load that is assessed when an investor leaves the fund. The back-end load usually declines or disappears the longer a shareholder remains invested in the fund or in another fund within the same family. (See Chapter Ten for further discussion of share classes.) While these alternative classes have garnered more new fund sales in recent years as investors have begun to show a preference for back-end loads and annual 12b-1 fees, assets in Class A with front-end loads continue to be much larger than assets in all other classes because of the historic dominance of fund sales in Class A.

The broker-dealer sales and service model is based on personal relationships between the broker-dealer's registered representatives (RRs) and their clients; the RRs are in turn supported by the relationship between the broker-dealer as a firm and a variety of fund sponsors through wholesalers. We will look at the RR-client relationship first, focusing on how it affects mutual fund sales. In its simplest form, the sales process starts with a meeting between the client and the RR. The two parties discuss the client's financial status, and this conversation gives rise to suggested investment purchases, which are made through the RR. The RR maintains an ongoing relationship with the client, monitoring existing investments and suggesting new investment products as appropriate.

An RR's fund recommendations to clients generally would be based on several factors. Top choices typically include firms with a broad spectrum of products as well as a long history with the distribution channel. Above-average performance is another essential factor, although consistency of performance holds greater value in the intermediary channel than the direct-marketed channel. Whether a fund sponsor has a large and skilled wholesale force—with the resources to support a presence in the broker-dealer channel—also could influence an RR's recommendation.

In recent years, competition among fund sponsors for shelf space at broker-dealers has become intense. In part, this derives from the proliferation of funds in the industry and, in part, from the explosion of financial information available directly to clients. Such competitive forces led to the rise in popularity of mutual fund wrap programs, which offer portfolios of funds that are assembled and managed for brokerage clients. In putting together these programs, most major broker-dealers perform significant research on mutual fund complexes; that research is used typically to equip their representatives with detailed opinions on individual funds. These opinions often evolve into formal or informal lists of select or preferred funds, which help to guide the recommendations of RRs. (For an illustration of a response by a full-service broker-dealer to these competitive factors, see "Merrill Lynch: Changing with the Times.")

In this competition for shelf space at broker-dealers, the central figure has been the fund wholesaler, who typically is an employee of the fund sponsor. The wholesaler works in the field, interacting directly with RRs by providing them with marketing materials, sales strategies, support for client seminars and a host of other items. The wholesaler typically is backed by a phone bank at the fund sponsor, which can answer questions from RRs and send out product information.

CALLOUT

Merrill Lynch: Changing with the Times

A giant in the brokerage industry, Merrill Lynch illustrates well the ways intermediaries have responded to the competitive challenges of a changing financial marketplace. As the largest wire house, the firm is a major force in the brokerage industry, accounting for about 15% to 20% of 1999 sales.[7] Merrill Lynch has long been known for providing a full suite of investment products sold through RRs to clients at full-service commissions. Faced with a host of new competitors, however, Merrill Lynch has made several significant—and bold—changes to its sales and service models in order to meet consumer demand more effectively and remain competitive.

During the 1990s, old-line brokerage firms faced a variety of pressures. An explosion of easily accessible financial information made it easier for investors to analyze and select stocks as well as mutual funds without a broker recommendation. Old-line brokerage firms lost market share to entities such as Charles Schwab & Co. and Fidelity Investments that empowered do-it-yourself investors by offering brokerage capabilities—other than advice—at discount prices via the Internet, telephone or at branch offices. Internet-only brokers, such as E-Trade and Ameritrade, added to the competition with their emphasis on low-cost web-based transactions. All of these competitors encroached on the territory traditionally held by full-service firms such as Merrill Lynch.

After considerable internal debate, Merrill Lynch launched an aggressive campaign to compete head-to-head with its new rivals. Merrill Lynch began by offering Unlimited Advantage, a flexible form of wrap account. Under this program, investors receive unlimited advice with a Merrill Lynch financial consultant and unlimited trading capability, all for a flat fee starting at 1.5% for accounts of at least $100,000. Clients of this service may also receive discounts on financial planning products such as insurance and trust products. By shifting the focus from transactions to asset management, the program represented a significant departure from the traditional model that had historically characterized Merrill Lynch, as well as the rest of the brokerage industry.

In 1999, the firm rolled out its own online brokerage service, Merrill Lynch Direct, with moderate commission rates. This initiative directly targeted the territory staked out by Schwab and Fidelity, as well as by other wire houses such as Morgan Stanley Dean Witter, which previously had launched an online brokerage service. Not only can self-directed clients of Merrill Lynch trade online at relatively low prices, but they also can invest in over 2,000 funds through the firm's newly launched supermarket. Moreover, Merrill Lynch has beefed up its Internet presence by widely promoting and distributing its research online to its customers.

However, the roster of competitors—in terms of both sponsor and product—has expanded beyond the traditional lineup of mutual funds sold by wholesalers. Direct distributors of mutual funds also are targeting broker-dealers. Several formerly no-load firms have begun introducing shares with various types of loads; these include companies such as Strong Funds, INVESCO, Gabelli and Scudder. Mutual fund wrap programs have reinforced this no-load threat to fund wholesalers. Many traditional no-load fund families participate in wrap programs, thus exposing RRs and their clients to a broader competitive universe. For example, in the 1990s, popular participants in wrap programs have included Janus and American Century, two well-known no-load complexes. Although these new forces have not displaced the top wholesalers from their leadership roles, they are beginning to divert new fund flows, especially from the smaller or weaker wholesaling firms.

More fundamentally, the role of the mutual fund wholesaler is being reshaped by three related trends. First, as the brokerage industry shifts its focus from episodic sales of products to customized relationships based on continuing advice, fund wholesalers are being forced to expand the scope of information they provide to RRs. The new information includes, for instance, how particular funds fit into an overall asset allocation strategy. Second, in this information age, consumers themselves may play a greater role in driving product sales. Promotional efforts by wholesalers attached to specific fund sponsors may be less effective in spurring RRs to sell particular products. Third, the Internet is increasingly the source of the same materials historically provided by wholesalers to RRs through visits, mail or phone calls. Accordingly, the personal ties between fund wholesalers and RRs may be eroding.

B. Other Intermediaries

While the various types of brokerage firms predominate in the intermediary channel, there are other important types of intermediaries: banks, insurance companies, registered investment advisers and financial planners.

1. Banks   Banks are a modest but steady source of mutual fund assets, accounting for 6% to 7% of mutual fund sales each year.[8] This statistic includes proprietary bank funds sold through bank trust departments, bank-affiliated brokers and nonaffiliated securities firms, as well as bank sales of independent funds such as those managed by American and Putnam. Until recently, banks were somewhat hamstrung in competing for mutual fund business by the Glass-Steagall Act, which established a partial legal wall between banks and securities dealers. As a result, banks were allowed to advise a mutual fund, but not to sponsor or underwrite a fund. Conversely, mutual fund sponsors were allowed to own a bank only if it was limited to certain functions such as fiduciary services or credit cards. When Congress repealed the Glass-Steagall Act in late 1999, bank affiliates were permitted to participate in all aspects of the mutual fund industry and vice versa—subject to functional regulation.

With approximately a 30% share of fund assets under management, banks appear to be substantial players in the arena of selling proprietary mutual funds. However, they are not significant contenders in the arena of equity funds, managing only about 2.4% of the assets in that fund segment. Rather, the fund assets of banks are concentrated overwhelmingly in low-risk asset categories, primarily money market funds, where they possess 27% of that fund segment.[9] One important way banks developed their mutual fund business was by converting trust accounts into mutual funds. But remaining trust assets are not generally attractive for conversion. Acquiring mutual fund management firms has been the other main way banks increased their assets under management. Such acquisitions may be a more viable option for continued expansion of both their overall and product-specific market shares. (See Chapter Ten for more on acquisitions of fund managers.)

The banking industry's dominant players are best positioned to move beyond proprietary funds to play a broader role in the mutual fund industry. Most large banks possess enviable brand name recognition, and many have poured significant resources into their asset management businesses (see Table 7.3). For example, Mellon Bank acquired

TABLE 7.3

Top ten fund companies, December 31, 2000 (bank proprietary funds)

Market Share by Bank Proprietary Fund Assets	
Bank of America	11.90%
Wells Fargo Bank	9.84
BankOne	9.76
Chase Manhattan	8.30
Northern Trust	5.41
J. P. Morgan Investment Management	4.94
U.S. Bancorp	4.61
Fleet Financial	4.38
State Street Bank	3.23
KeyCorp	2.97

Source: Strategic Insight.

the manager of the Dreyfus fund family in the early 1990s and later acquired the manager of the Founders Funds to broaden its product line. Known originally for its direct distribution of no-load funds, Dreyfus has since shifted its marketing focus toward financial planners and broker-dealers. Bank One, which acquired the manager of the Pegasus Funds through its purchase of First Chicago/NBD Corp., has directed significant resources toward building its fund family. This family, now called One Group, has successfully recruited within the mutual fund industry for investment personnel. Citigroup has heavily promoted the Salomon Smith Barney funds, which appear to receive more marketing attention than its CitiSelect Funds. At the same time, Citigroup has embraced open architecture by becoming a major distributor for traditional fund families. Finally, Chase Manhattan's 2000 acquisition of J. P. Morgan & Co makes it a significant competitor in the asset management arena because of Morgan's expertise in fund management. In early 2001, the firm consolidated its Chase Vista Funds under J. P. Morgan, the better-known name in asset management.

The vast majority of smaller regional banks have faced a more difficult challenge—especially those that have attempted to manage and distribute proprietary funds. Across the entire banking industry, a late entry into the field has been a significant disadvantage in gaining recognition and market share. While the growth of mutual funds began to pick up in the late 1980s, some banks did not become serious about entering the fund industry until the 1990s, and other banks were slowed down by the regulatory constraints applicable at that time. Smaller banks may also lack the investment talent and compensation structures to compete with the major fund complexes. Similarly, smaller banks may not have the internal resources to offer international or sector funds. Finally, the expenses of operating a fund complex can be significant as the level of technology rises rapidly in the fund industry. As a result, some smaller banks are reevaluating their commitment to fund management by either subcontracting their fund management functions to outside investment advisers or simply distributing funds managed by outside fund families.

2. Insurance companies   Insurance companies are a quiet giant within the intermediary channel. Insurers now directly manage about 7% of mutual fund assets, and their rate of growth has lagged the pace in the broker-dealer channel. However, insurers are taking significant steps toward expanding their product lines and acquiring established fund managers. In doing so, they are building on their longstanding relationships with both clients and distribution agents, as well as their experience with fund sponsors through the variable annuity (VA) business.

Many insurance companies became acquainted with the mutual fund industry through VAs, which provide a tax-deferred investment vehicle for retirement without any limit on the amount of contributions to VA accounts. While contributions to VAs are made with after-tax dollars, the assets grow tax free until they are distributed during retirement (earlier in the event of death or disability). VAs also come with some degree of insurance protection against death and sometimes disability before retirement. Almost all VAs protect against a decline in account value below the amount of the aggregate contribution. Many now protect investment gains at specified anniversary dates, and some provide guaranteed minimum rates of return. The annuity is considered "variable" because its value depends on the investment performance of a professionally managed portfolio of securities. The annuity owner is typically responsible for choosing among several subaccounts, which generally represent a range of investments from conservative money market funds, to high yield bond funds, to domestic and international equity funds.

Although VAs have been in existence since the 1950s, during the 1980s insurance companies looked to mutual fund sponsors to provide the investment options. The result was the development of close relationships between particular insurers and particular fund managers. In the 1990s, insurers moved toward VA products that offered their customers a wide choice among mutual fund sponsors. This movement was part of the general gravitation toward open architecture in the mutual fund industry. But the emphasis on VA products with funds from multiple sponsors increased competition among mutual fund sponsors and complicated their relationships with insurers.

Although VAs do provide for tax deferral of any investment earnings until distribution, they have one tax drawback: payouts above contributions are taxed at ordinary income rates even if much of the appreciation derives from capital gains. Yet VA sales remained robust despite federal legislation in 1993 that significantly increased the differential between the highest federal tax rate on ordinary income (39.6%) and the highest federal tax rate on long-term capital gains (20%). VAs have proven popular in the pre- and post-retiree markets, where both the tax-deferred growth and insurance wrapper have had enduring appeal. Nor has Congress imposed any income limits on eligibility for the tax benefits from VAs, in contrast to the complex income limits placed on eligibility for tax deductions or exclusions for individual retirement accounts. (See Chapter Eight.)

During the 1990s, the rate of VA sales growth surpassed that of mutual funds.[10] But a significant portion of recent VA sales have been transfers from one VA sponsor to another, in the form of exchanges made under Section 1035 of the Internal Revenue Code. That section allows a tax-free swap of an annuity for another annuity, which may be issued by the same or a different issuer. In fact, net cash flows in 1999 were only 28% of total VA sales, according to consulting firm Cerulli Associates,[11] and this trend seems likely to continue. VA owners have taken advantage of Section 1035 exchanges for several reasons. The VA marketplace now includes lower-cost offerings, including VAs without sales loads, which may be attractive to policyholders who have older contracts with higher-cost structures. Moreover, newer VAs may offer enhanced features such as larger death benefits or more diverse payout options.

Another reason for the rise in Section 1035 exchanges has been the expansion of investment options within VA contracts, which has led some owners of older VAs to swap contracts in order to broaden their subaccount choices. By mid-2000, 35% of all VA contracts offered 30 or more subaccounts. In 1997, only 6% of all VAs offered as many.[12] The types of available subaccounts have changed as well. Most dramatically, as the 1990s' bull market bestowed more rewards on growth-oriented investments, VA owners demanded more aggressive options in their subaccounts. At the same time, some insurers sought a more lucrative economic arrangement by hiring fund managers as subadvisers for their own VA funds instead of using the separate set of VA funds offered by many fund sponsors. This led to partnerships between insurance companies and name-brand fund managers, some of whom were dominating the top-performers list. In a powerful example of the industry's movement toward open architecture, insurers negotiated subadvisory arrangements with fund sponsors such as Alliance and Janus.

VA purchases are concentrated overwhelmingly in the intermediary channel, which accounted for 97% of all VA sales in 1999.[13] The commissions for sales of VAs are typically a little higher than those for intermediary sales of mutual fund shares. The direct marketing of VAs still accounts for only 3% of all VA sales, despite the offering of low-cost products by two industry giants—Fidelity and Vanguard. However, there is growing interest in low-cost VAs marketed through fee-based intermediaries such as financial planners and registered investment advisers, who charge an annual fee for advice instead of commissions on product sales. Since these VAs are sold without the traditional up-front commission, they can pass on lower costs to the consumer. In a related development, VAs may now be sold in an "unbundled" format with a menu of choices. In other words, the insurance contract that comes with the VA may be fairly basic in terms of its coverage. Then the client and adviser have the option of adding, and paying for, additional features, such as guaranteed levels of retirement payments. Variable annuities also are gaining an Internet presence gradually through a few start-up firms that are marketing VA information and research to financial intermediaries.

Besides VAs, insurance companies play broader roles in the mutual fund industry. Many fund managers are owned by insurance companies (see Table 7.4). Putnam, which has long been owned by the Marsh & McLennan Companies, is the largest such arrangement. During the 1990s, domestic insurers acquired some fund managers (e.g., Oppenheimer and Delaware Management), while foreign insurers acquired other fund managers (e.g., PIMCO and Scudder). More typically, fund management units were developed internally by large insurance companies such as Prudential and John Hancock.

Another route toward mutual fund distribution has been to develop and market funds under the insurer's name, with investment management subcontracted to a traditional fund sponsor. A notable example of this structure has been American Skandia, the U.S. arm of Skandia Worldwide. A relative newcomer to the industry, American

TABLE 7.4

Long-term fund assets managed by selected insurance-owned companies

Complex Name	Parent Company	Fund Assets ($ millions), 2000
Putnam Investments	Marsh McLennan	233,617.3
MFS Investment Management	Sun Life of Canada	93,405.0
Oppenheimer Funds	Massachusetts Mutual Life	80,656.7
PIMCO Advisors	Allianz	65,998.2
Alliance Fund Distributors	Axa Financial	54,746.6
Scudder Investor Services	Zurich Financial Services	40,740.2
Prudential Investments	Prudential Insurance	37,622.5
Kemper Funds	Zurich Financial Services	30,892.4
Liberty Funds Distributor	Liberty Financial	23,903.9
John Hancock Funds	John Hancock Insurance	23,020.4
USAA Investment Management Co.	USAA	21,854.6
MainStay Funds	New York Life	18,142.9
Delaware Management	Lincoln Financial Group	14,298.6
Hartford (The)	Hartford Life	10,298.7
ING Pilgrim Investments	ING Group	11,546.9
Phoenix Investment Partners	Phoenix Home Life Mutual	11,388.5
State Street Research	Metropolitan Life	9,838.5
AAL Capital Management Corp.	Aid Association for Lutherans	7,507.9
MassMutual	Massachusetts Mutual Life	6,191.0
American Skandia	Skandia Insurance Co., Ltd.	5,948.7
IDEX Management	Western Reserve Life	5,980.7
SunAmerica Mutual Funds	SunAmerica	5,468.1
Stein Roe Farnham	Liberty Financial	5,415.7
Enterprise Capital Management	Mutual of New York	4,510.6
Guardian Investor Services Co	The Guardian	3,898.4
Principal Financial Group	Principal Financial Group	3,682.8
SAFECO Securities	SAFECO	3,364.5
Nationwide Financial Services	Nationwide Insurance	3,406.6
Fortis Financial	Fortis	3,245.5
Sentinel Advisers	Provident Mutual	2,756.4
TIAA-CREF	TIAA-CREF	2,527.6
Aetna Funds	Aetna Life	2,548.1
Security Distributors	Security Benefit	1,541.1
North American Funds	American General	1,500.6
Conseco Capital Management	Conseco	730.8
Mimlic Asset Management Co.	Minnesota Life	541.7
Chubb Investment Advisory Corp.	JP Corp	228.0
FBL Investment Advisory Services	Farm Bureau Financial Services	244.7
O. N. Investment Group	Ohio National Life Insurance	45.7
Long-term fund assets managed by insurance-owned companies		843,257.4
Industry long-term fund assets in mutual fund industry		4,386,088.0
% of total		19.23%

Source: Financial Research Corporation.

Skandia aggressively marketed its broad collection of subadvised funds through financial planners and other smaller intermediaries inside and outside the VA wrapper. It is now considered a powerful example of the potential for this approach to distributing mutual funds.

3. Registered investment advisers and financial planners
Smaller members of the intermediary channel include financial planners and registered investment advisers (RIAs). Many of these firms were at the vanguard in terms of providing fee-based advice, although a minority of these firms still accept sales commissions. Moreover, the mutual fund supermarket (covered below) facilitated fund sales and account management for these smaller firms by offering a variety of products in one account together with streamlined reporting and professional record keeping. Indeed, supermarket pioneer Charles Schwab specifically targeted this portion of the intermediary channel and currently serves approximately 6,000 RIAs.

RIAs are relatively new to the intermediary fund market. They rose to prominence during the late 1980s and 1990s as more customers chose to pay for advice through annual fees rather than sales commissions. Typically, RIAs are small shops with assets under management ranging from $100 million to several hundred million. Many RIAs are ex-brokers from wire-house firms or other brokerages, who left to work in a different environment with more emphasis on money management. Some RIAs are independent, and others are affiliated with larger firms such as American Express Financial Advisers or Royal Alliance Associates. RIAs overlap to a considerable degree with financial planners, who often offer a broader range of services such as estate planning and tax advice. Financial planners may offer investment services themselves or recommend other investment advisers to their clients. Although some planners and RIAs focus on separate accounts of individual securities, the two groups are significant distributors of mutual funds. In fact, it is estimated that they control between $110 and $125 billion in mutual fund assets.[14]

By offering adviser independence and product variety, financial planners and RIAs have helped raise the bar for services provided by brokerage firms. Planners and RIAs are viewed typically as fairly independent, without perceived loyalty to specific products. They tend to focus on the no-load fund universe or purchase funds through a no-transaction-fee supermarket arrangement. Instead of receiving sales commissions or 12b-1 fees, planners and RIAs typically charge their clients an annual fee based on a percentage of the client's assets, often 1%.

The main exception to this pattern is commission-based financial planners who, similar to brokers, navigate a complicated web of client perceptions. As broker-dealers move toward providing fee-based advice versus commissioned trades in order to maintain their competitive edge, they increasingly overlap with the RIA/financial planning segment of the intermediary channel. Some observers suggest this migration will slow the expansion of this segment, as broker-dealers become more formidable competitors to RIAs and financial planners.

II. The Direct Channel

Mutual funds have been credited with democratizing investing in that they allow the average consumer easy access to a diversified portfolio of securities managed professionally at a modest cost. The direct distribution channel further empowers investors by enabling them to manage their own mutual fund purchases and sales through direct interaction with fund sponsors. This section discusses the history and current state of the direct marketing channel as well as the mutual fund supermarket (which can be used for direct purchases of mutual funds or purchases through an investment adviser).

A. Direct Marketers

The direct distribution model became popular with the advent of money market funds in the 1970s, as these were often advertised and sold directly to investors without any sales charges. Sponsors of money market funds were able to capitalize on the high interest rates of the 1970s and early 1980s by attracting clients from lower-paying bank accounts and offering convenient services such as check writing. In the dismal stock markets of the 1970s and early 1980s, money market funds helped fund sponsors gather investor assets, which in later years were often diversified among stock or bond funds within the same mutual fund complex.

Traditionally, broker-dealers not only provided transaction services to investors, but also served as sources of advice about the financial markets and the selection of mutual funds. The load attached to broker-sold funds was considered in part a fee for this advice. By contrast, the direct channel offered more limited guidance and sold what came to be known as no-load funds, or funds without a sales charge. While pure no-loads charge neither a sales load nor a 12b-1 fee, the National Association of Securities Dealers, Inc. (NASD) allows a fund to be called "no load" only if it has no sales loads and its 12b-1 fees do not exceed 25 basis points (bp) per year.

No-load fund complexes have sought to promote their lower costs deliberately as a means of attracting shareholders. For example, some no-load funds have from time to time capped fees to shareholders at a specified level and absorbed any additional costs themselves. This is an especially common practice for new funds as well as for money market or short-term bond funds, whose lower return potential makes them especially sensitive to costs. Other fund complexes have sought to attract investors by introducing low-fee funds for investors with higher account balances. For instance, Dreyfus's Basic funds and several of Fidelity's Spartan funds offer all-inclusive expense caps to shareholders who can meet required minimum investment amounts. In an all-inclusive fee, the fund sponsor promises that total expenses—advisory fee, transfer agency fee and other fund expenses—of the mutual fund will not exceed a specified number of basis points per year. Vanguard has made its name by offering low-cost funds, especially index funds, and recently has launched a new class with particularly low expense ratios for longtime shareholders with large accounts. (See "Vanguard Funds: The Low-Cost King.")

CALLOUT
Vanguard Funds: The Low-Cost King

In an industry that has seen its share of fads, Vanguard has long stood as a symbol of low costs and plain-vanilla products. Founded by John Bogle in 1975, the Vanguard Group is now the second largest mutual fund complex in the United States and has inspired a loyal following among many of its shareholders.

Low-cost funds have been Vanguard's hallmark—and one of its main rallying cries within the industry. Its ability to provide funds with low expense ratios depends on the company's unusual business model. In the Vanguard Group, the management company is actually owned by shareholders of its member funds. (The typical arrangement is to have the management company contract with the fund; in such an arrangement, the shareholders of the management company have little relationship to those of the funds.) The Vanguard Group provides the family's funds with management, administrative duties and marketing on an "at-cost" basis. The Vanguard Group also contracts out investment advice for most of its actively managed equity funds to third parties such as Wellington Management Company, LLP, at relatively low fees.

Vanguard's emphasis on low costs has gone hand in hand with its allegiance to index fund investing. One year after founding the company, Bogle opened what has become the largest or second largest U.S. mutual fund, the Vanguard 500 Index Fund. Much of the fund's growth came in the mid-1990s when a seemingly tireless bull market among large-cap stocks helped fuel the relative outperformance of the Standard & Poor's (S&P) 500. During those years, Vanguard was situated ideally for the explosion of interest in S&P 500 index funds, which became a core building block in the portfolio of many investors. Over the years, Vanguard has introduced a wide range of index funds that track everything from the entire U.S. stock and bond markets to foreign markets to specific investment styles such as growth and value. Although Vanguard offers actively managed funds, it has championed index funds as an investment strategy.

In November 2000, Vanguard took its emphasis on cost even further by introducing a new share class called Admiral, which is intended to reward long-time, large-dollar investors with fees even lower than the normal Vanguard fund. To qualify for the lower-cost structure, shareholders must meet one of the following descriptions: possess an account balance of $250,000; possess an account balance of at least $150,000, have established the account at least three years ago and be registered for online account access at the company's website; or possess an account balance of at least $50,000, have established the account at least 10 years ago and be registered for online account access at the company's website.

Once mutual fund sponsors began marketing directly to consumers, they stressed the convenience of their services as well as their low prices in an effort to compete with the personalized attention offered by broker-dealers. For example, fund sponsors in the direct channel offered to do business by mail or telephone through toll-free numbers; a few took calls around the clock, 365 days a year. Many shareholders of direct-marketed funds now use automated telephone services to collect account information, obtain quotes and place trades using push-button response systems. Technological advances allowed fund sponsors to route calls for optimal efficiency and provide their phone representatives with access to extensive databases containing customer account and contact information as well as market news. Such advances resulted in quicker response times and better-equipped, better-educated representatives.

Some direct marketers also maintain a modest number of walk-in offices, or investor centers, in key cities across the United States. These centers accept checks for fund purchases, handle investor problems and make available a broad array of disclosure documents and educational materials about funds as well as other products. Moreover, they provide the opportunity for customers to meet in person with financial representatives to discuss their asset allocation mix, tax objectives or other personal investment issues. Such investment centers have proved especially useful in opening new customer accounts and selling complex products like variable annuities.

The advent of the Internet in the 1990s created another sales and service model for the direct channel. At this juncture, retail fund investors are using the Internet primarily to gather market information, monitor performance, and compare products. In contrast to the customers of online brokers, customers of mutual funds conduct a modest percentage of fund purchases and redemptions online. Thus, the creation of websites by fund complexes is augmenting rather than replacing other communication channels, such as phones and branches. It appears that websites are providing retail customers with the answers to simple questions (e.g., account balances and fund prices), leaving more complex questions to phone conversations with live reps. (See Chapter Nine for more detail.)

During the late 1980s and 1990s, as the number of funds grew tremendously, investors became increasingly interested in obtaining investment guidance and advice. Direct marketers responded by providing investors with more educational materials, such as newsletters and asset allocation guides. The Internet has been invaluable in this pursuit by enabling fund sponsors to expand their educational efforts through such tools as live webcasts and portfolio manager chat sessions. At the same time, fund sponsors have provided online interactive tools to help the do-it-yourself audience plan for their investment goals. These include tools to calculate how to save enough to pay for college tuition or to maintain a certain standard of living in retirement. In addition, as explained later in this Chapter, some direct marketers now offer mutual fund wrap programs for an extra fee.

The growing appetite for advice has challenged the fundamental rationale of the direct market channel in mutual fund sales. The direct channel was designed originally for investors who desired low-cost products and autonomy in making investment decisions. It also could be an ideal channel for investors who had smaller portfolios that might not qualify for high levels of attention from intermediaries. In fact, the advent of no-load funds has resulted in increased cost sensitivity among investors—and within the fund industry itself. By virtue of their lower distribution costs, no-load funds put considerable cost pressure on their load fund competitors. The no-load challenge helped push the intermediary channel toward lowering front-end loads and introducing new fund classes with deferred sales charges (as discussed earlier in this Chapter). Nevertheless, the pure direct channel has been losing market share gradually to both the intermediary channel and the mutual fund supermarket (discussed below). For example, net sales of stock, bond and hybrid funds in the direct channel declined from 23% in 1990 to 18% in 1999.[15]

The relative decline in direct channel fund sales is partly a response to the growing appetite for advice. Although direct marketers now provide educational materials and planning tools, these fall short of personalized advice. Some potential customers of the direct channel have sought personalized advice from RIAs and financial planners; others have looked to broker-dealers, especially for large accounts such as individual retirement account rollovers. Another important factor has been the demand for greater convenience. In the pure direct model, investors who wished to own funds from a variety of families found themselves contending with multiple statements and other difficulties in managing their investments as an integrated portfolio. Rebalancing their desired exposures between stock and bond funds, for example, could involve executing purchases or sales in a cumbersome process involving several different fund complexes. Many investors wished for greater breadth in product line, including the ability to trade individual stocks and bonds. While portfolio integration and product diversification are offered by traditional intermediaries, the demand for these services helped spur the growth of the mutual fund supermarket as an adjunct to the direct channel.

B. *Mutual Fund Supermarkets*

Few other innovations have made as big an impact on the fund industry as the mutual fund supermarket. Today's popular version of the mutual fund supermarket was introduced by discount brokerage firm Charles Schwab in 1992 and has since transformed the way investors purchase and sell funds. Like the supermarket from which most people purchase food, fund supermarkets bring together a variety of similar products from different vendors. In other words, they allow investors to purchase and hold a broad range of funds from many different fund sponsors through a single brokerage account. Similar to the grocery version, fund supermarkets soared in popularity because of their ability to provide a high degree of convenience, breadth of product, ease of comparison and simplicity of transaction.

The mechanics of a supermarket are straightforward. In return for a "place" to market its funds, the fund or fund sponsor usually pays an annual fee of 25 to 35 bp to the company that operates the marketplace and services the customer accounts (called the supermarket operator). The supermarket operator also may produce various forms of advertising, either as part of this arrangement or for additional fees. For example, the supermarket operator may offer the fund or fund sponsor opportunities for cooperative marketing that link the fund supermarket with a specific fund sponsor. These opportunities may include print or website ads, direct mailings, portfolio manager road shows or conference calls.

The annual fee paid by the fund or fund sponsor covers the supermarket operator's charges for servicing and effecting transactions for shareholders of the fund. Thus, investors can buy and sell many funds in a supermarket NTF, which means "no transaction fee" or no trading costs. Outside this universe of NTF funds, supermarkets may allow investors to purchase a host of other funds for a transaction fee or for the fund's standard sales load. All of these fund positions usually can be housed in one brokerage account, which can also hold stocks or other types of investments. In a tremendous innovation for the direct distribution channel, supermarket operators then consolidate information on all of the customer's holdings and send out one integrated statement. Although fund supermarkets are generally operated by a broker, they are considered an adjunct to the direct market, since the broker typically provides no advice in connection with a supermarket transaction.

The Internet has become integral to the operations of the mutual fund supermarket. Supermarket operators typically offer interactive web-based tools that enable customers to sort through thousands of funds quickly and efficiently. Online trading is another tool that is typically available—even encouraged—by supermarket operators. The website of the supermarket operator also may be a source of valuable educational information on funds in the supermarket, as well as news and securities research from multiple third-party sources.

While many financial services firms have launched supermarkets, this segment is dominated by two platforms: Charles Schwab Co.'s Mutual Fund Marketplace and Fidelity Investments' Funds Network. These two platforms together hold more than 90% of supermarket fund assets,[16] with the rest split among 30 or so small firms. Assets within supermarkets reached $500 billion in 1999.[17]

Fund supermarkets are an especially welcome innovation for many smaller money management firms and niche funds. Supermarkets offer a distribution channel, sales support and customer service capabilities such as record keeping and handling client calls, all of which may be beyond the budget of smaller shops. The flipside is that the supermarket operator in essence owns the customer and most likely owns the potential for future asset growth. Only the operator of the supermarket typically knows the names of the shareholders in the fund sold by the sponsor through the supermarket. If the performance of a fund sponsor declines, it often has no way to communicate directly with shareholders of its funds.

III. *Cross Channel Trends*

Today's investor is better informed and more engaged than ever before. The Internet has democratized investment information, making it easy to compare fund returns as well as fees and services, and then just as easy to transact based on this information. As a result, the financial services industry has been challenged to develop new ways of meeting consumer demand for convenience, personalization and advice. This section explores how a combination of consumer demand and industry innovation is creating a dynamic landscape that necessitates creative product development and marketing strategies.

The key idea underlying most current trends is that the investor is in the driver's seat. Investors are shifting away from anything that resembles a one-size-fits-all approach and shifting toward demanding products and services on their terms. This shift has made a substantial impact on the mutual fund business. Most large fund sponsors have responded to this shift by distributing a broader array of financial services to their customers. Conversely, many smaller fund sponsors have responded by manufacturing new products that are distributed ultimately by larger players or fund supermarkets. Only a few firms remain focused exclusively on managing and selling their own mutual funds.

Although the pace of change is rapid, a few broad themes encapsulate many key developments in mutual fund distribution. This section focuses on three of these thematic areas:

1. Open architecture has pushed fund sponsors toward new ways of bolstering customer loyalty and increasing their businesses. We will look at advertising strategies
   employed to gain recognition among the myriad of fund choices and attract new
   assets. We will also look at account aggregation as a developing technology used to
   remain the customer's primary platform for all fund holdings.

2. Advice—delivered through a range of platforms and designed for widely varied investors—is a requisite offering for fund industry leaders. We will look at the customized products and services developed for high-net-worth investors. We also
   will look at the lower end of the advice spectrum, where fund sponsors are relying on Internet tools and packaged solutions.

3. A logical extension of the market for advice is needs-based marketing, which seeks
   to meet investor needs with targeted products and services. We will look at college
   planning, a need for most younger families. We will also look at wealth transfers, a
   need for high-net-worth-investors, especially in their later years.

A. Open Architecture

As we have seen, open architecture provides investors with centralized access to products from many fund sponsors; it is one of the most powerful forces in the mutual fund
industry, shaping every distribution channel. Given the proliferation of fund supermarkets, it is now very hard for any single fund complex to monopolize customers in the
direct marketing channel. Similarly, open architecture has opened up the intermediary
channel. In the broker-dealer world, preferred lists of funds include funds from a range
of complexes. In the insurance industry, variable annuities typically combine managed
portfolios from a variety of well-known fund sponsors. One of the chief attractions of
RIAs and financial planners is their independence in choosing among fund options for
their clients.

Within this environment of open architecture, fund sponsors must develop new
strategies: advertising approaches designed to rise above the clutter of fund choices
that can overwhelm investors, and aggregation strategies to remain the primary service
provider for customers with funds from multiple complexes.

1. Fund advertising Open architecture has contributed to an increasingly
complex financial marketplace, where customers have easy access to many products
from many financial services firms. To attract investors to their products, fund sponsors
have been increasing expenditures on advertising, with particular emphasis on top-
performing funds.

There has been a marked rise in advertising by financial services firms, including
fund sponsors, broker-dealers and banks. As illustrated in Table 7.5, financial services
advertising in 2000 exceeded $1.7 billion—its highest level ever—culminating a rising
trend during the 1990s. This 2000 amount represented a 25% growth rate over 1999
and is more than four times the amount spent for advertising in 1995. Within the aggregate amount for the year 2000, top spenders included major fund sponsors such as
Fidelity and Janus; full-service brokerages such as Merrill Lynch, Morgan Stanley Dean
Witter and Salomon Smith Barney; discount brokerage/fund supermarket operator

TABLE 7.5

Mutual fund industry measured advertising expenditures ($ millions)

	Television	Print	Total	As a % of Net Sales (basis points)
1990	$18	$112	$130	25.5 bp
1991	22	113	135	11.3
1992	27	127	154	7.8
1993	30	138	168	6.0
1994	19	187	206	14.4
1995	35	167	202	12.4
1996	140	220	360	12.7
1997	203	209	412	12.6
1998	176	184	360	11.6
1999	176	211	388	14.7
2000	247	268	514	17.5
All Investment Services Spending[a]				
1995	$140	$268	$408	—
1996	341	373	714	—
1997	466	404	870	—
1998	535	424	959	—
1999	773	543	1,316	—
2000	1,109	640	1,749	—

[a] Includes consumer-directed advertising by mutual funds, brokerage firms and non-FDIC-insured product advertising by banks and insurance companies.
Source: Competitrack Consumer Investment Report.

Charles Schwab; and online brokers Ameritrade, E-Trade and Datek.[18] This rise in advertising expenditures is to be expected, given the increased prominence of mutual funds and other financial products in the lives of ordinary Americans. At the same time, as the number of investment options available to potential customers has exploded, advertising has become a means to stand out in a crowded marketplace.

Given the plethora of mutual funds in today's marketplace, fund sponsors are seeking new ways to differentiate themselves. One strategy is to advertise "value-added" services such as advice. In 2000, the largest increase in advertising expenditures versus 1999 was in the advisory category, which includes financial planning, portfolio management, trust services, estate planning, tax preparation and wrap accounts. Spending increased 141% year over year in the advisory category.[19] By contrast, overall advertising spending in the fund industry increased 25% from 1999 to 2000. A vivid illustration was Merrill Lynch, which devoted 45% of its advertising budget to promoting its advisory services in 2000, a dramatic increase from 1999.

Another important tactic in today's cluttered marketplace is brand advertising, which focuses on establishing a firm's reputation for qualities such as trustworthiness, reliability and experience. While overall spending in this area dropped somewhat in

2000 versus 1999, brand advertising remains among the top three messages that major financial services firms typically seek to convey (the others being online capabilities and general mutual fund information). For example, in 2000, the industry's top spender, Schwab, devoted 39% of its budget to advertising brand. The advent of online trading has put renewed emphasis on reliability as a key aspect of brand. Financial service firms tout their high levels of continuous computer service and downplay any reports of systems downtime.

But there is an increasing tension between brand and performance advertising. In the mutual fund supermarket, for example, brand is rendered less important, whereas performance is often the major differentiating factor among funds. While performance advertising has always been characteristic of the fund industry, it became especially prominent in the late 1990s, when the bull market for stocks helped certain funds attain compelling return records. More specifically, droves of new shareholders bought growth-style funds focused on technology stocks as these funds garnered high double-digit or even triple-digit gains in 1998 and 1999, only to fall sharply in 2000.

Because of its dramatic power to attract investors, performance advertising by funds is regulated heavily by the SEC and NASD. (See Chapter Three for more on regulation of fund advertising.) Fund returns must be shown for 1-, 5- and 10-year periods (or the life of the fund for newer funds), with data current as of the most recent quarter end. Furthermore, performance ads for stock and bond funds must be accompanied by SEC-mandated text essentially stating that the performance data shown represents past performance, which may not be indicative of future returns. In 1999, as many fund sponsors sought to promote extraordinary returns of certain funds, especially those in existence for only a year or two, both the SEC and the NASD reminded financial services firms to evaluate performance advertising carefully. For example, the NASD issued a formal notice to its members reminding them not to overemphasize extraordinary short-term results and avoid the suggestion that such phenomenal results were repeatable. Similarly, after growth and tech funds fell sharply in late 2000, the regulators asked fund sponsors to make clear that one-year gains as of the end of the latest quarter might not continue through the next quarter.

Other forms of performance advertising promote third-party ratings or highlight individual fund managers. An important third-party rating provider is Morningstar, which ranks funds from one to five stars based on risk-adjusted past performance relative to peer groups. (See Chapter Two for further discussion on third-party mutual fund research.) The stars are extremely popular advertising content for fund sponsors that garner high ratings because funds with four and five stars typically account for over two-thirds of net sales of long-term funds. At the same time, fund managers as advertising spokespeople have become more prominent, with well-known, high-performing managers achieving near-superstar status. Fund sponsors such as Smith Barney and Warburg Pincus have built advertisements around the individual personalities of fund managers, as illustrated by the advertisement displayed in Figure 7.1.

Potential clients seem persuaded by many forms of performance advertising. Despite admonitions from regulators and commentators, investors are motivated increasingly by short-term performance. For example, the 50 top-selling equity funds in 2000 received over two-thirds of net mutual fund inflows that year; these inflows were based on average returns of nearly 70% for these 50 equity funds in 1999, more than double

FIGURE 7.1

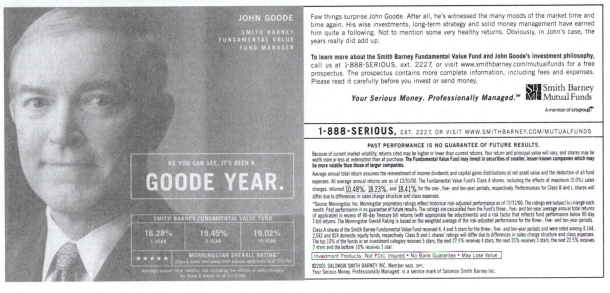

© 2001 Salomon Smith Barney, Inc. Reprinted with the permission of Salomon, Smith and Barney.

the returns of the average stock fund that year.[20] Thus, it is no surprise that fund complexes have viewed performance advertisements as one of their most powerful tools for attracting customers. However, this boom in performance advertising coincided with a powerful bull market in certain types of U.S. equities. The market correction of 2000 has reduced the emphasis on past performance and begun to reorient fund sponsors toward marketing more enduring attractions, such as diversification and advice.

2. Account aggregation   Open architecture has the power to reduce customer loyalty to any single fund complex. In a marketplace where investors can purchase mutual funds and other investment products through any number of platforms, investors can choose where to locate their accounts. Their decision often comes down to which firm offers the platform with the best service. Convenience and personalization are among the top service demands from customers today. In response to these demands, fund sponsors have provided investors with more convenient technologies, such as wireless trading, and more personalized disclosures, such as account statements with their own rates of return.

One of the most exciting and far-reaching efforts toward convenience and personalization is account aggregation (AA). AA allows an investor to view his or her online accounts at other institutions on the AA provider's website. From the customer perspective, AA greatly simplifies overall financial management by gathering and integrating all of a customer's online financial information in one place. From an industry perspective, aggregation is expected to strengthen relationships with clients by allowing financial services firms to consolidate all of the customer's information, which the customer can plug into analytical tools. Then, by marketing targeted products and services, firms can encourage such customers to consolidate and expand their investment assets at the firm.

While the technology has been in existence for some time, AA caught fire in 2000, as major financial institutions began providing the service to clients. Citigroup took the lead in the bank world with its My Accounts service introduced in mid-2000. Fidelity Investments was the pioneer among traditional fund sponsors when it rolled out Full View later that year. Both firms now offer clients the ability to bring together online information from virtually any account, including those for credit cards, retirement plans, banking or brokerage. AA also can include email accounts, news links and frequent flyer miles. Customers simply enter the email addresses and passwords of the accounts they wish to aggregate. Then customers can log onto a single site to view all these accounts.

Yodlee, based in California, is the dominant provider of the technology that enables AA. There are currently two techniques used to bring together customer data, both conditioned on a customer's consent to gathering such data. "Screen scraping" essentially sends out "bots" (robots) to a customer's web-based accounts and "scrapes" or brings back relevant data. Yodlee's proprietary technology is what allows the bot to make choices regarding what data to collect. However, visiting each site and gathering information for each customer is cumbersome. The alternative approach, which Yodlee and others champion, is to employ direct feeds from participating financial firms with lots of customer accounts, in order to speed the process of gathering data. As of early 2001, Yodlee's operation was a mix of one-third direct feed and two-thirds screen scraping.

Currently, the main attraction of AA is its ability to centralize data on a customer's assets and liabilities. In the near future, most firms plan to incorporate analytical tools that use the aggregated information. For example, Fidelity Investments is launching a service that allows customers of its fund supermarket to link their aggregated information directly with online financial planning tools. In the intermediary channel, Fidelity has joined with Putnam Investments, PFPC Inc. and Franklin Templeton to create an AA service targeted to professional advisers who do not use fund supermarkets, but instead transact directly with fund sponsors. The service will not only give advisers access to centralized trading, but it will also provide advisers with aggregated information on their client accounts.

Proponents of AA see more opportunities for highly specific marketing and product placement. For example, a site might offer customized portfolio analysis based on a client's aggregated data and then provide the user with the option of viewing specific investment recommendations for implementing the plan. More generally, AA tends to lengthen the amount of time users spend on a fund sponsor's web page, which expands opportunities to cross-sell products and services to these users.

Recognizing this potential, major banks, brokers and credit card issuers have launched or are planning to launch their own versions of AA. What remains to be seen is the extent to which investors embrace this technology and become comfortable with giving all their account information to one financial provider. Assuming a large number of investors do so, the financial services firms with the best AA are likely to become big winners in retaining customer loyalty and expanding assets under management.

B. Advice

As open architecture dramatically expanded the range of investment choices available to consumers, there has been a simultaneous explosion in investment information. Today's investors can easily gain access to data from journalists, financial websites and fund rating services—making it easier than ever before for investors to guide their own financial decisions. However, this information and product explosion has overwhelmed and confused many investors, especially those with relatively little experience in financial markets. Thus, although investors can perform research and handle investment planning on their own, a vast number prefer to consult with a financial professional— if for no other reason than to confirm their own conclusions. This preference has given rise to a large and growing demand for investment advice.

The demographics of U.S. investors and the bull stock market have been contributing factors to the growing demand for advice. The aging of the baby boomers has led to significant changes in the services they seek. As investors age, they tend to accumulate assets, especially in the rising U.S. stock market of the 1990s. Someone with over $120,000 in fund assets has more incentive to seek professional advice than someone with only $20,000 in fund assets. Similarly, as investors age, they face increasingly complex questions about retirement distribution and estate planning.

For all of these reasons, almost every fund sponsor has developed products or tools for giving advice or guidance to investors. Although the distinction between the two terms is not totally clear, advice usually aims at providing solutions to an investor's specific situation. Advice also may involve enacting those solutions on behalf of the investor, including ongoing discretionary management of his or her assets. Guidance is typically less directive in nature and less customized to the investor's specific situation. The investor typically initiates the quest for guidance and is in turn provided with options to evaluate and possibly implement.

In developing marketing strategies for advice, fund sponsors have distinguished between the high-dollar and low-dollar segments of the investor base by creating products and services for each group.

1. High-net-worth advice The high-net-worth population, often defined as investors with $1 million and more in investable financial assets, is a choice target for fund sponsors. These investors have the capacity to buy a lot of products, and their accounts tend to be the most profitable. Moreover, this is a growing population, making it an even more important marketing focus. The bull market of the 1990s and the tremendous boom in executive compensation have helped expand the number of wealthy households in the United States. The 1990s also saw the rise of the so-called 401(k) millionaires, who after years of investing found themselves with a large nest egg to manage. As their assets grow large, high-net-worth investors are demanding products offering professional money management that is responsive to their personal financial and tax needs.

Mutual fund wraps offer discretionary management of a portfolio of mutual funds. In this arrangement, a financial professional—such as a broker, RIA or a dedicated portfolio manager—selects and monitors a diversified collection of mutual funds and charges an annual advisory fee—typically in the range of 1.5% to 2.5%—in addition to the expenses of the underlying funds. Mutual fund wraps are a key factor in the intermediary channel. SEI Investments is the largest manager of mutual fund wrap assets, and its products are distributed typically through independent broker-dealers and RIAs. Other large players include American Express Financial Advisers, as well as brokerage firms Salomon Smith Barney and Merrill Lynch. In the intermediary world, one selling point for mutual fund wraps is that they are fee based rather than commission based, so they offer access to no-load funds that might not otherwise be available to the customers of intermediaries.

Although the direct marketing channel historically has shunned advice, a number of fund sponsors have developed mutual fund wrap programs. The largest such program in the direct channel is run by Fidelity Investments, which offers both programs limited to Fidelity funds and programs containing all funds in its mutual fund supermarket. The highest advisory fee for these wrap programs is 1.1% of assets under management (for accounts between $50,000 and $200,000), with substantial discounts for larger accounts. More along the lines of guidance than advice, Vanguard offers a service recommending a portfolio of mutual funds to its investors at a modest fee. But this is a recommendation at one point in time rather than a program for continuing management of a portfolio of mutual funds.

Across the fund industry, wrap accounts have been a significant source of inflows in recent years. As of year-end 2000, mutual fund wraps had assets of nearly $130 billion, which represented an increase of 47% over 1999 levels. Among managed product offerings, however, mutual fund wrap assets fall far short of those in separately managed accounts of individual securities. At the end of 2000, for example, assets were approximately $290 billion in consultant wraps, in which assets are invested in individual securities managed by separate account managers. Another $69 billion in assets were held in rep wrap accounts, where a registered representative selects and monitors individual securities for the client's account.[21]

Separate accounts are popular because of the desire for personalization and tax sensitivity among high-net-worth individuals. For these individuals, outside of their retirement accounts, tax liabilities resulting from the annual distributions paid by mutual funds have become a source of shareholder dissatisfaction. As discussed in Chapter Three, the Investment Company Act and the Internal Revenue Code effectively require mutual funds to pay out to their shareholders each year virtually all capital gains they realize. Funds typically realize capital gains through purchases and sales made in the normal course of portfolio management or, less frequently, when abnormally large shareholder redemptions force a manager to sell securities to meet the demand for cash. In either case, fund shareholders have little control over when they receive taxable distributions, although fund sponsors are increasingly disseminating advance estimates of such distributions to help fund shareholders in tax planning. The mutual fund industry's current solution to this problem—tax-managed funds with low annual distributions of capital gains—has been met with muted enthusiasm among high-net-worth investors, although the industry is supporting a legislative proposal to address part of this problem. In the meantime, many high-net-worth investors have gravitated toward separately managed accounts that hold individual stocks and bonds.

Similar to mutual funds, separate accounts provide investors with a portfolio of securities run by a professional manager. However, separate accounts differ from mutual funds in that the investor's monies are not pooled with those of other investors. Instead, the investor directly owns individual securities such as common stock or bonds (rather than a pro rata share of the fund's portfolio). Accordingly, the investor realizes capital gains only when the stock or bonds in his or her account are actually sold. In addition, supporters of separate accounts maintain that they are customized to the particular needs of the high-net-worth investor. In fact, except for very wealthy customers, most separate accounts are managed according to several models. Every customer in a model portfolio generally owns the same securities, although the customer retains the right to impose reasonable restrictions (e.g., no tobacco stocks).

Separate accounts used to be limited to truly high-net-worth investors. More recently, middle-class investors have gained access to this world through financial advisers and broker-dealers, some of which offer separate management for accounts as small as $25,000. Of course, such separate accounts are managed as clones according to standard models. The latest trend is for separate account management through Internet services, such as Folio*fn*. These services allow investors to construct their own portfolios based on either standard models or criteria selected by the investor (e.g., 20 large-cap and 20 small-cap stocks, each with a price to earnings ratio below 20). It is unclear whether separate accounts offered through the Internet will become popular. More fundamentally, it is unclear whether separate accounts based primarily on standard models will produce investment returns attractive to investors.

2. Smaller account advice   As mutual funds have penetrated an ever-larger segment of the population, investors with smaller accounts are clamoring for advice and guidance as well. For fund sponsors, however, this population presents substantial challenges. Because these investors have smaller account balances, it is not cost-effective for fund sponsors to offer high levels of customized, personalized service. Therefore, to serve this marketplace, fund sponsors have developed one-fund solutions and Internet-based tools.

With the influx of inexperienced investors in the 1990s, mutual fund sponsors emphasized products that were relatively simple and easy to understand. *Asset allocation funds* enable investors to buy one fund that invests across multiple asset classes, including equities, bonds and cash or money market instruments, rather than having to buy a fund from each asset category. Initially, fund sponsors tended to offer a single asset allocation fund that invested in each asset class according to a strict or flexible asset allocation policy. Today, many complexes offer two to four funds with varied allocation across the asset classes in order to provide investors with choices at different levels of risk.

T. Rowe Price's Personal Strategy funds, for example, consist of three offerings designed for varied risk tolerances and investor needs ranging from growth of capital to income. As is true for most such products, the portfolio managers of the Personal Strategy funds may change the mix between stocks and bonds, typically within specified ranges. However, the neutral asset allocation strategy for each of these funds reflects its investment goals. At the conservative end, the income-oriented fund holds roughly 40% in stocks, 40% in bonds and 20% in money market instruments. The most aggressive fund has a neutral mix of 80% stocks and 20% bonds and money market instruments.

Lifestyle funds are even simpler to use than asset allocation funds: they provide not only instant diversification by asset class, but also an asset mix that automatically shifts over time. This automatic shift eliminates the need for investors to change their fund choices as they age or get close to their goals. These products (sometimes structured as funds of funds) are designed for specific time horizons, over which period their asset mix gradually grows more conservative. For example, a lifestyle fund for investors with a 30-year time horizon to retirement would begin with a heavy allocation to stocks, which would gradually be reduced over the 30 years. Lifestyle funds have been marketed to relatively unsophisticated investors in retirement plans as a way to adjust their asset mix automatically to their stage in life.

Technology has provided fund sponsors with an attractive means of offering semi-customized solutions at a moderate cost as well as one-fund solutions. Many fund complex websites provide online asset allocation recommendations based on information about investment goals, time frames and risk tolerances. Such websites also frequently provide tools to screen mutual funds and view what passes for a select list of mutual funds. More sophisticated sites combine the two functionalities by proposing both an asset allocation strategy and recommended funds. Providing these online tools at no or minimal cost is increasingly considered a necessary supporting service for a fund sponsor of any size.

The data requested for these types of tools generally cover a similar range of topics. Investors are asked to create a personal profile that contains information such as date of birth, intended investment time frame, current asset allocation and past experience with various types of investments such as individual stocks or stock funds. These tools also try to assess an investor's risk tolerance by asking questions about the investor's potential response to down markets. For example, a typical question would ask what an investor's response would be to a market drop of 20% in a short-term period. The investor selects a response ranging from, "I would sell," to "I would hold," to "I would buy more." On the basis of the information that the investor enters into the computer, the fund's website provides a recommended asset allocation strategy, and the investor then has the option of receiving specific fund recommendations. Other online planning tools offered by fund complexes include those focused on specific goals such as purchasing a home, funding college or retiring at a certain age.

Third-party researchers, which are not affiliated with fund sponsors, also offer a range of planning tools from very simple calculators that estimate the future worth of an investor's portfolio to more comprehensive asset allocation and fund recommendations. For instance, besides providing financial news, stock quotes and market updates, Yahoo's portal allows investors to enter and track personal portfolios. Yahoo's tax center includes information such as tax rates, tax deadlines and state tax information. It also offers tax forms and provides online worksheets for filing taxes, either individually or with professional assistance. Financial websites such as TheStreet.com offer tools covering several areas of financial planning including investments, taxes and insurance purchases. In most cases, the site provides straightforward calculators combined with educational information. Morningstar runs one of the more robust third-party sites. Its tools not only create a recommended asset allocation and fund portfolio, akin to those recommended on mutual fund complex websites, but they also supply detailed analysis of fund portfolios in areas such as overlap among stock holdings, regional exposure and allocations across investment styles. Paying subscribers to Morningstar's site gain access to additional investment management tools, such as an individualized portfolio diagnosis, which is designed to point out weaknesses in an investor's portfolio and suggest improvements.

C. Needs-Based Marketing

Needs-based marketing seeks to meet particular customer needs with specific products and solutions. This, too, is a technique that fund sponsors are using to break through clutter in the marketplace and enable their products to stand out from the plethora of competitors. Needs-based marketing is an extension of advice-oriented products and services in that it indirectly assists investors by providing methods of achieving their financial goals. One important investor need is retirement savings, which is covered in Chapter Eight. Here we focus on college planning and wealth transfers.

1. College planning   College costs have doubled since 1980, and over the past decade they have increased at more than twice the average rate of U.S. household income, according to the College Board. In recognition of this trend, fund sponsors have offered tools and products to address the need for college planning. These can be viewed as another form of low-end advice.

Among the roster of typical Internet tools, for example, are those that calculate savings needs for college tuition. Typically, an investor enters the current age of the future student, the number of years before college, the number of years the child is expected to be in college and whether tuition is for a private or public institution. These pieces of data are then combined with a forecasted rate of return and college tuition inflation rate to determine the sum needed and the savings necessary to meet this goal. As a next step, some Internet tools then direct customers to information about products available for college funding.

The traditional route to college savings has been via custodial accounts established under the Uniform Transfer to Minors Act (UTMA) or Uniform Gift to Minors Act (UGMA). These acts enable a donor to establish an account on behalf of a minor, with the appointment of a custodian who is charged with managing the assets in a fiscally prudent fashion. The minor actually owns the account's securities and may take possession of them upon adulthood. The primary appeal of UTMA/UGMA accounts is that their income and capital gains generally are taxed at the child's rate, which is typically lower than that of the donor-custodian. However, such accounts do not offer the attraction of tax deferral before payout, in contrast to Education IRAs and Section 529 plans.

Education IRAs offer another solution to the need for college savings, albeit with some limits. These savings vehicles enable married couples with annual income of less than $160,000 and individual taxpayers with annual income less than $110,000 to contribute up to $500 per year toward a child's college education, which will grow tax free until the child reaches 18 years of age. Distributions can also be tax free if the beneficiary's qualified higher education expenses for the year equal or exceed the Education

IRA distribution that year. However, given the significant costs of higher education, the $500 limit and a number of other technical defects rendered the Education IRA virtually useless in the past. Congress made Education IRAs more attractive, effective in 2002, by raising the contribution limit to $2,000 per year and increasing the income eligibility range for married couples to a phase-out range of $190,000 to $220,000, and expanding tax-free distributions to include certain elementary and secondary school expenses.

College savers and fund sponsors alike have welcomed Section 529 plans as a solution that addresses the limitations of UTMA/UGMA accounts and Education IRAs. While state-sponsored prepaid tuition plans have existed since the late 1980s, tax legislation in 1996 and 1997 added a new option. Under Section 529 of the Internal Revenue Code, states may now offer college savings plans, which can be used to fund qualified higher education expenses at any accredited institution (e.g., college, vocational school) in the United States. In contrast to UTMA/UGMA plans, Section 529 plans allow assets to grow tax deferred until withdrawn, at which time the income and capital gains from the account used to pay for qualified higher education expenses are taxed at the child's tax rate for ordinary income. Effective in 2002, Congress went further by declaring that any distribution from a Section 529 plan used to pay for qualified higher educational expenses would be excluded from federal income taxation. In contrast to Education IRAs, every donor may contribute up to $50,000 in a lump sum to a Section 529 plan without becoming subject to gift taxes.

In a Section 529 plan, investors are not permitted to select their own securities, although they may choose from a variety of investment options offered by the plan. Rather, each state is responsible for overseeing the investment management of assets in a Section 529 plan; the states in turn have tapped large financial services providers such as TIAA-CREF, Fidelity Investments, Merrill Lynch and Salomon Smith Barney. Investment portfolios are generally managed conservatively, many using a mix of stock and bond funds that becomes less risky over time through changes to its asset allocation strategy (similar to the concept behind lifestyle funds), and many plans do not permit a contributor to choose the investment portfolio, often assigning a portfolio based on the age of the child. Each distribution channel offers its own approach to managing Section 529 plan assets. For example, within the intermediary channel, Merrill Lynch offers a Section 529 plan that contains 35 portfolios using funds from a range of sponsors. The plan charges a 1.75% annual fee, in part to select the portfolios of funds and in part to compensate the adviser for helping the customer with financial planning. By contrast, no-load firms such as Vanguard (which manages the Iowa plan, for example) uses the firm's own LifeStrategy funds with lower expenses.

2. Wealth transfers   With the increase in investor wealth, fund sponsors are positioning themselves not only to help investors increase their assets, but also to help investors transfer their wealth to the next generation and charities. This has resulted in new programs designed to assist in estate planning and new products intended to facilitate charitable giving.

Many financial firms have long offered trust services for their clients. Most sponsors of large fund complexes own limited-purpose trust companies, which are equipped to provide administrative, custodial and record keeping services as well as professional investment management for fiduciary accounts. In 2000, Charles Schwab took a step toward expanding its client base from smaller financial planner accounts toward larger fiduciary accounts through its acquisition of U.S. Trust, an established wealth manager. This merger allows Schwab to refer high-net-worth clients to U.S. Trust for specialized services such as separate account management as well as estate planning, trust management and private equity. But such referrals may pose a threat to the financial planners and RIAs who offer similar services and are the heaviest users of Schwab's fund supermarket.

Fund sponsors always have offered simple estate planning tools such as UGMA accounts, which allow donors to remove assets from their estates by earmarking them for a minor. Fund sponsors also have supplied educational materials and run seminars on estate planning. More recently, fund sponsors have recognized the importance of estate planning services for retaining their wealthier customers. In addition to offering investments for trusts, many now offer to draw up basic estate plans for a one-time fee. Other fund sponsors are increasing the sophistication of their wealth transfer services by providing higher levels of advice through specially trained phone and branch representatives, as well as through referrals to attorneys and other estate planning specialists.

To facilitate charitable giving, Fidelity Investments started its Charitable Gift Fund in 1992 and has since been joined by competitors such as Vanguard and Schwab. The Fidelity Charitable Gift Fund, with assets of $2.5 billion as of March 2001, remains the largest such fund. Such funds simplify charitable giving by creating what is in essence a foundation geared to middle-class investors. Individuals make irrevocable contributions of cash or appreciated securities to an account at the Charitable Gift Fund, garnering a tax deduction in the year of the gift. At any later time they choose, donors can recommend gifts from their accounts to any qualified charitable organization, subject to a veto by the trustees of the Charitable Gift Fund. Meanwhile, the original contribution is invested in a pool of several mutual funds and managed in a discretionary fashion according to one of several models selected by the donor—for example, growth, equity income or money market pools. Typical fees for investment management, as well as for services such as grant administration and record keeping, hover modestly above 1% of assets, with the cost declining for larger accounts. Donor-advised funds for the intermediary channel have recently been introduced as well by firms such as Eaton Vance. Such funds levy an additional fee that compensates the intermediary for providing advice on charitable giving as part of an overall financial plan.

REVIEW QUESTIONS

1. List and briefly describe five different types of firms in the intermediary channel.
2. What are the advantages and disadvantages of the mutual fund supermarket for a small sponsor of funds?
3. What is account aggregation, and what are the two methods for aggregating accounts?
4. What are the uses and limitations of performance advertising? What is the tension between performance and brand advertising?
5. What is a mutual fund wrap program? How does it differ from a separate account?

6. What are asset allocation funds and lifestyle funds? How are they different?

7. What are 529 college plans and charitable gift funds? Who chooses the underlying funds in these products?

DISCUSSION QUESTIONS

1. How have traditional broker-dealer services evolved in recent years, and what has prompted changes in their sales and service models?

2. What factors have reduced the percentage of new fund sales going to the pure direct distribution channel? Can any of these factors be overcome?

3. Define *open architecture*. Do you think it will increase or decrease in importance to the intermediary and direct distribution channels?

4. Compare and contrast the strategies that mutual fund complexes are using to provide advice to high-net-worth and smaller account clients.

5. What are the pros and cons of various options for college savings?

6. Visit the website of either a large mutual fund complex or a well-known third-party researcher such as those mentioned in the text. Provide an analysis of their online advice and guidance tools.

NOTES

1. Investment Company Institute, *Fact Book*.
2. Bernstein Research, *The State of Money Management in America* (New York: Sanford C. Bernstein & Co., 2000), 20.
3. VIP Forum, *What's in a Name? Building in an Era of Increased Competition* (Washington, D.C.: Corporate Executive Board, 2000), 8.
4. Bernstein Research, 115.
5. Cerulli Associates, *The State of National Full-Service Brokerage Industry* (Boston: Cerulli Associates, 2000), 31.
6. Ibid., 50.
7. Bernstein Research, 115.
8. Ibid., 118.
9. Ibid.
10. Ibid., 128.
11. Cerulli Associates, *The Cerulli Edge: Variable Annuity Issue* (July 2000), 10.
12. R. H. Carey, *The VARDS Report* (Financial Planning Resources, November 2000).
13. Bernstein Research, 127.
14. Ibid., 117.
15. B. Reid, *Perspective: The 1990s: A Decade of Expansion and Change in the U.S. Mutual Fund Industry* (Washington, D.C.: Investment Company Institute, July 2000), 11.
16. Cerulli Associates, *The Cerulli Edge: Variable Annuity Issue*, 4.
17. Reid, *Perspective: The 1990's*, 12.
18. Hill/Holliday with data from Cometitrack.
19. Ibid.
20. Analysis based on data from Strategic Insight.
21. Cerulli Associates, *Q4 2000 Summary* (January 2001), Exhibits 3-4.

····· **CASE STUDY**

Evaluating Strategies for Fund Distribution

Banks have become a significant player in the mutual fund business—as both sellers of fund products and creators of their own proprietary funds. In the 1980s, banks served primarily as selling agents for mutual funds advised by traditional investment management companies. Larger banks established broker-dealers to sell these funds in return for sales commissions and/or 12b-1 fees. Smaller banks sold these funds through the bank itself, which is permitted under federal banking and securities laws. By the 1990s, the larger banks began to create or expand their own line of mutual funds, which were sold through broker-dealer affiliates of the bank. For legal reasons, the underwriter of these funds was required to be an independent securities firm.

This case study is about a middle-size bank, which had recently established a relatively small line of its own propriety funds. The bank also acted as selling agent for a range of third-party funds, advised by traditional fund management companies. The case study involves the efforts of a bank executive in the mid-1990s to think through what the bank's mutual fund strategy should be and how the bank should implement this strategy.

Be prepared to answer the following questions.

Discussion Questions

1. What are the potential benefits to BayBank of entering the mutual fund business? Would entering this business pose a threat to BayBank's traditional banking business?
2. What comparative advantages would BayBank have over traditional fund companies, like Putnam or Fidelity, in developing a mutual fund business? What would be the barriers faced by any bank in successfully entering the mutual fund business?
3. Are there good reasons for BayBank to focus on developing its own full line of mutual funds? What would be the potential drawbacks of this strategy?
4. What would be the advantages of BayBank's focusing exclusively on offering third-party funds? What would be the potential drawbacks of this strategy?
5. What are the alternative strategies (other than those mentioned in questions 3 and 4) that could be pursued by BayBank? Evaluate the pros and cons of each alternative.

Bay Funds*

In early June 1994, Judy Benson, Senior Vice President of BayBank's Investment Management Group (BBIM), was in the process of preparing the 1995–1997 strategic plan for the organization's line of mutual funds. Sixteen months earlier, BayBank had entered the mutual fund business successfully by launching BayFunds, a family of proprietary mutual funds. Now, Benson faced a new set of marketing issues in formulating a growth plan to develop the business further. Foremost among the questions that concerned her were: (i) how to extend the line of funds offered to meet changing economic conditions and (ii) what mix of proprietary and third party funds would be most effective in attracting and retaining customers. As she listened to the latest recording on the 1-800-BAY-FUND line, she was reminded of the many challenges involved in managing this complex business:

> Thank you for calling BayBank. You can call us 24 hours a day. Federal regulations require us to remind you that mutual funds, including BayFunds, are not FDIC-insured, are not deposits or obligation of, or endorsed or guaranteed by, BayBank, and may involve investment risks, including the possible loss of principal. Please select one of the following four choices at any time . . .

Company Background

BayBank, Inc., headquartered in Boston, Massachusetts, was New England's fourth-largest banking organization in 1993 with assets of more than $10 billion. Its predecessor, BayState Corporation, was organized in 1928 as a bank holding company. Through acquisition and branching, BayState emerged as one of the state's leading bank franchises in the mid-1970s, holding an 11% share of Massachusetts' deposits. BayState's decentralized organization was composed of a number of separate banks; each one had a distinctive character and operation within a unique

* Copyright © 1994 by the President and Fellows of Harvard College. Harvard Business School Case 9-595-031. This case was prepared by Jamie Harper and Lisa Klein under the direction of Alvin Silk as the basis for class discussion rather than to illustrate either effective or ineffective handling of an administrative situation. Reprinted by permission of *Harvard Business School Review.* From, "BayFunds," by Alvin Silk, Lisa Klein, and Jamie Harper. Copyright © 1984 by the Harvard Business School Publishing Corporation; all rights reserved.

marketplace. Under William M. Crozier, Jr., chairman and chief executive officer since 1974, BayState underwent significant change. Bank mergers, a consolidation of data processing and other major operations, and new unified advertising resulted in a substantial increase in the organization's operating efficiency. In 1976, BayState adopted the BayBank name, highlighting its recent transformation and newly formed corporate identity.[1]

Crozier continued to build and strengthen BayBank's regional presence thereafter, using technology, for example, to advance the bank's retail distribution network. In the 1980s, BayBank launched one of the nation's most successful electronic banking programs that involved installing over a thousand automatic teller machines (ATMs) throughout the region. The ubiquitous green and blue logo reinforced BayBank's commitment to banking with a widely recognized symbol for convenient customer service.

In 1993, BayBank provided a full-range of commercial banking services to retail and corporate customers. The bank's extensive distribution system featured 201 full-service branches, a network of over 1,000 ATMs, and a 24-hour customer sales and service center (SCC) accessible by telephone. In 1993, BayBank's share of checking/NOW accounts in Eastern Massachusetts was 29%, almost three times that of the nearest competitor. Over 33% of the

households in Massachusetts maintained at least one account with BayBank. Eighteen percent of households indicated in a recent survey that BayBank was their primary bank. Exhibit 1 provides a comparison of BayBank's customers with those of other Massachusetts banks. BayBank's retail bank penetration led all other banks in Massachusetts. Shawmut National Corporation and Fleet Financial ranked second behind BayBank, each with a 17% market share; Bank of Boston held a 13% market share. The latter three banks, however, were considered strong competitors of BayBank given their larger asset bases, broad distribution systems throughout the region, and substantial financial resources.

Over 750,000 Massachusetts households had a BayBank relationship. Core deposits included transaction accounts (demand, NOW, savings), money market deposit accounts (MMDAs), and certificates of deposit (CDs). BayBank's rate of total deposit balance growth had decreased since 1988, partially due to the New England recession that was characterized by high unemployment and falling interest rates. This environment led customers to seek higher-yielding alternatives to bank deposit accounts, such as mutual funds (see Exhibit 2).

BayBank employed approximately 5,600 people (full-time equivalents) at year-end 1993. The organization's cul-

EXHIBIT 1

1993 Demographic profiles of customers of various Massachusetts banks

	State of Massachusetts	BayBank	Bank of Boston	Shawmut	Fleet	Thrifts	Other Commercial Banks
Median age	39	35	41	41	39	40	42
Median income	$35,000	$41,000	$40,000	$33,000	$33,000	$33,000	$38,000
Percent with college education or greater	42%	64%	51%	39%	37%	35%	36%
Percent with professional/ managerial occupations	47%	60%	47%	42%	48%	43%	45%
Number in sample citing primary bank [a]	3,939 [b]	699	205	266	306	1,285	330

Source: Company Records. U.S. Bureau of the Census, Census of Population, General Population Characteristics, United States (1990 CP-1-1), as reported in *Statistical Abstracts of the United States 1993*, Table 69.

a. 848 Households cited either no primary banking relationship or one of the following: other credit union, other finance company, other insurance company, mutual fund, out of state bank, or brokerage company.

b. There were approximately 2.3 million households in the state of Massachusetts in 1993—15% of which had annual household incomes of more than $75,000.

ture was one where setting goals and striving to meet them were highly valued and regularly practiced. BayBank's organizational structure consisted of three full-service commercial banks in Massachusetts and Connecticut and a number of subsidiaries that provided operational support. BayBank Investment Management, Inc. (BBIM) was incorporated and registered as an investment adviser with the Securities and Exchange Commission in the mid 1980s, but the predecessor division had been providing investment management advice to trust customers of the banking subsidiaries of BayBank for over 60 years. Currently, BBIM offered a range of investment products and services to a diverse group of corporate, municipal, and personal trust customers. Although BBIM had achieved a favorable long-term performance record, BayBank's investment and trust business had not achieved as strong a position as its retail bank.

Mutual Fund Industry

A mutual fund was an investment vehicle that pooled money from many individuals and organizations and typically invested that money jointly in stocks, bonds, or money market securities. Each day, the fund calculated the market value of the stocks in its portfolio. That total, divided by the number of outstanding shares in the mutual fund, yielded the net asset value (NAV) per share, which

measured how much each share of a mutual fund was worth. Mutual funds involved risk—their NAV could fluctuate daily as a result of market activity, portfolio trading, or changes in the interest rate or economic outlook. Mutual fund managers decide when to buy, sell, and hold investments in the securities that comprised the funds. The limitations on the scope of a fund manager's decision making authority varied and were governed by the investment guidelines for each mutual fund.

Mutual funds offered the individual investor several advantages over individual stock or bond market investments: professional fund management, minimized risk through diversification, liquidity, and fair pricing.[2] For such services, most mutual fund companies charged shareholders a management fee, typically 1% of assets under management; fees for a money market mutual fund were substantially lower than for an international equity fund. Many funds also could charge annual "12b-1" fees, ranging from 0.05% to 0.75% of assets per year to cover marketing expenses and sales "loads," up to 8.5%, which were one-time fees measured as a percentage of the initial investment or fund withdrawals, used to cover commissions to sales agents.[3] Mutual funds were also used by institutional investors (for example, in the investment of excess operating cash balances) and for defined contribution plans, such as the 401(k)s.

EXHIBIT 2

BayBank's deposit balance, 1989–1994

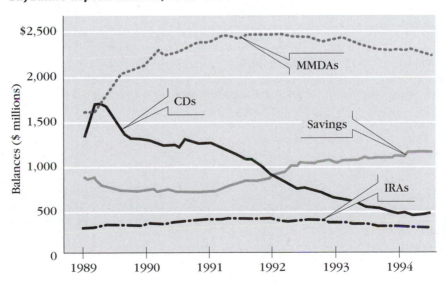

In 1993, there were about 4,500 mutual funds sold in the United States. The industry was highly concentrated with roughly 15 mutual fund complexes managing more than half of all mutual fund assets (see Exhibit 3). Well-established families of funds with familiar brand names were Fidelity Investments, Putnam, Franklin/Templeton, Vanguard, T. Rowe Price, and Dreyfus. Fidelity alone managed more than $200 billion, while Vanguard was well known as the low cost provider. These mutual fund companies were particularly strong in customer prospecting and many had established powerful reputations for successful funds management. Mutual fund complexes whose funds were sold directly (as opposed to the broker-dealer channel)—principally by print advertising and direct mail—had reached an effective saturation point in capturing additional market share and were looking for alternative distribution channels. Similarly, funds that relied on the broker-dealer network also were seeking to expand their distribution channels, since many investors were uncomfortable in receiving investment advice from a broker. In short, the advisory aspects of the distribution business—assessing customers' financial needs and risk tolerance, and the selecting, recommending, and reviewing investment

choices—represented an area of opportunity which currently was not being fully exploited by the existing system.

Achieving economies of both scale and scope was critical for fund performance and growth. Large funds could realize scale economies by distributing the marketing, service, and operation expenses over an extensive asset base. The scope advantages of offering an extensive product line of funds were driven by consumer preferences for a variety of funds to satisfy individual investment diversification goals. Industry leaders were aggressively developing additional support services for their product families in an effort to attract new customers as well as to retain existing ones.[4]

Mutual funds could be classified into three broad categories: money market, bond/fixed-income funds, and equity funds. *Money market funds* included some of the most conservative noninsured investments, since any money market mutual fund had to adhere to maximum fund maturity and quality standards. *Income funds* typically sought current income, as opposed to total return, and were typically used by individuals to supplement other sources of income. *Equity funds,* on the other hand, sought long-term growth and were typically positioned to

EXHIBIT 3

Overview of leading mutual fund companies

Mutual Fund Management Company	Parent Company	1993 Rank	1993 Assets ($ billion)	1992 Rank	1992 Assets ($ billion)
Fidelity	FMR Corporation	1	237	1	164
Vanguard	Vanguard Group	2	130	3	93
Merrill Lynch	Merrill Lynch & Co., Inc.	3	117	2	108
Capital Research	Primerica	4	101	6	62
Franklin/Templeton [a]	Franklin/Templeton Group	5	92	5	65
Dreyfus [b]	Dreyfus Corp.	6	74	4	76
Federated [c]	Federated Investors	7	68	9	45
Dean Witter InterCapital [d]	Dean Witter	8	59	7	53
Putnam	Marsh & McClennan Co., Inc.	9	59	11	41
Prudential	Prudential Insurance Co. of America	10	52	12	34

Source: Company records, *Hoover's Handbook of American Business 1994* (Austin, Texas: The Reference Press, 1993), "The Power of Mutual Funds," *Business Week,* January 18, 1993, p. 64; Timothy Middleton, "No Place Like Home," *Newsday,* March 14, 1994, p. 29.
a. 1992 ranking is for Franklin only, prior to late 1992 merger with Templeton.
b. Merged with Mellon Bank in 1993.
c. Sold by Aetna Life and Casualty in 1989 to management.
d. Spun off from Sears Roebuck, Inc., in 1993.

be used by individuals to meet long-term goals such as funding retirement or children's education. Within each of these three fund groups, there were several subcategories of fund types and each one had a specific investment objective. Well-established mutual fund companies offered extensive product lines that encompassed many of these sub-categories, including, for example, growth, asset allocation, and international coverage.

Demand for mutual funds increased dramatically during the 1980s. Assets grew at a rate of 17% compounded annually, as declining short-term interest rates motivated investors to move their financial resources out of bank deposits and into mutual funds, in search of higher yields.[5] By 1990, mutual funds had become the nation's third largest financial institution in terms of assets, trailing only commercial banks and life insurance companies. In 1993, total assets of mutual funds (including institutional assets) were roughly $2 trillion with 38% of assets in bond and income funds, 33% in equity funds, and 29% in money market funds. By 2000, the total mutual fund industry was projected to reach $3.6 trillion. Retirement plan assets were identified as one of the primary drivers of future industry growth. Mutual funds were expected to grow faster than the overall economy in the 1990s as a result of an anticipated increase in the savings rate and the entrance of the baby boomer generation into peak earning years.[6]

Bank Mutual Funds

Commercial banks entered the retail mutual fund market in earnest during the late 1980s. A fall-off in the growth rate of deposit balances and weak loan demand forced banks to seek alternative sources of income. Offering mutual funds enabled banks to retain customers who might otherwise depart in search of higher-yielding products. It also provided the banks with a new way to generate fee income through providing investment advice and selling funds.[7]

Initially, banks served only as a distribution channel for third-party funds. These funds were managed and marketed by mutual fund companies such as Fidelity or Putnam. Banks received a substantial part of the up-front sales load as compensation for selling the funds, as well as "trailer" income for retaining assets in the fund. In the early 1990s, banks began to take on the role of investment advisers for their own "proprietary" mutual funds. (An alternative strategy was to "private label" a fund. An outside fund company would manage and provide all support services, but a fund or class of an existing fund was created

with a bank's own "brand name.") Thus, banks were offering both proprietary and third-party funds. Most banks started their own funds with converted trust assets. Proprietary bank funds were typically small and included only the three broad categories of funds—money market, bond, and equity portfolios. Most banks carried third-party funds because they enabled them to offer more "sophisticated" types of mutual funds to meet diverse customer needs, reinforced a bank's claim to objectivity in managing customers' investment goals, and enhanced profitability. Moreover, the brand names of third-party funds attracted bank customers who were seeking a convenient and simple way to invest in mutual funds while also satisfying their banking needs. Although third-party funds provided banks with a substantial source of fee income though sales loads, overall program profitability depended in part on whether the proprietary funds were sold on a load or no-load basis. Exhibit 4 provides an overview of several of Boston's bank fund families.

In 1993, one-third of *all* mutual funds were available through at least one channel within a bank, while banks accounted for 13% of all fund sales. Roughly 100 banks in the United States together sold over 1,000 proprietary funds. Bank of America managed the leading family of proprietary bank funds which consisted of 24 classes of funds and $10.4 billion in assets in 1993. Total bank-managed assets invested in mutual funds were $216 billion in 1993 (11% of the total mutual fund market), up 34% from the preceding year. Money market funds comprised the majority of these assets (67%) while equity funds held a minority share (13%). The skew toward money market funds was driven by the heavy institutional clientele base of most bank proprietary funds. Many individual customers also favored money market funds because, like CDs, these portfolios were relatively safe investments whose value tended to be stable. Total proprietary fund assets were expected to grow to $400 billion by 2000.

Banks moving into the mutual funds business naturally looked to their existing customer base as their principal source of prospects. However, the majority of bank depositors tended to be unsophisticated about making investments. Roughly 75% of bank depositors had never purchased an investment product. As a result, they were often attracted to conservative, low risk funds. Bank customers who had some investment experience represented a particularly attractive target opportunity. However, these investors also were less likely to move funds out of the hands of existing managers. A 1988 study by the

EXHIBIT 4

Proprietary fund families offered by Boston's leading banks, 1993

	BayBank, Inc.	Fleet Financial Group	Bank of Boston	Shawmut
BHC assets ($ billions)	$10.10	$47.90	$40.60	$27.20
Deposits ($ billions)	8.8	31.1	24.1	15.2
No. branches in Massachusetts	200	177	188	159
Total no. branches in New England (as of 12/93)	202	398	326	491
Proprietary fund family	BayFunds	Galaxy Funds	1784 Funds	Shawmut Funds
Date funds introduced	1991	1990	1993	1993
No. funds	6	17	8	9
Total fund assets ($ millions as of 3/31/94)	$1,240	$4,154	$844	$1,060
Investment advisory fees ($ millions 1993)	2.8	16.3	N/A	3.5
Loads	None	None	None	Front-end for equity funds
Initial investment	$2,500	$2,500	$2,500	$2,500
Product mix				
Bond	19%	54%	21%	22%
Stock	9%	22%	13%	25%
Money market	72%	21%	65%	53%
Blend	0%	3%	1%	0%
No. Third-party funds	16%	N/A	N/A	12%

Source: Lipper Analytical Services, company records.

Investment Company Institute (ICI) found that 80% of mutual fund buyers surveyed used only one distribution channel for three-fourths of their mutual fund purchases, suggesting that consumers had stable preferences for methods of investing in mutual funds.[8] A recent study conducted by Fidelity Investments found that 32% of investors who already owned funds were likely to buy funds from their own banks.[9]

Bank mutual funds could offer a number of potential advantages to consumers:

Consumer Preferences	*Bank Service*
One stop shopping	Bundled services
Simplified money management	Personal service
Face-to-face contact	Heritage as fiduciary, conservative
Reduced risk through diversification	Informed guidance
Simplified purchasing process	Ongoing client communications
Guidance after purchase	Local presence

Banks that sold their own line of mutual funds were often criticized for their seeming lack of investment knowledge and experience. How would banks respond to a major downturn in the stock market? Federal regulators were also concerned that selling uninsured products on the banking floor and/or under the aegis of a bank could be confusing to consumers. Unlike traditional bank products, such as savings accounts and CDs, mutual funds were not covered by the Federal Deposit Insurance Corporation (FDIC). Furthermore, many banks used their own names or similar names to identify or brand their proprietary funds. This practice was one which those concerned about consumer protection believed might mislead customers and create an erroneous impression that their principal was protected by the FDIC or the bank.

The total mutual fund market in Massachusetts was strong among the state's households with an 11% penetration for money market mutual funds and 16% penetration for other mutual funds. This rate was greater than the national average, a reflection of the fact that Massachusetts had a higher than average percentage of its population earning more than $75,000 per year. The first mutual fund was started in Boston in 1929. Since then, the city had become a major center for mutual fund sales. Competition was fierce among Boston's leading fund companies: Fidelity Investments, Putnam, Eaton Vance, Colonial, Scudder, Pioneer, Keystone, and Mass Financial Services. By mid-1993, the four major banking organizations in New England had all introduced proprietary mutual funds. Fleet was the largest local competitor. Its Galaxy fund family, introduced in 1986, contained 15 funds and had over $3 billion in assets. Local banks considered their toughest competition to come from the Boston-based mutual fund companies, particularly when they were distributed as third-party funds along with a bank's own proprietary and private label funds.

Regulatory Environment

As banks dramatically expanded their brokerage and investment advisory activities, they faced increasing regulatory scrutiny from both federal banking agencies and Congress. However, no branch of the Federal Government had yet obtained jurisdiction over bank sales of uninsured investments. Banks that offered mutual funds, unlike brokerage firms and investment advisory services, were not required to register with the Securities and Exchange Commission (SEC). Moreover, banks were not subjected to either the registration and reporting requirements or the sales practice rules contained in the Federal securities laws.[10] Nonetheless, an investment adviser to a mutual fund (whether a bank, or a nonblank subsidiary such a BBIM) was subject to the SEC's governance. Accordingly, the SEC closely monitored banks' marketing of proprietary mutual funds and the National Association of Securities Dealers (NASD) had to approve certain types of advertising and sales literature for fund programs.

In early 1994, the federal regulatory agencies for banks and thrift institutions first issued joint guidelines on bank retail sales of mutual funds and other nondeposit investment products.[11] The guidelines outlined the steps banks should take in marketing their mutual fund products in order to minimize the potential for customer confusion over the risks they incurred when investing in these noninsured investment vehicles. Specifically, they contained explicit rules on the content, form, and timing of disclosures; advertising claims; the physical setting in which funds could be sold; and the qualifications, training, and compensation of personnel involved in making recommendations or referrals relative to the sale of mutual funds. The most stringent rules concerned the use of conspicuous verbal and written disclosures when selling, advertising, or otherwise marketing nondeposit investment products to retail customers.

Several Congressional representatives considered the banking agencies' guidelines to be insufficient, and introduced bills to regulate bank sales of mutual funds and other nondeposit investment products. In October 1993, Henry Gonzales, Chairman of the House of Representatives' Banking Committee, proposed legislation (the "Depository Institution Retail Investment Sales and Disclosure Act") that would transform several of the agency guidelines into enforceable laws and at the same time, make others even more restrictive. For example, the Gonzales bill would prevent any bank from using its name or logo (or a "similar" one) for its mutual funds and prohibit nonlicensed bank employees from receiving any compensation for customer referrals. In November 1993, John Dingell, Chairman of the Senate Subcommittee on Oversight and Investigations, introduced the "Securities Regulatory Equality Act of 1993." That bill sought to require that banks engaged in securities activities register with the SEC as a broker-dealer and be subject to the securities laws and regulations like other participants in the securities business. If passed, the bill would, among other things, force banks to make all proprietary fund sales through licensed investment professionals.

Currently, branch sales staffs were allowed to sell mutual funds, although few did. Certain programs, like BayBank's, allowed nonlicensed bank personnel to make customers aware of the availability of mutual funds, to "make available" (rather than proactively sell) money market mutual funds and to refer them to the bank's licensed personnel. However, the bill, if passed, would restrict nonlicensed bank personnel to making only referrals. Although Congress was not expected to act on either of these bills in 1994, it was likely that, in the longer term, pressure for increased consumer protection would lead to some strengthening of current regulations.

Industry Marketing Research

In recent years, a number of studies had been undertaken to explore consumer decision-making with respect to investments. This research helped to expand industry understanding of the investment-decision process. Earlier views were based primarily on standard economic models which emphasized a simple trade-off between risk and return. However, subsequent research indicated that these factors alone did not fully explain the variation in investment decisions observed.

A national consumer telephone survey conducted in 1992 examined attitudes toward the mutual fund investment decision, focusing on the selection criteria and information sources used by consumers in choosing among mutual funds.[12] As Exhibit 5 indicates, the majority of investors surveyed rated published performance rankings as both the most important information source and the principal selection criterion used in allocating their investment dollars. Investors tended to view information about a fund's relative historical performance as a "proxy for antic-

EXHIBIT 5

Importance of information sources and selection criteria in mutual fund investment decisions

Question: Please rate the importance of the following nine information sources when considering a mutual fund investment:

Information Source	Mean Rating [a]	Std. Deviation
Published performance rankings	4.57	0.73
Advertising	3.13	1.21
Commission-based financial advisers	2.60	1.59
Seminars	1.89	1.34
Recommendations of friends/family	1.74	1.05
Recommendations of business associates	1.56	0.85
Fee-based financial advisers	1.34	0.91
Books	1.17	0.63
Direct mail	1.11	0.42

Question: Please rate the importance of the following nine selection criteria in selecting a mutual fund investment:

Selection Criteria	Mean Rating	Std. Deviation
Investment performance track record	4.62	0.64
Fund manager reputation	4.00	0.77
Number of funds in family	3.95	1.06
Responsiveness to inquiries	2.30	1.08
Management fees	2.28	1.31
Investment management style	1.68	1.12
Additional services offered	1.38	0.92
Confidentiality	1.35	0.83
Community service record	1.09	0.48

Source: Adapted from Noel Capon, Gavan J. Fitzsimons, and Russ Alan Price, *An Individual Level Analysis of the Mutual Fund Industry,* Unpublished Working Paper, Columbia University, (1992). Table 1. Statistics reported above are derived from a national sample of 3,386 households contacted via telephone in March 1991.
a. Rated on 5-point scale: 1 = not at all important; 5 = extremely important

EXHIBIT 6

Investor groupings based on information sources and selection criteria

Information Source Groups	Selection Criteria Groups			
	Price-Insensitive Performance	Service-Substance	Price-Sensitive Performance	Totals
Commission-based advisees	32%[a]	1%	3%	37%
Advertising-driven investors	18%	0%	6%	24%
Knowledge-based investors	2%	4%	1%	8%
Ranking-only investors	17%	0%	14%	32%
Totals	70%	5%	25%	

Groups	Criteria for Assignment
Based on information source importance	
Commission-based advisees:	Ranked commission-based financial advisers as most important information source, on par with published performance. Advertising also ranked highly.
Advertising-driven investors:	Ranked advertising as high in importance as published rankings. Friends and family also very high.
Knowledge-based investors:	Ranked fee-based advisers as most important next to published rankings. Least reliant on advertising.
Ranking-only investors:	Published performance rankings are the most important source.
Based on selection criteria	
Price-insensitive performance:	Rankings close to sample mean, but less concern for management fees and responsiveness.
Service-substance:	Ranked responsiveness, management style, and confidentiality very high and track record lower than mean.
Price-sensitive performance:	Ranked track record, scope, management fees, and responsiveness very high.

Source: Adapted from Noel Capon, Gavan J. Fitzsimons, and Russ Alan Prince, *An Individual Level Analysis of the Mutual Fund Industry,* Unpublished Working Paper, Columbia University, (1992), Table 4.
a. Cell entries are the percentages of a national sample of 3,386 households classified into each of the subgroups indicated.

ipated future return."[13] Classifying investors on the basis of both the selection criteria and information sources used led to the segmentation scheme shown in Exhibit 6.

However, evidence from a recent empirical study examining investment behavior suggests that consumer response to past performance is asymmetrical. The 20-year study of 690 equity mutual funds found that while exceptionally high performing funds attracted large inflows of new money, poorly performing funds did not suffer from a similar investment outflow. In short, there was a great deal of inertia in the movement of funds. That is, consumers appeared to be hesitant to reallocate their moneys, once the initial investment decision was made. In addition, the study found that demand for specific funds was sensitive to fee

levels and, even more strongly, to the support services offered.[14]

BayFunds

In the early 1990s, under the leadership of William M. Crozier, Jr., Chairman of BayBank, and Jack Arena, Vice Chairman of BayBank (who was responsible for the entire Investment Services Group at BayBank, including BBIM, mutual funds, trust, private banking, and Capital Markets), BayBank began investigating the possibility of entering the mutual funds market. Several factors influenced the bank's decision to move forward. BayBank wanted to take advantage of the growing mutual fund market and the increasing recognition by customers that existing bank products alone would not allow them to build their savings sufficiently to satisfy long-term investment goals. Aware of the success other banks had experienced with mutual funds, BayBank believed that by also offering such funds, it could fill certain gaps in its overall product line and create cross-selling opportunities. Mutual funds could generate additional revenues from existing bank customers and aid in overall customer retention. They also offered long-term profit potential from earnings on fund sales and investment advisory services. The critical objectives for BayBank funds were:

1. **To leverage the BayBank franchise** The characteristics of BayBank's existing customer base closely resembled those of the typical mutual fund customer. Perceived as a stable institution with leading-edge service, BayBank believed it had the kind of trustworthy reputation customers valued most in a mutual fund provider.

2. **To increase fee income** Mature mutual funds had attractive gross contribution margins, ranging from 60% to 70%. They could also become a powerful vehicle for retaining customers who were eager to move their financial assets out of bank deposits.

3. **To provide an off balance sheet alternative for gathering the investment funds of retail customers** The mutual fund product line could allow BayBank to capture and retain the investment funds of retail customers who were becoming more sensitive about the interest rate environment and were seeking alternatives to traditional bank products.

In August 1991, BayBank introduced its first proprietary mutual fund, the BayFunds Money Market Portfolio, to its trust customers. Then, in February and March 1993, it rolled out BayFunds, a family of no-load funds, to the institutional and retail markets, respectively. The family included five proprietary funds and one private label fund, which covered the three broad categories of funds: three money market portfolios (one of which was a private label), two bond funds, and one equity portfolio. Also included in the new line of mutual fund products were 11 specialized third-party funds. The minimum investment required to open a BayFunds account was $2,500, although in order to invest through a BayBank IRA, only $500 was needed. Additional investments could be made in $100 increments.

The organization had invested in excess of five million dollars to develop and launch BayFunds. The startup costs included: systems development, training, marketing, advertising, legal expenses, and the building of a comprehensive compliance infrastructure. BayBank projected that its mutual fund business would break even on a cumulative basis by year three and be solidly in the black by year five.

The project represented a major effort within BayBank as it involved coordination among many different areas of the bank. Approximately 65 BayBank employees worked full time on BayFunds, most of whom had been hired specifically to support the initiative, including a sales force, a compliance group, and administrative support personnel. Approximately 3,000 other BayBank employees were also involved in the program. The operation of BayFunds required a complex organization structure. Exhibit 7 presents the BayFunds' organizational chart. Two divisions of BayBank played key roles in BayFunds. BBIM served as the funds' investment adviser while BayBank Systems, Inc. (BBIS) functioned as their shareholder-servicing agent.[15] In addition, Federated Management served as investment manager for the private label money market mutual fund.

Research on Demand for BayFunds

In the spring of 1992, BayBank commissioned a marketing research study to assess the demand for BayFunds. Telephone interviews with 700 BayBank retail CD and MMDA customers and 200 non-BayBank CD and MMDA customers were conducted in March and April 1992.[16] Data were collected on several issues, such as customers' attitudes toward BayFunds' service and delivery capabilities, third-party funds, and investment risk (see Exhibit 8). The study confirmed that BayBank's customer base represented an excellent potential market for mutual funds. Results suggested that 5%–25% of BayBank's CD and MMDA customers would be interested in BayFunds. While 26% of those surveyed already owned at least one type of mutual fund, approximately 40% said they would be either "very likely" or "somewhat likely" to invest in a BayBank money market, bond, or stock mutual fund in the future. When asked the reasons for not investing in one of the three types of BayFunds, the most frequently cited reason was satisfaction with one's existing investment portfolio mix. In addition, the study, combined with previous marketing research, suggested a preliminary segmentation of the target market for BayFunds.

BayBank identified as its primary retail target market those BayBank customers with household incomes over

EXHIBIT 7

BayFunds organizational structure

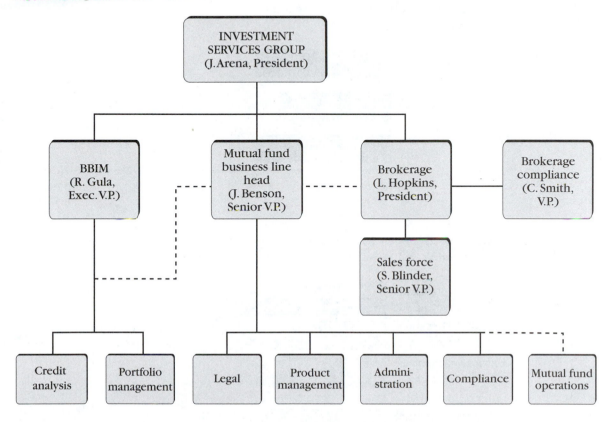

$75,000 ("affluent customers"), with emphasis on those between ages 35 and 54. BayBank already had about 39% of this "affluent customer" segment in Massachusetts as customers—the highest market share of any commercial bank in Massachusetts. The segment of the total population accounted for 79% of all mutual fund assets nationally. Over 40% of these target customers surveyed planned to open a new mutual fund account or make an additional purchase within the next 12 months. These customers held an average of $130,000 in mutual fund assets which generated $750 in annual mutual fund revenue.

BayBank customers with incomes between $50,000 and $75,000 were classified as the secondary retail target market. In this second group, customers below age 40, the "emerging affluent," were identified as being an especially high potential sub-group, as they were expected to move into the primary target market as they grew older and became wealthier. Non-BayBank customers in these demo-

graphic groups and current BayBank small-business customers were also identified as important markets.

BayBank initially estimated the total retail market for BayFunds in Massachusetts to be roughly 150,000–220,000 BayBank customers and 450,000–600,000 non-BayBank customers. The former figures included 135,000 BayBank customers in the primary "affluent" target group (representing 18.1% of BayBank checking customers) and 71,000 in the secondary "emerging affluent" group (representing 9.5% of BayBank checking customers). The latter figures for non-BayBank customers were based on estimates of the potential penetration of the "affluent" and "emerging affluent" customers in Massachusetts who did not currently have BayBank relationships.

Product Line

BayBank offered its retail customers a product line that covered the three major categories of mutual funds: money

EXHIBIT 8

Likelihood of Investing in Various Types of BayBank Mutual Funds if Yield Were Comparable to Industry Average

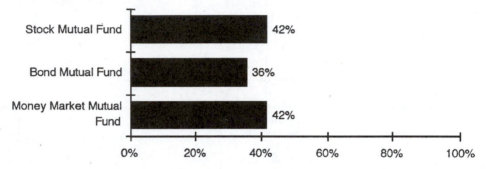

Stock Mutual Fund — 42%
Bond Mutual Fund — 36%
Money Market Mutual Fund — 42%

Effect of Different Service Enhancements on Likelihood of Investing in BayBank Mutual Funds

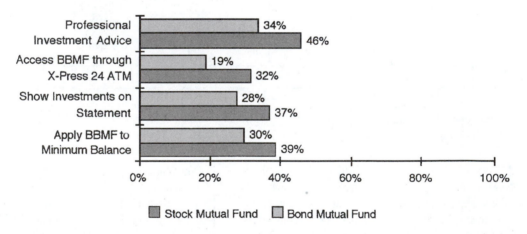

Professional Investment Advice — 34% / 46%
Access BBMF through X-Press 24 ATM — 19% / 32%
Show Investments on Statement — 28% / 37%
Apply BBMF to Minimum Balance — 30% / 39%

■ Stock Mutual Fund   □ Bond Mutual Fund

market, bond/fixed-income, and equity. The BayFunds product line was designed to meet a variety of consumers' financial goals, including regular monthly income, retirement investment, tax-free investment, and long-term capital growth (see Table A).

Exhibit 9 describes the investment objectives and anticipated customer profile for each of the six BayFunds. Combined, the six funds started with roughly $750 million in assets. Reaching a critical mass of $100 million per fund in invested capital soon after the launch was essential to profitability. BayBank's existing Money Market Portfolio and the Massachusetts Tax-Exempt Money Market Portfolio

exceeded the threshold level. Seed capital for the remaining four funds was drawn from several different existing pools of bank assets that were converted concurrent with the funds' launch.

"BayFunds" was selected as the name for BayBank's line of proprietary funds to foster an association between the bank and the funds and thereby leverage the positive image and reputation that BayBank had developed with respect to financial strength and convenience. BayBank took several steps to minimize the risk that the similarity of the bank and fund names might be a source of customer confusion over FDIC insurance of the funds:

TABLE A

BayBanks' proprietary funds

BayFunds	Fund Type	Primary Fund Objective
Money Market Portfolio	Money Market	Stability of principal
U.S. Treasury Money Market Portfolio	Money Market	Stability of principal
Massachusetts Tax-Exempt Money Market Portfolio[17]	Money Market	Stability of principal
Short Term Yield Portfolio	Bond	Current income consistent with preservation of capital
Bond Portfolio	Bond	Current income and capital appreciation
Equity Portfolio	Equity	Long-term capital appreciation

- Customers were asked to sign an acknowledgment of understanding at account opening that BayFunds were not federally insured;
- All literature and advertising disclosed that BayFunds were not FDIC insured;[18] and
- Comprehensive training was given to both the branch staff and investment specialists.

The effectiveness of these programs was assessed in a 1994 study in which BayBank surveyed 358 of its BayFunds customers to establish whether they correctly understood the rules, regulations, and risks surrounding its proprietary fund family. The results indicated that BayFunds customers had a high level of understanding of the risks associated with mutual funds: 82% of respondents indicated that their BayFunds investment was not FDIC-insured while 72% of respondents reported that all mutual funds—regardless of who offered them—were not covered by the FDIC.

BayBank intended to employ the BayFunds name with all its proprietary funds. Research by ICI indicated that, overwhelmingly, new mutual fund customers stay with one family of funds, typically the one in which they initially invested. Although such umbrella branding was permitted under existing regulations, federal legislation which would prevent the use of either identical or similar names by banks for their mutual fund families was under consideration.

In addition to BayFunds, at inception BayBank also marketed 11 complementary third-party funds, each with a distinct investment objective. As the mutual fund business has developed, BayBank has introduced 5 additional third-party funds to broaden its product line and meet the more specialized investment objectives of some of its target customers. Also, the third-party funds carried well-established

names including: Putnam (10), Kemper Financial Services (4), and Eaton Vance (2). Descriptions for the 16 third-party funds BayBank offered are given in Exhibit 10. Consumer research indicated that roughly 35%–50% of BayBank's customers (and 50%–60% of the bank's primary target customer group) would be interested in investing in third-party funds through BayBank.

BayBank offered several services to enhance the attractiveness of the BayFunds product line. First, BayFunds were available as companion products to various checking accounts. In order to facilitate the purchase and redemption of funds, customers could transfer money between the mutual funds and their deposit accounts. Relationship pricing was offered with one high-end checking account, BayPlus, which allowed customers to combine holdings in mutual funds and BayPlus accounts to satisfy minimum balances for all accounts. Second, depositors received a consolidated monthly statement summarizing BayBank checking and savings information along with BayFunds investment activity. BayFund shareholders also had access to 24-hour service, seven days a week, available through a toll-free number (1-800-BAY-FUND). By 1996, BayBank also contemplated using its ATM network to allow customers to perform certain BayFunds transactions.

Pricing

BayFunds' shareholders were charged an investment advisory fee to cover the management costs of the fund. Measured as a percentage of assets under management, this fee ranged from 0.20% and 0.70% based on the nature and complexity of each fund, with money market funds having the lowest fees. BayFunds retail customers were also charged a 0.25% shareholder servicing fee that covered all retail processing and statementing costs. Sales loads and

EXHIBIT 9

BayBank proprietary mutual fund portfolio

	Fund Objective	Customer Appeal
STABLE NET ASSET VALUE		
Money Market Portfolio	Seeks high current yields by investing in a wide range of money market instruments, including commercial paper, bank CDs, obligations issued by the U.S. Government and its agencies, and repurchase agreements. Average maturity of the portfolio cannot exceed 90 days.[a]	Savings vehicle, liquidity for emergencies, expected expenses (i.e. tax payment, down payment for auto, home), income, with no fluctuation in principal while earning a competitive yield.
BayFunds Shares— MA Municipal Cash Trust	Seeks a high level of income exempt from federal and Massachusetts taxes by investing in money market securities issued by the State of Massachusetts and its local governments. Average maturity of the portfolio cannot exceed 90 days.[a]	Investors partly concerned with federal and Massachusetts taxes who are seeking a savings vehicle and liquidity with no fluctuation in principal.
U.S. Treasury Money Market Portfolio	Seeks a high level of income by investing in U.S. Treasury and agency obligations, for which the repayment of principal and interest is guaranteed, as well as repurchase agreements backed by such obligations. Average maturity of the portfolio cannot exceed 90 days.[a]	Investors who are seeking safety associated with short-term U.S. Treasury securities, liquidity of a money market fund, and no fluctuation of principal.
FLUCTUATING NET ASSET VALUE		
Short Term Yield Portfolio	Seeks a higher yield than a money market account while maintaining a relatively steady NAV. Invests in U.S. Treasury and federal agency obligations, high quality corporate debt obligations, bank CDs, commercial paper, and repurchase agreements. Average maturity of the portfolio is approximately one to two years but cannot exceed three years.	Investors seeking higher yields than bank CDs and willing to accept modest fluctuations in NAV.
Bond Portfolio	Seeks to provide current income and capital appreciation while applying conservative investment standards. Invests in U.S. Treasury, federal agency, investment grade corporate debt instruments, and repurchase agreements. Average maturity of the portfolio cannot exceed 12 years; but depending on market conditions, may have a much shorter maturity.	Investors seeking high current income to provide for current expenses. May also be appropriate as a conservative long-term savings vehicle. Investors must be willing to accept fluctuating NAV.
Equity Portfolio	Seeks to provide long-term capital appreciation and to produce competitive performance rankings against a nationwide universe of equity portfolios. Invests in companies which display consistent and growing earnings, and are in solid financial condition.	Investors seeking long-term total return for future needs (i.e., college savings, retirement, savings for a home, and long-term savings). May be appropriate for IRA or 401k plan customers.

Source: Company records
a. Subject to rule 2a-7 of the SEC.

EXHIBIT 10

BAYBANK
MUTUAL FUNDS AT A GLANCE

Investment Objective	Mutual Funds (Non-FDIC Insured)	Tolerance for Risk	Time Perspective
MONEY MARKET MUTUAL FUNDS Seek to preserve the value of your investment and to provide current income.	• BayFunds Money Market Portfolio • BayFunds U.S. Treasury Money Market Portfolio • Massachusetts Municipal Cash Trust - BayFunds Shares	Low	Short-term (up to 3 years)
TAX-FREE INCOME FUNDS Seek to provide current income generally free from federal and Massachusetts income taxes consistent with safety of principal. Your return potential depends on the securities each fund holds and its average maturity.	• Eaton Vance Investment Trust – Massachusetts Limited Maturity Tax Free Fund • Eaton Vance Municipals Trust – Massachusetts Tax-Free Fund • Putnam Massachusetts Tax Exempt II	Low to Moderate	Short-term/ Intermediate-term (up to 5 years)
TAXABLE INCOME FUNDS Seek to provide current income consistent with safety of principal. Your return potential depends on the securities each fund holds and its average maturity.	• BayFunds Bond Portfolio • BayFunds Short Term Yield Portfolio • Kemper Investment Portfolios – Government Portfolio • Kemper Investment Portfolios – Short-Intermediate Government Portfolio • Putnam Adjustable-Rate U.S. Government Fund • Putnam U.S. Government Income Trust	Low to Moderate	Short-term/Intermediate-term (up to 5 years)
BALANCED FUNDS Seek income and long-term growth through a diversified mix of stocks and bonds.	• Eaton Vance Investors Fund • George Putnam Fund of Boston	Low to Moderate	Intermediate-term/ Long-term (3 years up to 10+ years)
GROWTH AND INCOME EQUITY Seek capital growth and current income through equity investments that typically pay above-average dividends.	• Eaton Vance Stock Fund • Putnam Fund for Growth and	Moderate	Intermediate-term/ Long-term (3 years up to 10+ years)
GROWTH EQUITY FUNDS Seek long-term capital growth; current income is secondary.	• BayFunds Equity Portfolio • Kemper Growth Portfolio • Putnam Voyager Fund	Moderate to High	Long-term (5 years up to 10+ years)
INTERNATIONAL AND GLOBAL FUNDS Seek long-term capital growth. Global Funds invest in domestic and foreign securities while International Funds are devoted exclusively to foreign securities.	• Kemper International Fund • Putnam Global Growth Fund	Moderate to High	Long-term (5 years up to 10+ years)

☎ **CALL 1-800-BAY-FAST (1-800-229-3278) 24 HOURS**

a In April 1994, BayBanks added a 16th proprietary fund to its family—the Putnam Asset Allocation Fund, which offered investors a choice of one of three different asset mixes.

WHAT ARE MUTUAL FUNDS?

Mutual funds offer a convenient and timesaving way for individuals to invest, without undertaking the responsibility of personally selecting and following specific stocks and bonds. Mutual funds pool the money of many investors and pursue a variety of investment objectives.

Each fund's portfolio manager invests assets in a portfolio of different securities pursuing a specific investment objective.

Many kinds of mutual funds are available to meet your investment objectives. The funds that are right for you depend upon your financial goals, the time you have to achieve them, your tolerance for risk, and the return you're seeking.

Mutual funds carry varying degrees of safety or risk, depending on their objectives and investments. Unlike CDs or savings accounts, *mutual funds are not insured by the FDIC* and do not have a guaranteed rate of return. Additionally, the principal value of non-money market mutual funds is likely to fluctuate, so when fund shares are sold they may be worth more or less than the investor paid for them.

While no investment is 100% secure, mutual funds reduce the overall risk inherent in investing because the funds direct your money into many different securities. This means that your return is not tied to any single stock or bond.

For easy tracking of your fund's performance, daily market prices for shares of most mutual funds are listed in major newspapers.

* See the "Supplemental Information" section on the inside back cover of this Catalog for important mutual fund information.

12b-1 fees were not levied by BayBank. While sales loads and 12b-1 fees were commonly charged by well-established non-bank fund providers–particularly those whose products where sold through the broker-dealer channels—BayBank believed that by not imposing such fees it would be able to compete effectively against its New England rivals and accelerate the penetration of its customer base. With the growth in third-party rating services, like Morningstar, Lipper, and Consumer Reports, consumers had become even more attuned to the impact of fees on returns and more skeptical of their influence on overall fund performance.

Sales and Distribution

Sales and service in the retail mutual fund business involved a number of processes that were typically delivered by registered mutual fund representatives (in person or by telephone), or branch personnel ("making available"), and supported by direct mail, telemarketing, print advertising, and statement stuffers. BayBank's distribution strategy emphasized the use of personal selling in combination with a variety of other communication channels. Several research studies indicated that mutual fund customers were uncomfortable in dealing with financial matters and wanted help from a trusted expert to sort through investment alternatives and to determine how different products could assist them in meeting their financial goals.[19] In addition to personal contact and guidance in the purchasing of mutual funds, many customers also wanted the flexibility and convenience of alternative distribution channels—such as branch offices for opening mutual fund accounts and telephone and mail access for conducting routine transactions.

The BayFunds retail sales and distribution structure, outlined in Exhibit 11, consisted principally of three components: investment specialists (ISs), BayBank's network of 200 branches, and the Customer Sales and Service Center (SSC). This distribution system was developed to meet the varying preferences of different target markets and to facilitate asset growth and business profitability. In 1992, BayBank began developing its new BayFunds salesforce and hired 32 registered ISs, professionals who have extensive experience in a variety of financial markets.[20] Twenty-nine of the ISs were assigned to a cluster of branches and were located off the banking floor at each of the branches. The other three ISs were assigned to the SSC. Five of the field ISs also served as team leaders, supervising the activities of a group of ISs. The team leaders reported directly

to a sales manager. This type of sales force and the attendant sales management process was new to the BayBank organization.

ISs sold both proprietary and third-party mutual funds to BayBank's primary target market. The sales mix for a typical IS was 60% in BayFunds money market portfolios, 29% in fluctuating BayFunds portfolios, and 11% in third-party funds. ISs worked closely with the branch personnel who were their primary source of referrals. Roughly 60%–70% of the remainder was spent providing investment guidance to customers face-to-face. The remainder was spent serving as the primary resource for branch personnel. ISs averaged $50,000 in annual earnings, receiving almost 75% of their compensation as salary and about 25% as a bonus for selling mutual funds. This compensation arrangement, with such a large salary component, was not the norm for the industry. However, BayBank had decided that this compensation mix was the best way to ensure that the customer was receiving the most appropriate and objective investment advice. ISs were compensated slightly more for selling third-party funds because they involved a more complicated sales process and because of the higher cash flow to the broker-dealer. That is, the up-front payments to BayBank from the fund managers allowed Bay-Bank to pay out larger commissions to its salesforce and, thereby, match its income and expenses at the time of sale.

Customer Service Managers (CSMs) and Sales and Service Associates (SSAs), located in the "platform" area of the branch, were only permitted to open money market mutual funds. They were not licensed to advise customers on any type of mutual fund, although they could refer customers interested in obtaining investment advice to the IS or to the SSC. CSMs and SSAs were encouraged to employ a "park and go" strategy, whereby they would open a money market account "at the door" and then refer the customer to the IS if he or she sought investment advice. Customer Service Representatives (CSRs), or tellers, could only make mutual fund referrals to the platform personnel; they were precluded by regulation from referring customers directly to the ISs. The branch sales staff was the critical link between the customers and the ISs. The branch sales staff received one-time bonuses for opening accounts and for making referrals to ISs, a policy consistent with the compensation practice for traditional bank products. Although SSAs received substantial training, many were still uncomfortable dealing with funds. It was difficult for them to service customers interested in non–money market mutual funds while simultaneously adhering to the strict federal

EXHIBIT 11

BayFunds sales and distribution strategy

	Distribution Channels		
	Investment Specialists	Branch	Sales and Service Center
Target segment	Affluent BayBank customers Household income $75K	All BayBank customers	Emerging affluent Bay-Bank customers
Product	All BMFs, third-party mutual funds Capital market and brokerage products	BBMFs—money market funds only	All BBMFs
Personnel	29 licensed ISs servicing branches	All SSAs and CSMs in branches	Sales center: • 3 investments specialists Service center: • Investment service specialists
Role	Act as customers' "financial counselor," explain products build trust, and help customers make decision Sell and open mutual funds	Answer questions, make BayFunds money market portfolios available Make referrals to IS for equity and bond portfolio sales Complete routine transactions (transfer, redemptions, purchases, etc.)	Sales center: • Generate awareness • Answer questions • Send out prospectuses and applications • Sell mutual funds • Follow up on leads • Open accounts (after customer receives prospectus) Service center: • Handle routine transactions (transfers, purchases, redemptions, information needs)
Relationship to other channels	Work with and train branch personnel to receive referrals	Make referrals to investment specialists	Receive referrals from branches and other groups in sales and service center

Source: Company records.

regulations that severely limited the amount and type of fund information they could provide to customers. SSAs were responsible for promoting many other BayBank products in addition to mutual funds. BayBank's product managers for credit cards and various deposit products, for example, aggressively competed for the branch staff's sales support.

The ISs and branches received extensive training prior to the BayFunds launch. The ISs, for example, were instructed in the mutual fund product line and in different selling techniques. Branch employees were trained to provide customers with information about mutual funds in general and specific BayFunds products so that they could increase the number of referrals made to ISs. BayBank believed that a strong on-going training program would ensure that its employees became increasingly confident in talking about mutual funds. A secondary benefit of the training was in customer (and bank) protection—to ensure that the customer understood the risks associated with the product he or she was purchasing.

The SSC marketing efforts were targeted at BayBank's emerging affluent customer segment and non-BayBank customers. In addition to the three ISs, several service specialists were based at the SSC to serve those customers who preferred to conduct business over the toll-free BayFunds phone service. Advertisements and direct mail for Bay-Funds instructed customers interested in mutual fund sales or service to call the ISs at the dedicated toll-free number (1-800-BAY-FUND).

Marketing Communication

BayBank spent $2 million in mass media advertising and direct marketing to launch BayFunds. In the future, marketing communications for BayFunds were expected to amount to about one-half the prior budget, and might be allocated differently.

The introductory campaign was aimed at both Bay-Bank and non-BayBank customers to create awareness of the bank's investment product offerings and capabilities, and specifically, to promote BayFunds (see Exhibit 12). The ads sought to communicate that BayBank was a credible mutual fund provider. The media advertising budget for BayFunds in its first year, summarized in Exhibit 13, emphasized local newspapers, magazines, and radio. The introductory campaign ran during March and April 1993 and was followed by a sustaining campaign for the remainder of the year. The newspaper and magazine ads described either the mutual fund product line or the role of the IS (see

Exhibits 14 and 15). The radio campaign focused on the availability and convenience of BayBank funds.

Direct marketing, consisting of detailed mutual fund information, was aimed at both the bank's primary and secondary retail audiences. BayBank sent out direct mailings coincident with the launch. These mailings were expected to produce a 2% response rate, generating 8,000 new accounts annually.

Marketing Challenges

By January 1994, total BayFunds assets had reached $1.2 billion (including both institutional and retail accounts), up 60% from the level at the launch date almost one year earlier. Retail asset balances grew from $18 million to $256 million over this same time period. BayFunds ranked 49th in size among the more than 100 bank proprietary fund groups and second in the region to Fleet's Galaxy fund family, which ranked 15th. Almost 14,000 retail BayFunds accounts had been opened since March 1993, of which 40% were money market fund accounts. The average account balances in each of the six portfolios remained fairly stable. The funds had been delivering returns fully competitive with their "peer" funds (see Exhibit 16).[21]

Having successfully launched BayFunds, Benson now faced a new challenge in formulating the strategy for Bay-Funds future growth. She viewed this as a critical juncture in the life of BayBank's newest investment product. Benson had observed during the past year that proprietary funds did not completely satisfy the investment needs of bank customers. Most banks were attempting to expand their limited range of proprietary stock and bond funds in response to recent marketing research showing that many holders of money market funds were considering broadening their investment portfolios. Benson was not sure if she could match the relatively broader proprietary fund offerings of other local competitors without a heavy subsidy for new funds lacking sufficient seed capital. Most proprietary funds were dominated by money market offerings, which were less profitable than long-term bond and equity funds. Furthermore, the typical bank proprietary fund had an asset base smaller than the industry average, which also translated into lower profitability. Thus, both demand and cost considerations favored companies that offered a broad array of mutual funds. BayBank, however, was currently not well positioned with its BayFunds product line to meet these market challenges. While overall BayFunds sales had been strong during the first year, Benson believed, based on recent sales of new accounts, that the Bay-

EXHIBIT 12

Print ad for BayFunds launch, March 1993

THE NEW WAY TO INVEST.

BayFunds

INTRODUCING SIX "NO-LOAD" MUTUAL FUNDS NOW AVAILABLE AT BAYBANK.

For whatever reasons you have to invest, it may pay you to consider the new BayFunds. With potentially higher yields, these mutual funds could be an appropriate alternative to many other types of investments.

BayFunds: A Choice for You

BayFunds is a family of six mutual funds. With "no-load," you'll pay no sales fees. Each fund has a different investment goal. As such, you're sure to find one that may answer your specific financial needs – for regular monthly income, retirement savings, tax-free income or long term capital growth.

The BayFunds Family of Mutual Funds

Fund Name	Fund Type	Investment Goals
BayFunds Money Market Portfolio	Money Market	Current income consistent with stability of principal
BayFunds U.S. Treasury Money Market Portfolio	Money Market	Current income consistent with stability of principal
BayFunds Short-Massachusetts Municipal Cash Trust	Money Market	Tax-free current income consistent with stability of principal
BayFunds Short Term Yield Portfolio	Bond Fund	High current income consistent with preservation of capital
BayFunds Bond Portfolio	Bond Fund	High current income and capital appreciation
BayFunds Equity Portfolio	Equity Fund	Long term capital appreciation

BayFunds: Invest Where You Bank 24 Hours a Day

Because BayFunds are available at BayBank, it's now as easy for you to buy and sell mutual funds as it is to do your banking, just around the corner.

You can open a BayFunds account with a minimum of $2,500. Or $500 for a BayBank IRA.

BayFunds on Your Bank Statement

For added convenience, as a BayBank customer, you will receive a summary of your BayFunds activity on the same statement with your checking and savings. You can see at a glance how your money is working for you.

Investment Specialists: Personal Advice When You Need It

By investing in mutual funds at BayBank, you can get assistance from licensed mutual fund Investment Specialists. Meet with them at a BayBank office, where they will answer your questions and advise you on how to reach your investment goals.

24 Hour Customer Service

Wherever you are at any time of day or night, if you have a question about BayFunds, you can call to arrange for an appointment with an Investment Specialist who will be glad to answer your questions or help you with any of your mutual fund purchases. Simply call 1.800 BAYFUND.

Find Out More About BayFunds Today

To receive more information about BayFunds, or to obtain a prospectus, visit any of over 200 nearby BayBank offices today. Or call 1.800 BAYFUND.

BayFunds™

THE WAY TO BANK.

EXHIBIT 13

1993 BayFunds advertising budget ($000)

	Budget
Print	
Spring	$862
Fall	170
Radio	140
Product of the month	60
Airport dioramas	35
Sales collateral	75
Direct mail & fulfillment	460
Applications	60
Brochures	180
Total budget	$2,042

Source: Company records.

Funds group had not made sufficient progress towards establishing BayBank's proprietary equity and fixed-income funds.

Moreover, in addition to refining BayBank's mutual fund product line, Benson needed to reassess her market segmentation strategies to ensure a fit between BayBank's strengths and the target customers' varying needs. While short-term growth in assets was certainly a goal, Benson understood that the critical long-term challenge was to develop a stable and profitable customer base. Benson also recognized that she needed to address two related issues that had grown in importance since BayFunds' introduction. First, how could BayFunds be further integrated into the BayBank system? And how could she effectively grow the retail business while, at the same time, coping with the uncertain regulatory climate?

Reexamining BayFunds Marketing Strategy

BayBank's strategy for launching BayFunds was based on the premise that it could successfully diversify by leveraging the bank's strong brand identity. By extending the Bay-Bank brand to its new mutual fund product line, the organization believed it could enhance BayBank's core reputation, expand the customer franchise, and grow the overall business. Convenience and technological superiority were the core associations typically evoked by the Bay-Bank name; they were the benefits BayBank regularly emphasized when marketing its existing products and services. Benson, however, wondered whether convenience and technology were the features that customers valued most when purchasing mutual funds, particularly since a substantial percentage of BayBank customers rarely visited a branch office where the majority of BayFunds sales were made.

Tracking studies of bank-managed mutual fund revealed that, unlike CDs, non–money market mutual funds tended to be held by customers for a considerable period of time with remarkably stable average balances. In effect, most customers viewed mutual funds as long-term savings vehicles and, thus, in order to select an appropriate fund or combination of funds, they needed to do a careful assessment of their financial needs, resources, and risk tolerance. Consequently, Benson wondered if marketing for BayFund shouldn't also emphasize this solution-driven sales approach. Historically, BayBank had concentrated on selling checking and savings account products and generating transactions and, therefore, was not accustomed to this more relationship-oriented sales process. How else could the overall strategy be adjusted to reflect the characteristics of BayFunds which made it markedly different from those of traditional bank products?

Integrating BayFunds into the core BayBank franchise was, therefore, a challenging task for Benson that was critical to the success of the bank's mutual funds program. As Benson explained, "We need to establish mutual funds as another core BayBank product and facilitate the sales process so that it is treated as another bank product." In an effort to achieve this goal, Benson wanted to include mutual funds in several of BayBank's packaged product offerings, an effort which would necessitate closer interaction with other product management teams. She believed that additional packaging strategies would enhance the worth of BayBank's existing product offerings and the positioning of BayBank as a full-service financial provider. Bay-Funds had been able to sell mutual funds to 10% of new BayPlus checking accounts. However, cross-selling with other BayBank products, such as payments and credit services, was less developed.

Managing in an Uncertain Regulatory Environment

During the first year of its operation, the BayFunds group spent 20% of its time addressing issues and requests emanating from regulatory bodies concerned with proprietary bank funds. New rules and standards were issued almost

EXHIBIT 14

BayFunds print ad

Mutual Funds Without The Mystique.

If you're interested in learning more about mutual funds and in making the investment decisions that are right for you, just speak to a BayBank Investment Specialist.

Every one of BayBank's licensed Investment Specialists has undergone very specialized training in mutual funds. That makes them highly skilled at answering your questions. Questions like these:

What are mutual funds? Mutual funds are a convenient and affordable way to participate in professionally managed and diversified portfolios. Mutual funds pool the money of many investors and pursue a variety of objectives. By investing in mutual funds, you gain the edge that only professional investment management provides.

How safe are mutual funds? Mutual funds carry varying degrees of safety or risk, depending on their objectives and investment practices. Unlike CDs or savings accounts, mutual funds are not insured by the FDIC and do not have a guaranteed rate of return. While no investment is 100% secure, mutual funds reduce the overall risk of investing because your funds are diversified across numerous stocks, bonds, or other securities and are managed by financial experts.

What types of mutual funds are available? Many types of mutual funds are available to meet your specific investment objectives. The funds that are right for you depend on your financial goals, the time you have to achieve them, and your tolerance for risk. Mutual funds can generally be classified into three categories:

MONEY MARKET: Money market funds are among the most conservative non-insured investments available. If you're looking for attractive current returns with minimal risk to principal, money market funds could be the right choice for you.

INCOME FUNDS: These funds seek high current income and capital appreciation. Income funds are designed for investors who can accept fluctuations in principal in return for potentially high current income and total return. You can choose from taxable and non-taxable funds.

EQUITY FUNDS: These funds seek to achieve long-term capital appreciation with current income as a secondary objective. Equity funds may be the ideal choice for investors who can accept some fluctuations in share price in return for potential long-term capital appreciation. Many people use equity funds to help meet long-term goals such as retirement or education.

How can BayBank help? With BayBank, it's as easy for you to buy and sell mutual funds as it is to do your everyday banking. We're just around the corner from where you live and work.

You can choose from a full selection of mutual funds available at BayBank, including BayFunds, a family of six no-load funds. Or choose from well-known mutual fund families such as Eaton Vance, Kemper Financial Services, and Putnam. One or more may be the right choice for reaching your investment objectives. A BayBank Investment Specialist will help you determine which funds meet your financial requirements.

For more answers to your questions about mutual funds, meet with a BayBank Investment Specialist at the nearest BayBank office. To speak to an Investment Specialist or to arrange for an appointment, simply call 1-800-BAY-FUND.

Call 1-800-BAY-FUND®

BayBank®

Day and night. Night and day.

EXHIBIT 15

BayFund print ad

A Savings Alternative.

BayFunds
Short Term Yield
Portfolio

Mutual
Funds At
BayBank

BayFunds

The BayFunds Short Term Yield Portfolio can offer a potentially higher yield than savings accounts.

If you're concerned about current interest rates, consider the BayFunds® Short Term Yield Portfolio. This mutual fund seeks a higher level of income than savings accounts and CDs. Remember, however, that no mutual fund is FDIC insured; and the value of the shares you purchase may vary. But over the long run, the BayFunds Short Term Yield Portfolio may provide more price stability than investments in higher-yielding, longer-term bonds.

Investing in BayFunds is affordable too. There's no sales charge (or "load"), and all you need is $2,500 to open an account. Or only $500 with a BayBank IRA or when you have automatic transfers made from your checking or savings account.

With BayFunds, you'll enjoy the best in investing and banking convenience – including professional advice from BayBank Investment Specialists and 24-hour customer service. Plus, BayBank customers can get a consolidated statement that summarizes BayFunds activity with their checking and savings.

To invest in the BayFunds Short Term Yield Portfolio, call 1-800-BAY-FUND or stop by your nearest BayBank office. For more complete information about the fund, including charges and expenses, ask for a prospectus and read it carefully before you invest or send money.

1-800-BAY-FUND

BayFunds®

Mutual funds, unlike traditional bank products, are not federally insured and do not offer a fixed rate of return. In addition, they involve certain risks, including the possible loss of principal. A rise in interest rates can result in a decline in the value of your investment. BayFunds are not deposits or obligations of or guaranteed by BayBank, and are not federally insured or guaranteed. Federated Securities Corp., Distributor.

EXHIBIT 16

BayFunds performance versus peers: total return—investment shares [a]

Fund Name	Quarter Ending 6/29/93	Quarter Ending 9/30/93	Quarter Ending 12/31/93	Quarter Ending 3/31/94	12 Months Ending 3/31/94
BayFunds U.S. Treasury Money Market Portfolio	0.64%	0.65%	0.65%	0.67%	2.64%
Peer group average [b]	0.63%	0.65%	0.65%	0.65%	2.61%
Number of funds in peer group	74	76	76	79	76
BayFunds Money Market Portfolio	0.60%	0.66%	0.66%	0.66%	2.70%
Peer group average [c]	0.71%	0.72%	0.73%	0.74%	2.94%
Number of funds in peer group	99	104	109	117	105
BayFunds Short Term Yield Portfolio	1.24%	1.68%	0.21%	11.50%	3.21%
Peer group average [d]	1.38%	1.61%	0.21%	0.11%	3.21%
Number of funds in peer group	95	90	100	106	86
BayFunds Bond Portfolio	2.68%	3.45%	(0.77%)	(1.19%)	3.40%
Peer group average [e]	2.42%	2.70%	(0.12%)	(2.71%)	2.30%
Number of funds in peer group	81	88	99	117	90
BayFunds Equity Portfolio	1.22%	6.48%	(0.46%)	(4.68%)	2.27%
Peer group average [f]	0.72%	5.01%	2.26%	(3.44%)	3.79%
Number of funds in peer group	416	435	475	467	394
Ranking in peer group	181	143	407	330	225

Source: Lipper Analytical Services, company records.
a. Peer groups defined and measured by Lipper Analytical Services.
b. U.S. Treasury Money Market Funds.
c. Money Market Institutional Funds.
d. Short Investment Grade Debt Funds.
e. Intermediate Investment Grade Debt Funds.
f. Lipper Growth Stock Funds.

every month, and they impacted almost every area of Bay-Bank's mutual fund business. Examinations by the SEC and various banking agencies required substantial preparation, and could be scheduled with as little as one day's notice. As a result, Benson believed that the BayFunds team needed to be proactive with respect to the mutual fund regulations and to anticipate potential regulatory and legislative action. Benson was in the process of recruiting someone who would assume responsibility for ensuring the bank's compliance with all the regulations.

1994–1995 Strategic Marketing Plan

Against this background, Benson began the task of formulating a marketing program for 1995. Benson was particu-larly interested in pursuing a plan for the bank's mutual funds program that would facilitate BayFunds becoming a core BayBank product, and achieving business line profitability by leveraging BayBank's strengths. Profitability depended on both asset retention and growth, as well as the mutual fund product mix. It was well known that the best prospects for mutual fund sales were the bank's existing customer base. While about 21% of BayBank customers already owned some type of mutual funds, less than 2% invested in BayFunds, suggesting that the potential for growth was enormous. To date, the majority of sales had been in money market funds, rather than bond or equity funds. As Exhibit 17 demonstrates, both the "source" (i.e., proprietary versus third party) and the type of mutual fund

EXHIBIT 17

Projected fee income comparison by mutual fund type and source [a]
Proprietary funds with investment management fee [b]

Year	Assets ($ millions) Year-End	Assets ($ millions) New	Product Mix 90/10 Fee Income ($)	Product Mix 70/30	Product Mix 50/50
1	1,000	0	2,175,000	2,525,000	2,875,000
2	1,300	300	5,002,500	5,107,500	5,212,500
3	1,600	300	6,307,500	7,322,500	8,337,500
4	1,900	300	7,612,500	8,837,500	10,062,500
5	2,200	300	8,917,500	10,352,500	11,787,500

Third-party funds with loads [c]

Year	Assets ($ millions) Year-end	Assets ($ millions) New	Product Mix 90/10 Fee income ($)	Product Mix 70/30	Product Mix 50/50
1	1,000		1,900,000	3,700,000	5,500,000
2	1,300	300	2,470,000	4,810,000	7,150,000
3	1,600	300	1,140,000	2,220,000	3,300,000
4	1,900	300	1,140,000	2,220,000	3,300,000
5	2,200	300	1,140,000	2,220,000	3,300,000

a. Product mix is ratio of money market funds to fluctuating NAV (equity and bond) funds.
b. Investment advisor fee of 40 basis points for money market funds, 75 basis points for fluctuating NAV funds. Calculations assume all new monies received at mid-year.
c. Front-end load of 20 basis points for money market funds, 200 basis points for fluctuating NAV funds. Loads applicable only to new monies to the funds. Calculations assume all new monies received

influenced product line profitability over time. At present, a significant portion of BayFunds' assets were vulnerable to factors such as market volatility, the high percentage of investment dollars in money market funds, and the runoff of existing 401(k) assets when employees terminated employment or retired. As a result, mutual fund product offerings, distribution channels, and compensation strategies had to be aligned with profitability objectives.

In developing the marketing plan, Benson identified several broad mutual fund initiatives she wished to pursue over the next 18 months (see Exhibit 18). The most controversial proposal advanced in the plan was expanding the bank's relationship with third-party vendors. To date, BayBank had offered third-party funds from Putnam, Kemper,

and Eaton Vance with the objective of providing its customers with more extensive investment options. Significant opportunities existed, however, for BayBank to expand and leverage these existing relationships by either adding new third-party mutual funds or by entering into more exclusive partnerships.

For vendors, BayBank's extensive retail distribution network offered access to a large untapped customer market. Thus, several fund providers had expressed interest in becoming the bank's "preferred provider" which would allow them, among other things, to enhance the position of their funds by working closely with the bank's mutual funds salesforce. For BayBank, further development of its third-party relationships would result in several benefits.

EXHIBIT 18

1994–1995 mutual fund intiatives

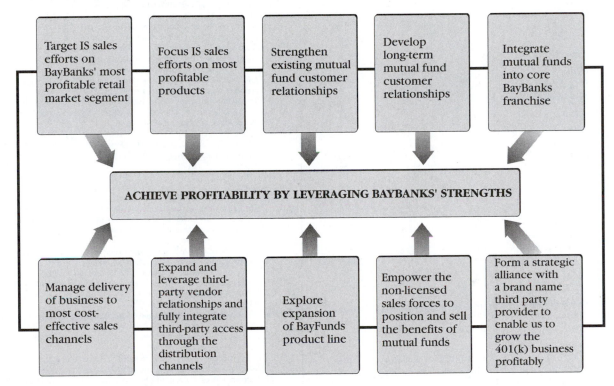

The organization could take advantage of vendors' expertise and resources in: training (for licensed and non-licensed personnel), regulatory compliance, strategic marketing, consumer education, and the development of customer-focused, solution-driven portfolios. Available at no out-of-pocket costs, these services could greatly reduce total marketing expenditures for mutual funds. All of the third-party vendors that BayBank considered as potential partners had strong, widely recognized brand names.

At various times in early 1994, Fidelity, Putnam, Kemper, and Federated had each approached BayBank about entering into some form of a strategic relationship. Benson wondered about the possibility of co-branding between BayBank and a well-established vendor. While the opportunities for BayBank appeared to be numerous, Benson had some concerns about developing closer ties with third-party vendors. Once familiar with the bank and its customer base, could the vendor then take those customers away from BayBank? She also wondered about the impact these types of arrangements might have on the future growth of BayBank's proprietary funds.

In addition to pursuing third-party partnerships, Benson placed a high priority on expanding marketing and strengthening customer relationships. Whatever product line mix was chosen, the organization had to pay careful attention to its target segments. To encourage greater asset retention and more profitable asset growth, the organization needed to focus on developing long-term customer relationships. As a result, the mutual fund marketing group had to shift from the product-oriented to a process-oriented sales approach, whereby sales staffs and investment specialists together would encourage customers to consider their overall financial goals and the benefits of long-term investing. Benson planned to modify BayFunds advertising strategy by increasing direct marketing and revising its advertising message to be more solutions focused. Exhibit 19 contains budgeted costs for a selection of the proposed marketing programs.

EXHIBIT 19

BayFunds marketing budget, 1994 and 1995 ($000)

	1994	1995
Advertising		
Print	$455	?
Direct mail	200	?
Product of the month	100	?
Seminars	100	?
New funds collateral	100	?
Sales support	75	?
Fulfillment	25	?
	$1,055	$750
Branch contests	$50	$80
Marketing research and		
* systems consulting*	$130	$155
Prospectuses and		
* collateral materials* [a]	$457	$515
Total budget	$1,692	$1,500

Source: Company records.
a. Internal training is included in BayBank's corporate overhead budget, which amounted to $1,674,000.00.

Benson was scheduled to present her proposed marketing plan for mutual funds to the senior executives of BayBank at a meeting to be held at the end of the month. In the course of working on her presentation, she came across the following press report:

> Widely regarded as the premier retail bank in New England, [BayBank] is pulling every available lever: its 203 branches in Massachusetts and Connecticut, its 24-hour telephone sales and service center, private banking and community business development officers, and newly-hired cadre of "investment specialists" dedicated to mutual fund sales. (Jeffrey Marshall, "Hitting the Ground Running," United States Banker, 1992).

After reading the press clipping, she asked herself: "Are we pulling all of the right levers at BayFunds?"

Notes

1. See Christine Remey and Gregory Dees, "BayBank Boston," HBS Case No. 9-393-095.
2. Raymond Sczudlo, "Mutual Funds: Opportunities and Risks," *Bankers Magazine,* March/April 1994, p. 26.
3. A 1993 regulation limited annual 12b-1 fees to 0.75% of assets under management with a per-account lifetime cap on these fees ranging from 6.5 to 7.25%, depending on other fees imposed. See Carole Gould, *The New York Times Guide to Mutual Funds* (New York: The New York Times Company, 1992), pp. 46–62.
4. J. William Bowen, "Strategies for Harnessing the Mutual Funds Boom," *Bankers Magazine,* March/April 1994, pp. 21–23.
5. The six-month Treasury bill was 8.8% in 1989 and 3.2% in 1993.
6. Baby boomers represented the 78 million persons born in the United States between 1946 and 1964.
7. Sczudlo, op. cit., p. 26.
8. Investment Company Institute, *The Environment for the Investment Company Industry in the 1990s* (Investment Company Institute, 1990).
9. Sczudlo, *op. cit.,* p. 26.
10. Attachment to the "Securities Regulatory Equality Act of 1993," prepared by John Dingell, November 4, 1993.
11. The four federal banking agencies—Board of Governors of the Federal Reserve System (Federal Reserve Board), the Federal Deposit Insurance Corporation (FDIC), the Office of the Comptroller of Currency (OCC) and the Office of Thrift Supervision (OTS)—had in the past issued separate guidelines that addressed various aspects of the retail sale of bank-managed mutual funds.
12. N. Capon, G. J. Fitzsimons, and R. A. Price, "An Individual Level Analysis of the Mutual Fund Investment Decision," unpublished Working Paper, Columbia University (1992): 1–8.
13. Ibid., p. 25.
14. E. Sirri and P. Tufano, "Buying and Selling Mutual Funds: Flows, Performance, Fees, and Services," *HBS Working Paper No. 93-017* (1993): 3.
15. For regulatory reasons, BayBank Boston, N.A. serves as the investment adviser to one of the BayFunds portfolios.
16. The criteria for participation included having at least $7,500 in any one CD or at least $7,500 in any MMDA account.
17. Federated Investors, a mutual fund manager and an affiliate of the distributor of BayFunds, created a second class of its existing fund, Massachusetts Municipal Cash Trust, for use in the BayFunds program, for which Federated management would serve as investment adviser. The Federated organization provides an array of services for BayFunds including administration distribution, and portfolio record keeping.
18. In fact, all BayBank mutual fund customers were informed 17 times in the first year that their BayFunds shares were not FDIC insured.
19. A study conducted in 1991 by the ICI revealed that only 28% of mutual fund investors were sufficiently comfortable with their own financial expertise to be willing to purchase mutual funds through direct marketing channels.
20. Anyone giving investment advice had to be registered with the NASD and be sponsored by a broker-dealer. At a minimum, all ISs had a Series 6 license which enabled them to advise on mutual funds and annuities only. Eventually, the ISs would all be Series 7 registered where they could advise on other investments besides mutual funds.
21. "Peer" funds are those designated by the investment community as closely comparable in investment objectives, management style, and risk profile for the purpose of fund comparisons.

Retirement Plans and the Fund Business

8

The retirement business is an additional distribution channel to the two channels—intermediary and direct—discussed in Chapter Seven. The retirement channel is partially intermediary and partially direct. This channel is intermediary in that the initial sale is made to the employer organization that determines which funds or fund complexes will be available to employees through the retirement plan. The retirement channel is direct in the sense that the eventual decision to buy particular funds is made by a plan's participants, sometimes numbering in the hundreds of thousands, who must choose among mutual funds as well as other investment alternatives offered by the retirement plan.

Retirement assets have become tremendously significant for financial intermediaries generally and for mutual funds particularly. U.S. retirement assets held in all types of investment vehicles more than tripled from $4.1 trillion in 1990 to $12.7 trillion in 1999 (see Figure 8.1). During this period, the mutual fund share of U.S. retirement assets almost quadrupled, from 5% to 19%. As a consequence, mutual fund assets held in retirement accounts, including individual retirement accounts (IRAs) and employer-sponsored retirement accounts, totaled over $2.4 trillion at the end of 1999, up from $207 billion held in 1990 (see Figure 8.2). This $2.4 trillion represented 35% of total mutual fund assets at the end of 1999, up from 19% in 1990.

What triggered this phenomenal growth in mutual fund retirement accounts? To begin with, there has been the demographic impact of the aging baby boom population. According to the U.S. government, baby boomers account for approximately 65 million of the 270 million people in the United States, and the number of people over age 65 is predicted to increase from 12.7% of the population in 2000 to 16.5% of the population in 2020. As baby boomers approach retirement, their financial focus inevitably has moved to concerns about the adequacy of their retirement income.

The second cause for this growth has been the dramatic shift to defined contribution (DC) plans, particularly 401(k) plans, from defined benefit (DB) plans over the past decade. The operation of both types of plans is detailed later in this Chapter. In short, in DC plans, participants typically choose among various investment options, usually including mutual funds. In DB plans, the employer chooses the investment vehicles for its plan's assets, rarely including mutual funds. Of particular significance to mutual funds has been the explosive growth of 401(k) plans, the most popular type of employer-sponsored DC plan. The assets in 401(k) plans have increased from less than $400 billion in 1990 to over $2 trillion in 2001. Since mutual fund complexes dominate the 401(k) market, its growth has been enormously important to the fund industry.

Third, the growth of IRAs has fueled the growth of the mutual fund industry. As this Chapter later explains, mutual funds were one of the key funding vehicles for the universal IRAs during the 1980s. Although contributions to IRAs were slowed by legislative

FIGURE 8.1

U.S. retirement assets, 1990–1999

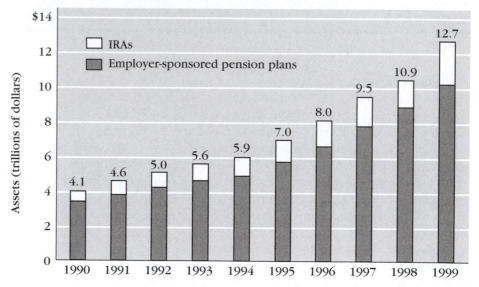

Source: ICI, *Fundamentals,* Vol. 9/No. 2, May 2000. Reprinted by permission of the Investment Company Institute.

FIGURE 8.2

Mutual fund retirement assets, 1990–1999

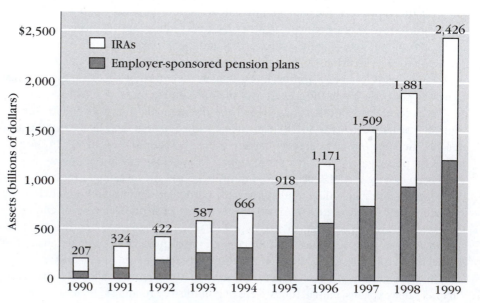

Source: ICI, *Fundamentals,* Vol. 9/No. 2, May 2000. Reprinted by permission of the Investment Company Institute.

restrictions during the late 1980s and early 1990s, they became more popular again in the late 1990s with the creation of the Spousal and Roth IRAs. Moreover, as employees left DC plans, through retirement or other forms of separation, they increasingly transferred assets in their DC accounts to IRAs. These so-called rollover IRAs often have gone into mutual funds. By the end of 1999, IRA assets totaled almost $2.5 trillion, an amount greater than DC plan assets and even slightly larger than DB plan assets (see Figure 8.3).

These trends toward DC plans and IRAs have spread equity ownership through mutual funds to millions of new investors, who in the process have become interested more broadly in mutual funds and financial markets. To understand these trends, this Chapter summarizes the structure of tax-qualified retirement plans in general, and the operation of 401(k) plans in particular, before it discusses in greater detail the dramatic shift to DC from DB plans. It then explains why the structure of 401(k) plans has favored mutual fund sponsors, which provide a broad array of investment options and other services to these plans. It next reviews the other types of DC plans—403(b), 457 and SIMPLE plans—as well as the various forms of IRAs and describes the role of mutual funds in each of those retirement markets. The Chapter finishes by outlining two key trends affecting the future of the retirement channel for mutual funds. It also provides an exercise on designing 401(k) plans for different types of companies.

I. Structure of Tax-Qualified Retirement Plans

A. Tax Benefits of Qualified Retirement Plans

In order to encourage employers to sponsor retirement programs for their employees, the Internal Revenue Code provides tax incentives for employers that establish retirement plans. To fully understand the popularity and impact of employer-sponsored

FIGURE 8.3

U.S. retirement asset holdings, 1999 ($ billions)

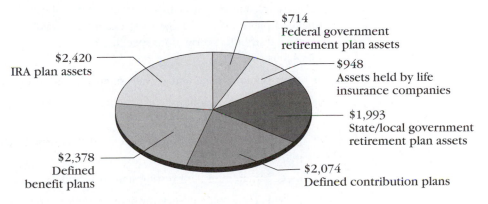

Source: EBRI, "Research Highlights, Retirement Data," October 2000. Reprinted by permission of Employee Benefit Research Institute, *Research Highlights, Retirement Data,* October 2000.

retirement programs, it is important to recognize the tax benefits provided by qualified plans. These are as follows:

- The employer's contributions to the plan are deductible in the tax year for which they are made.

- Participants realize no taxable income in the year employer contributions are made to their plans or their accounts with the plan.

- Participants do not recognize any taxable income on their own qualifying salary-reduction contributions to the plan or their plan accounts in the tax year for which such contributions are made.

- Earnings on contributions to the plan, from both the employer and participants, are accumulated tax free in the trust established to fund the plan.

- Participants realize taxable income only when they actually receive their retirement benefits as distributions from the plan.

To put the tax advantages of qualified plans in perspective, let's contrast the tax consequences of qualified and nonqualified retirement plans. In a qualified retirement plan, the employer receives a tax deduction for its contribution in the tax year for which they are made, although the employee does not recognize that contribution as taxable income in that year. Indeed, the employee does not recognize that contribution as taxable income until he or she receives a plan distribution on retirement. In nonqualified plans, by contrast, the realization of taxable income by the employee and the tax deduction by the employer occur in the same year. In other words, deferral of taxable income by the employee comes at the cost of delay in the tax deduction by the employer in a nonqualified plan. Alternatively, immediate tax deduction by the employer comes at the cost of immediate realization of taxable income by the employee in a nonqualified plan. Furthermore, unlike a qualified plan where earnings on contributions are accumulated tax free until distributed to participants, a nonqualified trust is treated as a grantor trust, and earnings therein are taxable to the employer in the year they are earned.

The tax benefits obtainable for qualified plans come with restrictions. Given the tax revenues "given up" by the Treasury in allowing employers to deduct plan contributions immediately while deferring recognition of taxable income by employees until retirement, Congress insists that two important social policy goals be furthered by qualified plans: plan coverage must extend as broadly as possible, and plan benefits must be distributed fairly. More specifically, in order to attain tax advantages, qualified plans must:

- meet minimum age and service standards and minimum coverage requirements;

- provide for contributions or benefits that do not discriminate in favor of highly compensated employees;

- provide for contributions or benefits that do not exceed certain employee compensation limits;

- meet certain minimum vesting standards; and

- provide for automatic survivor benefits under certain circumstances.

These tax benefits and restrictions apply to all qualified plans, including DB plans and the various types of DC plans. There are many types of employer-sponsored DC plans, including Savings (or Thrift) Plans, Profit-Sharing Plans, Money Purchase Pension Plans, Employee Stock Ownership Plans and 401(k) plans. The most popular type of DC plan is the 401(k) plan, named after a section of the Internal Revenue Code. Primarily corporate employers use the 401(k) plan. As discussed later in this Chapter, other types of salary-reduction DC plans are available to municipal and state employers (457 plans) and to nonprofit institutions like universities or hospitals (403(b) plans).

B. Operation of 401(k) Plans

401(k) plans allow employees to choose between current taxable compensation and a tax-deferred contribution to a qualified retirement plan. There are three principal types of contributions that can be made to a 401(k) plan:

- *Elective*—Tax-deferred employee contributions made by the plan sponsor on behalf of the employee in the form of salary reduction

- *Matching*—Employer contributions that match employee contributions up to a flat dollar amount or percentage of salary contributed

- *Nonelective*—Nonmatching contributions made by the plan sponsor from employer funds (usually made to satisfy nondiscrimination tests)

The annual pretax elective deferral limit for participants in 401(k) plans is $10,500 for 2001, which gradually rises to $15,000 by 2006. Additional contributions such as employer matches and profit-sharing contributions can bring the total contribution to the lower of $35,000, or 25% of the individual's compensation as of 2001 (beginning in 2002, $40,000 with no percentage of compensation cap). Moreover, beginning in 2002, employees over age 50 may make "catch-up" contributions of an additional $1,000 per year (increasing to $5,000 per year by 2006) that are not subject to these antidiscrimination rules. These contributions are intended to enable older workers to make up for their inability to maximize their contributions when younger and confronted by competing savings needs, such as their children's college education. Also beginning in 2002, but ending in 2006, lower-income workers (i.e., single filers earning less than $25,000 and joint filers earning less than $50,000) are entitled to receive a nonrefundable tax credit of up to 50% of their 401(k) contributions up to $2,000 per year (i.e., a tax credit of up to $1,000 per year). This tax credit should spur non–highly compensated employees (NCHEs) to make larger contributions to 401(k) plans, thereby enabling plans to meet antidiscrimination rules better. (See "2001 Pension Legislation.")

The antidiscrimination rules specific to employee salary-reduction contributions to 401(k) plans are designed to ensure that highly compensated employees (HCEs)—those generally earning more than $80,000 per year—do not contribute at a disproportionately higher rate than do NHCEs. Average contribution rates for the two groups of employees must be calculated and compared by the 401(k) plan administrator each year. The plan passes the test if HCEs contribute at an average rate no more than 125% higher than that for NHCEs, or if the average contribution rate for HCEs is less than two percentage points greater than the average rate for NHCEs. If the plan fails the test, a portion of the contributions made by HCEs must be returned to them so that the test can be passed. Failing the test is costly from both an administrative and employee relations point of view. Plan sponsors therefore go to great lengths to encourage NHCEs to

CALLOUT
2001 Pension Legislation

A. Scheduled increases in 401(k), 403(b), 457, SIMPLE and IRA: contribution limits

Year	401(k) & 403(b) Limit	457 Plan Limit	IRA Limit	SIMPLE Limit
Current	$10,500	$8,500	$2,000	$6,000
2002	$11,000	$11,000	$3,000	$7,000
2003	$12,000	$12,000	$3,000	$8,000
2004	$13,000	$13,000	$3,000	$9,000
2005	$14,000	$14,000	$4,000	$10,000
2006	$15,000	$15,000	$4,000	Indexed for inflation in $500 increments
2007	Indexed for inflation in $500 increments	Indexed for inflation in $500 increments	$4,000	
2008			$5,000	
2009			Indexed for inflation in $500 increments	
2010				

B. Scheduled increases in 401(k), 403(b), 457, SIMPLE and IRA: catch-up amounts

Year	401(k) & 403(b) Catch-up	457 Plan Catch-up	IRA Catch-up	SIMPLE Catch-up
Current	——	——	——	——
2002	$1,000	$1,000	$500	$500
2003	$2,000	$2,000	$500	$1,000
2004	$3,000	$3,000	$500	$1,500
2005	$4,000	$4,000	$500	$2,000
2006	$5,000	$5,000	$1,000	$2,500
2007	Indexed for inflation in $500 increments	Indexed for inflation in $500 increments	$1,000 in later years, not indexed for inflation	Indexed for inflation in $500 increments
2008				
2009				
2010				

C. Low-income tax credit for pension contributions

1. Applicable Contributions:
   All elective contributions to 401(k), 403(b), and governmental 457 plans, SIMPLE and traditional or Roth IRAs.
2. Eligible Taxpayers:
   Joint filers with adjusted gross income of $50,000 or less; heads of households with $37,000 or less; and individual filers with $25,000 or less.
3. Credit Limits:
   Maximum annual contribution eligible for non-refundable tax credit is $2,000; Maximum credit rate is 50% (with lower rates for those in higher range of income eligibility); Credit is in addition to exclusion from income or deduction that otherwise applies; Credit is in effect for years 2002–2006.

contribute at as high a rate as possible—through matching contributions and targeted employee communications programs, for example. Plan sponsors also welcome the recent developments described above—the relief from the antidiscrimination rules provided for catch-up contributions and the incentive to meet these rules provided by the lower-income tax credit.

C. *Defined Benefit (DB) vs. Defined Contribution (DC) Plans*

In DB plans, retirement benefits typically are set by a schedule based on the number of years worked by the participant and his or her average salary in the years immediately prior to retirement. To finance this benefit schedule, employers (and sometimes, but rarely, employees) make regular contributions to DB plans. Employers (or their investment managers) choose the investments for DB assets, and employees have no say in investing these assets. If the contributions to the DB plan and the investment performance of DB assets are together insufficient to meet the schedule of retirement benefits offered by a DB plan, the employer must make up the shortfall by making higher contributions to the plan. But if investment performance is better than expected, benefits remain the same and the employer's future contributions are lowered. If the employer sponsoring a DB plan goes bankrupt, participants in that employer's plan are guaranteed to receive only a modest level of "basic benefits" from a federal insurance program administered by the Pension Benefit Guaranty Corporation (PBGC). If an employee terminates employment with the employer sponsoring a DB plan, it is usually quite difficult for the employee to take with him or her any share of the plan's assets. This lack of portability is one of the biggest disadvantages of a DB plan, given the high level of mobility among today's workforce.

In DC plans, especially 401(k) plans, participants typically decide how much to contribute to the plan; the employer usually (but not always) contributes by matching some of the participant's contributions to the plan. In DC plans, employers establish the array of investment alternatives available in the plan, but the participants choose the investments for their own accounts. The retirement benefits of DC participants are determined by the amount of plan contributions and the performance of the investment alternatives chosen by the participants. In a DC plan, the employer is not obligated to provide any specific level of retirement benefits; the employer's obligation is limited to a specified level of contributions. If the retirement benefits of the employee are lower than desired because the plan investments selected by the employee did not perform well, the employee must make do with those benefits. But if the investments perform better than expected, the employee receives higher benefits. If the employee leaves an employer sponsoring a DC plan, the employee usually can receive his or her vested account balances as a lump sum, or transfer his or her account to an IRA or new employer's plan. The portability provided by DC plans is one of the principal advantages of this type of plan.

As mentioned already, the number of DC plans, as well as the assets held in those plans, continues to grow in relation to the number of DB plans and DB assets. In 1985, DB assets were twice that of DC assets. But DC assets caught up with DB assets in 1996 and are projected to exceed DB assets by more than 35% before the end of 2005 (see Figure 8.4). Over the past 20 years, the number of DB plans actually has shrunk, while the number of DC plans has increased to the point where they now represent over 90%

FIGURE 8.4

Defined benefit versus defined contribution assets, 1992–2005

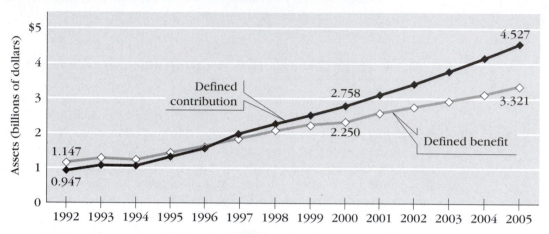

Source: For 1992–1996, EBRI tabulations based on U.S. Department of Labor, Pension and Welfare Benefits Administration, *Private Pension Plan Bulletin* (Winter 1999–2000); for 1997–2005, EBRI projections. Asset amounts shown exclude funds held by life insurance companies under allocated group insurance contracts for payment of retirement benefits. These excluded funds make up roughly 10 to15 percent of total private fund assets. From EBRI, "Research Highlights: Retirement and Health Data," January 2001. Reprinted by permission of Employee Benefit Research Institute, *Research Highlights, Retirement Data,* January 2001.

of the number of private sector qualified plans. Similarly, the number of employees covered under these different types of plans has changed dramatically. In 1975, about 44% of workers were covered by DB plans and only 18% by DC plans; by 2005, it is projected that only about 17% of workers will be covered by DB plans, but over 52% will be covered by DC plans.

Why has this happened? There are three principal reasons. First, federal laws and regulations, beginning with ERISA's enactment in 1974, have added to the cost and complexity of sponsoring DB plans (See "What Is ERISA?"). From an employer's perspective, changes such as mandatory funding requirements, high PBGC premiums and increased exposure to fiduciary claims have made DB plans increasingly unattractive.

Second, demographic changes have made DB plans less attractive to employees. The design of most DB plans is based on a model of lifetime employment at one company— a model that has been displaced by a model of job mobility. In an average month during 1999, for example, 2.7% of the workforce (or 4 million people) switched employers.[1] Under a typical DB plan, benefits are back-loaded, that is, they are based on a combination of years of tenure and final pay in an effort to provide long-term employees with adequate retirement income. But short-term employees receive significantly reduced benefits, with the result that the typical job hopper will receive substantially less under a DB plan than will a long-term employee of a single firm. This difference has been demonstrated in a study by Samwick and Skinner that compared the simulated retirement benefits of randomly chosen DB participants and DC participants. That study found DC participants to be increasingly better off than their DB counterparts as the number of job changes grew.[2] This back-loading, together with a lack of portability, has made DB plans quite unpopular among many employees, except for those working for large manufacturing firms where long-term tenure has been the norm.

CALLOUT
What Is ERISA?

ERISA is the Employee Retirement Income Security Act of 1974, as amended. It was signed into law on September 4, 1974, by President Gerald Ford. Its history goes back to 1962, when President John F. Kennedy appointed an advisory committee to study private pension plans. The report of that committee, which detailed significant shortcomings in the private pension system, led to a number of congressional investigations and the introduction of numerous bills to regulate private pension plans, culminating in the adoption of ERISA.

ERISA's main purposes were to broaden coverage under employer-sponsored retirement plans, better ensure that retirement benefits are distributed fairly among those who are covered, and protect the rights of participants and their beneficiaries to those benefits.

ERISA sought to achieve these purposes in three principal ways. First, it amended the Internal Revenue Code to stiffen the eligibility and vesting requirements that all plans must meet in order to obtain tax-favored status. Second, it imposed substantial funding requirements on DB plans to obtain tax-favored status, and it also enacted a federal insurance program to guarantee that at least basic DB plan benefits would be paid. Third, it adopted strict fiduciary standards that trustees, plan sponsors and other fiduciaries must follow when dealing with plan assets.

In many ways ERISA has been a resounding legislative success. It has, as intended, broadened the base of participants in the private pension system and made the rights of those participants to receive their benefits more secure. However, critics complain that it imposes unnecessary regulatory burdens—for example, by its broad prohibitions on transactions between retirement plans and their service providers.

The third reason was the shifting performance of the U.S. stock market during the 1970s and 1980s versus the 1990s. Under a DB plan, the risk and reward of investment performance remain with employers. Thus, the relatively low returns of the stock market during the 1970s and the early 1980s encouraged employers to move from DB to DC plans; they also wanted to control employer contributions by making them more predictable. Although some commentators insist that the primary reason for the shift was the pressure from employers to reduce costs, employers who continued to sponsor DB plans have benefited greatly from the higher investment returns in the 1990s. Because of the combination of the bull market of the 1990s and the tax rule that prevents an employer from making any contributions at all if its DB plan is more than 150% funded, fewer than half of U.S. employers sponsoring DB plans made any contribution at all to those plans in 1998. On the other hand, the bull market of the 1990s certainly helped increase the popularity of DC plans. Although DC plans effectively shift the risk of inadequate benefits to employees, positive returns appeared on DC participants' quarterly statements throughout most of the decade. It is interesting to ponder whether DC plans would have met with the same acceptance in the United States if introduced in a long down market, such as Japan saw during the 1990s.

II. Role of Mutual Funds in 401(k) Plans

This section discusses why mutual funds have benefited so much from the rapid growth in 401(k) plans, the investment options offered by mutual fund complexes to these plans and the range of other services provided by fund complexes to these plans.

A. *401(k) Growth and Mutual Funds*

Virtually nonexistent in 1985, 401(k) assets grew to more than $1.9 trillion at the end of 2000 and are projected to grow to $3.2 trillion by 2005, representing over two-thirds of total DC assets (see Figure 8.5). This growth in plan assets is paralleled by similar growth in the number of participants covered by 401(k) plans. Participants are expected to grow from 41 million in 2000 to almost 55 million by 2005. Similarly, by 2005, the number of 401(k) plans is expected to grow to over 435,000.

This phenomenal growth of 401(k) plans has been a key factor in fueling the growth of the mutual fund industry. Before the advent of 401(k) plans, banks and insurance companies dominated a retirement business that was predominantly DB in nature. This dominance carried over to the 401(k) market in its infancy as banks offered early 401(k) plans with the same type of commingled pool products they had previously developed for the small DB market. Insurance companies, on the other hand, developed guaranteed investment contracts (GICs) with fixed interest rates and separate accounts with equities for the 401(k) market. In 1985, as the 401(k) market began to grow, mutual funds held only 5% of the total assets in 401(k) plans; this percentage rose to only 9% by 1990 (see Figure 8.6).

However, as 401(k) plans experienced their growth spurt during the 1990s, mutual funds rapidly gained market share from other financial institutions. As shown in Figure 8.6, 45% of 401(k) assets in 1999 and 2000 were held in mutual funds, and that percentage is still rising. Furthermore, mutual fund sponsors administered substantial amounts of

FIGURE 8.5

401(k) Trends: asset growth, 1992–2005 ($ trillions)

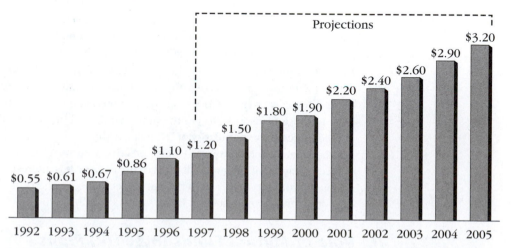

Source: For 1992-1996, Employee Benefit Research Institute tabulations based on U.S. Department of Labor, Pension and Welfare Benefits Administration, Private Pension Plan Bulletin (Winter 1999-2000), for 1997-2005, EBRI projections. Asset amounts shown exclude funds held by life insurance companies under allocated group insurance contracts for payment of retirement benefits. These excluded funds make up roughly 10 to 15 percent of total private fund assets. From EBRI, "Research Highlights, Retirement and Health Data," January 2001. Reprinted by permission of Employee Benefit Research Institute, *Research Highlights, Retirement Data,* January 2001.

FIGURE 8.6

Mutual fund share of 401(k) assets, 1985–2000

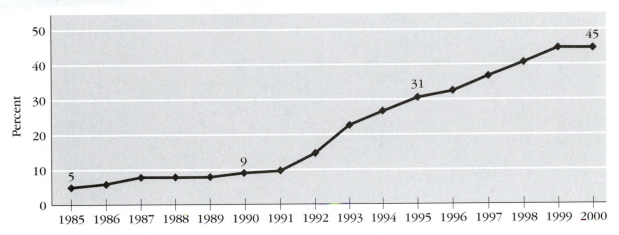

Sources: Investment Company Institute, Federal Reserve Board and Department of Labor. From *ICI Mutual Fund Fact Book,* 2001. Reprinted by permission of the Investment Company Institute.

other types of assets—for example, employer stock and GICs—held by 401(k) plans as well as mutual funds. Of the 10 largest players in the 401(k) marketplace, five were among the largest players in the mutual fund industry: Fidelity, Vanguard, Capital Research, Putnam and Janus (see Table 8.1).

Why have 401(k) plan sponsors migrated more and more to mutual complexes rather than banks and insurance companies? In general, banks and insurance companies were traditionally oriented toward DB plans, which primarily involve investing one aggregate pool pursuant to the guidelines of a relatively sophisticated set of plan trustees or investment committee members. Because the risk and reward of investment performance remain with the employer, it is the employer who is the buyer of DB investment management services. As such, DB plans are the quintessential institutional product. By contrast, once the employer chooses the provider for a DC plan, it is primarily a retail product involving hundreds or thousands of individual plan participants choosing among multiple investment alternatives. Mutual fund complexes were generally accustomed to distributing and servicing products designed for retail investors.

Specifically, mutual fund complexes provided an array of products and services that were attractive to plan sponsors and participants in a retail-like context. First, mutual funds are valued at the end of every business day and may be redeemed at that time. The prices of mutual funds appear each day in the newspaper. By contrast, the commingled pools of many banks and the pension accounts maintained by insurance companies traditionally were valued monthly or quarterly, and redemptions traditionally were limited to those valuation dates. Moreover, the prices of most commingled funds at banks and most pension accounts at insurance companies are not published daily in the newspapers.

Second, mutual fund complexes offer a broad array of product choices. As explained in Chapter Two, there are over 8,000 mutual funds, including broadly diversified and

TABLE 8.1

Top managers of defined contribution assets (by assets as of 12/31/00)

Firm	$ Millions
Fidelity	345,800
TIAA-CREF	277,636
State Street Global	178,646
Barclays Global	101,200
Vanguard	92,008
Capital Research	91,407
Deutsche Asset[a]	87,000
Putnam Investments	55,301
Prudential Insurance	54,308
Janus	50,554
Total of top 10	1,333,860
Total of top 25	1,744,292

Note: U.S. institutional, tax-exempt assets managed internally.
[a]As of December 31, 1999.
Source: Pensions & Investments, May 14, 2001.

narrow sector funds, as well as funds focused on different investment styles and geographical areas. As 401(k) plans have increased the number of investment options offered to plan participants, mutual fund complexes were the natural beneficiaries. While banks and insurance companies have increased their product array over the years, most have not kept pace with the incredible proliferation of choices available from mutual funds.

Third, mutual fund sponsors were used to applying technology to service large numbers of individual accounts. The leading providers of 401(k) record keeping include no-load complexes—such as Vanguard, T. Rowe Price and Fidelity—that made extensive investments in mail, phone and the Internet to deal directly with their customers. Except for the processing-oriented banks like State Street Bank & Trust, most banks did not develop the record keeping systems needed to service thousands of 401(k) plan participants. With a few exceptions, insurance companies generally serviced their customers through agents rather than through direct mail, phone or Internet.

Finally, there is a historical connection between the heavy marketing support of IRAs by fund sponsors during the early 1980s and the participant preference for mutual funds in 401(k) plans during the late 1980s. When tax deductions were available universally for IRA contributions from 1981 through 1986, many individual investors were introduced to mutual funds, which were available investment options through an IRA. After these deductions were restricted in 1986, interest in IRAs declined and interest surged in 401(k) plans, which had their own tax advantages. Therefore, it was logical for plan participants, who had invested their own retirement contributions in IRAs through mutual funds, to favor mutual funds again when investing their own retirement contributions through 401(k) plans.

B. Investment Options and Fund Expenses

In a 401(k) plan, an employer may choose to offer as few or as many investment alternatives as it pleases, provided that such alternatives are "prudent" within the meaning of the fiduciary rules of ERISA. However, an employer must offer at least three core investment alternatives in order to enjoy the benefit of a safe harbor established under Section 404(c) of ERISA by the Department of Labor (DOL). The safe harbor protects employers from liability on the performance of the specific investments chosen by the employee as long as the employer provides a reasonable array of investment alternatives and sufficient information about such alternatives. The three investment alternatives required to meet the DOL safe harbor must have materially different risk and return characteristics, and they must be well diversified within their asset classes. Three typical examples are a money market fund or other low-risk alternative such as a bank deposit or a fixed-rate contract offered by insurance companies known as a GIC; an income alternative such as a government or corporate bond fund; and a diversified stock fund.

Most 401(k) plans offer several stock funds, one or more bond funds, a "safe" choice such as a money market fund or stable value pool (which includes GICs), as well as employer stock. In terms of investment options actually chosen by participants, assets are frequently placed in equities. In fact, at the end of 1999, over 53% of 401(k) and other DC plan assets were allocated to equity funds and another 19% to company stock, so that the overall allocation to equities exceeded 70% (see Figure 8.7).

By the end of 1999, the average number of investment options available to 401(k) participants had increased to 10, up from 7 in 1995 (see Table 8.2). The number of options was correlated positively to plan size, with the smallest plans offering only 8 investment options, but the largest holding 34 on average in 1999. Because of this correlation, over 70% of participants now have access to at least 11 investment options, and 40% have access to at least 16.

This trend toward providing participants with more and more investment choices is expected to continue. Some large employers now offer 75 or more fund alternatives from the same complex. Other large employers have asked mutual fund sponsors to expand 401(k) plan offerings to include not only their own funds but also funds from other complexes, a development parallel to fund marketplaces in the direct channel. (See Chapter Seven.) A few plans sponsored by large employers, especially those with a substantial group of sophisticated professionals, have offered a "mutual fund window"—allowing access by participants to substantially all of the funds in a mutual fund complex.

Certain large employers are also asking for nonmutual fund investment products such as brokerage for individual stocks and stable value pools for bonds. "Stable value" pools contain specialized fixed income instruments with specified yields issued by insurance companies, banks and similar financial institutions; they differ from normal bonds in that they are not marked to market value on a daily basis. Instead, such pools typically are valued at book (historical cost with adjustments) because the issuer redeems at book value so long as (1) the redemption is at the direction of the plan participant and (2) the plan participant does not transfer the proceeds to a bond or similar

FIGURE 8.7

Average asset allocation for all plan balances, 1999

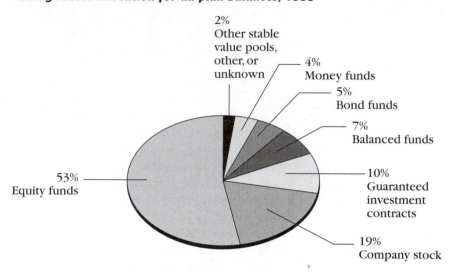

Source: Tabulations from EBRI/ICI Participant-Directed Retirement Plan Data Collection Project. From EBRI, "Research Highlights, Retirement Data," October 2000. Reprinted by permission of Employee Benefit Research Institute, *Research Highlights, Retirement Data,* October 2000.

"competing" fund available as an option under the plan (without a substantial waiting period).

In addition, employers have begun to ask for commingled pools—provided through bank affiliates of mutual fund managers—that are offered exclusively to participants in DC plans. So long as these commingled pools are offered only to retirement plans and their participants but not to the public at large, they do not need to register like mutual funds with the Securities and Exchange Commission (SEC). Nor do the daily prices of such commingled pools appear in the newspapers. Like mutual funds, however, such commingled pools are not taxable entities. They are also similar to mutual funds in that they may offer an unlimited variety of investment objectives and styles.

What is driving this trend toward broader investment choices in 401(k) plans? The mutual funds currently offered in the 401(k) market typically were created for taxable retail investors. As an increasingly greater portion of mutual fund assets are held in 401(k) plans, plan sponsors have begun to demand investment products geared more specifically to the 401(k) marketplace, including new mutual funds whose investment strategies take into account the tax-exempt status of 401(k) plans. As a consequence, the typical 401(k) plan today offers a blend of retail mutual funds and nonmutual fund products geared more specifically to the retirement plan marketplace.

At the same time, employers have demanded lower expenses for mutual funds in 401(k) plans than those charged for retail taxable funds. Almost all mutual funds offered to 401(k) participants are no-load; even funds with loads typically waive them for retirement plans. Without sales loads, the principal revenue stream from retirement investors to the fund sponsor is the advisory fee and, to a lesser extent, the transfer agent

TABLE 8.2

Average number of investment options available, by plan size

Plan Size (number of participants)	1995	1996	1997	1998	1999
0–49	5	6	7	7	8
50–99	6	7	8	8	9
100–499	6	7	8	9	11
500–2,499	8	8	10	11	13
2,500–4,999	8	9	12	13	15
5,000–9,999	9	10	12	14	18
10,000+	14	16	18	25	34
Overall	7	7	8	9	10

Source: Fidelity Investments, "Building Futures: How American Companies Are Helping Their Employees Retire—A Report on Corporate Defined Contribution Plans," 2001.

fee. As evidence of this pressure on fees, an SEC study on mutual fund fees (discussed in Chapter Ten) reported that the asset-weighted average expense ratio for retirement-oriented funds (i.e., the 50 mutual funds with the most 401(k) assets) is 24% below the average expense ratio for all funds (69 basis points versus 91 basis points). In part, this may be due to the fact that most of these funds are very large, since the SEC study also reported that funds with more than $1 billion in assets have average expense ratios that were 50% below the average expense ratio for smaller funds. This creates the possibility of an interesting dynamic: the more plan sponsors choose lower-expense funds, the larger those funds become, thereby increasing the likelihood that their expense ratios will decline even further.

Since plan fiduciaries must consider cost among other factors in choosing investment options for plans, the pressure on mutual fund expenses will continue. Large plan sponsors make two main points. First, they say that their DC plans deserve the lower prices they pay in the institutional market for their DB plans to reflect the economies of scale they are bringing to the investment product embodied in the mutual fund. Second, they maintain that they deserve a significant price break on the distribution portion of the mutual fund's expenses because they are bringing thousands of investors to the fund at once. In essence, these large plan sponsors are arguing that participants in large plans should pay less than do other shareholders in a fund. Such an argument cuts against the general concept of a mutual fund, where all shareholders pay fees at the same rate.

One possibility is the creation of a separate class of a mutual fund limited only to participants in large plans. (For more on classes, see Chapter Ten.) Although the advisory fee must be the same for all classes of the same fund, one class may have lower expenses than another because of lower servicing or distribution costs. However, to the extent that these large plans obtain the creation of new classes of mutual fund shares exclusively for them, the cost reductions they seek may prove illusory for two reasons. First, these plans often demand a higher level of service than do retail accounts. Second, the average 401(k) account size, although reasonable, is often not as large as the average retail account. The combination of a higher level of services plus a lower average account size leads to higher servicing and distribution costs, not lower ones.

Nevertheless, the pressure on fees is not going to evaporate, and mutual fund complexes will continue looking for new ways to drive down expense ratios in the retirement market. Among the possible solutions are the following:

- New mutual funds whose pricing structures take into account the institutional aspects of distributing investment products in the 401(k) marketplace

- New classes of funds that handle all transactions electronically to reduce transfer agency expenses for retirement accounts

- Commingled investment pools designed exclusively for DC plans, with institutional type of pricing and externalized record keeping offered through affiliates of the mutual fund manager

C. Other Services

The shareholder services provided by mutual funds match up well against the basic services needed by participants in 401(k) plans. As mentioned above, these services flow from the daily valuations performed by mutual funds to ensure that their shares are redeemable on demand. To handle high volumes of shareholder interactions, mutual funds also have developed extensive customer reporting and processing capabilities. The following functions are necessary to service most 401(k) plan participants:

- Daily contribution and distribution processing

- Daily exchange processing

- Daily processing of participant loans

- Quarterly or more frequent participant statements

- Telephone service capabilities

Beside these basic services to participants, 401(k) plans require basic services to plan sponsors. These include aggregation of individual participant data and activity at a plan level so that these aggregate statistics can be reported periodically to plan sponsors. Such plan-level reporting is necessary to enable the plan sponsor to meet its reporting obligations under ERISA. Moreover, fund complexes typically provide the plan sponsor with other services, such as tax reporting and nondiscrimination testing, which can be delivered through the fund complex's record keeping system.

These basic participant-level and plan-level services are sufficient for a 401(k) plan invested in mutual funds only. These 401(k) plans typically consist of newly created supplemental savings plans that are in addition to other DC plans, or DB plans, sponsored by employers. Such supplemental savings plans are designed to take advantage of the salary-reduction feature of 401(k) and offer employees an additional way to save for retirement. Limiting the investment options to mutual funds works fine for this group of 401(k) plans.

By contrast, another group of 401(k) plans consists of long-standing savings plans sponsored by large employers to which employees have traditionally made after-tax contributions, which have often been matched by employer contributions. The typical investment options under these plans include company stock and stable value investments. Through the use of 401(k) plans, employers may convert the employee contributions made to these savings plans from after-tax to pretax status, making them more attractive to employees. This group of 401(k) plans presents better business prospects to mutual fund complexes because of the significantly higher cash flows from such plans and the opportunity to convert some of the existing assets in such plans to mutual funds.

But the processing of company stock and stable value investments involves enormous operational efforts to make these investment options compatible with the daily processing requirements of mutual funds offered by the same plan. The processing requirements for mutual funds have three key elements. First, mutual funds must create and implement systems that are able to price thousands of portfolio securities in the overnight cycle. Second, mutual funds must create and implement additional systems that are able to record and process thousands of shareholder purchase, exchange and redemption transactions in the overnight cycle. Third, mutual funds must carry a sufficient cash position to handle shareholder redemptions on a daily basis. Absent such a cash position, a mutual fund would not be able to meet shareholder redemptions until it sold securities held in the fund and received the cash proceeds from settlement of the trade (e.g., three-day settlement period in the case of trades in U.S. equity securities).

Therefore, to provide 401(k) plans with daily valuation, exchange and redemption capabilities for all investment options, including company stock and stable value investments, mutual fund complexes have to "unitize" those non–mutual fund investment options in the same way as they do for mutual funds: by adding cash positions to those options to ensure daily liquidity and by accounting for those unitized funds on a daily basis in the same way as mutual funds. In other words, each company stock fund must be set up as a "mini–mutual fund" even though it holds only one equity security. Stable value pools are even more complicated, since they typically hold several non-publicly traded investment contracts with insurance companies, banks or other issuers. In effect, each stable value pool must be set up as a mini–mutual fund that invests exclusively in private placements, thereby requiring the establishment of direct connections with the issuers in order to obtain accurate daily prices and to process redemptions.

Another special set of services required by almost all types of 401(k) plans involves strong capabilities for communicating plan choices to employees. Such communications capabilities are not particularly important in a DB plan, where employees expect to receive the promised benefit at retirement regardless of the plan's investment returns. However, in a DC plan, particularly a participant-directed 401(k) plan, employees need to understand their investment choices and the potential impact of these choices on their retirement income. Additionally, strong employee communication capabilities are important to satisfy the nondiscrimination requirements of 401(k). As mentioned above, the level of pretax contributions by highly compensated employees to a 401(k) plan is dependent on the level of contributions made by NHCEs. For this reason, senior executives usually want to implement an effective communications strategy to influence rank-and-file employees not only to participate in the plan but also to contribute at a high rate. The informational requirements of Section 404(c), as discussed above, further heighten the need of the employer to mount an effective employee communications campaign. In effect, Section 404(c) obligates plan sponsors to educate plan participants about the plan and each of its investment options. The informational materials that mutual funds use to satisfy the SEC's disclosure rules for offerings to individual

CALLOUT

Profile Prospectus

In an attempt to satisfy the informational requirements of Section 404(c) of ERISA and the disclosure rules promulgated by the SEC under the federal securities laws, Fidelity Investments developed a format for summarizing the prospectuses of the Fidelity funds available under a particular DC plan. The intent was to provide a summary description of the funds' investment strategies, risk and return characteristics, operating expenses, historical performance and distribution practices—all in a standardized format designed to facilitate comparisons among all mutual funds offered by the plan. In 1995, the SEC issued a no-action letter confirming that such a summary satisfied the relevant disclosure rules.

This no-action letter was quickly followed by an industry effort to expand the concept of a summary disclosure document to a "profile prospectus" that could be used in the offering of mutual funds in all markets, not just the DC or 401(k) market. The SEC approved the profile prospectus in 1996 on a pilot basis, and adopted a Profile rule in 1998. As a result of these efforts, DC plan sponsors can now satisfy both 404(c) and SEC requirements by providing DC plan participants with a profile prospectus before enrolling in the plan or exchanging into a new mutual fund option under the plan. After confirmation of such a transaction to the plan participant, the plan sponsor or fund sponsor must provide the longer, statutory prospectus for the fund or funds selected by the participant. (For more information on the profile prospectus, see Chapter Three.)

investors are well suited to the communications needs in the 401(k) environment (See "Profile Prospectus").

Nevertheless, the 404(c) rules do create other problems. Plan sponsors have become increasingly concerned that by meeting the informational requirements of 404(c), they might be unintentionally giving investment advice to plan participants. Under ERISA, this would eliminate the employer's protection from liability otherwise provided by the Section 404(c) rules for the specific investment selected by any plan participant. The DOL helped resolve this concern by publishing an interpretive bulletin on educational materials in 1996. That bulletin allows employers and their service providers to disseminate educational materials to 401(k) plan participants without such dissemination constituting "investment advice." At the same time, the SEC provided additional comfort by announcing that plan sponsors who provided informational materials to participants to satisfy 404(c) did not risk becoming "investment advisers" under the federal securities laws.

But many employers had concerns beyond their own legal liabilities. They were concerned that many of their employees, when confronted with a lengthy menu of investment options, actually needed investment advice. These employers expected their fund providers to give such advice on the mutual funds they manage as well as all other plan investment options. This expectation posed a dilemma for the fund providers because ERISA prohibits a provider from giving investment advice to plan participants about its own investment products. Fortunately, the DOL interpretative bulletin resolved this dilemma by promulgating several safe harbors on what does *not* constitute "investment advice" under ERISA, regardless of the commonly understood meaning of these two words. These safe harbors included interactive planning tools that provide participants with model portfolios made up of the investment options available under a particular plan, so long as those portfolios were based on generally accepted investment principles. With the protection of these safe harbors, several fund complexes now generate a number of model portfolios, containing different combinations of mutual funds offered by a plan, based on the investment objectives and risk appetites of plan participants.

Other mutual fund complexes are taking a different route by entering into arrangements with independent firms that purport to provide a full array of investment advice services on mutual funds and other plan investment options. For example, Vanguard has entered into such an arrangement with Financial Engines, and Putnam Investments has entered into a similar arrangement with mPower. However, the plan sponsor or the plan participants themselves typically pay the independent firm's fees for such a full array of advice services. Payment of those fees by the mutual fund complex could create a prohibited transaction under ERISA.

Beyond advice services, plan sponsors continue to demand increasingly sophisticated multimedia employee communication strategies, including video and Internet capabilities. In particular, the utilization of the Internet for participant communications and transactions continues to grow each year at a significant rate. For example, Fidelity Investments reports that the total number of contacts made by plan participants through NetBenefits, Fidelity's Internet access channel for its 6.2 million record keeping and DC participants, grew from almost zero in 1996 to over 34 million in 1999 (see Table 8.3). While the number of telephone contacts was still larger (48.1 million) than the number of Internet contacts (34.4 million) in 1999, the number of telephone contacts was actually lower than in 1998, while the growth rate for Internet transactions from 1998 to 1999 was 197%. What type of inquiries did participants perform on the Internet? According to the Fidelity report, participants used the Internet channel predominantly for easy access to determine their account balances, although more sophisticated monetary transactions, including the ability to make exchanges among investment options, were available. This report is consistent with the observations on the use of the Internet in the retail mutual fund channel. (See Chapter Nine.) In both the retirement and retail channels, fund shareholders rely on the Internet to satisfy simple requests for information like account balances, leaving fund transactions to automated phone systems and more complex questions to calls with live representatives.

The ability to use the Internet to make mutual fund exchanges has led to concerns among some commentators that easy access might lead to an inappropriately high

TABLE 8.3

Total contact by participant access channel (millions)

Access Channel	1996	1997	1998	1999	Growth Rate, 1998–1999
Phone representatives	7.9	8.3	9.5	10.8	14%
Voice response systems	24.1	37.1	52.2	48.1	–8%
NetBenefits	0.3	1.7	11.6	34.4	197%

Source: Fidelity Investments, "Building Futures: How American Companies Are Helping Their Employees Retire—A Report on Corporate Defined Contribution Plans," 2001.

frequency of trading among plan participants. Certainly the delivery of services through the Internet will enable mutual fund complexes to reach their retirement customers more efficiently and less expensively. But the question on many observers' minds is the potential impact the Internet will have on the investment behavior of retirement participants. The fear is that the availability of online trading will change them from long-term investors to day traders. These issues were addressed in a study conducted jointly in 2000 by Choi and Laibson of Harvard and Metrick of Wharton.[3] The study analyzed the impact of Internet trading on the trading activity (i.e., exchange transactions among available investment options) of about 100,000 participants in two 401(k) plans that added Internet trading capabilities to preexisting telephone trading. The study reviewed trading activity for the first 18 months after market trading opened.

The authors reached a number of conclusions. First, Internet trading became the vehicle of choice, accounting for 60% of trading by the end of the study. Second, the overwhelming majority of participants who tried Internet trading continued to use it. Third, the transaction amounts involved in Internet trading were substantially lower than for telephone trading (possibly for demographic reasons). Finally, the study concluded that online trading caused a significant increase in exchanges among investment options over the long term: during the course of the study, exchange frequency doubled. However, and most important, the study also concluded that this increased trading activity was not the result of short-term trading (i.e., where the position was reversed within five days) or last-hour trading (i.e., where the trades placed in the hour before the market closes). Thus, the study suggests that while Internet access may increase the rate of exchanges among funds by 401(k) participants, it is not turning them into speculative day traders.

III. *Other Types of DC Plans*

Historically, 401(k) plans were limited to corporate sponsors. Comparable salary-reduction DC plans were available for tax-exempt employers and public schools (403(b) plans) and for state and local governments (457 plans). Insurance companies have traditionally dominated the smaller 403(b) and 457 plan markets, but the mutual fund industry has begun to make its presence felt in those markets. Over the past 10 years, legislative changes have made 403(b) and 457 plans more like 401(k) plans, but as discussed below, several historical differences continue to help distinguish these markets from the 401(k) market.

A. *403(b) Plans*

These DC plans are established pursuant to Section 403(b) of the Internal Revenue Code and are available only to employees of organizations exempt from tax under 501(c)(3) of the Internal Revenue Code, public educational systems and self-employed ministers. The big users are universities, hospitals and public school teachers. Historically, 403(b) plans could be invested only in nontransferable annuity contracts; and TIAA-CREF, an insurance company established solely for the purpose of providing retirement services to higher education employees, came to dominate the 403(b) market (See "TIAA-CREF and 403(b)"). That began to change in 1974, when ERISA amended the

CALLOUT
TIAA-CREF and 403(b)

TIAA-CREF is two separate but related institutions. TIAA is the Teachers Insurance and Annuity Company of America, a nonprofit stock life insurance company that offers fixed and variable annuities. TIAA was established in 1918 by the Carnegie Foundation, Andrew Carnegie's largest philanthropy, to provide retirement benefits for employees of private higher educational and research institutions. TIAA offers traditional fixed annuities. CREF is the College Retirement Equities Fund, which was established in 1982 and registered with the SEC as a mutual fund. CREF issues variable annuity contracts, the investment accounts of which are managed by TIAA-CREF Investment Management, LLC, a subsidiary of TIAA. Because CREF is registered with the SEC as a mutual fund, it offers a major feature not available with TIAA annuities: redemption on demand. Together, TIAA-CREF manages over $290 billion in assets, primarily through retirement products offered not only to faculty and other employees of educational institutions and research facilities, but also to employees of public colleges and K–12 teachers. TIAA-CREF currently dominates the higher education retirement marketplace.

The form of retirement plan that TIAA-CREF's customers most commonly use is the Section 403(b) tax-deferred annuity. However, as the financial markets and the income tax laws have changed, TIAA-CREF has expanded its products and services to accommodate the needs of its customers. One recent significant development is its involvement with state tuition savings plans across the country. (See Chapter Seven on these plans.) In addition, TIAA-CREF now offers various insurance products—including life insurance, group disability insurance and long-term care insurance—to its customer base. Finally, TIAA-CREF has now gone beyond its traditional customer base to offer its mutual funds and certain IRA products to the public at large. This expansion of its mission by TIAA-CREF in part results from a recent change in its federal income tax status from a tax-exempt entity to a taxable entity.

Internal Revenue Code to allow 403(b) plans to invest in mutual fund shares held in a custodial account for the eligible employee. Another boost was provided in 1988 when TIAA-CREF reached a settlement with the SEC that allowed participants to transfer previously nonredeemable amounts held in TIAA annuity contracts to 403(b) custodial accounts invested in mutual funds.

Section 403(b) plans are similar to 401(k) plans in most respects. Employees may reduce their salary in order to make contributions, or the employer may contribute for eligible employees, or both. The employee pretax contribution limits for 403(b) plans are generally the same as for 401(k) plans, as is the ability to make "catch-up" contributions (a benefit already available under 403(b) plans before 2002). In addition, under the recent legislation, lower-income workers in 403(b) plans can receive the same tax credit, of up to $1,000 per year, that applies to 401(k) plan participants with respect to their contributions during the five-year period ending in 2006.

However, 403(b) plans are different from 401(k) plans in two respects. First, contributions to 403(b) plans are not subject to the nondiscrimination rules that apply to 401(k) plans. Second, and perhaps more important, while a company typically chooses one primary provider for its 401(k) plan, a nonprofit organization often selects multiple 403(b) providers for its employees. In the 403(b) world, the typical arrangement includes not only different investment options offered by different investment firms but also different plans from which the participant can choose. For example, a teaching hospital might offer to its employees a "TIAA-CREF plan" and a "Vanguard plan," each of which contains a broad range of annuity or mutual fund options (or both). Sometimes the number of plans offered to participants in the 403(b) world is as high as 50, particularly in the case of some of the public universities.

This plan design significantly complicates the marketing of 403(b) plans. Vendors must first market their investments and other securities at the institutional level to the nonprofit employer. But success at the institutional level does not result in any sales directly. Instead, that success only gives the vendor access to the employees of the nonprofit, where a retail sale must subsequently be made to individual participants. In other words, the 403(b) market has two tiers: with access to the market determined at the institutional level and the ultimate sale made at the retail level.

Notwithstanding the complexity of the 403(b) market, the amount of mutual fund assets invested in mutual funds has grown significantly in recent years, from $15 billion in 1990 to over $280 billion in 1999. As a consequence, 403(b) assets now represent over 20% of the total amount of mutual fund assets in DC plans. In addition to the CREF portion of TIAA-CREF, other mutual fund complexes with a significant presence in the 403(b) market are Fidelity, Vanguard and T. Rowe Price. Large players from the insurance industry, in addition to the TIAA portion of TIAA-CREF, include VALIC, Aetna and Prudential.

B. 457 Plans

Section 457 plans include state and local retirement programs covering public employees and certain tax-exempt organizations not eligible for 403(b) plans. Section 457 plans are similar in operation to 401(k) plans, particularly in that they are funded through salary-reduction contributions made by eligible participants. Beginning in 2002, 457 plans will be subject to the same contribution limits (including the "catch-up" contribution limit) and the lower-income worker tax credit (up to $1,000 per year) that will apply to 401(k) plans. Furthermore, the 457 plan marketplace is more like the 401(k) marketplace than the 403(b) world in that a single record keeper typically administers multiple investment options from multiple investment firms for a state and local plan sponsor.

However, there are some differences between 457 plans and 401(k) plans. From a tax perspective, 457 plans are not subject to many of the complex rules, particularly the nondiscrimination rules, that apply to 401(k) plans. Nor are they subject to ERISA. They are therefore simpler for the governmental employer to implement and maintain than 401(k) plans.

The 457 plan marketplace remains relatively small, as does its impact on mutual funds. While there are virtually no data that currently track the 457 plan market, it appears that the overall size of that market did not exceed $100 billion in 1999. At the end of 1999, 457 plan assets invested in mutual funds totaled only $30 billion and were therefore dwarfed by 401(k) and 403(b) assets invested in mutual funds. The smaller presence of 457 plans in the overall DC marketplace is in part explained by the extent to which the state and local plan market is still dominated by DB plans. This is beginning to change, however. (See "Shift from DB to DC in the Governmental Plan Market.") As the governmental plan market shifts from DB to DC, the presence of mutual

CALLOUT
Shift from DB to DC in the Governmental Plan Market

The retirement systems maintained by state and local governments traditionally have been structured as DB plans. For example, a state government may promise, through its DB plan, to provide each employee with pension income that is based on the employee's final average compensation and years of employment by the governmental entity. The state government is responsible for funding its employees' retirement benefits under the DB plan, either on a pay-as-you-go basis (contributions are made to the plan as current benefits become payable to the retirees) or by making contributions to fund benefits before the benefits are payable. To the extent that the state government chooses to set money aside to fund the benefits from its DB plan, the state government can either manage the money itself (such as the California Public Employees' Retirement System, the nation's largest state pension fund) or hire professional investment managers to do so on its behalf. In either case, the state government guarantees a particular retirement benefit to its employees under such a DB arrangement, regardless of the performance of the underlying assets set aside to fund the promised benefit.

However, as of the beginning of 2001, at least eight states were offering participation in a DC retirement plan to all or some of their employees, partially in an effort to modernize their retirement systems. A DC plan in the public sector is structured as either a 401(k) or a 457 plan, and plan participants typically have the right to direct the investment of their accounts among various investment options offered under the DC plan. Plan participants can receive a distribution of the vested balance of their accounts when they leave employment and will have the ability to roll the distribution over to an IRA or certain other types of retirement plans. The potential advantages and disadvantages of DC plans are generally the same in the public sector as in the private sector. However, additional issues of transition costs arise when a public sector employer considers converting from an existing DB to a DC plan. Older employees may wind up with less retirement income in a DB to DC conversion because they will lose the benefit of back-loaded benefits that typically occurs in a DB plan, and they will not have enough time to accrue a similar level of benefits in their individual accounts under a DC plan. In other words, since DB plans typically provide benefits on the basis of final pay, which is typically much larger than career average pay, the bulk of DB benefits are earned in the last several years of an employee's career (and relatively little is earned in the early years of an employee's career). DC benefits, on the other hand, are earned more evenly over a participant's career. Relative to a DB plan, a DC plan therefore accrues more benefits to younger participants. The crossover point is somewhere between ages 45 and 55.

funds should grow as it has in the 401(k) and 403(b) segments of the overall DC plan marketplace.

At the beginning of 2001, the two largest 457 vendors were Fidelity Investments and ICMA Retirement Corporation. The ICMA Retirement Corporation is an affiliate of International City/County Management Association (ICMA), which originated as a trade association for city managers. The ICMA Retirement Corporation sponsors a master retirement program for state and local employees that offers investment choices from a menu of mutual funds and bank commingled pools. Other major players in the 457 plan market include Vanguard, American Century and T. Rowe Price among mutual fund complexes; Nationwide, Aetna and The Hartford among insurance companies; and Great Western among banks and thrifts.

C. Small Employer Plans

In contrast to large employers, a majority of small employers historically have not offered any type of retirement plan to their employees. About 80% of full-time employees working for companies with more than 100 workers do have employer-sponsored retirement plans, but only about 45% of full-time employees working for companies with fewer than 100 workers are covered by such plans. Although small employers had been eligible during the 1980s for various types of regulatory relief in sponsoring retirement plans, they still complained about the cost and red tape involved in complying with government requirements for such plans. In 1996, Congress responded by creating the Savings Incentive Match Plan for Employees (SIMPLE), a streamlined type of DC plan for employers with 100 or fewer employees. Under this type of plan, small employers may elect to establish either a SIMPLE 401(k) or a SIMPLE IRA. Both are designed to have lower costs and less administration than traditional plans.

The contribution limits are lower for SIMPLE plans than they are for 401(k) plans. Under a SIMPLE plan, participants may contribute $6,000 in 2001, which gradually rises to $10,000 by 2006. In addition, SIMPLE plan sponsors must either match employee contributions with a dollar-for-dollar contribution up to 3% of an employee's compensation or make a minimum 2% contribution for all their employees. The trade-off for this lower contribution limit and mandatory matching or minimum contribution is that SIMPLE plans are free from the antidiscrimination tests that apply to 401(k) plan contributions. The catch-up contribution for employees over age 50 is similarly lower under a SIMPLE plan than under a 401(k) plan. Beginning in 2002, employees over age 50 can contribute an additional $500 to a SIMPLE plan, increasing by the same amount each year until it reaches $2,500 in 2006. Like a 401(k) plan, lower-income employees who make a contribution to a SIMPLE plan may also receive a nonrefundable tax credit of up to $1,000 per year until 2006.

If an employer signs up for SIMPLE with a qualified financial institution, including a mutual fund sponsor, the employer has to transmit monthly payments to that institution only for employees who choose to participate. The employer must either make a limited matching contribution for participating employees or make a minimum contribution for all employees. Employees participating in a SIMPLE plan may establish their own retirement accounts with the financial institution and choose among its investment alternatives. The employees deal directly with the institution, which provides almost all reports and services required for the SIMPLE plan.

The sound policy behind SIMPLE has led to a high level of acceptance in the marketplace for this type of plan, particularly among very small employers (those with fewer than 10 employees). Mutual fund complexes responding to an Investment Company Institute survey estimated that by the end of 2000, they serviced over 250,000 small employers that had adopted SIMPLE plans covering over 1 million employees. In this same survey, mutual fund assets of SIMPLE plans were estimated to exceed $6.5 billion by the end of 2000.

While SIMPLE has made it easier for mutual fund complexes to service small employer plans, other obstacles continue to make it more difficult and less attractive for such complexes to market retirement plan services to small employers than to large employers. Principal among these are the low number of plan participants, geographical dispersion and the relative lack of financial sophistication of small employers. It is far more efficient for mutual fund complexes to capture 100,000 plan participants by selling services to two plans covering 50,000 employees each than to sell services to 2,000 plans covering 50 employees each. (Of course, a mutual fund complex will be required to supply a much broader array of services to the two larger plans.)

As discussed above, the utilization of the Internet for participant communications and transactions has greatly assisted mutual fund sponsors in implementing increasingly sophisticated multimedia strategies for employee communications. Now mutual fund sponsors and other service providers are also using the Internet to market retirement plan services to small employers. This is particularly true for mutual fund sponsors that directly market their services and therefore do not have large sales forces. In addition, independent "clearinghouses" have developed Internet sites that assist small employers in determining which mutual fund sponsor or other service provider is most suitable for their plan needs.

Nevertheless, utilization of the Internet is still far from universal, and marketing retirement plans to small employers remains a significant challenge. While the small employer market tests the limits of the direct marketers without a large sales force, it plays to the strength of the financial intermediary distribution channel. Financial intermediaries such as banks, broker-dealers, insurance companies and financial planners typically have large sales forces, with better access to small employers through branch offices in many locations. In other words, intermediary sales capabilities remain necessary to capture much of the less efficient small employer market for retirement plans. However, this extensive branch network comes with a cost, as an intermediary's sales force must be compensated for advising and servicing retirement plans for small employers. Such compensation usually takes the form of 12b-1 fees paid out by the mutual funds on an annual basis.

IV. IRAs

A. Legal History

The IRA was established under ERISA in 1974 in order to encourage taxpayers who were not covered by employer-sponsored plans to save for their retirement. In 1981, Congress expanded the IRA to allow tax-deductible contributions by all taxpayers, including those covered by employer-sponsored plans. As a result, contributions to IRAs soared. Fund sponsors and other financial institutions responded to this universal IRA by actively marketing IRAs to individual investors as a retail product. As a consequence, annual contributions to IRAs rose to over $38 billion by 1986. After 1986, however, Congress again restricted IRA tax deductions for taxpayers participating in an employer plan, except for those who also earned less than a certain amount of income. Because of these restrictions, fund sponsors and other financial institutions greatly reduced their marketing and advertising budgets for IRAs. As a consequence, IRA contributions declined to little more than $10 billion per year throughout the late 1980s and 1990s.

In 1997, Congress expanded the IRA market for mutual funds by expanding the eligibility for up-front tax deductions to the traditional IRA and by creating a new type of

IRA (the Roth IRA) with a back-end tax benefit. After a gradual phase-in of the new rules, a taxpayer with annual income of $50,000 or less ($80,000 or less for couples) may take a full tax deduction in the year of contribution of up to $2,000 to a traditional IRA even if the taxpayer participates in an employer plan. But like employer-sponsored plans, the amount contributed and the earnings thereon will be taxed when distributed at retirement. Alternatively, a taxpayer with annual income of $110,000 or less ($150,000 or less for couples) may now choose to contribute up to $2,000 a year to a back-end Roth IRA. While taxpayers will receive no deduction in the year of contribution to Roth IRAs, the earnings on assets in these IRAs are never taxed if they are held in the IRA for five years and distributed after age 59½ or for another qualifying reason.

At about the same time, Congress also increased the IRA market by expanding the opportunities for nonworking spouses—a relatively affluent group of over 13 million taxpayers, many of whom already own mutual funds. Historically, a nonworking spouse and working spouse could together make an annual IRA contribution of only $2,250. Moreover, the deductibility of that IRA contribution often depended on whether the working spouse was an eligible participant in an employer-based retirement plan. In 1996, however, Congress enacted legislation allowing a nonworking spouse to make an annual IRA contribution of $2,000 in addition to the $2,000 IRA contribution of the working spouse. In 1997, Congress provided further that the nonworking spouse may receive a full tax deduction for an IRA contribution, regardless of the working spouse's pension participation, as long as the couple's total income does not exceed $150,000 per year.

In 2001, Congress again made changes to the law that expanded the IRA market. The following are the most important changes for IRAs:

- The annual contribution limit increases for all types of IRAs from $2,000 to $3,000 in 2002 and incrementally thereafter until it reaches $5,000 in 2008.

- Similar to 401(k), individuals over age 50 are able to make "catch-up" contributions to IRAs of an additional $1,000 per year beginning in 2002 and increasing incrementally thereafter until the catch-up limit reaches $5,000 in 2006.

- Also similar to 401(k), lower-income workers are able to receive a refundable tax credit of up to $1,000 per year with respect to their IRA contributions beginning in 2002 and ending in 2006.

B. Growth of IRAs

The overall growth in IRAs has been staggering. As mentioned before, by the end of 1999, IRA assets totaled almost $2.5 trillion, an amount that exceeded the assets in DB plans or DC plans. The penetration of U.S. households is comparable to this asset growth. By 2000, over 42.5 million U.S. households, representing 41% of all U.S. households, owned an IRA. Nearly one-third of U.S. households (over 33 million) held traditional IRAs, and another 10% (about 10 million households) owned Roth IRAs. Growth in IRAs is expected to continue, with traditional IRA assets almost tripling by 2010 (see Figure 8.8). The keys to this growth are attracting new investors to contributory IRAs and continuing to attract 401(k) and other DC participants to rollover IRAs upon retirement or other separation from service.

FIGURE 8.8

Traditional IRA assets, 1999–2010 ($ billions)

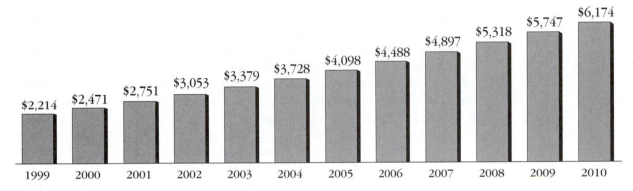

Source: Employee Benefits Research Institute, Investment Company Institute, Cerulli Associates, "The Cerulli Report on the Rollover IRA Market: Retirement Markets in Transition," 2000.

In particular, Roth IRAs represented almost one-quarter of all IRAs after only two years in existence. This growth spurt indicates the extent to which Roth IRAs have reinvigorated the contributory IRA market. In part, this has occurred because the passage of the Roth IRA led to vigorous marketing efforts by financial institutions, which had curtailed these efforts after the universal IRA was repealed in 1986. In part, this has occurred because the increased income limits for Roth IRAs allow a larger and wealthier population the opportunity to make IRA contributions than has been permitted since 1986. For both of these reasons, mutual fund sponsors are once again aggressively marketing contributory IRAs, and eligible Americans have responded enthusiastically.

Notwithstanding the positive impact made by the Roth IRA and the expanded rules for nonworking spouses, annual contributions to IRAs have not returned to the level from 1982 through 1986 with the universal IRA. Instead, most of the recent growth in IRAs has come from rollover IRAs. A *rollover IRA* is an IRA established with assets rolled over from an employer-sponsored retirement plan. The big push in rollover IRAs came in 1992, when Congress passed incentives for plan participants who leave employment to "roll over" the assets in their employer-sponsored plan accounts to an IRA instead of withdrawing those assets for consumption. The law now requires a plan administrator to withhold 20% of plan withdrawals for departing employees, unless those withdrawals are transferred directly from the plan to a rollover account at a qualified financial institution. A qualifying rollover is not subject to income tax until the participant actually takes retirement distributions from the IRA.

As a result of baby boom demographics and these tax incentives, the percentage of job changers who transfer their account balances to rollover IRAs increased to 40% by 1998. In 1999, lump-sum distributions from employer-sponsored plans of all types reached $300 billion, of which $200 billion was rolled over to IRAs. Most of the monies rolled over from qualified plans to IRAs come from DC plans, because DC plans are more likely to permit lump-sum distributions than DB plans, which tend to favor annuity or installment distributions. Rollovers to IRAs from 401(k) and other profit-sharing plans have always been permitted. Rollovers to IRAs from 403(b) plans have been permitted since 1992; beginning in 2002, rollovers to IRAs from 457 plans can be made as well. As a consequence, the growth of DC plans has fueled—and will continue to fuel—the growth in rollover IRAs. In fact, DC distributions rolled over to IRAs are projected to reach $467 billion by 2010 (see Figure 8.9).

Beginning in 2002, new portability rules allow transferability among different types of employer-sponsored plans. Before this change, transfers could be made only (directly or through a conduit rollover IRA) between the same kinds of plan—for example, 401(k) to 401(k) but not 403(b) to 401(k). In addition, the new rules allow for the transfer to employer plans of all accumulations in IRAs of the employee in excess of his or her after-tax contribution—from both contributory and rollover IRAs. Such transfers would, in effect, be the opposite of the typical transfer from an employer plan to a rollover IRA. These new rules are likely to have both a positive and a negative effect on IRAs. On the positive side, IRA holders will now be able to consolidate their contributory and rollover IRAs into a single IRA, which should provide a cost benefit to IRA providers through fewer IRAs but larger IRA balances. On the negative side, when some employees find a new job, they may move monies from their rollover IRA to the new employer's plan. Other such employees may move their accounts directly from their prior employer's plan to their new employer's plan, without the need to leave accumulations in a rollover IRA. However, it is still likely that most employees will prefer a rollover IRA upon eventual retirement because of the greater control and choice offered by an IRA relative to many employer-sponsored plans.

FIGURE 8.9

Rollover IRA and DC distributions, 1999–2010 ($ billions)

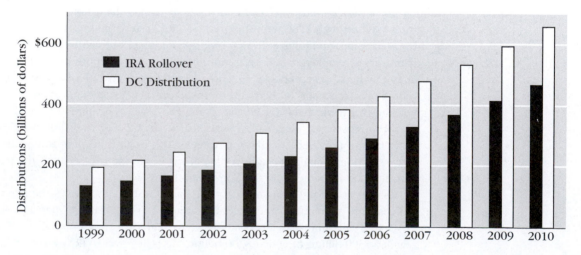

Source: Employee Benefits Research Institute, Investment Company Institute, Cerulli Associates, "The Cerulli Report on the Rollover IRA Market: Retirement Markets in Transition," 2000.

The potential magnitude of IRA rollovers from DC plans has attracted the attention of mutual fund sponsors for obvious reasons. This portion of the retirement market is particularly attractive since the likelihood that separated employees will roll over to an IRA increases significantly as their account size grows. As shown by Table 8.4, the percentage of retirement plan distributions that roll over to IRAs rises to the range of 75% to 85% for distributions between $50,000 and $99,999, and to over 90% for distributions over $100,000. For most fund sponsors, these large accounts are the most profitable to manage and service.

C. IRAs and Mutual Funds

As has been the case with 401(k) plans, the growth of IRAs has been a key factor in contributing to the growth of the mutual fund industry. Before the advent of IRAs, the only tax-advantaged way to allocate personal savings outside the employment context to retirement was through the purchase of insurance products, particularly annuities that allow for tax-free earnings growth (see Chapter Seven). But IRAs have an additional tax advantage in that they offer either a front-end tax deduction (regular IRA) or a back-end tax exclusion (Roth IRA). In other words, while both IRAs and insurance annuities allow for the tax-free building up of income during the deferral period, only IRAs offer the benefit of an upfront tax deduction or back-end tax exclusion.

Mutual funds eventually came to dominate the IRA marketplace for reasons that are similar to the reasons that mutual funds dominate the 401(k) marketplace. First, like 401(k) participants, IRA holders view the IRA as their own money—whether contributed on a regular basis annually or by way of a rollover. Therefore, they want to control the investment of their IRA assets by selecting particular mutual funds they like rather than turning over total investment discretion to any financial institution. Second, the broad range of investments available under a mutual fund IRA—particularly equity investments—dwarfs the investment choices available under an insurance annuity, which at the time IRAs were first enacted were almost exclusively limited to long-term fixed income investments that permitted no redemptions or exchanges. The attractiveness of using a mutual fund IRA to make equity investments only increased during the long bull market run of the 1990s. Third, the IRA is very much a retail account since no

TABLE 8.4

Relationship between size of lump-sum distributions and rollover rates

Distribution Size	Share of Dollars That Roll Over	Estimated Share of 401(k) Assets
Less than $5,000	17–30%	2%
$5,000–24,999	35–45	10
$25,000–29,999	65–75	13
$50,000–99,999	75–85	25
$100,000+	90+	50

Source: Hewitt Associates, Employee Benefit Research Institute, LIMRA and Bernstein estimates.

employer or other institution is involved. As is the case with 401(k) accounts, services typically made available to retail mutual fund customers—such as daily valuation, exchanges and redemptions, Internet access and the appearance of mutual fund prices in the daily press—all contributed to the attractiveness of mutual funds as an investment for IRAs. Finally, the success of mutual funds in the 401(k) marketplace strengthens the dominance of mutual funds in the IRA marketplace because 401(k) customers have become increasingly comfortable with mutual funds as the core of their retirement investment strategy. This comfort level has been reinforced by the portability of 401(k) plan accounts to rollover IRAs.

Thus, the dominance of mutual funds in the universal IRA marketplace helped establish the domination of mutual funds in the 401(k) market, which took off at about the same time that the universal IRA was repealed in 1986. In turn, the ensuing domination by mutual funds of the 401(k) market helped mutual funds gain dominance in the rollover IRA market as baby boomers began to retire and move their money from employer-sponsored plans into rollover IRAs. For all these reasons, 49% of all IRA assets in 1999 were invested in mutual funds, more than double the 23% rate held in mutual funds in 1989. As shown by Figure 8.10, banks and thrifts in particular have lost significant market share of IRA assets to mutual funds (and to brokerage firms as well).

V. *The Future of Retirement Plans*

The retirement market is now maturing, largely as a result of demographics. The first wave of the baby boom is now in its 50s and will begin to retire in significant numbers over the next 10 years. The population over age 65 will increase dramatically around

FIGURE 8.10

IRA market share

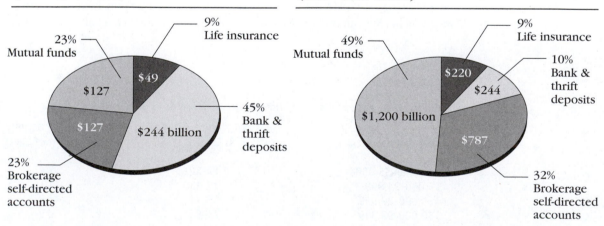

1989
(total = $546 billion)

1999
(total = $2.47 trillion)

Source: Investment Company Institute, *Mutual Fund Factbook,* 2000; and Paul Yakoboski, "IRA Assets Total More Than $2 Trillion," *EBRI Notes,* no. 5 (Employee Benefit Research Institute, May 2000): 1–3. From *EBRI Research Highlights: Retirement Data,* January 2001. Reprinted by permission of Employee Benefit Research Institute, *Research Highlights Retirement Data,* January 2001.

2010 and not level off again for almost 30 years. Over the next decade, these demographics will have two principal effects on the private retirement system: first, a greater emphasis on distribution planning, and second, possible reform of social security.

A. *Distribution Planning*

The current accumulation phase of the retirement marketplace will change to a distribution phase. In other words, more money will be coming out of retirement plans than going in as the baby boomers begin to retire in significant numbers. Financial decisions at retirement therefore will become critical, since two-thirds of retirees who received lump-sum distributions at retirement between 1995 and 2000 reinvested the entire amount (almost always in a rollover IRA) and an additional 26% reinvested some of the proceeds.[4] As a consequence, the rollover IRA will become an increasingly important part of the retirement system, as both an investment vehicle and a distribution vehicle. The rollover IRA enables baby boomers to consolidate their retirement accumulations in a single investment vehicle, where those accumulations can continue to grow tax free but with maximum flexibility in terms of receiving distributions. Distribution planning, not investment planning, will become the watchword of the next decade. Tax and estate planners will become as popular as investment planners. Accordingly, fund sponsors will have to expand their products and services significantly if they desire to remain the dominant player in the IRA marketplace.

On the service side, distribution planning includes a multitude of services that go beyond investment planning. For example, distribution planning for retirees includes an understanding of the complex minimum required distributions as well as a series of tools that enable retirees to meet these requirements with confidence. Fund sponsors must offer tools that integrate all income sources of retirees and all applicable distribution requirements in order to develop an efficient retirement plan. Moreover, fund sponsors must offer tools that take into account the special rules that apply to the distribution of company stock from a DC plan, as well as the tax rules that apply to the exercise of stock options that might otherwise terminate on retirement. Distribution planning also must include a series of tools that enable retirees and their legal advisers to determine the appropriate role of the rollover IRA in the retiree's estate plan. This requires the IRA custodian (usually an affiliate of the mutual fund sponsor) to be able to understand and implement distributions to complex beneficiaries, including various types of trusts.

On the product side, fund sponsors must focus on investment products that fit within the retirement income plan that ultimately flows from such a distribution planning service. Since preservation of income and protection against inflation are generally more important to retirees than to active employees, various types of bond funds—possibly including inflation-adjusted instruments—will be tailored to this market. Fixed annuities also should increase in popularity because of concerns that retirees have about outliving their retirement income. On the other hand, since the combination of the trend toward earlier retirement and the reality of increased life expectancies means that retirement income must cover a longer span, equity products will have to be developed for this market. As mentioned above, almost 45% of rollover IRAs established at retirement are invested in equities, and this percentage surely will grow. Variable annuities backed by equity mutual funds may be particularly attractive since the average retiree will now need at least 20 years of retirement income. (For more information on variable annuities, see Chapter Seven.) At the same time, retirement income plans that include equity mutual funds and well-designed systematic withdrawal plans will continue to serve the needs of many retirees.

In the past, investors have been confused by the enormously complex rules surrounding distributions from qualified plans and IRAs. In 2001, however, the IRS issued new rules that will make it much simpler for retirees to determine the minimum amount they must withdraw from their IRA (or qualified plan) each year. Most important, these new rules allow for the distribution of smaller annual amounts, thereby allowing retirees to retain the benefits of tax-free compounding on the larger amount remaining in the IRA. The new rules also are more flexible with regard to when the actual amount that needs to be distributed must be determined. Indeed, the new rules allow IRA beneficiaries to be changed to younger family members until one year after the IRA holder's death. These new rules should reinforce the increasing trend among retirees to consolidate their retirement accounts into a rollover IRA in order to simplify distribution planning.

B. Social Security Reform

The problem confronting Social Security in the United States is primarily a demographic one. Social Security was created as a pay-as-you-go system on the expectation that each retired generation would be followed by a working generation sufficiently large, and sufficiently productive, to pay for the Social Security benefits of retirees. But the prospective retirement of the baby boom generation is undermining this expectation. In 1950, 16.5 workers supported each retiree; in 2030, only 2.0 workers will support each retiree. Therefore, the payroll taxes collected each year to finance Social Security benefits will be insufficient to pay the full amount of those benefits each year beginning in about 2016, when the baby boomers will be retiring in full force.

Congress recognized this potential problem in 1983 by significantly increasing annual payroll taxes so they substantially exceeded the amount needed to pay current benefits. The excess amount has been credited to a "trust fund," which was intended partially to secure some of the additional monies needed to pay Social Security benefits when baby boomers retire. But the "trust fund" is merely a legal concept, not an actual lock box. In the past, the annual excess of contributions from the 12.4% payroll tax over benefit distributions to retirees have generally been used to finance other government programs that otherwise could have been paid for only by an increase in tax revenues or Treasury debt. The Treasury has financed these other programs by crediting the trust fund with special non-negotiable Treasury bonds. In the future, however, the Treasury will be obliged to find the resources to redeem these bonds in order to finance the annual deficit incurred by the trust fund from 2016 until about 2038, as higher outflows of Social Security benefits exceed inflows from payroll taxes. Around 2038, Social Security will technically be insolvent, with a shortfall by an amount equal to 25% to 30% of annual benefit obligations. Unfunded liabilities of Social Security in 2038 are estimated to approach $7 trillion (in 2001 dollars) unless reforms are implemented by Congress.

To address these long-term financing deficits of Social Security, Congress could logically take one of the several paths:

- Reduce the Social Security benefits of future retirees (including extending the age for retirement with full benefits).[5]

- Increase payroll taxes on current workers to finance the payment in full of expected Social Security benefits to future retirees.

- Divert general tax revenues from current non–Social Security programs to pay the full amount of the expected Social Security benefits.

Because none of these alternatives is politically attractive, Congress has been reluctant to confront the problem squarely. Some commentators have looked to Wall Street for a "miracle cure" by arguing that future Social Security benefits can be maintained without tax increases if the government invests the Social Security trust fund in the stock market. One drawback with such a cure is the possibility of the federal government's eventually owning or controlling a large equity stake in corporate America. Such a large stake could become the vehicle for political meddling with the world's most efficient market for capital allocation—for example, by prohibiting investments in "sin" stocks (e.g., tobacco and gambling) or stopping acquisitions of U.S. companies by foreign companies. For these reasons, others have argued for spreading the equity ownership stake among individual accounts that are controlled by each worker. Under such an individual account system, a small portion of the payroll taxes would be allocated to individual accounts and invested at the direction of each worker. The most popular proposal is to allow each worker to invest 2% of payroll taxes in an individual account, while leaving the remaining 10.4% of payroll taxes in the Social Security system to finance a guaranteed floor of benefits.

But that potential solution creates problems of its own—most important, the cost of administering a system of individual accounts for over 140 million American workers. The administrative cost of such a system would depend on its precise design. For example, it would be too costly for financial institutions to collect small monthly contributions from 140 million workers and invest them in a broad variety of options. A more viable approach would be for the federal government to continue to collect all payroll taxes and then allow workers to make one annual election directing a small portion of these taxes into one of several investment options. Moreover, there is much debate about the investment options that should be allowed for individual Social Security accounts. Should these investments be limited to U.S. Treasury securities and index funds, or should the investment choices be broader, as in most 401(k) plans? (Readings 8.1 and 8.2 provide more detail on the issues involved in the debate on Social Security reform.)

This debate, which is not close to resolution, raises questions about the potential impact of Social Security reform on the mutual fund industry. Assuming that the part of the resolution of Social Security's long-term deficits involves the establishment of some type of individual accounts, mutual funds are likely to become interested in providing such accounts if they are patterned after IRAs or employee accounts in 401(k) plans. The dominant role of mutual funds in both the IRA and 401(k) markets suggests that fund complexes might fare well in an individual account system for Social Security.

But there are at least two important arguments against this possibility. The first is potential cannibalization of the 401(k) and IRA markets. This could occur if workers reduce their 401(k) or IRA contributions, or both, to take into account the portion of their payroll taxes being directed to individual Social Security accounts. This could also happen in terms of asset allocation, with workers reducing the equity portion of their 401(k) and IRA accounts because a small portion of their Social Security contributions would be subject to investment risk. Thus, the advent of individual Social Security accounts might not result in a boom for mutual funds in terms of net cash flow and allocation to equities.

The second argument is the potential restrictions on the pricing of services to individual Social Security accounts. The pressures of the political process may prevent mutual funds from charging the full fee necessary to recoup their costs for managing and servicing these accounts, at least for the small ones. If individual accounts are available for only 2% in payroll taxes, the majority of such accounts will be quite small. Currently, two-thirds of workers covered by Social Security have earned income of less than $25,000 annually. Thus, an individual account system capturing 2% in payroll taxes would mean annual contributions of less than $500 for over 90 million workers.

In short, it is unclear whether Social Security reform will include the establishment of individual accounts or whether such accounts would present a profitable business opportunity for mutual fund sponsors.

REVIEW QUESTIONS

1. Why have employers wanted to shift from DB to DC plans? What is the difference in accounting treatment for pension liabilities of a public traded company sponsoring a DB plan versus a DC plan?

2. Why have employees accepted and often embraced the shift from DB to DC plans? What are the potential negative effects of this shift for employees?

3. What were the effects of the DOL's 404(c) regulations on investment options and educational materials in 401(k) plans?

4. Why have mutual funds come to displace banks and insurance companies as the dominant providers in the 401(k) market?

5. What are the differences and similarities among a 401(k) plan, a 457 plan and a 403(b) plan?

6. Would you be better off contributing $2,000 to a traditional front-end IRA than contributing $2,000 to your employer's 401(k) plan? State precisely the assumptions and conditions underlying your answer.

7. If you were a 30-year-old nonworking spouse in a family with a total annual income of $100,000, should you contribute $2,000 to a traditional front-end IRA or to the Roth back-end IRA? State precisely the assumptions and conditions underlying your answer.

8. If you and your spouse earned $90,000 per year, should you each invest in a back-end Roth IRA or in a variable annuity? Why?

DISCUSSION QUESTIONS

1. Is employer stock an appropriate investment alternative for DC plans? Should there be a limit to the amount of employer stock held in any participant's account?

2. How many funds is "too many" for a 401(k) plan? Should 401(k) plans allow trading in individual securities as well as mutual funds?

3. Should mutual fund sponsors provide advice to plan participants about investment choices? If so, what should be their liability for the advice?

4. Do you think that SIMPLE will lead most small employers to offer DC plans? What do you predict would be the objection of small employers to SIMPLE?

5. Why has the rollover IRA market grown so quickly? Do you think mutual funds will continue to play a significant role in that market?

6. What are the pros and cons for allowing a small portion of Social Security payroll taxes to be invested in individual accounts? If such accounts were allowed, would you suggest that mutual fund sponsors focus on offering such accounts?

NOTES

1. B. C. Fallick and C. A. Fleischman, *The Importance of Employer-to-Employer Flows in the U.S. Labor Market* (Washington, D.C.: Federal Reserve Board, April 2001).

2. A. A. Samwick and J. Skinner, "How Will Defined Contribution Plans Affect Retirement Income?" NBER Working Paper 6645, July 1998.

3. J. J. Choi, D. Laibson, and A. Metrick, "Does the Internet Increase Trading: Evidence from Investor Behavior in 401(k) Plans," Rodney L. White Institute for Financial Research, 15-00, July 2000.

4. See Investor Company Institute, "Defined Contribution Plan Distribution Choices at Retirement: A Survey of Employees Retiring Between 1995 and 2000," Fall 2000.

5. The normal retirement age for full benefits under Social Security will rise gradually from 65 to 67 by 2027.

READING 8.1

*Social Security: Ten Basic Questions Answered**

C. Eugene Steuerle

1. Why Is Reform Needed?

Social Security and other government entitlement programs for the elderly and near-elderly:

- *Provide benefits that are growing at unsustainably high rates.* Due to real growth in annual benefits combined with longer retirement, an average-income one-earner couple retiring at age 65 in 1960 could expect lifetime Social Security cash benefits to total $99,000 (in 1993 dollars). Today those benefits total $223,000, and in 25 years, $313,000.
- *Have an enormous impact on the federal budget.* These programs now comprise almost half of federal expenditures, and Social Security alone represents more than one-quarter of all federal expenditures other than interest on the national debt. By contrast, in the early 1950s, expenditures on retirement, disability, and health occupied less than 10 percent of federal expenditures.
- *Encourage ever longer retirement periods relative to working years,* thus reducing the nation's productivity and encouraging consumption.
- *Don't fully meet the needs of the very elderly among the poor.* Poverty rates among the very old are still high by many standards.
- *Treat second earners in families unfairly.* Lesser-earning spouses in a family may contribute a substantial amount to Social Security over a lifetime, but often don't earn enough over their careers to yield benefits greater than half of the primary worker's (an amount to which the lesser earning spouse is already entitled).
- *Reduce national saving* by reducing the workforce, transferring large sums from younger savers who work to older consumers who don't, and possibly displacing the need to save for retirement.

2. Is It Too Late to Repair the System?

No, with adequate forethought and preparation, reform can still guarantee that almost all future retirees will receive lifetime benefits at least as great as those of Ameri-

cans who retired before them. In general, benefits can be maintained but growth at its current promised rate cannot.

3. What Principles Should Guide Social Security Reform?

A viable program should:

- Keep all retirees out of poverty, which may involve redistributing benefits from the better-off to those with lower incomes and greater health problems.
- Ensure that people with equal levels of economic well-being pay equal amounts of taxes.
- Give individuals a fair return on their contributions so that insurance protection relates to premiums paid.
- Achieve economic efficiency and be cost effective.

4. What Budgetary Guidelines Also Make Sense?

Future voters and generations should have some say about how future tax resources are spent. Promises of excessive benefits should be avoided. Programs with related goals (such as Medicare and Social Security) should be considered as a whole.

5. What Is the Danger of Financing Social Security Through Long-Term Deficit Spending?

Failure to bring long-term revenues and expenditures into line will eventually raise interest and tax rates and still displace spending for other types of government programs.

6. What Are the Advantages of Coordinating Reforms Across Programs?

Worthwhile trade-offs would become more evident. One example might be increasing cash benefits for some poor elderly if more tightly controlled Medicare expenditures or premium increases are required for all elderly.

7. Why Is Reform Necessary Sooner Rather Than Later?

The longer we continue to delay dealing with Social Security's problems, the more likely legislation will center on cash-flow fixes (quick infusions into Social Security trust funds) rather than the needed long-term reforms. But

**Source:* C. Eugene Steuerle, Urban Institute, Washington, D.C. (www. urganinstitute.org/news/factsheets/SSreformFS.html). "Social Security: Ten Basic Questions Answered," by Eugene Steuerle. Reprinted by permission of the Urban Institute Press.

long-term reforms—such as gradually raising the retirement age—are often more appropriate.

8. Why Is It Important to Take a Lifetime Perspective on Social Security Reform?

Annual costs simply don't tell the whole story. Consider cost-of-living adjustments. If we are forced to cut lifetime benefits by 10 percent, it may be wiser to cut back on benefits for the young elderly than the old elderly, who are poorer and most hurt by the compounding effect of many annual adjustments. Similarly, for any lifetime benefit package, reducing years of expected support keeps annual benefits higher—a trade-off many Americans might prefer.

9. What Are the Pros And Cons of Reforming Social Security Through Privatization?

On the plus side, privatizing Social Security might increase individual saving through mandated saving accounts or greater incentives to hold private pension assets, and might also increase societal and government saving. On the negative side, privatization could result in reduced private saving (in other accounts) and increased borrowing. If privatization doesn't provide a sufficient basic guaranteed benefit, we could see many more poor elderly in the future, unless government were to step in and help.

10. How Does the U.S. Social Security Prospect Compare with Those of Other Countries?

In some ways the United States is lucky. Our population is aging more slowly than those of most other industrial countries. We thus have some chance to learn from other countries' experiences and decisions.

READING 8.2

*Grounds for Compromise: Competing Reform Proposals Are Closer Than They Appear**

C. Eugene Steuerle and Adam Carasso

In the spirit of politics, lawmakers tend to paint rival Social Security reform proposals in extremes: If one privatizes and another preserves, then never the twain shall meet. The polarized way in which proposals are debated, more than the actual substance of the proposals, makes compromise difficult. However, compromise doesn't have to be so daunting a task. Considerable overlap exists among reform proposals presented by lawmakers on both sides of the aisle. Agreement can be found in the following areas.

Save the Surplus

Democrats and Republicans began competing in 1999 to create the best "lock box" with which to protect Social Secu-

rity's surplus. Until then, it was common for Congress to allow deficits in other parts of the budget to exceed the size of the Social Security surplus. Now, almost all policymakers attempt to safeguard Social Security surpluses while trying to prevent budget deficits elsewhere. This dual "balanced budget and lock box" approach puts the federal government on record as trying to increase retirement saving through its own fiscal policy—not merely encouraging saving, but actually mandating it. This remarkable achievement is largely ignored because of the rancor of the reform debate.

Establish Individual Accounts

Individual accounts have become a mainstay of proposals by many policymakers, regardless of their ideology. Such accounts would give workers direct ownership of real assets—not just promises from the government that their benefits will be paid out of levies on future taxpayers. Even the amount of money being discussed to put in these

**Source:* C. Eugene Steuerle and Adam Carasso, Urban Institute, Washington, D.C., February 2001 (www.urbaninstitute.org/retirement/st/straight30.html). "Grounds for Compromise: Competing Reform Proposals Are Closer Than They Appear," by Eugene Steuerle and Adam Carasso, February 2001. Reprinted by permission of the Urban Institute Press.

accounts is similar. When fully implemented, for instance, many proposals would shift about 2 percent of taxable payroll (about 1 percent of GDP). Regardless of how these accounts are financed (some say from Social Security tax revenues and others say from income taxes and other general revenues), the real economic problem is how the additional resources are made available: a Social Security and non–Social Security spending cut, an increase in Social Security or income taxes, or some combination of these options.

Increase National Saving

Despite their political affiliation, many policymakers feel that increasing net national saving, not just having individuals put more money into one set of accounts by taking it from another, is an important aspect of Social Security reform. Whether more money is placed in trust funds or in individual accounts, most policymakers would like to see additional returns from saving generate economic growth that eases some of the burden of helping future retirees.

Meet Future Obligations

Policymakers of all political stripes also hint that they want Congress to more fully and immediately fund its future Social Security obligations. For example, if the Department of Treasury issues additional bonds to the Social Security program, many policymakers agree that the interest owed on the bonds should be paid out of general revenues and not be available for other government functions. This would reduce revenues available for other expenditures. Similarly, payments to individual accounts would be recognized immediately as a liability (unlike Social Security, which is not recognized as a liability until people retire and try to cash in on the government's promises). Such timely acknowledgement, however, will stress the federal government's cash flow, making a non–Social Security budget that

is deficit-free obtainable only with less spending or more taxes.

Depend on General Revenue

Many policymakers, regardless of political leaning, realize that reforming Social Security may require tapping general revenues. However, they come to this conclusion differently. Some suggest that general revenues will be needed to cover the principal and interest on the Treasury bonds issued on Social Security.

Other policymakers favoring individual accounts admit a reliance on general revenues. Some suggest funding the accounts directly from general revenues; others would finance them out of current Social Security taxes. But as taxes once meant for Social Security are diverted into individual accounts, general revenues will need to be used, at least temporarily, to shore up Social Security benefits that night otherwise be cut due to lost funds. Indeed, most policymakers realize that the transition to a new system may require significant amounts of general revenues to deal with the very large excess of Social Security liabilities over expected revenues. . . .

Given the common foundations of most reforms proposed by either party, reaching compromise on Social Security reform shouldn't be as difficult as the polarized reform debate suggests. This success of reform hinges mostly on the ability to recognize and building upon existing similarities.

Ironically, policymakers have formed consensus in one detrimental way: a tacit agreement to avoid discussing politically unpopular but necessary steps toward reform. To financially underpin the reforms politicians do want, the debate must also address topics like the need for workers to extend their careers in line with their increasing life spans. Here, agreement thwarts reform.

EXERCISE

Designing an Investment Array for a 401(k) Plan

As you now are aware, the employer-sponsor of a 401(k) plan has the obligation to design an appropriate array of investment choices for plan participants if it does not want to be legally responsible for participants' investment decisions. If that array is properly designed and participants are provided with adequate information about the available choices, the employer-sponsor obtains the protection of a regulatory safe harbor from ERISA liability for the investment choices of plan participants.

In designing an appropriate array of investment alternatives for a 401(k) plan, the employer-sponsor should take into account the characteristics of its workforce. These include the age and sophistication of its employees as well as their attitudes toward investing: employees may be insecure, comfortable or confident investors. In addition, to qualify for the protection of the regulatory safe harbor, an array must include a relatively "safe" choice such as a money market fund, a bank deposit or a stable value pool.

This exercise puts you in the position of a consultant to five employers, each the sponsor of a 401(k) plan. Your job is to assess the investment alternatives offered by the plan and the actual choices made by plan participants, with a view to making recommendations for improvements. Along with the different company profiles, your employer—Benefits, Inc.—has provided background information on general investment behavior and strategies for plan sponsors to help participants meet their investment needs.

Discussion Questions

1. How would you describe the participants in this company's plan in terms of their level of comfort with investment concepts and investment decision making?

2. Does the plan's current set of investment choices offer enough investment diversification to meet the needs of the plan participants? If so, why? If not, why not?

3. What changes, if any, would you recommend the company make in the menu of investment choices the plan offers to its participants?

4. What communications strategy would you recommend the company follow?

The Situation

Benefits, Inc. is a global management consulting firm that is highly regarded for creativity and innovation in the areas of retirement plan design, benefits administration and human resources. Benefits is known for its commitment to superior client service and has enjoyed tremendous growth over the past decade. In particular, it has seen a huge rise in demand for consulting services related to corporate retirement plans.

In recent years, many U.S. companies have shifted from defined benefit retirement plans to defined contribution plans, which are increasingly in the form of 401(k) plans. From the employer's perspective, an important aspect of a 401(k) plan is the "safe harbor" provision in the Department of Labor's 404(c) Regulation, which limits the liability of plan sponsors offering an investment menu to participants in defined contribution plans. If the plan provides a diversified array of reputable investment alternatives and adequate information about investment choices, the plan sponsor will generally be protected from liability for specific investment alternatives chosen by plan participants.

As part of their consulting services, Benefits often aids companies in establishing, administering and educating employees about 401(k) plans. Benefits' promotional materials for its clients include a paper on general strategies for plan sponsors to help participants meet their investment needs (see Exhibit 1). Currently, five plan sponsors have hired Benefits to evaluate and to make recommendations about improving their plans, with a focus on investment alternatives and education campaigns. (See Exhibits 2–6 for company profiles.)

EXHIBIT 1

Benefits, Inc.'s strategies for successful participant investing

Focusing on the Investor, Not the Investments

Every day, defined contribution plan participants make investment decisions that will affect their income in retirement. Some make these decisions easily; others are less confident that they are making appropriate choices. Benefits, Inc. understands that participants' investment decisions should be driven primarily by an accurate assessment of their retirement income needs and the time they have to accumulate the appropriate nest egg. (See Figure 1.) But Benefits also understands that participants' own personalities and attitudes toward investing are often a barrier that prevents them from doing the right thing. Benefits therefore attempts to target the plan design and communication programs it develops for its clients to take into account these behavioral differences. By understanding that there are different types of investors with varying concerns and needs, plan sponsors have an opportunity to provide employees with suitable investments—ones that improve the likelihood of being utilized effectively by participants.

This paper outlines strategies for successful participant investing, based on Benefits' many years of experience and research with regard to participant investment attitude and behavior. It presents information about:

- how participants invest and the different types of investors (insecure, comfortable, confident);
- the importance of investment diversification and the difference it can make to the participant;
- the investment options that match investor levels of sophistication; and
- what plan sponsors need to consider in evaluating their plan's investment structure.

Our objective is to help plan sponsors simplify investment decision making for employees by understanding how participants think, and by developing appropriate investment menus and well-thought-out communications programs.

Participants Matter Most

Defined contribution plans put the burden of making investment decisions entirely on the plan participants. But many participants have difficulty understanding investing. This may be because we often try to turn employees into *experts* who should be able to develop diversified portfolios, rather than *educating* them about investments

FIGURE 1

Recommended equity allocation percentages by age cohort for retirement plan holdings

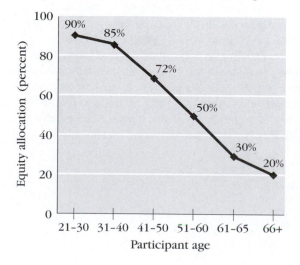

that match their retirement needs and time horizon while still taking into account their levels of comfort and understanding.

Benefits' customer-service philosophy is based on the premise that "*participants matter most.*" This means that we work with plan sponsors to:

- understand how employees think about investing;
- evaluate the investment mix of their plans;
- evaluate their plans and decide whether their investment options are simple and straightforward so that participants can understand them;
- develop communications programs that target different employee groups from the least confident investors to the most confident investors; and
- achieve desired participation levels, asset allocation and investment diversification results.

The cornerstone of these efforts should be an effective plan design that simplifies and demystifies investment decision making for participants and effectively guides then to proper investment allocation and diversification.

The rest of this paper will address:

- how plan sponsors can determine the most optimal investment plan design;
- some sample investment structures; and
- how plan sponsors can achieve more of their objectives through a well-designed, targeted communications campaign.

How Do Participants Invest?

In the early years of 401(k) plans, the emphasis was on participation—how to motivate the maximum number of employees to enroll. In recent years many plans have achieved high levels of participation and sponsors have turned their attention to ensuring the plans offer enough variety of investments and to helping participants achieve effective asset allocation and diversification. Over the long term, a properly allocated and diversified portfolio has tended to return more than one that is too heavily weighted in fixed income securities with less risk to principal and inflation protection, or too heavily invested in company stock, with greater industry and single security risk.

Benefits' research and experience with a diverse group of plan sponsors and participants have taught us:

- One can identify distinct groups of employees who think differently about investing and will respond to different investment messages.
- Well-diversified investment options can be packaged and presented in a way designed to appeal to these distinct groups.
- Successful communications campaigns can be built around extensive investment menus. In several cases, investments were packaged, targeted to the needs of distinct groups and accompanied by a communications campaign that delivered the right messages. The campaigns resulted in increased participation and improved asset allocation among participants.

The Importance of Diversification

Driven by a combination of management-initiated efforts to improve defined contribution plans and increasing employee bottom-up requests for a wider array and range of investment options, the average number of choices offered by Benefits, Inc. clients is now 10, compared to 3 or 4 choices 10 years ago. Indeed, many large companies offer 75 or more options. However, a concern is whether these additional options are being used properly.

What is diversification, what is proper diversification, and why worry about it? Diversification in the investment context is the combination into a single portfolio of several types of investments with sufficiently different characteristics so that they normally behave differently in any particular investment environment. (They may also behave differently over time through varying environments.) The purpose of diversification is to reduce the risk inherent in any one type of investment or of multiple but closely related investments. Risk in this context is the risk of a temporary decline of the investment's value or outright loss of value. More often than not, diversification is thought of in connection with protection against loss. But investment risk includes the loss of opportunity to offset the negative effects of inflation, as well as the opportunity for higher investment returns over time than many single types of investments can produce. Therefore, diversification can also be used to enhance opportunity for the long term within acceptable bounds of risk of loss.

Table 1 illustrates the effect and potential benefits of asset class diversification over time. It shows the historical returns of a mix of stock and bond mutual funds as the percentage invested in growth mutual funds increases. Note

TABLE 1

Returns for various asset class mixes over longer time horizons

% Investment			Average Annual Percentage Total Return Period Ending 12/31/00*					
	Growth Funds Average*	Fixed Income Funds Average*	1 Year	5 Years	10 Years	15 Years	20 Years	25 Years
Higher equity investment/ higher risk	0	100	7.1	4.7	5.8	6.3	8.2	8.3
	25	75	−1.9	7.7	8.4	8.3	9.6	10.1
	50	50	−3.8	10.6	11.1	10.3	10.9	11.8
	75	25	−5.7	13.6	13.7	12.3	12.3	13.5
	100	0	−7.5	16.5	16.4	14.3	13.7	15.3

*Based on Lipper Analytical Services, Inc. Fixed-Income Funds and Growth Funds averages as of 12/31/00. The 1-Year Growth Funds average covers over 1,475 mutual funds with a growth objective. The Fixed-Income Funds average includes over 5,585 funds.

that higher equity investment would have produced higher returns for all time periods shown, albeit with likely higher risk.

Many plan participants have long periods, say 15 to 25 years, of employment still ahead. With an average current plan balance of $31,000, a return of 8.2% over 20 years, assuming no further contributions, amounts to $150,000 achieved through a portfolio of only fixed income funds with presumable low risk. On the other hand, a much more aggressive portfolio that is 75% in growth funds and only 25% in fixed income returned 12.3% over the same period. Here the $31,000 grows to $315,500—an enormous difference. (Of course, a portfolio that was 100% in growth funds would have resulted in an even greater amount of money.) The higher volatility of a 75/25 mix may be too great for many investors, but certainly not for all. Most participants should probably be somewhere in between.

The difficulty, of course, is that there is no such thing as a one-size-fits-all diversification concept for all defined contribution plan participants because every investor is uniquely different from every other investor in terms of need, time and personality. In the defined benefit retirement world, the employee does not play a role in investment decision making. He or she is only a potential beneficiary, not an investor, and all retirees can expect to receive a financial benefit based on a uniform formula that is the same for everyone. In the defined contribution world, however, without guarantees or formulas, the investor is everything, and each individual's financial base in retirement is dependent on the investment decisions and actions he or she made years earlier.

Some plan participants may accumulate substantial assets and are able to retire comfortably due to good investment decisions, while others may end their careers with less retirement income. The employer will have satisfied its legal responsibility to both groups of employees if it has both provided enough good-quality investment options to allow all employees an opportunity to construct a portfolio with an appropriate level of risk and return for their particular circumstances, and if it has provided them with sufficient information about these investment options to construct such a portfolio properly. Given that all defined contribution plan options in a company are available to all employees, from the least to the most sophisticated and the most to the least risk averse, plan sponsors have no easy task in meeting these plan design and communication requirements.

Numerous quantitative methodologies adopted from pension fund management practices are available and can be helpful. However, we believe such tools don't effectively work to help certain groups of participants select the particular investment options that are best for them from within the range of choices offered by the plan.

Participants Are Not All Alike

Client research by Benefits, Inc. shows that plan participants may be usefully grouped into three major segments based on their attitudes toward, and sophistication with, investment concepts. Plan sponsors should consider positioning options to relate to the needs of each segment.

Insecure Investors

Insecure investors usually compose the largest single participant group. These individuals describe themselves as "beginner" investors. They express a lack of confidence and understanding in matters related to investing and doubt their ability to accumulate enough assets to retire. Their lack of confidence has pushed them into relatively safe investment choices such as money market, fixed income and stable value options. They tend to be the least well diversified. Some avoid participating in a 401(k) plan altogether because of their lack of confidence.

Options for Insecure Investors

Insecure investors need simple, easily understood choices that will not overwhelm them, but which still give them the diversification they need. The goal is to help them gain the potential of a more balanced investment program. The investment menu might include "ready-mix" options, such as asset allocation funds, that provide appropriate asset allocation within a single fund. Several ready-mix options could be offered, each targeted to investors with a defined risk level and/or horizon. For example, the menu might include a growth-oriented asset allocation fund with a mutual mix of 65% stocks and 35% bonds and an income-oriented asset allocation fund with a neutral mix of 65% bonds and 35% stocks.

Comfortable Investors

Other respondents from the Benefits research say they are comfortable with their current investment planning situation. These people make asset allocation decisions based on a sense of well-being about their financial security. They understand investing basics and the major types of investments. They believe they are saving enough money to retire and have not done a financial plan. However, many are risk averse and often not adequately diversified. This group often desires a limited selection of diversified individual fund choices and may be receptive to asset allocation offerings.

Options for Comfortable Investors

Investors in this group like to choose from an array of "mix-your-own" options. These are sometimes referred to as "core" options. Core options may include a broad spectrum of choice—from money market funds to aggressive equity funds. Core options may include a few broadly diversified funds that together constitute a broadly diversified portfolio. Such a portfolio might include a few equity funds such as growth & income, growth and diversified international. Such a portfolio may also include a fixed income fund or a stable value pool. (A stable value pool contains fixed income instruments with specified yields issued by an insurance company or bank, which do not fluctuate in value if certain conditions are met.) A "mix-your-own" or "core" menu might look as shown in Figure 2.

Confident Investors

Still other respondents provide a very confident investment self-profile. These people are willing to take risks when necessary. They are confident they know how to select investment options that meet their goals and consider themselves more investors than savers. Confident investors are not intimidated by a wide variety of investment choices or even a self-directed brokerage option.

Options for Confident Investors

These investors may find the "ready-mix" or even the "core" options too limiting. For their more sophisticated investors, plan sponsors should consider a third tier of expanded options. These are sometimes referred to as "window" or "extended" options, because they provide participants with a wide choice of investments beyond the core. A "mutual fund window" can allow access by participants to substantially all of the funds in a mutual fund

FIGURE 2

A "mix-your-own" or "core" menu investment objective spectrum

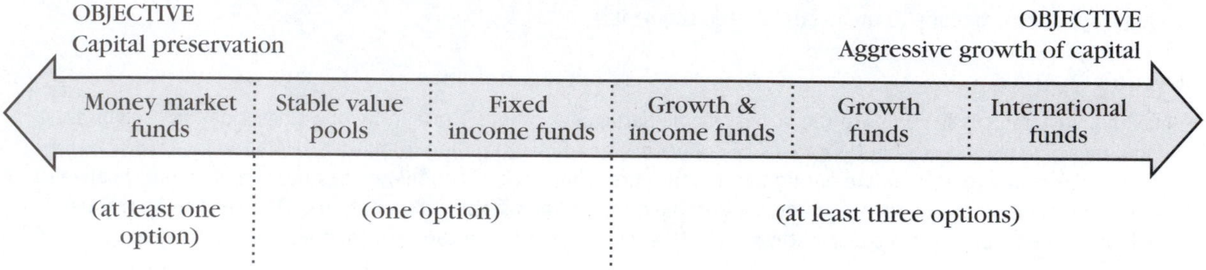

OBJECTIVE
Capital preservation

OBJECTIVE
Aggressive growth of capital

| Money market funds | Stable value pools | Fixed income funds | Growth & income funds | Growth funds | International funds |

(at least one option)   (one option)   (at least three options)

complex or all or a subset of funds offered by a mutual fund supermarket. Such a supermarket allows an investor to access through one brokerage account mutual funds from many different fund families. These window options may include specialty funds that invest in certain market sectors, like small-cap companies, or in particular types of stocks, like real estate or utilities. These window options could also include specialized international funds such as emerging markets, country and region funds.

Plan Investment Structure

The key to diversification and investment success is to be sure a plan menu offers sufficient conservative, moderate and aggressive investment options that allow for the creation of participant portfolios that are appropriate for each investor profile. A comprehensive plan menu, offering adequate opportunities for diversification for all participants, could be structured as in Table 2.

How Many Options?

Traditional advisers recommend that plans offer a certain number of investments to participants. At Benefits, Inc., we prefer an alternative approach—one that focuses on the investors, not the investments. This means that:

- Employees define their investment style.
- Plan sponsors provide investments that can meet every employee's needs.
- A comprehensive communications program assists employees with their selection of suitable diversified investment options.

TABLE 2

A comprehensive plan menu

Ready-Mix Options	Core Options	Extended Window Options
Asset allocation growth	Money market fund	All or substantially all of mutual funds
Asset allocation income	Stable value pools	in a single complex
	Bond fund	All or a subset of mutual funds in a fund supermarket
	Growth & income fund	Self-directed brokerage
	Growth fund	
	Aggressive growth fund	
	International fund	

Conclusion

There are many different types of investors in defined contribution plans, with varying concerns and anxieties. If plan participants are going to be successful investors, they have to be confident in their investment decisions. To this end, we need to work with plan sponsors to provide a menu of options that meet every participant's investment need—from the least sophisticated to the most sophisticated. In addition, we have to develop communications programs directed at various employee populations. With expanded investment options and targeted communications programs, we should be able to help investors make sound investment decisions that can help give them the security they need for retirement.

EXHIBIT 2

Company profile A: Cosmetics, Etc.

Cosmetics, Etc. is a well-known fashion accessories manufacturer. It is located mostly in five primary manufacturing sites in the South, with sales staff scattered across the U.S. It has about 3,000 employees.

Cosmetics, Etc. senior management's overall goal is to increase their plan's diversification, and they are considering several changes including plan design, fund options and communications strategy.

The profile of Cosmetics, Etc. employees:

- 25% manufacturing, 30% sales/marketing, 45% administration
- Average age 40, sales and marketing employees are younger
- Heavy stable value/money market investment orientation
- Most in two to three funds, with small balances in either equity fund
- Some language issues among manufacturing staff
- Relatively low salaries

Cosmetics, Etc.'s current plan investment menu includes four options, and requires that the company match be automatically invested in the Stable Value Pool. This requirement has resulted in a plan where 64% of plan assets are in Money Market and Stable Value, with the remaining 36% split between the two equity fund choices (see below).

Plan investment options and percentage allocation:

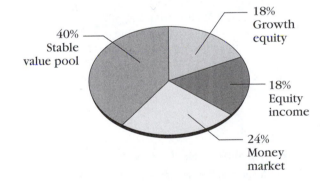

EXHIBIT 3

Company profile B: Financial Services, Inc.

Financial Services, Inc. is a financial services provider headquartered on the East Coast. It has five urban offices, with 50 small sites across the country, and about 3,600 employees.

The plan sponsor's goal is to increase diversification, increase participation and increase employee awareness and appreciation of the plan through better, basic investment education. The sponsor particularly wants to target clerical workers, whom it feels are most in need of investment education.

The profile of Financial Services employees:

- Majority of employees are clerical, with salary under $15,000, high school educated
- Small percentage of highly compensated employees with salaries over $100,000 and postgraduate education
- Plan participation rate is 63%, with 67% of plan participants under the age of 40 and 44% between ages 31 and 40
- 31% of participants have 1–2 funds, with no significant differences in investment choices by age

Average assets per participant: $22,406

Financial Services, Inc. faces some unique challenges in its retirement savings plan. Its current plan investment menu includes eight options. However, despite an attractive matching contribution (one dollar from the company for every two dollars of participant contribution to any investment option up to 6% of salary) and a commitment from the company to promote the 401(k) plan, participation lags at about 63%. About two-thirds of their employees are under the age of 40, and these people are not significantly more aggressively invested than their older colleagues. Allocations for the various plan options are shown below.

Plan investment options and percentage allocation:

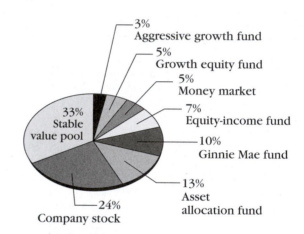

- 3% Aggressive growth fund
- 5% Growth equity fund
- 5% Money market
- 7% Equity-income fund
- 10% Ginnie Mae fund
- 13% Asset allocation fund
- 24% Company stock
- 33% Stable value pool

EXHIBIT 4

Company profile C: Health Insurance, Inc.

Health Insurance, Inc. is a diversified midwestern company that operates finance, insurance and real estate businesses. The company has about 5,600 employees located throughout the midwestern states.

The plan sponsor's goal is to increase diversification of the plan assets. The most important target is the female 30- to 40-year-old clerical workers who make up a significant portion of the plan's participants. Health Insurance feels that by reinforcing basic investment concepts to this core group, it can significantly improve the plan's asset allocation.

Health Insurance's employee profile:

- Predominantly female, 30–40 years old
- Clerical workers
- Mostly high school educated, some college
- 75% participation rate

Health Insurance provides dollar for dollar matching in the form of company stock, plus five other investment options. The assets in the plan are currently allocated as follows:

Plan investment options and percentage allocation:

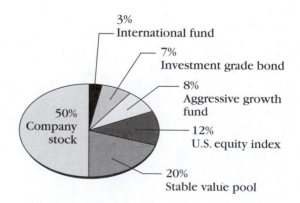

- 3% International fund
- 7% Investment grade bond
- 8% Aggressive growth fund
- 12% U.S. equity index
- 20% Stable value pool
- 50% Company stock

EXHIBIT 5

Company profile D: Smith & Jones

Smith & Jones is one of America's largest accounting firms, with 16,700 active participants in their plan. S&J is headquartered in the mid-Atlantic states and has multiple domestic and international offices.

The plan sponsor's goals are to increase employees' investment and retirement planning knowledge so that employees will be appropriately invested. The challenge is to reach their well-educated employees, who are uninformed investors and who have little time available for investment education.

The profile of Smith & Jones employees:

- Generally well-educated population but not investment sophisticated
- 15% administrative staff
- Average age of employee: 33; 67% of employees between 21–40 years old

The current plan investment menu includes seven options and has the following percentage allocations:

Plan investment options and percentage allocation:

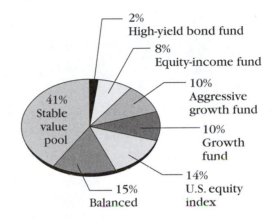

EXHIBIT 6

Company profile E: Petrochemical, Inc.

Petrochemical, Inc. is a huge multinational oil company, with over 40,000 employees in the United States.

The company has sponsored a defined benefit plan for many years that is designed to offer retirees a safety net level of benefits. The company recently added a defined contribution plan that is designed to supplement the DB plan. The plan sponsor's goals are to increase employees' understanding of a defined contribution plan as well as their investment and retirement planning knowledge so that employees will be appropriately invested. At the same time, the company wants to deal with the needs of two very different employee groups: a highly educated group that is overly invested in relatively high risk–high return choices, and a relatively unsophisticated group that is overly invested in bonds and money market funds.

The aggregate profile of Petroleum, Inc's employees is as follows:

- 40% are college educated and work as scientists, engineers or other professionals

- 45% have little or no college education and work primarily at the production sites
- 15% are administrative staff
- Average age of office worker: 40; average age of oil field worker: 28

The current plan investment menu includes four commingled pools, run by a trust company affiliated with a mutual fund sponsor, plus a brokerage option. The percentage allocations for plan assets are as follows:

Plan investment options and percentage allocation:

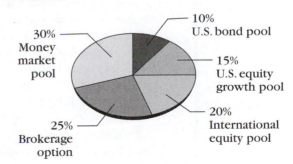

9 Servicing Fund Shareholders

On the surface, the servicing of mutual fund shareholders might seem like a straightforward topic. After all, most of us have experienced customer service as retail shoppers, bank depositors or utility consumers. Furthermore, all of us have experienced customer service by various methods: in person, by telephone or over the Internet. In the process, we have come to think of customer service as a function performed by employees of the same company whose products or services we purchase. This is not the case with respect to mutual funds, however. A separate entity from the mutual fund, called the "transfer agent," services shareholders of the fund. A transfer agent has its own employees and facilities; it may or may not be affiliated with the mutual fund's sponsor or adviser. The costs of servicing fund shareholders incurred by the transfer agent are billed primarily to the mutual fund under a contractual arrangement; these costs are included in the line item "other expenses" in the fee table near the front of every fund prospectus. In addition, some transfer agent expenses such as wire transfer or account fees may be billed directly to the accounts of individual shareholders.

Before beginning this Chapter, it is useful to review a few basic distinctions on servicing mutual fund shareholders. First, the servicing of shareholders is often intertwined with the act of selling to the same shareholders. A customer who calls to check on his or her fund holdings may also want to discuss buying another fund. Similarly, a broker-dealer may send material announcing a new fund in the same envelope with a customer's quarterly account statement. We discussed the selling of mutual funds in Chapter Seven. In this Chapter, we focus primarily on servicing customers after they have decided to buy shares in funds held outside of corporate and individual retirement plans. (See Chapter Eight for retirement plans.)

Second, servicing of fund shareholders is quite different in the broker-dealer context than in the direct marketing channel. In the context of a full-service broker-dealer, the customer is connected to a named representative who is primarily responsible for providing a complete range of services. By contrast, in the direct marketing channel, the customer is serviced by a wide variety of impersonal methods, including telephone representatives, automated telephone systems, direct mail and the Internet. An obvious disadvantage of these methods is the lack of highly personal service. In a partial response, some fund complexes in the direct marketing channel have adopted a team-based approach to servicing high-net-worth customers (e.g., with more than $1 million in investable assets). For example, a small team of registered representatives is assigned to service each high-net-worth customer, who may get to know the team members by name.

Third, servicing of fund shareholders is very different for retail investors as compared to institutional investors. As mentioned in Chapter Two, corporate treasurers, banks and other institutions invest for their own accounts, or for the accounts of multiple beneficiaries, in specially designed money market funds for cash management purposes. Such funds typically require a high minimum account size (e.g., $100,000 or even $1 million) and charge relatively low expenses (e.g., 0.20% or 20 basis points). Although this Chapter focuses primarily on retail investors, it is useful to understand the special servicing needs of institutional customers of such money market funds. When purchasing shares of such funds, these institutional investors want their monies invested and earning interest on the same day they are sent by Federal Reserve wire to the fund's transfer agent. Conversely, these institutional investors want their monies wired to their bank on the same day as the redemption request is made. In addition, since institutional investors often invest in mutual funds on behalf of multiple beneficiaries, these institutions want fund transfer agents to assist with maintaining customer subaccount records.

This Chapter explains the key functions of the transfer agency: maintaining records of shareholder accounts, processing fund transactions, transmitting account statements and fund reports, handling customer inquiries, tracking shareholder cash flows and monitoring fund compliance. It next reviews the structure of the transfer agency industry, including the main companies engaged in the business and the evolution of the technology used by transfer agents. It then discusses the role of mutual fund independent directors in choosing a transfer agent, pricing its services and measuring its performance. The Chapter ends with a case study of various strategies to control short-term shareholder trading in shares of a mutual fund investing primarily in Japanese securities.

I. *Functions of the Transfer Agent*

A. *Fund Purchases, Redemptions and Exchanges*

To give you a sense of how fund shareholders are serviced, let's follow a typical series of transactions beginning immediately after a prospective customer decides to purchase fund shares. In the first step, the customer completes and returns an application for opening a new account to the transfer agent. The application may be returned in a number of ways, including by mail, at a branch office (if one exists locally) or through the Internet. Once the transfer agent receives the application, the transfer agent determines whether it is in good order. Although the definition of "in good order" can vary somewhat among fund complexes, many core elements are consistent. The transfer agent always makes certain to obtain a social security number or taxpayer identification number (in the case of corporate accounts) for tax reporting purposes. The transfer agent also ensures that the initial funding amount complies with any account minimums specified in the fund's prospectus. If there is any issue with the application, the application is considered to be "not in good order." In that event, the establishment of the account and the purchase of fund shares may be delayed until the issue can be resolved with the customer.

Account setup via the Internet initially was complicated because the transfer agent needed a customer signature on paper. The passage of the Electronic Signatures in Global and National Commerce Act of 2000 simplified the establishment of new accounts through the Internet by enabling customers to use their social security number and personal identification number (PIN) in lieu of a physical signature on a piece of paper. (See Chapter Three.) This procedure allows customers to complete the fund purchase process entirely on the Internet. Some fund complexes also allow customers to set up accounts and make purchases over the phone, with the final paperwork sent in later.

Once the account has been established and ownership properly assigned or registered (e.g., individual, joint or partnership account), the next servicing function is to complete the purchase of fund shares by processing the customer's payment for the shares (see Figure 9.1). Payment usually occurs by check, Federal Reserve wire, electronic funds transfer or exchange between the customer's old fund and new fund choices. Transfer agents generally do not accept cash for fund purchases. When a customer purchases a fund by check, the checks are sent for clearance to a collecting bank. Since the customer purchases fund shares at the next determined net asset value (NAV), the transfer agent must make certain that the fund actually has the cash available to invest promptly after the customer purchases the shares. The check clearance and collection process involves presenting the customer's check to the financial institution on which the check was drawn. Since fund shareholders often reside in many parts of the country in different Federal Reserve districts and time zones, the time needed for the transfer agent to "collect" the cash can range from less than a day to as long as a day or two. Because of these and other systemic delays in the national check clearing system, transfer agents are constantly looking for ways to speed up the collection of "good funds" from locations all across the country. Recent enhancements to check imaging and electronic check transport technology are beginning to shorten the check collection period. Throughout the processing of a customer's payment for shares, the fund's transfer agent monitors the flow of monies because it is responsible for computing the number of shares that are to be purchased from which funds and the amount of money to be sent to the fund's bank account to pay for the purchase.

FIGURE 9.1

Direct mutual fund purchase by check

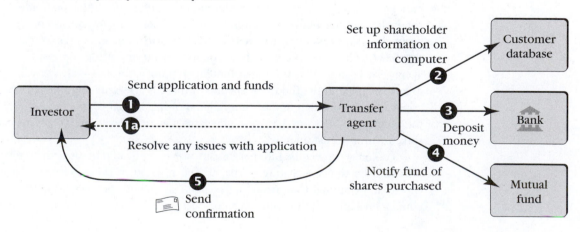

The opposite of a fund purchase is a redemption or sale of fund shares. The ability of a fund shareholder to redeem daily is one of the distinguishing characteristics of shares of a mutual fund versus other financial products (e.g., bank CDs or insurance policies). Although a mutual fund may close to purchases from new investors and may limit additional purchases from existing investors, it is still required to redeem its shares on every business day at one daily NAV, usually set at 4 P.M. Eastern Standard Time. Most fund redemptions involve an exchange out of one fund into another—for example, from a stock fund into a money market fund against which checks may be written. A redemption may also involve a request for payment by check, wire or electronic funds transfer, which is accomplished by the transfer agent through a cash management bank. (See "A Fund Redemption Through a Broker-Dealer.") Retirement distributions represent one of the more complicated redemption transactions because of numerous laws regarding the age at which distributions may start to occur (55), the age at which they must begin to occur (70½) and the minimum amounts that must be distributed from retirement accounts at various ages. In addition, there are detailed tax reporting rules with respect to various types of share redemptions from mutual funds. Accordingly, transfer agents have developed sophisticated systems that enable them to process and report all forms of fund redemptions accurately.

When customers effect a purchase by selling shares in one fund and using those sale proceeds to purchase shares in another fund, this is called an exchange. Exchanging shares from an existing fund to a new one in the same fund family is a relatively

CALLOUT
A Fund Redemption Through a Broker-Dealer

Jim Jones has spent the past 17 years investing in mutual funds through his broker and friend Andy Martinez for the express purpose of saving for his daughter Sarah's education. With the first $15,000 tuition bill about to arrive from the university, Jim calls Andy to discuss the best way to access the funds so that he can pay the bill when it arrives.

Andy offers a number of alternatives. The first option is to have the fund's transfer agent send a check for $15,000 directly to Jim. In this way, Jim could deposit the check in his local bank account and subsequently write a check from his bank account to pay the tuition. Although this option is appealing to Jim, it seems very time-consuming and potentially unreliable. Andy then offers to send the funds to Jim's bank by Federal Reserve wire. He explains that this is a quick way to receive the proceeds because the funds can be at Jim's bank account the following day. Jim likes this idea but becomes concerned when Andy mentions that this service might entail paying fees to the fund's transfer agent and his bank. Searching for the best alternative for Jim, Andy suggests using electronic funds transfer (EFT). He explains that EFT is a quick and reliable way to redeem funds and transfer the proceeds. As an added benefit, EFT generally does not carry a fee from either the fund's transfer agent or the receiving bank. Jim likes this idea and instructs Andy to sell enough shares to redeem $15,000 from his mutual fund account and to send the proceeds via EFT to his local bank account. Andy receives the appropriate authorization and instructions to have the fund's transfer agent process the EFT redemption.

Two days later, Jim, using his bank's Internet service, accesses his account and sees that it was credited with the proceeds from the $15,000 redemption the previous day. Jim is able to relax, knowing that he will be able to pay for Sarah's education as soon as the tuition bill arrives.

straightforward process. The customer gives the instruction to exchange shares to the fund's transfer agent through a phone representative, automated telephone system or the Internet. The exchange typically is processed during the overnight transaction processing cycle following receipt of the customer's request. Cash is transferred from one fund's bank account to the other fund's bank account early the next business day (see Figure 9.2). Exchanges between funds, even within the same complex, are generally considered taxable events unless they occur within a qualified retirement plan or tax-deferred vehicle such as a variable annuity. (See Chapter Seven.)

The requirement to allow for daily fund redemptions (including exchange redemptions) has substantial implications for mutual funds. Because of this redemption requirement, a mutual fund must invest most of its assets in liquid securities and must determine the NAV of its shares on each business day. In most fund complexes, the pricing and bookkeeping agent has the job of computing the NAV for each fund, and the transfer agent is responsible for disseminating the NAV. (See "Functions of the Pricing and Bookkeeping Agent.") Since the redemption requirement can, at times, have significant effects on cash flows and thus the overall management of a fund, the fund's portfolio manager closely monitors the velocity at which money is moving into and out of the fund. The case study at the end of this Chapter explores the challenges presented by "hot money"—short-term movement by fund shareholders in and out of funds.

B. Account Information and Fund Reports

Besides effecting the various types of shareholder transactions, the fund's transfer agent must provide fund shareholders with information about their accounts and their funds. When a customer purchases, redeems or transfers fund shares, the fund's transfer agent must send him or her a confirmation of that transaction. In addition, most fund complexes send confirmations of changes to nonmonetary information, such as address, account ownership and selected account features. On no less than a quarterly basis, each

FIGURE 9.2

Example of a $5,000 direct mutual fund exchange

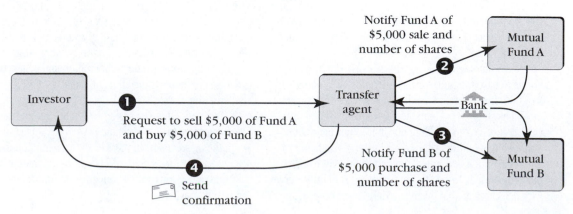

CALLOUT
Functions of the Pricing and Bookkeeping Agent

The pricing and bookkeeping agent is responsible for maintaining the fund's accounting records, pricing the fund's portfolio each day, calculating periodic distributions, determining the fund's cash availability, preparing financial statements and filing the fund's tax returns. A fund's accounting records are very similar to those of a small corporation, consisting of revenue, expenses, assets, liabilities and shareholder's equity. The pricing and bookkeeping agent is responsible for maintaining these records each day. The accounting records are the basis for calculating the fund's NAV, the price at which shareholders buy into and sell out of the fund, as well as for determining the distributions the fund makes to its shareholders.

A fund is required to be priced at least once each business day when orders to buy or sell fund shares are received. This is usually at the close of the New York Stock Exchange (NYSE) at 4:00 P.M. EST. The NAV is then sent to the National Association of Securities Dealers, Inc. (NASD) by 5:55 P.M. EST. The NASD disseminates the fund's NAV to newspapers and other electronic media. If a fund misses this deadline, it reports no NAV in the next day's newspaper, although it must still generate an NAV in time for fund transactions to be processed overnight during the nightly transaction processing cycle. (For more information on how to read data on fund prices in newspapers, see Chapter One.)

In order to calculate the fund's NAV, the pricing and bookkeeping agent needs to value the fund's portfolio, add in net other assets such as cash and receivables, less liabilities, and divide this sum by the number of outstanding fund shares. The value of a fund's portfolio is determined by using the quoted market price for securities for which market quotations are readily available or an estimate of value (fair value) as determined in good faith by the fund's board of directors for other securities (or amortized cost in the case of money market funds). The objective of the fair valuation process is to estimate the price that the fund could reasonably expect to receive if it would have wanted to sell the security in an orderly fashion. For instance, fair valuation of a security may occur when trading in that security is halted prior to the NYSE close. Fair valuation may also be used for securities traded in foreign markets if those markets close significantly earlier than the time of calculation of the fund's NAV and there is a "significant event" that may affect the current market value of those securities.

The fund's accounting records are also used to calculate a fund's distributions. As explained in Chapter Three, a mutual fund must annually distribute almost all of its investment income and capital gains to its shareholders in order to qualify for pass-through tax treatment. Since any undistributed income or gains is subject to federal tax, as a practical matter most funds distribute all of their income and gains within the time required under the Internal Revenue Code. Almost all money market funds and many bond funds declare income distributions daily. Other funds may make distributions monthly, quarterly or yearly. A distribution is calculated by taking undistributed income or gains (net income or gains, less prior distributions paid during the period) and dividing this amount by the number of fund shares outstanding.

Another key function performed by the pricing and bookkeeping agent is to calculate the fund's daily cash availability for its portfolio manager. This involves accumulating information from a variety of sources: the transfer agent for shareholder transactions, the custodian banks for trade settlement and income collection and the fund accounting records. This information on cash availability is provided to the fund's portfolio manager to assist him or her in timing securities sales or purchases for the fund's portfolio.

The pricing and bookkeeping agent also prepares the fund's financial statements. Every six months, each fund is required to publish and distribute to shareholders a report containing the fund's financial statements. The financial statements present net assets, results of operations, changes in net assets and financial highlights resulting from investing activity. In addition, the pricing and bookkeeping agent is responsible for preparing and filing the fund's tax returns.

shareholder receives an account statement reflecting the status of his or her position in the fund. Most fund complexes have made account statements user friendly by consolidating all of the customer's positions in the complex on one statement. For customers who hold more than the funds of just one fund family in a single account (e.g., within a fund supermarket or with a broker), the funds from all of the fund families are usually consolidated on a single statement (see Figure 9.3). Most fund complexes now are offering electronic delivery on the Internet of account statements, transaction confirmations and nonmonetary confirmations with an option to suppress the paper copy.

On an annual basis, transfer agents supply mutual fund shareholders with tax information. During the fall, the transfer agent works with the pricing and bookkeeping agent to obtain estimates of year-end distributions by funds in the complex. Toward the end of the calendar year, most fund complexes publish a schedule of estimated fund distributions to help fund shareholders begin to engage in tax planning. In January or February each year, the customer receives a summary of the prior year's reportable transactions for tax purposes. This tax statement includes a breakdown of all fund distributions into taxable and tax-exempt ordinary income, as well as long- and short-term capital gains. Contributions and distributions into or out of IRAs and other tax-sheltered retirement vehicles are also reported, as well as state tax reporting to the extent required. In most of the large mutual fund complexes, tax statements provide the average

FIGURE 9.3

Consolidated customer statement

Investment Report
June 1, 2000 — June 30, 2000

Trustworthy Investment Company

Brokerage Account   XXX-123456   JOHN DOE – INDIVIDUAL

Holdings (Symbol) as of June 30, 2000	Quantity June 30, 2000	Price per Unit June 30, 2000	Total Cost Basis	Total Value June 1, 2000	Total Value June 30, 2000
Mutual Funds 85% of holdings					
ALLIANCE GROWTH (AGRFX)	486.2540	42.19000	15,438.12	19,432.66	20,515.06
EATON VANCE HIGH INCOME (ECHIX)	245.6640	36.21000	6,591.22	8,495.06	8,895.49
FIDELITY JAPAN (FJPNX)	349.4140	23.66000	4,109.65	7,743.01	8,267.13
GLOBAL LATIN AMERICA (GLATX)	207.9860	15.39000	2,519.97	2,795.33	3,200.90
GLOBAL SOUTHEAST ASIA (GSEAX)	1,135.4700	15.51000	11,401.89	16,384.83	17,611.13
JANUS MERCURY (JAMRX)	215.6470	18.29000	1,564.57	3,526.21	3,944.18
PBHG MID CAP VALUE (PBMCX)	505.9160	31.26000	10,297.13	15,831.44	15,814.94
T. ROWE PRICE SCIENCE & TECH (PRSCX)	428.7440	29.24000	2,547.25	3,692.65	12,536.49
Core Account 15% of holdings					
Trustworthy Money Market	16,020.94	1.0000	not applicable		16,020.94
Total Market Value					106,806.26
Total Net Value					**106,806.26**

cost basis for nonretirement fund shares redeemed during the prior year to assist fund shareholders in calculating their capital gains on these shares for tax purposes.

Every six months, the Securities and Exchange Commission (SEC) requires each fund to publish a report containing the fund's financial statements, which are prepared by the pricing and bookkeeping agent. More important, this report contains a description of the fund's investment results and a discussion of its investment performance. The latter is often done in the form of an interview with the portfolio manager, explaining why the fund has performed well or poorly over the period. The transfer agent distributes these annual and semiannual reports to all fund shareholders. Approximately once a year, the transfer agent sends each fund shareholder an updated prospectus for any fund he or she holds. Periodically, the transfer agent sends to fund shareholders a proxy statement. Proxies ask the shareholders to vote on topics such as the election of fund directors or possibly a change in the fund's investment policies or fees.

As with account statements and trade confirmations, most fund complexes now offer fund shareholders the option of receiving these reports, prospectus updates and proxies online. Shareholders who exercise the online option must receive, through mail or email, a schedule of when these semiannual reports, prospectus updates and proxy statements will first be available on the fund complex's website. For fund shareholders who are not yet comfortable with the Internet, the SEC now allows a fund complex to mail one copy of such documents to all people who share the same address, unless they object to such "householding." Communicating with fund shareholders over the Internet or through combined mailings to households can result in substantial savings to funds, which can be passed on to fund shareholders in the form of lower transfer agency expenses.

Furthermore, most complexes that directly market their funds send out periodic newsletters and magazines to their fund customers. These periodicals contain articles about such topics as changes in tax laws, new investment trends and the introduction of new products or services. Similarly, fund complexes selling through brokers and other financial intermediaries provide informational material (in addition to the annual and semiannual report and the updated prospectus) on the performance of the funds, trends in investing and descriptions of new products or services. The broker passes along this material to the fund's shareholders.

C. *Customer Inquiries and Problem Resolution*

Probably the most challenging servicing function is handling customer inquiries and customer problems. These inquiries cover such a broad range of subjects (e.g., estate taxes, address changes and foreign stock prices) that it would be virtually impossible for any one representative to know enough to handle every situation well. For this reason, fund complexes have established and trained service teams to deal with questions from customers. These teams often are located in telephone service centers. Pioneered in the 1970s by Fidelity Investments and Vanguard, telephone service centers continue to be the predominant method of direct contact between shareholders and their mutual fund sponsor. Telephone centers also are used in the intermediary channel by complexes like Putnam and Franklin-Templeton to answer questions and provide support to registered representatives and other investment professionals selling the complex's funds.

Most fund complexes that perform their own customer service have more than one telephone customer service center. Often the call centers are established in multiple regions so that customer service can be achieved seamlessly, even in the event of a disaster or other contingency. Another key reason for multiple call centers is to gain access to different labor markets where availability and cost may be advantageous. When more than one call center exists, customers generally do not know where their call is being handled. Sophisticated telecommunications technology routes the customer's call to the most appropriate telephone service center. This routing is based on the current availability of representatives with the right skills to handle the customer's inquiry.

Not all customer service centers are organized in the same manner, but they tend to have some common characteristics. They normally perform several functions, such as sales, customer service and problem resolution. Supporting these multiple functions helps create a dynamic work environment, allows for job diversity and provides ongoing career progression for the representatives. However, because many customer service centers operate seven days a week, up to 24 hours a day, employees may burn out from regularly dealing with customer problems, making it a challenge to staff and retain employees at these centers. In fact, some customer service centers experience upwards of 30% employee turnover each year. Over the years, the investing public has become accustomed to ready access to qualified customer service agents anytime, anywhere. As a result, it would seem that the long hours of operation for call centers are probably here to stay. (See "Phone Representatives and a Typical Customer Inquiry.")

Technology plays a key role in supporting frontline service representatives when handling customer inquiries and customer problems. For example, sophisticated workstations store large amounts of data about the customer that are available at the representative's fingertips. Data-tracking systems allow a phone representative to ascertain quickly the progress in resolving a customer complaint instead of forcing the customer to wait or to be transferred to someone else. The imaging of most customer documents has allowed them to be stored efficiently and accessed promptly if needed. Imaging has enabled frontline service representatives to call up on their computer screens customer documents that in the past were stored in inaccessible paper files in the back office.

Most transfer agents for mutual fund complexes are offering and using the Internet as a technological platform for meeting customers' servicing needs. Many customers go to their fund complex's website to find answers about their account balances, fund prices or other straightforward subjects. (The Chapter later details this kind of customer "self-service.") But customers still tend to call live phone representatives on complex issues such as mutual fund taxation or account errors. Similarly, email has become an accepted medium for many customers. Although email exchanges are not instantaneous, many fund complexes strive to answer email inquiries within a short span of time (three to six hours).

D. Monitoring and Compliance

In addition to its obligations to service all customers effectively and efficiently, the transfer agent has certain responsibilities to the mutual fund and management company running the fund's portfolio. One responsibility is to ensure overall compliance

CALLOUT

Phone Representatives and a Typical Customer Inquiry

Comprehensive training of representatives is an important element of a successful customer service center. Training starts when the employee is newly hired. New hire training can last as long as 6 to 12 weeks. It generally encompasses product information, customer service skills, industry knowledge and readiness to pass industry exams. For certain roles in the customer service center, the NASD Series 6 or Series 7 license and a state-specific license (often called the Series 63) may be required. These licensing requirements are designed to ensure public investors that they are dealing with highly skilled professionals who have a good understanding of the mutual fund business.

Following is a dialogue in a typical customer inquiry handled by a call center. Although the customer service representative (Rep) is able to find the information requested by using her workstation, her knowledge of the mutual fund business is critical to having an intelligent exchange with the customer.

REP: Trustworthy Investments, this is Leia. May I help you?

CUSTOMER: Hi. I'd like to ask a few questions about the upcoming distribution from my Trustworthy Growth Fund. Can you help me?

REP: Sure. What would you like to know?

CUSTOMER: Well, last year, the Growth Fund made a distribution of $3.25 per share on December 15. Will it be making another similar distribution this year?

REP: Let me look that up. [She accesses the information using her workstation.] Yes, Growth Fund will be making a distribution again this year around December 15. And the amount of the distribution is estimated to be $2.70 per share.

CUSTOMER: Will the whole $2.70 be taxed at the same rate on my federal income tax?

REP: [Reading from the workstation screen.] No. The $2.70 per share will be divided into two parts: $2.30 will be taxed at the rate for long-term capital gains. That rate is now a maximum of 20%. The other $0.40 will be taxed at the rate for ordinary income. Although that rate will depend on your income tax bracket, it's likely to be higher than 20% for most shareholders of Growth Fund.

CUSTOMER: Okay. That'll help me estimate my taxes for this year. But when will I get the exact amount of my distribution from the Growth Fund?

REP: When the distribution is paid and declared, it will show up in your account. In addition, by the end of January, we'll send you a form 1099-DIV along with a detailed statement of your distributions from Growth Fund and all other funds in the Trustworthy complex that you owned during the year.

CUSTOMER: Great. Thanks for your help.

REP: You're welcome.

with each fund's prospectus in matters relating to shareholder activity and customer service. For example, a transfer agent is usually responsible for compliance with minimum balance requirements as outlined in the fund's prospectus. If accounts or transactions do not meet a specified size limit, the transfer agent must communicate the issue to the customer and take appropriate action. Because of the expense in handling small balance accounts, some funds require their shareholders to bring their balance to the minimum by depositing additional funds or consolidating disparate accounts.

Another responsibility of the transfer agent is to enforce any limits on the frequency of shareholder transactions, as specified in the fund's prospectus. Many funds limit the number of exchange transactions that a single customer can make during a specified period of time in order to constrain transfer agency expenses and brokerage costs that are incurred if a fund has to sell securities to meet redemptions. (See the case study at the end of this Chapter.) Transfer agents are also responsible for levying and collecting various account and transaction-related fees—for example, fees for annual account maintenance, check writing and bank wires, as well as custodian fees for Individual Retirement Accounts. More generally, transfer agents are typically under contract to maintain high levels of accuracy in processing shareholder transactions at a reasonable cost.

In the process of servicing large numbers of fund shareholders and performing large numbers of shareholder transactions, a transfer agent accumulates a significant amount of data on shareholder activity. This data have a myriad of uses, from reconciliation of money movement to tax and compliance reporting.

1. Shareholder transaction reporting   The thousands of shareholder transactions that are processed each day by the transfer agent must be reported and reconciled. Some key reports on shareholder transactions that the transfer agent prepares for the fund complex include:

- A report indicating the number of outstanding fund shares after all shareholder transaction activity has been posted. This is one of the most critical reports produced because knowing the correct number of outstanding shares is a precondition to calculating the fund's NAV.

- A report detailing the cash requirements for shareholder transactions, including exchanges among funds. This report is important as it serves as the basis for cash movement between the fund's bank accounts and its cash management banks.

- An exception report summarizing all shareholder transactions that may not have been correctly processed—for example, a check that is made payable to a fund for $5,000 but is processed and posted to the customer's fund account for only $500. Such a discrepancy in dollars deposited with a fund and dollars posted to a customer's account would show up on an exception report to be reconciled by the transfer agent.

2. Fund-level cash reporting   Each morning that a fund is open for business, the transfer agent must forward information about how much cash is available from shareholder transactions to the fund's pricing and bookkeeping agent, who combines this information with other data to determine the total amount of cash available to the fund. This amount is reported to the fund's portfolio manager, who must decide whether the fund has sufficient cash to purchase additional securities or whether the fund must sell securities to handle shareholder redemptions. The timeliness of this report on cash availability is critical for the effective management of the fund.

3. State registration fees   On a daily basis, transfer agents ensure that funds are in compliance with the various state laws governing their activities. Blue Sky laws are the most significant state laws that govern the offering and sale of fund shares within a particular state. Fund shares offered for sale in a particular state must be registered with that state, and a registration fee must be paid. The maximum number of shares that can be issued by a fund must also be approved by many states. To ensure compliance with Blue Sky laws, the transfer agent must monitor fund purchases and redemptions by state on a daily basis.

4. Backup tax withholding   Mutual funds are required to withhold and pay certain taxes on behalf of their shareholders. One such example is International Revenue Service (IRS) backup withholding for fund distributions and redemptions. Backup withholding is required when the shareholder does not provide a valid social security or taxpayer identification number to the fund. The transfer agent for the fund must withhold and forward these tax receipts to the IRS on a regular basis. Additionally, the transfer agent must submit tax return filings on behalf of the funds with the IRS on a quarterly basis.

5. General fund information   Most interactions between fund shareholders and a transfer agent are either over the phone or through the Internet. Therefore, it is critical that customer service representatives and fund websites promptly receive accurate information about the funds from either regular reports or responses to a specific query. Most fund transfer agents have developed large databases with sophisticated search capabilities to house such information. The information contained in these databases is very diverse, ranging from historical NAV information, to detailed proxy information, to fund performance and distribution history.

II. Transfer Agents as an Industry

Having reviewed the functions of the transfer agent, this section provides an overview of transfer agents as an industry: the organizational structure of the industry into external and internal transfer agents, and the industry's historic reliance on technology, including the emphasis since 1995 by the industry on the Internet.

A. External and Internal Transfer Agents

There are approximately 1,600 transfer agents in the United States today. A transfer agent must register under the Securities Exchange Act of 1934 with the SEC, which serves as the primary regulatory body governing transfer agent activities. Most transfer agents handle individual stocks issued by publicly traded companies, but a number focus mainly on mutual fund activity. (See Table 9.1 for a listing of full-service transfer agents, which provide the complete range of transfer agency services to various mutual fund complexes.)

Most of the providers in Table 9.1 are primarily external transfer agents—independent businesses that contract to deliver services to mutual funds—though some providers also service their own affiliated funds. Smaller and medium-size fund complexes often hire external transfer agents because such complexes cannot, or do not want to, make the large capital expenditures necessary to support extensive shareholder servicing. By contrast, most large fund sponsors own an internal transfer agent

TABLE 9.1

Full-service transfer agent providers, March 1999

Provider	Number of Fund Groups Serviced	Number of Shareholder Accounts Serviced
DST/BFDS/NFDS	179	14,500,000
First Data Investor		
Services Group	41	9,007,000
PFPC	100	5,087,000
Chase Global	90	1,716,000
Federated Investors	90	1,441,000
FIRSTAR	68	1,400,000
BISYS	44	410,000
Sunstone	11	191,000
Countrywide	34	57,000
IBT	30	36,000
United Fund Services	18	28,000
Forum Financial	13	18,000
MFS Company	6	18,000
Totals	**724**	**33,909,000**

Source: Strategic Insight, "Mutual Fund Industry Fee and Expense Benchmarks" (1999).

in order to control the delivery and quality of shareholder services. By far, the largest numbers of accounts are serviced by transfer agents internal to fund complexes. Some fund complexes use a combination of internal and external transfer agent service providers, resulting in shared responsibilities. In this combination model, an external transfer agent provides the back office processing, account servicing and the related computer systems, while personnel of the fund's internal transfer agent perform front-line customer service. This approach has the benefit of enabling the fund complex to retain control over the level of customer service, while not having to bear the full cost of performing all transfer agent activities.

The most comprehensive surveys of the transfer agent function for mutual funds are carried out by the Investment Company Institute (ICI), the trade organization for mutual funds. Most recently, the ICI has surveyed the transfer agent practices of almost 500 mutual funds representing over 70 fund complexes as they operated in 1999. This survey divides the categories of internal and external transfer agent each into two sub-categories. The category of internal transfer agent encompasses both the "fully internal" organization that is a captive of the fund complex and the "remote" organization that uses an outside service firm only for data processing. The category of external transfer agent encompasses both the "fully external" organization that is serviced totally outside the fund complex and the "hybrid" organization that outsources most shareholder servicing but retains limited functions such as telephone communications.

As shown by Table 9.2, most fund complexes in the ICI survey for 1999 are fully internal (30%) or "remote" (33%)—primarily internal but using an outside firm for data processing. By contrast, only 12% of the fund complexes in the ICI surveys are fully external and only 25% are "hybrid"—primarily external, but retaining limited functions

TABLE 9.2

Types of transfer agents used by funds included in the 1999 ICI survey

Type	Number	Percentage of Total
Fully internal	137	30%
Hybrid	115	25
Fully external	56	12
Remote	155	33
Total	463	100

such as telephone communications. These results may be explained by the fact that the participants in the ICI surveys tend to come more from the larger mutual fund complexes, which generally view shareholder servicing as a key element of competitive differentiation.

Both external and internal transfer agents address the needs of each mutual fund complex separately. With the advent of open architecture in the mutual fund industry, there is a broader need for a facility to process transactions between two mutual funds in different complexes. As explained in Chapter Seven, open architecture involves offering the customer through one account mutual funds from many different complexes. Such offerings are made by broker-dealers in their wrap programs and by the mutual fund supermarkets such as One Source (run by Charles Schwab). If an investor exchanges shares between two funds in different complexes, then some entity must sell shares in one fund, purchase shares in the other fund and move the cash between the fund complexes. The organization that helps to facilitate transfers between fund complexes is the National Securities Clearing Corporation (NSCC), a wholly owned subsidiary of The Depository Trust & Clearing Corporation. In general, the NSCC provides centralized clearance, settlement and information services to the financial services industry. In particular, it is the leading processor of mutual fund transactions between fund complexes.

The NSCC has centralized the processing of mutual fund transactions across the financial services industry through its Fund/SERV platform. This platform allows orders for purchases and sales of fund shares to be transmitted electronically between broker-dealers, banks and other financial intermediaries. Fund/SERV not only acts as the conduit for these orders, but it also supports confirmation, settlement, reconciliation and net money movement in connection with shareholder transactions between fund complexes. Without Fund/SERV, each mutual fund complex would have to go through the costly and inefficient process of establishing a reciprocal relationship with many other mutual fund complexes in order to support shareholder activity between them.

A complementary system called Networking was launched by NSCC in 1988. Networking was a significant advance in that it enabled standardized data on existing fund positions to flow across the financial services industry. For example, this system provides for the settlement of cash dividends and capital gains distributions from mutual funds in addition to reporting for tax purposes.

In short, the key benefits to the industry from the NSCC are as follows:

- The NSCC provides a single technological interface for the entire mutual fund industry when transactions and accounts need to move between institutions.

- The NSCC sets standards for the movement of transaction and account activity across the entire industry including net settlement and money movement.

- The NSCC provides a highly cost-effective way to conduct business, especially for smaller fund complexes that probably could not afford to support intercompany movement of transactions and accounts.

B. *Technology and Shareholder Servicing*

Technology has enabled fund transfer agents to improve the quality of customer service, enhance information flows to portfolio managers, cope with exploding volumes of transactions and introduce a broad array of new shareholder services. Moreover, technology has allowed the mutual fund industry to do all these things at a reasonable variable cost, after making substantial capital expenditures for the technology. Expensive labor-intensive functions have been replaced by automated systems that rely on ever cheaper hardware and communications channels.

In the 1960s and 1970s, advances in technology included the introduction of mainframe computers, online transaction processing and telecommunications connectivity. Mainframes and online processing made it feasible for mutual fund sponsors to manage the records of their shareholders. This was helpful to existing external and internal transfer agents for mutual funds and allowed some fund sponsors to establish in-house transfer agency services more easily. Advances in telecommunications made it possible to establish toll-free telephone numbers and route incoming calls to geographically distributed customer service centers, which could provide information and handle investor orders over the phone. In particular, these advances allowed direct-marketed fund complexes to offer telephone customer service during all business hours and later to offer such service up to 24 hours per day, seven days a week.

The 1980s saw the improvement of the voice response unit (VRU) with prerecorded answers to customer inquiries when linked to customer databases and trading systems using touchtone phones. This improvement began a trend toward customer self-service that continues today. New real-time data feeds, specifically geared to reflect transactions promptly, replaced batch service data feeds that occurred at the end of each day. These new feeds allowed transfer agents to monitor shareholder activity and update portfolio cash flows on a real-time basis. The use of mainframe computers to process enormous increases in trading volumes and customer transaction data, especially from 401(k) plans, increased dramatically. On the desktops of employees, "intelligent" personal computers replaced "dumb" terminals—which don't process data and input locally, but simply display the output of a program running on a server elsewhere. Toward the end of the 1980s, these multiple layers of systems began to be interconnected by local area networks (LANs) and wide area nationwide networks (WANs). These networks allowed for the integration of customer service functions, leading to automated work flow and problem tracking systems.

During the first half of the 1990s, the mutual fund industry began to rationalize some of this technological hodgepodge. The departmental systems that were convenient to use but difficult to manage grew into "enterprise servers"—large computers based on the UNIX operating system—with the capacity and stability to become the next generation of mainframes. Mainframes themselves became cheaper and better oriented to their new role as the repositories of huge databases. On the desktop, graphical user interfaces brought a standardization and ease of use that allowed PCs to be provided to all employees with a minimum of required training.

During the second half of the 1990s, Internet-based technology burst onto the scene and quickly became a force within the mutual fund industry. In 1995, the Internet was a 20-year-old technology, developed for the military and used primarily by the scientific and academic communities. But the broadening of the Internet has brought about dramatic changes in communications with current and prospective funds shareholders. Since 1995, web browsers installed on Internet-enabled PCs and hand-held devices have become the medium by which an increasing number of investors obtain information and conduct business.

According to the ICI, there has been a rapid growth in adoption of the Internet by mutual fund shareholders. In 1998, 62% of fund shareholders surveyed indicated that they had used the Internet; this percentage rose to 68% by 2000. Figure 9.4 from the same ICI survey shows differential Internet usage by marketing channels. Not surprisingly, fund shareholders in the direct market channel were the most likely to visit the website of their fund sponsor since such shareholders are accustomed to obtaining fund information for themselves. But the visit level was high even for shareholders of mutual funds in the intermediary (sales-force) channel, despite the normal reliance of such shareholders on their account representatives for fund information.

Despite this high overall acceptance of the Internet by mutual fund shareholders,

FIGURE 9.4

Visited websites of companies offering mutual funds, by source of fund ownership, 2000[1]

Percent of U.S. households owning mutual funds and using the Internet[2]

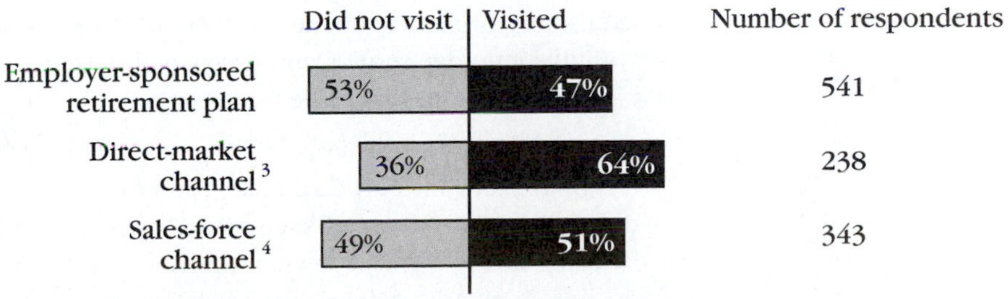

	Did not visit	Visited	Number of respondents
Employer-sponsored retirement plan	53%	47%	541
Direct-market channel [3]	36%	64%	238
Sales-force channel [4]	49%	51%	343

[1]Multiple responses included. Includes mutual fund companies and unaffiliated distributors, such as brokers, independent financial planners, insurance agents and bank or savings institution representatives (but not retirement sponsors).
[2]In the 12 months preceding the survey (April 1999 through March 2000). Excludes shareholders using the Internet only to send or receive email.
[3]Includes fund shares purchased directly from fund companies, through discount brokers and through brokerage firms only available online.
[4]Includes funds purchased from full-service brokers, insurance agents, financial planners and bank representatives.
Source: Investment Company Institute, "Mutual Fund Shareholders' Use of the Internet—Fundamentals," Investment Company Institute Research in Brief, Vol. 9, No. 3 (July 2000): Fig. 5. Reprinted by permission of the Investment Company Institute.

FIGURE 9.5

Use of the internet to conduct mutual fund transactions, 2000

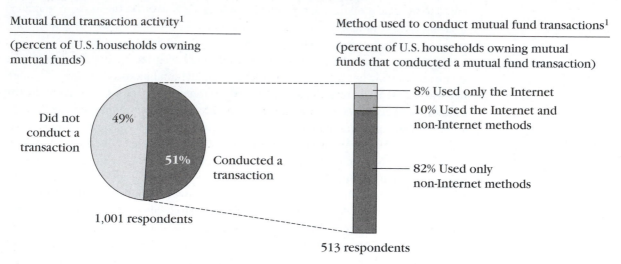

Mutual fund transaction activity[1]

(percent of U.S. households owning mutual funds)

Method used to conduct mutual fund transactions[1]

(percent of U.S. households owning mutual funds that conducted a mutual fund transaction)

Did not conduct a transaction — 49%

51% Conducted a transaction

1,001 respondents

8% Used only the Internet

10% Used the Internet and non-Internet methods

82% Used only non-Internet methods

513 respondents

[1]In the 12 months preceding the survey (April 1999–March 2000).
Source: Investment Company Institute, "Mutual Fund Shareholders' Use of the Internet—Fundamentals," Investment Company Institute Research in Brief, Vol. 9, No. 3 (July 2000): Fig. 9. Reprinted by permission of the Investment Company Institute.

only a few indicated that they had conducted a fund transaction (purchase, sale or exchanges) through the Internet. As shown by Figure 9.5, of those shareholders who conducted a mutual fund transaction, only 18% used the Internet in whole or in part.

Instead of effecting transactions on the Internet, mutual fund customers on average have tended to use the Internet as a vehicle for gathering information about various funds and determining appropriate investments. They also use the Internet to check on current account balances and view information about their accounts. By contrast, discount brokerage customers on average have embraced the web as a very efficient and timely way to perform brokerage transactions. In fact, over 80% of the transactions in some discount brokerage operations were effected through the Internet. These disparities in Internet usage result from three key differences between the mutual fund business and the discount brokerage business:

- ***Pricing.*** There is usually a significant financial advantage to customers for performing trades in individual stocks and bonds over the Internet. The Internet reduces the actual costs of such trades, and these savings are passed along to the investor in the form of lower commission rates. By contrast, most mutual funds do not carry any charges directly to customers for purchases, redemptions and exchanges. Therefore, there is little personal financial advantage to the customer for performing mutual fund transactions through the Internet.

- ***Activity levels.*** The average discount brokerage customer who trades stocks is much more active than the average mutual fund investor. As a result, such brokerage customers seem to value the convenience and flexibility afforded them by the Internet. The average mutual fund customer transacts only a few times per year—almost never a few times a day like many online brokerage traders. As a result, most fund shareholders are satisfied with the level of convenience and flexibility afforded by more traditional transactional methods like telephone systems.

- ***Speed.*** The active discount brokerage customer has a much greater need for timely execution of orders than does a mutual fund customer. The speed of Internet executions is critical to a discount brokerage customer who is trying to buy at the lowest price or sell at the highest price in a stock market with a lot of intraday trading volatility. But the same need for speedy executions does not apply to transactions for customers of mutual funds, since they generally price their shares only once per day. There is no pricing difference if a fund shareholder submits a purchase or redemption at 11 A.M. versus 2 P.M.

Although the Internet is gaining slow acceptance for effecting fund transactions, it is in the process of transforming the delivery of service to fund shareholders. Some of the groundbreaking innovations that have already occurred include a fully paperless account opening process, online access to daily fund prices and electronic delivery of customer reports, such as account statements, proxies, prospectuses and semiannual reports. The Internet already has begun to merge with other consumer media, so it is now possible for a customer service representative to have an interactive chat with a customer or help the customer navigate pages on the fund sponsor's website. The next generation of this capability will enable full voice and video communications between the transfer agent's representatives and fund shareholders.

A number of currently emerging technologies offer great promise to improve the overall service experience of fund shareholders. Voice recognition, which is already in use, enables a customer to speak commands to either a voice response unit or a voice-enabled Internet-connected device. As voice recognition improves, it will open up the use of the Internet to an older generation of fund shareholders who are not yet comfortable with computers. Furthermore, new developments in biometrics would allow the creation and storage of a voiceprint of the customer. In this way, the customer can avoid the inconvenience of using a PIN number for authentication and achieve a higher level of personal security.

Although knowledgeable customer service professionals will always be the most important components in the servicing functions of the mutual fund industry, technology will continue to change the nature of their work. Transaction processing, account queries, account setup and account maintenance increasingly will be conducted by investors independently. The role of the fund's transfer agent will focus on handling the more complex needs of customers: dispensing investment guidance and acting as a technological resource.

III. *Pricing and Service Quality*

The transfer agent supplies services to the fund pursuant to a contract. In most situations, this transfer agency contract must be approved annually by the directors of the funds in the complex. In negotiating the transfer agency contract, the fund directors typically are provided with industry-wide data on pricing of shareholder servicing. One of the best available sources is the ICI survey of transfer agency billing practices for 1999, described previously in this Chapter. In arriving at an appropriate level of

TABLE 9.3

Average dollar charge per account (all accounts), by fund type, 1999

Fund Type	Charges per Account
Fixed income	$22.00
Equity	20.32
Money market	24.92
All funds	**21.46**

transfer agency charges, the fund directors should take into account important distinctions among types of funds by investment objective and by distribution channel.

As Table 9.3 shows, the transfer agency fees on a dollar basis generally are highest for money market funds because they are the most service intensive; for example, every check written on a money market fund involves a fund redemption. The next highest transfer agency fees on a dollar basis are the fixed income funds because some offer check writing, and many declare income distributions daily. The lowest transfer agency fees on a dollar basis are for equity funds, which do not usually offer check writing or frequent income distributions. However, as shown by Table 9.4, the result is much different when the cost is expressed in basis point terms (i.e., the cost relative to the amount in the account). Fixed income funds have the lowest basis point charge because they tend to have the highest average account size. Conversely, equity funds have the highest basis point charge because they tend to have the smallest average account size. Money market funds tend to be in the middle in terms of basis point charge and average account size.

As shown by Table 9.5, transfer agency fees on a dollar basis are lowest in the affiliated broker channel, where fund shares are purchased through affiliates of the fund's sponsor (e.g., Merrill Lynch fund purchased through a Merrill Lynch broker). This is because their sales forces typically have integrated and automated servicing systems that allow their registered representatives to provide account and performance information

TABLE 9.4

Average basis point charge, by fund type and average account size, 1999

Average Account Size	Basis Point Charge		
	Fixed Income	Equity	Money Market
Less than $10,000	20	29	31
$10,001–15,000	18	19	23
$15,001–20,000	16	14	23
$20,001–30,000	11	13	18
Greater than $30,000	9	11	8
All funds	**13**	**19**	**17**

TABLE 9.5

Average dollar charge per account (all accounts), by distribution channel, 1999

Distribution Channel	Charges per Account
Broker (affiliated)	$15.74
Broker (independent)	22.36
Retail (direct)	25.49
Retail (captive)	20.08
Bank	29.20

on all securities holdings and transactions directly to fund shareholders (without significant intervention by the transfer agent). Conversely, transfer agent fees tend to be high on a dollar basis in the retail (direct) channel since the transfer agent is the main source of contact for fund shareholders. Although transfer agent fees appear to be highest on a dollar basis in the bank channel, the sample size may be too small to warrant valid conclusions. The two categories toward the middle of the range are "broker (independent)," where fund shares are purchased through a broker not affiliated with the fund sponsor (e.g., Mass Financial Services fund purchased through A. G. Edwards broker), and "retail (captive)," where fund shares are purchased through representatives who sell funds of only one sponsor (e.g., IDS funds purchased through IDS field representatives). Despite these significant differences on per account charges by dollars, the differences among distribution channels are much narrower on basis points per account, as shown in Table 9.6. This is primarily because the affiliated broker-dealer channel has relatively more small accounts, while the retail (direct) channel has relatively more large accounts.

Taking into account these differences among funds by investment objective and distribution channel, the directors of the funds must choose between an internal and

TABLE 9.6

Average basis point charge, by distribution channel and average account size, 1999

Average Account Size	Basis Point Charge[a]			
	Affiliated Broker-Dealer	Independent Broker-Dealer	Retail (Direct)	Retail (Captive)
Less than $10,000	27	31	26	29
$10,001–15,000	18	19	22	17
$15,001–20,000	11	17	20	13
$20,001–30,000	10	15	13	12
Greater than $30,000	5	9	13	8
All funds	**16**	**17**	**18**	**17**

[a]Bank channel data by basis points are not included in the survey.

external transfer agent for the complex. Most large complexes use internal transfer agents because they want to control the quality of customer service and are willing to invest in the technology needed to deliver that service. By contrast, most small complexes tend to hire external transfer agents because they cannot afford the large investment in technology, and they can obtain reasonable service levels from third-party vendors. As shown in Table 9.7, the dollar-based fees for external transfer agents are slightly lower on average than those for internal transfer agents, though not for money market funds. As shown by Table 9.8, the basis point charges for external transfer agents are also slightly lower on average than those for internal transfer agents (though not for the smallest and largest accounts). On the other hand, the services of internal transfer agents usually are more extensive and customized than the services of external transfer agents, which tend to offer a standardized menu of functions.

After choosing an internal or external transfer agent for the fund complex, the directors need to decide which services they want the transfer agent to perform and what prices to pay for those services. In most complexes, officials of the management company present each year for approval by fund directors a proposed schedule of services to be performed by the transfer agent as well as a proposed pricing schedule for those services. In negotiating a proposed pricing schedule, the fund directors generally attempt to obtain reasonably low prices, as well as an appropriate structure of those prices. The structure must reflect the fact that every mutual fund account has certain fixed servicing requirements such as sending quarterly statements and annual tax reports. However, there are tremendous variations among customers as to the extent to which they use discretionary account services, including the number of representative-assisted phone calls they place and the number of fund exchanges they make.

The most prevalent structure for transfer agent fees is a flat fee per account in a mutual fund. This pricing structure is simple to administer and accurately reflects the fixed costs associated with servicing every account, but it is not very sensitive to variations in service usage by different kinds of accounts. Another pricing structure is to charge transfer agent fees by transaction (e.g., $3.00 per representative-assisted phone call and

TABLE 9.7

Average dollar charge per account (all accounts), external and internal transfer agents, 1999

Agent Type	Charges per Account
External	
Fixed income	$21.30
Equity	19.59
Money market	26.90
Average	**20.97**
Internal	
Fixed income	$22.27
Equity	20.78
Money market	23.90
Average	**21.72**

TABLE 9.8

Average basis point charge, by transfer agent type, 1999

Average Account Size	Basis Point Charge	
	External	Internal
Less than $10,000	29	28
$10,001–15,000	18	19
$15,001–20,000	15	16
$20,001–30,000	13	13
Greater than $30,000	10	9
All funds	**16**	**17**

$.50 per automated phone call). While such a pricing structure captures well the costs associated with the variations in shareholder activity, it does not match well the fixed costs associated with servicing a fund account. For this reason, some funds pay a relatively low flat fee per account plus transactional charges. Moreover, any pricing structure involving transactional fees presents the administrative burden of counting transactions. For example, if a customer call includes inquiries about two existing fund positions, a redemption of a third fund position, a purchase of a fourth fund and an address change, it would be difficult for the transfer agent to record the number of transactions that occurred. To avoid this administrative burden, other funds pay a relatively low flat fee per account plus a basis point charge, expressed as a percentage of average fund assets, as a rough estimate of transactional activity by fund shareholders. Still other funds pay a transfer agent fee expressed entirely in basis points on average fund assets. In addition, a few funds use "variable" billing arrangements, in which the fund is charged a lower per account fee as the average number of shareholder accounts or net assets increases. Yet another approach used by some fund complexes with internal transfer agents is "allocated" costs, where the transfer agent fee for each fund is based on an allocated share of servicing costs plus an agreed-on profit margin.

Table 9.9 shows the relative use of the different types of billing practices by the mutual funds in the ICI survey for 1999. In the Table, the most prevalent category by far is

TABLE 9.9

Billing practice distribution as a percentage of funds in the ICI survey, 1999

Billing Practice	Percentage of Funds
Flat	48%
Flat plus	16
Variable	6
Allocated	7
Basis points	10
Other	13

the "flat fee" per account (48%), with the next most prevalent being the related variant of "flat plus" (16%), meaning a flat fee plus a transaction charge. On the other hand, the least prevalent types of billing practices are "variable" (6%), "allocated" (7%) and "basis points" (10%). The "other" category (13%) represents funds employing a combination of billing practices (except for flat plus, which has its own category).

Most servicing fees are charged to the fund and paid out of its assets to the transfer agent. However, mutual funds can and do levy special transactional charges on individual shareholders whose behavior differs sharply from the norm and imposes significant cost on other shareholders. For example, some transfer agents levy a charge per check on any shareholder who writes more than a specified number of checks during a certain period of time. Other transfer agents impose a maintenance fee on very small accounts since the cost of servicing these accounts is disproportionate to their size.

Another type of charge that is levied directly on the shareholder, and paid to the fund, is a redemption fee. This fee is paid by an individual shareholder if he or she redeems shares from the fund in less than a specified time frame. For example, a fund might levy a 1% redemption fee if a shareholder redeems from the fund within 90 days of purchasing fund shares. Such a redemption fee is not like a back-end load paid to the fund's distributor as a sales charge. Instead, a redemption fee is paid to the fund. It is designed to compensate the remaining shareholders for the fund's brokerage costs incurred by the fund in selling securities quickly in order to meet the redemption request. The transfer agent must collect the redemption fee as part of its services to the fund to ensure compliance with the prospectus.

After choosing a transfer agent and establishing a pricing structure, the fund's independent directors should establish procedures to measure and monitor the quality of service provided by the transfer agent. Although these procedures can take many forms, almost all involve some kind of periodic reports on service measures by the transfer agent to the fund's board of directors. Transfer agents are measured on both general attributes of service satisfaction and specific elements of their service delivery. For example, the metrics might cover a certain level of overall monetary transaction accuracy, the percentage of customer phone calls to be answered within a specified time frame or the average number of days to respond to customer inquiries. In a broader sense, the board might also want to understand the overall satisfaction of shareholders with fund services or the ranking of their transfer agent against competitors. In assessing these general and specific measures of customer services, fund directors often rely on surveys by independent firms. (See "Sample of Firms Measuring Mutual Fund Service.")

Measurement of shareholder satisfaction with customer service is a complex, multidimensional challenge. Fund shareholders are sensitive to a number of variables such as ease of use, accuracy of processing, timeliness of responses and skill of customer service representatives. Fund shareholders also tend to view customer service more favorably in periods of rising markets than falling markets. Moreover, since many fund shareholders maintain accounts at more than one mutual fund complex, as well as banks and other financial institutions, they have a broad perspective on overall service quality. As Figure 9.6 indicates, fund shareholders give generally high ratings to the overall service they receive from mutual fund complexes. Among types of fund complexes, direct marketing companies receive higher ratings than sales force companies.

CALLOUT
Sample of Firms Measuring Mutual Fund Service

CRC Research (Montreal, Canada): A division of U.S. research giant Maritz, with quantitative and qualitative research across industries. Provides annual satisfaction and loyalty study for mutual fund complexes with investment professionals as clients.

Dalbar (Boston): A financial services rating and research firm serving major institutions in mutual funds, insurance, retirement plans and brokerage. Known as the creator of customer satisfaction and service metrics that have become the standards for mutual funds and annuities.

Forrester Research (Cambridge, Massachusetts): A consultant firm known for its work on the Internet. Provides syndicated research studies for many industries, including financial services, on customer use of technology.

Intersearch: TNS Intersearch of (Horsham, Pennsylvania): A full-service international marketing research company, providing customized research to a broad range of industries. Areas of interest for mutual fund complexes include customer service, loyalty and value, product usage and attitude studies.

Market Facts (Arlington Heights, Illinois, Natick, Massachusetts): A full-service marketing research firm and a division of the British company Aegis. Offers proprietary research products that measure and track customer satisfaction and loyalty.

Market Matrix (Los Angeles): A market research firm specializing in financial services, with a focus on mutual funds and marketing materials. Performs an annual syndicated study on mutual fund sales literature.

Market Metrics (Quincy, Massachusetts): A focused research and consulting firm serving the mutual fund industry. Specializes in performance measurement that permits mutual fund complexes to assess their organization's position against their key competitors on issues like customer satisfaction.

MSI, International (King of Prussia, Pennsylvania): A full-service firm that offers research to many industries, including financial services. Offers quantitative and qualitative research to mutual fund complexes on subjects such as tracking customer interaction and problem resolution.

Roper Starch Worldwide (New York): Provides proprietary research services to corporations, government agencies, media and advertising agencies. Services include data collection, sampling, questionnaire development, coding and tabulation services.

Although the overall quality of services delivered to mutual fund shareholders is quite high, there are a number of areas for potential improvement. For example, as outlined in Figure 9.7, the most significant improvements in shareholder satisfaction for direct-marketed funds would occur if they handled all customer requests in a timely manner and had knowledgeable employees responding to customer inquiries.

FIGURE 9.6

Evaluation of overall service of mutual fund companies

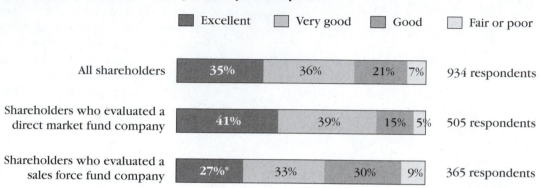

| | Excellent | Very good | Good | Fair or poor |

All shareholders — 35% | 36% | 21% | 7%   934 respondents

Shareholders who evaluated a direct market fund company — 41% | 39% | 15% | 5%   505 respondents

Shareholders who evaluated a sales force fund company — 27%* | 33% | 30% | 9%   365 respondents

*Direct market and sales force responses are statistically different at the 95% confidence level.
Source: Investment Company Institute, "Understanding Shareholder Service Needs" (Spring 1998), Figure 16. Reprinted by permission of the Investment Company Institute.

FIGURE 9.7

Opportunities for improving shareholder service for direct market fund companies

Percent change in quality rating if each improvement is made

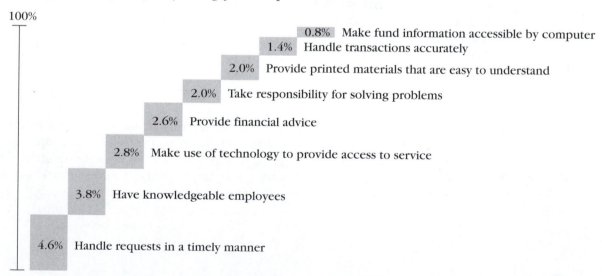

100%

0.8% Make fund information accessible by computer
1.4% Handle transactions accurately
2.0% Provide printed materials that are easy to understand
2.0% Take responsibility for solving problems
2.6% Provide financial advice
2.8% Make use of technology to provide access to service
3.8% Have knowledgeable employees
4.6% Handle requests in a timely manner

80% of shareholders who evaluated a direct market fund company rated the overall service of the company as either excellent or very good.

Source: Investment Company Institute, "Understanding Shareholder Service Needs" (Spring 1998), Figure 20. Reprinted by permission of the Investment Company Institute.

Most mutual fund executives have come to the conclusion that the quality of their customer service is critical to retaining the loyalty and support of fund shareholders. Although every fund manager strives to deliver excellent investment performance, there inevitably will be periods of relatively weak performance. However, it is feasible for a fund complex to provide consistently excellent customer service month after month, year after year. The challenge for the transfer agent of a mutual fund complex, whether internal or external, is to handle a huge volume of transactions and inquiries with a high level of accuracy and timeliness at a reasonable cost. In order to achieve these multiple objectives, a transfer agent must train a small army of phone representatives and give them access to extensive databases through computer workstations. At the same time, the transfer agent must invest heavily in technology to allow communications between the fund complex and fund shareholders through voice response and voice recognition systems as well as the Internet.

REVIEW QUESTIONS

1. What are the key responsibilities of the transfer agent hired by a fund complex?

2. What are the various types of redemptions of fund shares? If a fund shareholder wants cash quickly from a redemption, what would you recommend?

3. How are exchanges between funds in different fund complexes effected? What is the role of the NSCC?

4. What are the advantages and disadvantages of an internal versus external transfer agent? How should the fund's independent directors choose between the two?

5. What are the pros and cons of a transfer agent pricing structure based on the number of customer accounts? The number of shareholder transactions? The asset size of the fund?

6. Why would a fund sponsor close a mutual fund? If a sponsor announces that a mutual fund is closed, may existing shareholders still redeem and purchase their shares?

DISCUSSION QUESTIONS

1. When would you need the most staff members for customer servicing (hours during the day and months during the year)? How would you address the potential customer service needs in anticipation of a sharp market correction (such as the market correction in October 1987)?

2. Should individual shareholders, rather than the fund, be charged for check writing, wire transfers and exchanges? Should funds charge a redemption fee to an individual shareholder who leaves the fund after 30 days or nine months?

3. Why do mutual fund shareholders use the Internet less often for transactions than discount brokerage customers do? Do you think this differential will change over time?

4. What have been the most important technological developments to servicing of fund shareholders? What do you think will be the most significant future developments for such servicing?

5. How should fund directors evaluate the quality of services provided by the transfer agent? Do you think customer satisfaction on a service survey would be influenced by fund performance?

6. What factors account for the differences in servicing charges among funds? Should funds have a separate, lower-cost class for large accounts or accounts that are serviced only by the Internet?

CASE STUDY

Controlling Hot Money

A mutual fund may be thought of as a group of people who pool their money and hire someone to use it for the purpose the group has agreed on. Mutual fund shareholders agree to split the proceeds of their investment and also agree to split the costs of some basic services that they feel are important, such as customer phone service and fund annual reports. In a pooled investment, there are many different shareholders and many different relationships that must be considered: large investors, small investors, investors that are part of a retirement plan, and others. Each shareholder may have different servicing needs and preferences, but has agreed to pay for the average level of service required by the group.

The transfer agent of a fund incurs the ongoing costs of shareholder servicing such as transaction processing, updating account information and mailing confirmation statements, and these costs are charged directly to the fund. These ongoing servicing costs are spread on a pro rata basis to all shareholders of the fund, regardless of an individual shareholder's contribution to the costs. Because fund shareholders would have great difficulty coordinating among themselves, they rely instead on the fund's independent directors to protect shareholder interests and act as arbitrators when conflicts arise. Among other fiduciary tasks, the directors decide whether the services provided by the fund's transfer agent are worth the costs borne by all fund shareholders or whether some of these costs should be borne by a particular set of shareholders.

This case study presents one such dilemma for independent directors. It involves conflicts between different groups of shareholders of the same fund. A Japan Fund has recently experienced high cash flow volatility caused by short-term movement in and out of the fund by a small percentage of shareholders. The portfolio manager has been forced to spend more and more time managing this cash flow, and portfolio transactions have increased greatly as a result of the volatile cash flows. Also, increased shareholder activity has led to higher fund expenses for transfer agent services. See Exhibits 1–4.

The situation facing the directors of the Japan Fund is further complicated by the significant time difference between the U.S. and Japanese stock markets. The fund

EXHIBIT 1

Global Japan Fund: Expenses as of June 30, 1997

Shareholder Transaction Expenses	
Maximum sales charge on purchases (as % of offering price)	5%
Maximum sales charge on reinvested distributions	None
Deferred sales charge on redemptions	None
Exchange fee	None

Annual Fund Operating Expenses	
Management fee	0.80%
12b-1 fee	0.25%
Other expenses	0.52%
Total fund operating expenses	1.57%

Source: Global Japan Fund prospectus, June 30, 1997.

focuses on Japanese securities, which are primarily traded on stock exchanges in Japan. These exchanges operate during Japanese business hours (rather than U.S. business hours) and close long before the U.S. business day begins—typically 2 A.M. Eastern Time (ET). Most U.S. mutual funds are priced daily at 4 P.M. ET to coordinate with the close of the New York Stock Exchange (NYSE). This leaves a 14-hour window (except 13 hours when the U.S. is on daylight savings time) between the last trade in a Japanese security and the valuation point of that security for the purposes of determining the net asset value (NAV) of the fund.

EXHIBIT 2

Global Investment Company schedule for significant "other expenses" as of June 30, 1997

Transfer Agency (for shareholder transactions)	
Account fee	$10
Transaction fee	$12

Custodian (for Japan Fund transactions)	
Asset charge	2 bp
Transaction fee	$40

Pricing and Bookkeeping	
Asset charge	5 bp
Transaction fee	None

EXHIBIT 3

Listed equities: total institutional transaction costs by country for one-way transactions

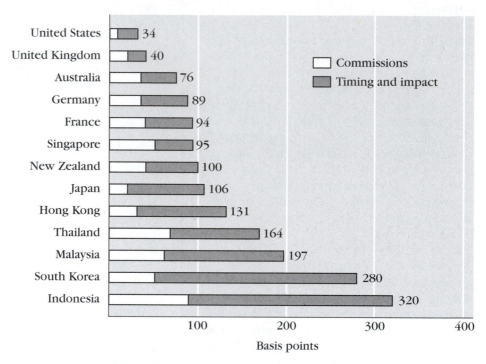

Note: For simplicity, transaction costs do not include taxes and exchange fees.
Source: Plexus Group.

At the next meeting of the fund's board of directors, you, as the chief financial officer for the investment adviser to the fund, are scheduled to make a presentation addressing these cash flow and pricing issues. The case study contains the material on both issues available to you. At your last staff meeting, you asked a select group of experienced employees to help you analyze the situation, evaluate alternatives and develop recommendations to present to the board.

Discussion Questions

After a review of the materials provided, the group has determined that answers to the following questions are necessary:

1. What is the impact of the short-term trading on the Japan Fund during August 1997? Identify and quantify, to the extent feasible, the various categories of costs that result from short-term trading on the fund. Which fund shareholders bear these costs of short-term trading?

2. What are the disadvantages (opportunity costs and administrative costs) of controlling "hot money" in the Japan Fund? Who bears these costs?

3. Assuming that action is warranted, what strategy will you propose to the Japan Fund directors that is likely to reduce substantially the short-term purchases and redemptions (or their impact) by shareholders while minimizing the disadvantages identified above? (Be specific and quantify your recommendation.) Alternatives may include:
    *   Restricting the number of transactions per account
    *   Restricting the manner in which redemption orders are taken
    *   Adding a redemption fee to the fund
    *   Adding a back-end load to the fund

4. What security prices is the fund using at 4 P.M. Eastern Time when NAV is determined? What other prices could be used? What other valuation time could be used?

5. Review the SEC's interpretation of its forward pricing rule included in the case study (see Exhibits 7 and 8).

EXHIBIT 4

Global Japan Fund sales data

Date	Gross Sales	Gross Redemptions	Net Sales
8/1/97	$540,003	$590,457	($50,454)
8/4/97	698,457	1,589,497	(891,040)
8/5/97	542,378	595,911	(53,533)
8/6/97	480,573	1,441,264	(960,691)
8/7/97	49,487	151,081	(101,594)
8/8/97	957,845	3,985,150	(3,027,305)
8/11/97	3,500,240	1,490,821	2,009,419
8/12/97	298,563	1,563,346	(1,264,783)
8/13/97	249,448	1,511,611	(1,262,163)
8/14/97	113,895	526,078	(412,183)
8/15/97	113,799	1,010,743	(896,944)
8/18/97	634,040	650,709	(16,669)
8/19/97	16,023	569,273	(553,250)
8/20/97	101,644	1,678,032	(1,576,388)
8/21/97	3,422,587	469,827	2,952,760
8/22/97	99,348	4,100,354	(4,001,006)
8/25/97	145,325	249,950	(104,625)
8/26/97	140,652	914,240	(773,588)
8/27/97	40,292	697,674	(657,382)
8/28/97	12,345	380,198	(367,853)
8/29/97	37,836	868,789	(830,953)
Total	12,194,780	25,035,005	(12,840,225)

Is the fund's current pricing policy a violation of the literal words or underlying concerns of this rule? If not, is it possible for investors to "game" the fund's pricing policy? If so, how?

6. Refer to Exhibit 10 for the price movements in Nikkei futures traded in Chicago during U.S. business hours on January 16, 1997. For that day, should you adjust the price of the Japan Fund or some or all of the securities it owns? Would you make a different valuation decision if the futures were up by the same amount or percent as they were down?

The Japan Fund

The Problem

Since the beginning of 1997, the U.S.-sold Japan Fund has experienced substantial cash inflows and outflows from investors, and portfolio manager David Smith has voiced his concern recently about the volatility. He also noted that extremely large shareholder orders seem to coincide more and more with news affecting Japan, and cash flow management is taking up a large percentage of his time that might otherwise be spent selecting securities.

Smith suspects some shareholders are trying to increase their profits by "timing" the market—quickly moving their money from one fund to another within the complex. Furthermore, he speculates that these investors might be attempting to profit from the methodology that the fund complex uses to compute the daily NAV of the fund by trading on stock price information that may become available between the time when the Japanese markets close and the time the fund values its holdings. Smith has requested that someone look into shareholder activity and analyze whether the pricing of the fund has encouraged or contributed to the cash flow volatility.

Background on the Japan Fund

Introduced on October 28, 1993, the Japan Fund is a non-diversified, SEC-registered mutual fund sold with a 5% sales load and a .25% 12b-1 fee to U.S. investors. The fund's investment objective is to achieve long-term growth primarily through investment in securities of Japanese companies. The fund may hold any type of equity or debt securities, although it is expected that equity securities normally will account for the majority of the fund's investments. The Japan Fund may also invest in indexed and debt-like securities whose value depends on the price of foreign currencies, securities indexes, other financial indicators or underlying interests. As of August 31, 1997, the fund had assets of $125 million and 12,500 shareholders with an average account size of $10,000. Currently, the average equity trade for the Japan Fund is 2,500 shares at $40 per share, and Smith tends to hold no more than 3% of the fund's assets in cash but occasionally may hold less for a day or two, depending on recent shareholder redemption activity.

The Japan Fund is managed by Global Management Company ("Global"), which also serves as manager of the following other mutual funds in the Global complex: Emerging Growth, Large-Cap Stock, Small-Cap Stock, S&P 500 Index, Diversified International, Emerging Markets, Europe, Latin America and High Income Bond. Shareholders of any fund in the Global complex may sell their fund shares and buy shares of other Global funds, subject to any restrictions detailed in each prospectus. The shares exchanged will carry credit for any sales charge previously paid by the investor in connection with their purchase. Each fund reserves the right to terminate or modify the exchange privilege at any time in the future.

Regional international funds, which are relatively new offerings for Global, seem to have gained in popularity. Assets in the funds increased at a fairly steady pace the prior year, and the complex now has a few funds (listed above) that each focus on a non-U.S. region or country. Although these focused funds carry higher risk than diversified international funds, they have the potential for higher returns. Because they are more concentrated than diversified international funds, country funds may appeal to investors who want to take more personal control of their investments, potentially including more active traders. As a result, Global anticipated that the Japan Fund might experience higher shareholder volatility, but the recent wave of cash that has been moving in and out of the Japan Fund seems to be especially high.

Short-Term Trading

Global has found that short-term trading is somewhat more likely to occur in aggressive or volatile funds or funds that are concentrated in one type of investment. Investors who are looking to place a "bet" have more difficulty doing it in a diversified fund, where the manager has more discretion to move money among market sectors and possibly asset classes. Since most sector and country funds have relatively small shareholder bases, a small number of shareholders making short-term trades can cause huge cash flow volatility relative to the size of the fund.

Short-term trades affect various categories of fund expenses that are paid by all shareholders in the fund. The fund's expenses, as detailed in Exhibits 1 and 2, include management fee, 12b-1 fees, transfer agent fees and other expenses, as well as brokerage commissions. Brokerage commissions are accounted for as an addition to the cost basis, or reduction in the proceeds from the sale, of the fund's portfolio securities and therefore reduce the capital gains (or increase the loss) realized by the fund.

Back-End Loads

Back-end loads are a sales commission levied by some load funds when an investor sells mutual fund shares. These back-end loads typically are structured as a contingent deferred sales charge (CDSC), which often start at 5% or 6% of money withdrawn within a year of buying the fund and then decline by a percentage point or so each year until they disappear. Back-end loads usually are set to compensate the distributor for marketing and selling the fund, especially to protect anticipated annual flows of 12b-1 fees. However, back-end loads may also be used to dissuade short-term traders; funds may set a high back-end load for money withdrawn within a very short time frame and then revert to the more general schedule of yearly declining load amounts referenced above.

Like most other mutual fund complexes, Global grants investors the privilege to exchange in and out of funds within the complex and also allows credit for any load paid when purchasing or redeeming one of the funds. For the purpose of calculating an applicable CDSC of Fund X, some complexes also give credit to investors for the holding period of shares purchased in other funds of the same complex if those shares are exchanged into Fund X.

Redemption Fees

Redemption fees are defined as fees paid to the fund (as opposed to loads, which are paid to the distributor). They may be imposed on all redemptions or on shares redeemed within a certain time period (e.g., 90 days) and are sometimes used to dissuade short-term trading and/or to compensate the remaining shareholders for the adverse effects of such trading. Redemption fees typically are charged on exchanges into other funds within the complex as well as account liquidations (i.e., leaving the complex). Some funds are introduced with redemption fees initially, while others have redemption fees added only after experiencing heavy cash flow volatility.

Global previously has determined that the level of a redemption fee should be based on the trading costs associated with the type of portfolio and has used estimates of turnover costs, including such factors as commissions, taxes and bid-offer spreads. The company feels that redemption fees based on a holding period are clear-cut and precise, but such fees may affect people who sell after a short period even though they did not buy the fund as a short-term or market-timing investment.

General Mutual Fund Pricing

Most mutual funds sold in the United States are priced daily as of 4 P.M. ET to correspond to the closing of the NYSE, although the time of pricing is left to the board of directors of the fund. Since there is no secondary market in fund shares, a daily price means that investors can be assured of having their orders executed within 24 hours (during normal business days). Although more frequent valuations are allowed, they may be prohibitively expensive for a fund manager from both an administrative and an operational perspective.

SEC rule 22c-1 (see Exhibit 7) links the time of the NAV calculation to shareholder trades by requiring that investor orders be executed at the next available share price after receipt of the order. For example, an investor who places an order at 11 A.M. to redeem 200 shares in the Japan Fund must be able to redeem those shares at the fund NAV calculated as of 4 P.M. ET that afternoon. However, an investor who places an order at 4:59 P.M. the same day to purchase $2,500 worth of shares in the Japan Fund will buy the shares at the NAV calculated as of 4 P.M. ET on the next day. (Exhibit 8 is a reprint of a response issued by the SEC to an inquiry from legal counsel to the Putnam Growth Fund on the timing of NAV calculations.)

Pricing of the Japan Fund

The Japan Fund is open for business each day the NYSE is open. Its NAV normally is calculated as of the close of business of the NYSE, which is usually 4 P.M. Eastern Time. The fund's NAV is the U.S. dollar value of a single share and is computed by adding up the value of the fund's investments, cash and other assets; subtracting its liabilities; and dividing the result by the number of shares outstanding. Foreign securities are translated to U.S. dollar values using the applicable foreign exchange rate.

At 4 P.M. ET, the last price offered for most securities held by the fund is 14 hours old, since the Japan exchanges close at 2 A.M. ET (earlier in the same day). Nevertheless, on most trading days, there is little change in Japanese stock market levels after Tokyo markets close at 2 A.M. ET and little activity in Japanese equity trading outside Japan. As a result, there typically is little change in the yen-denominated prices of Japanese equities from the market's close in Japan to the market's close in the United States. To the extent that the fund owns Japanese securities that trade with significant volume in the U.S. markets (including American Depository Receipts for Japanese stocks, which are usually listed on the NYSE), they will be valued at their last trading price in the U.S. market at 4 P.M. ET.

Occasionally, however, significant events that occur after Japan's business day is over can change Japanese equity values dramatically. When these unusual market events occur, the Japan Fund may value its Japanese investments at a level reflecting their value at the U.S. market close, which may be more or less than their value at the end of Japanese trading hours. The ability to make this kind of adjustment is recognized in the prospectus for the Japan Fund, which states that the fund's board of trustees may use valuations other than closing local market quotations if prices have been materially affected by events occurring after the closing of a local market.

Summary

Portfolio manager David Smith has called to check on the status of his request, and the board of directors' meeting is coming up in a few weeks. Your staff members have gathered relevant statistics, documents and articles (Exhibits 3–12), and are busy conducting analyses of the topics to be discussed.

EXHIBIT 5

Global Japan Fund: Redemption by holding period during the 46 months ended August 31, 1997

Months Following Purchase	Percent of Shareholders Redeemed Each Month
1	10.0%
2	1.0
3	1.0
4	9.0
5	9.0
6–12	2.0
13–46	0.5

EXHIBIT 6

Retail marketing memorandum

GLobaL investment company

Retail Marketing

Memorandum

TO:	Chief Financial Officer
FROM:	Heather Martin
DATE:	September 10, 1997
RE:	Japan Fund

Further to our discussion earlier today, I would like to argue strongly against the possible addition of fees or restrictions to the Japan Fund. In interacting directly with customers on a daily basis, I have the opportunity to observe firsthand their reactions to differing fees and restrictions on Global funds.

I find that additional fees on any fund are a deterrent to existing and potential customers. To the average investor, a fee is a fee whether it is front- or back-end, targeted to short-term traders or not. As you know, the Japan Fund currently has a front-end load, and a redemption fee would, in my opinion, significantly reduce new monies coming into the fund and may spur redemptions from current shareholders. While most investors do correctly perceive a load as a sales charge (whether front- or back-end), they perceive a redemption fee as an additional fee charged by the management company (even though it is paid to the fund).

Imposing a limited transaction policy or making the redemption process more difficult would also put off potential shareholders and may frustrate current shareholders once they decide to redeem. One of the attractive features of the Global complex is that investors can place, buy, sell or exchange orders for multiple funds with one phone call. Differentiating the Japan Fund by placing additional restrictions not found in other funds makes integrated servicing more difficult and more confusing to the customer. Anything that makes the redemption process for the Japan Fund more difficult than for other funds—even if disclosed in the prospectus and verbally reiterated during phone orders—has the potential to anger shareholders when they attempt to redeem and sour them on the entire Global complex.

Is short-term trading truly enough of a problem to warrant any of the actions mentioned above? In my opinion, the answer is clearly no.

Please feel free to contact me if you would like to discuss this further or have additional questions.

EXHIBIT 7

Pricing of redeemable securities for distribution, redemption and repurchase

SEC, Investment Company Act of 1940, Release No. IC-14244, File No. S7-39-84, 17 CFR Part 270, November 21, 1984 (excerpt)

Rule 22c-1(b), as amended in 1979, requires investment companies issuing redeemable securities to compute the net asset value of shares (i) not less frequently than once daily on each day (other than days when no order to purchase or sell is received and no tender for redemption is made) in which there is a sufficient degree of trading in the investment company's portfolio securities that the current net asset value of the fund's redeemable securities might be materially affected by changes in the value of the portfolio securities, and (ii) at such specific time during the day as determined by a majority of the board of directors of the investment company no less frequently than annually.[a]

Rule 22c-1 was originally adopted in 1968 to require forward pricing of investment company redeemable securities.[b] The rule requires that an open-end investment company, for purposes of sales, redemptions and repurchases of its redeemable securities, give investor orders the next computed price of the net asset value after receipt of the order. Prior to adoption of rule 22c-1, investor orders to purchase and redeem could be executed at a price computed before receipt of the order, allowing investors to lock-in a low price in a rising market and a higher price in a falling market. The forward pricing provision of rule 22c-1 was designed to eliminate these trading practices and the dilution to fund shareholders which occurred as a result of backward pricing.

[a]17 CFR 270.22c-1(b).
[b]ICA Release No. 5519 (October 16, 1968); 33 FR 16331 (November 7, 1986).

EXHIBIT 8

Putnam "no action" letter

SEC-Reply-1: Securities and Exchange Commission
Washington, D.C. 20549
January 23, 1981

Response of the Office of Chief Counsel
Division of Investment Management

Our Ref. No. 80-327-CC
The Putnam Growth Fund
Putnam International Equities Fund, Inc.
File Nos. 811-781 and 811-1403

Based on the representations contained in your letter, we would not recommend any action to the Commission under section 22(d) of the Investment Company Act of 1940 (the "1940 Act") or rules 22e-1 and 2a-4 under the 1940 Act if The Putnam Growth Fund and Putnam International Equities Fund, Inc. ("the Funds") value their assets at 4:00 P.M. New York time and use as the values of their portfolio securities which are principally traded on foreign securities exchanges the next preceding closing values of such securities on their respective exchanges except when an event has occurred since the time a value was so established that is likely to have resulted in a change in such value, in which case the fair value of the securities as of 4:00 P.M. New York time will be determined by the consideration of other factors. In addition, based on the representations contained in your letter, we would not recommend any action under the aforementioned provisions if each of the Funds, a substantial majority of whose portfolio securities are not principally traded on Japanese exchanges, does not price its shares for sale or redemption as of those Saturdays that the Japanese exchanges are open for business.

Stanley B. Judd

EXHIBIT 8 (CONT.)

Inquiry-1: Ropes & Gray
225 Franklin Street
Boston, MA 02110

Investment Company Act of 1940;
Section 22(d) and Rules 2a-4 and 22(c) (1)
October 22, 1980

Securities and Exchange Commission
Division of Investment Management
500 North Capital Street
Washington, D.C. 20549

Attention: Joel H. Goldberg, Associate Director
Stanley B. Judd, Assistant Chief Counsel

Re: The Putnam Growth Fund
Putnam International Equities Fund, Inc.

Gentlemen:

The purpose of this letter is to request confirmation by the staff of the Securities and Exchange Commission that it will not recommend action by the Commission under Section 22(d) of the Investment Company Act of 1940 (the "1940 Act") and Rules 22(c) (1) and 2a-4 under the 1940 Act if The Putnam Growth and Putnam International Equities Fund, Inc. value their assets invested in securities of companies principally traded in foreign companies in accordance with the procedure outlined below.

Facts:

The Putnam Growth Fund ("Putnam Growth") is a Massachusetts business trust which is registered under the 1940 Act as an open-end management company which had assets as of September 30, 1980, of approximately $690 million. The investment objective of Putnam Growth is to seek long-term growth of capital with current income as a secondary consideration. Under most conditions, common stocks have constituted a substantial majority of the Fund's investment. As of September 30, 1980, Putnam Growth had approximately $48 million, or less than 7%, invested in securities of issuers whose securities are primarily traded in foreign countries. As of that date, approximately 3% of the Fund's total assets were invested in securities of companies whose securities are principally traded on the Tokyo Stock Exchange. The Fund may invest up to 20% of its assets in securities of foreign issuers although to date the Fund has never invested in the aggregate more than 10% of its assets in such securities. Putnam Growth is owned by approximately 85,000 shareholders.

Putnam International Equities Fund, Inc. ("Putnam Equities") is a Massachusetts corporation which is registered under the Act as an open-end management company with assets as of September 30, 1980, of approximately $42 million. The investment objective of Putnam Equities is to seek capital appreciation by investing its assets primarily in common stocks. Up to 70% of Putnam Equities' assets may be invested from time to time in securities principally traded in foreign markets. As of September 30, 1980, investments of the Fund could be geographically divided as follows:

Australia	6.4%
England	2.4%
Germany	9.2%
Hong Kong	4.2%
Japan	26.4%
South Africa	6.9%
Switzerland	2.9%
Netherlands	4.6%
United States	37.0%

Putnam Equities is owned by approximately 13,000 shareholders.

Both Putnam Growth and Putnam Equities currently value their assets at 4:00 P.M. each day on which the New York Stock Exchange is open for trading. Securities which are principally traded in foreign countries are valued as of 4:00 P.M. New York time using as a basis for this valuation the next preceding closing values for such securities on the stock exchanges where such securities are principally traded. For many foreign securities there are American Depository Receipts ("ADRs") which reflect ownership in the underlying foreign security. Such ADRs are traded in the U.S. in the over-the-counter market and are valued daily as of approximately 4:00 P.M. New York time. *Where such ADRs exist and are actively traded, the Funds use such ADRs to value the underlying foreign security whether or not they in fact own the ADRs.

Both Putnam Growth and Putnam Equities are sold only in the United States. In the case of orders for purchases and sales through dealers, the applicable public offering price will be the net asset value determined as of the close of the New York Stock Exchange on the date the order was placed plus the applicable sales charge but only if the order is received by the dealer prior to the close of the Exchange and transmitted to the Fund's distributor prior to its close of business that date—normally 5:00 P.M. Boston time.

Both Putnam Growth and Putnam Equities are managed pursuant to contracts with The Putnam Management Company, Inc., which also acts as investment adviser to eleven other open-end and one closed-end investment companies. The pricing of the Funds' portfolios is done by Putnam Administrative Services Company, Inc., acting as agent for The Putnam Management Company, Inc.

The offices of Putnam Growth, Putnam Equities, The Putnam Management Company, Inc., and Putnam Administrative Services Company are not open for business on Saturday. No fund business is transacted on that day and there are no personnel regularly present to process orders to purchase shares or to determine prices of portfolio securities and make other calculations necessary to determine net asset value. To the extent necessary, investment matters on such days relating to foreign securities are generally followed by portfolio managers from their own homes. Mail addressed to the Funds or their shareholder servicing agent or principal underwriter at the street address is picked up Monday through Friday at the central post office in Boston and processed on those days. A clerical person picks up box mail each Saturday but the letters are not opened until Monday nor is there personnel present to open such mail on Saturday.

Discussion:

In response to comments of the Commission's staff in connection with certain registration statements of open-end investment companies which have recently or will soon become effective and in light of the response of the Commission's staff to the "no action letter" of Nomura Capital Fund of Japan and Nomura Index Fund of Japan of November 6, 1979 (the "Nomura Letter"), Putnam Growth and Putnam Equities have reviewed their pricing policies with respect to foreign securities. Such review has been made not only with respect to the practice of not pricing securities which are traded in the Japanese market on those Saturdays on which the Japanese Stock Exchange is open for trading but also generally with respect to the manner in which each Fund normally values its foreign securities on a regular business day. While each Fund believes that its procedures are appropriate and fair to all investors, we believe it is appropriate in light of the Nomura Letter to seek the views of the Commission's staff as to the current procedures followed by these two Funds.

Rule 22c-1(a) and (b) provides in part:

(a) No registered investment company issuing any redeemable security . . . shall sell, redeem, or repurchase any such security except at a price based on the current net asset value of such security which is next computed after receipt of a tender of such security for redemption or of an order to purchase or sell such security; . . .

(b) For the purposes of this rule, (1) the current net asset value of any such security shall be computed (i) no less frequently than once daily on each day (other than a day during which no such security was tendered for redemption and no order to purchase or sell such security was received by the investment company) in which there is a sufficient degree of trading in the investment company's portfolio securities that the current net asset value of the investment company's redeemable securities might be materially affected by changes in the value of the portfolio securities, and (ii) at such specific time during the day as determined by a majority of the board of directors of the investment company no less frequently than annually; . . .

Rule 2a-4 under the Act provides in part:

(a) The current net asset value of any redeemable security issued by a registered investment company used in computing periodically the current price for the purpose of distribution, redemption, and repurchase means

EXHIBIT 8 (CONT.)

an amount which reflects calculation, whether or not recorded in the books of account, made substantially in accordance with the following, with estimates used where necessary or appropriate:

(1) Portfolio securities with respect to which market quotations are readily available shall be valued at current market value, and other securities and assets shall be valued at fair value as determined in good faith by the board of directors of the registered company. . . .

As described above, Putnam Growth and Putnam Equities, at the time of their daily computations of net asset value at 4:00 P.M. New York time, utilized for the purposes of determining the proper security value of portfolio investments traded principally in foreign countries the market values for such securities as of close of trading on the principal exchanges where such securities are traded as of a time earlier in the day. For example, with respect to securities traded on the London Stock Exchange, trading has ceased as of 10:00 A.M. New York time.

We believe that the above procedure for valuing such foreign securities is consistent with the requirements of Rule 2a-4 (a) under the Act for either of two reasons. First, if one determines that portfolio securities traded in London and for which trading ceased approximately six hours earlier in the day are "portfolio securities with the respect to which market quotations are readily available" then one is required to use "current market values" for such securities in computing current net asset value. Since no securities have generally traded in London since 10:00 A.M. New York time, the only current market values available for determining the value of such securities as of 4:00 P.M. New York time are the closing prices on the London Stock Exchange earlier in the day. Pursuant to the provisions of Rule 2a-4, Putnam Growth and Putnam Equities estimate the prices as of 4:00 P.M. New York time utilizing the earlier day London closing values as the basis for such estimates. Second, if one determines that as of 4:00 P.M. New York time the London securities are not "portfolio securities with respect to which market quotations are readily available" one is then required to value such securities "at fair value as determined in good faith by the board of directors of the registered company." In this case, the Fund would in almost all instances use, for the purposes of fair valuation, the closing prices of such London securities of approximately six hours earlier and estimate that as of 4:00 P.M. New York time such values reflect fair value of such securities as of the time. In either case, the valuation made at 4:00 P.M. New York time is being estimated based on market values which reflect closing values as of earlier in the day. Such method would clearly seem to be permissible under Rule 2a-4.

If, however, some extraordinary event were to occur after the close of business on the London Stock Exchange but prior to the close of business on the New York Stock Exchange on the same day and the Funds' officers, to whom authority for pricing the respective Funds has been delegated, determine that such closing prices are no longer a reasonable estimate of such securities values as of 4:00 P.M. New York time, then there would be made a fair value determination of the value of such securities as of 4:00 P.M. using other appropriate indicia of value or valuation of the Funds' overall portfolio would be suspended until early the next morning at which time current portfolio quotations for such London securities could be obtained with the previous U.S. closing prices used for U.S. securities.

The above valuation procedures of Putnam Growth and Putnam Equities avoid the abuses which forward pricing, as set forth in Rule 22c-1, was intended to limit. For example, an investor who enters an order to purchase shares of either Putnam Growth or Putnam Equities at 3:00 P.M. New York time will not be circumventing the requirement of Rule 22c-1 that such shares be purchased at a price which is next computed after the order is received. This is true even with respect to foreign securities, values for which will be established as of 4:00 P.M. New York time. This is not any less true because the Fund utilizes prices reflecting closing stock exchange values earlier in the day since the determination that such prices continue to be valid is made in fact after the order has been received. In those rare circumstances when the earlier London or other foreign markets' closing values are no longer deemed by the Funds to be accurate as of 4:00 P.M. New York time the Funds' procedures for valuation as required by the Act would require that the Funds unitize fair value procedures for arriving at a 4:00 P.M. New York valuation and thus the valuation would continue to be made after the order had been received.

Further, the utilization of 4:00 P.M. New York time as the valuation time is not only for Putnam Growth but also for Putnam Equities which may have a majority of its securities traded in countries outside of the United States is appropriate and consistent with the Act and the rules thereunder. As stated in Rule 22c-1, it is required that directors/trustees of each Fund determine the specific time during the day when a fund must value its assets. The utilization by Putnam Equities of 4:00 P.M. New York time is not only consistent with the provisions of Rule 2a-4 for the reasons stated above but also permits the Fund's shareholders to have a net asset value fixed at a time consistent with other mutual funds and which permits the maximum public distribution of such prices. To pick another time, for example 10:00 A.M. New

York time (i.e., the close of business on the European markets) would mean that a shareholder who purchased his or her share at 11:00 A.M. New York time would not be given a value for such purchase until 10:00 A.M. the next day and would not be able to read the price per share received in a newspaper until the following day or two full days after the order was entered. This approach would not seem to be beneficial for shareholders and would tend to underscore the reasonableness of the director's decision that a 4:00 P.M. New York time on the day the order to purchase or sell shares is received is the proper time for valuing Putnam Equities' securities. . . .

If you need any additional information in connection with the forgoing, please do not hesitate to contact the undersigned. Also, in the event that you have any difficulty taking the position requested in this letter, I would appreciate the opportunity to discuss this matter with you further at your convenience.

Sincerely yours,
Edward P. Lawrence

Cc: Mr. Richard M. Cutler
Vice Chairman
The Putnam Funds

*As of September 30, 1980 approximately one-third of Putnam Growth's foreign investments and one-quarter of Putnam Equities' foreign investments reflect ownership by the Funds of ADRs.

EXHIBIT 9

"Fair-value" pricing for shares in funds to be reviewed by SEC
Charles Gasparino

The controversy surrounding "fair-value" pricing for mutual-fund shares has caught the eye of the fund industry's top cop.

The Securities and Exchange Commission, which regulates the $4.4 trillion mutual-fund business, plans to scrutinize the unusual pricing technique in the wake of last week's market turmoil and investor angst over the issue.

In fair-value pricing, fund companies largely disregard closing market prices of stocks and other securities to determine how much a mutual fund is worth. Instead, they rely on other bits of information, including the trading of futures tied to these securities, to determine stock prices and ultimately the price of mutual-fund portfolios.

At the moment, SEC rules allow fund companies to use this technique—instead of the more traditional approach of using closing share prices—to come up with a fund's net asset value, or NAV. However, following last week's upheaval in global markets, many investors are complaining that they bought or sold fund shares unaware that some fund companies, including giant Fidelity Investments, relied on the fair-value system. SEC officials now say they will reconsider the commission's policy.

"In light of the events of the last week," an SEC spokesman said in a statement, "the commission intends to review the operation of its rules of the pricing of fund shares in turbulent markets. We will be talking to the fund groups and may conduct examinations of the fund groups that use 'fair-market value' pricing methods. If it appears that the rules are not working in the best interest of fund shareholders, they will be revised."

In theory, SEC officials favor giving fund companies leeway in their pricing of fund shares. Gene Gohlke, an associate director with the SEC's Office of Compliance Inspections and Examinations, told a securities conference in New York Friday he believes fair-value pricing is a "reasonable approach," when market prices "might no longer be the best prices." The SEC, he said, had given its blessing to the practice in a "no-action" letter to Putnam Investments. Mr. Gohlke said Putnam wanted to be sure it wouldn't raise regulators' eyebrows if it considered post-closing events when pricing overseas stocks or bonds, or mutual funds with overseas holdings.

EXHIBIT 9 (CONT.)

But in light of what happened last week, SEC officials said they are no longer sure that when put in practice, fair value works to the benefit of investors. "We will review how the policy worked, and if it didn't work—if it hurt investors instead of helping them—we may change it," the spokesman added.

Though fund companies have used fair-value pricing for several years, it became an issue last week when markets throughout the world gyrated for several days. As investors sought to profit from depressed prices in international markets by buying shares of overseas funds, they discovered that some big fund companies weren't relying on the closing price of overseas markets. Instead, as the companies later explained, they were using a "fair-value" stock price to determine a fund's NAV, or price-per-share.

At the center of the storm was Boston-based Fidelity, the nation's largest fund company. Fidelity normally uses closing market prices to determine the value of stocks in its mutual-fund portfolios and, ultimately, the portfolios themselves. But last Tuesday, Fidelity calculated a two-cent rise in the NAV of its Hong Kong & China fund, based on the futures market and other factors it believed had an effect on the value of the stocks in the portfolio. Earlier in the day, however, many investors, unaware of fair-value pricing, had purchased the fund based on the close of the Hong Kong market, which fell about 14% before the day's opening in New York.

"I lost $50,000 in profits," said David DeVault, a retired dentist from Houston, who was one of the angry investors tripped up by the pricing system. "They say they used fair-value pricing, but nobody knew about it."

Officials at Fidelity defended the move, saying the fair-value method helps protect long-term investors from market speculators who might buy the fund in an effort to capitalize on short-term market distortions. They said the company's disclosure documents clearly spell out that they may use fair-value in determining stock and fund prices.

As for the SEC scrutiny of the matter, "we welcome it," said Jerry Lieberman, Fidelity's senior vice president and chief financial officer. "What we're doing is the right thing."

That, he said, is because speculators can spot a profitable short-term investment because of the time differences between overseas and U.S. markets. If, say, speculators believe that a rebounding U.S. market will help support prices in Hong Kong later, they might purchase shares of Fidelity's Hong Kong fund—as many did last week—only to flip it the following day at a big profit when the Hong Kong Markets recover.

That profit, Fidelity said, comes at the expense of long-term investors who don't gain as much from such short-term market movements. But Fidelity officials said that Tuesday evening, after U.S. Markets rebounded, they managed to stymie "market timers" by developing a fair-value price for the stocks in the Hong Kong fund that took into account futures trading foreshadowing a parallel recovery in Hong Kong. As a result, they said, the pricing was more accurate than the previous day's lower closing prices in Hong Kong.

Interestingly, Fidelity relies on fair-value pricing all of the time, one way or another, Mr. Lieberman said. Sometimes the fair value of a security is reflected in the close of the market; sometimes it reflects other factors such as futures trading or dealers' quotes.

To price bonds, many mutual funds actually rely on outside pricing services. These services use models that are programmed to add "variances" to prior-day prices, taking into account the difference in credit quality between the bond at issue and the Treasury security of similar maturity. In a pinch, when a bond is too hard to price that way, the model kicks it out; the pricing service has to turn to dealers instead.

Source: From *The Wall Street Journal,* issue of November 3, 1997. © 1997 Dow Jones & Company, Inc. All rights reserved.

EXHIBIT 10

Instances of 1997 intraday Nikkei 225* futures price movements more than 150 points as of Aug. 1997

Date	Chicago Nikkei Futures Open	Chicago Nikkei Futures Close	Previous Nikkei Close	Next Nikkei Open	Next Nikkei Close
01/13/97	18,050	17,895	18,119	18,061	18,093
01/15/97	18,025	18,225	18,093	18,126	18,144
01/16/97	18,160	17,900	18,144	18,097	18,090
01/21/97	17,385	17,640	17,358	17,441	18,014
01/23/97	17,950	17,760	17,909	17,894	17,689
02/12/97	18,460	18,660	18,410	18,505	18,688
03/05/97	18,290	18,450	18,274	18,342	18,041
03/06/97	18,050	17,820	18,041	18,001	18,199
03/07/97	18,250	18,030	18,199	18,196	18,114
03/24/97	18,025	18,300	18,044	18,117	18,440
04/24/97	18,650	18,440	18,698	18,648	18,613
05/05/97	19,720	19,890	19,515	19,617	20,181
05/08/97	20,030	20,185	20,062	20,097	19,803
05/09/97	19,910	19,660	19,803	19,731	20,144
05/12/97	20,030	20,280	20,144	20,207	20,129
06/23/97	20,400	20,220	20,436	20,383	20,342
07/22/97	20,175	20,340	20,157	20,244	20,131
08/08/97	19,570	19,200	19,604	19,462	18,824
08/15/97	19,430	19,050	19,326	19,213	19,041
08/20/97	19,195	19,375	19,252	19,320	19,157
08/21/97	19,150	18,900	19,157	19,074	18,650

Note: The Nikkei 225 stock average is a price-weighted benchmark that tracks the continuous price-only performance of 225 actively traded companies listed on the Tokyo Stock Exchange's first section.

EXHIBIT 11

Asian equity market trading hours: eastern time (May–September) versus local time

New Zealand (+16)	ET: 5:30 P.M.–11:30 P.M.
	Local: 9:30 A.M.–3:30 P.M.
Australia (+14)	ET: 8:00 P.M.–2:00 A.M.
	Local: 10:00 A.M.–4:00 P.M.
Japan (+13)*	ET: 8:00 P.M.–10:00 P.M. //
	11:30 P.M.–2:00 A.M.
	Local: 9:00 A.M.–11:00 P.M. // 12:30 P.M.–3:00 P.M.
Singapore (+12)	ET: 9:00 P.M.–12:30 A.M. //
	2:00 A.M.–5:00 A.M.
	Local: 9:00 A.M.–12:30 P.M. // 2:00 P.M.–5:00 P.M.
Taiwan (+12)	ET: 9:00 P.M.–12:00 A.M. (M–F)
	9:00 P.M.–11:00 A.M. (S)
	Local: 9:00 A.M.–12 Noon (M–F) 9:00 A.M.–11:00 A.M.(S)
Philippines (+12)	ET: 9:30 P.M.–12:10 A.M.
	Local: 9:30 A.M.–12:10 P.M.
Hong Kong (+12)	ET: 10:00 P.M.–12:30 A.M. //
	2:30 A.M.–3:55 A.M.
	Local: 10:00 A.M.–12:30 P.M. // 2:30 P.M.–3:55 P.M.
Thailand (+11)	ET: 11:00 P.M.–1:30 A.M. //
	3:30 A.M.–5:30 A.M.
	Local: 10:00 A.M.–12:30 P.M. // 2:30 P.M.–4:30 P.M.

* U.S. is on daylight savings time, but Japan is not.
// indicates an intra-day market close

EXHIBIT 12

Fund companies look for ways to discourage market timers

Some mutual fund companies are working harder to keep fast-moving, fickle investors out of their funds.

The companies are targeting "market timers," those investors who pour large amounts of "hot money" into a fund but can pull it out just as quickly, depending on market conditions.

Funds are cracking down on market timers as the popularity of fund supermarkets has allowed inexpensive or no-fee trades that are harder to track. Supermarkets put more funds at risk to the perils of momentum traders.

"There are fewer and fewer places market timers can go," said Patrick J. Carolan, senior account manager for GT Global, Inc. in San Francisco. "Companies are being a lot more careful."

Small fund companies view market timers as an industry scourge. While new investments help build assets, market-timer redemptions can quickly gobble up a fund's cash reserves, playing havoc with investment strategies. Funds less than $100 million in assets are particularly at risk.

Market timers don't affect bigger funds of $1 billion or more as much because such investments are only a small percentage of such a large fund.

To slow the pace of market timers, some companies have instituted delays, periods ranging between 90 days and one year, where investors are kept from making trades. Other deterrents include watching trading activity, preinvestment screening, and redemption fees. In some cases, trades have been killed and investors banned from funds.

"The gist of these actions is to slow down the velocity of trades," says Peter J. Moran, chief marketing officer at Turner Investment Partners, Inc. in Berwyn, Pa. "Market timers like mutual funds because there aren't many fees and it's convenient."

Source: Dow Jones News Service, June 27, 1997. © 1997, Dow Jones & Company, Inc.

Financial, Governance and Global Implications of Mutual Funds

IV

Part IV explores some of the broader implications of the fund industry in three chapters on the financial dynamics of mutual funds, their role in corporate governance, and their spread across the world.

Chapter Ten begins by analyzing the various types of expenses that mutual funds and their shareholders incur. It next reviews the numerous studies in the current debate on whether management fees paid by mutual funds are too high. It then explains the key factors driving the structure of the mutual fund industry over the past decade, including mergers and acquisitions. The Chapter ends with a case study of a merger between two fund complexes.

Chapter Eleven addresses the role of mutual funds as shareholders of public corporations. It outlines the legal framework for shareholders of such corporations, especially in proxy fights and takeover bids. It details the policies and practices of mutual funds in normal proxy solicitations, as well as situations involving institutional activism. The Chapter ends with a summary of shareholder rights in foreign countries and a case study of a proxy fight for a tobacco company.

Chapter Twelve discusses the internationalization of mutual funds. It reviews the special constraints and risk factors involved in international investing of mutual funds. It explains the main approaches taken by U.S. fund managers in overcoming the entry barriers to selling mutual funds in Europe, Asia and Latin America. The Chapter ends with a case study on the challenges confronting a U.S. fund manager trying to enter the defined contribution market in Canada.

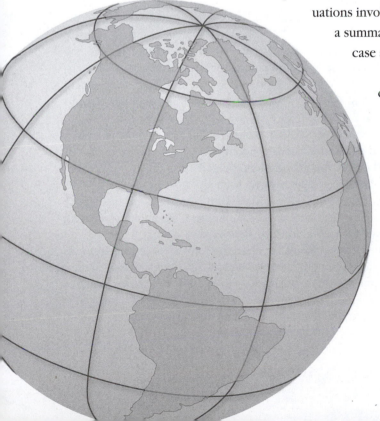

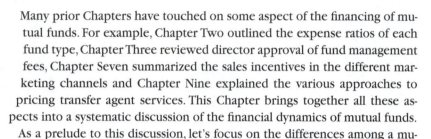

10 Financial Dynamics of Mutual Funds

Many prior Chapters have touched on some aspect of the financing of mutual funds. For example, Chapter Two outlined the expense ratios of each fund type, Chapter Three reviewed director approval of fund management fees, Chapter Seven summarized the sales incentives in the different marketing channels and Chapter Nine explained the various approaches to pricing transfer agent services. This Chapter brings together all these aspects into a systematic discussion of the financial dynamics of mutual funds.

As a prelude to this discussion, let's focus on the differences among a mutual fund, a fund management company and a fund distributor by looking again at Figure 10.1 (reproduced from Chapter One). As the diagram illustrates, a mutual fund is an unusual financial institution because both its management and distribution functions are housed in separate organizations; in other words, neither its managers nor its distributors are employees of the fund. A mutual fund is also unusual because it acts as a "pass-through" entity, distributing all gains, losses and income to the shareholders in the fund. Moreover, all operating expenses of the fund are taken out of fund assets and are effectively paid by the fund's shareholders. These operating expenses include paying the management company to invest the fund's assets, paying a transfer agent to keep shareholder records and paying other entities providing services to the fund such as the fund custodian and distributor.

The management company has its own income statement distinct from that of the fund. In exchange for investing the fund's assets, the management company receives revenues from the fund in the form of contractually agreed-on management fees. To perform this function, the management company employs portfolio managers, analysts, programmers, traders and support staff. The main expense items of the management company are for (in descending order) employee compensation, computer systems and space.

In many cases, the distribution company is an affiliate of the management company, although sometimes the fund distributor is independent of the management company. In exchange for selling fund shares, the distribution company may receive revenue in the form of sales charges (called sales loads) directly from investors or asset-based fees from the fund (called 12b-1 fees), or both. The distribution company's expenses arise mainly from marketing the fund to prospective shareholders, including advertising costs, production of sales material and commissions to the sales force.

This Chapter details the various types of expenses that investors in mutual funds pay, summarizes the studies on whether the management fees for fund advisers are too high, reviews the structural trends in the fund industry from 1990 to 2000 and analyzes the mergers and acquisitions of fund managers during this decade. The Chapter ends with a case study about the merger of two mutual fund complexes.

FIGURE 10.1

Structure of a mutual fund

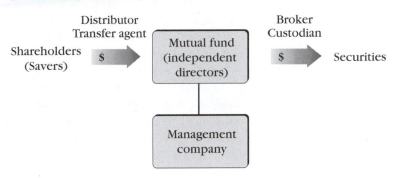

I. Expenses for Fund Investors

In reviewing the expenses of mutual fund investors, it is useful to distinguish between expenses paid directly by shareholders as individual investors and expenses paid by the fund itself (which are paid indirectly by all fund shareholders). In general, fees related to distribution and redemption are paid by shareholders at the time of a specific event, while fees related to management and service are paid by the fund on an annual basis. But this general rule has a few exceptions—most important, 12b-1 fees, which are continuing distribution charges borne by funds as a percentage of their assets.

Sales loads are the most significant fees charged to shareholders individually. Sales loads are paid to the fund distributor, usually affiliated with the fund management company, and mostly passed on to the broker who helped close the sale. The maximum sales load is 8½%, though as a practical matter, sales loads now average 4% or 5%. Historically, all sales loads were paid by shareholders when purchasing fund shares at the front end of their investment and therefore were called front-end loads.

Loaded funds have a net asset value (NAV) price and an "offering" price. The NAV is the underlying asset value of one share of the fund. The offering price is the price per share that includes the impact of the load. To illustrate, a fund with 4% load is listed in the newspaper at an NAV price of $96 and offering price of $100. For a $1,000 investment, an investor would purchase 10 shares ($1,000 purchase amount divided by the $100 offering price) with a value of $960 (10 shares multiplied by the $96 NAV) and would pay a $40 load. Most fund complexes give shareholders a credit for a front-end load paid to purchase shares of one fund if those shares are exchanged into shares of another front-end load fund in the same complex.

During the 1980s, fund complexes began to offer back-end loads, which the shareholder pays on redeeming fund shares. Most back-end loads decline the longer a shareholder stays in the fund. For instance, a shareholder might pay a 5% load after one year, a 4% load after two years, a 3% load after three years, a 2% load after four years, a 1% load after five years and no load thereafter. Such declining back-end loads are called CDSCs, which stands for contingent deferred sales charges. Back-end loads are charged on the lesser of either the initial investment or the value of the shares at the time of redemption.

In addition, most funds waive loads for various categories of investors. For instance, most funds waive loads for purchases of fund shares by retirement plans and trust accounts. Furthermore, load funds usually reduce their sales charges for purchases above certain dollar limits. For instance, a fund with a 4% load might reduce the load to 2% for purchases over $500,000 and reduce the load to 0% for purchases over $1 million.

In 1980, the Securities and Exchange Commission (SEC) allowed the fund (rather than each shareholder) to pay annual distribution charges called 12b-1 fees to the fund distributor. These 12b-1 fees are similar to periodic installment payments (accrued daily against fund assets), which can replace, in whole or in part, sales loads as a means of financing fund distribution. These 12b-1 fees usually range from 25 to 75 basis points (bp), plus an additional 25 bp "servicing" charge in some cases (25 bp = 0.25%). Thus, the maximum annual 12b-1 fee is actually 100 bp of fund assets. A 12b-1 plan (including service fees, if any) must be approved annually by the fund's independent directors, and the 12b-1 fees must appear in the fee table at the front of the fund's prospectus.

Although loads and 12b-1 fees are paid initially to the fund distributor, most of these loads and fees are passed through (or "reallowed") to the broker-dealers that actually distribute the fund's shares. For example, if the shares of a fund advised by a Boston fund manager are distributed by a Wall Street wire house, the fund's distributor owned by the Boston fund manager might reallow to the wire house 5% of the 6% load and 40 bp out of the 50 bp 12b-1 fee. The wire house in turn would pass on part of these loads and fees to the individual registered representative responsible for each investor account.

More recently, the fund industry has created funds with two or more classes of shares. Although all classes hold the same portfolio securities and have the same portfolio manager, each class has its own distribution and service arrangements, resulting in different class expenses. In a typical situation, Class A of the fund would have a high front-end sales load and a low 12b-1 fee. Class B would have no front-end load; instead, it would have a combination of a high 12b-1 fee and a back-end load in the form of a CDSC. In the Class B situation, the fund sponsor typically advances a large commission to the broker-dealer at the time fund shares are sold and then recoups that commission through the 12b-1 fees collected over several years. The CDSC is designed to protect that flow of 12b-1 fees to the fund sponsor in the case of a shareholder who leaves before paying sufficient 12b-1 fees to allow the fund sponsor to recoup its commission advance.

The Class B structure creates challenging financial issues for the fund sponsor. This structure carries inherent risk in that the fund's NAV could decline substantially, decreasing the amount of 12b-1 fees and CDSCs received by the sponsor, possibly below the amount it advanced to the broker-dealer. This is especially a risk for an equity fund sponsor, since equity assets are more volatile than other asset types. In recent years, many fund sponsors have sought relief from the risk that the CDSC arrangement entails by taking advantage of new methods of financial engineering developed by banks and investment banks. These methods enable fund sponsors to reduce or eliminate this risk by securitizing and selling the future cash flows from 12b-1 fees and CDSCs. For example, consider a fund sponsor that has just paid a broker a 4% commission for selling Class B shares of a growth fund. Rather than wait to recoup this commission via 12b-1 fees and/or CDSCs, the sponsor may sell the rights to these future cash flows to an unrelated party in exchange for a modestly lower payment today. This sale effectively protects the sponsor against the risk associated with a possible downturn in the equities market and consequential decline in cash flows from 12b-1 fees and CDSCs.

Beside Classes A and B, fund sponsors have developed classes with other pricing structures. Class C is sometimes described as a "level load" because it combines a high 12b-1 fee with a modest CDSC for one or two years. Class C typically imposes no front-end load, although the fund sponsor usually advances a small commission to the broker-dealer. A mutual fund could also offer a Class I, called the institutional class, with neither loads nor 12b-1 fees. This class is designed for institutions with very large accounts and financial planners who are collecting a separate fee from their customers. Set forth in Table 10.1 is a summary of the typical attributes of classes for an equity fund.

The 12b-1 fee (but not the sales load) is one of several components of a fund's expenses, often expressed in basis points as the fund's total expense ratio (the ratio of the fund's total expenses to its assets on an annualized basis). The most important component is the management fee paid by the fund to its investment manager. The management fee must be approved periodically by a majority of the fund's independent directors. Another fund expense is the transfer agent fee. This fee may be paid to a transfer agent affiliated with the fund manager or an external service provider. Other fund expenses include smaller amounts paid for fund audits, pricing and bookkeeping, custody charges, independent director fees, registration fees and sometimes proxy solicitations. By contrast, brokerage commissions are included as part of the capital costs of the fund's portfolio securities rather than as part of the fund's total expense ratio.

Some mutual funds, especially bond and money market funds, have "all-inclusive fees." In this arrangement, the management company charges a single fee of a specified amount (e.g., 50 bp) and assumes responsibilities for all fund expenses including transfer agency and other annual expenses as well as management costs. All-inclusive fees effectively shift the risks and rewards of controlling the fund's total expenses from the shareholders to the fund management company. Of the 100 largest mutual funds in

TABLE 10.1

Share classes for an equity fund

Share Class	12b-1 Fees	Front-End Sales Load	CDSC
Class A shares	0.25%	5.75%	None
Class B shares	1.0%	None	5% in the first year, declining 1% per year thereafter
Class C shares	1.0%	None	1% per year for initial two years
Class I shares	None	None	None

1997–1999, 19 had a single all-inclusive fee, according to the SEC. Alternatively, management companies may choose to impose voluntary caps on fund expenses. This has much the same effect as an all-inclusive fee, but with the difference that a voluntary expense cap, unlike a management fee, may be changed without shareholder approval. According to Lipper, 40% of stock funds and 52% of bond funds had some sort of voluntary expense cap in effect during the third quarter of 2000.

Fund sponsors impose other types of fees on shareholders, rather than on the fund, to modify their behavior and/or make them absorb certain fund expenses. Funds sometimes impose redemption fees on shareholders who leave the fund after a short period of time (e.g., 90 days or six months). (See the case study in Chapter Nine.) Such redemption fees go back to the fund (not to the distributor) to cover the transaction costs imposed on remaining shareholders by departing sellers. Fund managers increasingly use short-term redemption fees on shares held less than 90 or 180 days in an effort to reduce the amount of "hot" (frequently traded) money flowing in and out of a fund. Frequent trading in and out of a fund increases its transaction costs, which ultimately decrease total returns of the fund. Fund managers have found that implementing redemption fees has been an effective tool in curbing frequent trading. Similarly, some index funds impose fees on new purchasers to defray the fund's costs in acquiring more shares of companies in the index.

In addition, some fund sponsors charge fees for specified types of transactions, such as wire redemptions or fund exchanges, or for specific types of accounts. Most fund sponsors charge shareholders a fee for serving as the custodian for an individual retirement account or other retirement account, although such custodial fees may be waived for large accounts. Small account fees are another charge that shareholders may incur as individual investors. These fees, designed to offset in part the relatively higher costs of servicing smaller accounts, are payable by shareholders to the transfer agent. For example, a fund may deduct an annual maintenance fee of $12 from accounts with a value of less than $2,500 as of the last Friday in October. Some funds may waive this fee if the shareholder has aggregate assets in the complex above a certain amount (e.g., $50,000). To discourage the attraction of very small accounts, most funds have a minimum initial investment requirement. Further, most funds reserve the right to close any account that falls below the minimum balance and send the proceeds back to the investor if he or she fails to reestablish the minimum balance within a specified time period, such as 30 days after notification.

Any type of fund expense imposes a drag on fund returns actually received by fund shareholders. Given the mathematical realities of compounding over time, the difference between seemingly small variations in fund expenses can make quite large differences in returns over the long term, as illustrated by Figure 10.2.

Figure 10.2 illustrates the power of compounding annual expenses over the long term for three equity mutual funds, each with an assumed 11.5% annual return before expenses. Suppose $100,000 is invested with these three identically positioned equity funds: one with annual expenses of 0.50% (11.00% return net of fees), a second with annual expenses of 1.00% (10.50% return net of fees) and a third with annual expenses of 1.50% (10.00% return net of fees). The $100,000 invested in the fund with an expense ratio of 0.50% would be worth $806,231 after year 20. The $100,000 invested in the fund with an expense ratio of 1.00% would be worth $736,623 after year 20. The

FIGURE 10.2

Impact of fund expenses on investment returns over time

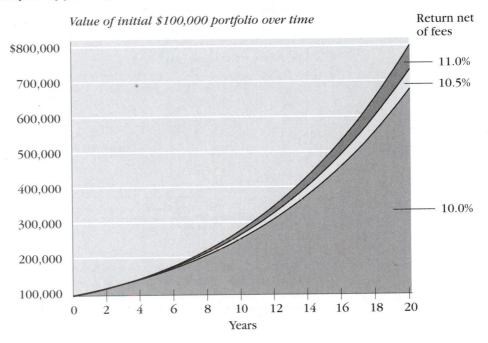

$100,000 invested in the fund with an expense ratio of 1.50% would be worth $672,750 after year 20. Thus, there would be a difference between the highest and lowest net return of $133,481, all due to fund expenses.

Since fund expenses are ultimately borne by fund investors, the SEC takes particular interest in the manner in which these expenses are disclosed. The SEC requires that all transaction and operating expenses charged by a fund be presented near the front of the prospectus in a relatively standardized format. This fee information is divided into three sections: shareholder transaction expenses (including sales loads and redemption fees), fund operating expenses (including management, transfer agency and 12b-1 fees) and a standard hypothetical illustrating the dollar amounts of fund expenses paid on a $10,000 investment in the fund over 1, 3, 5 and 10 years. Figures 10.3 and 10.4 are two examples taken from the T. Rowe Price Growth Stock Fund Prospectus (a no-load fund) and the Putnam Voyager Fund Prospectus (a loaded fund).

FIGURE 10.3

T. Rowe Price Growth Stock Fund: May 1, 2001, prospectus expense information

---

What fees or expenses will I pay?

The fund is 100% no load. There are no fees or charges to buy or sell fund shares, reinvest dividends, or exchange into other T. Rowe Price funds. There are no 12b-1 fees.

Table 2 *Fees and Expenses of the Fund**

	Annual fund operating expenses (expenses that are deducted from fund assets)
Management fee	0.57%
Other expenses	0.16%
Total annual fund operating expenses	0.73%

*   Redemption proceeds of less than $5,000 sent by wire are subject to a $5 fee paid to the fund. Accounts with less than a $2,000 balance (with certain exceptions) are subject to a $10 fee. See Transaction Procedures and Special Requirements - Account Maintenance and Small Account Fees.

Example. The following table gives you a rough idea of how expense ratios may translate into dollars and helps you to compare the cost of investing in this fund with that of other mutual funds. Although your actual costs may be higher or lower, the table shows how much you would pay if operating expenses remain the same, you invest $10,000, earn a 5% annual return, and hold the investment for the following periods and then redeem:

1 year	3 years	5 years	10 years
$75	$233	$406	$906

© T. Rowe Price Associates, Inc. Reprinted with the permission of T. Rowe Price.

FIGURE 10.4

Putnam Voyager Fund: November 30, 2000, prospectus expense information

FEES AND EXPENSES

This table summarizes the fees and expenses you may pay if you invest in the fund. Expenses are based on the fund's last fiscal year.

Shareholder Fees (fees paid directly from your investment)

	Class A	Class B	Class C	Class M
Maximum Sales Charge (Load) Imposed on Purchases (as a percentage of the offering price)	5.75%	NONE	NONE	3.50%
Maximum Deferred Sales Charge (Load) (as a percentage of the original purchase price or redemption proceeds, whichever is lower)	NONE*	5.00%	1.00%	NONE

Annual Fund Operating Expenses

(expenses that are deducted from fund assets)

	Management Fees	Distribution (12b-1) Fees	Other Expenses	Total Annual Fund Operating Expenses
Class A	0.45%	0.25%	0.16%	0.86%
Class B	0.45%	1.00%	0.16%	1.61%
Class C	0.45%	1.00%	0.16%	1.61%
Class M	0.45%	0.75%	0.16%	1.36%

*A deferred sales charge of up to 1% may be imposed on certain redemptions of class A shares bought without an initial sales charge.

EXAMPLE

The example translates the expenses shown in the preceding table into dollar amounts. By doing this, you can more easily compare the cost of investing in the fund to the cost of investing in other mutual funds. The example makes certain assumptions. It assumes that you invest $10,000 in the fund for the time periods shown and then, except as shown for class B and class C shares, redeem all your shares at the end of those periods. It also assumes a 5% return on your investment each year and that the fund's operating expenses remain the same. The example is hypothetical; your actual costs and returns may be higher or lower.

	1 year	3 years	5 years	10 years
Class A	$658	$834	$1,024	$1,575
Class B	$664	$808	$1,076	$1,710*
Class B (no redemption)	$164	$508	$876	$1,710*
Class C	$264	$508	$876	$1,911
Class C (no redemption)	$164	$508	$876	$1,911
Class M	$484	$766	$1,069	$1,928

*Reflects the conversion of class B shares to class A shares, which pay lower 12b-1 fees. Conversion occurs no more than eight years after purchase.

As revised May 14, 2001. © Putnam Investments. Reprinted with the permission of Putnam Investments.

II. The Debate on Management Fee Revenue

The management fee is the main source of revenues for investment advisers to mutual funds. Management fees, on average, are highest for stock funds and lowest for money market funds, with bond funds in the middle. According to Lipper, as of late 2000, the 25th to 75th percentile of management fees for equity funds ranged from 63 to 100 bp, respectively, with the median at 81 basis points. At the same date, the 25th to 75th percentile of management fees for bond funds ranged from 50 to 68 bp, respectively, with the median at 56 bp; and the 25th to 75th percentile of management fees for money market funds ranged from 32 to 50 bp, respectively, with the median at 45 bp.

In some fund complexes, management fees decline in terms of basis points as a fund's assets increase beyond a specified level (called "breakpoints"). For instance, an equity fund might have a management fee of 70 bp for the first $500 million of fund assets and 65 bp for fund assets above that threshold. Such breakpoints may represent an agreement between the independent directors and management company that there are potential economies of scale in managing a large fund as opposed to a small fund. In other complexes, breakpoints are based on the total assets in the complex or in a group of funds in the complex (e.g., all equity funds). Such breakpoints are predicated on the assumption that potential economies of scale derive from having common research or other services supporting all funds in the complex or all funds in the group. After reviewing the 100 largest funds for 1997–1999, the SEC found that 55 had breakpoints based on the fund's assets and 21 had breakpoints based on the fund complex's assets.

A relatively small number of mutual funds have management fees composed of a base rate plus or minus a performance fee. (See "Performance Fees as a Rarity.") Of the funds that do have a performance fee, most are equity funds. Performance fees serve to align the interest of fund shareholders with the interest of fund managers by increasing or decreasing the management fee on the basis of the fund's performance relative to a benchmark. Under SEC rules, a performance fee for a mutual fund must be linked to a published benchmark such as the S&P 500. A performance fee also must be symmetrical; it must go down and up by the same formula relative to the benchmark. For instance, a U.S. stock fund might have a base fee of 65 bp, with a performance fee of plus or minus up to 20 bp depending on the fund's performance relative to the performance of the S&P 500 index. By contrast, the typical management fee of "private" investment companies, usually called "hedge funds," is 1% of assets plus a performance fee. Moreover, the performance fee is typically 20% of net realized gains, without any penalty for net realized losses.

The operating expenses (excluding sales loads) of mutual funds have on average risen over the past decade, despite the rapid growth in fund assets. To fund critics, this growth of assets should have resulted in lower fund operating expenses based on economies of scale. On the other hand, a significant component of the operating expenses is now the 12b-1 fee, which is an alternative charge for distribution to sales loads. Since sales loads have declined from a maximum of 8½% to an average of 4% to 5%, this decline should be considered an offset against the increase in the operating expenses attributable to 12b-1 fees.

CALLOUT
Performance Fees as a Rarity

Fewer than 150 of the 8,000 mutual funds in existence at the end of 2000 had performance fees. Over half of these funds with performance fees were in three complexes: American Express (IDS), Fidelity and Vanguard. Performance fees were employed mainly in domestic growth funds, although a few international as well as growth and income funds had them. Performance fees usually are measured relative to an equity index—most frequently the S&P 500, though the American Express funds (IDS) measure their performance relative to Lipper peer groups. Most performance fees are measured over a period of trailing 12 months, with trailing 36 months as the second most common period for measurement. The differential required to reach the maximum or minimum performance fee is typically 10% above or below benchmark, although the total range is 2% to 15%.

If performance fees better align the interests of the fund's manager and the fund's shareholders, why are such fees used so rarely? An advocate of performance fees might argue that fund managers do not want their management revenues to be subject to the risk of underperforming a benchmark. But critics of performance fees argue that management fees are inherently dependent on performance since it tends to drive fund sales and fund asset levels. Three other points are worthy of consideration:

1. Performance fees can encourage inappropriate coasting or risk taking by fund managers, especially above the maximum or below the minimum. A fund manager above the top of a performance range may have an incentive to coast in order to protect the existing track record. Conversely, a fund manager deep in negative performance territory has no performance fee to lose by taking a huge speculative bet.

2. SEC rules on performance fees for any mutual fund are so rigid they tend to discourage their use. To earn a performance fee, a fund must not only beat an index but also must beat the index by an amount greater than all fund expenses including 12b-1 fees (but not loads). While other types of investment pools like hedge funds typically have much higher incentives for outperformance than penalties for underperformance, SEC rules require strictly symmetrical performance fees for mutual funds.

3. Press reports and fund measurement services generally do not separate out performance fees from total fund expenses. Accordingly, fee-sensitive investors may avoid funds with higher fees even if they result from good performance. On the other hand, less fee-sensitive investors may not give much weight to whether a fund adopts a performance fee.

Moreover, fund supporters note that fund operating expenses have financed a substantial expansion of shareholder services. For example, fund sponsors have invested heavily in technology to deliver web pages, combined statements and financial planning tools. In other words, any change in fund operating expenses should be evaluated relative to the significant increase in service benefits to fund shareholders over the past decade.

In general, the outcome of the fee debate depends heavily on the standard against which fund fees are judged. Fund operating expenses in Canada, Europe and the Far East are considerably higher than in the United States. But fund operating expenses are higher than the fees charged by U.S. money managers to defined benefit pension plans. More broadly, the profit margins of U.S. fund sponsors are higher than those in many industrial sectors, though roughly comparable to the profit margins in many high-technology and personal service companies.

A study of mutual fund fees by the Investment Company Institute (ICI), an industry trade group, found that the total cost of equity mutual fund ownership (including sales loads and 12b-1 fees) dropped by one-third from 1980 to 1997.[1] During this period, the average cost of each dollar invested in equity funds decreased to 1.49% from 2.25%, as shown in Figure 10.5.[2]

According to the ICI study, the main contributing factors to the lower total shareholder cost of equity fund ownership were competition in the marketplace, decreased costs of distribution and economies of scale passed along to shareholders. Regarding the competition factor, the ICI noted that investors in 1997 could choose among over 6,000 mutual funds (8,000 funds by 2000). During the 1980–1997 period, mutual funds exhibited a wide range of expense ratios, and investors tended to concentrate their purchases among lower-cost equity funds. As the ICI explained, a majority of fund investors now hold shares in relatively low-cost mutual funds.

The ICI measured distribution costs as the sum of 12b-1 fees and sales loads amortized over a period of years. Between 1980 and 1997, the distribution cost ratio for all funds declined from 1.49% to 0.61% of each dollar invested. Some of this decline reflected the shift by investors from load to no-load funds; in addition, the distribution costs of load funds fell significantly from 2.28% to 1.23% during this period.

To examine whether economies of scale were passed on to shareholders, the ICI focused on the 100 largest funds in 1997 that also were in existence in 1980. Assets of these funds grew rapidly over this period, with average assets per fund rising from $282 million to $5.8 billion. Over the same time period, the simple average expense ratios of these 100 funds declined 14.6 percent, from 82 bp to 70 bp. Moreover, the funds with the largest increases in assets generally posted the largest decreases in operating expense ratios.

Soon after the publication of the ICI paper, Morningstar, a leading third-party provider of mutual fund information, offered a critique of the ICI's conclusions. In Morningstar's view, the decrease in fund fees was explained primarily by the changes in the industry over the past two decades. For example, direct-marketed no-load funds are much more popular today than in 1980; as a result, the total fund universe is compara-

FIGURE 10.5

Total shareholder costs for equity funds

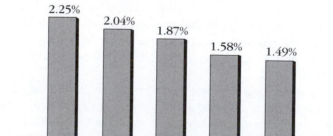

Source: Investment Company Institute, "Trends in the Ownership Cost of Equity Mutual Funds" (1998). Reprinted by permission of the Investment Company Institute.

tively less expensive. In addition, the types of mutual funds have changed since 1980, when almost every equity fund was actively managed and targeted to retail consumers. Today, 15% of equity fund assets are held by index and institutional funds, which charge lower management fees than actively managed retail funds. Finally, Morningstar noted that the ICI's decision to asset-weight its findings skewed its conclusions. The funds from three industry giants—Fidelity Investments, American Funds (Capital Research) and Vanguard—make up 35% of U.S. equity fund assets. Morningstar demonstrated (as seen in Figure 10.6) that if these fund complexes were excluded, the expense reductions in the ICI study would nearly disappear.[3]

In an attempt to resolve these differences of opinion in the private sector, the U.S. General Accounting Office (GAO) addressed the mutual fund fee debate in a study entitled "Mutual Fund Fees: Additional Disclosure Could Encourage Price Competition" (June 2000). The study analyzed a variety of topics related to fund fees such as competition in the mutual fund industry, expense trends in the industry and disclosure practices. Regarding competition in the mutual fund industry, the GAO study noted that industry was highly fragmented and that fund sponsors compete mainly on performance rather than on price.

To spot trends in fund expenses, the GAO conducted its own analysis using data on the 46 largest stock funds and the 31 largest bond funds in existence from 1990 to 1998. The GAO found that the average expense ratio as a percentage of assets for the 46 largest stock funds declined from 0.89% in 1990 to 0.71% in 1998, a decline of 20%.

FIGURE 10.6

Annual fund ownership costs, 1994 versus 1998

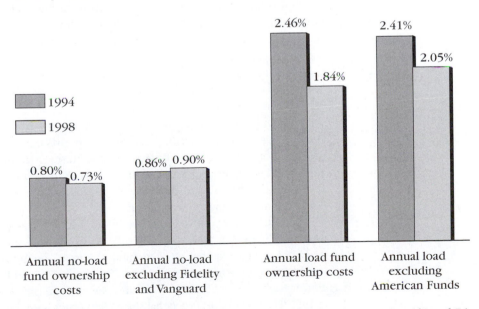

Source: Cooley, "Revisiting Fund Costs: Up or Down?" Morningstar Mutual Funds, Summary Section, Volume 34, Issue 6 (February 21, 1999).

Over the same time period, the expense ratios for the 31 largest bond funds fell from 0.66% to 0.64%, a decline of 3%. But the study found that expense ratios for both the 46 stock and 31 bond funds actually increased from 1990 to 1994, declining only after 1994.

The GAO study found a close correlation between asset growth in the 46 large equity funds and the likelihood of lower expenses in these funds. Specifically, the study found that the more that assets in these 46 large equity funds increased since 1990, the more likely they were to have a lower expense ratio in 1998. However, although the 46 largest equity funds grew more than 500% over the period of the study, a quarter of these funds did not decrease their expense ratios by at least 10%, and two funds even had a higher expense ratio. The GAO found a similar link between asset growth and expense reductions in fixed income funds.

The GAO report concluded by recommending that every investor in a fund receive information on his or her account statement disclosing the exact dollar amount of fees he or she paid. The report stated that many of those interviewed for the study felt that the standard fee table already presented at the front of every fund prospectus provided adequate disclosure of fees. However, the GAO maintained that it would be better for every mutual fund to itemize the actual dollar amount of fees that a shareholder paid over his or her actual holding period. As an alternative approach, the GAO suggested that every fund provide information about the actual dollar amount of fees that were paid during the period for preset investment amounts.

Defenders of current industry practice point to the fact that fund prospectuses already present absolute dollars of fund expenses based on a hypothetical $10,000 investment in the fund. Defenders also express concerns that customized individual disclosure would be costly to implement. Since the hypothetical $10,000 example is based on a full calendar year with no additional investment, it is quite simple to calculate. But a particular shareholder might invest various dollar amounts for various time periods in a given year. Providing a dollar- and time-weighted fee calculation for every shareholder account would entail substantial expenditures on additional computer and accounting systems.

In January 2001, the SEC's Division of Investment Management issued its "Report on Mutual Fund Fees and Expenses" ("SEC Report"). This SEC Report expressed concerns, especially on compliance costs, with the GAO's recommendation to provide every fund shareholder with disclosure of the exact dollar amount of fees paid during his or her actual holding period. Instead, the SEC Report supports the GAO's alternative approach of providing the dollar amount of fees paid for preset investment amounts in the fund's annual and semiannual reports "so that investors can evaluate the information alongside other key information about the fund's operating results, including management's discussion of the fund's performance."

The SEC Report based its conclusions on a staff analysis of expenses for all stock and bond funds for the following years: 1979, 1992, 1995 and 1999. It found that the weighted average expense ratios for funds declined from 99 bp in 1995 to 94 bp in 1999 but that these expenses increased from 73 bp in 1979 to 94 bp in 1999. The SEC Report explained that this difference in trends resulted from the SEC's adoption of Rule 12b-1 in 1980. The SEC Report noted that since 1980, funds with traditional front-end sales load had become less popular, as funds with 12b-1 fees and CDSCs became more popular. To

take into account this shift in popularity, the SEC Report also analyzed the total ownership costs of investing in funds, including loads and 12b-1 fees. The SEC Report found
that total ownership costs for loaded funds declined 18% between 1979 and 1999.

The SEC found that several factors were important in explaining variations among
funds with respect to operating expense ratios (the fund's total expenses minus 12b-1
fees divided by its average net assets). One factor was fund size: In 1999, a fund with assets of $1 billion had an operating expense ratio that was on average 66 bp lower than
a similar fund with assets of $1 million. A second factor was fund family size: In 1999, a
fund in a family with assets of $1 billion had an operating expense ratio that was on av-
erage 75 bp lower than a fund in a family with assets of $1 million. A third factor was
type of fund: Equity funds were more expensive than bond funds, while international
and specialty funds were more expensive than diversified domestic equity funds. On
the other hand, index funds and funds sold only to institutions had lower expense ratios than otherwise equivalent funds.

To explore the issue of economies of scale further, the SEC Report examined the
1,000 largest funds in 1999 with respect to their management expense ratios (fees paid
for investment advice and other services under a fund's management contract divided
by its average net assets). The SEC Report did not find any statistically significant relationship between the asset size of a fund and its management expense ratio. Rather, it
found a statistically significant relationship between the assets in a fund family and the
management expense ratio of that family's funds.

The SEC Report recommended that Rule 12b-1 be modified to accommodate
changes that have occurred since its adoption in 1980—for example, the creation of
multiclass funds and the advent of fund supermarkets. (See Chapter Seven.) It noted the
important role of independent directors in monitoring expenses of funds—a role that
would be enhanced by the SEC's recent initiatives to bolster the effectiveness of independent directors. (See Chapter Three.) The SEC Report also urged the fund industry to
expand its efforts to educate investors about identifying and comparing fund expenses.

III. *Structure of Fund Industry*

The fee debate is driven by the tremendous growth and change in the mutual fund industry over the past decade. Critics of current fee levels generally believe that this
growth should lead to economies of scale, which mutual fund complexes should pass
through to investors in the form of lower fees. Supporters of current fee levels tend to
emphasize the significant changes in fund and firm structure, which complicate any potential connection between growth in fund assets and economies of scale. Although it
may be impossible to draw exact conclusions about how such structural changes have
affected fee levels, it is nevertheless important to understand how the industry—both
funds and fund sponsors—differs today from what it was a decade ago.

As discussed below, changes in the composition of mutual funds during the 1990s
included the incredible growth of assets, the shifting popularity of asset classes, the introduction of numerous new funds and the evolving channels for fund distribution. At
the same time, the concentration of assets among fund sponsors remained relatively stable despite a decade of high levels of acquisition activity and the emergence of many
small competitors.

A. *Composition of Mutual Funds*

1. Asset growth   In 1990, the mutual fund industry was a relatively small industry among financial intermediaries, with just over $1 trillion in assets, or 12% of the total sector (see Table 10.2). By contrast, depository institutions had almost five times the assets, or 56% of the sector (of which commercial banks accounted for $3.3 trillion or 38%, and assets of life insurance companies equaled $1.4 trillion or 16%).

By the end of the 1990s, the mutual fund industry had become a major player among financial intermediaries, with almost $7 trillion in assets and 39% of the overall sector. Although mutual fund assets slightly lagged those of all depository institutions taken as a whole—at $7.6 trillion, or 43% overall—they exceeded commercial bank and life insurance assets of nearly $6 trillion, or 34%, and $3.1 trillion, or 18%, respectively. Thus, mutual funds, which grew at a compound annual rate of 23% from 1990 to 1999, were the fastest-growing segment of financial intermediaries, which in total grew at a compound annual rate of 8.1% over the same period.

What caused the tremendous growth in mutual fund assets during the 1990s? As discussed in prior Chapters, several factors played a role, including a prolonged bull market in U.S. stocks, an increase in the popularity of defined contribution retirement plans, the creation of attractive new fund products and the introduction of enhanced

TABLE 10.2

Assets of major institutions and financial intermediaries ($ millions)

	1990 (revised)	% of Total	1999	% of Total	% Change	Compound Annual Growth Rate
Depository institutions	$4,912,370	56.0	$7,560,620	42.8	53.9	4.9
Commercial banks[a]	3,337,480	38.1	5,994,080	33.9	79.6	6.7
Credit unions[b]	217,240	2.5	415,130	2.3	91.1	7.5
Savings institutions[c]	1,357,650	15.5	1,151,410	6.5	–15.2	–1.8
Life insurance	$1,367,370	15.6	$3,104,510	17.6	127.0	9.5
Investment institutions	$2,488,112	28.4	$7,004,779	39.6	181.5	12.2
Bank-administered trusts[d]	1,368,666	15.6	N.A.	N.A.	N.A.	N.A.
Closed-end investment companies	52,554	0.6	158,225	0.9	201.1	13.0
Mutual funds[e]	1,066,892	12.2	6,846,339	38.7	541.7	22.9
Total	$8,767,852	100.0	$17,669,909	100.0	101.5	8.1

[a]Includes U.S.-chartered commercial banks, foreign banking offices in the United States, bank holding companies and banks in affiliated areas.
[b]Includes only federal or federally insured state credit unions serving natural persons.
[c]Includes mutual savings banks, federal savings banks and savings and loan associations.
[d]Reflects only discretionary trusts and agencies.
[e]Includes short-term funds; excludes funds of funds.
Source: Federal Reserve Board, Federal Financial Institutions Examination Council, Investment Company Institute.

services to shareholders. Other factors contributing to asset growth include the broad variety of new products, distribution channels and pricing structures developed by the fund industry.

2. Asset composition   At the end of 1990, 47% of mutual fund assets were money market funds, and less than 23% were equity funds. By the end of the decade, equity funds represented almost 57% of assets, and money market funds dropped to a 27% share (see Figure 10.7). As noted above, money market funds charge a lower management fee on average than bond funds, which in turn charge a lower management fee on average than equity funds. Therefore, this dramatic shift from money market funds to equity funds should have significantly raised management fees on average for the industry, all other things being equal.

In addition, the composition of equity funds changed during the 1990–2000 period. According to Strategic Insight, broader investment objectives such as growth and growth & income experienced a decrease of 7.7 percentage points in share of equity funds during the decade. The decrease was offset by an increase in more specialized funds, with higher management fees, such as sector funds and international funds. In particular, emerging market and country funds went from a half-percent share of funds available in 1990 to almost 3% in 2000. At the same time, there was a substantial increase in lower management fee products such as index funds, which were almost nonexistent in 1989.

3. Number of funds   During the 1990s, fund choices grew alongside assets at a rapid pace as the number of mutual funds increased from around 3,000 to over 8,000 (see Figure 10.8).

Implications of this tremendous increase in the number of funds for management fees depend on the resulting trends in average and median fund size, as shown in Table 10.3 (which defines a fund to include each class of a multi-class fund). Table 10.3 shows that average fund size grew during the 1990s—for all funds from $330 million to $432

FIGURE 10.7

Mutual fund industry: Assets of funds by asset class, 1990 versus 2000 (billions of dollars)

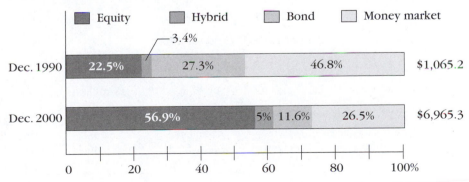

Source: Investment Company Institute. Reprinted by permission of the Investment Company Institute.

FIGURE 10.8

Mutual fund industry: Number of funds by asset class, 1990 versus 2000

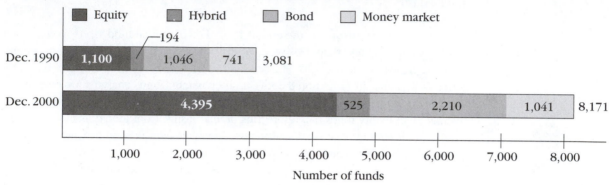

Source: Investment Company Institute. Reprinted by permission of the Investment Company Institute.

million and for equity funds from $205 million to $422 million. However, the median fund size dropped dramatically: for all funds, from $72 million to $43 million, and for equity funds from $46 to $37 million. These statistics show that the overwhelming majority of mutual funds in the industry were quite small, which tends to result in higher fund expenses. The SEC Report on mutual fund fees, discussed above, shows that as fund assets grow from $1 million to $1 billion, their operating expense ratio declines by 66 bp on average.

4. Distribution channels   Another factor that affects overall fee levels involves the distribution channels through which funds are sold. Load charges and fee structures differ by distribution channel, so any shift in the composition of assets by channel could have a significant impact on fund expenses. Table 10.4 shows the best available data on the composition of industry assets by distribution channel for 1990 versus 2000.

Table 10.4 shows a shift in fund assets away from the broker-dealer proprietary channel mainly to the direct and bank channels (and to a slight degree the institutional

TABLE 10.3

Size of funds*, 1990 vs. 2000

Date	Type of Funds	Median Fund Size ($ millions)	Average Fund Size ($ millions)	Maximum Fund Size ($ millions)
12/31/90	All funds	72	330	28,051
12/31/00	All funds	43	432	93,067
12/31/90	Equity funds	46	205	12,326
12/31/00	Equity funds	37	422	93,067

Source: Strategic Insight Simfund.
*Fund includes each class of a multi-class fund.

TABLE 10.4

Industry assets by distribution channel, 1990 versus 2000

	12/31/90	12/31/00
Direct marketer	25.0%	31.5%
Broker-dealer: Proprietary	25.0	13.3
Nonproprietary load	28.5	27.6
Bank proprietary	5.7	10.7
Institutional	14.3	15.7
Other smaller groups[a]	1.5	1.2
	100.0%	100.0%

[a]Includes insurance company, affinity group and exchange fund channels.
Source: Strategic Insight Simfund.

channel). Funds in the broker-dealer proprietary channel usually carry sales loads or 12b-1 fees, or both. Therefore, a relative decrease in assets in that channel should mean a decrease in the overall shareholder costs of mutual funds. Similarly, a relative increase in fund assets in the direct channel, which typically have no sales loads or 12b-1 fees, should mean a decrease in overall shareholder costs of mutual funds. However, according to ICI statistics, net sales of stock and bond funds (as distinguished from assets in money market funds) in the direct channel relative to sales of stock and bond funds in all channels dropped from 23% in 1990 to 18% in 1999.

It appears that much of the relative increase of fund assets in the direct channel was derived from retirement assets. Although Table 10.4 does not treat retirement as a distinct distribution channel, most of the largest providers of 401(k) services are direct marketers such as Fidelity, T. Rowe Price and Vanguard. (See Chapter Eight on retirement.) According to the ICI, in 1990 less than 20% of all mutual fund assets were held in retirement accounts; this figure grew to 36% by the end of 1999. Almost all funds sold to retirement plans in the direct channel charge neither sales loads nor 12b-1 fees; even funds with sales loads typically waive them for sales to retirement plans. Although most fund sponsors charge shareholders a fee for serving as custodian for retirement accounts, such fees are typically paid by shareholders individually and therefore do not affect fund expense ratios.

Table 10.4 also does not break out fund supermarkets as a source of fund assets by distribution channel. As with retirement assets, fund supermarket assets are embedded in the distribution channel data in Table 10.4, since mutual funds complexes may offer the same fund through other channels such as direct or proprietary as well as through supermarkets. (See Chapter Seven.) Fund assets derived from fund supermarkets went from almost nonexistent in 1990 to 7.4% of all long-term mutual fund assets (i.e., stock and bond funds) by the end of 1999, according to Sanford Bernstein Research. While funds sold through supermarkets do not usually carry a sales load to the shareholder, the distribution and servicing fees paid to the operator of the supermarket often come from the 12b-1 fees and/or transfer agency fees charged to the participating mutual funds. Indeed, some funds have created a separate class with higher 12b-1 fees and/or transfer agency fees to be sold mainly through fund supermarkets. Accordingly, the rise of fund supermarkets has tended to increase overall shareholder costs for the fund industry.

Finally, the relative increase in fund assets in the bank proprietary channel has tended to increase overall shareholder costs for mutual funds, since most funds in this channel charge sales loads or 12b-1 fees, or both. But this tendency is somewhat muted because the bank proprietary channel is heavily weighted toward money market funds, which have lower expense ratios than stock or bond funds.

B.   Profile of Fund Managers

Despite the huge growth of mutual funds, the marked shift in fund types and the creation of new distribution channels, the concentration of market share within the fund management industry remained remarkably stable during the 1990s. The industry has continued to be led by 10 fund managers with 45% to 55% of all mutual fund assets under management and 25 managers with 70% to 75% of all mutual fund assets under management. But many of the leaders changed places over the decade—some because of strong performances and others due to mergers and acquisitions. At the same time, the number of fund complexes overall has continued to increase as new fund managers have taken advantage of the mutual fund industry's low barriers to entry.

1. Overall industry concentration and turnover   In 1990, there were 464 mutual fund complexes, of which the top 10 managed 56% of total industry assets and the top 25 managed 76% of total assets. By the end of 2000, the mutual fund industry was modestly less concentrated at the top. There were 654 complexes at that date,[4] with the top 10 accounting for 46% of total assets and the top 25 accounting for 71% of total assets. The list of top 25 fund complexes has changed significantly, with some complexes dropping out and others stepping in, as shown in Table 10.5.

As Table 10.5 shows, many of the top complexes of 1990 were still in the top 10 in 2000, including well-known names like Fidelity, Merrill Lynch and Vanguard. But there was turnover within the ranks; several top players disappeared or changed places as a result of merger activity, while some new names like Janus rose from relatively unknown status into the top 10.

These changes at the top of the fund manager industry were the result of multiple factors. First, as explained earlier in this Chapter, there was a marked shift from bond and money market funds to equity funds during the 1990s. Accordingly, fund managers with a higher-than-average share of their assets in equity funds tended to grow more quickly than fund managers more oriented toward money market and bond funds. For instance, this factor appears to have helped American Funds with its strong equity line, while hurting Dreyfus with its concentration in money markets. Second, relative outperformance in equity funds, especially in growth funds during the late 1990s, was an important factor in change of rankings. For example, the high-performing Janus growth funds spurred its rise in the rankings, as the relative under-performance of Merrill Lynch's value-oriented funds hurt its ranking. A third factor was the ability of fund managers to expand through internal growth, especially through expansion in the rapidly growing field of 401(k) plans. This type of internal expansion, with particular emphasis on the 401(k) field, characterized the growth of both Vanguard and Putnam. A fourth

TABLE 10.5

25 Largest mutual fund complexes by assets under management

1990 Rank	Fund Group	Assets ($ billions)	Asset Share	2000 Rank	Fund Group	Assets ($ billions)	Asset Share	1990 Rank[a]
1	Fidelity Investments	108.3	10.2%	1	Fidelity Investments	822.9	11.8	1
2	Merrill Lynch	90.5	8.5	2	Vanguard Group	563.8	8.1	5
3	Shearson/IDS	75.2	7.0	3	Capital Research (American Funds)	359.8	5.2	10
4	Dreyfus Corp.	57.4	5.4	4	Putnam Funds	264.7	3.8	12
5	Vanguard Group	56.6	5.3	5	MSDW/Van Kampen	226.8	3.3	8, 35
6	Franklin	44.8	4.2	6	Janus/Berger	206.3	3.0	74
7	Federated	44.0	4.1	7	AMVESCAP PLC (AIM/INVESCO)	205.5	3.0	18, 62
8	Dean Witter	40.2	3.8	8	Merrill Lynch	184.9	2.7	2
9	Kemper	37.1	3.5	9	Franklin Templeton	172.9	2.5	6, 23
10	Capital Research (American Funds)	34.0	3.2	10	Salomon Smith Barney/Citi/Shearson	169.6	2.4	3[b], 26
Subtotal, Top 10:		**588.1**	**55.1%**			**3,177.3**	**45.6%**	
11	Prudential Mutual Funds	33.1	3.1	11	TIAA-CREF	165.5	2.4	—
12	Putnam Funds	26.4	2.5	12	Federated Investors/ Kaufman	160.3	2.3	7
13	PaineWebber	17.9	1.7	13	SchwabFunds/US Trust	137.4	2.0	29, 71
14	MFS	17.4	1.6	14	Dreyfus Corp.	129.4	1.9	4
15	T. Rowe Price	17.4	1.6	15	OppenheimerFunds/ MassMutual/DLB	128.4	1.8	16
16	Oppenheimer/Centennial	14.5	1.4	16	MFS	116.8	1.7	14
17	Scudder	13.7	1.3	17	American Express Funds/IDS	114.6	1.6	3[b]
18	AIM Group	12.4	1.2	18	Zurich Scudder (including Kemper)	113.8	1.6	9, 17
19	Goldman Sachs	12.4	1.2	19	Banc of America/Marsico	110.9	1.6	—
20	Alliance Capital Mgt	12.3	1.2	20	T. Rowe Price	110.0	1.6	15
21	SEI Financial Services	11.7	1.1	21	Alliance Capital Mgt/Bernstein	109.3	1.6	20, 88
22	American Capital	11.6	1.1	22	American Century (formerly 20th Century)	97.7	1.4	24
23	Templeton	8.0	0.8	23	Prudential Mutual Funds	97.5	1.4	11
24	Twentieth Century	7.9	0.7	24	Chase Global Mutual Funds/JP Morgan	91.5	1.3	c
25	Keystone Group	7.9	0.7	25	SEI Investments	84.9	1.2	21
Total, Top 25:		**812.9**	**76.2%**			**4,945.4**	**71.0%**	

[a]Rank given if fund group was in 1990 top 100.
[b]Combined rank for Shearson and IDS Funds.
[c]Neither had reported mutual fund assets as of 12/31/90.
Note: Variable annuity assets are included in figures for 2000 but not for 1990.
Source: Investment Company Institute. Reprinted by permission of the Investment Company Institute.

and final factor was the impact of merger and acquisition activity on the fund group rankings. Several of the fund complexes that remained in the top 10 during the 1990s did so through a merger with one or more middle-size firms. This was true when Franklin and Templeton merged in 1992. This was also true when Morgan Stanley, having acquired Van Kampen and Miller, Andersen and Sherrerd (MAS), merged with Dean Witter to form MSDW Advisers. Similarly, AMVESCAP PLC advanced into the top 10 partly through an acquisition-related strategy, combining the top-25 AIM Group with the smaller INVESCO Funds Group Inc. funds to reach the number 7 rank in assets in 2000.

At the same time, the success of the fund management industry, together with the ease of entry, attracted many new competitors. During the 1990s, 316 investment management firms entered the mutual fund industry. These new entrants more than replaced the 151 investment management firms, leaving the mutual fund industry through mergers or liquidations.[5] Although none of the new entrants was among the top 10 or 25 fund managers by the end of 2000, the fund assets managed by new entrants did amount to $757 billion, or 11% of total mutual fund assets in 2000, according to the ICI. Moreover, the aggregate market share of the number 15 through number 25 fund groups grew significantly over the decade, from 12.3% in 1990 to 16.8% in 2000. By 2000, the number 25 fund group managed assets of $84.9 billion, more than 10 times the $7.9 billion managed by the number 25 player in 1990.

2. Fund industry concentration   The sheer size of the assets managed by some U.S. fund complexes—almost $900 billion for the largest—can lead to the impression that the U.S. fund industry is dominated by a few giants and that smaller competitors have little chance to succeed. Certainly, the largest players in the mutual fund business have a significant market share. But is the industry truly more concentrated than others?

Economists look to quantitative measures to find an objective way of defining and measuring market concentration. One of the best-known measures is the Herfindahl-Hirschman Index (HHI), which describes market concentration in terms of a single number that can be compared across different parts of the economy. The HHI is calculated by squaring the market share of each firm competing in the market and then summing the resulting numbers. For example, for a market consisting of four firms with shares of 30%, 30%, 20% and 20%, the HHI is 2,600 ($30^2 + 30^2 + 20^2 + 20^2 = 2,600$). The theoretical maximum score for an industry with only one competitor would be 100^2, or 10,000.

The HHI takes into account the relative size and distribution of the firms in a market and approaches zero when a market consists of a large number of firms of relatively equal size. The HHI increases both as the number of firms in the market decreases and as the disparity in size between those firms increases. Markets in which the HHI is between 1,000 and 1,800 points are considered to be moderately concentrated, and those in which the HHI is in excess of 1,800 points are considered to be concentrated. During the 1990s, the HHI for the U.S. mutual fund industry saw a minor decrease from 396 to 352 based on assets under management,[6] indicating that the industry was, and still is, fairly unconcentrated according to this statistical measure.

Another fairly unconcentrated financial industry—domestic commercial banks (including thrifts)—has an HHI of 338, based on deposits of $3.4 trillion as of December

31, 2000.[7] A subset of that universe—domestic money center banks[8]— is much more concentrated, with an HHI of 1,676, based on deposits of $1.5 trillion. In comparison, the U.S. airline carrier industry has an HHI of 1,330, based on 2000 revenues.

The mutual fund industry's low concentration score reflects not only the large number of complexes that offer mutual funds, but also the relatively even distribution of market share across many different players. As Table 10.5 shows, the complexes ranked from numbers 5 to 10 in 2000 had market shares of between 2.4% and 3.3%. The next 15 complexes (making up the remainder of the top 25) had market shares of between 1.2% and 2.4% in terms of assets, averaging 1.7%. A 1.7% share translated to $119 billion in assets under management in 2000, giving these fund groups substantial resources to wage competitive battles. Competition between fund groups in this range is intense, with only a few tenths of a percent of market share separating many competitors.

Moreover, new entrants continue to start fund management businesses and expand rapidly, as the barriers to entering this business are quite low. To become a manager of a U.S. mutual fund, a firm must register as an investment adviser with the SEC and sponsor a fund that must also file a registration statement with the SEC. But the minimum seed capital for a new mutual fund is only $100,000, and there is no minimum capital required to set up shop as a registered investment adviser. A new fund manager can easily lease offices, computers and trading connections. Similarly, a new fund manager can hire one of several large banks or other external providers to perform almost all of the processing functions needed to run a mutual fund complex, such as handling customer transactions and inquiries, fund accounting and daily pricing and sending reports to fund shareholders and regulators (see Chapter Nine). Moreover, since the advent of fund supermarkets, new fund managers can obtain instant distribution by agreeing to pay the supermarket operator 25 bp or 35 bp on fund assets (see Chapter Seven). The new entrant can attract investor attention by launching a new type of fund (e.g., Internet funds) or attaining outstanding performance in an existing fund type—without offering a full line of fund products.

However, once a fund manager gathers a substantial amount of assets, it typically reaches a critical decision point. Should the firm remain a profitable manager of moderate size focused on a few types of mutual funds? Or should it embark on a plan to become one of the top 25 managers with a full product line? In making this decision, the firm must consider the key attributes that have vaulted these fund managers into the top tier. The top-tier players have built extensive distribution systems, either directly or through intermediaries. They have invested heavily in technology to provide a broad range of support services to their customers and portfolio managers. They have created a broad line of fund offerings, including specialized products like sector and international funds. They have developed, either themselves or through alliances, the ancillary services (e.g., employee record keeping) and products (e.g., stable value pools) necessary to compete in the defined contribution field. (See Chapter Eight.) Finally, most of the top-tier players have developed a recognized brand identity over a long period of time.

Thus, although starting a fund group takes a small capital outlay, there are formidable challenges to a firm that has the ambition to break into the top tier of the mutual fund business. Firms with such ambitions have two main choices: grow their own fund assets internally or expand fund assets through acquisitions. The three largest firms in the mutual fund industry—Fidelity, Vanguard and Capital Research (the manager of the

American Funds)—have tended to build their capacity from within. They are all independent firms specializing in fund management, avoiding major acquisitions and shunning potential acquirers. Putnam has also remained relatively self-contained, although it is owned by an insurance conglomerate rather than being completely independent.

For the rest of the top 10 firms, by contrast, mergers and acquisitions have been an important corporate strategy. As mentioned above, AMVESCAP PLC (the parent of AIM and INVESCO funds) and Franklin Templeton represent conglomerations of two or more firms focused on asset management. MSDW Advisors and SSB Citibank are also the result of mergers, but involving asset managers and other types of financial institutions. Merrill Lynch has built much of its U.S. fund business internally but has expanded outside the United States through acquisitions. Finally, the Janus/Berger fund group has seen both sides of the restructuring game: the Janus and Berger fund groups were acquired by Kansas City Southern in 1984 and 1992, respectively, and then spun out as a separate firm under the Stilwell Financial name in 2000.

Faced with the challenges of becoming (or remaining) top-tier players, many fund managers of moderate size have decided to combine with another firm within the fund management industry or be acquired by a larger entity: a U.S. or foreign financial institution.

IV. *Mergers and Acquisitions Involving Fund Sponsors*

Merger and acquisition (M&A) volume grew significantly across all types of financial services firms—and among fund sponsors and other asset managers in particular—during the 1990s, reaching a dramatic peak in 2000. Figure 10.9 plots the result of a study performed by Merrill Lynch analyzing the universe of M&A transactions announced between 1990 and 2000 where an asset manager was the target. This universe was refined to focus on the 144 publicly reported mergers and acquisitions with a reported value of at least $25 million where either the acquiring firm or the target was considered a fund sponsor. For the study, a fund sponsor was defined as an asset management firm where at least 20% of its assets under management were related to retail mutual fund products.

The total number of M&A transactions involving fund sponsors and their total value grew over the decade, along with the stock market and the financial services industry in general. At the 2000 peak, 32 M&A transactions took place involving fund sponsors, with a total value of $22.4 billion. The transaction volume in 2000 made the fund industry one of the most active areas for M&A in the financial services sector. The $22.4 billion in fund sponsor M&A transactions announced in 2000 capped a long growth trend and represented over 34% of the $64.5 billion total in fund sponsor M&A for the 11 years from 1990 through 2000 combined.

Figure 10.9 breaks down M&A transactions into three types: U.S. domestic transactions, cross-border transactions and foreign transactions. As the chart shows, U.S. domestic transactions—those involving a U.S. fund sponsor and another U.S. firm—predominated in the early part of the 1990s and continued throughout the decade. Indeed, domestic transactions account for the largest number of deals overall: 63 of the 144 M&A transactions in the study period were within the United States. However, cross-border transactions—those involving a U.S. firm and a foreign firm (of which

FIGURE 10.9

Fund sponsor M&A transactions by type: Annual dollar value ($ billions), 1990–2000

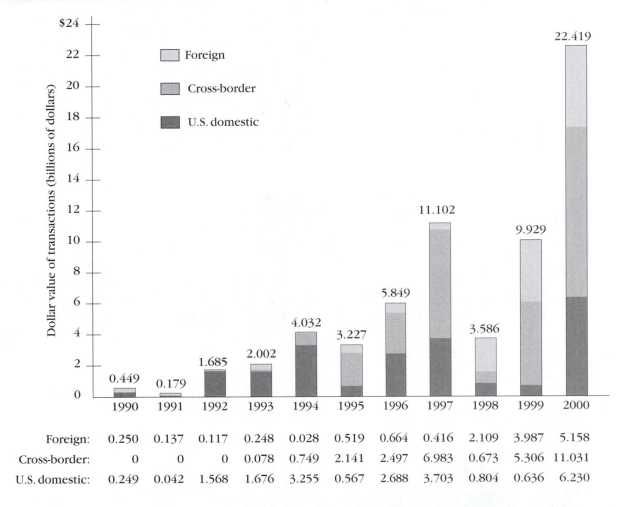

	1990	1991	1992	1993	1994	1995	1996	1997	1998	1999	2000
Foreign:	0.250	0.137	0.117	0.248	0.028	0.519	0.664	0.416	2.109	3.987	5.158
Cross-border:	0	0	0	0.078	0.749	2.141	2.497	6.983	0.673	5.306	11.031
U.S. domestic:	0.249	0.042	1.568	1.676	3.255	0.567	2.688	3.703	0.804	0.636	6.230

For purposes of this analysis in 1992, Templeton was classified as a U.S. fund sponsor because, although its head office was offshore, its fund assets were primarily in the United States.
Source: Merrill Lynch, Thompson Financial Securities Data and SNL Securities. Reprinted by permission.

either one, or both, may be a fund sponsor)—were the fastest-growing segment, increasing from little or no activity in 1990 to represent nearly half of 2000's total in aggregate transaction value. Finally, transactions exclusively involving foreign firms (i.e., no U.S. fund sponsor) made up the smallest segment of global M&A activity for 1990 through 2000, accounting for 21% of the total aggregate transaction value over the period.

In the next three sections, we discuss in more detail U.S. domestic transactions by industry type, the main types of cross-border transactions and the price trends across all types of M&A activity over the 1990s. We do not discuss merger and acquisition activity between two foreign, that is, non-U.S., firms, because this subject is beyond the scope of this book. The supplemental information at the end of this Chapter lists both selected domestic transactions and selected cross-border transactions involving fund sponsors.

A. U.S. Domestic Transactions: Interindustry and Intraindustry Mergers

Let's begin by reviewing M&A transactions within the United States. These can be divided into three subcategories, based on the industries of the parties involved: (1) M&A between two fund sponsors, (2) interindustry M&A (fund sponsors as acquirers) and (3) interindustry M&A (fund sponsors as targets for nonfund companies). Figure 10.10 shows the share by dollar value of total fund sponsor M&A transactions from 1990 through 2000 for each of these three transaction types.

FIGURE 10.10

Fund industry M&A: Total dollar value by transaction type, 1990–2000

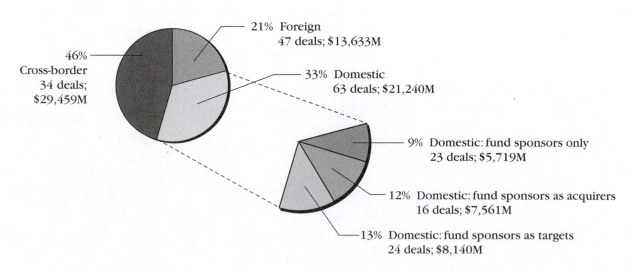

21% Foreign
47 deals; $13,633M

46% Cross-border
34 deals; $29,459M

33% Domestic
63 deals; $21,240M

9% Domestic: fund sponsors only
23 deals; $5,719M

12% Domestic: fund sponsors as acquirers
16 deals; $7,561M

13% Domestic: fund sponsors as targets
24 deals; $8,140M

Source: Merrill Lynch. Reprinted by permission.

1. Mergers between two fund sponsors   Consolidation within the fund industry—one fund sponsor combining with another—has become an ongoing trend in the mutual fund business. In the early 1990s, this was the typical type of transaction for fund sponsors, representing half of the 28 domestic M&A transactions from 1990 through 1995 and 45% of the dollar volume for that period. Later in the decade, interindustry mergers took on a larger share, but mergers among fund sponsors continued.

Several factors influence fund sponsors in deciding whether to pursue M&A as a corporate strategy. A fund sponsor that is strong in a particular fund type may want to develop more strength across its product line—a bond fund expert expanding its equity lineup, for example. This may be especially important for a sponsor with a narrow specialty area that may be left behind if the market changes. Fund customers may quickly abandon a fund manager that specializes in a particular fund type (e.g., international funds or technology funds) if that investment area falls out of favor. Another underlying motivation for many M&A transactions is a belief that a larger organization may be able to run more efficiently and achieve economies of scale as assets under management grow. Rather than develop additional fund management capabilities in-house, a fund manager may find it worthwhile to combine with or acquire the manager of another fund group.

A look at the top mutual fund complexes in 1990 and 2000 (see Table 10.5) provides a prominent example of a merger motivated heavily by product line considerations: the Franklin fund family, the number six group in 1990, joined forces with the number 23 Templeton funds in 1992 and appeared in 2000's rankings as the Franklin Templeton group. The combination of these two fund families resulted in a more diverse product line, as the Franklin funds, with a strong name in U.S. bond management, acquired the Templeton range of international equity funds. A similar product line expansion occurred a few years later in 1994, when American Century (then known as Twentieth Century) supplemented its line of equity funds by acquiring the Benham group, which specialized in fixed income fund management. Both mergers combined fairly well-known brand names into single complexes, positioning the fund sponsors more strongly as diversified asset managers. However, neither merger involved a significant crossover between distribution channels: Franklin and Templeton both made their names in the intermediary channel offering load funds, while Twentieth Century and Benham both were no-load, direct-marketed fund complexes. Thus, product diversification more than channel diversification was the result of these mergers.

Intraindustry mergers between fund groups continued though the 1990s, although none of the later mergers involved groups with the same industry prominence as the Franklin-Templeton transaction in 1992. Examples of the smaller intraindustry mergers of the late 1990s include the acquisition of Flagship Resources—a specialist in municipal bond funds—by the Nuveen fund organization in 1996, and the acquisition of Edgemont Asset Management Corp.—sponsor of the well-known Kaufmann Fund—by Federated Investors in 2000.

Thus, mergers within the fund industry usually involve a name-brand fund group acquiring or merging with another in order to strengthen its brand identity or to expand an existing product line. But two organizations have taken a different approach, building a diversified set of businesses through acquisition without starting from a strong fund management organization. These two firms—United Asset Management (UAM) and Affiliated Managers Group—have followed a strategy of acquiring relatively small asset managers and collecting them under a single corporate umbrella, without necessarily combining their day-to-day operations or activities. UAM actually began operations in 1980 and had assembled a portfolio of 25 managers by the end of 1999. UAM's strategy involved obtaining 100% of the equity in firms it acquired and sharing profits contractually with its subsidiary companies. Ultimately, however, UAM's agglomeration of businesses became unwieldy; by the end of the decade, UAM had become a target and was itself acquired by Old Mutual Plc, a British and South African insurer.[9]

UAM's experience highlights an important fact about investment management mergers and acquisitions: the individuals who manage money for the acquired firm, often including the firm's founders, are extremely important to the firm's success. Unless these individuals can be convinced to stay with a firm after an acquisition and continue to build relationships, the firm is certain to change and risks losing the forces that made it successful. Although UAM provided incentives to the key employees of the acquired firms through revenue sharing and other arrangements, without equity ownership the key individuals of the acquired firms may have had less incentive to develop their businesses after the acquisition. Affiliated Managers Group tries to avoid this situation by acquiring less than 100%—typically between 51% and 70%—of the acquired firm's equity, leaving the rest with management of the acquired firm. Affiliated Managers encourages the acquired firm to distribute the retained equity widely among junior managers as well as senior managers, providing a growth incentive for the next generation of managers as well as the founders and senior managers who built the firm's track record. By the end of 2000, the Affiliated Managers Group had assembled 15 asset managers specializing mostly in equity investments, including the advisers of the Tweedy, Browne funds and the Essex funds.

2. Interindustry mergers: Fund sponsors as acquirers In the late 1990s, fund sponsors increasingly reached out to acquire nonfund financial firms to supplement their mutual fund businesses. In an effort to attract and retain assets from high-net-worth customers, many of these fund sponsors sought to increase their ability to handle better the broader financial needs of such customers by expanding into related businesses, such as customized money management for individuals or institutions outside mutual funds. Managing money for high-net-worth customers often requires a level of customer service that differs from typical mutual fund distribution as well as different approaches to investment management. These differences spurred some fund sponsors to obtain both customer service and investment management capabilities though acquisitions rather than building them internally.

Some of the most prominent transactions of this type occurred in 2000: the acquisition of Sanford C. Bernstein, Inc. by Alliance Capital Group and the acquisition of Fiduciary Trust Company International by Franklin Resources (the parent of the Franklin Templeton Funds).[10] In both transactions, a fund sponsor acquired a firm with expertise in nonmutual fund management for the high-net-worth market. The larger of the two transactions, with a price tag of $3.5 billion, was the acquisition of Sanford Bernstein, a well-respected asset manager specializing in managing separate accounts for institutions and wealthy individuals, by Alliance, a subsidiary of a diversified financial firm with mutual fund product lines and variable annuities (sourced through AXA Financial). Bernstein's strong money management capabilities, particularly in the value style of equity investing, added to Alliance's range of investment disciplines as well as providing specialized skills in managing money for high-net-worth investors. In the smaller Fiduciary Trust acquisition, with a price tag of $825 million, Franklin obtained not only investment management of high quality but also servicing capacity for a private banking clientele.

More generally, when fund sponsors expand into other financial services through mergers and acquisitions, they almost always acquire institutional or high-net-worth asset managers. Of the 16 domestic acquisitions by fund sponsors from 1990 through 2000, 15 involved other asset managers (rather than banks or insurance companies, for example). Two main factors contribute to this strong bent of fund sponsors toward investment management firms when making acquisitions outside the fund industry. The first factor is the cost of acquiring different types of financial firms. Although mutual fund sponsors seem to be giants when viewed in terms of assets under management, they are smaller in terms of market capitalization than many other financial services firms. For example, Stilwell Financial (which includes the Janus and Berger fund families) was the number six fund firm in 2000, with assets under management of $206 billion. Yet its market capitalization at the end of 2000 was only $8.6 billion, smaller than the fourteenth largest U.S. commercial bank and the twenty-first largest U.S. insurance company as of that date—Comerica and Lincoln National, respectively. With their relatively small market caps, many fund sponsors simply do not have the capital to make substantial acquisitions in other parts of financial services outside asset management. In addition, the largest three fund sponsors—Fidelity, Vanguard and Capital Research—have no publicly traded stock, which deprives them of an important form of currency for making acquisitions.

The second factor behind the strong tendency of fund sponsors to acquire other types of asset managers is the relatively high profit margins available from most forms of asset management. Asset managers have lower costs for "bricks and mortar" and lower capital needs than other financial service firms such as banks. At the same time, asset management is one of the highest growth segments in financial services. As a result, asset managers enjoyed higher operating returns on equity than most other financial services firms, averaging 32% for the five years ended in 2000 compared to a financial services average of 19%. Thus, fund sponsors enjoying high-margin businesses in the 1990s were reluctant to reduce their returns on equity by expanding into higher-volume, lower-margin areas. Asset managers for high-net-worth customers were one of the few parts of the financial services sector offering fund sponsors comparable returns on equity in the 1990s.

3. Interindustry M&A: Fund sponsors as targets for nonfund companies
While mutual fund sponsors tend to acquire other asset managers, both groups make attractive targets for firms in other parts of the financial services sector. Traditional financial services businesses such as banking and insurance inhabit relatively mature market segments with lower growth prospects, contrasting sharply with the rapid growth experienced by fund sponsors in the 1990s. Asset managers were the highest potential growth segment of financial services at the end of 2000, as illustrated in Figure 10.11. Based on annualized earnings growth forecast by Wall Street to exceed 16% as of the end of 2000, asset managers were expected to increase their businesses

FIGURE 10.11

*Projected five-year annualized earnings growth rates by
segment at 12/31/00*

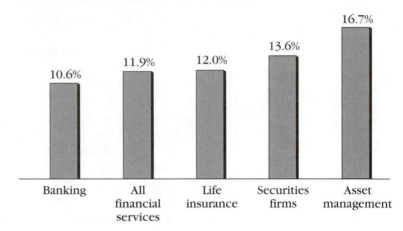

Sources: Factset Research Systems, Inc., Thompson Financial/First Call and Merrill Lynch. Reprinted
by permission.

significantly faster than other financial firms such as life insurers (12.0%) or banks
(10.6%). Although the rate of earnings growth for asset managers will probably be
lower in 2001 than forecast in 2000, the rate of earnings growth for other financial institutions will also be lower than forecast. This differential makes asset managers attractive for other financial firms seeking to expand into businesses with higher revenue
and earnings growth potential.

Asset managers also receive most of their revenue in the form of asset-based fees—
mostly from management fees, which typically are based on a percentage of assets
under management. Such fee-based income is considered more stable than the other
sources of income available to many financial services firms and tends to be rewarded
by the stock market with a higher price/earnings ratio. For brokerage and investment
banking firms, fee-based income is typically more stable, and less subject to stock market vagaries, than revenues from sources like stock commissions, underwriting fees for
initial public offerings and proprietary trading. For a banking institution, management
fee income offers a revenue source that is relatively independent of loan volume and interest rate spreads that drive much of a commercial bank's business. Thus, the acquisition of a fund sponsor by an investment or commercial bank provides an appealing
opportunity to reduce the volatility of the acquirer's income statement.

Morgan Stanley Dean Witter (MSDW) is an example of a firm that has tried to avoid
being overly dependent on revenues related to the stock market, as are most broker-
dealers. MSDW rose to fifth place in market share among fund sponsors in 2000 (see
Table 10.5) partly though a series of acquisitions; it now includes under its umbrella the
former Morgan Stanley and Dean Witter funds, as well as the Van Kampen and MAS
(Miller, Andersen and Sherrerd) funds. Expanding its mutual fund business was part of
a broader effort by MSDW, a financial services firm rooted in the brokerage industry, to
diversify its revenue sources away from the volatile brokerage business. The acquisi-

tions were also motivated by the potential to take advantage of MSDW's existing infrastructure to distribute more investment products. This motivation was reinforced by the growth of mutual fund wrap programs, in which a broker or adviser chooses a portfolio of mutual funds for their clients. (See Chapter Seven.) By expanding their in-house offerings to include mutual funds with a variety of brand identities, firms like MSDW may be able to increase the representation of their own proprietary funds within such mutual fund wrap programs.

A notable acquisition of a fund sponsor by a firm from another part of the financial world was the acquisition of Dreyfus by Mellon in 1993, in which a major banking organization sought to join the fund industry by acquiring a fund sponsor in the top tier. In the early 1990s, however, regulators were still working under the Glass-Steagall Act's restrictions on bank expansion into other financial activities, so the Mellon-Dreyfus merger was subjected to a lengthy regulatory review. This kind of cross-industry transaction was easier to accomplish later in the decade as the regulatory barriers between banking and securities activities were eroding. Thus, the acquisition of a 45% interest in the American Century group by JP Morgan in 1997 was met with far less regulatory resistance. Mellon and JP Morgan are both examples of banks that have generally expanded beyond traditional lending, emphasizing processing and servicing in the case of Mellon and securities underwriting and trading in the case of JP Morgan. For banks that are determined to expand out of traditional lending into asset management, acquiring a fund sponsor has been an attractive alternative in light of the difficulties in building internally a first-rate mutual fund business within a reasonable time period.

In addition to brokerage firms and banks, insurance companies were major acquirers of fund sponsors in the 1990s. For example, Liberty Financial (a subsidiary of Liberty Mutual) acquired the Colonial fund group, a well-known load fund sponsor, in 1994 and the Wanger Asset Management group in 2000. Similarly, the ReliaStar insurance group acquired the sponsor of the Pilgrim Funds in 1999 and the Lexington funds in 2000.[11] The high growth potential of funds was a major factor in the expansion of insurance companies into the fund business. As Figure 10.11 shows, since the growth rate of life insurance is expected to be substantially lower than the growth rate of asset management, higher-growth (and higher-margin) fund sponsors are especially attractive to insurance companies. Insurance executives also saw the need to diversify their product offerings to take greater advantage of favorable equity markets. Since traditional insurance products such as term and whole life policies are at a relative disadvantage during periods of strong stock market performance, many insurers emphasized products like variable annuities combining insurance with equity features. (See Chapter Seven.) Given that marketing emphasis, insurers wanted their own fund managers to run at least some of the mutual funds underlying their variable annuities.

B. *Cross-Border Transactions: U.S. Firms as Targets and Acquirers*

Figure 10.12 highlights another segment of fund sponsor M&A activity from 1990 through 2000: cross-border mergers and acquisitions (defined as M&A involving U.S. and non-U.S. parties). Cross-border transactions grew from nonexistent in 1990 to represent the largest segment of fund sponsor M&A in 2000, as shown previously in Figure 10.9. Between 1990 and 2000, cross-border transactions represented 46% of fund

FIGURE 10.12

Fund industry M&A: Total dollar value by transaction type, 1990–2000

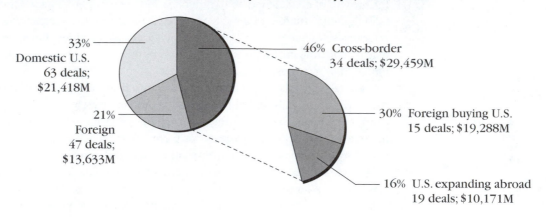

33%
Domestic U.S.
63 deals;
$21,418M

46% Cross-border
34 deals; $29,459M

21%
Foreign
47 deals;
$13,633M

30% Foreign buying U.S.
15 deals; $19,288M

16% U.S. expanding abroad
19 deals; $10,171M

Source: Merrill Lynch. Reprinted by permission.

sponsor M&A by dollar value and 34 of 144 transactions (about 24% of the number of transactions). Cross-border transactions were a larger percentage by dollar value than in terms of number of transactions because cross-border M&A deals are larger on average than domestic transactions, reflecting the scale needed to implement an international fund management strategy.

This acceleration of cross-border M&A grows out of the difficulties that fund managers face in trying to build a global franchise. As explained more fully in Chapter Twelve, differences in legal, accounting and tax regulations require a fund sponsor to create different funds to be offered in almost every country or region. Globalization presents a much greater challenge for fund sponsors than for other types of businesses. An umbrella manufacturer, for example, might be able to locate its factory in one country and sell the umbrellas made there all over the world, since the need for umbrellas is pretty much the same in rainy cities everywhere. But a fund sponsor generally will not be able to offer the same mutual fund to investors in the United States, the Far East and Europe. If fund sponsors want to offer their products worldwide, they must not only develop distribution and service relationships in each market, but must also create separate lines of funds (often managed as copies, or "clones," of each other) for each market. Faced with this daunting task in many geographical areas, fund sponsors wishing to expand outside their home markets often use M&A transactions as a way to acquire a local presence quickly.

To understand cross-border transactions better, we will divide them geographically into (1) transactions where a foreign firm is buying into the United States and (2) transactions where a U.S. firm is expanding abroad. As Figure 10.12 shows, foreign firms buying into the United States had a larger share of total transaction value from 1990 to 2000 ($19.3 billion) than U.S. firms expanding abroad ($10.2 billion).

1. U.S. fund sponsors as targets for foreign firms   The 1990s saw a wave of acquisitions of U.S. fund sponsors by foreign firms with historical roots as banks and insurers. Major M&A transactions leading up to the year 2000 included the acquisition of the Kemper and Scudder fund families by the Zurich Insurance Group in 1995 and 1997[12], the acquisition of the Montgomery Funds by Commerzbank in 1997, the acquisition of Warburg Pincus Asset Management by Credit Suisse in 1999 and the acquisition of bond experts PIMCO by Germany's Allianz in 1999. The year 2000 saw four cross-border M&A transactions targeting U.S. fund sponsors with values of at least $1 billion: Unicredito Italiano, a banking organization, bought the Pioneer Group for $1.2 billion; CDC Asset Management Europe, also principally a banking institution, acquired Nvest LP (the manager of the New England Funds, among others) for $2.2 billion; the U.K. and South African insurer Old Mutual Plc acquired UAM (as previously discussed) for $2.2 billion; and German financial services giant Allianz added the Nicholas-Applegate fund group to its U.S. lineup for a price tag of $1.6 billion.[13]

Most of these transactions involve large European financial services firms seeking to establish or solidify a position in the U.S. fund industry. As a general rule, such European firms are used to operating in multiple sectors of the financial services field, crossing lines between banking, insurance and money management. This breadth reflects Europe's regulatory history: with no equivalent of the Glass-Steagall Act separating banking and securities activities, major European firms tend to follow a more diversified or universal approach to financial services. Nevertheless, firms with a substantial banking or insurance business in Europe are subject to many of the same pressures to expand their money management activities that U.S. firms do: in Europe as in the United States, banking and insurance are relatively slow-growth and low-margin businesses compared to money management.

The dominance of European firms as acquirers is noteworthy; for example, there were no major acquisitions of U.S. fund sponsors by the Japanese during the 1990s. In part, this reflects the economic slump that took hold in Japan during the decade, which left Japanese firms facing inward without the capital for major foreign acquisitions. But the dominance of European acquirers also reflects widespread enthusiasm for globalization among European firms at the end of the 1990s and into 2000. Many of these firms, especially those with a substantial continental presence, felt a need to move beyond their European roots to establish themselves as global organizations. In the view of many European executives, a global presence in financial services requires a presence in the United States. Rather than taking the time to build a U.S. mutual fund line from scratch, these European firms opted for acquisitions as a quicker route to establishing a meaningful U.S. position.

The most geographically ambivalent fund sponsor is AMVESCAP PLC, which began as a European acquirer but now could be considered a U.S. acquirer. Starting from a base in the U.K. as fund sponsor INVESCO PLC,[14] this firm acquired the U.S. equity and money market fund specialist AIM Management in 1996 for $2.2 billion and quickly established itself as a multinational fund sponsor with headquarters in the United States. Changing its name to AMVESCAP PLC, the firm continued to acquire other asset managers across the globe—including a $1.1 billion acquisition of LGT Asset Management[15] in 1998, a $1.5 billion acquisition of U.K. fund sponsor Perpetual Plc in 2000 and a $1.8 billion acquisition of Trimark Financial—the sixth largest fund organization in Canada at the time—in 2000. By the end of the decade, AMVESCAP PLC had become number seven in market share in the U.S. fund industry, while continuing to expand abroad.

2. U.S. financial firms expanding abroad   The largest of the cross-border transactions, and one of the largest M&A deals in the asset management industry, was the acquisition of the U.K.-based fund sponsor Mercury Asset Management by Merrill Lynch in 1997 for $5.1 billion. This deal was a major strategic move by Merrill to establish a strong presence in Europe as a fund sponsor to complement its existing underwriting business there and to leverage Mercury's role as an asset manager on a global basis. Several other broad-based U.S. financial firms acquired European fund sponsors in smaller transactions—for example, the acquisition of the U.K. fund manager Newton Management Ltd. by Mellon Bank in 1998, the acquisition of BT Funds management subsidiaries in Europe by U.S. insurer the Principal Financial Group in 1999, the acquisition of U.K. fund manager Johnson Fry Holdings PLC by Legg Mason, Inc. in 1999 and the acquisition of U.K. fund sponsor Gartmore Investment Management by Nationwide Insurance Company in 2000.

Thus, most U.S. financial firms outside the fund industry have chosen to expand into Europe though acquisitions instead of internal growth of overseas units. Moreover, such financial firms often acquired firms in the United Kingdom, which is traditionally the first step abroad for U.S. financial organizations. This contrasts with the foreign firms acquiring U.S. fund sponsors, which tended to be from continental Europe. This difference reflects both the huge size of financial firms on the Continent and their consequential strength as acquirers, as well as the more pluralistic investment culture in the United Kingdom where the existence of more midsize players makes them easier acquisition targets.

Although cross-border acquisitions by nonfund financial firms accelerated in the late 1990s, the largest fund firms have tended to grow abroad internally or by nurturing sister organizations rather than through acquisition. Fidelity Investments, through its sister company Fidelity International Ltd., has built a strong franchise in the United Kingdom and is expanding into continental Europe. Fidelity also is growing internally its mutual fund business in Japan and other parts of the Far East. Similarly, through a joint venture, T. Rowe Price has long been affiliated with Rowe Price Fleming, a U.K. based fund manager. In 2000, T. Rowe finally made its joint venture, Rowe Price Fleming, into a wholly owned subsidiary of the U.S. firm by purchasing the remaining 50% interest following the sale of the rest of Fleming to Chase Manhattan, and renaming the subsidiary T. Rowe Price International.

Other large U.S. fund sponsors have focused on particular aspects of asset management overseas. For example, Vanguard has begun to offer index funds in selected countries including the United Kingdom and Australia. Capital Research has become a well-regarded manager of institutional pension assets in Europe and Asia. Putnam has been successful in joint ventures with local financial institutions in Italy and Japan.

This trend toward internal growth overseas by the largest U.S. fund sponsors is driven by many factors. One key factor is that such fund sponsors have the resources, the expertise and the stamina to develop a local set of funds in multiple foreign jurisdictions. A second key factor is that such fund sponsors, having demonstrated the ability to grow assets internally, are unwilling to pay the high prices required to acquire fund sponsors abroad.

C. Pricing Trends in Asset Management M&A

The result of rising global interest among financial services companies has been the steady growth in both average transaction value and acquisition multiples paid over the past decade. Although it is often difficult to determine transaction values versus the target's underlying financials because most of the deals are privately negotiated, Figures 10.13 and 10.14 show publicly available data collected on 43 acquisitions of asset managers from July 1990 to June 2001. They illustrate the most commonly cited acquisition pricing metrics: transaction value as a percentage of assets under management (AUM) and transaction value as a multiple of earnings before interest, taxes, depreciation and amortization (EBITDA).

Although often cited in press articles and company news releases, transaction value as a percentage of AUM is not the most relevant metric for acquirers of asset management companies. The more meaningful measure for buyers is transaction value as a multiple of EBITDA (EBITDA multiple). This is an important measure of a company's core earnings, excluding accounting, financing and tax factors, that are *not* related to the operation of the company's business. By using the EBITDA multiple as a valuation measure, potential acquirers are better able to assess the firm's ability to generate cash flow streams. Asset managers have very different fee schedules depending on the customer, product and market segment. An asset manager such as BlackRock, whose clients are primarily institutional investors with fixed income portfolios, charges clients much lower rates than a firm such as W.P. Stewart, which caters to high-net-worth investors with customized equity portfolios.

FIGURE 10.13

Transaction value as percentage of AUM for 43 acquisitions, 1990–2001

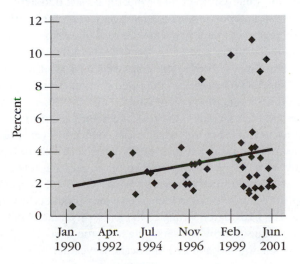

Source: Merrill Lynch. Reprinted by permission.

FIGURE 10.14

Transaction value as multiple of last 12 months EBITDA for 43 acquisitions, 1990–2001

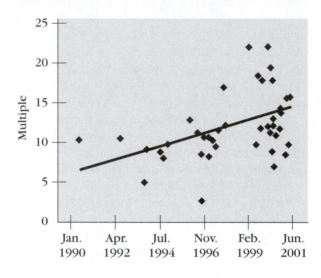

Source: Merrill Lynch. Reprinted by permission.

Thus, potential buyers should be focused on the cash flow generation from the asset base and fee structure of the target asset manager, as well as the operating margins of the manager. A separate analysis of the data suggests that buyers do factor these into their evaluation of potential acquisitions as EBITDA has a much higher correlation to transaction value than a target's AUM. In the 43 transactions studied, the R^2 for EBITDA as a determinant of transaction value was 0.81 versus 0.46 for AUM as a determinant of transaction value. On the other hand, the largest transactions do not always command the highest multiples in the asset management sector. For the 43 M&A transactions covered by this study, there was a low correlation between deal size and EBITDA multiple paid by the acquirer.

To illustrate the high prices commanded by asset managers toward the end of the 1990s, let's consider three of the priciest transactions in terms of EBITDA announced during the decade, as shown in Table 10.6.

The first transaction in the table, ReliaStar's acquisition of Lexington, demonstrates that a relatively small asset manager can command a very high EBITDA multiple even in a domestic deal if the manager offers an attractive client base and a good strategic fit. Lexington offered a diverse client roster comprising retail (48% of AUM), institutional (33% of AUM) and high-net-worth private clients (19% of AUM). Over 70% of Lexington's AUM were invested in higher-fee equity products. On the heels of a disappointing year in 1999, Lexington struggled to increase its retail franchise on its own and realized that an acquisition by ReliaStar might be the best strategy. With only $3.6 billion in AUM, Lexington did not have the scale to weather market downturns. A Minneapolis-based life insurance company, ReliaStar saw an opportunity to develop its retail busi-

TABLE 10.6

Expensive M&A transaction (as a multiple of EBITDA)

Date Announced	Buyer	Target	Transaction Value ($ billions)	EBITDA Multiple
02/29/00	ReliaStar Financial	Lexington Global Asset Management	0.05	22x
05/15/00	UniCredito Italiano	Pioneer Group	1.2	18x
11/19/97	Merrill Lynch	Mercury Asset Management Group plc	5.1	17x

ness through an acquisition of Lexington. Lexington's client base and investment skills fit well with ReliaStar's Pilgrim and Northstar mutual funds. Lexington's retail, institutional and 780 high-net-worth private clients (with average assets over $900,000) also presented attractive cross-selling opportunities.

The other two transactions involve cross-border acquisitions at high EBITDA multiples. The second example shown in Table 10.6 involved Italian financial services giant UniCredito Italiano and Boston-based Pioneer Group. UniCredito acquired Pioneer to gain access to the fast-growing U.S. retail market. Pioneer's brand name, investment management capabilities and retail marketing skills prompted UniCredito to pay the highest price in an auction process. With attractive growth prospects in the U.S. mutual fund industry and no substantial U.S. position, UniCredito regarded this acquisition as a strategic imperative. Pioneer, in turn, was interested in an acquisition because the company had run into problems with its unrelated activities outside the United States, including an African gold mine and Russian bank.

In the third transaction shown in Table 10.6, Merrill Lynch acquired Mercury Asset Management Group in the largest asset management acquisition of the past decade. The deal expanded Merrill's global asset management division by adding one of the largest institutional and retail franchises in the United Kingdom. Mercury managed approximately $177 billion for over half the companies included in the FTSE-100 index, 25 of the largest 50 Japanese corporate pension funds and 5 of the 10 largest pension funds in the world. For Merrill Lynch, the transaction was an ideal strategic fit as it expanded the firm's product range, added scale and strengthened its platform for overseas growth in asset management. For Mercury, the transaction was attractively priced and offered the potential to link up with a global powerhouse in financial services.

In summary, M&A activities involving fund sponsors evidenced several significant trends over the past decade. In the early 1990s, transactions among U.S. financial firms were the main focus, including intraindustry merger activity between fund sponsors and acquisitions of fund sponsors by other financial institutions. At the same time, a few small companies also pursued an aggregation strategy of assembling a stable of fund families and asset managers. Later in the decade, all of these types of M&A activities continued and were joined by some additional trends. Domestically within the United States, fund sponsors began to take more of a role as acquirers of other asset management firms focused on high-net-worth investors. Internationally, the pace of cross-border transactions accelerated dramatically, with European financial institutions making substantial acquisitions of U.S. fund sponsors. Some U.S. financial firms bought asset managers in Europe, although the largest U.S. fund sponsors sought to expand internationally through internal growth. As the decade proceeded, acquirers paid higher and higher prices for fund sponsors and other asset managers in anticipation of continued strong growth of revenues and assets. Whether these high acquisition premiums paid for asset managers were justified will become apparent over the next decade.

REVIEW QUESTIONS

1. Compare the fee information in Figures 10.3 and 10.4 for T. Rowe Price Growth Stock Fund and Putnam Voyager Fund. What is the distribution strategy, and how is it financed, for each fund?

2. In choosing among funds, should investors be more sensitive to the relative level of fees and expenses in stock funds versus bond or money market funds? What does your answer imply about a cost-control approach for fund sponsors?

3. How can investors and brokers or financial planners learn about the fees and expenses of each class in multiple class funds? Which is better for an investor in an equity fund: Class A with a 4% front-end load and 40 bp annual 12b-1 fee, or Class B with a 100 bp annual 12b-1 fee and a CDSC beginning at 4% and declining to zero after six years?

4. What have been the key reasons why the overall expenses of U.S. mutual funds appear to have risen over the last decade? Which is more important in understanding trends in mutual fund fees: the number of funds, the average assets per fund or the median assets per fund? Why?

5. What have been the main types of U.S. companies acquired by U.S. fund sponsors during the 1990s? Why were these types of acquisition targets attractive to U.S. fund sponsors?

6. What have been the main types of foreign companies acquiring U.S. fund sponsors during the 1990s? What factors have motivated these foreign acquirers?

DISCUSSION QUESTIONS

1. Sales loads are sometimes ignored in calculating fund performance, but 12b-1 fees are always included as a fund expense in performance calculations. Is this differential treatment justified?

2. Do you believe that mutual funds or fund complexes realize economies of scale at some asset level? If so, at what level? Will a mutual fund or a fund complex encounter diseconomies of scale if it becomes very large?

3. Should the SEC encourage or discourage performance fees for fund managers? What specific changes would you suggest with regard to the rules governing performance fees?

4. Do you think the structure of the U.S. fund management industry will become more or less concentrated over the next decade? What types of U.S. fund managers are likely to be acquired in the future?

5. What are the main choices in building a global franchise in the asset management industry? Why have U.S. and European firms typically taken different approaches to building such a global franchise?

6. What's the difference between EBITDA and AUM as a valuation metric? How can the prices paid for fund sponsors in the late 1990s be justified in terms of either metric?

NOTES

1. Investment Company Institute, "Trends in the Ownership Cost of Equity Mutual Funds" (1998).
2. The ICI has also published statistics in its 2001 Mutual Fund Fact Book comparing the sales-weighted average of shareholder costs for individual funds between 1990 and 1998. These statistics showed declines of 1.81% to 1.35% for equity (including hybrid) funds, 1.71% to 1.09% for bond funds and 0.53% to 0.42% for money market funds.
3. Morningstar Mutual Funds, "Revisiting Fund Costs: Up or Down?" February 21, 1999.
4. According to Strategic Insight Simfund.
5. Brian Reid, "The 1990s: A Decade of Expansion and Change in the U.S. Mutual Fund Industry," Investment Company Institute, Vol. 6 / No. 3, July 2000.
6. Analysis based on assets under management for all mutual fund complexes as reported by the Investment Company Institute.
7. Based on data provided by SNL Securities and Merrill Lynch.
8. As defined by Hoovers, Inc., an online business network.
9. Nvest pursued a similar strategy to UAM and was ultimately acquired as well.
10. Charles Schwab & Co. initiated a similar expansion into private account management in 1999 when it acquired U.S. Trust, a well-known firm specializing in providing financial services to wealthy clients. Although this transaction had many similarities to the Bernstein and Fiduciary Trust acquisitions, the transaction was not included in Merrill Lynch's study because a majority of U.S. Trust's revenues were driven by net interest income from banking functions rather than fees from asset management.
11. The asset management businesses of Liberty Financial are slated to be acquired by Fleet Financial in late 2001, and ReliaStar was subsequently acquired by ING, a Dutch financial conglomerate.
12. In September 2001, Deutsche Bank, a German financial services firm, agreed to acquire Zurich's Scudder group (the former Kemper and Scudder fund families).
13. Includes the present value of the earnout discounted at 14%, according to Merrill Lynch.
14. INVESCO PLC changed its name from Britannia Arrow Holdings in 1990.
15. Sponsor of the GT Global funds group and Chancellor LGT funds.

Summary of Transactions Involving Fund Managers

Selected Domestic Transactions

Date Announced	Target Name	Classification	Acquiror Name	Classification	Value of Transaction ($mil)
1990 6/8/90	Newbold's Asset Management Inc	U.S. Fund Sponsor	United Asset Management Corp	U.S. Fund Sponsor	63.0
6/19/90	United Asset Management Corp	U.S. Fund Sponsor	Investor Group	U.S. Other	28.0
7/31/90	Oppenheimer Management Corp	U.S. Fund Sponsor	Investor Group	U.S. Other	157.5
					248.5
1991 4/9/91	First Pac Advisors-Advisory	U.S. Institutional/HNW	United Asset Management Corp	U.S. Fund Sponsor	42.0
					42.0
1992 7/31/92	NWQ Investment Management Co	U.S. Institutional/HNW	United Asset Management Corp	U.S. Fund Sponsor	100.3
7/31/92	Templeton Galbraith & Hanberge	U.S. Fund Sponsor (Bahamas)	Franklin Resources Inc	U.S. Fund Sponsor	786.0
10/13/92	Van Kampen Merritt Cos Inc	U.S. Fund Sponsor	CDV Acquisition Corp	U.S. Other	395.0
11/23/92	Equitable Capital Management	U.S. Fund Sponsor	Alliance Capital Management LP	U.S. Fund Sponsor	286.8
					1,568.1
1993 3/22/93	AH Overseas Investments Inc	U.S. Fund Sponsor	Phoenix Home Life Mutual	U.S. Insurance	54.2
3/29/93	New England Investment Cos Inc	U.S. Fund Sponsor	Reich & Tang (New England)	U.S. Fund Sponsor	352.0
5/14/93	Mutual of Omaha Ins-Mutual	U.S. Fund Sponsor	Pioneer Group Inc	U.S. Fund Sponsor	26.5
6/9/93	Shields Asset Management Inc	U.S. Fund Sponsor	Alliance Capital Management LP	U.S. Fund Sponsor	70.0
10/18/93	Lieber & Co.	U.S. Fund Sponsor	First Union	U.S. Bank	127.0
12/6/93	Dreyfus Corp.	U.S. Fund Sponsor	Mellon Bank	U.S. Bank	1,046.0
					1,675.7
1994 2/28/94	Cadence Capital Mgmt, 3 others	U.S. Institutional/HNW	Thomson Advisory Group LP	U.S. Fund Sponsor	872.4
3/9/94	Thomson Advisory Group LP	U.S. Fund Sponsor	PIMCO Advisors LP	U.S. Fund Sponsor	140.0
4/22/94	Benham Management Intl Inc	U.S. Fund Sponsor	Twentieth Century Cos Inc	U.S. Fund Sponsor	150.0
4/29/94	Alliance Capital Management LP	U.S. Fund Sponsor	Equitable Life Assurance	U.S. Insurance	50.0
6/16/94	BlackRock Financial Management	U.S. Fund Sponsor	PNC Bank Corp, Pittsburgh, PA	U.S. Bank	240.0
8/24/94	American Capital Management	U.S. Fund Sponsor	Van Kampen Merritt Cos Inc	U.S. Fund Sponsor	429.2
10/10/94	Colonial Group Inc	U.S. Fund Sponsor	Liberty Financial Cos Inc	U.S. Fund Sponsor	378.0
10/10/94	Transamerica Fund Management	U.S. Fund Sponsor	John Hancock Mutual Funds	U.S. Insurance	100.0
11/11/94	Provident Investment Counsel	U.S. Fund Sponsor	United Asset Management Corp	U.S. Fund Sponsor	357.3
12/7/94	Pilgrim Group Inc	U.S. Fund Sponsor	Express America Holdings Corp	U.S. Fund Sponsor	28.0
12/12/94	Delaware Management Holdings	U.S. Fund Sponsor	Lincoln National Corp	U.S. Insurance	510.0
					3,254.9
1995 6/23/95	Harris Associates	U.S. Fund Sponsor	New England Investment Cos	U.S. Fund Sponsor	175.0
6/28/95	Miller Anderson & Sherrerd	U.S. Fund Sponsor	Morgan Stanely Asset Mgmt	U.S. Brokerage	350.0
8/18/95	Quest for Value Funds	U.S. Fund Sponsor	Oppenheimer Management Corp.	U.S. Fund Sponsor	41.8
					566.8
1996 4/11/96	Broadway & Seymour-Ast Mgmt	U.S. Other	Fidelity Investments (FMR Corp)	U.S. Fund Sponsor	30.0
6/24/96	Van Kampen/American Capital	U.S. Fund Sponsor	Morgan Stanley Group Inc	U.S. Brokerage	1,175.0
6/25/96	Heine Securities Corp	U.S. Fund Sponsor	Franklin Resources Inc	U.S. Fund Sponsor	717.1
7/10/96	Chancellor Capital Management	U.S. Institutional/HNW	LGT Asset Management	U.S. Fund Sponsor	300.0
7/16/96	Flagship Resources Inc	U.S. Fund Sponsor	John Nuveen Co (St Paul Cos)	U.S. Fund Sponsor	83.0
9/6/96	Keystone Investments Inc	U.S. Fund Sponsor	First Union Corp, Charlotte, NC	U.S. Bank	289.0
9/24/96	Jurika & Voyles Inc	U.S. Institutional/HNW	New England Investment Cos LP	U.S. Fund Sponsor	95.0
					2,689.1
1997 2/14/97	Oppenheimer Capital LP	U.S. Institutional/HNW	PIMCO Advisors LP	U.S. Fund Sponsor	265.0
2/14/97	Voyageur Funds Inc	U.S. Fund Sponsor	Lincoln National Corp	U.S. Insurance	69.0
2/27/97	GMG/Seneca Capital Management	U.S. Institutional/HNW	Phoenix Duff & Phelps Corp	U.S. Fund Sponsor	36.2
6/9/97	Pasadena Capital Corp	U.S. Fund Sponsor	Phoenix Duff & Phelps Corp	U.S. Fund Sponsor	180.0
7/15/97	Rittenhouse Financial Services	U.S. Institutional/HNW	John Nuveen Co (St Paul Cos)	U.S. Fund Sponsor	145.0
7/30/97	American Century Cos	U.S. Fund Sponsor	JP Morgan & Co Inc	U.S. Bank	900.0
8/14/97	Columbia Management Co.	U.S. Fund Sponsor	Fleet Financial Group Inc, MA	U.S. Bank	611.0
8/15/97	Tweedy, Browne Co.	U.S. Fund Sponsor	Affiliated Mgrs. Group	U.S. Fund Sponsor	300.0
11/5/97	Oppenheimer Capital LP	U.S. Institutional/HNW	PIMCO Advisors LP	U.S. Fund Sponsor	792.8
12/9/97	Brandywine Asset Management	U.S. Fund Sponsor	Legg Mason Inc	U.S. Brokerage	129.0
12/11/97	Founders Asset Management Inc	U.S. Fund Sponsor	Mellon Bank Corp, Pittsburg, PA	U.S. Bank	275.0
					3,703.0
1998 1/15/98	Essex Investment Management	U.S. Institutional/HNW	Affiliated Managers Group Inc	U.S. Fund Sponsor	120.1
6/11/98	Crabbe Huson Group Inc	U.S. Fund Sponsor	Liberty Financial Cos.	U.S. Fund Sponsor	96.0
12/18/98	Rorer Asset Management	U.S. Institutional/HNW	Affiliated Managers Group Inc	U.S. Fund Sponsor	100.0
11/10/98	Marsico Capital Management	U.S. Fund Sponsor	Bank of America Corp, Charlotte, NC	U.S. Bank	150.0
12/8/98	Trinity Investment Management	U.S. Institutional/HNW	Oppenheimer Funds	U.S. Fund Sponsor	175.0
12/16/98	Zweig Group	U.S. Fund Sponsor	Phoenix Investment Partners	U.S. Fund Sponsor	164.0
					805.1

Merrill Lynch, Appendix to "Study on Trends in the Fund Management M&A Environment," 2001.

Selected Domestic Transactions (continued)

	Date Announced	Target Name	Classification	Acquiror Name	Classification	Value of Transaction ($mil)
1999	5/13/99	OFFITBANK Holdings Inc.	U.S. Fund Sponsor	Wachovia Corp	U.S. Bank	199.9
	7/22/99	Pilgrim Capital Corp	U.S. Fund Sponsor	ReliaStar Financial Corp	U.S. Insurance	258.0
	10/18/99	Frontier Capital	U.S. Institutional/HNW	Affiliated Managers Group	U.S. Fund Sponsor	150.0
	10/21/99	Money Management Associates LP	U.S. Fund Sponsor	Friedman Billings Ramsey Group	U.S. Brokerage	27.5
						635.4
2000	2/28/00	Legend Group	U.S. Fund Sponsor	Waddell & Reed Financial Inc	U.S. Fund Sponsor	75.0
	3/1/00	Lexington Global Asset Mgrs	U.S. Fund Sponsor	ReliaStar Financial Corp	U.S. Insurance	47.5
	6/7/00	Wanger Asset Management Ltd	U.S. Fund Sponsor	Liberty Financial Cos Inc	U.S. Fund Sponsor	450.0
	6/20/00	Sanford C Bernstein & Co Inc	U.S. Institutional/HNW	Alliance Capital Management	U.S. Fund Sponsor	3,513.0
	6/28/00	Marsico Capital Management	U.S. Fund Sponsor	Bank of America, San Francisco	U.S. Bank	950.0
	10/20/00	Edgemont Asset Management Corp	U.S. Fund Sponsor	Federated Investors	U.S. Fund Sponsor	370.0
	10/25/00	Fiduciary Trust Co Intl	U.S. Institutional/HNW	Franklin Resources Inc	U.S. Fund Sponsor	825.0
						6,230.5

Selected Cross-Border Transactions

	Date Announced	Target Name	Classification	Acquiror Name	Classification	Value of Transaction ($mil)
1990						0.0
						0.0
1991						0.0
						0.0
1992						0.0
						0.0
1993	3/9/93	John Govett & Co Ltd (Berkeley)	Foreign Fund Sponsor	Bear Stearns Cos Inc	U.S. Brokerage	48.2
	10/8/93	Beutel Goodman & Co	Foreign Fund Sponsor	Duff & Phelps Corp	U.S. Fund Sponsor	29.9
						78.1
1994	8/31/94	Brinson Partners Inc	U.S. Fund Sponsor	Schweizerischer Bankverein	Foreign Multiline	750.0
						750.0
1995	4/11/95	Kemper Corporation	U.S. Fund Sponsor	Zurich Group	Foreign Insurance	2,000.0
	10/24/95	Cursitor Eaton Ast Mgmt, Cursit	Foreign Institutional/HNW	Alliance Capital Management LP	U.S. Fund Sponsor	141.5
						2,141.5
1996	3/4/96	Aberdeen Trust Holdings PLC	Foreign Fund Sponsor	Phoenix Home Life Mutual	U.S. Insurance	37.5
	5/13/96	AFP Habitat (Inversiones Previ)	Foreign Fund Sponsor	Citicorp	U.S. Multiline	80.0
	11/4/96	AIM Management Group Inc	U.S. Fund Sponsor	Invesco PLC	Foreign Fund Sponsor	2,200.0
	11/20/96	Altamira Management Ltd	Foreign Fund Sponsor	TA Associates	U.S. Institutional/HNW	179.1
						2,496.6
1997	3/25/97	Montgomery Asset Management	U.S. Fund Sponsor	Commerzbank	Foreign Bank	250.0
	5/28/97	Credit Lyonnais Intl Asset Mgmt	Foreign Fund Sponsor	Nicholas-Applegate Capital	U.S. Fund Sponsor	30.0
	6/27/97	Scudder, Stevens & Clark	U.S. Fund Sponsor	Zurich Group	Foreign Insurance	1,629.0
	11/19/97	Mercury Asset Management Group	Foreign Fund Sponsor	Merrill Lynch & Co Inc	U.S. Brokerage	5,074.4
						6,983.4
1998	4/13/98	Nelson Money Managers Plc	Foreign Institutional/HNW	Kansas City Southern (Stilwell)	U.S. Fund Sponsor	32.0
	5/8/98	Weiss, Peck & Greer	U.S. Fund Sponsor	Robeco	Foreign Fund Sponsor	400.0
	6/1/98	Reinhardt Werba Bowen Inc	U.S. Institutional/HNW	Assante Capital Management Inc	Foreign Fund Sponsor	30.0
	7/24/98	Newton Management Ltd	Foreign Fund Sponsor	Dreyfus Corp	U.S. Bank	210.5
						672.5
1999	2/15/99	Warburg Pincus Asset Mgmt	U.S. Fund Sponsor	Credit Suisse Asset Management	Foreign Multiline	650.0
	6/18/99	BTFund Mgmt, BT Invest Svcs	Foreign Fund Sponsor	Principal Financial Group Inc	U.S. Insurance	1,303.7
	6/18/99	BT Funds Management NZ	Foreign Fund Sponsor	Principal Financial Group Inc	U.S. Insurance	67.2
	10/18/99	Johnson Fry Holdings PLC	Foreign Fund Sponsor	Legg Mason (UK) Holdings Ltd	U.S. Brokerage	70.0
	10/31/99	PIMCO Advisors LP	U.S. Fund Sponsor	Allianz AG	Foreign Multiline	3,216.0
						5,306.9
2000	3/10/00	Perigee Inc	Foreign Fund Sponsor	Legg Mason Inc	U.S. Brokerage	208.0
	3/30/00	Gartmore Investment Management	Foreign Fund Sponsor	Nationwide Mutual Insurance Co	U.S. Insurance	1,635.2
	4/11/00	Rowe Price-Fleming Internation	Foreign Fund Sponsor	T Rowe Price Associates Inc	U.S. Fund Sponsor	780.0
	5/15/00	Pioneer Group Inc	U.S. Fund Sponsor	Unicredito Italiano	Foreign Bank	1,226.3
	5/16/00	Tilney Holdings Ltd	Foreign Institutional/HNW	Forstmann-Leff & Associates	U.S. Fund Sponsor	52.3
	6/16/00	NVEST LP	U.S. Fund Sponsor	CDC Asset Management Europe	Foreign Bank	2,186.2
	6/19/00	United Asset Management Corp	U.S. Fund Sponsor	Old Mutual PLC	Foreign Insurance	2,201.5
	7/26/00	Bissett & Assoc Invt Mgmt Ltd	Foreign Fund Sponsor	Franklin Resources, Inc.	U.S. Fund Sponsor	97.4
	8/16/00	MasterLink Securities Inv Trust	Foreign Fund Sponsor	Prudential Ins. Co. of America	U.S. Insurance	95.0
	8/31/00	Glenwood Financial Group	U.S. Fund Sponsor	E.D.F. Man Group Plc	Foreign Fund Sponsor	110.0
	10/18/00	Alleghany Asset Management Inc.	U.S. Fund Sponsor	ABN-AMRO Holding, NV	Foreign Bank	825.0
	10/18/00	Nicholas-Applegate Capt Mgmt	U.S. Fund Sponsor	Allianz AG	Foreign Multiline	1,613.8
						11,030.7

::::: **CASE STUDY**

Balancing Interests in a Fund Merger

Over the past few years, the merger activity in the mutual fund industry has sharply accelerated. Some of the mergers involved fund companies trying to fill out their line of products. An illustration is the acquisition of Templeton's management company, which has a strong reputation for international stock funds, by Franklin's management company, with its heavy emphasis on bond funds. Other mergers involved institutionally oriented securities firms seeking more distribution to retail investors. An illustration is the acquisition of Dean Witter, a retail wire house, by Morgan Stanley, with its institutional client base. Still others involve banks that want to gain a foothold in the mutual fund industry. An illustration is the acquisition of Dreyfus, an investment manager for a broad line of mutual funds, by Mellon National Bank. The following case study discusses several mergers in the mutual fund industry and the early results of the consolidations.

The acquisition of a fund management company raises difficult questions because, under the Investment Company Act of 1940, a change in control of an investment adviser to a mutual fund automatically terminates the advisory contract. Thus, the acquirer must obtain approval of a new or renewed advisory contract from the independent directors of the relevant funds as well as the shareholders of those funds. In reality, the acquirer is buying the assistance of the prior adviser in obtaining these director and shareholder approvals. In 1970, Congress enacted special rules for any acquisition of a mutual fund adviser, requiring that such an acquisition not impose "an unfair burden" on the mutual funds involved and further that at least 75% of the directors of such funds be independent for at least three years after such acquisition.

After an investment manager for one set of mutual funds acquires an investment manager for another set of mutual funds and obtains the necessary director and shareholder approvals, the acquiring investment manager often reexamines the resulting product line. There may be overlap between mutual funds previously advised by the investment manager and mutual funds in the new complex. Alternatively, there may be small funds in the prior or new complex that have never been successful. Either case may lead to the possibility of fund mergers, which must be approved by the independent directors of both funds, as well as the shareholders of the fund being merged out of existence.

This case study presents this type of situation. American Guardian has recently acquired Best Management and now wants to consider merging two funds: one from American Guardian's prior complex and the other from the Best complex. At the year-end board meetings for both fund complexes, executives of Best American (the name of the combined management firm) must make recommendations on merging these two funds. Since fund mergers require director and shareholder votes, the rationale for the merger is extremely important. It must make sense for all major stakeholders: Best American, the independent directors and shareholders of both funds, as well as the brokers who sell them.

Discussion Questions

As a respected member of the CFO's staff, you have been requested to attend the preboard meeting of Best American executives to map out a strategy. After reviewing the materials provided, you should be prepared to answer the following questions:

1. a. What should be the advisory fee of the combined fund? Is a breakpoint a good idea?
    b. What would you recommend regarding the choice of portfolio manager?
2. a. What should be the proposal for distribution fees—sales loads and 12b-1 fees—for the combined fund?
    b. What changes, if any, should be made to the brokers' compensation structure?
3. a. How much asset growth is needed to pay for the sales force expansion?
    b. What level of fund sales would you project for next year?
4. a. What service fees should be proposed for the combined fund?
    b. Should the fund use an external or internal transfer agent?
    c. How much investment in service development seems reasonable over the next few years?
5. In light of the answers to the above questions, what does the combined P&L look like (see Exhibit 2 in the case study materials)?
6. Should Best American offer a Class B pricing structure—declining back-end load with 12b-1 fee—for the combined fund?

EXHIBIT 1

Fund characteristics

	American Guardian (Patriot Growth)	Best Management (Western Growth)	Industry Median
Distribution channel	Intermediary	Intermediary	
Type of funds sold	Domestic equity growth/capital appreciation Class A	Domestic equity growth/capital appreciation Class A	
Transfer agent	Outsourced	Internal	
Size of fund	$3.0B	$2.5B	
Current fees			
Advisory fees	58 bp	44 bp	52 bp
12b-1 fees	25 bp (25 bp to broker-dealer)	35 bp (30 bp to broker-dealer)	25 bp (25 bp to broker-dealer)
Service fees	15 bp	19 bp	17 bp
Total expense ratio	98 bp	98 bp	94 bp
Load structure			
Front end	5% (4.5% to broker-dealer)	5% (4.5% to broker-dealer)	5% (4.5% to broker-dealer)

a. What factors should management consider in this decision?

b. How would you price the Class B share so that it would be comparable to Class A? Exhibit 3 provides a comparison of Class A and Class B pricing for a competitor which has both classes of funds but which has a different pricing structure than either American Guardian or Best Management.

You should frame your answers in the context of each major stakeholder for these important decisions. You should state why the proposed merger and resulting business decisions make sense for:

• The independent directors of both funds,
• The shareholders of both funds,
• The brokerage firms that sell both funds, and
• Best American

Best American Management

Earlier this year, two mutual fund management companies, American Guardian, Inc. and Best Management, Inc. entered into an agreement under which American Guardian would purchase all of the issued and outstanding stock of Best Management and merge Best Management into American Guardian. Although the companies are now combined, there are still two separate boards of directors for the funds. Each fund complex retained the same independent board members previously elected by the shareholders, but company-appointed directors were reevaluated and will be consistent for both boards. The combined entity, Best American Management, is now in the process of reviewing existing products and services and looking for opportunities to leverage its increased size.

American Guardian was a 30-year old Boston-based mutual fund complex. This fairly staid, conservative company was well known but had not been particularly innovative in fund distribution or shareholder servicing. It had historically chosen to distribute mainly through broker-dealers and outsourced its transfer agent process. The relatively new CEO of American Guardian firmly believed that

EXHIBIT 2

1996 Proforma P&L

	American Patriot Growth $000	bp	Best Western Growth $000	bp	Newly merged fund (1-year forward) $000	bp
Annualized average assets	3,000,000		2,500,000			
Projected gross sales	0		250,000			
Revenue:						
Sales loads, net (50 bp on sales)	0	0	1,250	5		
Management fees	17,400	58	11,000	44		
Subtotal net advisory fees	17,400	58	12,250	49		
12b-1 fees, net	0	0	1,250	5		
Fund accounting/transfer agent fees	4,500	15	4,750	19		
Subtotal service fees	4,500	15	4,750	19		
Total revenue	21,900	73	18,250	73		
Expense:						
Fund management	7,500	25	6,250	25		
Sales support	3,000	10	3,750	15		
Fund accounting/transfer agent	4,500	15	6,250	25		
Subtotal operations expense						
Total expense	15,000	50	16,250	65		
Pretax income	6,900	23	2,000	8		
After tax income (40% tax rate)	4,140	14	1,200	5		
After tax margin	18.9%		6.6%			

in today's highly competitive environment, mutual fund complexes must "grow or die." He saw an acquisition as a necessary step to ensure that his firm's products and services would be attractive to investors and their advisers in the future.

Best Management was a fast-growing Boston-based mutual fund complex. The 15-year old company was recognized as a leader in the use of technology, having invested millions in upgrading its internal transfer agent–shareholder servicing affiliate. Rapid growth had begun to strain the firm's capabilities, however, and further investment in shareholder servicing was needed for coming years.

Both complexes had several funds, and a review of Best American Management's newly combined product line reveals that a few of the funds have very similar investment objectives and holdings. In particular, there are now two

domestic equity growth funds sold through the intermediary channel. The possibility of merging these two funds, American Patriot Growth and Best Western Growth, is currently under discussion by Best American management.

American Patriot Growth, Class A (front-end load), has $3 billion in assets and has outperformed 45% of its peers over the past three years. The fee structure consists of a 58 bp advisory fee, a 25 bp 12b-1 fee (all of which is paid out to the selling broker-dealer) and a 15 bp transfer agent–service fee. Total fees are slightly above the industry median for this type of fund (see Exhibit 1). In addition, the fund carries a 5% load, 4.5% of which is retained by the broker who sold the fund. Gross sales for the most recent 12 months are negligible. Fund profitability for American Patriot Growth is forecast to be positive for the year (see Exhibit 2).

Best Western Growth, Class A (front-end load), has

EXHIBIT 3

Comparison of share class pricing for competitor X

A Share		Initial investment	$10,000			Sales charge	4.00%		12b-1 fees		0.40%
		Growth rate	8%			Commission	3.75%		Broker re-allowance		0.20%
		NPV discount rate	10%						Advisory fee + other exp.		0.70%

	Year 1	Year 2	Year 3	Year 4	Year 5	Year 6	Year 7	Year 8	Year 9	Year 10
Beginning investment (after load)	$9,600	$10,262	$10,971	$11,727	$12,537	$13,402	$14,326	$15,315	$16,372	$17,501
Net appreciation	$662	$708	$757	$809	$865	$925	$989	$1,057	$1,130	$1,208
Shareholder ending value	$10,262	$10,971	$11,727	$12,537	$13,402	$14,326	$15,315	$16,372	$17,501	$18,709
Sales charge	$400	$0	$0	$0	$0	$0	$0	$0	$0	$0
12b-1 fees	$40	$42	$45	$49	$52	$55	$59	$63	$68	$72
NPV of distribution-related expenses	$436	$471	$505	$538	$571	$602	$632	$662	$691	$719
NPV of distribution-related expenses retained	$43	$61	$78	$94	$110	$126	$141	$156	$170	$184
Sales charge commissions	$375	$0	$0	$0	$0	$0	$0	$0	$0	$0
12b-1 trailer	$20	$21	$23	$24	$26	$28	$30	$32	$34	$36
NPV of broker compensation	$393	$411	$428	$444	$460	$476	$491	$506	$520	$534

B Share		Initial investment	$10,000		CDSC	4,3.5,3,		12b-1 fees*			1.00%
		Growth rate	8%			2.5,2,1,0%		Broker re-allowance			0.20%
		NPV discount rate	10%		Commission	3.75%		Advisory fee + other exp.			0.70%

	Year 1	Year 2	Year 3	Year 4	Year 5	Year 6	Year 7	Year 8	Year 9	Year 10
Beginning investment	$10,000	$10,630	$11,300	$12,012	$12,768	$13,573	$14,428	$15,337	$16,395	$17,526
Net appreciation	$630	$670	$712	$757	$804	$855	$909	$1,058	$1,131	$1,209
Shareholder ending value	$10,630	$11,300	$12,012	$12,768	$13,573	$14,428	$15,337	$16,395	$17,526	$18,736
CDSC on redemption	$400	$350	$300	$250	$200	$100	$0	$0	$0	$0
Ending value with redemption	$10,230	$10,950	$11,712	$12,518	$13,373	$14,328	$15,337	$16,395	$17,526	$18,736
12b-1 fees	$103	$110	$117	$124	$132	$140	$149	$63	$68	$73
NPV of distr-related expenses with redemption	$94	$184	$272	$357	$438	$517	$594	$623	$652	$680
	$457	$474	$497	$527	$563	$574	$594	$623	$652	$680
NPV of distr-related expenses retained with redemption	($300)	($227)	($157)	($90)	($24)	$39	$100	$115	$129	$143
	$64	$62	$68	$81	$100	$95	$100	$115	$129	$143
Sales charge commissions	$375	$0	$0	$0	$0	$0	$0	$0	$0	$0
12b-1 trailer	$21	$22	$23	$25	$26	$28	$30	$32	$34	$36
NPV of broker compensation	$394	$412	$429	$446	$463	$478	$494	$509	$523	$537

*converts to the A Share12b-1 schedule at the beginning of year 8

above-average performance and has received favorable press coverage recently. The fund has $2.5 billion in assets and has beaten 72% of its competitors in the prior three years. Best's fee structure for domestic equities consists of a 44 bp advisory fee, 35 bp 12b-1 fee (30 of which is paid out to the selling broker-dealer) and a 19 bp transfer agent–service fee. Total fees for the fund are above the industry median (see Exhibit 1). Best Western Growth also carries the same load structure that American Patriot Growth does. Currently, gross sales are running at 10% of assets, and Best Western Growth is forecast to produce a marginal profit for the year (see Exhibit 2).

Because there has been increased attention on fees throughout the industry, both broker-sold funds have come under some adverse scrutiny of late for their total expense ratios of nearly 1% (100 bp). Management of the new firm has been considering introducing a break point pricing structure to the advisory fee of a potentially combined fund to help address this issue. For example, one idea being considered (after establishing a base advisory fee) is a reduction of 1 bp of advisory fee once combined assets reach $6 billion and an additional 1 bp for every $3 billion increase in assets thereafter.

Since both funds are distributed through the intermediary channel, any merged fund would also be sold through the existing network of broker-dealers. American Guardian's funds were primarily sold through Merrill Lynch and Dean Witter. Although Best Management also had a good relationship with Merrill Lynch, the majority of sales were made through Smith Barney. In general, brokers receive at least 25 bp 12b-1 fee on Class A securities from most fund companies, in addition to the front-end load of 4.5%. Any attempt to reduce these fees would likely be met with resistance and might hinder the brokers' willingness to promote the fund(s).

As summarized in Exhibit 2, both funds currently incur 25 bp of investment management expense, which includes portfolio management, research, trading and investment support. The portfolio manager of American Patriot Growth has been with the fund for many years. He has indicated a willingness to shift into a different role with the combined firm, should management so desire. The impact of his total compensation and related expenses on the fund management expense is approximately 2 bp. The portfolio manager of Best Western Growth is viewed as a rising star within the industry. She is very popular with the brokerage firms and has a good performance record for the short term and longer term. The impact of her total expense on the fund management expense is approximately 1.5 bp.

American Patriot Growth most recently spent 10 bp on sales support, while Best Western Growth spent approximately 15 bp. These expenses consist of a wholesaling sales force and other support for the brokers who sell the fund. American Patriot Growth has three wholesalers, and Best Western Growth has five. The senior sales executive

for the combined firm believes that all of them will stay on and hopes to be able to add two more wholesalers to gather additional assets.

Best Western Growth spends considerably more than American Patriot Growth on servicing (25 bp versus 17 bp) due to the fact that it has chosen an internal transfer agent strategy, while American Patriot Growth uses an external third-party servicing agent. American Patriot Growth's service quality is considered to be adequate, and Best Western Growth's is above average. The head of operations, who was with Best Management, has estimated that he could service American Patriot Growth with an incremental spending level of half that incurred by Patriot Growth in the last year. However, the expected cost to continue developing their internal servicing capability is substantial. After combining these servicing resources, he estimates that operations expense will grow in line with the expected growth in assets for the next three to five years.

At the December board meetings, company executives must present their recommendations for changes to these funds. This week's Funds' Operations meeting will focus on merging the two similar domestic equity funds. Since fund mergers require director and shareholder votes, the rationale for the merger is extremely important. It must make sense for all major stakeholders: Best American, the shareholders of both funds and the brokers that sell them.

EXHIBIT 4

When your manager sells out, should you?*

James M. Clash

A wave of consolidation is washing over the mutual fund business. So far this year funds totaling more than $125 billion in assets have changed hands. To hear the consolidators tell it, mergers are good because they bring fund investors economies of scale and breadth of choice within a fund family. Will these promises be fulfilled? It is instructive to consider some of the bigger recent mergers. The results are not encouraging.

Take the Dreyfus funds, purchased in December 1993 by Pittsburgh's Mellon Bank. In the three years before the merger, the 12 domestic stock funds at Dreyfus performed, on average, on a par with the S&P 500 index. In the three years since, these funds, on average, have underperformed the index by a stunning seven percentage points a year.

Then there's the American Capital/Van Kampen merger in August 1994. In the 26 months prior to the marriage, the 11 stock funds here outperformed the S&P 500 index by an average of two points annually. In the 26 months since the merger, the funds have underperformed, by two points annually. (See Table 1)

Do fund shareholders at least benefit from economies of scale? Not really. Average expenses at both the Dreyfus and American Capital families are just about where they were before they changed hands, notwithstanding that assets are up.

Even the Templeton family seems to be suffering from postmerger letdown. These mostly international funds, founded by the revered investor John Templeton, are still market beaters, but they have seen a sharp falloff in how much they beat their benchmarks.

San Mateo, California–based Franklin Resources bought control of the Templeton Family for $786 million on Oct. 30, 1992. The move gave Franklin, then primarily a bond fund firm, an instant international equity presence—and reputation—that helped market the combined firm's assets.

Templeton's two star managers, Mark Mobius and Mark Holowesko, signed what were essentially four-year employment contracts and were given fat cash bonuses and salary increases. Sir John Templeton, already cutting back from daily operations, bowed out almost entirely when the acquisition was finalized.

Not long after the merger, trouble began. Templeton's managers were not happy with the new bonus structure; suddenly their bonuses weren't linked just to their equity performance but to Franklin bond mangers' performances, too. Templeton Chief Executive Thomas Hansberger quit in 1993 to found a rival institutional firm, Hansberger's Global Investors, and took a bunch of Templeton staffers with him. Recently there has been further attrition as employment contracts begin to expire.

What has all this meant to Templeton's shareholders? All four of Templeton's big open-end international equity funds with at least four years on each side of the merger (a combined $27 billion in assets) show postmerger return declines against their respective benchmarks. (See Table 2.) The average drop in relative annual performance: a stunning six percentage points.

What about the hoped-for economies of scale? They didn't happen. While average assets in these four Templeton funds have more than doubled, expenses have not gone down. They have increased by a third, from an average $0.84. per $100 of assets annually to an average of $1.12.

This is not to say that the Templeton funds are a disaster for investors. Even with the relative petering out of their returns, the four still beat their Morgan Stanley benchmarks for international funds. But the simple fact is that they are not the winners they once were.

Mark Holowesko, president of the global equity group at Templeton, explains the postmerger weakening of performance as a consequence of too small a dose of Japanese stocks. He says expenses are up because the funds are invested in more countries, some of them—like Russia and Poland—very expensive to research. Holowesko says he plans to stay. Templeton's departure was not as traumatic as it may have seemed; the founder had already ceded most stock picking decisions in the late 1980s.

There has always been a question about whether fund buyouts are good for shareholders of the acquired firms. But this year, with a record half-dozen big fund acquisitions announced—including $50 billion-plus American Capital/Van Kampen by Morgan Stanley, and $57 billion AIM Management Group by INVESCO Funds Group Inc.—the stakes have risen.

TABLE 1

Dreyfus and Amcap

Fund family	Average Return		Average Expenses (per $100)		Average Assets ($ millions)	
	Before	*After*	*Before*	*After*	*Before*	*After*
Mellon/Dreyfus	−0.1	−7.2	$1.11	$1.14	$481	$535
American Capital/Van Kampen	1.8	−1.7	1.30	1.35	477	648

Mellon/Dreyfus: Premerger Dec. 31, 1990, to Nov. 30, 1993. Postmerger Nov. 30, 1993, to Oct. 31, 1996.
American Capital/Van Kampen: Premerger June 30, 1992, to Aug. 31, 1994. Postmerger Aug. 31, 1994, to Oct. 31, 1996.
All numbers are annual averages. Returns are domestic equity, against the S&P 500 index, in percentage points.
Note: These two families, consisting mainly of U.S. stock funds, petered out after recent mergers.
Source: Morningstar, Inc.

TABLE 2

Templeton

Fund family	Average Return		Average Expenses (per $100)		Average Assets ($ millions)	
	Before	*After*	*Before*	*After*	*Before*	*After*
Templeton Global Small Cos I	5.8	0.4	$1.05	$1.29	$858	$1,326
Templeton Growth I	7.7	1.9	0.74	1.03	2,581	5,815
Templeton World I	4.6	2.9	0.74	1.02	4,187	5,334
Templeton Foreign I	13.8	1.1	0.83	1.12	937	5,391

Premerger Oct. 31, 1988, to Oct. 31, 1992. Postmerger October 31, 1992, to Oct. 31, 1996.
All numbers are annual averages. Returns are in percentage points versus Morgan Stanley World Index, *except Templeton Foreign (versus Morgan Stanley EAFE).*
Note: These Templeton international stock funds, representing $27 billion in combined assets, have cooled significantly versus their comparison indexes since Franklin bought Templeton in 1992. But they've all managed to beat their benchmarks.
Source: Morningstar, Inc.

Arguments for consolidation are simple. First, lower expenses should be realized through economies of scale from combining back-office operations. Second, increased purchasing clout with a larger asset pool should result in better access to Wall Street research. Finally, if the fund family being acquired is small, consolidation can free money managers from diversions like marketing so they can spend more time picking stocks.

Arguments against consolidation are less tangible, James Margard, chief equity strategist at $3 billion Rainier Investment Management, a pension fund manager in Seattle, maintains that stock pickers are much sharper when they're independent. "They got complacent once they cash out and buy the big sail boat," says Margard, who has been approached by several firms interested in gobbling up his 15-year-old company, which runs the excellent mutual fund Rainier Core Equity Portfolio. So far, he has resisted. "My investors are better off when I'm hungry," he says.

There's also the potential for disharmony when two corporations merge, and it can affect the performance of money managers, even causing some to quit. When Merrill Lynch bought $9 billion Hotchkis & Wiley this year, most of the bond department left.

What should you do if your fund company sells out? If the portfolio manager of a fund you are in stays put, it probably makes sense to give the new owners a chance. But keep a close eye on the situation. Franklin just paid some $610 million for Heines Securities, operator of the excellent Mutual Series fund run by Michael Price. Supposedly Price's attention has been secured by a five-year contract and up to $193 million in performance incentives. But Price can go part-time after just one year, so his heart may not be in the job after that.

The other thing to watch for is the cost of ownership. If expenses climb, consider departing. The hitherto no-load Mutual Series funds have often been on the *Forbes* Best Buy list for U.S. equity funds. They will have a hard time staying there; effective Nov. 1, Franklin began charging a sales commission of up to 4.5%.

Mutual Funds as Institutional Investors

Mutual funds have become substantial owners of the common stocks of publicly traded corporations in recent years. As a result, mutual funds in the aggregate possess significant voting power over certain corporate actions, such as elections of directors or corporate mergers. In particular, mutual funds may become potential swing votes during battles for corporate control waged by others through proxy fights or takeover bids.

This Chapter begins by reviewing statistics on mutual funds and other institutional investors as stockholders of publicly traded companies.[1] It then describes the rights mutual funds have as stockholders[2] of U.S. companies and the regulatory regime governing the exercise of those rights. It goes on to explain the voting guidelines and practices of most mutual funds, as well as the limited role they play as institutional activists in the United States. It also outlines the corporate governance issues faced by U.S. mutual funds that own publicly traded common stock of foreign companies. This Chapter concludes with a case study in which an investment adviser to a mutual fund complex is asked to vote in two related proxy fights.

I. The Increasing Importance of Mutual Funds as Stockholders

A. Growth of Stock Ownership by Institutional Investors

Within the past two decades, institutional investors have come to own a majority of the common stock of most publicly traded American companies. Institutional investors include mutual funds, pension plans, insurance companies, banks and foundations. As Table 11.1 details, the average aggregate share of institutional holdings in the largest 1,000 U.S. corporations (by market capitalization) increased significantly over the past decade. Similarly, as Table 11.2 details, the concentration of institutional ownership in the largest U.S. corporations has generally increased over the past decade. However, both tables show a modest decline between 1995 and 3Q 1999 in certain brackets.

B. Growth of Equity Mutual Funds

Equity mutual funds, in particular, have acquired a larger percentage of the outstanding common stock of U.S. publicly traded companies, especially during the past few years. This trend over the past decade is quantified in Table 11.3. As of 1999, the relative share of mutual fund holdings had grown to 17.8% of the total equities outstanding in the United States, larger than any other category of institutional investor.

TABLE 11.1

Institutional investor concentration of ownership in the largest 1,000 U.S. corporations by bracket, 1990–3Q 1999

Top Corporations	Average Institutional Holdings		
	1990	1995	3Q 1999
1–50	50.1%	52.9%	58.2%
51–100	59.2	61.8	56.6
101–250	54.7	58.4	62.5
251–500	51.1	59.0	60.2
501–750	47.5	59.4	57.4
751–1000	44.6	52.5	52.3

Source: The Conference Board, "Institutional Investment Report." Calculated from the Brancato Report (1990–1995) and Thompson Financial (1999) databases. Reprinted by permission of The Conference Board.

Within the category of equity mutual funds, Fidelity Investments is the largest owner of U.S. equity, followed by Vanguard, Capital Group (which includes American Funds and Capital Guardian Trust Company), Putnam and Janus (which is owned by the same firm that owns Berger). The largest 10 equity mutual fund complexes in total held 55% of all equity assets held by the U.S. mutual fund industry, as shown by Table 11.4.

This substantial growth in institutional ownership of U.S. equity assets has broad implications for the governance of publicly traded U.S. companies. The concentration of ownership in the hands of sophisticated institutional investors, together with the Securities and Exchange Commission's (SEC) adoption of stockholder reporting and

TABLE 11.2

Institutional investor concentration of ownership in the largest 1,000 U.S. corporations by percentage of holdings, 1990–3Q 1999

% of Equity Held by Institutional Investors	% of the Top 1,000 U.S. Companies		
	1990	1995	3Q 1999
Over 90%	0.3%	4.2%	5.5%
Over 80%	3.0	15.8	17.6
Over 70%	15.9	31.0	37.3
Over 60%	33.4	50.1	54.2
Over 50%	50.4	65.0	66.6
Over 40%	65.4	75.7	75.9
Over 30%	78.9	86.5	84.1
Over 20%	88.5	92.9	89.1

Source: The Conference Board, "Institutional Investment Report." Calculated from the Brancato Report (1990–1995), and Thompson Financial (1999) databases. Reprinted by permission of The Conference Board.

TABLE 11.3

Share of total U.S. equities outstanding, by investor type, 1989–1999

	1990	1995	1999
Households	51.0%	48.5%	42.4%
Institutions	49.0	51.5	57.6
(Type of Institution, by percent of institutional holdings)			
Mutual funds	6.6	12.1	17.8
Private pension funds	16.8	14.6	13.2
Public pension funds	7.6	9.3	10.8
Foreign	6.9	6.2	6.4
Life insurance companies	2.3	3.7	5.0
Bank personal trusts	5.4	2.6	1.8
Other insurance companies	2.3	1.6	1.1
State and local governments	0.1	0.3	0.7
Closed-end funds	0.5	0.4	0.2
Other	0.6	0.7	0.6

Source: The Securities Industry Association Fact Book (2001).

TABLE 11.4

Top 10 firms managing equity mutual fund assets, year end 2000

Rank	Parent Firm	Equity Fund Assets ($ millions)[a]
1	Fidelity Investments	611,659
2	Vanguard	386,269
3	The Capital Group (American Funds + Capital Guardian)	337,452
4	Marsh McLennan (Putnam)	235,848
5	Stilwell (Janus + Berger)	215,719
6	TIAA-CREF	156,500
7	AmvesCap (AIM + Invesco)	151,791
8	Morgan Stanley Dean Witter (various)	136,848
9	Franklin Resources Inc. (Franklin + Templeton)	115,247
10	Sun Life of Canada (MFS)	114,427
	Top 10 parent firms	2,461,759
	As percentage of industry	55%
	Total industry equity mutual funds[b]	4,496,433

[a]Includes variable annuity assets, which are based on "actual adviser" (not subadviser) as reported by Strategic Insight.
[b]Total equity assets reported by Strategic Insight differ from those reported by the Investment Company Institute and shown elsewhere in this book.
Sources: Strategic Insight Simfund and Simfund VA; parent firms assigned by author for analytic purposes.

communication rules, enables corporate management, as well as those seeking to change corporate policy or effect a change in control, to identify and solicit the support of key stockholders. Yet most institutional investors focus on managing portfolios with equity holdings in a large number of publicly traded companies and typically avoid involvement in the operations of these companies. Instead, institutional investors generally let top executives and directors run these companies, subject to the rewards and punishment of stock price movements. Whether institutional investors, and mutual funds in particular, should be doing more or less in terms of monitoring corporate governance and whether such efforts are likely to have a significant market impact is a subject of intense debate. We will focus on this debate later in this Chapter, after describing the legal and policy context in which mutual funds exercise their rights as stockholders.

II. Legal Framework

A. General Role of Stockholders

To understand the role of mutual funds in the corporate governance process, it is important to review the traditional role of public stockholders in this process. Stockholders do not directly control the company's policies or business strategy. Instead, they elect a board of directors to represent their interests and provide strategic direction for the company; the board, in turn, appoints management to operate the company day to day. Stockholders retain a voice in corporate governance through the exercise of limited but important rights: election of directors as well as approval of significant corporate events, such as authorization of shares for issuance, mergers with other corporations and adoption of certain stock option plans.

Under state corporate law, companies are required to call a meeting of stockholders at least once a year, as well as whenever stockholder approval of a significant corporate action is required. Ordinarily, most stockholders do not attend such meetings; rather, they complete ballots, known as proxies, that direct management to vote for or against the proposals on the ballot.

Operating under this traditional framework for corporate governance, the stockholders of publicly traded companies were usually passive during most of the twentieth century. Annual meetings generally were sleepy affairs, where public stockholders regularly approved agenda items with little comment or dissent. Although stockholders owned the company, they were atomized and diffuse (other than management and a few insiders) so that they typically were not significant players in changing or influencing the decisions of company executives. While communication among stockholders was difficult and expensive, stockholders had an easier way of expressing their displeasure with management. If stockholders disagreed with the policies pursued by the top management of a publicly traded company, they simply sold the stock (this is known as the "Wall Street Rule").

Today, most actively managed mutual funds still adhere to the Wall Street Rule. Its efficacy is undeniable in sending clear signals through stock price movements as to whether management is winning or losing the battle for investor support. Stock prices have enormous influence on the ability of a company to raise additional capital, make acquisitions using stock as payment as well as attract and retain top talent through stock options. The increased use of stock options as compensation, while controversial in light of the large sums generated for management in certain situations, was pushed by institutional investors precisely because of the desire to align the interests of management with the interests of investors. Selling a stock, or avoiding buying a stock, is the quickest and most direct way to express displeasure with management. But there are times when selling shares is not desirable or not a viable option—for instance, when an institutional investor holds a very large position in a thinly traded stock.

Under state corporate law, shareholders are free to sell their shares to anyone unless the corporate charter or bylaws impose reasonable restrictions on sale. Such restrictions are used typically to maintain control in closely held companies that are not publicly traded. But a few publicly traded companies have two classes of shares: one with greater voting power for the founding family and another with weaker voting rights for everyone else.[3] Similarly, shareholders generally are permitted to sell shares at any mutually agreeable price. In certain situations, however, control shareholders receiving a premium above the market price for selling their shares have been required to share such a premium with minority shareholders.[4]

The recent rise of stockholder activism gave institutional investors like mutual funds an alternative to just selling their shares if they were dissatisfied with a company's performance. Because of the substantial increase in battles for corporate control, institutional investors have enhanced their understanding of their rights as stockholders and learned how to exercise those rights more effectively. Institutional investors have become particularly knowledgeable about the regulatory framework for proxy fights, shareholder resolutions and takeover bids.

B. The Regulatory Framework for Proxy Fights, Shareholder Resolutions and Takeover Bids

In their role as stockholders, mutual funds benefit from and are subject to various rights and restrictions created by corporate charters and stock exchange rules as well as state and federal law. The starting point in any battle for corporate control is the company's charter and by-laws, which delineate the scope of shareholder activity in important areas such as voting power and access to corporate information, subject to the minimum rights guaranteed to stockholders under applicable state law. State corporate law requires a majority (or two-thirds in a few states) to approve a range of fundamental corporate changes. Such changes typically include authorization of additional shares, merger with another company, amendments to the corporate charter and liquidation of the company.

Most states allow companies incorporated in that state to adopt "anti-takeover" measures, such as shareholder rights plans (commonly known as "poison pills.")[5] These measures generally improve a board's ability to control the timing and the ultimate success of any attempt to take over a company through a tender offer or merger. Anti-takeover devices, such as poison pills, spread rapidly during the 1980s in response to the substantial number of hostile takeover attempts during that era. Whether anti-takeover devices enhance or harm stockholder value maximization is an issue subject to substantial debate (outlined later in this Chapter). The ability of a board to thwart a takeover, even if a majority of stockholders would favor the takeover proposal, has raised significant questions about the degree of management accountability in these situations. In practice, however, anti-takeover devices rarely end up precluding a takeover entirely, as boards often bow to stockholder pressure and solicit the most attractive price possible. Ultimately, most acquisitions are negotiated (even if initially contentious or unwanted); although an initial bidder may fail, it still can put the company "in play," which ultimately may cause it to be acquired by someone else.

Stockholders are not the only ones affected by takeovers. The political reaction against the aftermath of some takeovers in the 1980s, such as plant closings and layoffs, prompted adoption of "stakeholder constituency" statutes in a few states. These statutes permit (but do not require) boards of directors to "take into account" the consequences for constituencies beyond the company's stockholders, such as employees, customers, and local communities, when evaluating whether to support a proposed acquisition. The provisions in these statutes are so vague and discretionary that they allow a board of directors to reject a takeover bid by taking into account the interests of the local community and then ignore these interests when accepting a subsequent takeover bid at a higher price.

In other states, stockholders retain some protection against a partial takeover, for less than all the shares of a company, through "control share statutes." These statutes prevent an acquirer from engaging in transactions with the target company for several years after a takeover unless the acquirer obtains more than 80% of the company's stock in the initial takeover. Thus, by not tendering their shares in response to an initial takeover bid, minority stockholders such as mutual funds with substantial share positions can effectively deter such a takeover or bring about an increase in the purchase price.

Absent an acquisition attempt, minority stockholders rarely have an opportunity to force a change in management through a proxy vote. Incumbent management usually controls enough votes, directly and through the proxy solicitation process, to reelect directors and retain their officer positions. Moreover, many companies have adopted boards with staggered terms[6] to provide continuity in direction and delay a change in control through a proxy contest. However, from time to time, a substantial stockholder or potential acquirer nominates an alternative slate of directors and solicits proxies in support of this alternative slate. In such a proxy fight, both incumbent management and insurgents typically court large institutional investors like mutual funds and solicit their views on company strategy.

Federal securities laws require public companies to provide substantial disclosure when seeking stockholder approval of corporate actions through solicitations of proxies or other consents. The proxy rules of the SEC assist stockholders by providing them with sufficient information about the items to be voted on, as well as adequate time to consider this information and cast their votes. Company management is usually the only party soliciting proxies from stockholders for the election of directors and other items such as a charter amendment. However, the SEC allows stockholders not affiliated with management to send out proxy statements opposing management's proposals, advocating their own proposals and/or nominating their own slate of directors. In such situations, the SEC's rules require substantial disclosures to all shareholders about the proposals and slates of these insurgents.

In addition, minority shareholders can have their proposals included in the company's proxy statement and sent out to all stockholders under the SEC's proxy rules. In effect, these rules allow minority stockholders to avoid the costs of a proxy solicitation by sending out their proposals to other stockholders at the expense of the company. Such stockholder proposals have covered a broad range of subjects, from the compensation of a company's executives to its policies on environmental matters to its deployment of a poison pill. The company must include such a stockholder proposal in its proxy statement unless the proposal goes beyond the legitimate purview of stockholders as defined by the SEC—for example, if the proposal relates to elements of the day-to-day operations of the company, which are beyond the jurisdiction of shareholders under state law. A company may also exclude a proposal that relates to a political issue beyond the control of management. However, an otherwise excludable stockholder proposal can sometimes be included in a company's proxy statement if the proposal is couched in terms of a mere recommendation to the company's directors—for example, recommending, rather than mandating, the rescission of a poison pill.

As with proxy fights, in the takeover arena federal securities laws establish disclosure obligations and procedural ground rules in order to level the playing field for all parties. The SEC rules require bidders in tender offers to make specific disclosures about the terms, conditions and financing arrangements for their bids, and to disseminate such disclosures to all shareholders. The SEC also requires the directors of the target company to issue a public statement on their position in response to a takeover bid.

Beyond disclosure, the SEC establishes a fair and orderly process for resolving tender offers. The SEC's rules on tender offers set forth a timetable for bidders to make their offers, management to respond to these bids and stockholders to tender their shares. The SEC rules allow tendering stockholders to withdraw shares already submitted if a competing bid is made or an existing bid is revised. The SEC rules also establish a procedure for allocating the purchase of shares by a bidder when its partial tender offer is oversubscribed.

Beside the states and the SEC, the New York Stock Exchange (NYSE) and the National Association of Securities Dealers, Inc. (NASD) have adopted corporate governance rules that apply to companies whose securities trade on the NYSE or NASDAQ, respectively. The NYSE and NASD require their listed companies to obtain stockholder approval before issuing substantial blocks of stock, effecting significant mergers or acquisitions, or adopting stock-related incentive plans for their employees. The importance of these rules has increased in recent years alongside the explosive growth in stock option plans. The NYSE and NASD rules are among the few mechanisms that permit stockholders to vote on the adoption of stock option or other stock-related plans for employee compensation.[7] The impact of substantial stock option grants and the controversy over repricing options have led many institutional investors to adopt policies governing their approval or disapproval of such plans. (These are discussed later in this Chapter).

III. Voting Policies and Practices of Mutual Funds

The SEC heavily regulates mutual funds and their advisers with respect to most aspects of their business. (See Chapter Three.) In their role as investors, mutual funds are subject to a variety of restrictions on how much stock of a particular company or industry they may own and how liquid their aggregate holdings must be. Every fund must disclose its complete holdings twice a year in reports to fund stockholders, and any fund adviser managing more than $100 million in the aggregate from all accounts must disclose quarterly a total list of equity securities owned by the funds and other accounts managed by the adviser. In addition, if the funds and other accounts managed by the investment adviser hold more than 5% of the voting securities of a publicly traded company, the adviser must file periodic disclosure reports with the SEC on such holdings. These filings are a source of valuable information on mutual fund holdings for participants in takeovers and proxy fights.

Yet the SEC currently imposes no specific restrictions or obligations on mutual funds or their advisers with respect to their activities on proxy voting or takeover bids. These activities are formally subject only to the general fiduciary duties of fund advisers and directors. Former SEC Chairman Arthur Levitt did provide informal guidance to mutual fund advisers and directors on how active they should be in proxy voting and takeover issues. Following is an excerpt from his speech, "Mutual Fund Directors: On the Front Line for Investors" (March 21, 1994):

> Mutual fund management must decide how active it should be and under what circumstances. I recognize that funds that invest in a large number of companies cannot possibly take an active role in every matter submitted to shareholders. The costs would far exceed the benefits. But when a shareholder vote raises issues that are tied directly to a stock's price, the case for involvement is obvious.
>
> Directors should look carefully at whether it is in investors' interest that a fund exercise its franchise in matters as critical as anti-takeover measures, proxy fights for control of a portfolio company, and elections. Funds also may find it advisable to consider executive compensation proposals, when those proposals are submitted to shareholders for approval.
>
> Fund directors should ask the adviser about its policies for participating in the governance process. What kind of system does the adviser have for identifying issues that might require shareholder activism? How does the adviser reach its decision on how to cast its ballot?
>
> I am not suggesting that directors generally should be involved in determining how a fund votes its shares in a particular matter. Rather, as in other areas, directors should ask the hard questions about overall policies and their implementation.

In the spring of 2000, the SEC proposed that mutual fund complexes disclose their voting and vote reporting policies, as well as information on conflicts of interest arising from owning stock in a company with which the adviser does business. Although the SEC chose to delay the adoption of these regulations for further study, the trend at the SEC seems to be toward more scrutiny of mutual fund voting policies and practices.

In contrast to the SEC's minimal guidance on proxy voting by mutual funds, the Department of Labor (DOL), which regulates investment of retirement assets through the

Employee Retirement and Income Security Act (ERISA), has provided specific guidance for proxy voting by pension funds that manage retirement assets under ERISA. In general, the DOL considers the proxy vote a valuable retirement plan asset. Accordingly, investment managers are required to vote in the best interests of the plan participants on issues that affect the value of the plan's investments. In addition, the DOL requires that investment managers maintain written proxy voting policies and keep accurate records with regard to individual proxy votes cast. The DOL requires that proxy votes be cast at all U.S. company meetings but permits investment managers to consider the expense, delay and trading restrictions that may render voting proxies for foreign meetings inadvisable.

A. *Proxy Voting Guidelines*

Despite the absence of SEC rules on fund participation in the governance process of publicly traded companies, mutual fund complexes routinely vote their proxies on items submitted to stockholders for approval. (Such proxy voting should be considered part of the normal exercise of fiduciary duties, as distinct from institutional activism, discussed below.) In voting proxies, fund advisers generally follow written guidelines that have been approved by the independent directors of the funds. The fund adviser typically processes and votes all proxies for shares held by the funds in accordance with these guidelines. On an annual basis, the fund adviser usually submits a report on proxy voting matters to the board of directors of the funds or a committee of the board.

Proxy voting guidelines are designed to cover the main issues that tend to appear frequently on proxy ballots; they are updated periodically to reflect recent developments in the corporate governance arena. These proxy guidelines are designed to direct the funds' votes in favor of matters that enhance stockholder value. While the fund's investment adviser usually votes all proxies in accordance with these policies, the adviser occasionally makes exceptions to the guidelines in light of unusual or unforeseen circumstances when such exceptions are in the best interest of the fund. In addition, from time to time, specific proxies raise novel issues that are not covered by the proxy guidelines and must be quickly resolved by the fund's adviser.

Proxy voting guidelines typically focus on three areas: general stockholder rights, anti-takeover measures and executive compensation plans. First, the guidelines of most fund complexes provide for votes against proposals that would reduce or eliminate the rights of stockholders in the corporate governance process. These would include, for example, proposals to eliminate important shareholder rights, such as the right of stockholders to call special stockholder meetings or initiate changes in corporate bylaws. Mutual funds also generally vote against measures allowing the company to buy back from, or sell shares to, one stockholder at a preferential price (so-called greenmail).[8]

Second, proxy guidelines usually provide that mutual funds should vote against anti-takeover measures because they are perceived as reducing the likelihood that stockholders will receive a premium over the current stock price through a merger or takeover offer. Such anti-takeover measures include, for example, supermajority-voting requirements for merger proposals as well as staggered boards that delay an acquirer from controlling the board for a few years. A company's board may adopt a poison pill without stockholder approval, but stockholders have often put forward their own proposals recommending the elimination of poison pills. Most fund complexes support these stockholder proposals, although a few complexes accept poison pills with reasonable time limits (e.g., five years) since it is unclear whether poison pills increase or decrease stockholder returns.

Third, stockholders are allowed to vote on a narrow slice of executive compensation—most important, the adoption of plans for awarding stock options and restricted shares. Shareholders also must approve executive performance criteria that are required in order for a company to receive a tax deduction for an executive's compensation of over $1 million in any one year.[9] Although mutual fund managers generally support stock-based incentive plans, they are concerned about the design of these plans and their potential effects on existing stockholders. For example, mutual fund guidelines support grants of stock options or restricted stock in reasonable amounts where the grants are conditioned on the company's achievement of specified financial objectives. On the other hand, mutual fund guidelines generally require a vote against a plan that provides for "mega-grants" of stocks not tied to financial performance criteria or stock option plans where the critical terms may be changed at any time in the total discretion of the company's directors. Similarly, mutual fund guidelines generally support the allocation of a significant percentage of the company's shares to stock-related compensation programs—for example, up to 10% of a company's total outstanding shares (and perhaps 15% or 20% for high-tech companies). Above these percentages, however, many fund managers become concerned that these programs are diluting the financial interests of all other shareholders in the company's profits. (Reading 11.1 contains excerpts from the program guidelines for executive compensation of TIAA-CREF, which manages defined contribution plans for employees of universities, as well as other nonprofit organizations, and also offers mutual funds to investors.)

Most advisers to mutual funds keep their policies and voting practices confidential—a practice that the SEC may change. A few fund advisers have begun to make limited disclosure of their voting policies in order to inform corporate executives of what will and will not garner the adviser's support. Some mutual fund advisers—like Barclays Global Investors, a large manager of indexed mutual funds—provide portfolio companies with a summary of their voting policies. Other advisers choose to explain their voting policies through face-to-face discussions with portfolio companies. A small group of advisers, such as the Calvert Group, an investment manager of "socially responsible" funds, widely disseminates portions of their proxy guidelines on their website.

B. *Proxy Decision Making by Mutual Funds*

In most cases, mutual fund advisers vote to support the recommendations of company management. This is true not only for management's proposed slate of directors, which routinely receive the support of 99% of those voting, but also for management proposals on other subjects. For instance, during the 2000 proxy season, management proposals on proxy statements were supported on average by 85% of the stockholders who voted; proposals opposed by management were opposed on average by 74% of the stockholders who voted. This high level of consensus between stockholders and management is not surprising, at least for actively managed mutual funds. Owning the stock of a company ordinarily indicates a belief in the ability of the company's management; supporting management's position in voting matters often follows as a matter of course.

From time to time, however, investment advisers to mutual funds may disagree with management over a proposal—such as the terms of a stock-related incentive plan, the attraction of a takeover bid or a proxy fight between an outside organization and company management. Furthermore, if a stockholder resolution raises a significant corporate issue, investment advisers to mutual funds will diligently consider whether to support the stockholder or management on such a resolution.

Mutual fund advisers may wish to communicate with other institutional investors regarding corporate governance issues in general and proxy proposals in specific. In 1992, the SEC liberalized its rules in connection with communications among stockholders. Under the current rules, an investment adviser to a mutual fund is permitted to discuss specific proposals with other institutional investors as long as they do not agree to act in concert and no one solicits a proxy from another. Despite the rule changes, mutual fund advisers—a fairly competitive lot—do not regularly discuss their views on pending proxy proposals with other fund advisers or institutional investors, although they may exchange views on a particularly controversial proposal. Nor do fund advisers participate in discussions among stockholders through Internet chatrooms. Instead, most fund advisers gauge the market's receptivity to a management proposal by monitoring the trading in the company's stock immediately following a proposal and listening carefully to the content and tone of the questions asked of management during analyst conference calls.

Fund advisers, like many other institutional investors, subscribe to various proxy voting and research services. The main proxy research services in the United States are the Investor Responsibility Research Center (IRRC), Institutional Shareholder Services (ISS) and Proxy Monitor. These firms provide in-depth analyses with respect to nonroutine proxy matters, together with proxy voting administration and record keeping services; ISS and Proxy Monitor also provide voting recommendations along with their analyses. These firms have grown in importance as mutual fund advisers and other institutional investors search for objective analyses of contested matters. A few commentators contend that the vote recommendations of the proxy research services have significantly influenced the outcome of certain recent proxy fights, especially when a company's stockholder base was heavily weighted toward public pension funds and index funds. While proxy research services provide helpful analysis and recommendations, they usually supplement internal research by mutual fund advisers, who typically make independent decisions on controversial proxy issues.

A significant influence on the voting decisions of mutual fund managers is the lobbying efforts by portfolio companies. Public companies employ investor-relations personnel and proxy-solicitation firms to identify large shareholders and communicate with them on proxy matters in order to obtain their support for management proposals.[10] For example, companies experiencing takeovers, proxy fights or stockholder-proposed resolutions frequently meet with mutual fund advisers to explain their positions and seek support. Similarly, a company that intends to propose controversial items for approval at its annual meeting may consult with mutual fund advisers to assess their receptivity to such items.

The utility of the proxy rules, the necessity for management to communicate clearly with stockholders and the willingness of institutional investors to consider challenges to management were all highlighted in the 1995–1997 proxy fight involving the Student Loan Marketing Association—previously called "Sallie Mae." Sallie Mae is the largest provider of financing for student loans in the United States, probably including loans taken out by many readers of this book. (See "The Battle for Control of Sallie Mae.")

IV. *Institutional Activism and Mutual Funds*

As illustrated by the above discussion, mutual fund advisers usually play an important, although often passive, role in corporate governance, evaluating management and stockholder proposals and voting in accordance with policies designed to further the interests of their funds. In recent years, however, mutual fund advisers have encountered an increasing number of proposals from stockholder activists, and in limited circumstances they have been among the activists pushing for such proposals. We use the terms "activism" and "institutional activism" to refer to conduct beyond diligently reviewing and voting on proxy issues submitted to stockholders by company management or by a party opposed to management.

A. *The Rise of Institutional Activism*

As the equity holdings of institutional investors have increased, some of these institutions, recognizing their potential ability to influence companies, have become unwilling to remain passive stockholders in all situations. Moreover, institutions pursuing strategies of investing in accordance with an index are not generally in a position simply to sell the stock if they are dissatisfied with management policies or a company's performance. The result is the phenomenon of increasing institutional activism toward publicly traded companies.

The initial stockholder activists were primarily affiliated with religious groups, educational organizations and philanthropic endowments. In the 1970s, these entities began pressuring some of the companies whose stock was held in their portfolios[11] over social issues related to South African apartheid, armaments manufacture and product safety. The 1980s witnessed the advent of the current brand of institutional activism more focused on the corporate governance process and corporate financial performance. Many factors contributed to this change in focus: first, corporate raiders and leveraged buyout specialists demonstrated the utility of exercising shareholder rights in situations of weak company performance; second, some institutions became concerned that corporate executives were insulating themselves from takeovers; and third, the Wall Street Rule proved less useful for holders of very large positions or those with indexed portfolios. In addition, certain pension funds sponsored by state and local governments began to make corporate governance a priority on their agendas.

These factors have encouraged some institutional stockholders to pressure for change in corporate policies through proactive methods—as compared to being simply reactive to issues raised by company management or those seeking to oust company management. This so-called activist phenomenon has been most regularly and dramatically represented through the activities of a relatively small group of public pen-

CALLOUT
The Battle for Control of Sallie Mae

Sallie Mae began its existence in 1972 as a federally sponsored enterprise to create a source of financing and guarantees for student loans. The growth in higher education enrollment and cost led to an enormous expansion in Sallie Mae's activities, which prompted congressional review of its operations and mandate. In 1996, Congress voted to privatize Sallie Mae so that it would be free of government control and subsidy. This review and subsequent vote for privatization triggered one of the most intense proxy battles of the 1990s.

In 1995, a group of dissident stockholders and former management established the Committee to Restore Value (CRV), based on the belief that incumbent management was not prepared to take full advantage of the freedom of privatization to increase Sallie Mae's business. The CRV initially was successful in electing a sizable minority of its candidates to Sallie Mae's board. In 1997, concluding that it could not reverse management's rejection of its proposals to change Sallie Mae's business strategy, the CRV decided that it would seek to oust the remaining directors and, in turn, management.

To obtain majority control of Sallie Mae's board, the CRV had to gain the support of Sallie Mae's stockholders, many of whom were institutional investors unaccustomed to supporting dissident slates in proxy fights. But the CRV was aided by a well-conceived business strategy for Sallie Mae, as well as the credibility of its leader, Albert Lord, the former chief operating officer of Sallie Mae. The CRV also took advantage of SEC rules requiring Sallie Mae to circulate to its stockholders the CRV's proxy solicitation materials, and the CRV used SEC filings to identify the institutional holders of Sallie Mae's stock.

Ownership of a substantial portion of Sallie Mae was concentrated in the hands of relatively few institutional investors. Institutions such as Capital Research and Management, Fidelity Management & Research, Scudder, Stevens and Clark and Boston Partners held substantial positions, the voting of which could determine the outcome of the battle. Both the CRV and Sallie Mae management held extensive meetings with Sallie Mae's stockholders, seeking support for their competing slates of directors. In addition, both parties met with Institutional Shareholder Services (ISS), a proxy research firm that disseminates voting recommendations in proxy battles to its institutional investor subscriber base.

At the first meeting of stockholders, neither the CRV nor the Sallie Mae management slate won a majority of votes. The meeting was adjourned, and both sides fanned out seeking additional stockholder support. Throughout the spring and summer of 1997, each side met with investors pressing their case, took out advertisements in the *Wall Street Journal* and distributed numerous press releases outlining the merits of their competing plans. Matters came to a head a week before the scheduled vote in July 1997, when ISS published a report withdrawing its support for management and recommending that stockholders support the dissidents. This change, combined with the CRV's efforts in convincing major stockholders to support its slate, propelled the CRV to victory.

The CRV's ability to wage a successful proxy fight demonstrated to institutional investors that they need not automatically follow the Wall Street Rule if management was unwilling to change a weak business plan and the insurgents had a good business strategy with credible leaders. Over time, the stockholders of Sallie Mae were well served: its stock price rose by more than 150% after the onset of the proxy fight in 1997 through the end of 2000 and significantly exceeded the return of the S&P 500 for that period.

sion plans, such as the California Public Employees' Retirement System (CalPERS), the State of Wisconsin Investment Board and the New York State Common Retirement Fund. By contrast, investment advisers to mutual funds usually have not become shareholder activists on a regular basis. From time to time, however, investment advisers to large mutual funds have become quietly involved in an effort to persuade corporate executives to change their policies. Reading 11.2 explains the approach taken by most institutional investors toward stockholder activism.

B. Types of Institutional Activism

Institutional activists can be divided into three groups: those who seek to implement sound corporate governance, those who target underperforming companies and those who advocate a social or political agenda. In practice, the first two groups tend to converge on companies that have substantially underperformed their peers or a market index. The last group focuses on companies whose businesses or corporate policies are viewed as detrimental to the social welfare in some fashion.

Let's begin with a little sense of perspective. The main risk for senior executives at companies that underperform is not institutional activism; it is garnering the attention of potential acquirers. Underperforming companies are often targets of merger proposals, tender offers or proxy contests for board control. However, battles for corporate control are expensive and time-consuming; therefore, they are rarely pursued by institutional investors, even among those who advocate stockholder activism. Institutional investors are not in the business of operating or controlling companies; they are portfolio investors in the business of seeking to maximize the returns on a relatively diversified pool of securities holdings.

Investment advisers to mutual funds, like most other institutional investors, rarely initiate proxy fights or propose alternative slates of directors, and they almost never launch a takeover attempt. Most fund advisers would rather adhere to the Wall Street Rule by selling the stock than attempting to restructure companies or oust management. By selling or refusing to buy the stock of underperforming companies, fund managers can impose a discipline on company executives by reducing their stock-based compensation and exposing the company to potential bidders for corporate control. Nevertheless, on certain occasions, a few mutual fund advisers have become active participants in corporate control contests. For example, the Mutual Series Fund, most notably during the tenure of investor Michael Price, has included within its investment strategies attempts to promote change at underperforming companies. Typically, Mutual Series has amassed a large stock position in an ailing company and then pressed company management for changes to boost the stock price or put itself up for sale. For example, many credit Price with having influenced the Chase Manhattan Bank's decision in 1995 to merge into Chemical Bank. At the time of the merger, Price's funds owned approximately 6% of Chase's outstanding shares.

In the limited number of situations where mutual fund advisers become activists, they tend to follow the type of cost-benefit analysis described in Reading 11.2. Fund advisers are most likely to become activists when the issue involves a potential increase in a company's stock price since that would directly contribute to the fund's financial return. Similarly, fund advisers tend to object to mergers or asset sales if the advisers believe that the pricing is unfair to stockholders. By contrast, fund advisers generally will not become activists with regard to procedural issues, like requiring confidential voting or appointing a nonexecutive board chairman, because the connection between such procedural reforms and financial performance is weak.

Former SEC commissioner Paul Carey, in a speech to the mutual fund industry's trade association in December 1999, supported the cost-benefit analysis laid out in Reading 11.2. In noting that fund advisers generally vote their proxies and ordinarily follow the Wall Street Rule, Commissioner Carey stated:

> Should fund advisers do more? Sometimes, fund advisers may not do more because they have concluded that doing more is not in the best interest of the fund. Clearly, fund advisers must engage in a cost-benefit analysis, and weigh the costs of possible courses of action against the potential benefits to the fund. In some cases, the costs of engaging company management on an issue may outweigh the potential benefits that may accrue to the fund. Fund advisers should not expend resources if they have no reasonable expectation that doing so will provide a net benefit to the fund.

Once fund advisers decide to become activists, they tend to choose the least costly and least time-consuming tactics available. Therefore, they generally avoid proxy fights and lengthy litigation. The strategy of choice is informal jawboning, where a group of institutional investors meet with top executives of a company, and subsequently perhaps its outside directors, to press for change. For example, informal jawboning by institutional investors including fund managers is reported to have played a significant role in the ouster of CEOs at American Express, IBM and Westinghouse in the early 1990s.[12] For a more detailed account of jawboning by a mutual fund manager, see "T. Rowe Price Opposition to Cort Deal."

C. *Active Fund Managers versus Index Fund Managers*

Investment advisers to actively managed funds devote tremendous resources to researching companies and industries. As part of that research, employees of such fund advisers meet regularly with company executives to discuss business results and trends. The analyst assigned to a company usually has detailed knowledge about the company's business strategy and financial performance, as well as the quality of its management. Therefore, in the limited situations where such fund advisers decide to become activist, they can formulate a customized approach tailored to the strengths and weaknesses of the company at issue.

By contrast, investment advisers that run index mutual funds devote minimal resources to researching the companies in their portfolios. By definition, index managers invest passively in a portfolio of many stocks, the composition of which changes based on decisions of third-party publishers of stock indexes, such as Standard & Poor's. The index manager has little influence over its portfolio once its benchmark is established; such a manager cannot follow the Wall Street Rule because index managers have no ability to sell the stock of underperforming companies which are in the index. This inability prevents index managers from influencing company management by putting downward pressure on the company's stock price. Nor do index managers as a matter of course meet with company management teams. This reduces their ability to influence corporate policy through expressing their views to management.

CALLOUT
T. Rowe Price Opposition to Cort Deal

In March 1999, the management of Cort Business Services and its largest stockholder, Citicorp Venture Capital, announced that they had reached an agreement to sell the company to a leveraged buyout group. The price, $24.00 in cash and $2.50 in stock, represented a 58% premium to the stock price immediately before the announcement. But Cort, a lessor of office equipment to small businesses, had seen its stock price fall from $48.00 a share in March 1998 to $16.75 a share immediately before the proposed sale. The announcement caused the stock price to increase significantly. With Cort's main stockholder supporting the transaction, it appeared that the sale would close without controversy.

A funny thing happened on the way to the closing. T. Rowe Price, a large mutual fund complex, took the virtually unprecedented step of issuing a press release on August 10, 1999, one week before the stockholders' meeting, opposing the sale. T. Rowe Price announced that it would vote against the sale on the grounds that the price was inadequate in light of Cort's earnings, growth prospects and industry leadership. This announcement, along with private objections from other large holders, prompted the buyer to revise its offer on August 12, 1999, by increasing the price to $25.00 in cash and $3.00 in stock, but to no avail. The stockhold-

ers' meeting, on August 18, 1999, was held but adjourned, as approval of the sale was not obtained. Citing major stockholder opposition and difficulties in obtaining financing, Cort announced on November 4, 1999, that the buyer had withdrawn its bid.

Three months later, a company owned by Warren Buffett announced that it had reached an agreement to buy Cort at a price of $28.00 a share in cash. Although equal in price to the revised proposal that had been rejected, the Buffet bid proved more attractive to Cort's stockholders because it was payable all in cash—as opposed to partially in stock whose value would be questionable—and was not subject to financing risk. By holding firm against the earlier bid, Cort's stockholders obtained a more attractive proposal than what had been initially offered to them.

The Cort example illustrates well the potential benefits of informal jawboning. T. Rowe Price was the largest stockholder after Citicorp Venture Capital; accordingly, its funds stood to benefit significantly from any action taken to prevent consummation of the "low-ball" original offer. As an active manager of equities, T. Rowe Price presumably had been following Cort's business closely, and thus was able to conclude that the terms of the original offer were inadequate. The cost of opposing the transaction was small: T. Rowe Price simply published a press release announcing its opposition. Through this press release, T. Rowe Price was able to send a strong signal to other institutional investors that it was dissatisfied with the original offer.

However, index managers have a systematic interest in the overall performance of U.S. companies, and they do retain some influence over company management through voting on proxy issues. For example, TIAA-CREF, which has a large portion of indexed assets, has been a leader in initiating a program of stockholder resolutions on poison pills. TIAA-CREF also was a vocal opponent of a stock recapitalization plan proposed by Ford Motor Co. to its stockholders in 2000. Moreover, a few index fund managers, recognizing the limited options to escape an underperforming stock holding, attempt to influence company management by urging improvements in corporate governance. For instance, CalPERS publishes annually a list of companies it views as suffering from inadequate performance or governance. This list attracts considerable media attention, although its impact on corporate results is unclear. As discussed later in this Chapter, it is still an open question whether index fund managers, without substantial research staffs and without regular company contacts, can effectively identify policies or initiatives to help underperforming companies in a timely manner.

V. *Mutual Funds and Social Activism*

As mentioned above, one group of activists has social rather than primarily financial agendas for U.S. companies. In the view of these activists, U.S. companies should help achieve social goals such as saving animals, protecting wilderness or alleviating poverty. Let's consider whether these social goals are appropriate for most mutual funds and then for the subset of funds specifically geared to socially responsible investing.

Social activists who attempt to change corporate policies or challenge corporate practices take many different tacks in pursuit of their goals, but all are motivated by one fundamental principle: corporations shouldn't be solely profit-maximizing entities; rather, they have an obligation to take into account their impact on social issues. Activists seek to influence companies through a variety of means—including litigation, picketing and public relations offensives—in an effort to encourage a company to alter its social policies in some fashion.

Mutual funds, as stockholders with the ability to influence corporate management, are sometimes the focus of activists seeking support for social causes. For many years, activists have sought to include proposals recommending changes in corporate social policies in corporate proxy statements for consideration at the annual stockholders' meeting. For instance, shareholders have made proposals to include more women and African Americans on corporate boards and to prohibit a company from doing any business with countries accused of human rights violations. Companies generally have sought to exclude such social proposals as an improper interference in ordinary business matters or as not a proper subject for stockholder review, with varying levels of support from the SEC. When those proposals are included on the proxy ballot, the success rate for purely social proposals, as opposed to business or financial proposals, has been very low. On average, social issues receive less than 8% of stockholder support; if they fail to attract sufficient percentages of votes as specified by the SEC rules (i.e., between 3% and 10%, depending on the time period), they cannot be reintroduced at the next shareholders' meeting.

Although the issues raised by these activists may address important social policy questions, advisers to mutual funds in general tend not to support such proposals unless a direct financial benefit would be obtained, or financial harm avoided, by a company's stockholders. Most advisers of mutual funds are not charged with the mission of pursuing any social policies; they are supposed to invest their customers' savings in accordance with the fund's stated objectives and policies in order to earn as good a financial return as practical. In fact, advisers to mutual funds that voted or invested based on social, not financial, grounds could expose themselves to claims of breach of fiduciary duty if the social grounds were not properly disclosed to customers. An adviser to a mutual fund that substituted its view of a social agenda for the goal of maximizing the fund's financial returns would undoubtedly come under considerable criticism.

However, mutual fund advisers do take into account the potential financial impact of social issues on a company's business and prospects. For example, a fund adviser will consider the potential effects of a company's environmental policies on its earnings and stock price. Conversely, an adviser to a mutual fund might conclude that a company's stock price was much lower than its earnings power because its product line was socially disfavored. For example, a fund manager who bought tobacco stocks in early 2000 would have reaped a significant financial gain for fund shareholders during the rest of that year.

Although most mutual funds do not invest based on a certain social agenda, in recent years the phenomenon of socially responsible investing has blossomed in response to the demands of a distinct minority of investors seeking to invest their money in a manner consistent with their social values or political views. Socially responsible investing can be divided into three forms: screening, activism and community building. Community-building investments, such as loans to disadvantaged entrepreneurs or subsidies for low-income housing, generally cannot be conducted through mutual funds with their high liquidity requirements. But screening and activism have found mutual funds to be a convenient vehicle to attract sympathetic customers and implement their social vision.

Screening is practiced by "socially responsible investing" (SRI) funds. Such funds generally seek returns from a portfolio that does not include the securities of companies that receive a substantial amount of their revenue from activities related to tobacco, alcohol, gambling, weapons production, animal testing or other controversial practices. Screening involves either not investing in certain companies because of their products or practices (e.g., tobacco or gambling) or deliberately investing in certain types of companies (e.g., renewable energy) that match investors' social goals. At the end of 2000, funds with SRI as a stated objective amounted to approximately $12 billion in assets, according to Morningstar, Inc. This represents a growing sector of the mutual fund industry, although a tiny fraction of the industry's total assets of approximately $7 trillion.

Socially responsible activism by investors generally involves the efforts of stockholders of a company to change corporate behavior, such as urging adoption of environmental or labor practices or boycotting certain countries or activities. Some SRI funds that screen their investments also take the additional step of lobbying the companies in which they invest to adopt or avoid practices they favor or oppose. The oldest SRI funds, like the Domini Social Equity Fund and the Calvert Group of funds, tend to combine social investment screens with advocacy efforts. More recent entrants to SRI funds, like TIAA-CREF and Vanguard, simply offer screened funds to their customers.

Whether SRI funds can provide competitive investment returns has been the subject of considerable debate. The social screens, as well as changes in company policies, can result in divestment or avoidance of stock purchases that would otherwise be financially sound. On the other hand, the increasing trend of professional investment management firms offering SRI products, together with the bull market of the 1990s, has resulted in a few SRI funds that have outperformed the broader market. These funds have tended to concentrate on stocks of technology companies, which often avoid practices and business areas that generate social controversy. Although technology companies performed extraordinarily well during most of the late 1990s, they generally underperformed in 2000, and so, consequently, did these SRI funds.

VI. *Empirical Studies on Shareholder Activism*

Underlying the policy debate about merits of institutional activism is the empirical question: Does such activism have a significant impact on corporations that are the target of that activism? The short answer is that it's unclear. A longer answer is given by Bernard Black in Reading 11.3, which reviews the academic literature on this subject.

In an attempt to provide an intermediate-level answer, let us review a few points that emerge from this debate on the impact of institutional activism.[13] To begin, the studies summarized in Reading 11.3 do not usually include proxy fights or takeover bids since these are rare events for institutional investors. In addition, these studies are all premised on the efficient markets theory (see Chapter One), so they assume that the impact from shareholder activism can be measured by looking at a change in stock price after a specific event, such as a pension fund's submission of a stockholder proposal.

These economic studies tend to show no or little positive price effects from proposals to change general governance procedures, such as the introduction of confidential voting or the appointment of an external board chairman (separate from the CEO). Although most studies find no or insignificant price effects from proposals to have a majority of independent directors on a corporate board, there are exceptions in the academic literature and many anecdotes about the importance of independent directors in takeover situations. By contrast, the studies on campaigns to remove anti-takeover amendments tend to show positive price effects over the long term, though the short-term effects are ambiguous. Many stockholder proposals have aimed at rescinding poison pills, but the effects of these efforts on stock prices are particularly confused because the merits of poison pills are themselves the subject of heated debate.[14]

The studies tend to show more positive price effects from an announcement of a successful negotiation about a stockholder proposal between an institutional investor and a target company than the public submission or subsequent vote on a controversial proposal. Some commentators argue that such negotiated settlements have more positive price effects because company managements agree to settlements only if proposals increase stockholder values. Others argue that such positive price effects derive mainly from the market's perception that negotiated settlements signal management's general willingness to respond to stockholder concerns.

A separate category of studies has focused on whether institutional activism has resulted in discernible corporate responses, as opposed to stock price changes. Again, in general, the results are mixed. There appears to be no significant correlation between institutional activism and CEO turnover; however, there does appear to be a significant correlation between institutional activism and corporate restructurings such as asset sales or spin-offs. But there is a further debate about whether these restructurings were caused by stockholder activism itself or whether the restructuring occurred because activists focused on underperforming companies, which tend to have a relatively high incidence of corporate restructuring.

Of course, certain types of stockholder activism are not aimed at improving the target company's financial performance; therefore, it would be inappropriate to look for price effects from such stockholder activism. Filing a stockholder resolution that urges an oil company to cease its exploration activities is unlikely to affect the company's stock price positively, but it may further the social agenda of the proponent. A limited group of such nonfinancial resolutions or requests can get a good reception in corporate circles. For example, a majority of the firms pressured by TIAA-CREF to name female or minority board members did so or are in the process of doing so. On the other hand, firms faced with stockholder proposals to cap the compensation of senior executives do not usually change such compensation.

More broadly, institutional activism has been defended on the ground that it has brought about salutary, though intangible, improvements in the corporate culture of the United States. For example, institutional activism has probably been a factor contributing to the enhanced sensitivity of company directors to issues raised by their shareholders. Moreover, stockholder activism by public pension plans has probably made advisers to mutual funds more sensitive to their fiduciary obligations to vote proxies diligently.

What are the policy implications of all these studies? Most commentators would agree that the mixed evidence on target impact means that institutional investors should proceed carefully by looking at the estimated costs and benefits of each instance of stockholder activism. Such a careful look is especially warranted because of the "free rider" problem inherent in institutional activism: its costs are borne by one or two stockholders, while all other stockholders reap its benefits.

A few critics would severely restrict stockholder activism because of their belief that the financial impact of activism on target companies is doubtful. These critics emphasize the dominant role in stockholder activism of public pension plans as opposed to mutual funds and other private investors. In the view of these critics, this dominance suggests that much stockholder activism is motivated more by the political or personal goals of public pension plan officials than by the financial interests of their pension beneficiaries. However, the supporters of stockholder activism by public pension plans emphasize that the corporate targets of their activism are selected on the basis of low scores on objective financial measures and not on the basis of any political criteria. They also note that the costs of stockholder activism are minuscule relative to the size of such public pension plans; for example, the annual cost of CalPERS' stockholder activism program is roughly $500,000 per year, or .002% of the plan's assets. Moreover, supporters point to a few studies showing positive financial results from activism by CalPERS and TIAA-CREF; critics, of course, challenge the methodological validity of these studies.

Similarly, there is no agreement on whether institutional activism should be permitted or encouraged on issues other than those designed to increase the financial return to company stockholders; as discussed above, these issues include environmental, labor and ethical concerns about corporate conduct. The critics maintain that social policy concerns should be resolved in a legislative or regulatory forum rather than in the corporate governance process. These critics would say, for instance, that stockholder activism should not extend to emissions standards utilized by car companies; instead, these companies should abide by the emissions standards set by Congress and the Environmental Protection Agency after public debate. On the other hand, supporters of social activism by institutional investors maintain that stockholders are only one of several stakeholders in a company, which should take into account the interests of their employees, customers and local communities. In their view, Congress and the EPA set only the minimum emissions standards for cars; a car company may choose to meet higher standards in light of community as well as stockholder interests.

In sum, the large increase in institutional ownership of publicly traded companies has significantly changed the dynamics of corporate governance in the United States. However, there is no consensus on the effects or merits of institutional activism. At present, most advisers to mutual funds diligently vote on all issues put to a stockholders' vote, including proposals by other stockholders as well as management. But these advisers become involved in stockholder activism only in unusual circumstances and generally prefer to follow the Wall Street Rule by selling a company's shares if they are dissatisfied with the company's performance.

VII. *Corporate Governance Outside the United States*

Over the past two decades, U.S. mutual fund complexes have increasingly invested in non-U.S. equities. In 2000, the assets of U.S. mutual funds with an international or global objective amounted to over $560 billion. In investing outside the United States, a U.S. fund manager faces a number of challenges in dealing with the corporate governance process of non-U.S. issuers. (Chapter Twelve reviews the other constraints and risk factors involved with foreign investing by U.S. mutual funds.) In short, the equity markets outside the United States tend to be less developed and provide fewer protections to investors than the very liquid and heavily regulated equity markets in the United States. Dominant local shareholders, including national governments, often seek to limit the rights of minority shareholders, including U.S. mutual funds. At the same time, the different relationship that exists between a company's board of directors and its shareholders may hinder the ability of U.S. mutual funds to assert what rights they have in foreign jurisdictions. Moreover, inadequate proxy disclosure often makes it difficult for U.S. investors to evaluate the activities and proxy proposals of foreign companies. Finally, a host of operational and logistical challenges create obstacles for U.S. mutual funds seeking to submit proxy votes to foreign shareholder meetings.

The discussion below is not intended to be comprehensive; rather, for illustrative purposes, we will focus on specific markets within some of the main investment regions of the world: in Europe, we will focus on France, in Asia on Japan and in the emerging markets on Brazil.

A. *Dominant Shareholder Groups*

The presence of dominant local shareholders characterizes the governance structure of many foreign companies. The dominant shareholders typically seek to preserve their influence by relying on a variety of structures designed to frustrate the exercise of rights by minority shareholders and "outside" investors.

France, for example, has a strong tradition of government involvement in the economy. Accordingly, the state maintains several devices to influence corporate decision making, which undermine minority shareholder rights. In many industries that the government has partially privatized, such as the energy, telecommunications and banking sectors, the state retains a "golden share," with greater voting power in the company than is proportionate with its equity holding. In certain companies, the golden share allows the state to protect the company from a takeover by investors outside the European Union (EU). For example, in 1999, the French government threatened to use its golden share in the event a non-EU suitor made a takeover bid for Elf Aquitaine, the French oil company. The golden share may also prohibit the company's sale of strategic assets, or the acquisition of more than 5% of the company's voting shares, without the government's consent.

Traditionally, Japan's industrial organization has been characterized by the prevalence of the *keiretsu*, a group of interrelated firms including suppliers or product chains, usually affiliated with a commercial bank and/or insurance company. Members of a *keiretsu* generally retain large holdings in each other's stock in an interlocking system of cross-holdings. The *keiretsu* system was touted during the 1980s as providing an effective form of management accountability, because the large shareholders in the *keiretsu* had the knowledge and power to monitor management's decisions. During the 1990s, however, the *keiretsu* system impeded needed reforms by preventing takeovers and making restructurings more difficult. As the Japanese recession has continued for over a decade, the *keiretsu* system has been on the decline as many companies have been forced to sell down their crossholdings.

Many public companies in Brazil have multiple-class capital structures, with voting power concentrated in one class held by a dominant group and other classes held by public shareholders. In particular, influential Brazilian families, corporate conglomerates and the Brazilian government retain voting control of large sections of the economy. According to the proxy research firm ISS, 70% of Brazil's common (voting) shares are held by these three groups. All of these groups have from time to time blocked the exercise of rights by minority shareholders, including U.S. mutual funds, by using multiple-class voting structures to retain control and resist efforts aimed at corporate reforms.

B. *Legal Relationship Between Company Board and Shareholders*

In addition to the influence of dominant local shareholders, the legal relationship between a company board and its shareholders may limit the rights of the minority shareholders. In general, under U.S. state corporate law, a company's directors owe a fiduciary duty primarily to its shareholders. By contrast, in many non-U.S. legal systems, the board may be required to consider the interests of other stakeholders in the enterprise, including the company's labor unions and local suppliers, as well as community groups and local government. The interests of these groups may, on occasion, come into conflict with the interests of minority shareholders.

For example, under French law, the board of directors represents "the company" and must act in its best interests; French courts have ruled that the best interests of the company go beyond and are distinct from the interests of shareholders. Even the president of France once complained that French workers were being asked to sacrifice in order "to safeguard the investment benefits of Scottish widows and California pensioners."[15] Similarly, Japanese law does not require the company board to represent the interests of shareholders. Courts have ruled that directors have only an indirect duty to shareholders as the ultimate owners of the company. However, Japanese stock exchanges do provide limited oversight of companies listed on such exchanges. Similarly, directors are supposed to represent multiple constituencies under Brazilian law. Furthermore, under the Brazilian Corporation Law, a "controlling shareholder," as well as a corporate director, owes a duty toward the corporation, other shareholders, corporate employees and the community in which the corporation operates.

The structure and composition of company boards may make their directors particularly unlikely to protect the interests of foreign institutional shareholders. In France, boards of directors are overwhelmingly French and often include a significant number of government representatives, even though non-French investors own as much as 40% of the shares in the companies that make up the country's CAC-40 Index.[16] In Japan, the size of company boards is often quite large, numbering as many as 40 or 50 individuals. The vast majority of Japanese board members are "inside" directors affiliated with the company; consequently, even if independent directors are present, their ability to protect the interests of minority shareholders is limited. In Brazil, many companies have two or even three governing bodies. The administrative council is elected by shareholders but must be composed of individuals who reside in Brazil. The supervisory board is an independent audit committee containing nonaffiliated auditors and elected by shareholders. Brazilian companies may also establish what is called a board of directors, but it actually resembles an executive committee comprising senior executives with ultimate responsibility for managing the company.

Even if shareholders enjoy certain rights in theory, in many countries these rights can be difficult to enforce in practice. For example, French law allows a minority shareholder to submit proposals to a shareholders' meeting only if that shareholder holds a large percentage of the company's stock (usually at least 5% of the company's share capital). In Brazil, foreign minority shareholders having no immovable assets in the country may enforce their rights in the Brazilian courts only if they make an advance deposit sufficient to cover the legal fees and court costs of the defendant, should the defendant be successful at trial. In Japan, with its cultural bent against litigation, it is extremely difficult for shareholders to obtain judicial assistance in asserting whatever rights they have as shareholders of publicly listed companies.

C. *Inadequate Proxy Disclosure*

The quality of the proxy information provided to shareholders in most other countries is generally much less comprehensive than in the United States. In many countries, companies provide only the most basic information describing the proposals to be voted on at a shareholders' meeting. There is generally very little or no disclosure information related to executive compensation, a valuable aspect of U.S. proxy statements. Nor is there much information about a company's pension liabilities, interested transactions or business segments in any disclosure documents distributed by most foreign issuers. Moreover, in many countries, proxy information need be published only in a local newspaper or financial publication a few days before the meeting rather than delivered to all shareholders prior to the meeting. Accordingly, many U.S. institutions, including mutual funds, find it difficult to obtain proxy information on a timely basis or to make an informed voting decision based on the information available.

Mutual funds may purchase shares of foreign companies that trade in the United States, through either direct listings on a U.S. exchange or an American Depository Receipt (ADR) program. For the relatively limited number of foreign companies that list their shares for trading directly on a U.S. exchange, the U.S. securities laws generally require these companies to disclose on a regular basis detailed information regarding their activities to a similar extent as would be the case for a domestic U.S. issuer. In particular, U.S. law requires publicly listed companies to send detailed proxy-related information, together with an annual report, to each shareholder in advance of a company's annual shareholders' meeting. These same proxy solicitation requirements, with certain informational exceptions,[17] apply to the approximately 400 foreign companies that have registered their shares directly for trading on a U.S. exchange.[18]

However, the shares of a much larger number of foreign companies—close to 2,000—are available for trading in the United States only through ADR programs. ADRs are essentially derivative securities representing beneficial interests in the shares of a foreign issuer that are held in trust by a U.S. bank (the ADR sponsor). ADRs are typically traded in the United States on one of the national exchanges or in the over-the-counter market. Foreign issuers that make their shares available in the United States only through ADR programs are entirely exempt from the SEC's proxy rules, although the SEC does require ADR sponsors to make available in the United States English translations of any materials (including proxies) that must be publicly distributed in the underlying issuer's local market. Similarly, none of the major U.S. stock exchanges require the ADR sponsors to provide any more proxy information to U.S. investors than is provided to investors in the issuer's local market. At times, however, ADR sponsors have successfully negotiated for undertakings from foreign issuers to provide supplemental company information—or at least translations of existing information—to the sponsors for dissemination to U.S. investors.

D. *Operational and Logistical Challenges to Exercising Shareholder Rights*

In addition to the substantive disadvantages that U.S. shareholders often face overseas, a variety of operational challenges can frustrate the exercise of shareholder rights abroad.[19] For example, in the United States, most institutional shareholders are able to submit their proxy votes electronically through a system called Proxy Edge. Outside the United States, by contrast, there currently exists no method for voting shares electronically. Rather, U.S. institutional investors deliver voting instructions through cumbersome manual processes that often involve sending instructions through the mail or by facsimile transmission. Further delays in the delivery of materials and translation process may give foreign investors very little time in advance of the meeting to make an informed decision. Consequently, many mutual funds rely on proxy research services such as IRRC and ISS to supply translations and analyses of proxy material for shareholders' meetings of foreign companies.

In deciding whether to vote, institutional investors must consider the possible negative effects of "shareblocking" requirements that are prevalent through much of Europe and South America. These requirements effectively prohibit the sale of shares once they are voted until the conclusion of the shareholders' meeting. In France, for example, the practice of shareblocking often restricts the liquidity of voted shares for up to 10 business days in advance of the company meeting.

Even in markets that do not practice shareblocking, a number of other impediments to voting exist. In some markets, shareholders (or their representatives) must attend a company meeting in person in order to vote their shares; in other markets, shareholders possessing bearer or "street name" shares are required to undertake a cumbersome "re-registration" process in order to submit votes. In Japan, most publicly listed companies end their fiscal year on March 31 and hold their annual meeting on the same date at the same time. Although this practice was established to thwart the activities of the *sokaiya*—Japanese gangsters who threatened to disrupt company meetings—it impedes foreign shareholders, such as U.S. mutual funds, from attending more than one company meeting.

E.   Recent Improvements

Notwithstanding the difficulties outlined above, many U.S. institutional investors attempt to exercise their voting rights in many markets around the world. As in the United States, mutual fund complexes are rarely activist overseas, although an institution may become involved when fundamental factors affecting the value of its investments are at issue. Indeed, as their foreign holdings increase in size, institutional investors have recently become more successful in certain situations in asserting their rights as shareholders. For example, in 1997, institutional investors in the French company Eramet, including Fidelity Investments and TIAA-CREF, successfully forced the company to abandon a politically motivated and financially damaging plan to dispose of assets engineered by the French government, its majority shareholder.

In Europe, the establishment of the single-currency zone has quickened the pace of cross-border mergers and led to a more shareholder-friendly environment. In 2000, the European Court of Justice invalidated the Italian government's ability to exercise its "golden shares" in Telecom Italia S.A. But in 2001 a senior E.U. official ruled that European governments can maintain golden shares in formerly state-owned enterprises as long as they do not use those shares to discriminate against foreign companies. Also in 2001, a French court struck down a friendly bid to acquire Schneider Electric S.A. because the price offered for the voting shares of the founding family was higher than the price offered for the preferred shares with a privileged dividend but no voting rights. In one of the most bitterly contested European takeover battles of recent years, a Dutch court agreed to investigate whether a March 1999 agreement between the luxury goods maker, the Gucci Group, and a French retail empire, Pinault-Printemps-Redoute (PPR), injured minority shareholders' interests by diluting their ownership shares and effectively blocking a takeover bid for Gucci by French luxury goods maker LVMH Moet Hennessey Louis Vuitton. For more detail on the long-running battle between Gucci management and LVMH, see "The War of the Handbags."

The E.U. has been debating whether to adopt a new pan-European law that would ease cross-border takeovers. Because of objections, led by Germany, the European Parliament in 2001 rejected a proposal that would have required European countries to obtain advance shareholder approval of poison pills and other anti-takeover measures. The role of shareholders in regard to such measures will continue to be governed by different rules in each European country.

More broadly, government and business leaders in many countries have realized they must improve the corporate governance process for locally traded companies in order to attract equity capital and improve investment returns. For instance, a study of 495 companies in 25 emerging markets found a high correlation between corporate

CALLOUT
The War of the Handbags

One of the most bitter cross-border takeover battles corporate Europe has ever seen began in early 1999. French luxury goods company LVMH Moet Hennessey Louis Vuitton (LVMH) had been steadily increasing its stock holdings in a rival Italian luxury goods maker, the Gucci Group, and by January 1999 LVMH had accumulated 34% of all shares outstanding— without making a formal bid for the whole company. When LVMH asked for an additional seat on Gucci's board to reflect its rising ownership stake, Gucci management responded to what they regarded as a "creeping takeover" with defensive maneuvers that soon set off a flurry of lawsuits. The media quickly dubbed this takeover fight "The War of the Handbags."

Most important, in March 1999, Gucci decided to issue 39 million new shares to be purchased by French luxury retailer Pinault-Printemps-Redoute (PPR). The issuance of the new shares, purchased by PPR at $75 a share pursuant to a "poison pill" defense, had the effect of reducing LVMH's holdings of Gucci's shares outstanding from 34% to 20%. In turn, PPR's purchase gave that company a 40% portion of the new total of Gucci shares outstanding.

One result was that an April 1999 bid by LVMH of $85 a share for Gucci did not go forward. LVMH demanded that Gucci again issue millions of new shares in order to dilute PPR's ongoing voting power on the Gucci board. Gucci flatly rejected LVMH's demand.

Since then, neither LVMH nor PPR has publicly offered either to buy out other Gucci shareholders or sell their own stakes to their rival. Instead, they have re-mained the two largest shareholders of the firm while pursuing legal struggles for control. The dispute has been complicated by commercial rivalry and personal animosity between LVMH's principal owner, Bernard Arnault, and his long-time rival François Pinault, who owns 43% of PPR.

LVMH has filed suit claiming that Gucci's March 1999 share issuance and sale to PPR violated minority shareholders' rights by diluting the voting strength and reducing the economic value of outstanding Gucci shares. (More peripheral fronts in the handbag wars include a regulatory complaint by Gucci against LVMH to the European Commission's competition authorities in Brussels and a complaint by LVMH against Gucci to the U.S. SEC.) The case was being litigated in the Dutch courts since Gucci is incorporated in the Netherlands. Under pressure from the Dutch courts, the parties reached a settlement in September 2001: PPR will obtain majority control of Gucci and LVMH will realize a substantial capital gain on its Gucci holdings.

Despite the settlement of the case, the War of the Handbags gives cross-border investors pause for reflection on what may be called corporate governance risk. Both the legal structure that allowed LVMH to acquire more than a third of Gucci without making a bid for all shares and Gucci management's willingness to block a takeover by diluting outstanding share holdings fall well short of legal norms and industry standards protecting minority shareholders in the U.K. equity markets. Unless the EU's pending takeover rules do more to protect minority shareholders, the legacy of the Gucci case may be a hesitation to invest and a higher standard of due diligence before mutual funds acquire significant share positions in continental European companies.

governance and share price performance. The study, done by CLSA Emerging Markets for calendar year 2000, defined the seven key aspects of corporate governance as discipline, independence, transparency, accountability, fairness, responsibility and social awareness. The largest 100 companies covered by the study fell by 8.7% on average in 2000, but the stocks of the 25 companies rated the highest in corporate governance rose 3.3% on average, while the stocks of the 25 companies rated the lowest in corporate governance fell by 23.4% on average.

These local movements toward better corporate governance are supported by industry groups of institutional investors, such as the Investment Company Institute and the International Corporate Governance Network, which are pressing for reforms around the world. Similarly, multilateral agencies like the Organization for Economic Cooperation and Development and the World Bank are adopting "best-practice" codes for corporate governance. These codes often focus on financial transparency and disclosure issues, as these agencies try to persuade countries to use the best practices in corporate governance as a way to attract international capital.

REVIEW QUESTIONS

1. What is the Wall Street Rule? Do managers of mutual funds still abide by the Rule?

2. What is a poison pill? How can a poison pill help or hurt shareholders of a publicly held company?

3. If you were a manager of a mutual fund, what position would you take in voting on stock option plans: for, against or a third position?

4. How would you define institutional activism? What is the free-rider problem confronted by an institutional activist?

5. Are index funds in a better or worse position to engage in institutional activism than other mutual funds? Why?

6. What is a socially responsible mutual fund? How would such a fund use screens?

DISCUSSION QUESTIONS

1. Suppose the Exxon proxy statement contains a stockholder proposal recommending that "Exxon's directors adopt a no oil spill policy to the maximum extent feasible." How should you vote as the manager of the Value Mutual Fund, which owns 3% of Exxon's outstanding common stock? Why?

2. A new independent director, a distinguished business school professor, suggests that the policies of all equity funds in the complex be revised (after approval by the funds' customers if required). At present, the fundamental policy limits each such equity fund to acquiring less than 5% of the outstanding common stock of any publicly traded company, and the complex's internal management policies limit all equity funds in the complex together to acquiring less than 15% of the outstanding common stock of any publicly traded company. The new director suggests that these percentages be changed to 10% and 35%, respectively. What are the arguments for and against these suggestions?

3. A mutual fund that is the largest stockholder in a class is permitted to take control of a class action filed by other plaintiffs' lawyers.[20] Suppose a software company is sued for allegedly failing to disclose promptly that its new Internet browser had significant bugs. The suit is brought by a plaintiffs' law firm on behalf of a class consisting of all buyers of that company's stock during April, just before the company disclosed the bugs. The Growth Fund bought 2% of the software company's common stock on April 1 at $100 per share. The stock dropped immediately to $80 per share after the company disclosed the bugs and stayed at $80 per share. At the time of the acquisition, the stock of the software company constituted ½% of the growth fund's total assets of $1 billion. Should you as the investment manager of the Growth Fund take over control of the class action?

NOTES

1. Mutual funds have also become substantial owners of corporate bonds in recent years, but bondholders generally have no say in the governance of the companies issuing the bonds. Therefore, this Chapter does not address the role of mutual funds as institutional investors in bonds.

2. To minimize confusion, we refer in this Chapter to shareholders of a fund as "customers" and reserve the word "stockholders" for the role of funds relative to publicly traded companies.

3. For example, the Ford family owns 40% of voting stock of the company yet only approximately 5% of the total market value of outstanding common stock (as of May 10, 2001).

4. See, e.g., *Feldman* v. *Pearlman*, 219 F.2d 173 (2d Cir. 1955).

5. Typically, a poison pill provides that if a person acquires more than 15% or 20% of a company's common stock, then the remaining stockholders of the company would receive the right to acquire a large number of company shares at a minimal price (e.g., all shareholders other than the bidder would receive 100 shares at 1 cent per share) unless the pill is waived by the board of directors. Given the extreme dilution caused by poison pills, would-be acquirers rarely trigger a poison pill but rather negotiate with the board to waive it.

6. A staggered board elects only a minority of its members (typically one-third) in any given year (typically for three-year terms). Thus, a staggered board prevents a potential acquirer from acquiring control of a company by proposing a dissident slate of directors that could displace an entire board at one meeting.

7. Federal securities law requires only disclosure of the amount of stock option grants and holdings in the annual proxy statement, but does not require stockholder approval of stock option compensation. State law generally requires that stockholders approve any increase in the number of shares authorized for issuance, which can limit a board's ability to adopt stock option plans. To avoid future stockholder votes, however, most companies include in their charters upon incorporation an authorized number of shares substantially in excess of the amount expected to be issued in order to accommodate stock splits and stock acquisitions as well as stock option grants. Therefore, without the NYSE or NASD requirements for shareholder approval of issuance, companies would be unrestricted from issuing up to the full amount of authorized shares.

8. "Greenmail" refers to the practice of purchasing a hostile raider's position at a premium to the market price, a practice employed by companies under siege in order to eliminate a potential hostile takeover. Institutional investors widely decried the practice because they were not offered the premium price, yet had to bear its cost in the form of increased company debt or reduced company cash.

9. NYSE and NASD rules are the source of a stockholder approval requirement for the adoption of stock option plans; stockholder approval of such plans in order to deduct executive compensation above $1 million per year arose out of a congressional desire to mandate some form of stockholder approval of high levels of executive compensation. Stockholders, however, have no vote on overall compensation of corporate executives, an area within the province of a company's board of directors.

10. The SEC's adoption of Regulation FD, designed to provide a more level playing field for individual and institutional investors in terms of access to corporate management, has encouraged some companies to limit their interactions with institutional investors. The efficiency and effectiveness of direct communication with large stockholders, however, is unlikely to result in a dramatic reduction in communi-

cation between institutional investors and management, since management is usually mindful of its obligations not to disclose improperly material nonpublic information.

11. Activist investors often purchase small amounts of stock in order to achieve standing to make proposals, attend stockholder meetings and wage public relations campaigns. The SEC, in order to weed out proposals from very small holders, requires a stockholder seeking to advance a proxy proposal to have owned, for at least one year, either $2,000 in market value, or 1%, of the company's outstanding shares. This de minimis ownership threshold, however, is not a serious impediment to activists.

12. "Shareholders Exercise New Power with Nation's Biggest Companies," *New York Times*, February 1, 1993, p. A1.

13. For full references in Reading 11.3 , see http://papers.ssrn.com/sol3/papers.cfm?abstract_id=182169) and sources cited in Jonathan M. Karpoff, "Does Shareholder Activism Work? A Survey of Empirical Findings" (unpublished manuscript, on file with Yale Law School, April 22, 1998). See also Stuart L. Gillan and Laura T. Starks, "A Survey of Shareholder Activism: Motivation and Empirical Evidence," *Contemporary Finance Digest* (Autumn 1998).

14. Studies generally show that once a takeover bid is made for a target company, the existence of a poison pill tends to increase the price ultimately received by the target's shareholders. However, a company's adoption of a poison pill tends to reduce the likelihood of a takeover bid being made for the target and may reduce the initial price offered if a takeover bid is made.

15. "Resisting Those Ugly Americans; Contempt in France for U.S. Funds and Investors," *New York Times*, Business section, January 9, 2000, p. 1.

16. "Ambivalent," *The Economist*, October, 7, 2000.

17. For example, foreign issuers need not comply with the information items in the U.S. proxy rules on interested transactions unless required to do so by their home country.

18. The vast majority of directly listed companies are domiciled in Canada. The United States maintains a reciprocal disclosure arrangement with Canadian securities regulators, based on the similarity of the two countries' regulatory and disclosure systems. Under the agreement, a disclosure document used in one country is accepted in the other country so long as minimum standards are met.

19. Investing in foreign companies through ADRs does not alleviate any of these operational issues and may in fact exacerbate some of them to the extent that the ADR structure actually increases the number of intermediaries that materials need to pass through before they reach the actual beneficial owner of the securities. In addition, because the ordinary shares that underlie ADRs are typically registered with the company through an omnibus account, attempting to vote these shares can frequently trigger cumbersome requirements to re-register shares in the names of individual investors before a company will permit the shares to be voted. This often seems to be a problem when an investor is attempting to take a more activist role, such as opposing a major corporate transaction or introducing a shareholder proposal.

20. In the 1990s, Congress passed a statute allowing one of the largest shareholders of a company to be a "presumptive plaintiff" in a class action against the company. The presumptive plaintiff may choose to control the class action, including hiring counsel, approving briefs, and negotiating settlements.

READING 11.1

TIAA-CREF's Executive Compensation Program Guidelines

The Role of Stock

Shareholder interests are vitally affected by stock-based compensation plans. Inherently, they provide the greatest opportunities for incentives, and for abuse. Failure of advisory and regulatory organizations to require realistic accounting of the cost of stock-based plans to measure this real cost to the company, and thus to shareholders, has contributed to excesses that encourage extremes and reduce the usefulness to shareholders of these plans. As public policy, TIAA-CREF advocates comprehensive disclosure and more realistic accounting of stock-based plans, the cost of which should be charged to the income statement. Further, we suggest the following guidelines for consideration by companies in which we hold an investment position:

- The provisions of stock-based plans should be fully disclosed to shareholders. This disclosure should include the size of grants, potential value to recipients and cost to the company, and plan provisions that could have a material impact on the number and value of shares distributed. Information on grants to and holdings by individual members of management, where required, should be accompanied by disclosure of the extent to which these individuals have hedged or otherwise reduced their exposure to changes in the price of the company's stock.
- All plans that provide for the distribution of stock or stock options to employees and/or directors should be submitted to shareholders for approval.
- All stock-based plans should specifically prohibit or severely restrict "mega-grants," which are grants of stock or stock options of a value at the time of grant greater than a reasonable and explainable multiple of recipient's total cash compensation.
- Grants of stock or stock options should not be timed to take advantage of nonpublic information with significant positive short-term implications for stock price.

We support the use of fixed price options that are reasonable in size. In certain circumstances, it may be desirable for a company to explore alternatives that may more closely link pay to performance, such as performance-based options, which set performance hurdles to achieve

vesting; premium (out-of-the-money) options, with vesting dependent on attainment of a predetermined appreciation of stock; and indexed options—i.e., those with a strike price tied to an index. Accounting rules should provide a level playing field for consideration of these alternatives; fixed price options should not receive more favorable accounting treatment.

Restricted stock awards, which can be simple and straightforward, have certain advantages over option programs, as long as they are reasonable in size. Restricted stock more closely aligns the interests of executives with shareholders (as opposed to option holders), and the value to the recipient and cost to the corporation can be computed easily and tracked continuously.

TIAA-CREF expects that all stock-based plans for which executives and directors are eligible, and any plan that could result in significant dilution, will be submitted to shareholders for approval. TIAA-CREF has developed decision-rules to guide its voting of proxies related to these proposals.

Stock-Based Award Voting Guidelines
Issue: Potential Dilution from Stock-Based Plans

Red Flag: Total potential dilution from existing and proposed compensation plans exceeds 15% over duration of plan(s) or 2% in any one year.

Override: Increase threshold to 25% for plans proposed by companies in human-capital-intensive industries in which coverage extends through at least middle management levels. Increase threshold to 20% for firms at the lower range of market equity capitalization.

Comment: The two override conditions are each designed to address a specific consideration. The first addresses the needs of human-capital-intensive industries where generous stock-based grants may be necessary to retain personnel and where significant contributions are made by individuals outside the ranks of senior management. The second override addresses the need to provide packages with sufficient value at lower capitalization firms, since a given level of dilution has lower economic value the lower the market capitalization of the firm.

Issue: *Excessive Run Rate from Actual Grants*

Red Flag: In the most recent three years, potential dilution from stock and stock option grants averaged in excess of 2% per year.

Override: Increase threshold to 3% for plans proposed by companies in human-capital-intensive industries.

Comment: The "potential dilution" test described above is a snapshot at a given point in time. That test can miss excessive transfer over time of stock ownership, through stock plans, to executives and employees at companies that repeatedly return to the well for more options. This red flag for excessive run rates is based on actual grants at companies requesting shareholder approval for additional share authorizations for employee stock plans.

Issue: *Reload Options*

Red Flag: Proposal provides for granting reload options.

Override: Plan (i) limits the frequency with which options can be reloaded; (ii) provides for a reload only if market price increases by a specified percent; and (iii) prohibits resale of shares purchased for which options were reloaded.

Comment: Reload options are automatically "reloaded" after exercise at the then current market price. They enable the individual receiving them to reap the maximum potential benefit from option awards by allowing him or her to "lock in" increases in stock price that occur over the duration of the option with no attendant risk. This creates an additional divergence of interests between the outside shareholders and the option recipient.

Issue: *"Evergreen" Option Plans*

Red Flag: Plan contains an "evergreen" feature that has no termination date and reserves a specified percentage of the outstanding shares for award each year.

Override: None.

Issue: *Option Mega-grants*

Red Flag: Option grants that are excessive in relation to other forms of compensation, are out of proportion to compensation of other executives of the corporation, and/or are abnormal compared to awards of peer group CEOs are permitted and have been made.

Override: Clear and credible rationale for such awards given by an independent compensation committee, provided the proposed plan specifically prohibits mega-grants.

Issue: *Option Pricing*

Red Flag: Unspecified exercise price or exercise price below 85% of fair market value on the date of the grant.

Override: None.

Issue: *Restricted Stock*

Red Flag: A plan limited to restricted stock exceeds 3% dilution, or, for an omnibus plan that potentially would allow award of restricted stock exceeding this level, the company has made grants of restricted stock exceeding 1% of outstanding shares over the last three years.

Override: Arguments for higher dilution from restricted stock may be considered on a case-by-case basis for small-cap companies.

Issue: *Coverage*

Red Flag: Plan is limited to a small number of senior employees.

Override: Permits awards to a small number of employees at firms at the lower range of market equity capitalization.

Issue: *Repricing Options*

Red Flag: An option plan gives the company the ability to lower the exercise price of options already awarded where the market price of the stock has declined below the original exercise price ("underwater options").

Override: The company has not repriced options in the past or has excluded senior executives from any repricing and has tied any repricing to a significant reduction in the total number of outstanding options.

Comment: Repricing options after a decline in the stock price undermines the rationale for establishing an option plan in the first place. Repricing gives management a benefit unavailable to shareholders and thereby reduces the alignment of interests between shareholders and management.

Issue: *Excess Discretion*

Red Flag: Significant terms of awards—such as coverage, option price, or type of award provided for the proposed plan—are not specified in the proposal.

Override: None.

READING 11.2

Institutional Investors: The Reluctant Activists

Robert C. Pozen

In 1991, when the police unions were upset by the lyrics of a rap song by Ice-T, they lobbied institutional investors to vote against the directors of Time Warner Inc., the company that had released the song. Because institutional investors now own a majority of the voting stock of publicly traded companies in the United States, they have an influence on the way these companies are run. And given their influence, institutional investors are under increasing pressure to become activist shareholders on behalf of national competitiveness and various social causes.

At the same time, institutional investors have been criticized for intervening in the corporate governance process. As Charles Wohlstetter, former chairman and CEO of Contel, wrote about public pension plans in "The Fight for Good Governance" (HBR, January–February 1993), "In sum, we have a group of people with increasing control of the Fortune '500' who have no proven skills in management, no experience at selecting directors, no believable judgment in how much should be spent for research or marketing—in fact, no experience except that which they have accumulated controlling other people's money."

While Wohlstetter's claims are exaggerated, how do institutional investors act? What factors do they weigh when deciding to become activists? When should they vote with management, and when should they champion the cause of a competing interest? And—perhaps most important—what should corporate executives know about the way institutional investors make these decisions?

Most institutional investors do not set out to become activist shareholders, nor do they want to get involved with a company's operational issues. For most institutions, the approach to shareholder activism is straightforward: to decide whether and when to become active, an institutional investor compares the expected costs of a course of action with the expected benefits. The costs of activism depend primarily on the tools with which the institution exerts influence, from the high costs of waging a formal proxy fight to the low costs of holding informal discussions with management. The benefits depend partly on the probability of success and partly on the issue at hand, with more potential benefit from proposals directly affecting stock price and less from proposals for procedural reforms. If corporate executives understood what motivates the decision making of institutional investors, they would realize that institutions share their concerns about strategic positioning, succession planning, and long-term profitability. Corporate executives would also recognize institutions as their natural allies in responding to the legion of requests to pursue social or political agendas.

A Cost-Benefit Analysis of Shareholder Activism

Institutional investors have a fiduciary duty to try to achieve their client's objectives. Although these objectives vary, clients generally place their savings with institutional investors to earn higher returns than they could by investing on their own, to reduce risk by holding an interest in a large and varied pool of securities, and to maintain some degree of liquidity. Given their responsibility to clients, institutional investors must justify their activism in terms of achieving these objectives. That means becoming an active shareholder only if the expected benefits to clients—that is, increasing financial returns without taking large risks or unduly sacrificing liquidity—exceed the expected costs. While this approach sounds good in theory, in practice it is difficult to predict the results of institutional activism.

Measuring the Benefits of Activism. The best indicator of having achieved benefits for clients is an increase in a portfolio company's stock price. The next best indicator is an earnings increase, which is ultimately reflected in a higher stock price and/or higher dividend.

But the results of activism are not always so easy to interpret. Many forms of institutional activism involve trying to establish better procedures for corporate governance, such as a recent successful effort by the California Public Employees' Retirement System (CalPERS) to have the compensation committee of Advanced Micro Devices (AMD) be composed entirely of independent directors. While such procedural reforms are difficult to link directly to financial

returns, they can be beneficial to an institution's clients if the new procedures lead to decisions that are more favorable to a company's shareholders. For example, with all independent directors, AMD's compensation committee is likely to align executive compensation more closely with shareholder returns through stock options or other devices.

If the price of a company's stock increases after an institutional investor's intervention, there is still the question of whether or not this intervention actually caused the price increase. Consider the case of Lens, Inc., a small activist-oriented institutional investment fund, and Robert Monks, its founder, who in late 1990 began pressuring Sears, Roebuck and Company to focus on its core business rather than attempt to combine a financial supermarket with a department store. After almost two years of pressure, Sears announced that it would concentrate on its retail business and sell Coldwell Banker, its real estate operations, as well as 20% of Dean Witter and Allstate, its principal financial holdings. Lens claimed that its efforts generated more than $1 billion in shareholder value because the price of Sears stock rose sharply over the two years. But the rise in the stock price generally followed the rise in the S&P500 during the same period. Only two points are clear from Lens' efforts: the company's stock substantially lagged the S&P500 before the campaign began, and the stock rose almost $4 on the day Sears announced it was selling its financial businesses. (See "Chronology of an Institutional Shareholder Campaign" at the end of this [reading].)

Measuring the Costs of Activism.

The cost side of an institutional investor's cost-benefit analysis involves estimating the expenses of activism for these institutions and for their clients. These expenses are heavily influenced by the duties spelled out in the advisory contract between the money manager and the institution's board and by the more liberal requirements of the 1992 revisions to the SEC's proxy rules.

Most advisory contracts require money managers to perform normal proxy activity: reading proxy statements, making careful voting decisions, and sending reports to an oversight board. These contracts typically do not address the question of who pays for proxy activism undertaken by the institutional investor on behalf of its clients. In some cases, a money manager may justify imposing a charge on the clients' fund in addition to the advisory fee that clients pay to the money manager. For example, proxy activism may require hiring outside experts, such as appraisers,

who will evaluate mineral rights held by a company proposing to go private. In other cases, such as travel expenses for meetings with company directors, the cost of activism is typically covered by the advisory fee.

Most such fees, however, are set on the assumption that institutional investors will usually function as passive money managers rather than as activists. The advisory fees of equity mutual funds average around 70 basis points (0.70%) per year, with a maximum performance fee of 10 to 20 basis points (0.10% to 0.20%). In other words, the fees do not cover heavy intervention on the part of the money manager. In contrast, advisory fees for a venture capital fund are typically composed of a 1% or 2% base fee plus 10% to 20% of all profits. This much higher fee is based on the assumption that venture fund managers will be actively involved with most of their portfolio companies.

An institutional investor can usually make a reasonable estimate of the out-of-pocket expenses associated with proxy activism. These include SEC filings of proxy solicitation materials; printing, mailing, and advertising these materials; professional fees for lawyers, proxy solicitors, and various consultants; and the extensive time and effort of the involved senior officials. The wild card is litigation. If a portfolio company sues one or more institutional investors for breach of a proxy rule or for acting in concert, the legal bills will be substantial regardless of the outcome. Litigation can also eat up lots of management time. The costs of litigation are hard to justify for institutional investors, since in most cases the benefits of activism are very difficult to predict.

By reducing the threat of litigation and the amount of necessary filings, the new SEC rules have significantly lowered the cost of proxy activism for institutional investors. According to these rules, an institutional investor, without any filings or mailings, can discuss voting issues with an unlimited number of other shareholders as long as the institutional investor does not solicit proxies from any of them. In late 1992, for example, the executive director of the Council of Institutional Investors called a number of council members to discuss the problems of Westinghouse's credit subsidiary, which had incurred large losses through aggressive lending. Representatives from several of these institutional investors then met with the management of Westinghouse to press for governance changes. The result of this very low-cost campaign: Westinghouse agreed to dismantle its poison pill, which would have deterred any large acquirer of Westinghouse stock by allowing all other shareholders to buy the company's stock very cheaply. Westinghouse also agreed to eliminate its staggered board, which would have prevented any potential insurgent from attaining control of a majority of the company's directors in one annual election.

The new SEC rules also allow an institutional investor to solicit proxies from a few large shareholders without mailing proxy statements to all shareholders. This focused approach was taken by Eagle Asset Management, a large holder of Centel and a virulent critic of its proposed merger with Sprint. Eagle mailed a 20-page booklet to Centel's 200 largest shareholders and lobbied them to vote against the merger. Eagle lost by less than 1% of the vote after spending only $250,000, much less than it would have spent on a series of mailings to all 5,000 Centel shareholders.

While the new SEC rules allow institutional investors to take on proxy issues without taking on tremendous expense, the rules do not solve the "free rider" problem. When an institutional investor spends substantial sums in pressuring a company to change its policies, the benefits of such activism are reaped by all stockholders, not just the clients of the active institution. While the value of Sears's shares as a whole may have risen by over $1 billion, how much of that gain was captured by Lens for its clients? And was that gain worth the expense of the battle?

As a practical matter, it is virtually impossible for the activist institutional investor to force all other benefiting shareholders to contribute to the effort. An activist institution can attempt to persuade a few large shareholders to share the costs of opposing a management initiative or of supporting a shareholder proposal. To take advantage of the new exemptions from proxy filings, however, an institutional investor cannot act in concert with other shareholders if together they hold more than 5% of a class of the portfolio company's voting stock. But the new SEC rules do not define "acting in concert," and the case law is very murky; no one really knows what this critical phrase means.

We do know that the new SEC rules have allowed more communication among institutional investors but have led to a more explicit rejection by them of group activity. If an institutional investor, for example, holds a large position in a company's stock and objects to a proposal on that company's ballot, the institution is likely to call other large holders to explain its objection. At the end of this conversation, however, both parties should state clearly that they will not be voting together or buying or selling securities together.

What's Worth Fighting For?

An institutional investor trying to decide whether or not to be an activist shareholder can use this cost-benefit approach to develop a ranking of voting issues and of the modes of proxy intervention. Voting issues can be ranked according to the potential benefits for institutional clients.

Stock Price. The highest potential benefits for clients come from voting issues in which stock price is directly at stake. Institutional activism that raises a company's stock price increases the financial returns for the institution's clients. In late 1987, for example, Hong Kong and Shanghai Bank, the majority shareholder of Marine Midland Bank, proposed to acquire the minority's shares in a cashout merger. Fidelity Investments thought the proposed price was too low, hired its own appraiser, and approached the special committee of independent directors of Marine Midland. As a result of this intervention, Hong Kong and Shanghai increased its offer by over $13 per share; this price increase directly delivered $12 million to the Fidelity funds as well as many millions of dollars to Marine Midland's other shareholders.

Antitakeover Measures. The adoption of most antitakeover measures tends to lower a company's stock price. To avoid these adverse price effects, the logic of cost-benefit analysis dictates that institutional investors should be prepared to devote some resources to opposing such measures. A possible exception is the poison pill, where companies may be able to demonstrate the need for a defensive position for a limited time. For example, as part of an informal settlement with institutional investors, Raytheon and Consolidated Freightways each announced that it would phase out its poison pill on a specified date within a few years and would not extend the poison pill or adopt a new one without the approval of a majority of shareholders.

Executive Compensation. Compensation packages heavily based on a company's financial performance usually correlate with positive returns for shareholders, although the adoption of a performance-based compensation package does not have the same immediate price effects as the adoption of an antitakeover measure. Institutional investors can vote directly on compensation issues only if a company is seeking approval of a stock option plan, a restricted stock plan, or a performance plan in order to deduct annual compensation of over $1 million under the

1993 tax act. Accordingly, it makes sense for institutions to vote for such a plan if properly designed and to lobby against nonperformance-based plans. Last March [1993], for example, the State of Wisconsin Pension Board urged the 160 largest shareholders of Paramount Communications to withhold their votes for members of Paramount's compensation committee because of the inverse relationship between executive pay and shareholder returns over the last five years. Although relatively few votes were withheld, the board reportedly believes that its campaign was an important factor in shaking things up at Paramount.

Governance Structures.
It is difficult to prove the financial benefits of good governance structures such as the establishment of separate audit, compensation, and nominating committees composed entirely of independent directors, or shareholder rights to vote cumulatively or to call special shareholder meetings. If a company has a smart and strong CEO with appropriate compensation incentives, it may do well for years without these structures. But these structures are important safety valves when crises arise, when CEO succession is an issue, or when the business begins to go downhill. It is in the interest of institutional investors to make modest efforts toward promoting good governance structures as part of a long-term investment philosophy.

Procedural Frills.
Some institutional investors have advocated procedural reforms that have not been shown to increase shareholder value or to play an important safety-valve function. One example is the shareholder advisory committee, which is either useless or will try to make decisions and thereby confuse the role of the board. Another example is the push for a chairman separate from the CEO: although this separation may be fruitful for a particular company, there is no evidence that as a general rule it benefits public companies.

Weighing the Modes of Institutional Activism
Using a cost-benefit analysis, institutional investors can also rank different types of proxy intervention, the tools of institutional activism.

Proxy Fights for Control.
Proxy control fights, especially if they are successful, can have a positive effect on a company's share price. Yet institutional investors almost never initiate such fights because the costs are very high, and most institutional investors are legally prohibited from reaping the benefits of acquiring control of a company. Moreover, institutional investors have neither the staff nor the expertise to exercise operating control over even a handful of portfolio companies.

Proxy Campaigns Against Management Proposals.
From time to time, institutional investors have been willing to incur the substantial costs of proxy campaigns against management proposals directly affecting share price, such as the opposition to the proposed merger of Centel and Sprint. But most of the opposition to antitakeover amendments has come from dissidents seeking to acquire control of the company. Without the potential benefits of acquiring control, institutional investors have generally been unwilling to launch proxy campaigns against antitakeover proposals. Institutions tend to be even more reluctant to expend large sums to defeat objectionable management proposals for compensation plans or governance procedures because, unlike issues that directly affect stock price, these have a weaker link to financial returns for institutional clients.

Shareholder Resolutions.
Shareholders who follow the SEC's procedural requirements can place a proposal on a company's ballot. Sponsorship of a shareholder resolution is inexpensive because it is distributed at the company's expense as part of the proxy statement. As long as the resolution sponsor does not ask for proxy authorization it may gather support orally without any SEC filings. As a result, shareholder resolutions have become a favorite mode of institutional intervention on a broad range of issues, including rescission of poison pills, performance measures for executive compensation, and expanded roles for independent directors. In 1987, the College Retirement Equities Fund (CREF) proposed a resolution calling for a shareholder vote at the next annual meeting to repeal poison pills at over a dozen companies. CREF's campaign reportedly involved total out-of-pocket expenses of less than $10,000 plus a modest amount of staff time and resources. At this price, a shareholder resolution could meet the cost-benefit test even if the benefits cannot be guaranteed.

Informal Jawboning.
Even less expensive than a shareholder resolution is informal jawboning—direct discussions with management or public announcements by shareholders seeking improvements in a company's governance structure, changes in overall business strategy, or

resolution of management succession issues. The costs of informal jawboning are limited to communications, travel expenses, and the time of the institution's representatives, but the benefits can be dramatic. For example, J.P. Morgan and Alliance met with the new CEO of American Express to protest its retention of James Robinson as the company's chairman; a few days later, Robinson resigned. Portfolio managers at Wellington Management and Loomis, Sayles publicly expressed concern about the failure of the Chrysler board to name a successor to Lee Iacocca; in less than a week, the board named Robert Eaton the next CEO.

Explanatory Letters. The cheapest mode of institutional activism is voting "no" or withholding a vote and writing a letter explaining why to a company's CEO and/or directors. Companies are often willing to redesign their proposals in response to the reasonable concerns of a large shareholder. For example, Fidelity Investments usually votes against the adoption of stock option plans that give the company's directors total discretion on the pricing and timing of options issuance. After receiving letters from Fidelity explaining its position, many companies have been willing to incorporate pricing and timing criteria into their stock option plans.

Expansionists and Contractionists: Two Activist Philosophies. Many corporate executives are Contractionists. Like Charles Wohlstetter, they believe that institutional investors are intervening too frequently and too intensively in corporate decision-making and that institutional investors will ultimately try to micromanage their companies. Contractionists would be surprised to learn that their views are largely shared by institutional investors that take a cost-benefit approach to activism. Since these institutions are organized and paid as passive portfolio managers, they could not possibly become active in a large number of companies. In 1992, Fidelity Investments voted proxies for almost 3,000 companies but became actively involved in fewer than 12. Even CalPERS, the most outspoken of the public pension plans, becomes actively involved in fewer than 30 companies each year.

According to Contractionists, if institutional investors are dissatisfied with decisions of company management, they should follow the Wall Street Rule of voting with their feet by selling that company's stock. In fact, most institutional investors dissatisfied with company management will sell the stock, because the expected benefits of activism do not warrant the expected costs. The Wall Street Rule is not viable, however, for those institutions employing a passive index

strategy: approximately 10% of all institutional equity assets. Indexed investors, who in effect match their portfolios to market indicators, continued to be big holders of IBM, at one time a huge component of the S&P 500, even as the computer company turned in several years of dismal financial performance. By contrast, several nonindexed institutions bailed out of IBM when the company did not respond adequately to the trend away from mainframe computers.

Even the most nonindexed institutions will become corporate activists only when company management proposes to take some action that portfolio managers view as depressing shareholder values over the long run. For example, institutional investors protested when Time, Inc., rejected a highly priced purchase offer from Paramount's Martin S. Davis and instead acquired Warner Communications, along with a very rich personal arrangement for Steve Ross, Warner's chairman.

Indexed investors will monitor the financial performance of the large holdings and will initiate discussions with management if that performance has been dismal over a period of three to five years. Since indexed investors cannot easily sell out, they will press these dismal performers on major structural issues rather than operational details. Such investors have successfully urged companies to refocus their core business strategies at Eastman Kodak, Sears, and U.S. Steel, and to replace their CEOs at General Motors, Goodyear, and IBM.

Corporate executives can avoid institutional activism by achieving good financial performance over the long term and explaining any short-term problems to their institutional shareholders. Although corporate executives complain that institutional investors do not understand the need for current expenditures to produce future benefits, institutions are actually big buyers of companies with large research budgets. But all research is not automatically good. If a company like Kodak spends millions on research that does not lead to enough successful products, institutional investors will lose faith in the research effort and company management.

Corporate executives should also be reluctant to make proposals to curtail the procedural rights of shareholders or to adopt antitakeover measures. Institutional investors strongly believe that the corporate governance process must serve as an effective means of holding management accountable. And although the takeover binges of the 1980s undoubtedly involved abuses of the governance process, the 1990s are a very different decade, without midnight raids and with much less junk bond financing. Moreover, the latest round of state antitakeover laws already provides corporate management with adequate protection against the abuses of the 1980s.

Most important, corporate executives should increase their efforts to talk directly with institutional investors about their shared goals. While many executives focus their communications efforts on Wall Street analysts, meeting periodically with their large institutional shareholders is equally critical. These meetings are often too important to be delegated to the investor relations office; they should include the CEO and the CFO. Ideally, these meetings should allow the company officials to sound out new ideas and portfolio managers to articulate their perceptions of the company. As Lockheed treasurer Walter Skowronski reported last June about a series of such meetings, "Rational and commonsensical approaches by Lockheed met with rational and commonsensical responses from investors; the process was self-reinforcing over time."

At the opposite pole from Contractionists are the Expansionists, who want institutional investors to play a larger role in corporate decision-making. Most Expansionists are professors, public officials, or leaders of organized interest groups. Social Expansionists want institutional investors to push U.S. companies along the Japanese-German model. Corporate executives should understand that, with a few exceptions, the proposals of neither the Social nor Block Expansionists pass the cost-benefit test for institutional investors.

Social Expansionists.

Social Expansionists want U.S. corporations to take an active role in resolving a variety of social issues, such as protecting animal rights or cleaning up the environment. Given the nature of individual shareholding in most U.S. corporations, Social Expansionists turn to institutional investors as the only hope for pressuring corporations to get involved. However, the goals of Social Expansionists are fundamentally different from those of most institutional clients, who are generally seeking high financial returns. Therefore, executives can often gain support from institutional investors in opposing social issues unless these institutions are subject to contrary instructions from their clients or if pursuing these issues would create financial liabilities for the company.

Most clients of an institutional investor have not chosen it because of its societal views or expertise; they have chosen it because they believe it is likely to fulfill their financial goals. Accordingly, it would be an act of hubris for an institutional investor to vote its social preferences unless specifically directed to do so by its clients. For example, directions may come though a city ordinance

prohibiting pension investments in South Africa, or through client selection of a "green" fund with limitations on investments stated in its prospectus.

Consider an institutional investor confronted with a request to vote against the incumbent directors of Time Warner because it released a song by Ice-T that seemed to condone attacks against the police. On the one hand, the police unions argued that this rap would encourage youths to beat up and shoot police officers. On the other hand, the civil libertarians defended Ice-T's First Amendment right to express his opinion of the police. Should an institutional investor resolve these complex issues in the context of shareholder election of corporate directors, or should government officials resolve these issues in the context of a public forum?

An institutional investor may actively oppose the social actions of a U.S. company if they affect the financial performance of that company. An industrial company's practices of disposing of toxic wastes, for example, may be financially material if these practices create a large contingent liability. But an institutional investor will probably not support efforts by Social Expansionists to stop an industrial practice that is perfectly legal and poses no significant financial threat to the company. If Social Expansionists disagree with the current law on such an industrial practice, they should try to persuade the relevant agency or legislature to change the rules.

Block Expansionists.

Block Expansionists have a different objective. They want institutional investors to acquire more than 25% of the voting shares of U.S. companies and become intensively involved with the management of those companies through board representation. In the view of the Block Expansionists, such intensive institutional involvement in U.S. companies would significantly enhance the economic competitiveness of U.S. industry. Block Expansionists explicitly or implicitly base their position on the success of the German and Japanese systems of corporate governance, in which very large shareholders keep close tabs on corporate managers.

Most executives would disagree with the Block Expansionist agenda, as would most institutional investors. If institutions acquired very large positions in a few U.S. companies, they would jeopardize the diversification objectives of their clients by dramatically increasing the risk of large loss. This extra risk could be justified only if intensive institutional involvement with management decisions would likely cause these portfolio companies to achieve much higher financial returns. But most institutional investors have neither the expertise nor the resources to increase significantly the likelihood of achieving such extra-ordinary returns on a regular basis through intensive involvement with management decisions.

An expansive role for institutional investors is also inconsistent with the liquidity objectives of their clients. If institutions held more than 25% of a company's stock, they would have a very difficult time getting out of that stock. Furthermore, if an institutional investor had representatives on a company's board, securities law restrictions on insider trading and short-swing profits would severely impede the ability of that institution to sell that company's stock. While Block Expansionists may applaud locked-in stock positions as "patient capital," institutions want fairly liquid positions in order to meet redemption requests from clients or to reduce exposure to a particular industry.

To implement their ideas on a broad scale, Block Expansionists would have to persuade Congress to relax the current limits on institutional inventors substantially. Corporate executives would undoubtedly oppose such a relaxation as a threat to management control, and they would find allies in most institutional investors. Most institutions are not interested in regularly running the affairs of U.S. companies along the Japanese or German model. They are troubled by the specter of a few large banks or funds controlling the boards of the *Fortune* "500." Most institutions want to maintain the diversification and liquidity of a portfolio investor, as long as they can occasionally hold accountable the management of a poorly performing company.

Conclusions

As executives have watched institutional investors acquire an increasing percentage of their companies' shares, many have come to fear a slippery slope of institutional intervention from questions about the wisdom of a merger one minute to advice about plant location or new product development the next. But institutional investors are not interested in day-to-day management of any portfolio company; they are reluctant activists. In a perfect world, institutions would never need to intervene in corporate governance because all their portfolio companies would be good performers. Even in this imperfect world, institutions overcome their built-in inertia only if the particular type of activism passes the cost-benefit test. Given the rigors of this test, activism turns out to be the best strategy in very few cases.

If corporate executives come to understand the modus operandi of institutional investors, these executives will realize that they do not need to worry about institutions taking control of U.S. corporations. In situations where

company performance is down or a ballot proposal is controversial, executives should discuss these issues with the institutional shareholders as early as possible. In most other situations, executives can avoid institutional activism altogether by turning in good financial performance over the long term and designing proposals to enhance long-term shareholder values.

Chronology of an Institutional Shareholder Campaign

One of the best examples of the new brand of jawboning is Lens, Inc.'s efforts from 1990 to 1992 to pressure Sears, Roebuck and Company into changing its business mix and governance structure. Lens is a private company founded by Robert Monks, a wealthy investor who had previously headed the pension program at the U.S. Department of Labor. Lens has attempted to raise capital from institutional investors to take large positions in public companies and improve their financial results through active intervention. But Lens' capital-raising efforts have so far been unsuccessful, and it has never owned more than $3 million in Sears stock.

Lens believed that because there was no synergy between Sears' retail and financial businesses, Sears should focus on one core business. Lens also believed that Sears' board, which was dominated by insiders, was not sufficiently accountable to shareholders. Moreover, the trustees of the company's Employee Stock Ownership Plan (ESOP), which held 25% of the Sears voting stock, were the company's CEO and other Sears affiliates.

This situation met all of Lens' criteria for becoming an activist shareholder. The issues concerned the overall structure and direction of Sears; the obstacles to shareholder value of the company's stock provided Lens with potential allies. Moreover, there were five board seats open at the next election. Since Sears allowed its shareholders to concentrate their votes on one candidate, a practice known as cumulative voting, Lens could elect one director by winning the support of only 16% of Sears' shareholders.

Below is a chronology of Lens' jawboning campaign and the price of Sears stock on each date (also see Figure 1):

11/1/90 ($24.87): Lens writes to Sears to suggest that Lens founder Robert Monks be considered as a management nominee for the Sears board.

2/1/91 ($25.87): When Sears refuses to nominate Monks to the management slate, he is nominated by a shareholder associated with Monks. Sears reduces the size of its board, so that Monks needs the support of 24%

of the company's shareholders to win a seat under cumulative voting.

5/9/91 ($39.50): Monks is not elected to the board, but he receives over 12% of the vote, primarily from institutional investors. Shortly after the election, the board decides to remove Sears' CEO from the board's nominating committee and to appoint independent trustees for the ESOP.

11/1/91 ($36.75): Individual and institutional shareholders sympathetic to Lens' critique of Sears propose five advisory resolutions to be voted on at the annual meeting scheduled for May 1992. Before that meeting, Lens solicits support for the resolutions by sending letters, making phone calls, and running a full-page advertisement in the *Wall Street Journal*.

5/14/92 ($43.25): At Sears' annual meeting, these five resolutions receive the following percentage of the votes cast:

    Declassify the board: 41.2%

    Establish confidential voting: 40.9%

    Separate roles of CEO and chairman: 27.4%

    Study divestiture: 23.7%

    Institute a minimum level of stock ownership for directors: 19.3%

7/1/92 ($39.50): During the summer, Sears experiences various difficulties, including fraud charges at auto repair facilities and Hurricane Andrew losses at its Allstate unit. As part of a settlement of litigation brought by shareholders other than Lens, Sears appoints two new outside directors to its board, one the chairman of Philip Morris and the other the former CEO of Kellogg.

9/29/92 ($44.75): Sears announces that it will concentrate on its retail business, while selling all of Coldwell Banker as well as 20% of Dean Witter and Allstate. Sears stock rises $3 and ⅞.

Given its very small holding in Sears, Lens was not in a position to benefit from the stock price increase as much as institutions with larger stakes in the company. These other institutional investors were "free riders" on Lens' efforts to refocus Sears, through which Lens claims to have generated more than $1 billion in shareholder value for an expenditure of less than $500,000.

Others might debate that dramatic conclusion. While the price of Sears stock rose over the two years of Lens' jawboning efforts, so did the S&P 500. Lens' campaign clearly had some influence on the course of events at Sears during the period. It's impossible, however, to determine precisely how much of an effect Lens' activism had on Sears' decision-making or on the company's stock price. Perhaps Sears would ultimately have decided to focus on its retail business without the nomination of Monks or the divestiture resolution. In deciding to sell off its financial services businesses, perhaps the company was responding more to a general sense of shareholder dissatisfaction than to the specific votes on the advisory resolutions. Perhaps Sears actually moved more slowly than it would have in order to avoid the appearance of caving in to Lens' demands.

FIGURE 1

Sears stock rises during Lens' efforts: So does the S&P 500

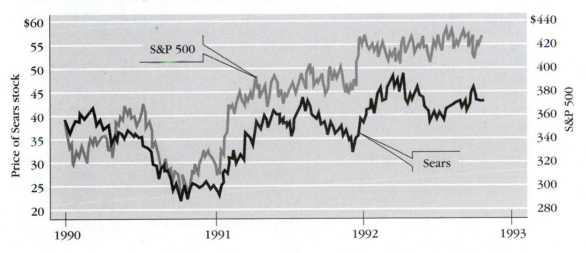

READING 11.3

Shareholder Activism and Corporate Governance in the United States (excerpt)

Bernard S. Black

Does Institutional Investor Activism Improve Company Performance?

It's hard to be against institutional investor activism. But does the muted activism found in the United States really matter—does it affect the bottom line performance? Studies of this question are beginning to accumulate. On the whole, they offer no convincing evidence that shareholder activism affects bottom line performance. To be sure, discerning an effect of activism on performance is not easy. Institutional activism could have a positive effect that is economically significant, yet still buried in the noise of other factors that affect performance. Still, the general absence of convincing evidence of a relationship between activism and firm performance suggests that activism has, at most, a minor impact on firm performance.

One question that researchers have asked is whether firms with a high level of institutional ownership, and therefore the possibility for accompanying monitoring, outperform firms with lower institutional ownership. There is no strong evidence of a correlation between firm performance and percentage of shares owned by institutions. Some studies report that firms with high institutional ownership *underperform* other firms (Carvell and Strebel 1987; Edelman and Baker 1987)—the so-called "neglected firm" effect. But two recent studies fail to find this effect (Beard and Sias 1997; Brennan, Chordia and Subramanyam 1997). McConnell and Servaes 1990 report a correlation between Tobin's q, which is in part a measure of management skill, and institutional ownership. But this could reflect institutions buying shares in firms with high Tobin's q, which also tend to be high-growth firms, rather than the institutions' improving the performance of firms that they own.

A second question researchers have asked is whether activism targeted at particular firms affects performance. Daily, Johnson, Elstrand and Dalton 1996 is representative of a number of studies that fail to find a relationship be-

tween firm performance and institutional investor activism. They find no significant contemporaneous or lagged correlation between firm performance (measured by abnormal stock price returns, return on assets, or return on equity), and ownership by institutions as a whole, ownership by activist institutions (those who have submitted shareholder proposals), or actual submission of a shareholder proposal. See also Del Guercio and Hawkins 1997; Gillan and Starks 1997; Karpoff, Malatesta and Walkling 1996; Smith 1996; Wahal 1996.

Nesbitt 1994 is an exception. He reports positive long-term stock price returns to firms targeted by CalPERS. However, Del Guercio and Hawkins 1997 find similar positive returns to poorly performing firms in general, including firms targeted by CalPERS, firms targeted by other institutions and firms not targeted for shareholder proposals. Wahal 1996 also finds mean reversion in stock price returns for firms targeted by CalPERS and eight other activist institutions. This suggests that market inefficiency, or failure of the asset pricing model to fully capture risk factors for these firms, are more likely explanations than activism for the "rebound" effect that Nesbitt finds.

A second exception is Opler and Sokobin's 1997 study of firms that are on the "focus list" of the Council of Institutional Investors (CII), an umbrella organization for large institutional investors. They find significant above-market performance in the year after targeting. They find no mean reversion in their control sample, in contrast to Del Guercio and Hawkins 1997 and Wahal 1996. Further research is needed to determine whether Opler and Sokobin's choice of control sample explains their failure to find a rebound effect. There are also general questions about the reliability of measures of long-term stock price returns (Barber and Lyon 1997; Kothari and Warner 1997). My personal judgment is that Opler and Sokobin's results are suspect, partly because they are too strong. The 12% mean (9% median) abnormal returns they find are implausibly large, given the mild nature of CII listing—which may or may not result in targeted activism by CII's members, which may or may not succeed.

Published in *The New Palgrave Dictionary of Economics and the Law*, vol. 3, pp. 459–465, 1998. Copyright © 1998 by Peter Newman. From *The New Palgrave Dictionary of Economics and Law*, edited by Peter Newman. Reprinted by permission of St. Martin's Press, LLC.

A third approach is to look for abnormal stock price returns around the date when a formal shareholder proposal is announced, or the date when a company announces acquiescence to an informal proposal. There is no consistent evidence of short-term abnormal returns to targeted firms (Del Guercio and Hawkins 1997; Gillan and Starks 1997; Karpoff, Malatesta and Walkling 1996; Smith 1996; Strickland, Wiles and Zenner 1996; Wahal 1996).

There are a few exceptions to this general pattern. Del Guercio and Hawkins 1997 and Smith 1996 find significant *negative* returns when a proposal to eliminate a takeover defense is announced. Strickland, Wiles and Zenner 1996 and Wahal 1996 find significant *positive* returns for successful "jawboning" efforts, which, because they are successful, don't lead to formal shareholder proposals. Smith reports significant positive returns for *non*-takeover related proposals. Smith also reports significant and positive announcement period returns, averaging 1.1%, for firms that subsequently accede to a CalPERS proposal, but significant negative announcement period returns, averaging 1.2%, for firms that continue to resist the proposal.

Taking these studies as a whole, one cannot conclude that activism has a large effect, and I am left in doubt as to whether it has any effect. The statistically significant results that exist lack an obvious pattern, and could reflect data mining. The clarity of the signal is also suspect. The appearance of a formal proposal could reflect management intransigence, which caused informal negotiations to fail. Conversely, the success of informal negotiations could signal that management is attentive to shareholder interests and thus produce a positive stock price reaction that isn't related to the governance issue on which agreement was reached.

These studies' mostly neutral results may also reflect event date uncertainty. This uncertainty arises partly because shareholder proposals are often discussed informally with management before being formally announced, partly because the voting outcome is unknown when the proposal is made, and partly because shareholder proposals aren't newsworthy enough to be consistently reported in standard sources, such as the Dow Jones News Service.

A fourth approach is to ask whether discrete corporate events occur more frequently at firms that have been targeted for governance efforts. Studies that take this approach—the reader should expect this by now—produce mixed results. There is no significant correlation between activism and subsequent CEO turnover (Del Guercio and Hawkins 1997; Karpoff, Malatesta and Walkling 1996;

Smith 1996) or subsequent takeover, whether friendly or hostile (Del Guercio and Hawkins 1997; Smith 1996).

Del Guercio and Hawkins 1997 find that targeted control firms have a higher incidence of some events during the next three years, most notably assets sales, spinoffs, restructurings, and employee layoffs (taken as a single group of events), and that some activist institutions, notably CalPERS, have more impact than others. They also find that *successful* shareholder proposals and proposals targeted at takeover defenses (successful or not), are associated with higher incidence of takeovers. This is consistent with (i) a strong shareholder vote for a proposal indicating shareholder displeasure with management, and signaling to prospective acquirers that shareholders will support a takeover bid; and (ii) shareholders targeting firms that are already attractive takeover targets for takeover-related proposals. Bizjak and Marquette 1997 find that shareholder proposals to rescind a poison pill increase the likelihood that the targeted firm will modify or rescind its pill. But the firms' response may be more a sop to shareholders than an important substantive change, because the firms can adopt a new poison pill if they become the target of a takeover bid.

These studies of management response to a shareholder proposal face a study design problem. Institutions target poorly performing firms for shareholder proposals. These firms are already more likely to become takeover targets or experience top management turnover, because of their poor performance. So a well-designed study must use a control group of equally poorly performing companies in the same industry that weren't targeted by shareholders. If the performance measures that a study uses to find a control group are less sophisticated than the measures that institutions use to select their targets, the study could find a correlation between activism and a governance event, when the true correlation is between the criteria that led the firm to be targeted for activism and the governance event. For example, the correlation that Del Guercio and Hawkins 1997 find between targeting and some governance events could be due to their use of a single measure, return on assets, to identify control firms.

A fifth approach, used by Wagster and Prevost 1996, is to examine the stock price reaction of firms that had already been targeted when the SEC liberalized its proxy rules in 1991–1992—a regulatory change that increased the potential effectiveness of shareholder activism. They find no significant reaction to announcements of these regulatory changes.

Even if institutional investor activism doesn't directly affect target firms, it could change corporate culture, and therefore affect the performance of all firms. This possibility can't be tested directly. But we can ask whether particular governance changes that the institutions support affect performance. Empirical evidence is available for three such changes: board composition; creation of nominating and compensation committees staffed entirely by independent directors; and separation of the positions of board chairman and chief executive officer.

Institutions strongly support corporate boards dominated by independent directors. But there is no compelling evidence that greater board independence improves performance, and some evidence that inside and affiliated directors play useful roles (on independent directors, see the review by Bhagat and Black 1997; on affiliated directors, see Klein 1997a). Westphal 1997 discusses how CEOs adapt to, and can substantially neutralize, the greater structural independence of boards of directors. Activist institutions generally support creation of nominating and compensation committees staffed entirely by independent

directors. But Klein 1997b finds no evidence that the existence of these committees or their staffing affects firm performance. Many institutions also support separating the positions of chairman of the board and chief executive officer. But here too, there's no convincing evidence that this governance change affects performance (Brickley, Coles and Jarrell 1997).

The review above of evidence on the importance of shareholder activism has focused on visible activism. There may be gains from the mostly invisible jawboning of particular companies to change strategy or CEO, both for the few companies that become the targets of these efforts, and for other companies that change strategy or CEO to avoid being singled out for their slowness. The data to assess this activity quantitatively don't exist, so one must rely on anecdote. Optimists about the effects of shareholder activism think these gains are large (e.g., Gordon 1997b). Pessimists, myself included, tend to think that these efforts are valuable, but doubt whether they have large overall efficiency effects (e.g., Black and Coffee 1994; Coffee 1997). . . .

••••• CASE STUDY:

Fund Voting in a Proxy Fight

Institutional activism takes many forms, as we have seen. In most situations, mutual funds are drawn into the fray by the actions of others. Company management may put forward a proposal or initiate a structural change, or an opposition group may propose to buy the company or change the company's business strategy. This case study presents such a situation where mutual funds and other institutional investors were drawn into a battle between an insurgent group and company management.

This case study involves two related initiatives by an insurgent group in relation to RJR Nabisco. RJR Nabisco is a conglomerate with both a tobacco business (RJR) and a food business (Nabisco). The tobacco business was subject to a broad range of legal suits along with other tobacco companies. The insurgent group, led by Bennett LeBow and Carl Icahn, owned slightly less than 5% of the voting stock of RJR Nabisco. The remainder of the stock was heavily concentrated in the hands of mutual funds and other institutional investors.

In the first initiative (First Act), the insurgent group put forth two shareholder proposals: to spin off the Nabisco food business from the tobacco business and to restore the right of shareholders to call a special shareholders' meeting. Subsequently, in a second initiative (Second Act), the insurgent group proposed a slate of directors to replace the incumbent directors of RJR Nabisco.

In reviewing this case study and Exhibit 3, "What Burns Holes in LeBow's Pockets?" assume that you are the manager of two mutual funds—Growth Fund and Environmental Growth Fund—each owning 1% of outstanding common stock of RJR Nabisco, which is trading at $30 per share. The Growth Fund is a $10 billion fund, and the Environmental Growth Fund is a $1 billion fund. The investment objective of the Growth Fund is to seek capital appreciation over the long term, and the investment objective of the Environmental Growth Fund is the same, while taking into account all aspects of environmental concerns.

Discussion Questions

You have been asked to vote shares of the two mutual funds on the above two shareholder resolutions and the election of directors. For each fund, please answer the following questions:

1. How will you vote? Will you vote the same for each fund?
2. What is the rationale for your vote? What is the difference between voting on shareholder resolutions and voting on director elections?
3. How would you evaluate the potential and probable benefits to your fund from engaging in shareholder activism on these votes? Quantify your answer to the extent feasible.
4. What strategies or tactics would you utilize in support of your position? Would you talk to the insurgents, company management and/or other institutional in-

EXHIBIT 1

Ownership information (February 6, 1996)

Beneficial Ownership		Type of Shares	Votes per Share	Shares Outstanding
Officers & directors	0.45%	Common stock	1.00	272,807,942
Institutions	64.33%	Series C conversion preferred stock	0.20	26,675,000
Wachovia Bank of North Carolina, N.A.	1.07%	ESOP convertible preferred stock	0.20	15,003,379

Source: Proxy Statement, CDA Investment Technologies.
Note: The company has three types of voting stock. Each share of common stock entitles shareholders to one vote. Each share of Series C conversion preferred stock and ESOP convertible preferred stock entitles shareholders to one-fifth of a vote.

vestors? Would you be prepared to solicit proxies or participate in any group actions?

RJR Nabisco Holdings Corp.*

First Act

Approval of the following shareholder resolutions submitted by Brooke Group, Ltd., a publicly traded company of the New York Stock Exchange, requires the written consent of a majority of RJR Nabisco Holdings Corp. common stock outstanding.

Brooke Group has initiated a consent solicitation through which shareholders are being asked to approve two proposals. The first item seeks adoption of a nonbinding resolution requesting that the board spin off the remaining 80.5 percent of Nabisco common stock immediately. The second resolution is a binding bylaw amendment proposal in which shareholders will vote on whether to restore the right to call a special meeting by written request of holders of 25 percent of the common stock outstanding. Brooke Group, which is controlled by Chairman and CEO Bennett LeBow, owns approximately 4.8 percent of RJR's outstanding common stock.

Item 1: Approve Resolution to Spin Off Nabisco

This resolution is a nonbinding proposal through which shareholders would ask the board to spin off the remaining 80.5 percent share of Nabisco common stock in order to enhance the value of shareholders' investment by separating the company's food and tobacco businesses.

RJR Management

RJR's board opposes the proposal, arguing that while it sees value in ultimately spinning off the remaining Nabisco stock to shareholders, it believes that the timing is wrong. RJR argues that a negative environment from litigation against tobacco companies could attract further litigation claiming that the spin-off is a fraudulent conveyance, meaning that the spin-off is intended to frustrate potential creditors rather than to effect a valid business strategy. Moreover, if the spin-off is viewed as not having a valid business purpose, it might not be tax-free to shareholders. The company also claimed that an injunction against the spin-off could block further dividend increases and stock

buyback programs that could otherwise enhance shareholder value. Another reason for delaying a spin-off was RJR's perceived commitment to security holders that a spin-off would be delayed for a period of time in order to ensure the company's investment grade credit rating and overall financial integrity. RJR also questioned the integrity of proponents, Mr. LeBow and Carl Icahn, who are well known for their involvement in financing corporate takeovers and their association with companies that have filed for bankruptcy protection.

Background

RJR implemented a partial spin-off of Nabisco in 1994 and used the proceeds to reduce the substantial debt burden that was its legacy from its debt-financed takeover by Kravis, Kohlberg and Roberts (KKR) in the mid-1980s. Following the partial spin-off, RJR retained an 80.5 percent stake in Nabisco. A shareholder proposal submitted at the 1995 annual meeting by a religious organization requested that the company engage in a full spin-off in order to achieve a full separation of the food and tobacco businesses. The board opposed the proposal as not being in the best interest of shareholders and because it would violate a board resolution in which it committed to not engaging in any distributions of stock of subsidiary before December 31, 1996—and not before December 31, 1998, if such a distribution would cause the company's senior debt rating to be downgraded. The company also argued that it was taking other steps that would benefit shareholders, including a one-for-five reverse stock dividend intended to improve the market for RJR common stock, the introduction of a $0.375 quarterly dividend, and an exchange offer involving debt securities of RJR and Nabisco, Inc. The spin-off proposal was defeated and received little support from RJR shareholders.

Brooke Group approached RJR in May 1995 about a possible combination of its struggling Liggett tobacco business with RJR's tobacco operations in a merger that Brooke Group believed would permit RJR to spin off the remaining shares of Nabisco to RJR shareholders in a legally defensible transaction. Brooke Group reportedly asked for a 20 percent stake in the combined tobacco company and $350 million in preferred stock. RJR ultimately rejected the proposed transaction and may have also turned down a subsequent offer to buy Liggett from Brooke Group outright.

In August 1995, after talks broke down between Brooke Group and RJR, Brooke Group's wholly owned subsidiary, New Valley Corp., made a Hart-Scott-Rodino Act (H-S-R) filing to buy 15 percent of the company's outstanding common stock. Later that month, the board amended the company's bylaws to eliminate the right of shareholders to call a special meeting in response to a perceived threat of a takeover by LeBow and Icahn. On October 30, 1995, LeBow sent a letter to RJR announcing Brooke Group's intent to conduct a consent solicitation in which shareholders would be asked to vote in favor of a nonbinding resolution to spin off the remainder of Nabisco immediately. On November 20, 1995, Brooke Group made the necessary filings to preserve its right to run a slate of directors at the company's spring annual meeting.

RJR and Brooke Group Positions on a Spin-Off

Brooke Group argues that the RJR board's fear of personal liability from litigation surrounding a potential spin-off is keeping Nabisco from being spun off and that the failure to carry out a separation of the food company is hurting the overall company's earnings and stock performance. Brooke notes that since RJR's initial public offering (February 1, 1991) through the date of the New Valley H-S-R filing, the company has had meager total returns of −0.5 percent, compared to 9.8 percent for the S&P Tobacco index and 9.8 percent for fellow food and tobacco products company Philip Morris. For the one-year period through the H-S-R filing RJR suffered a loss of 12 percent, while the S&P Tobacco index returned 28.6 percent and Philip Morris generated a 32.8 percent return for its shareholders. LeBow has stated that Brooke Group only wants to see RJR spin off Nabisco to increase his estimated $150 million investment in the company's stock and is not seeking to take control of RJR. Brooke Group cites recent studies and statistics demonstrating the apparent benefits of corporate spin-offs to shareholders. Brooke Group also expresses considerable doubt as to predictions of an improving litigation environment that will produce a more favorable time for a spin-off.

RJR does not refute Brooke Group's criticism of the company's past performance, but asserts that the litigation environment makes an immediate spin-off too risky. The company notes that the industry is currently faced with several lawsuits (*Castano, Engle, and Broin*) in which courts have upheld class certifications that could result in massive class action lawsuits against the industry, as well as a handful of state attorneys general cases in which states (including Florida, Mississippi, Minnesota, Maryland, and West

Virginia) are seeking reimbursements for Medicaid expenses arising from alleged injuries and deaths due to smoking. The company believes that in the current environment, a spin-off would attract protracted litigation to prevent RJR from shielding Nabisco from a potential megaverdict arising from any of these cases. RJR CEO Steven Goldstone has publicly stated that he thinks that the company may make sufficient progress in these cases by mid-1998 that will make a spin-off less risky at that time.

RJR cautions shareholders not to throw their support behind Messrs. LeBow and Icahn given their reputation as corporate raiders and their involvement in certain companies which ended up in bankruptcy at some point, including SkyBox International Inc. (LeBow), MAI Systems Inc. (LeBow), and TWA (Icahn). RJR asserts that Brooke Group was forced by the company to disclose its attempts to work a deal to combine Liggett with RJR Tobacco and efforts by LeBow to form a consortium to take a controlling interest in RJR. . . .

Amendment of the Bylaw and RJR's Corporate Governance

RJR Management

Mr. Goldstone acknowledged that the elimination of shareholders' right to call a special meeting is an unpopular move with many of the company's institutional shareholders. However, he claims that most shareholders RJR has contacted do not intend to support the LeBow bylaw amendment, given the concerns expressed by the company that the dissidents' agenda is really to take over RJR and not to improve the company's corporate governance. Goldstone said the board believed that this one potential defense against Mr. LeBow and Mr. Icahn is necessary given that relative to other S&P 500 companies, RJR has erected relatively few antitakeover defenses. He noted that the company does not maintain a poison pill, maintains cumulative voting in the election of directors, allows shareholders to act by written consent with a vote representing a majority of shares outstanding, and elects its board annually. RJR argues that the move to restrict the right to call a special meeting is aimed solely at the LeBow/Icahn solicitation and prevents the possibility of the dissidents calling a special meeting to vote on a takeover of RJR with support as low as 25.1 percent of shares outstanding. RJR also asserts that Brooke Group's corporate governance profile contains similar voting requirements to those adopted by RJR.

EXHIBIT 2

Ownership information (April 8, 1996)

Beneficial Ownership		Type of Shares	Votes per Share	Shares Outstanding
Officers & directors	0.46%	Common stock	1.00	272,982,782
Institutions	70.71%	Series C conversion preferred stock	0.20	26,675,000
Wachovia Bank of North Carolina, N.A.	1.07%	ESOP convertible preferred stock	0.20	15,003,379

Source: Proxy Statement, CDA Investment Technologies.
Note: The company has three types of voting stock: common stock entitles its holder to one stock, and ESOP convertible preferred stock. Each share of common stock entitles its holder to one vote. Each share of Series C conversion preferred stock and ESOP convertible preferred stock entitles its holder to one-fifth of a vote. Wachovia Bank of North Carolina, N.A. beneficially owns 100 percent of the company's ESOP convertible preferred stock. Bennett LeBow and Carl Icahn together own approximately 6.6 percent of the outstanding stock.

Brooke Group

Brooke Group complains that the bylaw amendment removing the right of shareholders, but not the board's right, to call special meetings was done in secrecy after Brooke Group met with RJR management and made known its intention to increase its stake in RJR. Brooke Group believes institutional shareholders will support its effort to restore their previous right to call a special meeting.

Second Act

Item 1: Elect Directors

Mr. LeBow's Brooke Group has nominated a ten-member slate to replace the current board of RJR. The LeBow slate has a three-prong platform:
- Effect an immediate spin-off of Nabisco.
- Increase the company's 1996 annual tobacco dividend from $1.50 to $2.00 per share and maintain a payout ratio of 60 percent of net cash flow.
- Revitalize the tobacco company under Ronald Fulford, former executive chairman of Imperial Tobacco, a subsidiary of Hanson PLC.

In addition, as a result of the terms of the recent Liggett Group Inc. tobacco litigation settlement of the Castano class action lawsuit and the settlement of a number of state attorneys' general suits against the industry to recover expenses of treating Medicaid patients, Mr. LeBow would offer RJR shareholders a first opportunity to consider a merger between Liggett and RJR that purportedly would extend the settlement to RJR and free the company from all current and future addiction-based liability claims.

The Brooke Group slate comprises ten nominees, five of whom (Bennett LeBow, Rouben Chakalian, Richard Lampen, Arnold Burns, and Barry Ridings) are employees or directors of Brooke Group or some affiliated organization. Mr. Chakalian has been president and CEO of Liggett since June 1994. Liggett is the manufacturer of Chesterfields and Eve cigarettes. Also providing the slate with tobacco industry experience is Peter Strauss, who was for three years (through December 1994) senior vice president, trade marketing (domestic) and international operations for the American Tobacco Co., which was merged into Brown & Williamson, a subsidiary of B.A.T. Industries, in 1994.

In addition to Mr. Strauss, the outside directors include shareholder advocate and former California Public Employees' Retirement System (CalPERS) CEO Dale Hanson, attorney Robert Frome, investment banker Barry Ridings, business professor William Starbuck, and Frederick Zuckerman, a former senior executive of IBM, RJR Nabisco, and Chrysler.

Cognizant that RJR and some shareholders are suspicious of Mr. LeBow's motives, Brooke Group's nominees have pledged that if they have not declared a spin-off of the remaining Nabisco shares held by the company within six months of their election, they will call a special meeting for the election of new directors. Brooke Group has also stated that it will not participate in the management of RJR Nabisco.

In addition, Brooke Group's slate has also pledged to adhere to a number of corporate governance policies, including the following:

- Any corporate transaction between RJR Tobacco and its subsidiaries and Brooke Group or its affiliates valued at more than $2 million (i.e., a Liggett/RJR merger) would require approval by a special committee of independent directors and RJR shareholders.
- No adoption of a staggered board or poison pill.
- Adoption of confidential voting for future stockholder votes. . . .

EXHIBIT 3

What burns holes in LeBow's pockets?

Jonathan R. Laing

The voice crackles with excitement that's only accentuated by the scratchy connection from a car phone. "We've got a great message that institutional investors are really starting to turn on to," gushes Bennett S. LeBow, the one-time tanktown takeover artist who's now in the biggest battle of his life and clearly relishing it. "I'm an experienced fighter, and come April 17, I think a lot of people are going to get the surprise of their life."

That's the day, of course, he hopes to oust the board of giant RJR Nabisco Holdings at the company's annual meeting and install himself and his hand-picked slate of nine others as directors. LeBow is merely the latest barbarian at the gate of this once venerable tobacco and food concern. But his platform of breaking up the company to unlock value has seductive appeal to shareholders who've been saddled with years of disappointing earnings and slack stock performance following Kohlberg Kravis Roberts' $29 billion leveraged buyout of the firm in 1989.

LeBow's plan calls for RJR to immediately spin off to current shareholders the 81% stake it still holds in Nabisco food operation. Then, LeBow figures, the food company's stock, freed of the immense litigation risks facing Reynolds and other tobacco companies, would bolt upward.

But it's difficult to imagine a more unlikely champion of shareholder value. Over the years, LeBow himself has proven a less-than-adept corporate manager. Two of his major corporation acquisitions of the mid-'Eighties, the computer concern MAI Systems and Western Union, ended up filing for Chapter 11 bankruptcy protection in 1993 while still under his tutelage. Heavy losses were inflicted on shareholders. LeBow denies any responsibility for this sad pass. He claims both MAI and Western Union were in trouble, high-risk companies that he was, unfortunately, unable to save.

His current publicly traded company, Brooke Group Ltd., is hardly in the pink of health. This despite the fact that Brooke's stock rocketed from $4 a share to $14 in a matter of weeks last fall after LeBow first announced his campaign to bust up RJR. The stock currently trades at around $9. Brooke's major operating unit, Liggett, is in free fall as a result of its shrinking share of the U.S. cigarette business. Liggett now holds about 2% of the market, and it is plagued by declining volume, poor distribution, a loss of pricing power for its important discount brands, and antiquated plants and equipment.

Meanwhile, the parent company Brooke is asphyxiating on some $400 million in consolidated debt that recently had to be restructured. As of last September 30 [1995], Brooke boasted a negative net worth of more than $325 million. And that number is likely to grow. In a notification of late filing last week, Brooke reported that it expects to post a net loss of $32 million for 1995. With performance like this, Brooke has another shot at being *Fortune* magazine's "Least Admired" company in the U.S., an accolade it last won in 1994.

The deplorable operating results of LeBow-controlled companies never stopped him from enriching himself at the expense of fellow investors. Over the years he has feasted royally even as his companies hemorrhaged red ink. His combined annual compensation at Brooke at its various units exceeds $2 million. He also has never been averse to making sweetheart deals between his public companies and the private entities he controls. Brooke, for example, spent some $10 million in 1992 to buy LeBow's management company, which benefited from having

Brooke buy back shares from him in a deal that was not offered to other shareholders. In a sense, LeBow green-mailed his own company.

And, when it comes to maneuvering in bankruptcy court, few financiers shake and bake with the agility of LeBow. Though a minority shareholder of Western Union, or New Valley, as the company was renamed in 1991, LeBow wound up maintaining control of the company when it shocked the investment world by emerging from bankruptcy in 1995 with a cash kitty of $300 million after paying off all its creditors. An unexpected windfall from the sale of New Valley's funds-transfer business had made a minor bonanza out of what was expected to be a lugubrious court-ordered liquidation in which creditors and shareholders would be hosed.

Other equity holders cried foul and sued, charging that LeBow and Brooke had manipulated the bankruptcy process to their own benefit. But to no avail. Today, LeBow uses New Valley as his personal investment arm despite the fact that Brooke owns but 42% of the company's common.

Lavish Lifestyle

Lastly, LeBow has few qualms about using his debt-laden companies as personal banks for streams of loans to finance his lavish lifestyle of multiple homes and occasional hijinks. He outdid himself in 1989 when he chartered a plan to fly 150 friends to a $3 million party in London to christen his private yacht, which was modeled on one built for Queen Victoria. LeBow's guests reportedly were put up at Claridge's Hotel and were met at the harbor by a uniformed marching band.

At one point, LeBow's borrowing got so out of control that Brooke shareholders successfully sued to force LeBow to pay back some $16 million in outstanding loans, waive his right to $6.25 million in preferred dividends and limit increases on his annual salary for the next four years.

LeBow remains unrepentant. As he told *Barron*'s last week, "The point to remember is that I would have paid every dime of the loans with contracted interest anyway. The lawsuit just accelerated the payback. Look, those were the swinging 'Eighties when everybody was living high. And by the way, you should know that RJR Chairman Mike Harper took some $40 million from the company last year, if you add up his salary, incentive compensation, bonuses, and other benefits. We'll fax you the numbers."

Of course, LeBow was stretching the truth a tad in his spirited rejoinder. The loans he was forced to repay all occurred in the Calvinist 'Nineties rather than the spendthrift 'Eighties. And the proffered fax on Harper's compensation got the magic $40 million level only by lumping together two and a half years of Harper's salary, bonuses, option awards, insurance benefits, and perks. Clearly, all is fair in love and takeover battles.

LeBow's career of self-dealing has clearly paid off. His nearly 60% interest in Brooke alone has a current market value of more than $90 million.

Characteristically, he's mounting his epic proxy battle for control of multibillion-dollar RJR on the cheap. His partner in the effort, long-time raider Carl Icahn, put up some $350 million of the $500 million the pair used to accumulate its 18 million-share, or 6.6%, position in RJR's common. LeBow's contribution consists of $80 million supplied by New Valley—seemingly his sole remaining source of corporate liquidity—leveraged with some $70 million in margin debt. Both Icahn and LeBow are slightly underwater on their positions, based on RJR's recent trading level of around $31.

Yet the proxy fight being mounted by LeBow and Brooke can't be dismissed out of hand. Certainly RJR is taking the effort seriously, firing volley after volley of full-page ads in the *New York Times* and *The Wall Street Journal* trumpeting various claimed depredations of "LeBow—LeBogus" or "LeBow—LeBankrupt" and carpet-bombing its shareholders with all manner of anti-LeBow propaganda.

In February, the LeBow team shocked RJR by winning a consent solicitation of the company's shareholders in which more than half of RJR's outstanding shares voted in favor of a nonbinding resolution that the food unit should be immediately spun off. "It's the first time any *Fortune* 1000 company has ever lost such a solicitation," LeBow crowed to *Barron's*.

Perhaps even more worrisome from RJR's standpoint, Brooke also won a binding bylaw change that would allow any RJR shareholder to call a special shareholder meeting with the backing of just 25% of RJR's outstanding shares. This means that LeBow and Brooke can continue to push for changes in the composition of the RJR board and the like, even if they lose the proxy fight at the April 17 annual meeting. And they would no longer need a majority of the shares outstanding to pass new resolutions, as is needed in consent solicitations. Just a majority of the shares present and voting would suffice.

Moreover, last month LeBow thought he'd pulled off a considerable coup that would virtually insure a Brooke victory in the proxy battle. Breaking with previously sacrosanct tobacco-industry practice, LeBow's Liggett settled a clutch of major outstanding tobacco liability suits. The Bucks involved were small, some 12% a year of Liggett's anemic pretax income, but the symbolism of the act was huge.

LeBow, of course, extracted a key concession from the plaintiffs' lawyers. They agreed that if LeBow were to win the proxy fight, they would allow the bust-up of RJR and the spin-off of the food unit to proceed without tying the deal up in court. Thus, RJR could no longer claim that any spin-off would automatically trigger suits from plaintiff's lawyers.

LeBow badly miscalculated, however. News of the Liggett settlement sent RJR and the other tobacco stocks careening lower. Industry giant Philip Morris slipped more than 10% in a matter of days, helping vaporize more than $10 billion in the tobacco industry's stock value. Investors panicked at the thought that Liggett's deal would, in the words of leading cigarette analyst Gary Black of Sanford Bernstein, "unleash a new flood of litigation." And who knew what damaging industry memos would surface now that Liggett was consorting with the enemy?

As a result, LeBow has likely cost Brooke victory in the proxy fight by alienating a number of large institutional shareholders in RJR who had backed Brooke's February consent solicitation. At least that's what Black and other analysts are hearing in their independent soundings of institutions. The doors at Fidelity and other major institutions are no longer open to LeBow, though he denies this is the case.

It's doubtful that LeBow would win the proxy fight anyway. For it's one thing to use LeBow to send a message to RJR management and quite another to actually hand over control of a major company to someone with as tainted a reputation as his. RJR's huge cash flow might prove too tempting.

RJR officials argue persuasively that LeBow has a hidden agenda in trying to take over RJR. They say his real intent is to unload the ailing Liggett on RJR at a fancy price.

There's plenty of evidence to back this contention. LeBow concedes that he began his saber rattling at RJR only late last summer after the company spurned his proposal to merge Liggett into RJR's tobacco company for a price nearly four times what RJR considered Liggett's fair market value. So much for boosting RJR's shareholder value. Likewise, the briefing books that various Brooke nominees for RJR directorships received last December included financial tables assuming the two tobacco operations would be merged.

If Brooke fails in its effort to dump Liggett on RJR, which now seems likely, its business could continue to deteriorate and it, too, could someday join that long list of companies that LeBow has driven into bankruptcy court. That's what several sophisticated short-sellers are betting.

But any setback for LeBow would only be temporary, one suspects. For in bankruptcy court he would have his fellow Brooke investors and creditors just where he wants them.

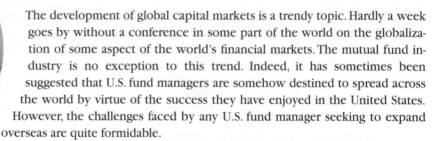

12 | Internationalization of Mutual Funds

The development of global capital markets is a trendy topic. Hardly a week goes by without a conference in some part of the world on the globalization of some aspect of the world's financial markets. The mutual fund industry is no exception to this trend. Indeed, it has sometimes been suggested that U.S. fund managers are somehow destined to spread across the world by virtue of the success they have enjoyed in the United States. However, the challenges faced by any U.S. fund manager seeking to expand overseas are quite formidable.

In thinking about the internationalization of mutual funds, it is important to distinguish between overseas investment by mutual funds and cross-border efforts by fund management companies to gather assets from overseas investors. In general, overseas investment by U.S. mutual funds has grown significantly over the past decade, aided in part by a growing trend among nations to open up their capital markets to higher levels of foreign investment. By contrast, most U.S. fund management companies have experienced only mixed success in their efforts to gather assets from overseas investors. U.S. managers have been stymied in these efforts by the lack of a truly global market for mutual funds. Because the level of integration among the world's markets for mutual fund products is still very low, each local market tends to limit itself to those types of mutual funds that are tailored specifically to meet the unique requirements of that market. Local limitations not only give local players a competitive (or "home court") advantage, but also make it more difficult for global players to take advantage of their larger size to achieve lower costs or better returns.

This Chapter first explores the general environment for international investing and the specific advantages of U.S. mutual funds in overcoming the difficulties of operating internationally. Then it discusses the various approaches taken by U.S. fund managers to gathering global assets and the barriers to such asset gathering in four main areas: Europe, Japan, Southeast Asia and the Americas (excluding the United States). The Chapter ends with a case study of a U.S. fund manager who is attempting to enter the defined contribution market for mutual funds in Canada.

• • • • •
• • • • •

I. Overseas Investing by U.S. Mutual Funds

A. The International Investment Environment

Until the early 1990s, overseas investment by U.S. investors was relatively modest. However, since that time, U.S. investors generally have been building up their portfolios of international securities (see Table 12.1), although net purchases of foreign securities

530

TABLE 12.1

U.S. holdings of foreign securities ($ billions)

Year	Foreign Stocks	Foreign Bonds	Total
1990	197.6	115.4	313.0
1991	279.0	130.4	409.4
1992	314.3	147.2	461.5
1993	543.9	230.1	774.0
1994	627.5	242.3	869.8
1995	776.8	299.4	1,076.2
1996	1,002.9	366.3	1,369.2
1997	1,207.8	427.7	1,635.5
1998	1,476.2	462.6	1,938.8
1999	2,026.6	479.4	2,506.0
2000	1,787.0	533.7	2,320.7

Source: Federal Reserve Flow of Funds.

have leveled off recently and were even slightly negative in 1999 (see Table 12.2). Overseas investment activity by U.S. mutual funds has mirrored this growth trend. As shown in Figure 12.1, from 1990 to 2000, the number of registered U.S. mutual funds with an international or global investment objective grew from 196 to 1,155, an increase of 489%. At the same time, total net assets invested in these funds grew from $41.3 billion to $563.3 billion, an increase of 1,264%. However, the number of international and global funds has plateaued over the past few years, while the assets of such funds have peaked and actually fell in 2000.

TABLE 12.2

U.S. net purchases of foreign securities ($ billions)

Year	Foreign Stocks	Foreign Bonds	Total
1990	9.2	22.5	31.7
1991	32.0	14.8	46.8
1992	32.3	19.6	51.9
1993	62.7	80.4	143.1
1994	48.1	9.2	57.3
1995	50.3	48.4	98.7
1996	59.3	51.4	110.7
1997	40.9	48.2	89.1
1998	(8.0)	18.7	10.7
1999	(15.6)	5.7	(9.9)
2000	9.5	3.9	13.4

Note: Gross: purchases plus sales; net: purchases minus sales.
Source: SIA Foreign Activity Report.

FIGURE 12.1

U.S. registered mutual funds with international or global objectives

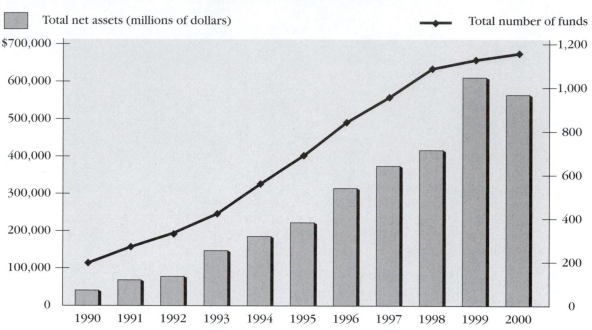

Source: Investment Company Institute. Reprinted by permission of the Investment Company Institute.

The growth in international investing by mutual funds and other U.S. investors has been made possible by a growing willingness on the part of nations to open up their capital markets to greater levels of foreign investment. Eliminating or reducing restrictions on cross-border capital flows usually confers significant benefits on the nations that do so—most important, by increasing market liquidity and lowering the cost of capital.[1] In practice, however, the extent to which eliminating capital controls can benefit a country's economy depends heavily on the overall state of development of that country's financial system. In general, the less developed a country's financial infrastructure is, the more vulnerable is its economy to short-term financial shocks. This vulnerability has led some countries to attempt to insulate themselves from global economic pressures by regulating the level or types of foreign investment in their financial markets (e.g., a country may try to capture the benefit of inflows and reduce the risk of sudden outflows).

During the Asian financial crisis of 1998 and 1999, for example, foreign "speculators" sometimes were cited as the main culprits responsible for the extreme devaluations experienced by Asian currencies. Although there is much evidence to suggest that more fundamental factors were the primary causes of the crisis, the perception that the damage was tied to foreign speculation led one country, Malaysia, to reimpose currency controls. Other countries also regulate foreign investment in ways that are designed to encourage long-term investment in the country and to discourage short-term investment—so-called hot money. For example, until quite recently, Chile used a system of foreign capital registration that imposed tax disincentives on foreign investors who were unwilling to commit capital to the country for a period of at least five years. Such national barriers to the free flow of capital present special challenges to mutual funds, which must stand ready to redeem their shares every business day.

Although some countries continue to take the position that capital controls can be used successfully to encourage the "right kind" of foreign investment in their developing economies, the advantages of maintaining open capital markets have generally gained widespread acceptance around the world. In the past 20 years, many nations (particularly in Eastern and Western Europe, as well as in large portions of Asia and Latin America) have entirely eliminated capital controls. Even among nations that continue to regulate foreign capital flows, there has been a trend toward reducing and simplifying these regulatory requirements as a means of encouraging greater levels of foreign investment. Even Chile has recently taken steps to eliminate its system of tax disincentives on foreign investors who invest in the country for less than five years.[2] This trend has allowed mutual funds to invest in countries like Mexico and Korea, which at one time were available to fund investors mainly through closed-end investment companies.[3]

This opening up of the world's capital markets has coincided with an increasing reliance by businesses on publicly issued debt and equity securities—as opposed to bank loans and other sources of private capital—as their primary source of raising capital. For example, bank lending constituted two-thirds of private capital flows to emerging markets in the early 1980s, but it is projected to be less than 8% in 2001.[4] Similarly, issuance of corporate debt in Europe went from just $8.7 billion in 1980 to $690 billion in 2000, while the value of European stock markets went from barely $200 billion in 1979 to $7.4 trillion in early 1999.[5]

Together, these trends have greatly increased the number of attractive overseas investment opportunities available to U.S. investors. The size of this opportunity is too large for U.S. investors to ignore completely. As shown in Figure 12.2, although the U.S. capital markets are by far the largest in the world, U.S. securities still accounted for just under 50% of total equity and fixed income market capitalization in the world in 2000. As recently as 1990, moreover, the total value of the Japanese equity market was larger than that of the U.S. equity market. Therefore, investors who focus their investment activities solely on the U.S. markets are excluding a substantial portion of the world's capital markets from their investment portfolio.[6]

In the long run, investing overseas can play an important role in helping investors to optimize the risk/return ratio of their portfolios. The usual argument offered in support of overseas investing is that it allows investors to diversify their portfolios. That is, because the performances of various securities markets around the world do not move in synch (i.e., there is a low correlation among the world's capital markets), investing overseas allows investors to decrease the risk of their overall portfolio by investing in some markets whose good performance can offset bad performance in other markets. But the benefits of international diversification have recently been called into question by studies showing that the degree of convergence among the world's equity markets is increasing. In particular, one study shows the degree of correlation among world equity markets is particularly high during periods of increased market volatility.[7] For

FIGURE 12.2

Share of global equity markets capitalization

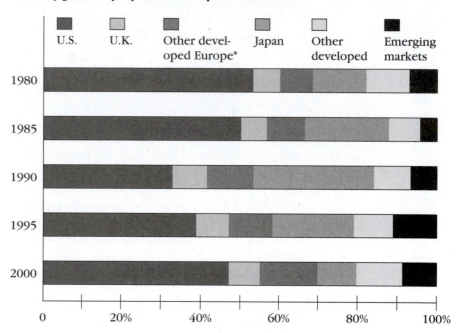

*Includes Germany, France, Switzerland, Netherlands and Italy.
Source: SIA Factbook.

example, the Russian ruble crisis of 1999 caused significant declines in securities markets around the world, even in markets with seemingly little relationship to the Russian economy such as the United States and Argentina. Such studies have led certain commentators to question whether the added costs and risks of overseas investment are worthwhile if the benefits of international risk diversification are so modest.[8]

It might be more accurate, however, to conclude that these studies suggest that simply investing one's portfolio across a number of different countries cannot ensure risk diversification. Risk diversification is more subtle and difficult to achieve than a simple formula for geographic allocation. For example, some recent research indicates that global sector (i.e., industry) factors have become more important than local market (i.e., country) factors in driving global share price performance (as shown by Figure 12.3). This is particularly so in developed markets, although stock-specific (i.e., company-specific) factors remain by far the most important factor in all types of markets.[9] Such research suggests that an adverse development affecting one industry in one part of the world is becoming more likely to have an adverse impact on the share prices of all companies in that industry, regardless of where their shares are traded. This global ripple effect is particularly true in highly globalized industries, such as oil and gas or chemicals, and less so in more localized industries, such as real estate or retailing.

All of these studies show that achieving an optimal state of risk diversification is dependent on many factors, which require careful analysis of the interdependencies

FIGURE 12.3

Shift toward the global sector from the local market

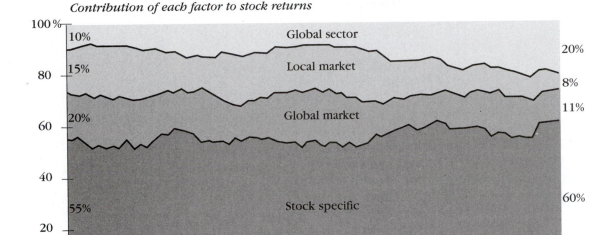

Contribution of each factor to stock returns

Note: Excludes emerging markets.
Source: Reprinted by permission. Goldman Sachs Global Investment Research.

within a portfolio. Nevertheless, if this analysis is done properly, a portfolio that is open to the possibility of international investing has a better chance of achieving an optimal risk/return ratio than it would if its investment universe was arbitrarily limited to the capital markets of one country. Figure 12.4 shows the risk/return relationship for portfolios made up of varying combinations of the Standard & Poor's (S&P) 500 Index and Morgan Stanley Capital International (MSCI) EAFE Index (EAFE stands for Europe, Australasia and the Far East), using 30 years of data from 1970 to 2000. On one end, the portfolio consists of 100% S&P 500 securities, and on the opposite end, the portfolio consists of 100% EAFE securities. The specified points in between represent portfolios with varying combinations of the two indexes in 10% increments. As shown by the plotted line, an analysis of the combined performance of the EAFE and S&P 500 indexes over the past 30 years suggests that the risk/return ratios for U.S. investors are optimized at a point where approximately 20% of an investor's portfolio is allocated to overseas investments, as indicated by the arrow and dark data point.

B. *Mutual Funds Overseas as Investment Vehicles*

Mutual funds have become a preferred investment vehicle for U.S. investors who are seeking to diversify their investments overseas. This is because investing overseas is

FIGURE 12.4

Diversified global portfolio with optimal risk/return relationship: Portfolio risk and return for various portfolio combinations of S&P 500 and EAFE indexes, 1970–2000

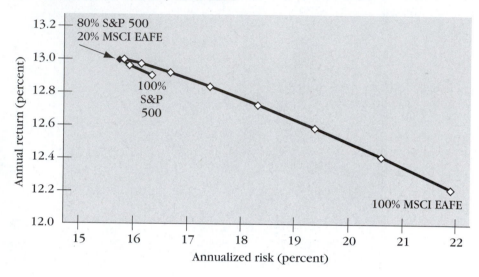

Source: Ibbotson Analyzer.

subject to a number of investment, political and operational risks that most individual investors are ill equipped to manage on their own.

1. Investment issues. As compared to the United States, the process of researching foreign securities is generally more difficult. In many countries, the principle of full, fair and timely disclosure of material information to the market is not as firmly established as it is in the United States, making reliable information about issuers more difficult to obtain.[10] In addition, the executives of many foreign companies are only gradually becoming comfortable with visits or phone calls from securities analysts and may not be as forthcoming in providing information as U.S. executives. Moreover, the concepts of shareholder rights and institutional activism are not as well developed in many foreign countries as in the United States.[11]

2. Trading costs. Trading in overseas securities markets is usually more difficult and costly than trading in U.S. markets. Although the securities markets in major financial centers such as London and Tokyo are relatively efficient, the securities markets of most foreign countries are generally not as liquid as those in the United States. Accordingly, investors may find it more difficult to sell a significant number of shares at a reasonable price in such markets. In some countries, investors are still charged fixed commission rates. In other countries with negotiated commission rates, individual investors are still charged much higher equity commission rates than charged in the United States.

3. Regulatory issues. Investors seeking to trade in overseas markets can face regulatory hurdles not encountered in the United States. For example, in certain countries, such as Taiwan, foreign investors must obtain advance regulatory approval in order to buy shares of local companies. Other countries impose restrictions on the number of shares in a company that foreign investors can hold, or they limit foreign investors to purchasing certain classes of shares with restricted voting rights. In addition, in some markets (particularly emerging markets), the regulatory rules to prevent abusive market practices (such as insider trading or market manipulation) are generally less effective than the regulatory regime in the United States.

4. Currency risk. Cross-border investing introduces the element of currency risk not encountered with domestic investments. This risk arises from the fact that while a U.S. investor normally will invest using U.S. dollars, the investor's portfolio of foreign securities generally will be priced in the local currency. Consequently, exchange rate fluctuations can have a significant impact on the investor's total return.[12]

5. Political risk. Investors in overseas markets are exposed to different and frequently more challenging political environments, including the risk of sudden changes in government policy toward foreign investors. A recent example is Venezuela, which in 1994 abruptly imposed a total ban (since lifted) on the repatriation of foreign capital. Even in relatively stable and developed nations, such as Canada, unexpected political developments can sometimes give rise to unforeseen market risk. In 1995, for example, Canada's securities markets (and the value of its currency) experienced extremely high volatility at a time when the secessionist vote in Quebec came to within less than 1% of succeeding. In addition, many foreign governments are more willing than the U.S. government to intervene in their stock markets when market behavior does not suit government policy (e.g., Hong Kong in 1998).

6. Operational risk. Finally, overseas investors must confront a host of operational issues. For example, the lack of a well-developed financial infrastructure (particularly in some emerging markets) can expose investors to significant risk by making it more difficult to sell securities quickly. A classic example is India, where until quite recently all securities transactions were based on an antiquated paper-based settlement system. This system led to long delays (in some cases exceeding six months) in settling and registering securities transactions, as well as a high incidence of fraudulent shares trading in the market. Another extreme example is Russia, where the lack of an independent, centralized securities registration system not only leads to lengthy delays in settling securities transactions, but also leaves investors vulnerable to having a company eliminate all evidence of their ownership interest simply by deleting the investor from the company's share register.[13]

Mutual funds cannot insulate investors entirely from the risks of international investing. However, investing overseas through mutual funds does permit individual investors to achieve a far greater degree of risk diversification and liquidity than generally would be possible in a portfolio of individual securities holdings. Perhaps more important, fund management companies are far better equipped than most individuals to monitor, manage and mitigate the risks of international investing. For example, mutual fund managers are able to devote greater resources to the international research process and, consequently, to make more informed investment decisions than would be practical for most individual investors. Similarly, many large fund management companies maintain global trading operations—staffed on close to a 24-hour basis by professional traders—that are far more capable than the typical investor of managing the challenges of overseas trading. In addition, fund management companies have greater resources available to them for monitoring political and other developments, enabling them to detect developing issues more quickly and to take steps to mitigate losses more effectively.

Moreover, as large institutional investors, fund management companies can put pressure on local financial institutions and other market players to achieve a higher level of customer service than would be provided to individual investors. For example, fund managers work closely with their custodian banks to establish and monitor extensive global custody networks. These networks are responsible for providing settlement, registration and safekeeping services for a mutual fund's overseas investments. (See "Foreign Custody of Mutual Fund Assets.") They have also become a primary source of information regarding investment risks and other developments in many foreign markets. It is safe to say that mutual funds receive a much higher level of operational support from their custodian banks than would be made available generally to an individual investor. In part, this is due to the fact that mutual funds and their custodians are subject to exacting regulatory standards with respect to foreign custody of assets. In large part, this is due to the degree of influence on custodial networks that fund management companies are able to exercise as large institutional investors.

In short, mutual funds have become a preferred vehicle for investing overseas by U.S. investors because they give individual investors access to a high level of diversification, daily redemption, operational controls and professional management that would not otherwise be available to most individuals. Although these are the same attributes that make mutual funds attractive for investors who invest domestically, they are particularly valuable to international investors in light of the increased risks and challenges associated with investing overseas.

Fund sponsors have responded to the growing demand for overseas investment by developing a variety of mutual funds that allow investors to tailor their portfolios to individual risk tolerances and investment objectives. Most fund sponsors offer investors a choice between so-called global funds (which can invest anywhere in the world, including the United States) and so-called international funds (which concentrate on investing exclusively outside the United States). Most fund companies further distinguish between international funds that restrict their investments to countries with more highly developed economies and established capital markets and funds that invest in riskier emerging markets. Fund sponsors have also developed a number of more specialized types of international funds, including:

- *Regional funds* that focus on particular geographic regions of the world (such as Europe, Latin America or Southeast Asia); and

- *Single-country funds* that focus exclusively on a single country (e.g., India, Japan or France).

The SEC recently adopted new "name-test" rules, effective in mid-2002, regulating the investment policies of funds whose names suggest they will focus on a particular type of investment or industry. (See Chapter Three.) As applied to international funds, the SEC's rules require any fund whose name suggests that it will focus on a particular country or geographic region to invest at least 80% of its assets in investments that are "tied economically" to the particular country or region suggested by the fund's name. The SEC rules also require such funds to disclose in their prospectuses the specific criteria that will be used to determine if a particular investment meets the "tied economi-

CALLOUT
Foreign Custody of Mutual Fund Assets

Mutual funds are subject to extensive regulations relating to the custody of their foreign assets. Until 1998, a Securities and Exchange Commission (SEC) rule required that a mutual fund's board of directors, after consideration of a number of factors, approve every foreign custodian and subcustodian of the mutual fund as being in the "best interests" of the fund and its shareholders. This rule led to a practice of providing fund boards with voluminous amounts of highly detailed information relating to the global network of foreign subcustodians used by a fund's U.S. custodian bank. In recognition of the fact that fund directors had neither the time nor the expertise to perform effectively the role required of them by the rule, the SEC began working on an initiative in 1990 that would redefine the directors' roles and permit them to delegate responsibility for day-to-day oversight of funds' global custody networks to a "foreign custody manager" (subject to certain conditions designed to ensure that these networks would continue to meet high standards for safety and reliability).

Although fund managers and the custodian banks were in broad agreement with the goals of the SEC's initiative, the debate over the exact terms and conditions of the new rule proved unusually long and difficult. In essence, the debate centered around the issue of how to apportion responsibility for ensuring that a fund's foreign subcustody arrangements would comply with the requirements of the new rule. Fund managers argued that establishing and maintaining global custody networks is a function manifestly within the special expertise of the U.S. custodian banks and therefore that these custodians should be held primarily responsible for ensuring that the subcustodians in their networks meet the standard of care required by the new rule. Custodian banks, for their part, argued that they can be only as good as the trading, settlement and custody environments in which they operate, that this type of "infrastructure risk" is an investment risk to be considered in making a decision to place assets in a particular country

and that it is therefore the fund manager's ultimate responsibility to determine if a fund's assets would be subject to the requisite standard of care. In particular, custodian banks objected to being held responsible for any risks associated with the use of locally organized, mandatory securities depositories (which technically are treated as subcustodians under applicable SEC regulations), when, practically speaking, the banks have little or no control over the establishment or use of a depository in a particular market. (A depository is a centralized clearing and settlement agency established by the government or the national stock exchange.) Eventually, the debate was resolved by developing different regulatory standards for foreign securities depositories and subcustodian banks.

In general, the SEC's new rule permits a fund's board to delegate responsibility for the day-to-day supervision of a fund's foreign subcustodians to a "foreign custody manager" (FCM)—typically, the fund's global custodian bank—subject to these conditions:

- A finding by the board that it is "reasonable to rely" on the FCM to perform the duties specified by the Rule;
- An agreement by the FCM to exercise "reasonable care, prudence and diligence" in the performance of its duties as an FCM; and
- The transmission of certain periodic reports by the FCM to the board.

FCMs are responsible for choosing the fund's foreign subcustodians, subject, in each case, to a determination by the FCM that the subcustodian will exercise "reasonable care, based on the standards applicable to custodians in the relevant market." The SEC's new rule imposes a number of requirements on the FCM to monitor its foreign subcustodians on a continuous basis and take steps to remove assets from any subcustodian that fails to meet the rule's requirements. In addition, the new rule imposes certain minimum requirements relating to the terms of the legal contracts between a fund's custodian and its foreign subcustodians.

For foreign securities depositories, the SEC adopted a different approach. Instead of requiring the appointment of an FCM that would be responsible for making "reasonable care" determinations, the SEC defined certain objective criteria that would have to be met in order

(continued)

for a securities depository to be considered an "eligible securities depository" for mutual fund assets. The new rule assigns responsibility to the custodian banks:

- To determine if the objective criteria are met;
- To monitor foreign depositories used by their networks for continued compliance with the objective criteria of the rule; and
- To provide a report giving an "analysis of the custody risks associated with the use of each eligible

securities depository" to fund boards or their managers.

The SEC's new rule did not explicitly define the responsibilities of the fund manager when it receives such a report by a custodian bank on a foreign securities depository. However, the SEC implied in its adopting release that such a report should be considered by the fund manager as one of many factors in deciding whether to buy securities in a particular country.

cally" standard. Thus, a Japan fund or Latin American fund would be subject to the SEC's 80% name test.

Furthermore, the SEC indicated that funds using the term "foreign" in their names would be subject to an 80% name-test requirement for securities that are "tied economically" to countries outside the United States. By contrast, the SEC did not subject international or global funds to the 80% name test. In the past, the SEC used to require any fund using the term "international" in its name to diversify its investments among at least three countries and not to invest in the United States. Funds using the term "global" in their names were required to follow the same country diversification standards but were permitted to invest in the United States. The SEC dropped this long-standing policy in 1998. In the adopting release for the new name-test rule, however, the SEC indicated in a footnote that it would continue to expect funds using "global" and "international" in their names to diversify their investments among a number of different countries.

C. Managing an International or Global Mutual Fund

In running international or global mutual funds, portfolio managers try to outperform both the relevant index and/or peer group. (For more detail, see Chapter Two.) In the international arena, the most prevalent index is the MSCI EAFE. It is designed to represent the developed securities markets other than the United States and Canada; it includes approximately 1,000 securities of companies representing 21 countries. By contrast, the MSCI Emerging Market Free Index is designed to represent the emerging (not developed) markets; it includes securities of more than 800 companies representing 26 emerging countries. A broader index is the MSCI All-Country World Free (ex–United States), which is designed to represent the developed and emerging markets; it includes securities of more than 1,725 companies representing 48 countries (including Canada and 26 emerging markets). In addition, there are separate indexes for Latin America, Southeast Asia and other geographic areas.

The manner in which a portfolio manager invests the assets of his or her mutual funds tends to be influenced significantly by the composition of the securities in the index that is used in measuring the fund's performance. Because a fund's performance is usually judged by comparison to the performance of the index (sometimes called the benchmark), most fund managers keep close track of precisely how much of their portfolios are over- or underweight in relation to the index by country, industry sector and individual security. This information is of crucial importance in helping active portfolio managers understand precisely where they have placed "bets" in their efforts to outperform the benchmark. (See Chapter Five.) Accordingly, it is very important to fund managers that the securities index used as a fund's benchmark accurately reflects the investment universe in which the fund operates. In other words, the securities included in the index, and the relative weightings assigned to each such security, should reflect accurately the securities that actually are available for the fund manager to purchase and sell.

As a result, fund management companies pay close attention to the methodologies that index providers use to construct their indexes and occasionally pressure the providers to make changes to these methodologies. For example, index providers typically assign a weighting to each company in an index on the basis of the company's total market capitalization. Fund managers complain, however, that this methodology may not accurately reflect the true availability of the security to the investing public; the reality for many companies (particularly in emerging markets) is that large blocks of the company's outstanding stock are not traded because they are tied up in the hands of a small number of insiders or through corporate cross-holdings. In addition, large government holdings or restrictive regulations on foreigners can have the effect of reducing the number of shares that actually are available for investment by U.S. fund managers. This issue is of particular importance for indexes that track emerging markets, where securities tend to be more thinly traded. Inappropriate index weightings can distort market prices in emerging markets as fund managers bid up the price of scarce securities in an effort to keep these securities from being underrepresented in the fund's portfolio as compared to the benchmark index.

Therefore, a number of the major index providers have begun studying or implementing proposals to reweight their indexes on the basis of some measure of the "public float" (the number of shares freely available and publicly traded) as opposed to simply using total market capitalization. During 2001, MSCI overhauled its international indexes in two significant respects. First, it eliminated from these indexes the portion of a company's stock that is not in the public float—that is, not available to investors because the stock is held by a founding family, national government or cross-owners, for example. This free-float adjustment will reduce the weighting of certain international stocks in these indexes—for example, those of many telecommunications companies where a substantial block is still held by the government after a partial privatization. Second, MSCI broadened the market capitalization of its indexes to include 85% of the stock in the free float from each industry (up from 60% previously). This increased percentage of the free float is likely to lead to a substantial expansion of the number of companies included in the MSCI indexes—for example, as many as 300 companies could be added to MSCI EAFE. Such dramatic shifts in the MSCI indexes may result in high transaction costs being incurred by mutual funds and other institutional investors as they adjust to the new composition of these indexes. To reduce such transaction costs, MSCI will move gradually toward the new indexes over a transition period.(See "Changes to International Indexes.")

CALLOUT
Changes to International Indexes

Changes to the makeup of a securities index can sometimes have a significant impact on a security's market price, as portfolio managers buy and sell shares in an effort to rebalance their portfolios in light of a change to the index. Indeed, the failure to make changes to indexes carefully has been the source of some occasional tension between fund managers and index providers. In 1998, for example, MSCI ruffled some feathers with its decision to remove Malaysia entirely from several of its widely used indexes that track Southeast Asia (e.g., Emerging Markets and Far East Ex-Japan) in response to the sudden imposition of currency controls in Malaysia. Not unreasonably, MSCI decided that Malaysia should be removed from its indexes because the imposition of currency controls effectively had closed the country to foreign investment. Nevertheless, this decision created some real difficulties for the portfolio managers of funds with existing investments in Malaysia that could not be liquidated and repatriated. As a result, a number of emerging market funds were in the uncomfortable position of having a locked-in exposure to Malaysia, even though their benchmark index had just excluded Malaysia from its performance results. After receiving vociferous complaints from fund managers, MSCI addressed the issue by offering to create a series of parallel indexes that would continue to include Malaysia. The situation was resolved more permanently in 2000 when MSCI announced that it would reinstate Malaysia in its indexes after Malaysia had lifted its currency controls. Even this decision was not entirely without controversy, however, since Malaysia has continued to impose a 10% "levy" on any capital gains repatriated from the country. Thus, the performance of a fund's Malaysian securities can be subject to a 10% drag on actual performance, although that drag is not necessarily reflected in the performance of the benchmark index.

Similar issues and controversies have surrounded MSCI's treatment of Taiwan in its indexes. Historically, MSCI has given Taiwan a discounted weighting—equal to only 50% of the country's total market capitalization—in the MSCI indexes to reflect the fact that capital flows into and out of that country are highly restricted. Taiwan maintains an onerous system of regulating foreign investment. Under this system, a foreign investor must submit an application to the government in order to receive an investment quota, which imposes considerable restrictions on the investor's ability to move capital into and out of the country. Particularly for mutual funds, which must be concerned with maintaining a high degree of liquidity in order to meet daily redemptions, these restrictions are a significant constraint on investment flexibility. In 2000, however, MSCI announced its intention to increase Taiwan's weighting in its indexes to 100% in three incremental stages over an 18-month period. MSCI's announcement was the result of extensive negotiations between the Taiwanese government and MSCI on reducing Taiwan's foreign investment restrictions to the point where the country could be considered "free" for purposes of according it full weight in the MSCI indexes. Although MSCI did succeed in persuading the Taiwan government to increase the maximum size of its investment quotas and streamline some of its requirements with respect to capital flows, the basic framework of the country's foreign investment regulations remained in place. MSCI's announcement was therefore greeted with some consternation by the investment community. There was considerable skepticism as to whether the reforms implemented by the government were sufficient and permanent enough to qualify the country as a truly "free" capital market. This concern was heightened because a fully weighted Taiwan would make the country one of the largest Asian markets in the MSCI indexes outside Japan.

FIGURE 12.5

Worldwide assets of open-end investment companies

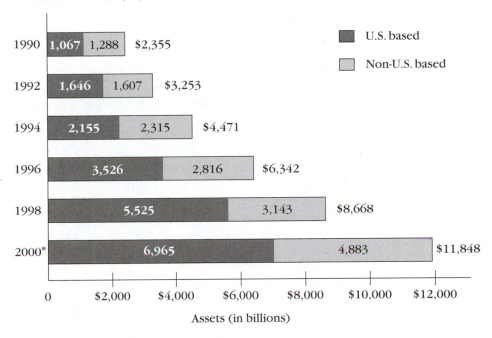

*Most non-U.S. figures as of September 30, 2000.
Sources:* Investment Company Institute, European Federation of Investment Funds and Companies.

 ## II. Cross-Border Asset-Gathering Activities

Globally, the demand for mutual fund products has grown substantially. As shown in Figure 12.5, over the past 10 years, assets invested in mutual funds domiciled outside the United States have grown from approximately $1.3 trillion to approximately $4.9 trillion, an increase of over 279%. A number of powerful factors are driving this growth. First, as noted above, an increasing number of businesses are relying on publicly traded equity and debt securities over private and bank finance as their main sources of capital. Second, a newly prosperous middle class, for whom mutual funds are an excellent savings vehicle, is beginning to emerge in many countries. Finally, and perhaps most important, many countries (including Japan and most of Europe) have rapidly aging populations that are putting a strain on these countries' pension systems. As a result, many countries are undertaking reforms to supplement their existing state-sponsored retirement programs with proposals to privatize pension fund management and introduce defined contribution systems, with participants choosing among investment options. This global trend toward pension privatization and defined contribution systems represents a potentially massive asset-gathering opportunity for the fund management industry.

As the market for mutual funds in the United States has begun to mature, many U.S. fund management companies have begun to look overseas as a key source of future growth opportunities. This enthusiasm for overseas markets is understandable given the tremendous untapped potential of many of these markets. One measure of this potential, pictured in Figure 12.6, shows that mutual fund assets as a percentage of gross domestic product (GDP) in most countries are far below the levels that have been attained in the United States. In Japan, for example, if mutual fund assets were the same percentage of GDP as in the United States, fund assets would be $3.2 trillion versus $500 billion today. In practice, however, most overseas markets tend to be dominated by local players. In Germany, for example, the large universal banks control over 70% of the mutual fund market.[14] In Japan, the three largest broker-dealers control over 65% of the market for Japanese investment trusts.[15] This level of local dominance is due to many factors, especially the low level of integration among the world's markets for mutual funds. Because most countries apply different (and frequently incompatible) tax regimes, accounting standards and regulatory requirements to mutual funds, it is virtually impossible to create a single global mutual fund that could be sold to investors in all countries. In addition, cultural differences and trade barriers are still quite significant around the world in the financial services arena. Moreover, most investors prefer to invest in funds that are denominated in their local currency in order to avoid currency risk. As a result, most local mutual fund markets tend to be limited to products that are tailored specifically to meet the needs and expectations of that market. These limits give local fund management companies, which have a long-established presence in the local market, a distinct competitive advantage over U.S. fund managers.

To offset this "home court" advantage, a U.S. fund manager company seeking to penetrate a foreign market usually must be willing to make a long-term commitment to

FIGURE 12.6

Potential global growth

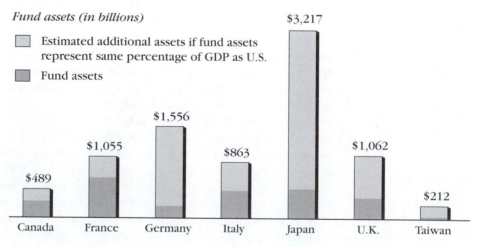

Note: Estimated additional assets are based on fund assets as of September 30, 1999, and 1999 GDP.
Sources: Investment Company Institute, Haver Analytics, European Federation of Investment Funds and Companies.

that market by establishing a significant local business presence and developing a local line of funds meeting the regulatory requirements and investor tastes in that market. The need to establish local funds in many different jurisdictions hampers the ability of large global players to take advantage of their size to compete locally on the basis of lower cost or superior performance. The challenge for a U.S. fund manager with global aspirations is to develop a business model that allows the firm to distribute products that are competitive in each local market, while at the same time achieving the economies of scale necessary to manage an investment management business efficiently and profitably. Although there is no perfect way to structure a global mutual fund business to meet this challenge, there are three plausible models.

A. *Three Models for a Global Mutual Fund Business*

The first such model is *mutual recognition*. Mutual recognition is a regulatory arrangement whereby a fund organized in one jurisdiction (the "home country") may be distributed in multiple jurisdictions (the "host countries") without the need to re-register the fund in each host country jurisdiction. Mutual recognition is difficult to achieve because it is premised on the willingness of each participating jurisdiction to recognize the legitimacy and adequacy of the regulatory regimes established in each of the other jurisdictions. Not surprisingly, given the supranational political framework provided by the European Union (EU), Europe has been the pioneer in developing a regional mutual recognition regime for mutual funds. As a means of establishing a truly global market for mutual funds, however, mutual recognition is not yet a realistic possibility because most officials are extremely reluctant to relinquish the level of control over their ability to regulate financial services that is necessary to make a mutual recognition regime work. As discussed in more detail below, even the EU has encountered difficulties in reconciling the ideal of mutual recognition with the desires of local governments to regulate mutual funds within their borders. In the United States, the SEC generally has rejected mutual recognition, preferring instead to follow the approach of "national treatment." That is, the SEC will treat a foreign firm that registers a U.S. mutual fund under U.S. laws in the same manner as the SEC would treat a U.S. firm registering a U.S. mutual fund under U.S. laws. Such national treatment represents the general rule across the globe, with mutual recognition the rare exception.

Given the prevalence of national treatment, the second business model that fund management companies with global aspirations use is the *master-feeder fund*. This is a structure where multiple "feeder funds," each of which can be designed to meet the needs of the targeted local market, invest in a single "master fund." In theory, this allows for greater economies of scale because it permits a single portfolio of assets managed by a single portfolio manager (the master fund) to support a number of funds in different distribution channels (the feeder funds). In practice, however, the multilayered master-feeder structure is complex and suffers from high accounting as well as administrative costs. In addition, there are legal hurdles, with master-feeder funds receiving only limited acceptance in many jurisdictions due to governmental concerns about the potential for using such structures to circumvent local regulations and tax laws. In both the United States and Europe, for example, master-feeder fund structures generally are prohibited in circumstances where the master fund would be organized outside the jurisdiction of the feeder fund's home country.

Given the difficulties in implementing one set of master-feeder funds across the world, the third business model used by global fund management companies is *cloning*. Cloning is a process whereby multiple funds with essentially identical investment policies are managed in parallel so as to have virtually identical investment portfolios. In theory, cloning allows a single portfolio manager to manage multiple funds, each of which can be designed to meet the distribution requirements of a targeted market, as though they were a single portfolio. In practice, however, it is difficult to maintain funds that are perfect clones of each other. Local regulatory requirements frequently oblige funds to follow slightly different investment policies—for instance, diversification policies that set different maximum limits on the amount of a fund's assets that can be invested in a particular security. In addition, each fund has its own level of available cash to invest on any given day as a result of different levels of shareholder activity. This requires frequent "reallocations" among the portfolios of cloned funds—thereby increasing transactional costs. Moreover, even among funds with identical investment portfolios, different expense ratios and tax rates can result in significant performance variations, a fact that can be difficult to explain to shareholders of the laggard fund.

In the absence of perfect cloning, most fund management companies generally have pursued a number of strategies designed to maximize the number of portfolios that a portfolio manager can manage efficiently. For example, some firms employ "templating," a technique that permits a portfolio manager to manage multiple portfolios using a single "investment template" that allows an investment decision by the portfolio manager to be allocated automatically among each of his or her funds—with adjustments for local regulations or differential cash flows. Although this technique does not result in funds that are perfect clones of each other, it does improve a portfolio manager's ability to manage a larger number of funds more efficiently and also helps to ensure that the performance variations among the manager's funds will not diverge by too much.

Besides templating, global fund management companies have pursued strategies of centralizing as many nondistribution functions as possible in order to achieve greater economies of scale and lower operating costs. For example, many fund management companies have centralized their portfolio management and trading operations in a limited number of financial service centers (such as London, Tokyo or Singapore). In addition, many global companies employ trading techniques such as "bunching" and "interfunding" to net together purchase and sale orders in a manner that reduces transaction costs for all their managed funds. Similarly, many firms strive to centralize as much of their back office fund accounting, shareholder servicing and record keeping operations as possible. For firms with global operations, this often means dealing with the complexities of developing multilingual and multicurrency capabilities in their service centers.

In devising their global strategies, most fund management companies take a practical approach and employ variations of mutual recognition, master-feeder and cloning in different markets depending on which model seems to work best under the circumstances. Thus, management firms will take advantage of mutual recognition regimes in regions where they are well established, such as Europe; use master-feeder funds when possible in offshore markets where regulatory issues are not so restrictive; and establish locally registered clone funds in countries where the cost of doing so can be justified by either the size of the market opportunity or the openness of the market to foreign competition. In general, however, it is safe to say that various forms of the cloning model, coupled with a strategy of centralizing as many nondistribution operations as is feasible, is the most common approach taken by fund management companies with global aspirations.

B. Regional Considerations

Following is a regional analysis of the factors that are driving asset-gathering strategies around the world. It is not intended to be a comprehensive survey of the world's markets for mutual funds; rather it is designed to illustrate the variety of situations that global fund sponsors confront in different geographic areas.

1. Europe   Under the framework of the EU's Directive, "Undertakings for Collective Investment in Transferable Securities" (UCITS), Europe has developed one of the most advanced mutual recognition schemes in the world. As a result, a mutual fund registered in Luxembourg or Ireland may be sold throughout the EU. At the same time, most of the EU's member nations have rapidly aging populations; such demographics undermine the long-term viability of the region's traditionally heavy reliance on government-sponsored "pay as you go" social security systems. As a result, many European countries are pursuing pension reforms actively, including the introduction of privatized defined contribution pension plans. Together, these factors make Europe one of the leading current and potential markets for mutual funds in the world.

Adopted by the EU in 1985, the UCITS Directive establishes certain minimum regulatory standards for UCITS and mandates that any fund organized as a UCITS under the laws of one EU country may be offered for sale in any other member country merely by filing a notice with the regulatory authorities of the host country (the so-called single passport). Responsibility for enforcing the regulatory standards set forth in the UCITS Directive is the sole responsibility of the home country. However, each host country retains jurisdiction over marketing practices in the host country, including advertising and areas "which do not fall within the field governed by this Directive."

Coupled with the introduction of a single currency (the euro) for most of the EU in 1999, the UCITS Directive goes a long way toward integrating European markets for mutual funds. At the beginning of 2001, there were more than 20,000 mutual funds in Europe. From 1995 to 2000, their total holdings tripled from 1.2 trillion euros to 3.6 trillion euros. Half that asset gain came during 1999 and 2000, as mutual funds became the fastest-growing segment of Eurozone savings vehicles.[16]

Nevertheless, even after 15 years, it would be premature to declare that the EU has succeeded in creating a truly single market for mutual funds in Europe. In practice, many EU regulators use their host country authority to undermine the usefulness of the UCITS Directive's single passport by imposing burdensome notice and reporting obligations on UCITS that seek to register in-country as well as their own unique (and occasionally inconsistent) requirements with respect to issues such as performance advertising and disclosure requirements. Moreover, even in situations where local regulatory differences can be reconciled, each member nation still has its own unique set of tax laws and established marketing practices that must be taken into account in designing products that will sell in that market. Thus, even in a relatively integrated region such as Europe, some local customization of product is still necessary before a UCITS can be distributed successfully in any particular country.[17] As a result, it is estimated that only 30% of UCITS actually are sold in Europe on a cross-border basis and that European mutual funds on average have roughly half the assets and 50% higher total expense ratios than U.S. mutual funds.[18]

Most fund management companies take advantage of the UCITS Directive's single passport by establishing a family of funds in one EU jurisdiction (typically Luxembourg or Ireland) and then working with the local regulatory authorities of targeted markets to open up these markets one by one. This approach sometimes requires lengthy negotiations with the regulators and the creation of country-specific supplements to the funds' disclosure documents. In the long run, this practice eventually may evolve into a truly single European market for mutual funds. For the moment, however, it would be more accurate to characterize Europe as a series of individual markets that can be targeted using a single product line. Moreover, a truly pan-European mutual fund market will probably not occur until the region achieves a higher degree of monetary integration and tax harmonization.

The EU's efforts at coordinating a regional response to pension system reform are far less advanced than its efforts at creating a single market for mutual funds. This is hardly surprising given the fact that the economic, social and political issues involved are much more complex. Currently, there are a number of regulatory requirements that impede the ability of fund management companies to develop European-wide retirement plan strategies. For example, investment restrictions are inconsistent from country to country and sometimes impose local content requirements (such as mandating a minimum level of investment in local government debt). Other European countries allow pension assets to be invested only by locally organized and regulated management companies.

Nevertheless, the EU is taking steps that are aimed at encouraging member nations to reform their pension systems in ways that would permit the more efficient management of pension assets on a cross-border basis and reduce barriers to cross-border mobility of labor and capital. In October 2000, the European Commission issued a proposal for a Directive on Occupational Pensions. If actually adopted, the proposed Directive would establish European-wide investment standards for the management of pension fund assets, which would move toward the functional principles embodied in the "prudent person" rule. These standards would restrict (though not eliminate) the ability of member nations to impose quantitative investment limits and local content requirements on pension funds. Establishing a framework for cross-border management of pension funds, the proposed Directive would further require member nations to allow investment managers established in other EU countries to manage local pension fund assets. The European Commission also has issued a nonbinding communiqué suggesting that any attempts to apply discriminatory tax practices against individual participants in another member nation's pension system would be incompatible with a member nation's obligations under the EU's founding treaty. The communiqué goes on to encourage member nations to establish tax deferral for occupational pension schemes as a universal principle, so as to bring about portability of pension plans among member nations. However, any legislative proposal to "harmonize" taxes within the EU would be extremely controversial as it raises fundamental questions relating to national control of budgets.

The EU's proposed Directive on Occupational Pensions could form the basis for a significant asset-gathering opportunity for fund management companies. If UCITS are established as the preferred financing vehicle for Europe's emerging market for defined contribution pension schemes, then mutual funds might come to dominate this market as they do the market for defined contribution plans in the United States. But this is by no means an ensured result. Given the complexity and controversy that is likely to surround the EU's proposals, their prospects for adoption are uncertain. In the meantime, each of the EU's member countries will most likely choose to rely on a mixture of responses that evolve over time in a series of incremental reforms. Although some EU countries have begun implementing pension reforms, many EU countries continue to require locally organized investment managers and funding vehicles for their pension schemes, and still others maintain local content requirements as well as other burdensome investment restrictions. Accordingly, it may be some time before the elimination of the regulatory requirements that currently serve as impediments to the ability of fund management firms to develop European-wide strategies for gathering retirement plan assets.

2. Japan   Like Europe, Japan is facing an urgent need to reform its pension system in the face of an aging population. In addition, Japan has a large middle class and one of the highest savings rates in the world. Together, these facts should make Japan one of the largest markets for mutual funds in the world. Efforts to realize this potential, however, have been complicated by the fact that the Japanese economy was largely stagnant throughout most of the 1990s. In addition, growth of the mutual fund industry in Japan has been hampered by a history of "churning" (i.e., trading customers in and out of funds on a short-term basis in order to generate commission revenues) by the broker-dealers who dominate fund distribution in Japan. Although some progress has been made to reduce this practice (such as the introduction of new trailer fee structures that create incentives to maintain assets within a fund), efforts to educate Japanese investors on the benefits of using mutual funds as long-term savings vehicles still face an uphill battle.

Until the 1990s, Japan's mutual fund industry essentially was closed to foreign competition through a series of regulatory practices that effectively prohibited foreign firms from obtaining the necessary licenses to manage locally registered investment trusts (the Japanese equivalent of a mutual fund). Subject to a number of restrictions, foreign firms were permitted to sell offshore funds (those organized outside of Japan) in Japan through local broker-dealers. Such offshore funds could not be denominated in Japanese yen, making them quite unattractive to Japanese investors.

In the past decade, however, the Japanese government gradually has begun to lift its restrictions on foreign competition, granting the first investment trust manager's license to a foreign firm in 1990. This trend accelerated in 1996, after the Japanese government announced a series of proposals to deregulate the financial services industry in Japan (the so-called Big Bang initiative).[19] As part of Big Bang, a number of significant initiatives to deregulate investment trusts were enacted by the government at the end of 1998. First, the 1998 reforms increased the number of distribution channels available for investment trusts by expanding the types of financial institutions that are permitted to distribute investment trusts. Second, the 1998 reforms streamlined a number of the regulatory procedures and requirements for establishing an investment trust business in Japan. Third, the 1998 reforms included initiatives designed to encourage greater financial innovation, such as the creation of an alternative structure for investment trusts similar to the "corporate" structure commonly used for mutual funds in the United States and permitting the sale of privately placed investment trusts. Fourth, and of particular significance for foreign fund managers, the 1998 reforms eliminated restrictions that had previously been imposed on the ability of investment trust management companies to delegate investment discretion to overseas affiliates. Finally, the 1998 reforms eased a number of restrictions applicable to the sale of offshore funds in Japan—most significantly, by eliminating the prohibition on offshore funds being denominated in Japanese yen.

Together, these reform efforts have opened up some significant market opportunities for foreign fund managers in Japan. As a result, a number of global fund managers have made substantial investments in Japan, establishing or expanding their offices in Japan and developing new families of Japanese investment trusts targeted at the Japanese retail market. Other global fund managers are pursuing strategies of entering into joint ventures and other alliances with Japanese financial institutions. Finally, a few global fund managers have experienced considerable short-term success by registering offshore funds (including U.S. bond funds) in Japan and distributing them to Japanese investors through local broker-dealers.

Another Big Bang initiative of considerable interest to global fund managers is the Japanese government's efforts to reform the country's pension system. This includes an initiative to supplement Japan's existing pension system by creating defined contribution plans loosely patterned after the 401(k) model used in the United States. From the fund management industry's perspective, it is fair to say that the Japanese government's progress on this initiative has so far been somewhat disappointing. In particular, the government's efforts have run into political opposition and concerns about the size of the country's national debt relative to its GDP.[20] As a result, passage of the enabling legislation for defined contribution plans was subject to numerous delays until finally being passed in June 2001. More important, the legislation was watered down in a number of ways that diminish the role that defined contribution plans would play in Japan's overall pension system. For example, the amounts of annual contributions to these plans will be significantly lower than in the United States, where the annual limit on employee contributions to 401(k) plans is rising from $10,500 in 2001 to $15,000 in 2006. By contrast, the total annual contribution limits to Japan's version of the 401(k) plan will be $1,800 for company employees already in a pension scheme, $3,600 for company employees covered only by a lump-sum severance plan and $6,800 for self-employed workers (all at an exchange rate of $1 = 120 yen). Moreover, most of these contributions will probably flow into a virtually guaranteed investment option that every Japanese defined contribution plan must offer.

3. Southeast Asia As compared to Europe and Japan, the economies and financial infrastructures of most Southeast Asian nations are generally in a much earlier stage of economic development. For that reason, the debate still rages over how open the financial service sectors of these countries should be to foreign competition. In addition, the economies of many Southeast Asian countries are only beginning to emerge from the severe dislocations caused by the Asian financial crisis of the late 1990s. The emerging middle class in the region has been particularly hard hit by the crisis, thus diminishing the size of the potential market opportunity for fund management firms for the time being. Nevertheless, in the long run, Southeast Asia remains a potentially significant market for global fund managers, particularly if the region's leaders respond to the financial crisis by recognizing the need to modernize their financial systems. Although overall progress has so far been modest, a few countries have been taking steps toward reform that may ultimately create growth opportunities for their mutual fund markets.

In South Korea, for example, the investment advisory and investment trust management industry has long been closed to foreign competition. As a result, the market is dominated by a small number of local "investment trust companies" (ITCs), which focus primarily on selling closed-end bond funds structured as investment trusts. Beginning in 1996, however, the South Korean government greatly expanded the number of ITC licenses that it was willing to grant and offered foreigners the opportunity to acquire ownership interests in ITCs of up to 30%. At approximately the same time, the government opened up the market to offshore funds that meet certain stringent requirements and are sold in South Korea through local broker-dealers on an exclusive basis. In 1998, the Korean government opened up the market further by authorizing the creation of a new type of closed-end mutual fund modeled after the corporate structure used in the United States. These new funds, called securities investment companies (SICs), are managed by Investment Trust Management Companies (ITMCs). Unlike ITCs, ITMCs may be 100% owned by a foreign company. While the capital requirements for ITMCs are slightly lower than the capital requirements for ITCs, they are still high at KRW7 billion (approximately US$5.6m at an exchange rate of KRW1,250 = US$1). ITMCs also are subject to significant local staffing requirements. More fundamentally, foreign firms have found it difficult to challenge local dominance of the ITC market successfully because the 30% ownership limitation means that foreign firms can access the ITC market only through a joint venture in which they do not have a controlling interest. The other product options available to foreign firms—offshore funds and the new SICs—have not yet attained widespread acceptance in the Korean market.

Like Korea, the mutual fund market in Taiwan remains heavily regulated and not especially hospitable to foreign entrants. In Taiwan, the only entities that can manage locally registered mutual funds are securities investment trust enterprises (SITEs). Although foreign fund management companies may establish a wholly owned SITE in Taiwan, the regulatory requirements for doing so are not particularly attractive. First, the minimum capital requirement for a SITE is NT$300 million (approximately US$9m at an exchange rate of NT$33.33 = US$1.00), which is prohibitively high for many fund management companies. Taiwan imposes additional burdensome requirements on local staffing—requiring each SITE to maintain a local investment management and research operation focused on Taiwan equities and placing restrictions on the ability of a SITE to delegate functions to offshore affiliates. Moreover, Taiwan requires a SITE's initial product offering to be a Taiwan equity fund and generally is reluctant to approve many funds that would invest outside Taiwan (so-called outbound funds) even after this initial product offering requirement has been satisfied.[21] As an alternative to establishing a SITE, foreign firms may establish securities investment consulting enterprises (SICEs) in Taiwan. Although SICEs have much lower capitalization requirements than SITEs (NT$10 million), their legal authority is generally limited to offering Taiwanese investors advice on the purchase of certain approved offshore funds or individual securities.[22]

Unlike Korea or Taiwan, Hong Kong maintains a uniquely open market for foreign financial institutions as a result of its long-established status as an international free trade zone. In Hong Kong's retail market, most global fund managers have long been permitted to sell offshore funds (typically European-style UCITS) rather than developing a local product line, and these offshore funds have gained a high degree of acceptance in the marketplace. More recently, Hong Kong has implemented legislation for so-called mandatory provident funds (MPFs), which is a form of privatized defined contribution pension plan designed to supplement Hong Kong's existing occupational pension and social security systems. Under the MPF legislation, Hong Kong residents are required by law to contribute 5% of their wages (subject to an annual cap) to the MPF system. The financing vehicles for the MPF system are locally organized mutual funds that must meet stringent requirements. Although the MPF scheme does appear to present a good opportunity for global fund managers, it imposes some constraints on permissible investments, including a 30% local investment requirement. The MPF legislation also requires that at least one investment option under each MPF plan be a "capital preservation product" offering a guaranteed minimum rate of return, a feature that favors insurance company-type products over mutual funds. Moreover, the cap on mandatory contributions to the MPF plans has been set at the equivalent of approximately US$3000 per year, thus reducing the amount of assets that will flow into the MPF funds.

The Hong Kong market for mutual funds is much more open than that of mainland China, which is beginning to allow foreign firms to participate in local joint ventures. (See "China Fund Market.")

4. North and South America   Like Southeast Asia, Latin America is a region where the opportunities for global fund managers remain relatively limited in the near term, but in the longer term, there are a number of potentially attractive markets. These opportunities arise because there is considerable wealth in Latin America, and many countries in the region are following Chile's lead in privatizing their state-sponsored retirement pension systems. Currently, however, most of Latin America's wealth remains heavily concentrated in the hands of a relatively small number of individuals, who are not very interested in investing in locally organized mutual funds.[23] In addition, the regulatory regimes in many Latin American countries are relatively hostile to foreign entrants into the local market. For instance, many Latin American countries continue to maintain very strict regulations on outward investment of capital, thus limiting the opportunities for global fund managers to sell products that would invest internationally.

Nevertheless, some Latin American countries have begun to take steps to open up their markets that over time are likely to create opportunities for foreign fund managers. In Chile, for example, local pension managers have hired foreign firms to act as subadvisers on non-Chilean investments in the defined contribution plan accounts that are part of a mandatory system for privatized social security. In February 1999, the Chilean government raised the statutory limit on non-Chilean investments by such pension plans from 12% (of which 6% could be invested in foreign equity securities and offshore funds) to 16% (of which 10% can be invested in equity securities and offshore funds); the Chilean parliament currently is reviewing a proposal to increase the statutory limit to 35%. At the same time, Chile has enacted a law to allow offshore mutual

CALLOUT
China Fund Market

Under the World Trade Organization (WTO) agreement expected to be adopted in 2001 or 2002, China will permit joint ventures (JVs) with partial foreign ownership to engage in fund management on the condition that the foreign partner may hold a maximum 33% share of equity for the first two years of WTO admission and up to 49% in the third year. The draft JV measure reportedly requires each JV fund company to have a minimum registered capital of Rmb75 million (US$9 million) and a minimum foreign participation of 25%. Foreign partners would be required to have a minimum of US$2.5 billion under management and maintain a representative office within China.

The realities of the Chinese market make the JV strategy the most viable method of entry for the foreseeable future. Solely owned foreign asset management firms are not likely to be allowed in the next five years, because the Chinese regulators want to give China's immature domestic industry time to grow strong enough to compete. The biggest advantage of partnering with a Chinese domestic firm is to leave the job of getting through the red tape of the Chinese bureaucrats with the local partner. Another advantage of setting up a joint venture is the ability to leverage a local partner's brand name and local market expertise.

For the next five years, the Chinese partner will be interested in the foreign partner's expertise in the fund industry. The foreign partner will likely take on a coaching role in terms of staff training and fund operations, while the Chinese partners can help their foreign counterparts learn more about the local investment culture and market trends. In terms of distribution, the foreign partner can take advantage of its local partner's relationships with established distribution channels. However, the drawback to relying on these relationships is a loss of a certain amount of bargaining power over trailer fees paid to the local distributors.

Fleming Investment Management Ltd. (now a subsidiary of J.P. Morgan Chase) signed a technical cooperation agreement with Shanghai-based Hua'an Fund Management Ltd. Hua'an was among the first five fund management firms approved by the Chinese authorities, and now controls two funds worth about Rmb8 billion (US$966 million). Also, Schroder Investment Management (Hong Kong) Ltd. finalized a deal with China Asset Management Co., one of the 10 domestic fund companies to cooperate on staff training and fund operations. Dresdner Asset Management Ltd. has also been engaged to provide consulting services to Guotai Asset Management Co.

However, certain types of companies will be better off in the longer term by deploying a more proprietary strategy, as illustrated by the Chinese experience in other industries. Between 1980 and 1990, JV companies in China accounted for more than 90% of the foreign direct investment (FDI) companies. By year-end 1998, wholly owned foreign companies constituted more than 28% of the total FDI companies, and that number was growing faster than JVs. The major advantages of the proprietary strategy are the long-term benefits of proprietary brand name, market share and full control.

A combination proprietary-partnership strategy can be used as groundwork for universal banks if a proprietary operation is desirable in the long run. Currently, Chinese banks are banned from directly entering the securities business. However, multinational universal banks are not subject to this ban. By year-end 1999, 87 foreign financial institutions from 22 countries had established 182 operational financial facilities in China, accounting for 2% of the total assets of China's banking industry. There are 25 foreign banks allowed to deal with local renminbi business. Geographical restrictions on foreign banks will be lifted five years after WTO admission. At that time, universal banks may leverage their bank branches across China as valuable cross-selling platforms for proprietary investment products.

Another related strategy would be to establish strategic alliances with local banks. Such alliances may work for asset management firms without a banking presence in China that do not want to set up a JV. An example of this strategy is being pursued by State Street Global Advisors, which recently signed a strategic alliance agreement with Industrial and Commercial Bank of China (ICBC), China's largest commercial bank, with a 38% total market share as well as 33% of the total custody market. Under the agreement, State Street will provide ICBC global market knowledge and experience, while ICBC will give support to State Street for its Chinese market initiatives. The two sides will cooperate initially on foreign exchange trading, custody and securities lending business. State Street will also advise ICBC's custody department on the launch of new open-end funds.

Source: Based on an article in Cerulli Edge (4th Quarter 2000).

funds to be registered locally. This is the first step toward permitting offshore mutual funds to be sold to retail investors in Chile through local intermediaries.

Like Chile, Argentina has established a defined contribution pension system to privatize social security. This system is a potentially significant source of assets for foreign firms as subadvisers to local pension fund managers. However, to this point, foreign investments by local pension fund managers have been extremely limited because such managers are subject to minimum return requirements that create a strong incentive to concentrate investments in local fixed income securities. Moreover, investments in offshore mutual funds are barred effectively under current regulations that require any foreign securities to be rated and listed on a recognized stock exchange. Although the regulators are considering initiatives to change these requirements, local opposition is strong and the prospects are uncertain given Argentina's difficult economic situation. For mutual fund opportunities in Mexico, see "Mexico After NAFTA."

In contrast to Latin America, Canada has established a vibrant marketplace for mutual funds. In addition, Canada has a well-developed equity culture with a high percentage of Canadian investors holding long-term investments in equity funds. These factors, coupled with Canada's relatively open attitude toward foreign entrants into the marketplace, make Canada an attractive growth opportunity for global fund management firms. From 1990 to 2000, Canada's mutual fund industry grew from $21.4 billion

CALLOUT
Mexico After NAFTA

The North American Free Trade Agreement (NAFTA) opened the door to Mexico for U.S. financial firms that virtually had been shut out of Mexico's rapidly growing financial market. But it is unclear whether U.S. fund managers will actually walk through those doors.

Before NAFTA, a U.S. firm was not allowed to sell mutual funds to Mexican investors directly or indirectly. A U.S. firm could not engage in cross-border sales by offering SEC registered funds on Mexican soil. Nor could a U.S. firm establish a Mexican subsidiary to sell customized Mexican funds—funds specially designed for Mexican investors and registered with the Mexican counterpart of the SEC.

By contrast, before NAFTA, a Mexican firm was permitted to sponsor a customized U.S. fund for sale to U.S. investors simply by filing two registration statements with the SEC: one for the firm under the Investment Advisers Act and the second for the fund under the Investment Company Act. The SEC has no capital requirement

for a foreign investment adviser and a capital requirement of only $100,000 for a U.S. registered fund.

This disparity was remedied in principle by NAFTA. It allowed U.S. firms to establish wholly owned subsidiaries to sponsor and advise customized funds for Mexican investors, subject to the same regulations as Mexican fund managers. These U.S. firms may choose to have their own distributors sell these customized funds or, alternatively, to rely on Mexican brokers to distribute these funds.

Although U.S. fund managers now have regulatory parity with Mexican fund managers, there are still practical barriers to entry to the Mexican fund market. Most important, Mexican mutual funds are generally prohibited from making significant investments in non-Mexican securities. As a result, foreign firms do not have a chance to offer their expertise in U.S., European or Asian funds to Mexican fund investors. Of course, U.S. managers could try to sell to Mexican investors a set of mutual funds investing only in Mexican stocks and bonds, but that would be the Latin American version of carrying coals to Newcastle.

in size to $280.4 billion (using an exchange rate of C$1.00 = US$.6676), an increase of 1,213%. Over the same time frame, the share of the Canadian mutual fund market held by non-Canadian firms grew from 3.4% to 24.7%.

Growth in the Canadian mutual fund market has recently been fueled by the growing popularity of the Registered Retirement Saving Plans (RRSP), a tax-deferred individual retirement savings account similar to the IRA in the United States. From a global asset management firm's perspective, the attractiveness of creating funds designed for the RRSP market was initially curtailed by the fact that RRSP funds are subject to a 20% limit on their ability to invest outside Canada. Effective January 1, 2001, however, this limit was raised to 30%. In addition, the Canadian tax authorities have recently been permitting the mutual fund industry to circumvent the foreign investment limit by developing RRSP-eligible funds whose primary assets are forward contracts (issued by Canadian financial institutions) linked to the investment performance of underlying funds with overseas investment objectives. Other opportunities for fund management companies arise because Canadian corporations are beginning to turn to defined contribution plans in place of their more traditional defined benefit plans. However, the growth of the DC pension plans in Canada has been somewhat slower than expected.

Canadian regulatory authorities and industry groups have worked with the SEC to adopt innovative regulations that ease some of the issues encountered by investors who move from one country to another. In 2000, for example, the SEC adopted a rule that permits regulated Canadian broker-dealers to continue to service certain qualified retirement plan accounts of Canadian citizens who establish residence in the United States without needing to register again as broker-dealers in the United States. The SEC adopted related rules permitting foreign securities and mutual funds to be sold to such accounts without having to register such investments in the United States.[24] In 1996, the SEC also issued a no-action letter that recognized that investors in Canadian mutual funds who purchase their shares while in Canada and later move to the United States need not be counted as "U.S. persons" for purposes of applying the registration requirements for mutual funds under the Investment Company Act of 1940.[25] Regulatory initiatives of this type eventually could form the basis for establishing a limited form of mutual recognition between Canadian and U.S. securities regulators, although it seems unlikely that the mutual fund markets in both countries will ever attain the level of integration that has already been achieved in the EU.

In sum, the continuing trend toward globalization of the world's financial markets has created significant long-term and near-term market opportunities for mutual funds. From the investment perspective, realization of this potential is already well advanced in the form of a growing acceptance by U.S. investors of international investing as part of a well-diversified investment portfolio and a corresponding increase in international mutual fund offerings by U.S. fund management companies. From the perspective of gathering assets from investors on a cross-border basis, however, the realization of a truly global market for mutual funds is still beyond the horizon. Nevertheless, U.S. fund managers have begun to implement asset gathering strategies in many parts of the world, and they are likely to have new opportunities for asset gathering as defined contribution plans spread internationally. Although the challenges of entering many foreign fund markets are formidable, they are not insurmountable. Over time, the trend toward global financial markets should help to reduce barriers to entry, allowing the existence of truly global firms as fund managers despite the absence of universally available mutual funds as products.

REVIEW QUESTIONS

1. What are the benefits of international diversification for a U.S. investor? What are the relevant factors to actually achieving these benefits?

2. Going back to the discussion in Chapter One, what are the pros and cons of investing in mutual funds versus investing in individual securities? Which of these arguments are significantly different for funds that invest in international versus domestic securities?

3. What is the difference between a global and an international mutual fund? What is the difference between a mutual fund and a closed-end investment company investing in Korea?

4. What are the current barriers to a truly global market for asset gathering through mutual funds? Are these barriers likely to go away any time soon?

5. What strategies might global fund management companies use to overcome the barriers noted in your answer to question 4? What are the drawbacks to each strategy?

6. What is the significance of the development of defined contribution plans to the mutual fund industry in Europe, Asia and Latin America?

DISCUSSION QUESTIONS

1. Should government policy, particularly in countries with developing economies, strive to encourage or discourage foreign investment in their securities markets? What are the pros and cons of attempting to regulate capital flows into or out of a country?

2. If you think broadly about diversification, how much of your own capital is located in the United States? (Count not only your financial assets but also your real assets and human capital.) Why worry about international diversification when the U.S. economy and stock markets have been so strong?

3. In Europe, to what extent has the EU's Directive on UCITS been successful at creating a single market for mutual funds in Europe? Will a common currency inevitably lead to a pan-European market for mutual funds in the EU, or does the EU need a common tax regime to support pan-European mutual funds?

4. In Japan, should global firms rely for fund sales on Japanese brokers, which continue to dominate fund distribution? Or, should global firms form joint ventures with Japanese banks or insurers to distribute mutual funds? Or, should global firms build their own distribution networks (branches or direct) in Japan for their own funds?

5. Do you think global fund managers would drive local competitors out of the mutual funds business in Southeast Asia or Latin America? What has been the actual experience of foreign firms in Europe, Japan and North America? How could government concerns about preserving local competitors be reconciled with policies favoring free trade in financial services?

6. What is the role of foreign fund managers in the defined contribution plans of Hong Kong, Chile and Canada? Which role presents the biggest potential for foreign fund managers? What are the barriers to actually realizing this potential?

NOTES

1. For a comprehensive study of the benefits of trade and investment liberalization, and associated issues, see Organization for Economic Co-Operation and Development, *Open Markets Matter: The Benefits of Trade and Investment Liberalization* (Source: OECD/Studies/Trade, April 1998, vol. 1, no. 4) and *Trade, Investment and Development: Reaping the Full Benefits of Open Markets* (Source: OECD/Studies/Trade, August 1999, vol. 1, no. 8)

2. In January 2000, Brazil also announced a major restructuring of its foreign investment regulations that eliminated many of the restrictions that previously had been imposed on the types of foreign investors who could invest in Brazil and on the types of securities that these foreign investors could purchase.

3. As explained in Chapter Three, a closed-end investment company does not stand ready to redeem its shares each business day. Its shares may be sold in the same manner as shares of stock are sold on a stock exchange.

4. Statistics from Institute of International Finance (IIF) in Washington, D.C.

5. Includes all corporate debt issued within the EU and corporate debt issued outside the EU by companies based in the EU. Excludes private placements and mortgage and asset-backed debt. Sources are Datastream, Thompson Financial Securities Data Corp. and Salomon Smith Barney.

6. It is also worth noting that even investors who invest only in the United States may have greater exposure to foreign markets than they might think because a number of large U.S. corporations (e.g., Intel, Coca Cola and IBM) derive a large portion of their revenues from overseas operations.

7. Kirt C. Butler and Domingo Castelo Joaquin, "Are the Gains from International Portfolio Diversification Exaggerated? The Influence of Downside Risk in Bear Markets," working paper, March 29, 2000; available on-line through http://courses.bus.msu.edu/fi/fi860/.

8. See, e.g., Mark Hulpert, "Deflating the Promise of Global Diversification," *New York Times,* July 9, 2000, sec. 3, p. 22; Craig Karmin, "Think Again: When the Conventional Wisdom May Not Be So Wise After All: 11: Investing Overseas Reduces the Riskiness of a Portfolio," *Wall Street Journal,* January 29, 2001, sec. R, p. 15; and Jonathan Fuerbringer, "Hedging Your Bets? Look Homeward, Investor," *New York Times,* February 4, 2001, sec. 3, p. 1.

9. See Stefano Cavaglia, Christopher Brightman, and Michael Aked, "The Increasing Importance of Industry Factors," *Financial Analysts Journal* (September—October 2000): 41; Alain Kerneis and Neil Williams, *Strategy Focus—Global Portfolio Strategy,* Goldman Sachs Global Equity Research Report (August 2, 2000); and Robin Brooks and Luis Catao, "The New Economy and Global Stock Returns," IMF working paper 216, December 2000. See also Michael R. Sesit, "Global Diversification Gets Harder to Achieve as Sectors Are Linked Across Countries, Regions," *Wall Street Journal,* August 2, 2000, sec. C, p. 12, and "Dancing in Step—Individual Markets Being Driven by Global Rather Than Local Factors," *The Economist,* March 24, 2001, p. 90.

10. For example, although accounting standards in most large, industrialized countries are reasonable, many foreign issuers follow accounting standards that allow these companies to provide less information on a less timely basis than would be the case under generally accepted accounting principles in the United States. Significant differences include accounting for pension liabilities, mergers/acquisitions and segment reporting.

11. See Chapter Eleven for a more complete discussion of issues faced by mutual funds attempting to exercise their voting rights as overseas investors.

12. For example, if a Japanese security achieves a total return of 12% over a one-year period but the value of the Japanese yen declines 5% against the U.S. dollar over the same period, the total return realized by a U.S. investor will be 7%, not 12%. Some mutual funds attempt to neutralize this risk for investors by using various hedging instruments, such as currency swaps. However, such hedging activities can impose significant transaction and opportunity costs on a fund and rarely provide a perfect hedge against exchange rate fluctuations.

13. Operational issues also can arise from time zone differences. For example, the shares of every U.S. mutual fund must be priced daily—for most funds at 4 P.M. Eastern Time—to coordinate with the close of the major U.S. stock exchanges. This requirement presents challenges to fund investing primarily in foreign markets that operate in different time zones. (See the discussion of fair value pricing in Chapter Nine.)

14. Cerulli Associates, Inc., *The Cerulli Report, Global Asset Gathering Strategies,* Vol. 2: *Country Profiles* (1999), p. 99.

15. Cerulli Associates, Inc., *The Cerulli Report, Japanese Asset Management* (2001), Exhibit 126, p. 255.

16. Pozen, "Continental Shift: The Securitization of Europe," *Foreign Affairs* (May–June 2001): 12.

17. Recently the EU has been debating certain amendments to the UCITS Directive that are intended to increase its flexibility. In particular, the amended Directive would increase the ability of UCITS to invest in certain types of money market instruments and derivative securities, allow UCITS to establish overseas subsidiaries and amend the diversification requirements to give index funds greater flexibility to track their indexes. The amended Directive would also give UCITS a limited ability to organize themselves using fund-of-fund structures, but the use of master-feeder structures would still generally be prohibited. More controversially, the EU is also debating additional amendments to the UCITS Directive that would address some of the issues that have emerged as impediments to the creation of a pan-European mutual fund market. These include a proposal that would establish a single passport for the EU firms that manage UCITS and a proposal that would permit UCITS to be sold throughout Europe on the basis of a single form of simplified prospectus.

18. Vania Schleef, *Moody's Global Fund Update: Cross-Border Distribution of Funds: Hurdles and Developments,* Moody's Investors Service—Global Credit Research (Moody's Special Comment, dated August 2000). See also Pozen, "Continental Shift," 12.

19. Compared to the other leading economies in the world, Japan's financial sector has been characterized by a low level of competition and a comparatively heavy reliance on direct, privately placed bank financing (particularly from banks that are part of the same *keiretsu* industrial grouping as the borrower) as its main source of capital. These attributes have resulted in a relatively low level of innovation in Japanese capital markets, hampering the ability of Japanese financial institutions to respond quickly or decisively to financial dislocations. The "Big Bang" reform initiatives included proposals designed to address these issues by lowering transaction costs, increasing competition among financial institutions, encouraging greater financial innovation, promoting greater transparency in corporate accounting practices and streamlining the regulatory process. At the same time, the Japanese government instituted a number of significant initiatives to open up the country's financial markets to greater levels of foreign competition. These included initiatives to liberalize Japan's relatively restrictive regulations on foreign exchange and other cross-border capital transactions. In addition, in 1995, the Japanese government entered into a bilateral trade agreement with the United States to open a number of financial services markets in Japan, including the asset management sector. These undertakings were later formalized in a multilateral context as part of Japan's commitments to the 1997 WTO trade agreement on financial services.

20. For example, labor unions in Japan generally oppose efforts to establish defined contribution pension plans, which they view as a secondary priority relative to the need to address the substantially underfunded defined benefit pension plan liabilities of Japanese corporations. In addition, the powerful tax authorities in Japan have been lukewarm in their support of defined contribution pension plans, because in their view, the tax incentives that are typically built into defined contribution plans will reduce tax revenues at a time when Japan is running record budget deficits.

21. Recently, the Taiwanese government established quotas as to how many outbound funds it would approve in any fiscal year.

22. Any offshore fund to which an SICE wishes to provide advice must be registered with the Taiwanese government and meet stringent criteria. Although this local registration requirement has been somewhat loosely enforced in the past, the government has recently been cracking down on the sale of unregistered offshore funds in Taiwan and reducing the number of offshore funds that it will approve.

23. A number of fund management companies have developed offshore fund products targeted at high-net-worth Latin American investors. Typically, these fund products are organized in offshore jurisdictions (such as the Cayman Islands or Bermuda) as a means of minimizing tax liabilities. Because such jurisdictions also have relatively less restrictive regulatory regimes, it is often possible to structure such offshore funds as master-feeders, with the offshore funds feeding into a larger master fund product line having better economies of scale.

24. SEC Rule Release, Offer and Sale of Securities to Canadian Tax-Deferred Retirement Savings Accounts, Release Nos. 33-7860, 34-42905, IC-24491; File No. S7-10-99, International Series Release No. 1226, 2000 SEC LEXIS 1193 (June 7, 2000).

25. SEC No-Action Letter, Investment Funds Institute of Canada (available March 4, 1996).

CASE STUDY

Transferring a Fund Business to a Foreign Country

U.S. firms may not sell U.S. registered mutual funds in most foreign countries. This is because each country tends to impose its own regulatory, accounting and tax requirements on mutual funds sold there. As a result, U.S. firms must establish clone funds customized to meet the requirements of each country.

This case study examines what should be a relatively easy international transfer: the export of a mutual fund–related defined contribution retirement system to Canada. After all, Canada is contiguous to the United States, and most Canadians speak English. Canadian mutual funds operate in a similar fashion to broker-dealer-sold funds in the United States, and Canadian defined contribution plans have features of both 401(k) and individual retirement account (IRA) plans in the United States. Furthermore, both Canada and the United States follow the Anglo-Saxon tradition of jurisprudence.

Nevertheless, as the case study demonstrates, even small differences in securities and pension laws between two countries can result in major challenges with respect to developing the computer systems needed to support defined contribution plans. For this reason, the questions for the case study are divided between regulatory and operational issues. In preparing for the case study, you may also wish to review Chapter Eight on the retirement business in the United States.

Questions

After reviewing results of the studies that you commissioned in the case, you should be prepared to answer the following questions.

Regulatory Questions

1. What are the principal securities law differences in Canada that will affect the Canadian business and how will they affect:
   a. product offerings?
   b. employee communications?
   c. TMC's responsibilities to educate or advise employees concerning their investments?

2. How does the "know your customer" requirement make the Canadian environment different from the U.S. environment?
3. Assuming that the Canadian retirement business will be based on telephone service, how will you design a compliance system?
   a. What information do you need to know?
   b. How should it be collected?
   c. How will you update that information and keep track of each investor's personal circumstances?
   d. What procedures will the phone representatives follow when a customer calls in a trade?
   e. How will you design customer applications, confirmations and statements to support the know your customer process?

Operational Questions

1. What are the important differences between CanHolder and Colossus? With respect to adaptability to the Canadian Know Your Customer requirements?
2. Which will be better suited for the Canadian environment? Which seems more likely to be ready six months from now?
3. What do you need to be able to deliver in six months? Assuming that you can persuade AmPride Canada to either a delay or a phased launch, you will not need the entire system in place at one time.
   a. What would you propose to do: (1) delay and test the entire system or (2) deliver the system on a just-in-time basis?
   b. Would your answer vary if AmPride Canada's number one priority was to ensure a flawless rollout rather than to launch within six months?

The Management Company

Background

Your firm, The Management Company (TMC), is a global mutual fund firm. It has established a mutual fund operation in Canada, selling Canadian mutual funds through Canadian dealers to their clients. TMC-Canada has met with significant success, establishing the TMC name and building an efficient customer service (or transfer agency) operation, among other things. TMC-Canada's operations currently revolve around a transfer agency system called CanHolder. CanHolder is a computer system licensed from a Canadian firm, Canadian Data Services Corp. (CDS), that tracks investor account data, including purchases, withdrawals, exchanges and dividends. Data are entered into CanHolder by telephone representatives taking instructions from full-service brokers (often called "dealers" in Canada) and by electronic feed from brokerage firms. Recently, CanHolder was updated to allow brokers to transact through a secure website, and the broker's clients now have account look-up features on the web.

TMC-Canada's biggest sales season is the "registered retirement savings plan" (RRSP) season, starting on January 1 and ending 60 days later. Canadians are allowed to invest up to $13,500 on a pretax basis in their RRSP. Most Canadian investors take advantage of RRSPs or a similar account. Many of them do so individually and through employer-sponsored RRSPs. These are particularly popular, as the employer often makes matching or partial matching contributions. TMC-Canada has reported to management of TMC in the United States that the employer-sponsored RRSP marketplace offers significant opportunities for TMC-Canada.

Although Canada is TMC's first offshore defined contribution retirement business opportunity, TMC intends to establish defined contribution retirement businesses in England, Australia, Hong Kong and Japan. It intends to offer customer service by telephone and mail, with investment vehicles in the form of mutual funds in each country. It assumes that the basic record-keeping and reporting functions in each country are similar. The system or systems will have to accept employee and employer contributions and track share purchases, exchanges and withdrawals. Dividends paid by the underlying mutual funds must be posted and the cost basis of each investment tracked over time. Each country will have local requirements that vary. They are as yet unknown, although work is now underway to determine local requirements in Canada.

TMC's U.S. retirement business has developed an enormous capacity for computing customer transactions—more than enough to handle the incremental transactions anticipated by a global retirement business—but the computer systems were necessarily programmed to satisfy the U.S. environment. Identifying the Canadian-U.S. differences will be an important part of your task. You have been asked to evaluate whether you should build separate systems for each of the four foreign countries, or whether you should modify the U.S. system for each country. Your first assignment is Canada, and you need a system that will be operational in six months.

TMC-Canada currently operates only CanHolder, which

was designed to run on a small scale. It is currently running on a series of minicomputers, and its nightly run is relatively slow. Even with recent enhancements—in the form of additional computing capacity—the nightly run for CanHolder still takes three hours. Yet local management will tell you that it is inexpensive to operate and to change. CanHolder will have to be changed because it was not designed as a retirement system; it simply does not provide the necessary basics, such as employer contributions functionality. Enhancing CanHolder's functionality as a transfer agent system requires TMC-Canada to rely on CDS, the owner of the software, to deliver enhancements. Some of management take a jaundiced view of CDS, known as "Can-Do-Slowly," around TMC.

The U.S. retirement record-keeping system is called "Colossus." Designed in the United States, Colossus does not have any Canadian-specific capability. Yet Colossus is a proven workhorse. U.S. management has undying faith in the system. Colossus resides on mainframe computers and was designed to process enormous transaction volume. It can handle single U.S. retirement plans that have more employees in them than there are participants in the Canadian defined contribution marketplace. Nothing can slow the system. It is as reliable as it is expensive to modify.

Your sales force reports back that they have just signed their first client. It is a subsidiary of a U.S. multinational, AmPride Worldwide, Inc., with facilities in each of your global target markets. (AmPride's slogan is, "The American way all the way!") Your senior management reports the Canadian account, AmPride Canada, was won along with the U.S. account. Your firm won the $1 billion U.S. business because AmPride was "overwhelmed" by Colossus, and you were the only firm in the U.S. bidding process that was building a Canadian retirement company. At the final sales pitch, TMC's chairman personally guaranteed that the Canadian business would offer nothing less than "TMS Quality" to AmPride Canada. That seemed to clinch the deal. Press releases quickly followed.

AmPride understands that you will not be ready to take AmPride Canada's monthly payroll for six months. Employee statements will be prepared quarterly, and AmPride has accepted TMC's standard format. AmPride is considering limiting trades to four per year and expects none during the first quarter. AmPride Canada's head of human resources will be traveling for two weeks. She expects you to present your system to her on her return. AmPride's head of human resources is reported by your senior management to be well aware that you are still in the design phase, and she is said to have only one priority: to launch within six months at all costs. You must decide whether to base your business on CanHolder or Colossus.

Knowing little about the Canadian defined contribution environment, you commission a series of studies: (1) an overview of the Canadian defined contribution marketplace by Maple Leaf Consultants, (2) a memorandum from TMC's legal department on differences between Canada and the United States from a regulatory perspective and (3) a study of the functionality needed for a defined contribution computer system in Canada, including a "gap" analysis for each of CanHolder and Colossus.

Commissioned Study 1

A Maple Leaf Consulting Report to the Management Company: The Canadian Defined Contribution Marketplace

I. Industry Overview

A. Mutual Fund Industry.   Much has been written in recent years about the size and growth prospects of the Canadian mutual fund industry. As of year-end 2000, the industry had approximately $280 billion in assets, compared to only $21 billion just 10 years ago, in 1990 (these and all future amounts converted using an exchange rate of C$1.00 = US$.6676). Our forecasts call for industry assets to exceed $521 billion by the year 2005. Canada is plainly a significant marketplace for mutual funds, although small in comparison to the $3 trillion U.S. fund marketplace.

Canada restricts mutual fund offerings to funds whose prospectuses have been filed with the Canadian securities administrators. These funds must be Canadian and must comply with Canada's mutual funds regulation. Foreign funds, including U.S. mutual funds, may not be sold in Canada.

The Canadian mutual fund industry may be divided into three distribution channels. Half of the assets (51%) are held by dealers and financial planners, while the remainder is broken out between the banks (24%) and other channels, including direct sellers (8%), discount brokers (5%) and dedicated sales forces (12%).

Half of Canadian mutual fund investment takes place inside various types of retirement savings plans registered with the Canada Customs and Revenue Agency. This is probably the result of a number of factors, including the significance of tax deferral in a country with marginal tax

rates of over 50%, the ease of mutual fund investing and Canadian investors' increasing familiarity with mutual funds. Canadian mutual funds will continue to increase in popularity as an investment choice for both Canadian individual registered retirement savings plans (known as RRSPs) and employer-sponsored group savings plans. RRSPs are the Canadian equivalent of an Individual Retirement Account (or IRA). Generally, there are both similarities between the Canadian and U.S. equivalents and very important differences.

A large number of Canadians use vehicles other than individual RRSPs for a significant portion of their savings. Frequently, these people rely on savings schemes provided by their employers. These savings schemes have traditionally been pension plans—either defined benefit (DB Plans) or defined contribution (DC Plans). More recently, there has been a sharp increase in the number of alternative employer-sponsored savings schemes, such as group retirement savings plans (Group RRSPs), deferred profit-sharing plans (DPSPs), employee profit-sharing plans (EPSPs), employer savings plans (ESPs) and similar vehicles. As these DC Plans have become more prevalent, mutual fund companies are becoming more important participants in this segment of the market.

B. How Big Is the Canadian DC Plan Market?   Canada is still early in the process of developing the DC Plan marketplace. At present, the main Canadian vehicles for employer-sponsored savings are DB Plans, in which the employer makes all the contributions, makes the investment decisions, takes all the investment risk and pays benefits to the employees according to a predetermined formula, regardless of the actual returns in the pension plan. DB Plans account for the majority of employer-sponsored savings plans, with more than $351 billion, or approximately 89% of the total amount invested in all employer-sponsored savings plans. Their growth has leveled off in recent years, and most projections call for no real growth in the next decade. This stagnancy will result in a sharp decline in market share as employee savings continue to grow through other vehicles.

The diminishing popularity of DB Plans has been paralleled by the increasing prevalence of various defined contribution schemes, including, most significantly, DC Plans, Group RRSPs and similar options. Currently, DC Plans account for $28 billion, or 7% of the market, while Group RRSPs make up $16 billion, or 4% of the market. Growth projections are very strong.

Growth of DC Plans and Group RRSPs will come from two sources: first, new plans that are established for employees with no current employer savings plan, and second, from the winding up and conversion of existing DB Plans. Estimates show assets in DC Plans growing to approximately $57 billion by 2005 and close to $108 billion, or more than 12% of the market, by 2010. Group RRSPs should enjoy almost as substantial a growth rate, more than doubling to $36 billion by 2005 and shooting up to close to $67 billion (or almost 8% of the market) by 2010. Clearly, there is a lot of money at stake, with even more to come.

Traditionally, the chief providers of DC Plans have been insurance companies. However, bank-owned trust companies now control 46% of the market, followed by insurance companies (37%), fund sponsors (11%) and investment dealers (6%). Mergers and acquisitions have also reduced the number of players in this market.

With the shift from defined benefit to defined contribution schemes, which are frequently individual, self-directed vehicles, the competition for assets is likely to intensify further. Mutual fund companies and investment dealers, who have extensive experience catering to individual investors, are likely to challenge vigorously the traditional institutional providers, such as insurance and trust companies.

This shift represents an important new business opportunity for Canadian and foreign mutual fund firms, but it carries with it a variety of regulatory and practical challenges. In order to understand these challenges better, it is important to survey the Canadian DC Plan environment briefly.

II. Canadian Employer-Sponsored Savings Plans

A. Shift to DC Plans.

There are a wide variety of different workplace savings schemes in use in Canada. Traditionally, such schemes were primarily limited to DB Plans, but in recent years the growth has been in DC Plans (which are sometimes called money purchase pension plans). This shift in pension plans has been augmented by the increasing popularity of a variety of nonpension plans, such as Group RRSPs, DPSPs, EPSPs and ESPs. Some of these are tax-sheltered plans registered with the Canada Customs and Revenue Agency (e.g., Group RRSPs), while others are simple taxable savings plans (e.g., Employer Savings Plans). What all these plans have in common is that they are established and administered by the employer through the workplace. Generally, participation in the

plans is dependent on the employee's meeting certain conditions, such as having attained a minimum length of service and being in good standing. In a typical plan, employees may make contributions through regular payroll deductions and sometimes by lump sums as well. Often, part or all of the employee contribution may be matched by the employer, and in some cases the employer may make the entire amount of contributions on behalf of the employee, with no need for the employee to make any contribution.

B. What Are They?

The types of employer-sponsored savings schemes are limited only by the creativity of employers and, in the case of registered plans, the tolerance of the Canada Customs and Revenue Agency. Each plan must be examined carefully to ensure that its particular features are properly understood, because plans with similar names can have important differences.

Some of the more common types of employer-sponsored savings plans are as follows:

Pension Plan (Defined Benefit). The DB Plan is the classic employer-sponsored savings plan. Typically, the employer will determine all aspects of employee eligibility and entitlement, including the level of benefits. The employer will also take complete responsibility for making contributions to the plan and making all investment decisions for the pension plan assets. More important, the employer will assume all investment risk: if the plan earns less than what is required to provide the promised levels of payments to employees, then the employer will be liable for the shortfall; conversely, if the plan earns more than what is required to provide the promised levels of payments to employees, then the employer may (depending on the plan's particular provisions and subject to resolving legal issues about surplus entitlement) be able to enjoy the benefit of any excess gains.

Pension Plan (Defined Contribution). A defined contribution pension plan is very similar to a defined benefit pension plan, except for one fundamental difference: the employee assumes all investment risk. Employees are promised a certain level of contributions rather than a specific level of final benefit. (Note that defined contribution *pension* plans ought to be distinguished from defined contribution plans in general. The broader phrase, *defined contribution plan,* includes both pooled investment vehicles, such as defined contribution pension plans, as well as individual investment vehicles, such as Group RRSPs and similar plans.)

Group Retirement Savings Plan. Group RRSPs are the major alternative to traditional pension schemes. A Group RRSP is, in fact, something of a misnomer, since *there is no true group plan.* In U.S. 401(k) plans, the employer-sponsored plan is a single separate trust for the benefit of all employees. The Canadian employer DC Plan consists of a series of individual RRSP trusts, one per employee; the employer provides a single prototype plan (registered with Revenue Canada) on which all the individual RRSP trusts are modeled. From a legal perspective, the individual RRSP accounts are similar to self-directed RRSPs in a nongroup context, except that each trust will have the same features and available investment options, since each trust in a Group RRSP is derived from the same template. This individual characterization is a fundamental difference from U.S. 401(k) plans and from DB Plans in both the United States and Canada: whereas 401(k) and DB Plans are collective investment vehicles, Group RRSPs are *individually administered trusts.* From a practical perspective, the benefits to an individual in using an employer-sponsored group RRSP instead of an individual RRSP boils down to: employer contributions, automatic monthly payroll deductions, employer-sponsored educational materials and a prescreened menu of investment alternatives that narrow the selection process.

Deferred Profit-Sharing Plans. There are additional retirement plans in the Canadian marketplace, and employee participants in a Group RRSP may well also participate in one or more of these other plans. A popular adduct to the RRSP is the Deferred Profit Sharing Plan (or DPSP). DPSPs are individual accounts, although they exist within a form of umbrella known as a deferred profit-sharing plan. Like RRSPs, DPSPs are tax-sheltered investment vehicles, but they are subject to different rules and restrictions. For instance, only employer contributions are permitted; that is, individual participants cannot contribute to their own DPSP accounts. DPSPs may, however, be similar to Group RRSPs in that the individual participants may be entitled to make their own investment selections, although it is common for a DPSP to require all investments to be allocated to the employer's stock or another limited alternative.

Employee Profit-Sharing Plans. An EPSP is similar to a DPSP in that it is an individual account that exists within a form of umbrella known as an employee profit-sharing plan. Like a DPSP, the ostensible purpose of an EPSP is to provide an incentive to employees by giving them some participation in their employer's profits. It is also similar to a DPSP in that investment choices may be very limited or may be entirely restricted—for example, only employer's stock. It differs from a DPSP, however, in that it is not tax sheltered, and employee contributions are permitted.

Share Purchase Plans. There are a variety of different plans through which employees may be able to acquire shares of their employer's stock, frequently on very favorable terms. The investment option in these plans is limited to employer-issued securities and does not include pooled investment vehicles such as mutual funds; in this way, share purchase plans are fundamentally different from the other types of plans listed here.

Employer Savings Plans. This is a catchall description for a variety of other employer-sponsored savings schemes that do not fit into any of the above categories. ESPs are typically not tax sheltered, but they are still administered by the employer, and participation is limited to employees. Like Group RRSPs and DPSPs, individual participants are typically entitled to make their own investment choices, subject to any particular restrictions imposed by the plan.

For the purpose of analyzing the registration requirements arising under securities laws, the key difference between these various plans is whether they are truly pooled investment vehicles, such as pension plans, or are individual, self-directed accounts, such as Group RRSPs, DPSPs, EPSPs and ESPs.

III. The Basic Business Requirements
A. What Type of Functionality Is Required?

The marketplace will demand that TMC-Canada offer all types of plans, whether Group RRSPs, DPSPs, EPSPs and ESPs. Each employee's investments in each plan will need to be reported on a combined statement. The marketplace is increasingly driven by employers looking to outsource the employee benefit function. Indeed, the proliferation of types of retirement plans offers a niche for providing advice on plan structure and, our surveys show, advice on what types of pools (funds) or other investment options (e.g., company stock) should be in the plan. TMC has earned a reputation as a highly skilled outsource vendor. Maple Leaf believes that this is TMC's natural niche in Canada. A survey of human resources (HR) managers determined that the typical Canadian HR director is aware of the Colossus system. The typical HR director is looking to move to an outsource solution where a third party supplies telephone service on a continuous basis to employees, sends employee statements, performs tax reporting and shoulders all administrative and legal burdens. Most HR directors either want or are willing to offer mutual funds as the investment option for benefit plans. Nearly all are looking to offer DC Plans or to add DC Plans to their existing DB Plan.

B. What Types of Products Are Required?

Canada's late-blooming DC Plan marketplace is quickly learning by observing the state of the art in the United States. Accordingly, most HR directors expect that their DC Plan administrator will offer a wide array of funds and will allow the employer to select funds from various sponsors.

IV. Conclusion

TMC-Canada is well positioned to launch a DC Plan administration business in Canada. To do so successfully and to capture market share, it will need to offer more than the competition. It will need to offer a wide array of investment products as well as a high level of service.

Commissioned Study 2
The Management Company Legal Department

To:	Dudley Doright, TMC General Counsel
From:	John Dean, TMC Associate Counsel
Date:	June 30, 2001
Subject:	TMC-Canada Key U.S./Canadian Legal Differences

Question Presented: You have asked me to determine whether there are important differences between Canada and the United States applicable to a defined contribution retirement business. Specifically, you have asked me to focus on whether Canadian law regulates DC Plans in a manner similar to the United States and whether there are any new responsibilities that TMC will encounter in Canada.

I. The Canadian DC Plan Investment Process
A. Relevant Regulations and Differences from U.S. Regulation.
There are various bodies of applicable regulations in Canada, including securities regulations. This stands in contrast to the United States, which largely exempts U.S. 401(k) plans from securities laws on the theory that the supervisory function of the Department

of Labor and the protections of the Employee Retirement Income Security Act of 1974 (ERISA) provide a sufficient and unified regulatory environment. The Securities Act of 1933, which applies to U.S. public securities offerings, and the Investment Company Act of 1940, which governs U.S. mutual funds, do not apply to ERISA plans. This means that U.S. 401(k) plans are exempt from SEC oversight, although mutual funds offered through the plans are SEC regulated. As a practical matter, this means that employee participants in U.S. 401(k) plans are not required to receive prospectuses for U.S. mutual funds that are held in their plans. Prospectuses must be given by the mutual fund firm to the employer/plan sponsor acting as trustee of the plan. The U.S. theory is that the employer acts as a plan fiduciary and serves to protect employees.

Further, U.S. law limits the responsibility of the employer and the plan administrator for investment selection. So long as neither explicitly offers investment advice, the risk of investment decision making can be shifted to the employee. ERISA [section 404(c)] provides a safe harbor for employers that offers a balanced range of mutual fund investment options to their employees. Having done that much, the employer has no duty to advise the employee on investment selection. The plan administrator, or another supplier, must be a registered broker-dealer, but the broker-dealer has no duty to advise either. The broker-dealer's duty is to give suitable advice, if it chooses to make a recommendation. If the broker-dealer acts as a discount broker and makes no recommendations, it need not get involved in the suitability of the employee's investment selections.

The theory behind the regulatory scheme in Canada is different. In Canada, there is no equivalent to ERISA, and there is no trustee acting for the employees. Each employee has his or her own RRSP or other DC Plan. Canada's securities laws are applied to protect these investors much the same as they would in any other mutual fund transaction.

Virtually all Canadian mutual fund transactions take place in one of two contexts: (1) the traditional individual, retail broker-client relationship or (2) a large-scale institutional environment. An example of the latter might be a DC Plan investing in a fund. Although various private placement exemptions from securities laws may apply to large-scale institutional trades, retail trades are the subject of Canadian securities regulation.

The individual retail relationship typically involves a personal one-on-one relationship with a dealer; to place a trade, the individual calls his or her registered dealer, who then places the order for the individual's account.

The problem with Group RRSPs (and similar vehicles) is that they don't fit well into either of these traditional relationships. They are neither as individual and personal as the traditional retail broker-client scheme nor as impersonal and sophisticated as the traditional institutional scheme. An individual investing through his or her own account typically works within what has been described above as a "retail" relationship; this relationship places him or her squarely within the scope of the various provincial securities acts. The individual investing within a Group RRSP has a relationship that is clearly individual, as opposed to institutional, yet it is not as direct and personal as a classic retail relationship. This results in a degree of regulatory tension.

B. Group RRSP Investing. Although participation in a Group RRSP is unlike being a member of a DB Plan, it is also unlike traditional individual investing where someone calls a stockbroker and buys a publicly traded security. This is the primary source of regulatory tension. Although the legal characterization of a Group RRSP participant is that of an individual investor, the reality is that the nature of the investor/registrant relationships and their working arrangements are relatively unique and largely dissimilar to either the traditional retail or institutional relationships.

The typical Group RRSP established with a mutual fund company begins with negotiations between the employer company and the mutual fund firm. The two parties agree to work together, determine what sorts of plans will be offered, design the particular features of the various plans, identify the investment options that will be made available to participants and allocate the various administrative and operational responsibilities. In due course, introductory materials are prepared and distributed to employees to advise them of their new Group RRSP, its key features and how they participate in it. The individual employees should then be required to open an account with the mutual fund company. This is the stage at which, from a regulatory perspective, the process passes from the traditional world of institutional, employer-administered pension-like savings schemes into the realm of a more traditional individual securities trading relationship.

Once the account has been opened, the employee will generally conduct his or her transactions directly with the mutual fund company, either by regular payroll deductions or through phone instructions to the fund company. (This presents a new problem for TMC: direct dealing with investors. Now we will be the dealer, unlike our mainline funds business, where someone else is the dealer.) The vast majority of transactions are small purchases made by means of payroll deduction, often accompanied by a company matching contribution or a partial match. The employer (or its agent) will process the regular payroll and make a record of the amount of the deduction made for each employee. This record, which is typically in the form of a tape or other computer file, is sent to the mutual fund company, which processes the information and makes purchases for each individual's account in accordance with his or her previously provided instructions. In addition to these payroll deduction transactions, employees can typically provide phone instructions to transfer amounts between funds, redeem a portion of their investments or make a lump-sum purchase.

C. The Key Differences in Administration. One of the most important differences between a U.S. 401(k) plan and a Canadian Group RRSP scheme is that in a Group RRSP, the employee must establish individual relationships with the dealers and other market participants. This is a fundamental change. The significance of this change is that Canadian dealers have a duty to provide advice to their clients concerning the suitability of their transactions, subject to exceptions, which we think will not apply. The key exception requires that we can make no recommendations on the purchase of any security. This would constrain us from advising on the funds to include in the Group RRSP. You have told us this is a key service. If so, we will acquire a duty to determine suitability. This "suitability" duty requires the dealer to know his or her customer's individual circumstances and evaluate each transaction in light of these circumstances. This is a very challenging responsibility to administer in the DC Plan administration environment.

In a DC Plan, the bulk of transactions occur by way of payroll deductions. This is fundamentally different from the typical retail brokerage trade: the investor makes the purchase without ever speaking to a broker, and, in fact, interposing anybody between the creation of the payroll tape and the purchase of the fund units is inconsistent with what both employers and employees expect and demand. Their desire is to have a process that is as automated as possible to maximize efficiency and minimize cost. Whereas the traditional retail broker-client relationship is quite personal and involves direct contact, the Group RRSP environment is more institutional. Technically, the relationship is an individual one, yet as a practical matter, there is little need or desire for personal interaction.

II. Canadian Requirements

A. Basic Registration Principles.

The basic regulatory scheme under Canadian securities law is well established. Essentially, the rule is that one can trade securities only if registered to do so. This basic requirement is set out in section 25 of the Securities Act (Ontario) (the "Act") and comparable provisions in the legislation of other jurisdictions. The type of securities being traded determines the nature of the registration required.

In addition, each distribution of securities (which includes the issuance of new mutual fund units on a purchase) must be undertaken pursuant to a prospectus.

Since registration is necessary, a variety of obligations arise, including requirements to ensure suitability of investments for the client (the so-called know-your-client obligations). These know-your-client obligations are a fundamental part of the securities regulatory framework and are written in unequivocal terms. The registrant (e.g., the dealer) has a positive duty to ensure the suitability of investments made by his or her clients. In the context of DC Plans, TMC will be the dealer.

B. "Know Your Customer"—Canadian Rules.

The law in Canada has not specifically addressed the DC Plan environment. Still, by statute, the provinces have imposed an affirmative suitability regime. The Ontario Securities Act Rule, for example, provides that each dealer "shall make such inquiries as . . . are appropriate in view of the nature of the client's investments and of the type of transaction being effected for the client's account, to ascertain the general investment needs and objectives of the client and the suitability of a proposed purchase or sale of a security for that client" (ON Rule 31–505: 1.5(1)(b),[1].

Cases interpreting a prior, similar Ontario regulation have found that the regulation creates a *limited but specific* statutory duty. That duty is discharged when the broker diligently makes a recommendation. Should the client then elect not to follow the recommendation and a loss is incurred, the broker will not be liable. See *Srdarev* v. *McLeod Young Weir Ltd.* In *Srdarev,* the investor failed to recover losses because the facts demonstrated careful advice from his broker that the investor consciously ignored.

The most interesting Canadian case is *Varcoe* v. *Sterling.* Varcoe was a sophisticated investor who lost a small

fortune trading futures in his own account that he managed himself. The Court found no advisory relationship between Varcoe and his dealer. The dealer never suggested that Varcoe trade futures in any way. Varcoe recovered his losses from the dealer nonetheless after demonstrating that the dealer failed to meet his duty to advise Varcoe of the unsuitable nature of Varcoe's trading. This failure to advise was demonstrated by the dealer's failure to warn Varcoe of his losses while they were arising through a so-called margin call. Varcoe traded futures and was obliged to maintain a deposit with his dealer equal to a percentage of his losses. As Varcoe's losses mounted, the dealer typically would have called Varcoe to ask for additional cash deposits. These "margin calls" would have had the effect of warning Varcoe of the magnitude of his losses. The Court found that since margin calls were customary and part of the dealer's procedures manual, failure to make margin calls was a breach of the dealer's duty. The Court stated, "If industry and the regulatory authorities permit member brokers to ignore or violate their own rules and blame losses on the cupidity of the customer, then it falls to the Court to provide a remedy."

The Court's remedy was to allow recovery for all losses over and above the client's trading limit, established at the time the account was opened, and to deny counterclaims for negative balances in the client's account.

The *Varcoe* case involved a Toronto Stock Exchange regulated broker that failed to follow its procedures or to make any effort at a suitability determination. The Court in *Varcoe* stated that the suitability role of a nondiscretionary broker was fairly specific. The Court stated that so long as a broker "applies the skill and knowledge relied upon and advises fully, honestly and in good faith, the broker . . . is not responsible if the transaction proves unfavorable." Moreover, if the client does not follow the advice or if the broker disagrees with the client's decision, the broker has no duty to refuse the order.

C. "Know Your Customer": U.S. Rules.

In the United States, TMC acts as a service provider to DC Plans that invest in mutual funds. TMC's role as broker is limited to acting as an order taker. The law in the United States is fairly clear. The NASD Rules of Conduct impose a suitability duty only when a broker makes recommendations. The NASD rule states that "in recommending to a customer the purchase . . . of a security, a member shall have reasonable grounds for believing that the recommendation is suitable for such customer." U.S. courts generally find no duty in the broker to determine suitability or to prevent unsuitable trading, so long as the broker does not have investment discretion or affirmative knowledge that trading is unsuitable.

A second U.S. commodities case is worth noting, if only because it stands in contrast to the state of the law in Canada. In *Puckett v. Ruffenach, Bromagen & Hertz, Inc.* 1991 WL 191654 (Miss.), Mr. Puckett managed to lose $2 million trading futures. The Court noted that the futures commission merchant provided no advice, knew Puckett's trading was foolish and offered no warnings. The Court found no duty at common law to intervene in Puckett's debacle and no contractual responsibility, even assuming that it was customary for futures commission merchants to do so as an industry practice and even assuming further that the futures commission merchant failed to follow internal procedures and ignored information about the client's tolerance for losses on its account application. The Court stated, "If society is to be free, it must demand of every person who, completely on his own, makes a mistake that he has no legal right to shift from his shoulders onto another's the suffering it causes."

III. Conclusion

TMC-Canada will need to design a know-your-customer compliance system for Canada. This will be new territory for TMC. I am sure none of our U.S. computer or phone systems are designed to track the sort of background information that will be needed. Ultimately, the business unit will have to design a practical solution.

Commissioned Study 3

Project:	Global Pension Recordkeeping System—Canada
SDM Module:	PPI
Deliverable:	Project Charter
Version: 2.0	Publication Date: 6/30/01
GPRS Doc ID:	CB010

Prepared by the GPRS Strategy Team.

1 Introduction

1.1 Business Problem/Opportunity. As the pension plan industry expands worldwide, TMC has domestic and international companies that are positioned to take advantage of the growing market. As more pension plan business is managed by TMC, a cohesive technology strategy becomes an imminent requirement to support the rapidly growing business, as well as accommodate a global retirement plan technology infrastructure. The effort to plan a global strategy and build a supporting system infrastructure has been named the Global Pension Recordkeeping Strategy/System (GPRS). GPRS is projected to be very costly. Therefore, an alternative system solution has also been considered: enhancements to CanHolder.

Through the integrated efforts of TMC Systems, TMC-Canada and TMC, this project ultimately will deliver Canada-specific business functions supported by a core system as well as external subsystem interfaces.

Although the GPRS project eventually is intended for the end-to-end international solution, which includes other countries, such as the United Kingdom and countries in Asia, the focus of this document will be on the Canada implementation from a cost-benefit perspective.

2 Objectives and Scope
2.1 Objectives.

2.1.1 Business Objectives.
- Provide TMC-Canada with an internal system that will ensure control over strategic business direction, product design, costs, services provided and pricing.
- Proactively manage volume of new business and allow for system scalability for increasing capacity.
- Ensure a higher level of quality service to pension plan providers and sponsors.

2.1.2 Project Objectives.
- Manage the increasing volume of pension plan business efficiently and cost-effectively.
- Provide a system infrastructure that is flexible enough to add record-keeping processes and functions from other countries as TMC expands its business worldwide.
- Implement the end-to-end Pension Recordkeeping System solution in Canada (and the United Kingdom and countries in Asia in the future).

2.2 Scope. The full scope of the project is to provide system recommendations and solutions that allow TMC-Canada to implement all record-keeping and administration functions associated with the delivery and servicing of retirement products.

3 Summary of Relative Advantages of CanHolder and Colossus

3.1 Narrative of the GPRS system project.

In April 2000 we began to examine whether the CanHolder transfer agency system (the home-grown Canadian record-keeping system) could be used by a single group plan in Canada and, if so, whether it was adequate for future business growth in Canada. It is immediately apparent that Can-Holder is not adequate as a global pension record-keeping system, but it may be considered as a viable solution for Canada.

At the same time, we began to review Colossus. It is also apparent that Colossus has the potential to become the core for a global pension record-keeping solution, providing a range of functions for multiple countries, provided that country-specific applications were to be developed. Colossus would require country-specific applications to be used in Canada. We also believe that the cost of a mainframe computer—projected to be in excess of $2.5 million—precludes using Colossus in a mainframe environment. Nor will a mainframe be needed. Two mini-computers, one for backup, collectively cost $300,000 and have ample computing capacity. Accordingly, Colossus will have to be adapted to a PC/minicomputer environment.

3.2 Key Functionality Needs.

We have identified two critical systems needs for the Canadian business: foreign content rebalancing and "know-your-customer" support functionality. We immediately compared the relative merits of both systems regarding these criteria.

4 Foreign Content Rebalancing

4.1 Scope.

In Canada, investment in foreign property, including mutual funds that hold foreign property, is restricted for registered plans such as RRSPs (including LIRAs [Locked In Retirement Account] and spousals), DPSPs, EPSPs and MPPs (Money Purchase Plan). From January 2001, foreign content must not exceed 30% of the assets in the registered plan, determined at the time of purchase on a cost basis. Foreign securities are foreign content for this purpose. Mutual funds that hold in excess of 30% foreign property are themselves considered foreign property when held by a registered plan.

If the foreign holdings in a registered plan are more than 30% of the plan's cost, then Revenue Canada will penalize the participant. If the participant holds funds over 30% foreign based in their registered plan, they will be fined monthly 1% of the value of the foreign content hold-ings in excess of the permitted 30%. The foreign content rules require compliance on the last day of each month, and violations during the month will not trigger the penalty. The formula used to calculate foreign content in a plan is the adjusted cost base (ACB), which is: cost of (purchases − redemptions +/− interfund transfers + income distributions).

4.2 Assumptions and Constraints.

TMC-Canada has made a business decision to rebalance registered accounts to 30% foreign content holdings on a monthly basis to ensure that participants never exceed the 30% foreign content holdings and incur a tax penalty. This practice has been widely adopted by the competitors as well.

The following assumptions have been made:
- Month end is defined as the last business day of the month.
- System calendars must reflect Canadian holidays.
- Registered plans (RRSPs, including LIRA and Spousal, DPSPs and DCPPs) are the only types of retirement plans that restrict investment in a foreign fund.
- At fund setup, the retirement system (whether Colossus or CanHolder) will allow the funds to be designated as either domestic or foreign.
- At enrollment, participant accounts are set up for automatic rebalance to the domestic fund that has the highest market value for that month. However, participants may request that their foreign content excess be exchanged into a domestic fund other than the one with the highest market value. This would involve only a choice of at least one fund.
- The month-end rebalancing program will not prevent participants from making exchanges into their foreign funds prior to month end or from making full or partial withdrawals that will alter the plan's content. However, when an exchange or withdrawal is initiated by telephone, there will be a warning on the workstation that the foreign content threshold may be exceeded and that this transaction will activate automatic month-end rebalancing. TMC-Canada will not allow participants to be out of balance by month end.
- The foreign content limit may be subject to change, so there must be the flexibility to change the 30% to another amount.
- The TMC-Canada retirement system will calculate adjusted cost basis on a transaction-by-transaction basis and store the information.

- The percentage of foreign content in the plan will be displayed on the workstation so the Employee Service Centre representatives can advise the participant. If the participant requests the breakdown by fund, this will be available on the representatives' screens.

4.3 CanHolder and Foreign Content Rebalancing.

4.3.1 CanHolder System Functionality. The current CanHolder system automatically rebalances participants' accounts to 30% on a daily basis. This functionality was developed to support the TMC-Canada mutual fund business. TMC-Canada already offers an individual RRSP through brokers. These RRSPs are also subject to the foreign content requirement.

4.3.2 CanHolder System Description. The CanHolder system is currently rebalancing all registered plans on a daily basis if a transaction has occurred. The accounts are "rebalanced" by shifting assets from a fund that is foreign property to a fund that is not foreign property, meaning to a domestic fund that holds at least 70% Canadian securities. The CanHolder system transfers the excess foreign property amounts automatically to the TMC-Canada domestic fund option with the highest market value at the time. If, however, the participant specifies that he or she wants the rebalanced amounts to be invested in a specifically designated domestic fund, then the CanHolder system will automatically rebalance excess foreign content amounts to the designated fund or to more than one fund. If the participant specifies, he or she has an option of having his or her foreign fund rebalanced to one domestic fund.

4.4 Colossus and Foreign Content Rebalancing.

4.4.1 Colossus System Functionality. The Colossus system has no foreign content rebalancing capacity. Were Colossus to be selected, a systems enhancement would be necessary, and the solution functionality recommended would not be the same as that currently available on CanHolder.

4.4.2 Colossus Enhancements. The Colossus enhancements to accomplish foreign content rebalancing should be cost-effective. Foreign content rebalancing necessarily involves rebalancing a portion of a registered plan. It is anticipated that initially plan balances will be small and the foreign content transactions will be even smaller. This implies a very large number of small transactions, which would be an inefficient and costly use of Colossus. Therefore, TMC-Canada has decided to rebalance on the Colossus system monthly, thereby eliminating high transaction volumes involving small amounts of money.

During plan enrollment, participants are advised that TMC-Canada will automatically rebalance their accounts monthly to the domestic fund in their plan with the highest market value at the end of the month. Although this is the preferred procedure from an operational perspective, TMC-Canada must also provide the participant with the option of choosing the domestic fund where excess foreign dollars will be transferred. This feature will be too costly to automate and will require a manual process. Accordingly, this would be done only if there was a specific request and the participant would be able to choose only one domestic fund for rebalancing.

4.4.3 Proposed Solution. The following solution is possible within six months, the time frame specified by TMC in the AmPride negotiations.

Monthly, TMC-Canada will run a program to extract from all registered plans the adjusted cost base (ACB) of every fund within each participant's plan. (The ACB calculation will be a Colossus function.) The program will also select a foreign fund indicator for each account. The program will sort the data by participant plan and calculate the percentage invested in Canadian funds versus the percentage invested in foreign funds. When a participant's account is over 30% foreign content threshold, TMC-Canada will *manually* create the transactions to rebalance the account; an exchange out of the foreign fund, and an exchange into the Canadian fund with the highest market value (or chosen by participant) will be created. These transactions will be loaded into Colossus, and the accounts will be rebalanced in that night's batch cycle.

4.4.4 Data and Additional Functionality Needed in Colossus **Data Needed.**
- Daily calculation of adjusted cost base (ACB) by participant by plan
- Default for foreign rebalancing to go to the domestic fund with the highest market value
- Workstation field for inputting a rebalancing fund choice (if the participant chooses one)

- An exchange screen display of which fund will receive excess foreign content for each participant
- A withdrawal screen notice for when a withdrawal may put the foreign fund content above the threshold
- An update for the user-defined table to include the four-digit fund number of the foreign content spill fund
- Two new transaction codes—rebalance exchange in and rebalance exchange out—to distinguish these transactions from nonrebalancing exchanges
- The foreign fund indicator (stored on the fund file as a field)
- A display of the ACB for each plan on the account balance information screen adjacent to market value
- The percentage of each participant's money that is in foreign funds, displayed on the workstation

Additional Functionality Needed

- Storage and calculation of ACB for every fund within a participant's plans
- Default setup on Colossus that tells TMC-Canada that each time a participant is over the 30% foreign content where the fund should be rebalanced to, based on the domestic fund at the end of the month with the highest market value
- A field on Colossus for participants to choose where their foreign content will be rebalanced to if they insist on choosing (available on the workstation for the employee service center to input if the participant requests)
- An indicator to distinguish between foreign or domestic when funds are set up on Colossus
- At the end of the month, a transaction file, back to Colossus, from the local side for all interfund transfers that are a result of any plans being over 30% foreign content

4.5 Conclusion. The CanHolder System can service the foreign content rebalancing requirements of TMC-Canada without enhancement. It will have a daily rebalancing capability and the ability to offer multiple investment options (i.e., spill funds) on an automated basis.

Colossus can be adapted to provide a partially automated foreign content solution within six months. The system will operate only monthly. This is adequate but less sophisticated. It will also not allow accounts to maintain a constant foreign content exposure, as exposure will fluctuate during the month. The cost for the Colossus enhancements will be $75,000. Full automation will be achievable, after the six-month deadline, for an additional $25,000.

5 Know Your Client and Risk Class for Funds

5.1 Scope. The Canadian securities administrators require that mutual fund companies track retirement plan members' investment profile. Thus, TMC-Canada is required to inform a member if his or her choices of investments are outside his or her chosen risk level. Investment profile information is not carried on either CanHolder or Colossus today. Modifications will be required to carry and store investment risk information as well as other directives. This information, which will reside at the participant/plan level, must be stored and tracked for each member within each plan. A warning must be issued if the member is outside his or her chosen risk level.

5.2 Assumptions and Constraints. The TMC-Canada system will need to deliver the following functions:

- Store investor profile information for each member within each plan.
- Store risk class for each fund.
- View and maintain the investor profile information on the workstation.
- Track and monitor anything that may affect the member's portfolio.
- Warn a member if he or she is outside the chosen level of risk.
- Trigger a Risk Warning record for the "outside the member's chosen risk level" event.
- Create an Audit report (Investment Profile Audit Report) that contains all members warned from the workstation and the reason for the warning.
- Create a Warning report for front-end investment mix changes that are determined to cause a member to be outside his or her chosen risk level.

5.3 CanHolder and KYC. CanHolder has no KYC (Know Your Client) functionality at present and will not offer an automated solution within the six-month timeframe.

Experience has shown that CanHolder's software owner, Canadian Data Services, is not able to enhance its systems in a timely way to meet TMC's needs and time frames. CDS has estimated that a fully automated solution would be at least a six-month project and that they would propose to allocate staff to the project in three months when other initiatives within CDS are expected to be completed. Accordingly, if CanHolder is TMC-Canada's system, KYC will be manual and after the fact, at least for the first nine months or so.

TMC will be able to download transaction data and then compare the data to asset allocations and customer profile rankings using largely manual processes and spreadsheets. Written warnings could then be mailed to customers recommending that they rebalance their portfolios to meet their risk profile. CanHolder will not allow real-time KYC assessments at the time of the transaction.

5.4 Colossus and KYC.
Colossus can be enhanced within the six-month time frame to provide an automated and real-time solution for KYC. Colossus can be modified using internal systems resources:

- To provide TMC-Canada with the ability to store member investment profile information for each member within each plan that he or she belongs to.
- To provide an automated process for tracking anything that might affect a member's portfolio. This automated process will determine whether a member's current level of risk is within his or her chosen risk level. It will also trigger a Risk Warning record in the event that a participant's portfolio exceeds the chosen risk level.
- To modify fund tables to include a fund risk indicator for each fund.
- To provide the capability of viewing and maintaining a member's Investor Profile, Investment Knowledge and Net Worth information on the workstation at the participant level.
- To provide a pop-up warning screen on the workstation. This would be used to notify a member that he or she is outside his or her chosen level of risk.
- To provide a front-end process that will detect investment mix changes that place a member outside his or her chosen risk level. This event (out of participant's risk level) will trigger a Risk Warning record on the workstation.

5.5 Conclusion.
Use of CanHolder will necessitate a manual process of monitoring KYC. This is a practicable and low-cost approach, given the immediate needs of the TMC retirement business and the small number of accounts in the AmPride plans. This manual approach will not be capable of supporting large transaction volumes and will need to be replaced eventually. (We estimate that the manual system will be able to handle no more than 10 employers and, depending on their number of employees, as few as five.) This manual process will be very labor intensive and will cost $200,000 per year to support on a fully loaded basis (assuming two full-time employees).

Automating CanHolder will take some time. CDS will not take us on for 12 months, and the project will take an additional 12 months. You should plan on manual processing for 2 years, just to be safe. Their initial cost estimate for a customer software enhancement to support KYC fully is $150,000.

Colossus offers the potential for an automated KYC system within the immediate six-month time frame. Colossus will be capable of performing KYC on a real-time basis and in large volumes. The enhancement will cost $100,000. We fully expect the system to handle any number of employees.

6 Modifying Colossus from a Mainframe to a Mini
Colossus was designed for and resides on a mainframe. The Canadian-specific enhancements to Colossus mandate working on the system offline. In order not to interfere with the U.S. business, a copy of the Colossus source code will be made and modified offline. At the same time, the code will be rewritten in its entirety to suit a PC/mini environment. This project will require a significant programming resource. At the same time, the rewritten code will need to be tested in the new environment.

Our summary conclusion is that Colossus can be rewritten from Cobalt to Unix over a five-month period and that testing will take the balance of a month. Once accomplished, Colossus will be easily copied for use in other countries, and a key step in establishing a GPRS will have been accomplished. The cost of this process—rewriting from Cobalt to Unix in order to run on minicomputers—will be $250,000. It is reasonable to expect that the rewritten system will be unstable during its first three to six months, with brief systems interruptions arising from time to time until all weaknesses have been identified through use. The impact of this instability may mean occasional delays in processing customer transactions. This risk can be avoided only through a further two-month trial run of the system.

Notes

1. Rule 31–505 provides that, in lieu of complying with the rule, a member of The Investment Dealers Association of Canada (IDA) may comply with any IDA regulation covering the same subject matter. For purposes of this case study, assume that TMC—Canada is not an IDA member and is not in a position to become one.

Index